CANON LAW, RELIGION, AND POLITICS

CANON LAW, RELIGION, AND POLITICS

Liber Amicorum Robert Somerville

Edited by Uta-Renate Blumenthal, Anders Winroth & Peter Landau

The Catholic University of America Press
Washington, D.C.

The paper used in this publication meets the minimum requirements of American National Standards for Information Science—Permanence of Paper for Printed Library Materials, ANSI Z39.48-1984.
∞

LIBRARY OF CONGRESS
CATALOGING-IN-PUBLICATION DATA

Canon law, religion, and politics : liber amicorum Robert Somerville / edited by Uta-Renate Blumenthal, Anders Winroth, and Peter Landau.
p. cm.
Includes bibliographical references and index.
ISBN 978-0-8132-1975-2 (cloth : alk. paper)
1. Lord's Supper (Canon law) 2. Canon law—Sources. 3. Councils and synods (Canon law) 4. Church history—Middle Ages, 600–1500. 5. Papacy—History. 6. Somerville, Robert, 1940– 7. Catholic Church—Doctrines. I. Blumenthal, Uta-Renate, 1935– II. Winroth, Anders. III. Landau, Peter.
KBU3085.C36 2012

262.9—dc23 2012004530

Contents

Preface

Robert Somerville, Professor of History at Columbia University and Ada Byron Bampton Tremaine Professor of Religion at Columbia, has taught there since 1969, except for 1975–1976, when he was at the University of Pennsylvania. He came to New York from Yale University, after a year there as Teaching Fellow and Research Associate in the Department of Religious Studies and the Institute of Medieval Canon Law, a research center directed by Stephan Kuttner. Stephan Kuttner's influence and friendship characterize Robert Somerville's extraordinary scholarly work to this day. At Columbia University he has educated generations of undergraduate and graduate students in both the Department of History and in the Department of Religion, where he served as Chair as well as Acting Chair on several occasions. To no one's surprise, Robert Somerville also devoted much of his indefatigable energy to Butler Library as a member of many advisory committees, in particular those connected with ancient and medieval history.

Robert Somerville has established here as well as abroad his position as the preeminent expert on medieval church councils, law, and papal history. His scholarly honors are legion, including a fellowship in the Medieval Academy of America and of the Commission Internationale de Diplomatique. He is a member of the American Academy of Arts & Sciences and a corresponding member of the Monumenta Germaniae Historica in Munich as well as of the Bavarian Academy of Sciences (Bayerische Akademie der Wissenschaften) and has received numerous awards, including two John Simon Guggenheim Memorial Fellowships.

Between the councils of the ancient Church and the Council of Trent there stands a continuous history of church councils, in the East as well as in the West, called to deal with matters of discipline as well as doctrine. Many of these councils remained largely overlooked until Robert Somerville began to explore their canons and decrees which have left significant deposits in medieval canon law and in the history of the papacy. He discovered numerous papal and conciliar documents in manuscripts even from periods that had been thought to have been thoroughly mined. All of the councils which Somerville examined now look quite different; they reveal historic reality and significant doctrinal and political developments far more clearly. His primary focus was the eleventh and twelfth centuries, when papal councils constituted the chief means of government for a reformed Church and its incipient centralization. His 1972 publication examined and critically edited the decrees of the Council of Clermont (1095) celebrated by Pope Urban II. This was the famous council at which Urban proclaimed the Crusades to the Holy Land. After his *Pope Alexander III and the Council of Tours (1163)* had appeared in 1977, he turned to papal diplomatics and published, in 1982, *Scotia pontificia,* which contains calendars or editions of all letters known to have been sent by the pope before 1198 to addressees in Scotland. The book was awarded the Haskins Medal of the Medieval Academy of America, which is the most prestigious book prize among North American medievalists. In his next book he continued his study of late eleventh-century councils and papal letters with *Urban II, The Collectio Britannica, and the Council of Melfi (1089),* which was published in 1996 with the collaboration of Stephan Kuttner. Somerville's most recent work, *Pope Urban II's Council of Piacenza, March 1–7, 1095,* his analysis and edition of the decrees and *acta* of Urban's councils of Piacenza (1095) and of Rome (1099) has just come out. As the reference to the canonical collection *Britannica* in the title of his volume on the Council of Melfi highlights, canon law manuscripts, mainly from the eleventh and twelfth centuries, but certainly not excluding those of the humanists of the sixteenth and seventeenth centuries, constitute a major source of information for Robert Somerville's masterful investigations and reconstructions of councils. As he once confided, he ideally wanted to examine every twelfth-century manuscript still extant in European libraries, always on the hunt for texts that would illuminate the ecclesiastical and political history of this period. The study of medieval canon law is a discipline that calls for a high level of competence in several subjects: history, philology, theology, jurisprudence. As a result, it is also a discipline that most medievalists now neglect, but they do so at their peril. Thanks to Robert Somerville's researches, the mass of often unpublished canon law manuscripts can now no longer be overlooked as part and parcel of medieval history. The impact of his work is profound.

We would like to thank the Catholic University of America Press and in particular its director, Dr. Trevor Lipscombe, for accepting the book as well as especially his predecessor, Professor David McGonagle, who guided the submission, Theresa B. Walker, the responsible editor at the Press, and Susan Needham, the very helpful copy editor. Last but not least, we are much indebted to Beatrice Terrien for enthusiastic support and advice; and to Professors Walter Goffart, University of Toronto (emeritus), and John Wei, Grinnell College, for their assistance with translation and copy-editing. We are grateful to Alexa Selph for compiling the general index. Finally, we would like to thank one another for a happy collaboration.

URB, AW & PL

Introduction

The essays published in this volume in honor of Robert Somerville reflect the admiration, gratitude, and friendship of his former students and of scholars some of whom have known him since his days as a graduate student in the manuscript room of the Biblioteca Apostolica Vaticana. They mirror Somerville's influence and his eminent status in the fields of medieval canon law, theology, and political history, not only in connection with the eleventh and twelfth centuries, but also later centuries, when the rediscovery of Roman law had led to the sophisticated developments of the *ius commune* and its practical application among the jurists *utriusque iuris*. The essays dedicated to him fall thematically into three sections, corresponding to areas of Robert Somerville's own interests and research. Under the broad heading 'Canon Law' papers address issues relating to the compilation and transmission primarily of pre-Gratian canonical collections. Under this title, Greta Austin continues the analysis begun by Somerville and Martin Brett of the links between the Ivonian *Panormia* and the collection—or, as she shows, collections—in MS Paris, Bibliothèque de l'Arsenal 713, suggesting that this codex might contain a combination of what originally were two distinct canonical compilations. Austin based her conclusions on textual links to either Ivo's *Decretum* or his *Panormia*. Uta-Renate Blumenthal focuses on Roman legal texts in the *Caesaraugustana*, a collection from Catalonia or southern France, that depends on Anselm of Lucca as well as on Ivo of Chartres and once again on the Arsenal manuscript, but also uses new Roman sources such as Justinian's *Digest*. Kathleen G. Cushing closely examines the broader relationship between penitentials and the treatment of penance in canon law collections in Italy on the basis of MS Padua, Biblioteca del seminario vescovile 529, a manuscript of the *Liber Decretorum* of Burchard of Worms. The two extant manuscripts of the *Collectio Burdegalensis* from the late 1070s and originating in southwestern France are compared and analyzed by Herbert Schneider, who concludes that they must preserve different stages of an abbreviation of the work of Burchard of Worms with a strong pro-Gregorian tendency. It is difficult to exaggerate the influence of Burchard's work, a fact that shows very clearly how wrong it would be to separate the quarrel over investitures between Pope Gregory VII and Emperor Henry IV from the preceding ecclesiastical reforms, even if we cannot always pinpoint direct links. The contribution of Franck Roumy among the essays in the first section is the most obvious—but certainly not the only—example of international collaboration in the circle of Robert Somerville. The French scholar analyzes the *Collectio Sinemuriensis* in MS New York, Columbia University, Western MS 82 (s. XII in), a manuscript discovered by Franck Roumy at an auction at the Hôtel Drouot in Paris a few years ago, and thanks to his contacts with Somerville, eventually acquired by Columbia University. Roger E. Reynolds directs attention to the astonishingly wide influence of eastern patristic fathers on south Italian collections, presenting detailed lists supplementing the rich sources made available in Fowler-Magerl's *Clavis canonum*. A century after the intense canonistic activities of the eleventh- and early twelfth-century Church reform, jurists had largely replaced theologians in the field of law, as Bruce C. Brasington shows with his edition of a twelfth-century '*Summula*' on anathema and excommunication, inc.: *Differentia est*. The practical side of canon law and its elaboration and use in the court system come to the fore in several essays under the same heading. Anna Trumbore Jones discusses the 'Power of an Absent Pope: Privileges, Forgery and Papal Authority in Aquitaine, 877–1050' showing the seemingly undiminished authority of the papacy even in the tenth century. Peter Landau presents evidence for the early civil procedure in the courts by analyzing 'Treatises in Durham during the Twelfth Century.'

The brief second section of this collection of essays contains under the general heading 'Religion' two papers on the Eucharistic controversies, going back to the Carolingian period and reinvigorated in northern France and across the Channel in England in the eleventh and twelfth centuries. Charles R. Shrader presents a critical bibliography and detailed description of all the surviving manuscripts of the Eucharistic Treatises of Heriger of Lobbes (Laubach). Martin Brett edits Ernulf of Canterbury's *De corpore et sanguine Domini*. Both learned authors, Heriger in the tenth and Ernulf in the eleventh and early twelfth century, defended the realist understanding of Christ's presence in the sacrament unlike Berengar of Tours, who has been studied by Robert Somerville.

The third and last section of essays focuses on politics, once again in conjunction with the evolution and application of canon law by individual institutions such as monasteries and bishoprics, ecclesiastical and secular courts, universities, propagandists, and last not least the papacy. Alison I. Beach analyzes the political interplay between reformed monasteries and bishoprics in the eleventh and twelfth centuries based on the Chronicle of Petershausen. Detlev Jasper edits polemical writings defending Pope Gregory VII's deposition and excommunication of 1076 by means of a compilation of assumed or at least distorted historical precedents. Edward Peters shows how Gervase of Tilbury relied on canon law more than a hundred years later to admonish the excommunicated and therefore deposed Emperor Otto IV. The contribution of Giles Constable, 'Charter Evidence for Pope Urban II's Preaching of the First Crusade,' uses charters from the 1090s referring to Urban's presence at Clermont (November 1095) in order to balance the less objective narrative accounts of this event that were mostly written in the early twelfth century. His significant conclusion is that the charters 'support the view that the goals of going to Jerusalem and helping the Christians in the east were linked from the beginning to the crusade.' The use of Roman law by the papacy under Pope Innocent II and the contradictory prohibition of the study of Roman law at several of the councils of Innocent—as highlighted in some of Somerville's studies—is the focus of the essay of Kenneth Pennington. A comparison between the use and enforceability of diocesan statutes in England and France from 1200 to 1500 is the wide-ranging topic addressed by Charles Donahue Jr. It is hard to miss the nearly contemporary ring of the paper of James A. Brundage, learnedly and amusingly describing and analyzing the competition between the faculties of theology and of canon law at thirteenth-century universities. The same could be said of the essay by Elizabeth Makowski, describing the English echo to the 1298 decree of Pope Boniface VIII *Periculoso* that prescribed strict enclosure for nuns of every order and throughout Europe.

Abbreviations

Abh. Akad.	*Abhandlungen der ... preussischen, bayerischen* etc. *Akademie der Wissenschaften, philosophisch-historische Klasse*
AHC	*Annuarium Historiae Conciliorum*
AHP	*Archivum Historiae Pontificum*
AKKR	*Archiv für katholisches Kirchenrecht*
BAV	Biblioteca Apostolica Vaticana
BD	Burchard of Worms, *Decretum;* see LD
Berlin SBPK	Berlin, Staatsbibliothek Stiftung Preussischer Kulturbesitz
BIMAE	*Bibliotheca iuridica medii aevi*
BMCL	*Bulletin for Medieval Canon Law n.s.*
BN	Bibliothèque Nationale Paris
C	*Causa,* see *Decretum* (subdivision of part two)
CA	*Collectio Caesaraugustana*
Can. Coll.	Lotte Kéry, *Canonical Collections of the Early Middle Ages (ca. 400–1140): A Bibliographical Guide to the Manuscripts and Literature* (Washington D.C. 1999)
CB	*Collectio Britannica*
CC	see CCL
CCCM	*Corpus Christianorum, Continuatio mediaevalis*
CCL	*Corpus Christianorum, Series latina*
CP	*Chronik des Klosters Petershausen*
CIC	*Corpus iuris civilis,* ed. T. Mommsen, P. Krüger, R. Schöll, and W. Kroll (3 vols.; Berlin 1872–1895)
Fowler-Magerl, *Clavis*	Linda Fowler-Magerl, *Clavis Canonum: Selected Canon Law Collections before 1140* (Hannover 2005)
Cod.	*Codex,* see CIC (part three)

1 Comp., 2 Comp.,…5 Comp.	*Compilatio prima (-quinta)*, ed. E. Friedberg, *Quinque Compilationes antiquae* (Leipzig 1882)
CSEL	*Corpus scriptorum ecclesiasticorum latinorum*
D	*Distinctio*, see *Decretum* (subdivision of part one, three)
DA	*Deutsches Archiv zur Erforschung des Mittelalters*
Decretum	*Decretum Gratiani*, ed. E. Friedberg, *Corpus iuris canonici* 1 (Leipzig 1879)
Dig.	*Digesta*, see CIC (part two)
DPS	*Diversorum patrum sententie sive Collectio LXXIV titulorum = Collection in 74 Titles*
DThC	*Dictionnaire de théologie catholique*
GC	Gallia Christiana
HJb	*Historisches Jahrbuch*
HLF	*Histoire littéraire de la France*
ID	Ivo of Chartres, *Decretum*
Institutes	CIC (part one)
IP	Ivo of Chartres, *Panormia*
JEH	*Journal of Ecclesiastical History*
JK, JE, JL	Jaffé, *Regesta pontificum romanorum*…ed. secundam curaverunt F. Kaltenbrunner (JK), P. Ewald (JE), S. Loewenfeld (JL)
JMH	*Journal of Medieval History*
LD	Burchard of Worms, *Liber decretorum;* see BD
Lex.MA	*Lexikon des Mittelalters* (9 vols.; Stuttgart/Weimar 1977–1999)
Mansi	J. D. Mansi, ed., *Sacrorum conciliorum nova et amplissima collectio*…(Florence and Venice 1759–1798)
MC	Montecassino, Archivio della Badia
MGH	Monumenta Germaniae historica
—Capit.	Capitularia
—Epp.	Epistolae (in Quart)
—Ldl	Libelli de lite imperatorum et pontificum
—SS	Scriptores
—SS rer. Germ.	Scriptores rerum Germanicarum in usum scholarum

MIC	*Monumenta iuris canonici*
NA	*Neues Archiv der Gesellschaft für ältere deutsche Geschichtsforschung*
Nachrichten	*Nachrichten der ... Akademie ...* (identified by city)
ÖAKR	*Österreichisches Archiv für Kirchenrecht*
Pflugk-Harttung	J. von Pflugk-Harttung, *Acta pontificum Romanorum inedita* (3 vols.; Tübingen/Stuttgart 1881–1886)
PL	*Patrologia Latina*, ed. J.-P. Migne (Paris 1844–1855, 1862–1865)
Proceedings	*Proceedings of the Second (Third ... etc.) International Congress of Medieval Canon Law* identified by place, ed. MIC
QF	*Quellen und Forschungen aus italienischen Archiven und Bibliotheken*
RDC	*Revue de droit canonique*
RHD	*Revue historique de droit français et étranger* (4e série unless otherwise indicated)
RHE	*Revue d'histoire ecclésiastique*
RIDC	*Rivista internazionale del diritto comune*
RQ	*Römische Quartalschrift für christliche Altertumskunde und für Kirchengeschichte*
RSCI	*Rivista di storia della Chiesa in Italia*
Sb.	*Sitzungberichte der ... Akademie ...* (identified by city)
SG	*Studia Gratiana*
TRHS	*Transactions of the Royal Historical Society*
TUI	*Tractatus universi iuris*, ed. G. Ziletti (18 vols.; Venice 1583–1586)
Vall.	Bibliotheca Vallicelliana, Rome
X	*Liber Extra (Decretales Gregorii IX)*, ed. E. Friedberg, *Corpus Iuris canonici* 2 (Leipzig 1881, part 1)
ZRG Kan. Abt.	*Zeitschrift der Savigny-Stiftung für Rechtsgeschichte, Kanonistische Abteilung*
ZRG Rom. Abt.	*Zeitschrift der Savigny-Stiftung für Rechtsgeschichte, Romanistische Abteilung*

PART ONE ⇷ CANON LAW

GRETA AUSTIN

1 Were There Two Arsenal Collections?

Arsenal 713B and the Ivonian *Panormia*

The so-called Arsenal Collection played an important role in providing canons to at least three late eleventh- and early twelfth-century collections: the *Decretum* and the *Panormia* attributed to Ivo, bishop of Chartres (d. 1115), and the *Collectio Caesaraugustana*. The Arsenal Collection is preserved only in one manuscript, that of Paris, Bibliothèque de l'Arsenal MS 713. It appears in the second part of the composite manuscript, from folios 117 to 192, which Somerville dubbed '713B.'[1] To describe this set of materials as a 'collection' almost seems like a misnomer, at least upon first glance. It consists of many canons written in a small hand, without any immediately transparent organizing principle, and with few line breaks or spaces.

Although early modern editors knew about Arsenal 713B, only in the last twenty years have scholars studied the manuscript seriously. Robert Somerville and Martin Brett brought to light the significance of Arsenal 713B. Somerville has mined Arsenal 713B for the texts and information it provides about the eleventh-century reform movements and the reforming popes, particularly Pope Urban II. When Somerville investigated Pope Urban II's letters as preserved in the *Collectio Britannica*,[2] he concluded

I thank Robert Somerville, who first introduced me to Arsenal 713B and who provided invaluable guidance in explaining it to me. I am also grateful to Martin Brett, who commented on a version of this article, and who generously loaned me his extensive draft collations and a copy of his annotated copy of Arsenal 713B. Thanks are also due to Christof Rolker, for discussing Arsenal II and this article and for generously making available an advance copy of chapters of his book, *Canon Law and the Letters of Ivo of Chartres* (Cambridge, 2010). The errors that remain are solely my own.

1. For what is known of the manuscript's history, see Robert Somerville, with the collaboration of Stephan Kuttner, *Pope Urban II, the Collectio Britannica, and the Council of Melfi* (1089) (Oxford, 1996) 16.

2. In what follows, the *Collectio Britannica* will be abbreviated as CB, Arsenal 713B as LP,

that 'the compiler of MS 713B made extensive use of a collection very similar to CB, but which contained fuller inscriptions and better texts than in the surviving version of that book.'[3]

Part of the collection copied in Arsenal 713B was, in its original form, probably made as a preliminary step to making the Ivonian *Decretum*.[4] Martin Brett found that Arsenal 713B contains long rows of canons which also occur in the Ivonian *Decretum*—canons which were not taken from Burchard's collection by the same name. Brett demonstrated that these rows of canons in Arsenal were probably not copied from the *Decretum*. Rather, these sequences comprise a preliminary working collection which Ivo utilized in making the *Decretum*. As Brett writes, Arsenal 713B probably represents 'in part a moment in the compilation of the *Decretum*.... It must preserve almost the last stage before a complete *Decretum* was copied out.'[5] At the same time, Arsenal 713B itself does not represent that 'last stage,' but was itself a later copy.[6] Arsenal 713B thus does not preserve exactly what Ivo used.

Furthermore, some earlier form of Arsenal 713B contributed canons to the Ivonian *Panormia*. The *Panormia* editors dramatically cut down the number of canons in the Ivonian *Decretum*, and then added approximately 130 more canons.[7] The *Collection in Four Books* provided about 40 of these 130.[8] Brett identified Arsenal as the source of another 57 canons which were new to the *Panormia*.[9] Furthermore, these *Panormia* canons occur in particular sections in Arsenal, sections which do not have 'sequences shared with the *Decretum*.'[10] These canons were already 'sorted thoroughly by topic' in these sections, which appear to be part of 'the preparation for a larger enterprise.'[11] Brett's discussion can be read as suggesting that the sections of Arsenal which contributed to the *Panormia* were compiled sep-

Burchard's *Decretum* as BD, Ivo's *Decretum* as ID, and the Ivonian *Panormia* as IP. For the texts of ID, the working edition made by Martin Brett has been consulted, and for the texts of IP, the working edition of Brett and Bruce Brasington has been checked; both are available on-line at http://project.knowledgeforge.net/ivo/ [last accessed November 15, 2011].

3. On the use of the *Collectio Britannica*, see in particular Robert Somerville, 'Papal Excerpts in Arsenal MS 713B: Alexander II and Urban II,' in *Proceedings Munich 1992*, 169–84, especially at 173. On the *Britannica*, see now Christof Rolker, 'History and Canon Law in the *Collectio Britannica*: A New Date for London, BL Add. 8873,' in *Bishops, Texts and the Use of Canon Law around 1100: Essays in Honour of Martin Brett*, ed. Bruce Brasington and Kathleen Cushing (Aldershot 2008), 141–52.

4. Martin Brett, 'The Sources and Influence of Arsenal MS 713,' *Proceedings Munich 1992*, 149–67. In this paragraph and the next, parenthetical citations to page numbers are to this article.

5. Brett, 'Sources and Influence,' 155.

6. Ibid.

7. Ibid,157.

8. Ibid.

9. Ibid.

10. Ibid., 156.

11. Ibid., 157.

arately from the long sections which contributed to the Ivonian *Decretum*.

Following Brett's lead, Christof Rolker distinguished between the *Decretum* sections in the Arsenal manuscript and the *Panormia* ones as 'Arsenal I' and 'Arsenal II' respectively. Rolker suggests that 'the second Arsenal collection is presently only known from blocks of texts interpolated among the preparatory collection of the *Decretum* in the Arsenal 713 manuscript.'[12] Arsenal II may have been a separate collection from 'Arsenal I,' although eventually both were copied together into the Arsenal 713B manuscript.

About fifteen years ago, Professor Somerville asked the author to investigate further the relationship between the Ivonian *Panormia* and Arsenal 713B. This article begins this project by building on Rolker and Brett's work. Here I examine the sections of the Arsenal manuscript in which the *Panormia* canons occur. A striking number of the Urban II extracts analyzed by Somerville in *Pope Urban II, the Collectio Britannica and the Council of Melfi (1089)* occur in these sections of Arsenal.[13] It is appropriate, in a volume in honor of Professor Somerville, to consider the *Panormia* sections of Arsenal, since they play an important role in transmitting texts of eleventh-century reforming popes. This article, by identifying the particular sections in which *Panormia* canons are clustered in Arsenal 713B and studying their contents, asks whether these sections provide evidence for a separate, later Arsenal II collection. Is the so-called "Arsenal Collection" actually two separate collections, Arsenal I and Arsenal II, which were then mixed up and copied together into Arsenal 713B?

The Panormia Canons in Arsenal 713B

Following Brett, Rolker proposes that some sections of 713B may represent (in a later form) a second, independent collection, 'Arsenal II.' The so-called Arsenal Collection as preserved in the Arsenal 713B manuscript would consist of two separate collections which had been combined: Arsenal I, interspersed with sections of Arsenal II. Rolker did not identify these sections. Upon investigating Arsenal 713B, it becomes clear that nearly all of the canons that are shared uniquely with the *Panormia* appear in five distinct sections of Arsenal 713B. These sections represent blocks of material with very few or no canons in common with ID.[14] Many canons

12. Rolker, *Canon Law and the Letters of Ivo of Chartres* 124.

13. See Somerville, *Pope Urban II*, appendix I, 299–300.

14. If there are ID canons, there are no more than three canons in these sections. Furthermore, some sections in Arsenal 713 which lack ID canons did not provide canons to IP, such as the stretch of canons at LP fol. 158r–v.

in these sections also occur in the *Collectio Britannica*.[15] Some of these sections follow blank folios or begin new quires. In almost all cases, they occur between longer blocks of ID material.

fol. 125r (LP 142–150)[16]*: 9 canons, with 1 IP canon*
—IP 3.163 in this section
fol. 131r–135v (*LP 253–334*)[17]*: 82 canons, with 9 IP canons*[18]
—IP 3.52–54, 3.84–89 in this section (not in sequential order)
fol. 136v/137r–138v (*LP 356–388*)[19]*: 33 canons, with 10 IP canons*
—IP 2.134–135, 3.154–55, 3.166, 5.110–11, 8.3, 8.77–78 in this section (not in sequential order)
fol. 139v–140r (*LP 407–419*)[20]*: 13 canons, with 1 IP canon*
—IP 3.3 in this section
fol. 149rv–152r (*LP 0653–731*)[21]*: 87 canons, with 31 unique to IP*
—IP 3.90–96, 97–99, 101–15, 122, 133–45 in this section (not in sequential order), although eight of these have parallels in ID.[22]

15. Commenting on these sections, Brett notes 'the sources are often those used for the *Decretum;* most obviously a source very close indeed to the *Collectio Britannica* as it survives in the unique manuscript, and partially in the *Decretum,* has been excerpted on a considerable scale. Every section of the collection is represented, though the *Varia,* Gelasius, Pelagius, Alexander II and Urban II have been exploited at considerable length, and John VIII, Stephen V and Leo IV very modestly. The texts are sometimes better than those of the defective *Britannica* manuscript ...' Brett, 'Sources and Influence' 156.

16. Folios 123v and 124r–v are blank. A series from ID book 16 begins at the bottom of fol. 125r, after the Arsenal II canons. The scribe used a lighter brown ink on fol. 125r than that on fol. 121–123r. Furthermore, this section begins a new quire (quire 1 is fol. 117–124, quire 2 is fol. 125–130). I thank Dr. Patricia Stirnemann of the Institut de recherche et d'histoire des texts for her analysis of the Arsenal manuscript in February 1998. The comments on the quire structure of the manuscript reflect my notes from that meeting.

17. This section begins a new quire (131–138), and the ink is darker than on the previous folios (fol. 130r). The previous quire (125–130) ends with half of fol. 130r blank and all of fol. 130v blank. Canons from ID book 4 begin near the bottom of fol. 135v, and, according to Dr. Stirnemann, there is a change in the hand of the scribe here.

18. This section and the next one may well be one long Arsenal II section. See n. 19 *infra.*

19. Canons from ID book 4 (4.71) begin on the bottom third of fol. 135v and continue to ID 4.83 on the bottom of fol. 136r. There is non-ID material, along with IP canons at the top of fol. 137r, followed by ID 4.84–85–86, and then some canons not from ID 4. A canon shared with the *Britannica* breaks off midway on fol. 138v, followed by a number of blank lines. Then another *Britannica* canon appears near the bottom of the page. On fol. 139r the ID book 4 canons resume.

20. This section does not correspond to a new quire. It begins after a series of ID book 4 canons break off (ID 4.87–104, fol. 139r). A row of ID book 5 canons begins without indication of a change (such as a line break, paragraph break or large initial) midway on fol. 140r.

21. This section occurs in the middle of a quire (fol. 146–53). It begins after a series of canons from ID book 14, three lines from the bottom of the page (fol. 149r). There is nothing to indicate a new section. It clearly ends when canons from ID book 8 begins near the bottom of fol. 152v.

22. IP 3.91, 3.94, 3.106, 3.108, 3.112, 3.133, 3.143, 3.145. See Brett, 'Creeping up on the *Panormia*'

That Arsenal II could have been scattered among Arsenal I is entirely possible. As Brett points out, Arsenal 713B appears to have been copied from a set of loose pages and/or quires which had became disordered.[23] Canons on very different topics and issues sometimes appear close together in Arsenal 713B. For instance, canons shared with Ivo's *Decretum* books 5, 4, and 14 are found together in Arsenal 713B at fol. 139v–146r. The material which contributed to Arsenal I is closely related to that which contributed to Arsenal II—especially the material shared with the extant copy of the *Britannica*. It is possible that the distinction between Arsenal I and Arsenal II could have been lost, both because the collections drew upon very similar sources and also because they were probably copied onto loose quires.[24]

In addition to these five 'Arsenal II' sections, described above, there are four individual canons otherwise unique to *Panormia* which occur in Arsenal in the middle of sequences of Ivonian *Decretum* canons. If Arsenal II existed, one might not expect to find these canons shared with the *Panormia* in the middle of *Decretum* sections of Arsenal 713B. Brett, however, has provided an elegant solution: that at least two of these canons attest to an earlier, and fuller, version of an Ivonian *Decretum* than any extant manuscript of that collection today.[25] In other words, these canons originally appeared in a *Decretum*, and the *Panormia* compiler took them from the sequence in the *Decretum*, rather than from Arsenal II. This explanation can

in *Grundlagen des Rechts: Festschrift für Peter Landau zum 65. Geburtstag*, ed. Richard Helmholz, Paul Mikat, and Michael Stolleis (Paderborn 2000) 237–39. Furthermore, there are three other canons in this Arsenal section with parallels in IP, but probably all three in IP were derived from ID rather than from Arsenal:

a. IP 5.9 has a parallel in LP 706, f. 151r, but see also ID 6.231] BD 2.186; *Ars.* differs from IP and ID: quolibet sacerdote ID, IP] quilibet sacerdos *Ars.*; accusato ID, IP] accusatus *Ars.*; illato veritatem dicant ID, IP] aprobent illato veritatem *Ars.*

b. IP 4.97 has a parallel at LP 708, fol. 151r, but see also ID 6.276] BD 2.202; *Ars.* lacks the opening Placuit ut which appears in ID and IP (although Qa, the *Panormia* which appears as the first part of Arsenal 713, also lacks this phrase); *Ars.* has ab illo requirantur where ID/IP have requirantur ab illo; and *Ars.* has excommunicationem for accusationem.

c. IP 6.95–96 have a parallel at LP 735, fol. 152r–v, but see ID 8.303 (ID 8.302 also occurs in Arsenal at fol. 152r).

23. See Brett, 'Sources and Influence' 154, who discusses the possibility, for the ID series in Arsenal I, of 'separate sheets (or quires)' being used to make a pre-sorted collection of canons to be added to Burchard's *Decretum*. Brett suggests that 'some of these loose sheets survived long enough to be copied into the Arsenal manuscript.'

24. Perhaps the Arsenal 713 copyists occasionally tried to arrange some of the material topically. For instance, the section which would seem to be part of Arsenal II on fol. 125r discusses the unfree, and the ID section which follows on 125v continues with related issues about the unfree and about manumission. This may, however, simply be a coincidence.

25. On the use of the *Collectio Britannica*, see Robert Somerville, 'Papal Excerpts' 173 and *Pope Urban II* 18–21.

be extended to all four canons, all of which interrupt sequences of *Decretum* canons. It seems likely that the *Panormia* compilers would have taken these individual canons from a fuller *Decretum*, and not from Arsenal II.[26]

Why Might There Be Some Ivonian *Decretum* Canons in Arsenal II?

What is harder to explain is the presence of Ivonian *Decretum* material in Arsenal II. The hypothesis here is that Arsenal I was made as a preparatory step for the *Decretum*, and that Arsenal II was created as a separate collection. One would expect that Arsenal II would generally lack *Decretum* canons. Yet Arsenal II *does* include a handful of canons which also occur in Ivo's *Decretum*. It is thus important to look at the *Decretum* canons in these sections, in order to understand whether these work against the argument for Arsenal II.

First of all, a number of *Decretum* canons can be explained, at the very beginning and ends of these sections, as 'transitional' texts, and in fact there are some of these.[27] Identifying where Arsenal II might begin and end involves some guesswork, and possibly the sections of text bleed over into each other, especially since the originals of these canons in Arsenal 713B were written on loose quires, which could have 'contaminated' each other.

Second, Arsenal II is distanced from Arsenal I, inasmuch as some of

26. There are four IP canons in Arsenal which do not occur in sections with other IP canons. They are in Arsenal at fol. 122r, 129r, 169r, and 171r. Brett proposes, of the ones at 122r and 169r, that these were in a fuller version of ID: LP 114 (fol. 122r), IP 1.106, which interrupts a sequence of canons from ID book 1, and LP 1046 (fol. 169r), IP 7.18, which, along with a handful of other miscellaneous canons, is sandwiched in a series of canons from ID book 8. See Brett, 'Sources and Influence' 151, n. 9; see also idem, 'Creeping up on the *Panormia*' 225, n. 76 and 253, n. 130. The same explanation can be extended to the other two canons. IP 3.81 occurs in Arsenal at fol. 129r (LP 236), in a series of ID book 5 canons, and IP 3.57 occurs on fol. 171r (LP 1098), along with a number of ID book 9 canons. It seems very likely that these canons were *not* part of Arsenal II, but rather represent a longer, fuller version of ID to which both Arsenal and the *Panormia* witness.

27. On fol. 131r of Arsenal, ID 2.94partim–ID 2.95–ID 2.96 (not in BD) = LP 257–59 occur at the beginning of the Arsenal II section. These could be stray canons which did not originally belong to Arsenal II. Similarly, the series of canons from ID 5.33 and onwards bleeds into the end of the section, where 5.33 appears on 139v, followed by two non-ID canons on 140r, and then by the series of ID 5.34–39a. Finally, two ID book 8 canons appear at the very end of the section at fol. 152r–v (LP 734, cf. ID 8.302, and LP 735, cf. IP 6.95–96] ID 8.303). These canons, however, occur at the end of this section. It is possible that such sheets from two different sets of collections were overlaid on each other or even that there were cases of 'eye-skip' in copying the canons.

There is one final, difficult case. Three ID canons, ID 4.84–86, interrupt one "Arsenal II" section. These ID book 4 canons belong properly with the series of ID book 4 canons which surround this section. Here it seems possible that loose sheets with canons from ID book 4 were mixed in with Arsenal II texts, since ID book 4 appears in this section and the previous one.

Arsenal II's Ivonian *Decretum* canons are actually canons from Burchard's *Decretum* taken into Ivo's collection of the same name. As noted above, the Ivonian *Decretum* often contains long, nearly continuous sections of Burchard's *Decretum*, often sandwiched between chunks of material which occurs in Arsenal 713B.[28] As Brett demonstrates, Arsenal I systematically excludes the Burchardian material, and includes only the Ivonian *Decretum* sections which are not from Burchard. Yet Arsenal II incorporates a handful of Ivonian *Decretum* canons derived originally from Burchard.[29] The presence of these Burchardian/Ivonian *Decretum* canons thus might point to an Arsenal II compiler who worked at some distance from Arsenal I and who distinctly did *not* avoid Burchardian material. Furthermore, the presence of Burchard's *Decretum* canons suggests that Arsenal II may not have been made specifically for the *Panormia*. In the final version of the *Panormia*, the *Panormia* compilers worked to eliminate doublets in the Ivonian *Decretum* and to include the canon not from Burchard.[30]

Third, some Arsenal canons with parallels in the *Decretum* seem to have come from sources other than the Decretum, because the Arsenal II canons have different readings than the Decretum. Sometimes the *Decretum* canon is longer than the text in Arsenal II (although all such conclusions should be reached with caution, given that Arsenal 713B is a later copy).[31] And sometimes the inscription in Arsenal II differs significantly

28. Thus, for instance, it is unclear whether IP 5.9 was taken from ID 6.231 (= BD 2.186), or from LP 706 (fol. 151r). Similarly, it is unclear whether IP 4.97 was taken from ID 6.276 (= BD 2.202) or LP 708, fol. 151r. As noted above, however, it seems more likely that IP came from ID rather than from Arsenal.

29. For instance, we see the following:
LP 145a (fol. 125r), cf. IP 3.46] ID 6.126] BD 2.25
LP 275 (fol. 132r), cf. ID 15.87] BD 19.74
LP 293 (fol. 133r), cf. IP 3.151] ID 6.150] BD 2.49
LP 409 (fol. 139v), cf. IP 2.91] ID 4.64] BD 3.220c, in which ID is longer than the Arsenal text
LP 682 (fol. 150r), cf. ID 6.234] BD 2.189

30. See Greta Austin, 'Editorial concerns in the Ivonian *Panormia*: The case of repetitious canons in book 8' ZRG KA 89 (2003) 82–106.

31. The canons in which the parallel canon in ID is longer are presented in Table 1.2.

IP	LP	Arsenal 713 fol.	ID
	256	131r	2.102 (ID is shorter than LP); 2.103 (ID is longer than LP)
	274	132r	6.50 (ID is longer than LP)
	294	133r	See 5.310 (ID is longer than LP)
	317	135r	16.172b (ID is longer than LP)
	318	135r	16.183mid (ID is longer than LP)
7.7mid	325	135r	See 8.43mid (ID and IP are longer than LP)
	711	151r	See 6.425b (ID is longer than LP)
	730	152r	See 6.382 (ID is longer than LP)

from that in Ivo's *Decretum*, although these may result simply from the fuller and sometimes better texts and inscriptions in Arsenal.[32] This suggests that Arsenal II took the canon independently from a different source and not from the Ivonian *Decretum* and/or Arsenal I.

Fourth, one might expect to find a few *Decretum* canons occasionally appearing in both Arsenal I and Arsenal II, because the Arsenal II compiler utilized the same sources as Arsenal I—above all, the *Collectio Britannica*. In fact, this is the case. Arsenal 713 contains some 'doublets': canons that appear in Arsenal I and again in Arsenal II. For instance, ID 1.304 appears twice in Arsenal—once in a block of ID book 1 canons (LP 141, at fol. 123r), and once in a non-ID section, at fol. 134r (LP 302). In fact, the existence of Arsenal II would help to explain such repetitions. A different compiler making Arsenal II would be more likely to reproduce canons already in Arsenal I, than if the same compiler created the so-called Arsenal Collection at one time.[33]

Thus, some Ivonian *Decretum* canons with parallels in Arsenal II can be explained as canons which were both taken from an earlier form of the *Collectio Britannica*. The Ivonian *Decretum* canons in Arsenal II often can be found in the extant *Britannica*.[34] What may well have happened is that

32. See, e.g., LP 289 (fol. 132v), and ID 8.292; not only do the inscriptions differ, but Arsenal is considerably longer. Similarly, LP 144 (fol. 125r) differs from ID 7.154, in text and inscription. ID has *cap.* 2, with the previous canon attributed *Constitutio quinta, cap. 1 Ex libro Constitutionum*, whereas Arsenal 713 has the attribution *Novellarum constitutio v* (note that *Clavis* omits *v*). There are also variants between texts. ID begins *Sin autem servitutem effugiens, veniat*, whereas Ars reads *Si servitutem effugiens veniens;* Arsenal 713 omits *figuram*, and reads *trahere* for ID's *retrahere*. ID 7.154 is Julian's *Epitome* 4.2. The text of the *Novellae*, however, differs significantly from Arsenal 713B; Arsenal probably was taken from the *Epitome*.

33. See also ID 1.304] IP 6.126, which appears twice in Arsenal, once as LP 141 in a sequence of ID book 1 canons (fol. 123r) and again in a section of non-ID canons (LP 302, fol. 134r); virtually the same is true for ID 1.136] IP 6.124, which occurs both in Arsenal in a long row of ID book 1 canons at fol. 119r-v (LP 80), and at fol. 134r (LP 303).

34. See, e.g.,

IP	LP	Ars. 713 fol.	ID	CB
	257a–b	131r	2.94part (mid)	Varia I C 10a–b (ii), fol. 92v [LO 5.10]
	258	131r	2.95	Bon 17, fol. 142r [LO 7.17]
	259	131r	2.96	Bon 7, fol. 138v [LO 7.7]
	265	131v	6.406	Urb II 38b, fol. 149v [LO 8.38b, first part]
3.51	283	132v	6.410	Urb II 47 (ii), fol. 152v [LO 8.52]
	308	134v	6.414	Varia I B 22, fol. 74rv [LO 4.22]
	317	135r	16.172b	Varia I A 13d, fol. 54v [LO 3.12d]
	318	135r	Cf. 16.183d	Varia I A 22c, fol. 56r [LO 3.21c]
3.164	376	137v–138r	6.353	Gel 15, fol. 12r [LO 1.15]
3.165*	378	138r	6.354*	Gel 17a, fol. 12v [LO 1.17]

* ID and IP are shorter than Ars. and CB.

the Arsenal II compiler went back to his version of a *Britannica* to find material and then copied some canons already in the Ivonian *Decretum*. This would not be surprising, inasmuch as the Ivonian *Decretum* is enormous, and the compiler might not have remembered every single canon in it. Among these canons which appear both in Arsenal II as well as in the Ivonian *Decretum* (and, through that collection, the *Panormia*) is the controversial canon attributed in Arsenal (LP 283, fol. 132v) to Urban II at the Council of Melfi, but attributed in ID 6.410 to *decretum Gregorii VII et Urbani II*, and attributed in many *Panormia* manuscripts (IP 3.51) to *decretis Gregorii VII et Urbani II*.[35] This canon appears in the middle of what would be called 'Arsenal II'—sections in Arsenal 713 which provided canons to IP. The text may have entered the *Decretum* book 6 directly from the *Britannica*, but it might have been copied again from the *Britannica* in the process of making Arsenal II.

Furthermore, those *Britannica* canons which are found in both ID and in the Arsenal II sections are generally ones which Arsenal I did not include. Many are canons from the Ivonian *Decretum* book 6, of which Arsenal I contains no long series of canons.

If all of the above types of Ivonian *Decretum* canons in Arsenal II are explained in this way, then there is only one Ivonian *Decretum* canon in the Arsenal II sections. This canon could easily have been included simply by coincidence.[36] In other words, if a later compiler made Arsenal II, it would not be remarkable for him to replicate some canons already in ID. What is remarkable is simply that he repeated so little.

Arsenal II

Some factors suggest that Arsenal II was not made directly for the *Panormia*.[37] The *Panormia* compiler demonstrated his familiarity with the Ivonian *Decretum* by avoiding doublets.[38] So the maker of the *Panormia* would presumably have noticed doublets in a preparatory collection like Arsenal I. Yet a different compiler might not have been as aware (or even have cared as much) about overlap with the Ivonian *Decretum*. Another factor distancing Arsenal II from Arsenal II is that Arsenal II occasionally included canons from Burchard's *Decretum*, whereas Arsenal I noticeably omits Burchardian material. Furthermore, many Arsenal II canons were

35. At least two IP manuscripts omit 'II.'

36. LP 379 (fol. 138r), IP 7.153, a Roman law text.

37. Personal communication from Christof Rolker, December 3, 2009.

38. Austin, 'Editorial concerns in the Ivonian *Panormia*.'

not incorporated into the *Panormia*, and this fact might also distance Arsenal II a step from the *Panormia* compilers.

The existence of a separate collection, Arsenal II, would explain better how the *Panormia* compilers could have selected new material from an apparently undifferentiated mass of material, if there were only ever one Arsenal Collection (of which Arsenal 713B is a later copy). It is difficult to imagine how the *Panormia* compiler could have navigated a collection that looked anything like the existing manuscript, and plucked out the material which was not already in the massive Ivonian *Decretum*. But, if the *Panormia* compiler had a separate collection with which to work, the task would have been much simpler.

There are still some mysteries surrounding Arsenal I and II. Why and how Arsenal I and II came to be copied together will need to be investigated further, as will the question of whether Arsenal II was available to Ivo in making the *Decretum*. The sections of Arsenal which do not contain *Panormia* or Ivonian *Decretum* canons still need to be studied in order to see whether they also might be parts of Arsenal II. These sections strongly resemble the Arsenal II sections, in that they also draw largely upon the *Britannica* and generally exclude Ivonian *Decretum* canons. On the other hand, perhaps these sections also were part of a fuller Ivonian *Decretum* which Arsenal preserves.

Another puzzling fact is that Arsenal I and Arsenal II are very closely related to each other. Both drew upon very similar sources, including the *Collectio Britannica*. Both contributed to collections which included Ivo's *Prologue* and which have been closely associated with Ivo. Perhaps these very similarities led them to be copied together. Arsenal I and II might have been copied together at a quite early date; the *Caesaraugustana* seems to have drawn upon both Arsenal I and Arsenal II.[39] Some factors suggest that Arsenal II was compiled later than Arsenal I; for instance, Arsenal II was utilized only by the *Panormia* and apparently not (as is demonstrated above) by Ivo in making the *Decretum*. Yet one fact suggests that Arsenal II might be contemporary with Ivo: there is one canon in Ivo's *Prologue* which occurs only in Arsenal II and then the *Panormia*.[40] This slender thread, however, is not enough to date the collection, particularly since Arsenal II might have derived the canon from the *Prologue*.

39. Brett, 'Sources and Influence' 163–64. There are parallels between the *Caesaraugustana* and Arsenal fol. 131v–33 (= ID 1.176–83), i.e., Arsenal I; but there are also parallels in Arsenal II at fol. 134r–v (e.g., *Caesaraugustana* 10.38–39, 10.50–51).

40. The text begins 'Felix tertius natione Romanus' and ends 'menses .v. dies .xxiii.' See Ivo of

Conclusion

It seems very possible the so-called Arsenal Collection began as two separate collections, Arsenal I and Arsenal II, which supplied canons independently to the Ivonian *Decretum* and to the *Panormia*. Arsenal I and II were probably written on loose leaves. These eventually were co-mingled and copied together, without distinct breaks between sections, into the extant Arsenal 713B manuscript.

There are still other directions for future study. At least one of the *Panormia* canons from Arsenal II is important for understanding the manuscript stemma of the *Panormia*. IP 8.3 (LP 383, fol. 138v) is omitted in many *Panormia* manuscripts, and its presence or absence, Brett writes, 'forms an invaluable diagnostic test.'[41] Perhaps this canon is a clue to unpacking Arsenal I and II further, since this Arsenal II canon does not occur in a number of *Panormia* manuscripts.

Furthermore, Arsenal 713B provides evidence for a fuller *Decretum* than any of the extant copies. Among the many issues which remain to be studied further is the nature of that longer *Decretum*, particularly the canons which are folded into blocks of Ivonian *Decretum* material and which may have been present in an earlier form of the *Decretum*, as discussed above. A text which Somerville has studied, JL 5383, occurs in a series of *Decretum* canons on Arsenal fol. 148v, in between ID 14.57 and 14.58. This suggests that JL 5383 might have occurred in a copy of the *Decretum* which has now been lost. If JL 5383 actually was present in the *Decretum* in the form in which it appears in Arsenal, this could have important implications for the dating of Ivo's *Prologue* and the much-debated question of the relationship between the *Prologue* and the Ivonian compilations.[42]

The Arsenal manuscript provides a fascinating window onto the process of making canon law collections. The so-called Arsenal Collection thus proves to be an even more complicated collection than it looks. The

---

Chartres, *Prologue*, in *Ways of Mercy: The Prologue of Ivo of Chartres: edition and analysis*, ed. Bruce Brasington (Münster 2004) 133.

The canon occurs in Arsenal 713 at fol. 132v (LP 282) and IP 3.52. I do not intend here to wade into the question of whether the *Prologus* was an independent treatise or whether it was composed for the Ivonian collections. As Rolker points out, it is unclear whether Arsenal II "was a common source for *Prologus* and *Panormia* or whether it depends on the *Prologus*": Rolker, *Canon Law and the Letters of Ivo of Chartres* 122 n. 200.

41. Brett, 'Creeping up on the *Panormia*' 216.

42. See Somerville, *Pope Urban II* 104–15, especially 109–10.

name 'Arsenal Collection' may be misleading, because it suggests one coherent collection of materials. The evidence suggests that the materials in Arsenal 713B probably were copied from what was originally two separate collections. To understand the materials in Arsenal 713B is, as Robert Somerville and Martin Brett first made clear, a vitally important project. Arsenal 713B allows us to see how canonical collections with crucial texts for the papal reform movements came into being in this seminal period.

UTA-RENATE BLUMENTHAL

2 The *Collectio Canonum Caesaraugustana* and Roman Legal Sources

In the light of the formidable, well-known difficulties in dealing with the oldest version of the *Caesaraugustana*, even a small step forward might assist further research.[1] This paper, therefore, will venture to examine the collection's interest in Roman law, law that had been invigorated a good generation earlier by the rediscovery of Justinian's *Digest*.[2] The *Collectio Britannica* (CB), studied recently and partially edited in such exemplary manner by Robert Somerville, is the chief and possibly the only extant witness for the earliest of scholarly efforts on the part of canonists to ap-

For help with access to the sources as microfilms or photocopies I am especially indebted to Linda Fowler-Magerl, Martin Bertram, Robert Somerville, and Jörg Müller. I am also most grateful to Martin Brett, who read a draft of this paper and generously provided comments. All errors are my own.

1. Paul Fournier, 'La collection canonique dite <<Caesaraugustana>>,' RHD 45 (1921) 53–79; repr. in *Mélanges de droit canonique*, ed. Theo Kölzer, vol. 2, 815–841; Fowler-Magerl, *Clavis* 239–42; Kéry, *Can. Coll.* 260–62; Linda Fowler-Magerl, 'The Version of the *Collectio Caesaraugustana* in Barcelona, Archivo de la Corona de Aragón, MS San Cugat 63,' in *Ritual, Text and Law: Studies in Medieval Canon Law and Liturgy Presented to Roger E. Reynolds*, ed. Kathleen G. Cushing and Richard F. Gyug (Aldershot and Burlington, VT 2004) 269–80; Martin Brett, 'The Sources and Influence of Paris, Bibliothèque de l'Arsenal MS 713,' *Proceedings Munich 1992*, 149–67, especially 160–67. Fowler-Magerl, *Clavis* 240, in a misprint refers to MS Salamanca 2664 instead of 2644. A similar error occurred in Kéry, *Can. Coll.* 261. I am very grateful to Carlos Larrainzar and Enrique de León, who checked the manuscript. See *Catálogo de manuscritos de la Biblioteca Universitaria de Salamanca II* (Salamanca 2002) 1060–61.

2. Max Conrat (Cohn), *Geschichte der Quellen und Literatur des Römischen Rechts* (Leipzig 1891; repr. Aalen 1963) 390–93; Carlo Guido Mor, 'I testi di diritto Giustinianeo nelle due redazioni della collezione canonica "Cesaraugustana",' *Studi in onore de Francesco Scaduto* 2 (Firenze 1936) 417–37. Conrat used manuscripts of the later recension for his remarks. Cf. Wolfgang P. Müller, 'The Recovery of Justinian's Digest in the Middle Ages', BMCL 20 (1990) 3–29, and the hypotheses of Charles M. Radding and Antonio Ciarelli, *The Corpus Iuris Civilis in the Middle Ages: Manuscripts and Transmission from the Sixth Century to the Juristic Revival* (Leiden/Boston 2007) 18–25, regarding the work of Conrat.

proach the *Digest* or Pandects in the eleventh century.[3] Ivo of Chartres extensively used the CB selections, but his great successor Gratian's attitude to Roman law in his *Decretum* is still debated.[4] The archetype of the earlier *Caesaraugustana*, however, was clearly in line with Ivo's work on which it depended heavily,[5] and reflects a practical and very positive attitude to the new Roman law, not to mention the 'old' Roman law that had been part of canonical collections at least since the eighth century. Over time it has become increasingly obvious that even before the period of the Bolognese glossators (c. 1125) scholars in southern France as well as in the region of the Pyrenees were intensely interested in the use of the rediscovered Roman law. Nevertheless, we know very little regarding the *Caesaraugustana* in this context, although it originated in the very same region as the *Exceptiones legum romanorum Petri.*[6] The *Exceptiones* contain excerpts from a later version of the Caesaraugustana—MS Paris BN lat. 3876 and its twin, MS Vatican BAV lat. 5715. These particular codices, therefore, attracted the attention of Max Conrat, who did not distinguish between the different recensions, as well as of Carlo Guido Mor, the editor of the *Exceptiones*, but they were hardly studied in their own right. They were merely of inter-

3. Paul Ewald, 'Die Papstbriefe der Brittischen Sammlung,' NA 5 (1879) 277–414 and 505–96; Max Conrat (Cohn), *Der Pandekten- und Institutionenauszug der Brittischen Dekretalensammlung: Quelle des Ivo* (Berlin 1887); for recent discussions see Robert Somerville (with the collaboration of Stephan Kuttner), *Pope Urban II, the Collectio Britannica and the Council of Melfi (1089)* (Oxford 1996) 8–172; Christof Rolker, 'History and Canon Law in the *Collectio Britannica*: A New Date for London, BL Add. 8873,' in *Bishops, Texts and the Use of Canon Law Around 1100: Essays in Honour of Martin Brett*, ed. Bruce C. Brasington and Kathleen G. Cushing (Aldershot and Burlington, VT 2008) 141–52; Antonia Fiori, 'La Collectio Britannica e la riemersione del Digesto,' RIDC 9 (1998) 81–121; Fowler-Magerl, *Clavis* 184–86; Kéry, *Can. Coll.* 237–38. See, however, Wolfgang Kaiser, 'Nachvergleichung von Novellen- und Codexzitaten in einer frühmittelalterlichen Sammlung mit Exzerpten aus dem Register Gregors d. Gr.,' ZRG Rom. Abt. 125 (2008) 603–644, especially p. 604 for earlier traces.

4. Anders Winroth, *The Making of Gratian's Decretum* (Cambridge 2000) 146–74, and idem, 'Recent Work on the Making of Gratian's *Decretum*,' BMCL 26 (2004–2006) 1–29; Carlos Larrainzar, 'El borrador de la "concordia" de Graziano: Sankt Gallen, Stiftsbibliothek MS 673,' *Ius ecclesiae: Rivista internazionale di diritto canonico* 9 (1999) 593–666; José M. Viejo-Ximénez, 'La ricezione del diritto romano nel diritto canonico,' *La cultura giuridico-canonica medioevale*, ed. Enrique de León and Nicolas Alvarez de la Asturias (Milan 2003) 157–203; Kenneth Pennington, 'The "Big Bang": Roman Law in the Early Twelfth-Century,' RIDC 18 (2007) 43–70.

5. Paul Fournier, 'Les collections canoniques attribuées à Yves de Chartres,' BEC 58 (1897) 416–26; idem, 'Caesaraugustana,' 822–23.

6. Fournier, '*Caesaraugustana*,' 72–73 and Mor, 'Testi' 421–22 as well as Carlo Guido Mor's edition of the *Exceptiones: Scritti giuridici preirneriani* (Milan 1938) 9. André Gouron, 'Sur la patrie et la datation du "Livre de Tubingue" et des "Exceptiones Petri",' RIDC 14 (2003) 15–39; Hermann Lange, *Römisches Recht im Mittelalter*, 1 (Frankfurt 1997) 387–95; Uta-Renate Blumenthal, 'A New Manuscript of the *Exceptiones legum Romanorum Petri*,' ZRG Kan. Abt. 96 (2010) 111–26.

est because some of their texts were included in the *Exceptiones Petri*.[7] As a matter of fact, one text even links the earliest extant manuscripts of the *Caesaraugustana* with the *Exceptiones*: CA 1.62 = Cod. 1.14.9; it is a unique passage not found in other collections:

Leges sanctissime, que constringunt omnium vitas, intelligi ab omnibus debent ut universi, prescripto eorum manifestius cognito, vel inhibita declinent, vel promissa sectentur. (CA 1.62, fol. 6ra)[8]

The same abbreviated *Codex* excerpt—abbreviated in the same manner but as far as we can tell probably farther removed from the original—shows up also as the first *capitulum* of the *Exceptiones* and, moreover, constitutes one of the few chapters not derived from the two sources of the *Exceptiones*, the *Liber Tubingensis* and the *Ashburnhamensis*.[9]

The passage from the *Codex* could well serve as the headline for the overall efforts in the south of France and northern Spain in the early twelfth century. The text quoted and its connection to both the *Exceptiones* and the *Caesaraugustana* seem to provide at first also an intriguing hint—that it might be possible to come closer to an actual date for both of these works. The *Exceptiones Petri* originated in the region of Die/Valence in southern France in the circle of the reformed canons of Saint-Ruf who, at the time of Pope Gregory VII, began to expand into Aragón and Catalonia. Paul Fournier suggested a date 'postérieur de peu d'années à 1110' for the *Caesaraugustana*.[10] It is possible that he was right, as so often he was.

7. Conrat, *Geschichte* 390–92; Mor, *Scritti* 9; Mor, 'Testi' 421–22. The texts derived from the *Caesaraugustana* of MS Paris BN lat. 3876 are: 5.53b; 5.60c; 5.60d; 10.1a; 10.1c; 10.62d; 15.a; 15.c; 15.d; 15.e; 15.f; 15.g; 15.h; 15.i; 15.l; 15.m. The numbers 15.a–15.m indicate texts inserted by a contemporary hand separately on a much smaller folio sewn into the manuscript.

8. The rubric reads: 'Quod sacre leges ab omnibus sciri debent; the inscription: Imperatores Val. et Marcio augusti ad Palladium prefecto pretorio.'—I used the chapter numbers and the abbreviation CA for MS Salamanca 2644 given by Linda Fowler-Magerl (*Clavis* 239–44) and collated texts with MS Paris BN lat. 3875. Her work was absolutely essential for this paper and was used with gratitude and admiration.—MS Paris BN lat. 3875 shares two variants with the original as well as with the *Exceptiones*: 'sacratissime' and 'permissa,' yet more evidence for the priority of the Parisian codex. See also the following note.

9. 'Leges sacratissime que constringunt omnium vitas, intelligi ab omnibus debent, ut universi, scripto earum manifestius precognito, vel inibita declinent vel permissa sectentur,' ed. Mor, *Scritti* 52 with the rubric *De admonitione super leges* and the inscription: *Imperatores Valerius* [!] *et Marcus A.A ad Palladium*. Cod. 1.14.9 reads: 'Impp. Valentinianus [!] et Marcianus AA. ad Palladium pp. Leges sacratissimae, quae constringunt omnium vitas, intellegi ab omnibus debent, ut universi praescripto earum manifestius cognito vel inhibita declinent vel permissa sectentur si quid vero in isdem legibus latum fortassis obscurius fuerit, oportet id imperatoria interpretatione patefieri duritiamque legum nostrae humanitati incongruam emendari.' It is noteworthy that the reference to imperial interpretation has been omitted.

10. 'Caesaraugustana,' 57–58 or 819–20.

At least as far as Roman legal texts of the oldest extant version of the *Caesaraugustana* are concerned, Fournier's inclination to assume an influence of the *Polycarpus*, dated 1104–13 or 1111–13, also is probably correct. In the sections analyzed more closely for this paper, the *Polycarpus* could in most instances be eliminated as a source, in favor of the canonical collection A of Anselm of Lucca. Still, in addition to the title of the first book, *De auctoritate et ratio*—it corresponds to the title of *Polycarpus* 1.27, as Hermann Hüffer noted long ago—a few other instances remain where the more sophisticated collection could well have been the source of canons in CA and thus influence the dating.[11] As for the *Exceptiones Petri*, they are not very helpful here, for their date is also still debated even if the work cannot be earlier than c. 1120–25. Thus we are once again left with the decree of Pope Paschal II (JL 6613) from the Council of Benevento held in October 1108 and the date of the *Polycarpus* as indicators; these suggest an approximate date of 1115 for the oldest version of the *Caesaraugustana*.[12] Martin Brett's significant discovery in the context of his studies of the manuscript Paris, Bibliothèque de l'Arsenal 713, that a copy of the Arsenal codex was not only used in the compilation of the *Decretum* and *Tripartita* attributed to Ivo of Chartres, but also was used directly by the anonymous author of the *Caesaraugustana*, adds yet another puzzle to the unknowns that surround the enigmatic collection.[13] He concluded that 'at present any date for the *Caesaraugustana* between 1108 and c. 1140 was possible.'[14] The Arsenal collection appears to predate both the *Decretum* and the *Panormia* attributed to Ivo,[15] but it is conceivable, according to Brett, that the *Caesaraugustana*

11. It is assumed here that the Coll. 3L depended on the *Polycarpus*. Giuseppe Motta's excellent edition leaves the question of such a dependence open (G. Motta, ed., *Collectio canonum trium librorum* [MIC series B, vol. 8, parts 1 and 2, 2005 and 2008] part 1, XXXVII–XL). Hermann Hüffer, *Beiträge zur Geschichte der Quellen des Kirchenrechts* (Münster 1862, repr. Aalen 1965) 81. It is probable that CA 9.57 depends on Pol. 4.35.31 (a central passage in CA was omitted by homoteleuton); CA 7.23 where Pol. 3.12.37 agrees with CA against Anselm A; possibly CA 10.3 depends on Pol. 6.4.71 and CA 10.10 on Pol. 6.4.70. Among parallel transmissions Ivo D underlies most likely also CA 10.12a, b, and c—Ivo D 8.20, 8.21, 8.22 and CA 10.23—Ivo D 8.1 and CA 10.24—Ivo D 8.44.—I have used *Polycarpus* in the edition at: http://www.mgh.de/polycarp; Fowler-Magerl, *Clavis* 229–32; Kéry, *Can. Coll.* 266–69.

12. Uta-Renate Blumenthal, *The Early Councils of Pope Paschal II 1100–1110* (Toronto 1978) 102–6; Linda Fowler-Magerl, 'Vier französische und spanische vorgratianische Kanonessammlungen', in *Aspekte europäischer Rechtsgeschichte: Festschrift für Helmut Coing zum 70. Geburtstag* (Ius commune, Sonderheft 17; Frankfurt 1982) 123–46, p. 145 indicated that JL 6613 is also found on fol. 84r in MS San Cugat 63. The text is also present in MS Paris BN lat. 4283 (Fowler-Magerl, *Clavis* 203–4).

13. Brett, 'Sources and Influence,' 149–67, especially 160–67. Ivo's texts have been consulted at: http://www.project.knowledgeforge.net/ivo/.

14. Brett, 'Arsenal,' 166–67.

15. Martin Brett commented regarding this complex issue. He currently thinks that the

could 'provide a *terminus ante quem* for the emergence of the Arsenal collection as we now have it.' The date he tentatively indicated for the completion of the *Panormia,* no later than 1115, and perhaps earlier,[16] would still allow for the *Caesaraugustana* to be dated c. 1115, given that the collection shares texts directly with MS Arsenal 713 as well as with Ivo's *Decretum* and the *Tripartita,* albeit not with the *Panormia.*[17]

The date of the *Caesaraugustana* is of interest primarily because of its approach to Roman law in the pre-Bolognese period. The most important sources for the collection as well as for its Roman legal texts have long been known. They are in the first place Ivo's *Decretum* (D), the *Collectio canonum* of Anselm of Lucca (Ans. Luc.) and the collection of Deusdedit. Fortunately, we can now add to them the collection in MS Paris, Bibl. de l'Arsenal 713, and probably a manuscript like MS Vatican, BAV, Vat. lat. 3830, albeit not this codex itself. Paul Fournier, Carlo Guido Mor, Eloy Tejero, and Martin Brett have published long series of texts illustrating the dependence of the *Caesaraugustana* on the *Decretum* attributed to Ivo, and, in the case of Brett's seminal article, also its dependence on the Arsenal manuscript.[18] In the context of Roman law only a few remarks regarding these collections can be added here. Unfortunately, they will highlight familiar analytical problems rather than provide in every instance the desired clarity. Given that the *Caesaraugustana* includes at the very least 80 canons from the Arsenal codex, it is surprising that examples of a direct derivation from either the *Decretum* or the Arsenal manuscript among secular legal texts are so rare. Rarer still are instances when it is possible to distinguish whether 'Ivo's' works or the Arsenal collection are closest to the text preserved in the two oldest extant manuscripts of the *Caesaraugustana* (MS Paris, BN lat. 3875 and MS Salamanca, BU 2644). One example of this problem is the inscription preceding CA 1.25a, *Institutionum*

Decretum excerpts in Arsenal 'represent a version more "primitive" than the extant one and that the parallels with the *Panormia* reflect the use of a collection earlier than the *Panormia*... but that the Arsenal manuscript itself could easily be later than either.'

16. Brett, 'Arsenal' 165.

17. Brett, 'Arsenal' 162. Detlev Jasper, *Das Papstwahldekret von 1059* (Sigmaringen 1986) 10–11 n. 38, pointed out that the form of the election decree of 1059 found in the late 'second' recension of the *Caesaraugustana* depended on the *Panormia,* but so do many of the texts in MS Paris, BN lat. 3876, as Martin Brett commented. The decree, albeit included in the Salamanca manuscript (CA 4.72), is not found in MS Paris, BN lat. 3875. Cf. n. 21 below.

18. Fournier, 'Collections,' 418–25 or in the reprint 599–606; Brett, 'Arsenal' 163–67. All Roman legal canons mentioned below as found in the *Decretum* are also included in the *Panormia* and in *Tripartita* B. Brett noted that both *Tripartita* A and B are among the sources of CA (p.163) but Trip. A was apparently not used for Roman legal texts; see also Mor, 'Testi' 436–37 for Ivo's *Decretum;* Fowler-Magerl, *Clavis* 192–93 for Arsenal 713 and pp. 193–202 for Ivo.

lib. 1 *tit.* 2, linking the text to Ivo, *Decretum* 16.184 rather than to its double, Ivo D 4.194 with the inscription *Constitutionum lib.* 1 *tit.* 1. The canon is found in MS Arsenal 713 on fol. 143v with the same wording as in Ivo D 16.184 = CA 1.25 a+b,[19] but with the explicit...*postea lege lata,* whereas the Salamanca manuscript of the *Caesaraugustana* and Ivo D 16.184 conclude with:...*postea lege data.*[20] So far, Ivo D 16.184 emerges as the likely source. The trouble is that the other early CA manuscript, Paris, BN lat. 3875 (fol. 4v), reads like Arsenal 713:...*postea lege lata,* as does Ivo D 4.194 and *Panormia* 2.160, where, however, the editor, Martin Brett and his collaborators, also indicate a few manuscripts with the final word:...*data!* Evidently, at this point of the editorial process the distinction between *data* and *lata* is not helpful as a means of source identification. All that can be said regarding CA 1.25 a+b, therefore, is that the text depends on either Ivo D 16.184 or Arsenal 713. Two excerpts from the *Codex* immediately following as CA 1.26a (Cod. 8.52.1) and CA 1.26b (Cod. 8.2.2) in the *Caesaraugustana* also do not help to find a definite answer. The texts of the canons are common to seven and, respectively, twelve other collections, as *Clavis* shows, but both the inscription for 1.26b (*tit.* 2) and its explicit (... *vincat aut legem*) indicate that only Ivo D 4.201 and 4.202 or Arsenal 713 (#537 and #538, fol. 144r) could have been the source for the two texts.[21] A single variant: *memento* instead of *momento* as in Cod. 8.2.2, does link the *Caesaraugustana* and Arsenal 713, but without further evidence it would be hasty to decide between the two candidates. It might be tempting as well as logical to think of Ivo's *Decretum,* used for the two preceding canons—and, as Fournier has shown, constituting 47 out of 64 canons of CA book 1—as a source for 1.26a and b as well, but two canons from the *Digest* following immediately: CA 1.27 (Dig. 1.18.12) and CA 1.28 (Dig. 1.3.37) are unique to the *Caesaraugustana* and without parallels in any other contemporary collection, Ivo included. They thus warn against the assumption that the anonymous author always relied on pre-existing canonical compilations. *Codex* 1.14.9—referred to earlier (CA 1.62)—underlines this fact, as do other unique texts throughout the collection.

It is noteworthy that no Roman legal texts in the *Caesaraugustana* are found after book 10 that is, in books 11 to 15, which underwent a series of

19. Fowler-Magerl, *Clavis,* divided the text into two sections. The web preliminary working edition of Ivo D shows no division.

20. I am most grateful to Robert Somerville for the loan of a microfilm of MS Arsenal 713.

21. The differences are slight, but they confirm Martin Brett's finding that MS Paris BN lat. 3875 is often closer to the original source than the Salamanca codex is; the latter has *consuetudinem longam* instead of *longam consuetudinem* like IV D 4.201 and the original.

revisions and recombinations. In books 2, 3, and 4 no canons from Roman law seem to be based on collections attributed to Ivo of Chartres. However, in book 5 of the *Caesaraugustana* with the title *De iudiciis ecclesiasticis*, Ivo's *Decretum* D 16.181a, b, c and e, appears to be the probable source for canons CA 5.90a, b, c and d. 'Ivo' in turn derived the sequence of *Digest* 22.5.6, 9, 16, 17, and 18 from the *Collectio Britannica* (3.19e, f, g); this confirms Conrat's generally accepted argument that some of the texts from Justinian's *Digest* found in CB arrived in the *Caesaraugustana* by way of Ivo's *Decretum*.[22] CA 5.90a (Dig. 22.5.6 and 4) with the inscription *Pandectarum libro xxi titulo ii* proves once again that MS London BL Add. 8873 is not the archetype of CB. All other transmissions of this canon share with Ivo the inscription *item* found in the London codex of CB. One other exception for this brief series in book 5 is remotely possible. The second version of the *Polycarpus* (5.1.61 MS Paris BN lat. 3882, fol. 90vb) carries the inscription *Digestorum 22 de testibus, Licinius Rufinus lib. 2 regularum*, corresponding to the text of the Mommsen/Krueger edition, and the rubric of the same text in *Caesaraugustana* 5.66b: *De testibus*, could perhaps suggest a relationship between the two collections, although the excerpt in CA 5.66b has been much abbreviated. As Fournier has shown the abbreviation of texts is rather typical for the *Caesaraugustana* and in this case cannot be used as indicator.[23] However, since the brief rubric is so close to the text of the canon and because of the late date of *Polycarpus* II, Ivo's *Decretum* 16.154 may be accepted as source for CA 5.66b with reasonable confidence. For the sake of completeness it should also be mentioned that CA book 10, examined in detail by Tejero, contains several Roman law citations that were derived from either Ivo D or Bibliothèque de l'Arsenal 713, but again the evidence is ambiguous and details will here be omitted. In addition, book 10 of CA also includes three original excerpts from the *Institutiones*.[24] On the whole, the Roman legal texts related to Ivo's *Decretum* or the Arsenal collection are found in the *Caesaraugustana* scattered among citations from ecclesiastical law, revealing a professional interest in secular, that is,

22. Conrat, *Geschichte* 390. The problematic history of Roman legal texts in CA is also evident in the work of Laborans. See Norbert Martin, '"Mare uitreum" (Neapel, Bibl. naz. MS XII A 27): Eine Quelle der 'Compilatio decretorum' des Kardinals Laborans,' BMCL n.s. 15 (1985) 51–59.

23. Fournier, 'Collections' 418 (599) for examples.

24. CA 10.14a–c—Ivo D 9.1a, 1c, 1d = Arsenal #836a, c, d, fol. 157v–158r; CA 10.91 shares the inscription with Ivo D 8.34 and Arsenal #885; CA 10.92—Ivo D 8.35 = Arsenal #886; CA 10.93—Ivo D 8.70 = Arsenal #919c.—Eloy Tejero, 'El matrimonio en la *Collectio Caesaraugustana*,' *Proceedings Cambridge* 1988, pp. 115–34. Unique excerpts from *Institutiones* I.10, 3, and 6 are CA 10.68a, b, and c.

Table 2.1

CA 7.18	Ans. Luc. 4.19	Cod. 1. 2, l. 22
CA 7.19a	Ans. Luc. 4.20a	Cod. 1. 3, l. 32
CA 7.19b	Ans. Luc. 4.20b	Cod. 1. 3, 6 and 7
CA 7.20	Ans. Luc. 4.21	Cod. 1. 2, l. 5
CA 7.21	Ans. Luc. 4.22	Cod. 1. 2, l. 21
CA 7.22	Ans. Luc. 4.23	Cod. 1. 3, l. 10
CA 7.23	Ans. Luc. 4.38	Cod. 1. 2, l. 23
CA 7.24	Ans. Luc. 4.53	Cod. 1. 2, l. 12

imperial, legislation and the support that this source could lend—or the challenges it could extend—to familiar canonical sources.

While the compiler thus created a mosaic of highlights as his use of Roman law could be described, he also did produce two noteworthy uninterrupted sequences of Roman law texts on the basis of canons in the *Collectio canonum* of Anselm of Lucca and from the *Novels* in the form of the *Epitome Iuliani*. Book 7 of the *Caesaraugustana, De sacrilegiis et de privilegiis ecclesiarum*, is dominated by a long series of Roman legal texts that are present in the same form and sequence in the canonical collection of Anselm of Lucca A.[25] Nonetheless, CA 7.81, 7.84, 7.87, and 7.88 may appear to be derived from Ivo D 3.184, 185, 187, and 188 respectively; but, as will be seen, this is an erroneous assumption. The collection *Polycarpus I* (Pol.) could be eliminated as a conceivable source, although in two instances (CA 7.22 and CA 7.23) parallel texts are transmitted there (Pol. 6.14.4 and Pol. 3.12.37). In the first case the elimination was possible because of a different inscription as well as a much shorter text in Pol., and in the second because it is most unlikely—albeit not impossible—that the compiler in the midst of his series of *Codex* excerpts from the *Collectio canonum* of Anselm would have switched to the *Polycarpus* (see Table 2.1).

In the final item it is a shared error in the inscription: *Imperatores Valerianus et Marcus augusti prefecto pretorio* as against *Valentinus et Marcianus* in other collections with the same text in agreement with the *Codex*, that indicates the continued reliance on Anselm (MS Vat. lat. 1363 fol. 87r) despite the larger break in Anselm's sequence. Paul Fournier, noting that 33

25. Fowler-Magerl, *Clavis* 139–48 and 227; Kéry, *Coll. Can.* 218–26. I have used a microfilm of MS Vatican, BAV Vat. lat. 1363. The parallel was first noted by Mor, 'Testi' 422.

chapters of the 103 chapters in book 7 of the *Caesaraugustana* were derived from Anselm, suggested at the same time that the compiler did not use 'la recension primitive' of Anselm's *Collectio canonum*, but rather the slightly later revision of the collection in MS Vatican, BAV Barb. lat. 535.[26] In the present context no significant variants from Anselm's text in recension A (MS Vat. lat. 1363 and Thaner's edition) and CA have emerged. It is striking to see in the Roman legal texts of the *Caesaraugustana* a division into two basic types of source groups. One consists of texts ultimately derived from the *Collectio Britannica* and transmitted in most cases through Ivo's *Decretum* as seen earlier, and the other group consists of excerpts from far earlier medieval compilations such as the *Lex romana canonice compta*, the *Excerpta Bobiensia* and the *Anselmo dedicata*. The latter are transmitted primarily by way of Anselm's collection. There is usually little overlap, in the sense of the two basic source types interacting with each other within a single book, if the seeming reliance on Ivo D 3.184, 185, 187, and 188 in book 7 of CA is disregarded for the moment. This may explain in part why the *Caesaraugustana* often appears so poorly organized and why there are duplications in the treatment of topics like penance. One is certainly led to conclude that more than one author or compiler was at work although the archetype of the collection has not been preserved.

In book 7 as well as 9 of the collection, an unusual collection of excerpts from the Justinian *Novels* in the form of the *Epitome Iuliani* must have been the source for the second sequential block of romanist texts to be noted in the *Caesaraugustana*, unless the *Epitome* itself was used. Fowler-Magerl's invaluable *Clavis* revealed a similar set of texts in an eleventh- and twelfth-century manuscript. The composite MS BAV Vat. lat. 3830, containing mostly excerpts from the *Decretum* of Burchard and from the *Collectio in V libris* from northern/central Italy, is dated mid-eleventh and twelfth century.[27] It is an intriguing but difficult manuscript. In the late seventeenth or early eighteenth century it was part of the 'biblioteca segreta' at Castello S. Angelo, but none of its several hands wrote in romanesca and there is no way to establish its original 'home.'[28] The first quire has been lost, quires

26. Fournier, 'Caesaraugustana' 824–25 (62–63). For a description of the manuscript see Fowler-Magerl, *Clavis* 157–58.

27. Gero Dolezalek in collaboration with Martin Bertram, *Vatican Library: Manuscripts of Canon and Roman Law: Continuation of the Catalogue published by Stephan Kuttner and Reinhard Elze in 1986 and 1987*. A preliminary printout of this volume can be consulted for MS Vat. lat. 3830 at http://www.abdn.ac.uk/~law379/CatalogueVatLat31374990; Fowler-Magerl, *Clavis* 98–99 with a description of the rearrangement of the original quires of the codex. The sequence given below is based on her analysis.

28. Paola Supino Martini, *Roma e l'area grafica romanesca* (Alessandria 1987) 315–16.

six and eight are incomplete, and the attribution of an *Epistola de simoniaca heresi* on fol. 17r–19v to Humbert of Silva Candida remains unfortunately an implausible hypothesis.[29] Among its varied content we also find excerpts from the *Epitome Iuliani* on fol. 4r–6r as well as fol. 25r–39r and 40r–53r (*recte* 25r–32v, 48r–53r, 40r–53r, 40r–47v, 33r–39r), evidently all written in the same eleventh-century hand. The imperial constitutions were excerpted in this manuscript and in books 7 and 9 of the *Caesaraugustana* as appears in Table 2.2.

The table indicates that several items could not be found in the microfilm of the Vatican codex, or presumably in the manuscript given its present state of preservation. Federico Patetta, to whom we owe a list of the constitutions in the *Epitome Iuliani* in Vat. lat. 3830, usually noted carefully whether the decrees were complete or whether sections were missing.[30] If his list is correct, then the manuscript contained complete transcriptions of Novels or Constitutions IV, VI, and VII, but it was without the Novels XLVIII (XLIX) 189 and LXI (LXII).3 [207].[31] In any event, textual comparisons leave no doubt that Vat. lat. 3830 cannot have been the formal source of the excerpts found in the *Caesaraugustana* either with the inscription *In Novellis* or, when suitable, with *Idem* or *Idem ibidem*. The *Caesaraugustana* text is much closer to the original. Nonetheless, it is intriguing to note the similarity in the set of excerpts from the imperial constitutions, especially when they are compared with Ivo's texts in the *Decretum* derived from Novel VII of the *Epitome Iuliani*: D 3.183 (= Ep. Iul. 32), D 3.184 (= Ep. Iul. 33), D 3.185 (= Ep. Iul. 36), D 3.186 (= Ep. Iul. 37), D 187 (= Ep. Iul. 39) and D 3.188 (= Ep. Iul. 40 combined with 42). The differences are noteworthy. Not only are there many omissions in Ivo's sequence (completely missing are *capitula* 34, 35, 38, and 41 of the *Epitome*), but most texts found in Ivo are also far briefer than the corresponding canons in CA. There are numerous and significant variants as well.[32] It is not so easy to dismiss the possibility that book seven of the *Decretum* of Ivo of Chartres influenced or even served as a source for texts from Novel IV in CA 9.39 (= Ep. Iul. IV.2[13]) and CA 9.42 (= Ep. Iul. IV.8[19]). A comparison of Haenel's edition of Constitutio IV.2 [13] with *Caesaraugustana* 9.39 (inc.: *Qui monachus fieri vult*) reveals that this canon (explicit . . . *de lib-*

29. Fowler-Magerl, *Clavis* 98–99; Kéry, *Can. Coll.* 198–99.

30. Federico Patetta, 'Contributi' (cited according to *Studi*) 24–27.

31. Gustav Haenel, *Iuliani Epitome latina Novellarum Justiniani* (Leipzig 1873).

32. The explicit of Ivo D 3.183 reads '. . . perpetuo exilio tradi oportet,' for instance. The remainder of Const. VII is, however, found in Ivo D 17.137, the very last capitulum of the *Decretum*.

Table 2.2

Caesaraugustana	BAV, Vat. lat. 3830	*Epitome Iuliani*
CA 7.80	fol. 29r–30r	Const. VII.1 [32]
CA 7.81	fol. 30r; #106	Const. VII.2 [33]
CA 7.82	fol. 30r–31v; #107	Const. VII.3 [34]
CA 7.83	fol. 31v; #108	Const. VII.4 [35]
CA 7.84	fol. 31v–32v #109	Const. VII.5 [36]*
CA 7.85	fol.32v	Const. VII.6 [37]
CA 7.86	fol. 32v; #111	Const. VII.7 [38]
CA 7.87	fol. 32v; #112	Const. VII.8 [39]
CA 7.88	fol. 48r; #113	Const. VII.9 [40]
CA 7.89	fol. 48r; #114	Const. VII.10[41]**
CA 7.90	fol. 48v; #116	Const. VII.12[43]
CA 7.91	fol. 49rv; #118	Const. XIV.1 [50]
CA 7.92		Const. XLVIII (XLIX)[189]
CA 7.93		Const. LXI (LXII).3 [207]
CA 9.39	fol. 25rv; #87	Const. IV.2 [13]
CA 9.40a	fol. 25v; #88	Const. IV.4 [15]
CA 9.40b	fol. 25v; #90	Const. IV.5 [16]
CA 9.41	fol. 26r; #92	Const. IV.7 [18]
CA 9.42	fol. 26r	Const. IV.8 [19]
CA 9.68	fol. 26r–26v	Const. IV.10 [21]
CA 9.69a	fol. 28v–29r; #102	Const. VI.6 [29]
CA 9.69b		Const. VI.6 [29]

*The concluding lines omitted by CA (explicit: . . . *neque sortem quam dedit*) read: . . . neque usuras, quas forte stipulatus est, exigat, deinde etiam ipsam rem cum suis emolumentis venerabili loco retituat, sed et in hoc casu adversus oeconomos, vel alios administratores venerabilium locorum actionibus creditori competentibus. Omnia enim, quae diximus, etiam in mulierum monasteriis vel asceteriis obtinere oportet.

**The section missing in CA, Const. VII.11 [42], is found in MS Vat. lat. 3830 on fol. 48rv, #115.

ertina conversione [*orig. conditione*]) has been much abbreviated in contrast to Ivo's *Decretum* 7.153, which contains the complete text of the original, ending. . . *domino reddi oportet*. This is the reverse of what was seen in connection with Constitutio VII, where the *Caesaraugustana* was both more complete and closer to the original. Still, the case for Constitutio IV is not as clear as it appears at first, for CA 9.39 adds after the explicit from cap. 2 [13] a final sentence of its own: *Et si recesserit bona eius ibi remaneant*. This short clause in effect summarizes the major point of some of the chapters of this novel omitted by CA. These chapters essentially stipulated that a monastery would stay in possession of the property originally given to it by a member, whatever the circumstances of a monk's or nun's leaving a house. Ivo's work included these sections in full as D 7.155, 7.156, and 7.157 in the legal sequence. The compiler of the *Caesaraugustana* could therefore have had either the 'original' or Ivo's *Decretum* in front of him and briefly summarized the sense of the *capitula* he omitted.

To sum up, with regard to the excerpts from Constitution VII found in the *Caesaraugustana*, Ivo of Chartres could be eliminated as a source, even for texts that the two collections have in common. Two segments of the same constitution are not part of Ivo's works. They are shared only by the *Caesaraugustana*, MS Vat. lat. 3830, and the *Lex romana canonice compta*, or, as the collection should properly be called, *Capitula legis Romanae*:[33] CA 7.82 (Ep. Iul. VII.3 [34]) and CA 7.89 (Ep. Iul. VII. 10 [41]). Wolfgang Kaiser's analysis of the *Epitome Iuliani* and their early medieval transmission generally excluded manuscripts younger than the end of the ninth century.[34] Thus MS Vat. lat. 3830 in the pertinent sections from the first half of the eleventh century was omitted. Patetta and Mor linked Roman legal texts in the Vatican codex to MS Rome, Biblioteca Vallicelliana T. XVIII, which Mor described as a 'compilazione parallela, ma indipendente, a quella del manoscritto vaticano 3830.'[35] Unfortunately the relevant section of the *Vallicellianus* only preserved rubrics, but the content has been reconstructed through the *Collectio in IX libris* in MS BAV Vat. lat. 1349 and the assistance of passages found in MS Rome, Biblioteca Casanatense 2010.[36] Codex Vat. lat. 1349 in turn influenced the *Collectio in V libris* (MS Vat. lat. 1339), which is also directly reflected among secular legal sources in the *Caesaraugustana* (CA 4.31, fol. 23ra).[37] The precise relationship of texts

33. Wolfgang Kaiser, *Die Epitome Iuliani: Beiträge zum römischen recht im frühen Mittelalter und zum byzantinischen Rechtsunterricht* (Studien zur europäischen Rechtsgeschichte 175; Frankfurt 2004) 493–522 with important corrections to Carlo Guido Mor, ed., *Lex Romana canonice compta* (Pavia 1927).

34. Kaiser, *Epitome* 8.

35. Carlo Guido Mor, 'La recezione del diritto romano nelle collezioni canoniche dei secoli IX–XI in Italia e Oltr'Alpe,' *Acta Congressus iuridici internationalis... Romae 1934* (Rome 1935) vol. 2, 284–307, p. 289. This cursory overview, however, is not necessarily reliable, because Mor maintained also that the *Brevis libellus de rebus ecclesiae* was similar to MS. Vat. lat. 3830. According to Conrat (*Geschichte* 148), however, the novels used for the *Brevis libellus* were not included in the *Epitome Iuliani*.

36. Kaiser, *Epitome* 20; Fowler-Magerl, *Clavis* 79–82; Kéry, *Can. Coll.* 196–97.

37. Kaiser, *Epitome* 630–37; Fowler-Magerl, *Clavis* 82–85; Douglas Adamson and Roger E. Reynolds, *Collectio Toletana: A Canon Law Derivative of the South Italian Collection in Five Books*

Table 2.3

CA 1.27 (fol. 3rb)	Dig. 1.18.12
CA 1.28 (fol. 3rb)	Dig. 1.3.37
CA 1.62 (fol. 6ra)	Cod. 1.14.9
CA 2.53 (fol. 9vb)	Dig. 1.4.2
CA 2.57.2 (fol. 10ra)	Dig. 1.3.20
CA 5.65 (fol. 40ra–b)	Ep. Iul. 325 (LXXXIII.2)
CA 5.66° (fol. 40rb–va)	Ep. Iul. 326 and 327 (LXXXIII.3, 4)
CA 5.66b (fol. 40va)	Ep. Iul. 328 and 329* (LXXXIII 5, 6)
CA 5.66c (fol. 40va)	Ep. Iul. 330 (LXXXIII. 7)
CA 7.92 (fol. 59rb)	Ep. Iul. 189 (XLVIII[XLIX].2)
CA 7.93 (fol. 59rb–va)	Ep. Iul. 207 (LXI [LXII].3)

*This text is not unique, but is here part of a series not found elsewhere in this sequence.

from the *Epitome Iuliani* in the *Caesaraugustana,* in MS Vat. lat. 3830 and the Vallicellianus cannot be elucidated here. However, given that the text in particular of Constitutio VII is fragmented and disorganized in other canonical collections, even in the *Capitula legis romane,* not to mention Ivo's *Decretum* and Deusdedit's *Collectio canonum,* but is found almost in its entirety and in the original sequence in the *Caesaraugustana,* strongly suggests the possibility that the author was working from a complete copy of the *Epitome.*[38] At the same time the compiler had access to the *Digest,* the *Codex,* and the *Institutiones,* for the Justinian passages listed in Table 2.3—with the omission here of Constitutio VII and other texts common to CA and MS Vat. lat. 3830 indicated in Table 2.2—are unique to the collection and not derived from earlier compilations. The texts are few, especially if one would omit the *Epitome,* but nevertheless this range of romanist sources is remarkable in a work that predates the glossators, does not come from Italy, and quotes texts from the *Collectio Britannica* only through the intermediary of the *Decretum* of Ivo of Chartres.

(Toronto 2008); Kéry, *Can. Coll.* 157–60, who notes the use of material from Burchard's *Decretum* in MS Vat. lat. 3830.

38. Const. VII.11 [42] is found in CA as 4.30 (fol. 23ra). There are variants and two additional phrases at the end.

KATHLEEN G. CUSHING

3 Law, Penance, and the 'Gregorian' Reform

The Case of Padua, Biblioteca del seminario vescovile MS 529

The *Liber decretorum* of Bishop Burchard of Worms was one of the most important canon law collections in the eleventh and early twelfth centuries until the compilations associated with Ivo of Chartres came into widespread use. Its popularity is borne out not just by its subsequent use as a formal source but also by its widespread transmission; the *Liber decretorum* (hereafter LD) remains extant in more than 80 copies in addition to some 20 fragments, some of which consist of single leaves. Compiled between 1012 and 1022, LD was soon thereafter transmitted, and Burchard himself may have had a role in its early dissemination. The collection—in the form of the Frankfurt manuscript—moved rapidly beyond Worms to southern Germany, to Burgundy, and to Italy.[1]

Burchard's collection was especially valued in Italy, and nearly half the extant manuscripts are of Italian origin.[2] It is known, for instance, that

I am grateful to Adriaan Gaastra for his help in identifying the penitential transmission; he bears no responsibility for my interpretations or conclusions. An earlier version of this article was presented at the International Medieval Congress at Leeds in July 2009. I am grateful to Martin Brett, Peter Landau, John Wei, Rob Meens, and Sarah Hamilton for their comments.

1. Greta Austin, *Shaping Church Law around the Year 1000: The Decretum of Burchard of Worms* (Aldershot 2009) 26–31 with a comprehensive bibliography.

For the reader's assistance, a list of manuscript abbreviations used in the present article can be found at the end of the Appendix.

2. The classic work on the transmission of Burchard is Otto Meyer, 'Überlieferung and Verbreitung des Dekrets des Burchard von Worms,' ZRG, Kan. Abt. 24 (1935) 141–83, which was extended by Hubert Mordek, 'Handschriftenforschungen in Italien,' QF 51 (1971) 626–51; Gérard Fransen, 'Le *Décret* de Burchard de Worms: Valeur du texte de l'édition. Essai de classement des manuscrits,' ZRG Kan. Abt. 63 (1977) 1–19; idem, 'Le *Décret* de Burchard' in Gérard Fransen and Theo Kölzer, eds., *Decretorum libri XX* (Cologne 1548; repr. Aalen 1992) 19–42; Hartmut Hoffmann and Rudolf Pokorny, *Das Dekret des Bischofs Burchard von Worms: Textstufen—Frühe*

Abbot Rudolf I of Nonantola (1002–1035) had acquired a copy and that another was at the Cathedral of Parma by the mid-eleventh century. The early use of Burchard in Italy can also be seen in minor canonical collections such as the *Collectio capitula veronensis* (second quarter of the eleventh century), in the *Collectio canonum* of Biblioteca Apostolica Vaticana, Vat. lat. 3830 (mid-eleventh century), in the *Collectio canonum Barberiniana* (begun between 1050 and 1073 and augmented in two later stages), in the *Collection in 183 Titles* (after 1063),[3] and Joseph Ryan long ago argued for its wider circulation in Italy before 1050, given the use of the collection made by Peter Damian in his letters.[4] As well as being copied as a unique collection, LD was combined, especially in central and southern Italy, with the *Collection in Five Books* (5L) and its derivatives, later with the *Diversorum patrum sententie*, and with other penitential and liturgical collections, a number of which date from the mid-eleventh century onwards.[5]

In his important article on the Gregorians' view of Burchard, Detlev Jasper noted that if it actually had been the reformers' intention to supplant LD, they failed abysmally in Italy.[6] In this article in honor of Robert Somerville, who long ago took on the role of my long-distance, unofficial and unpaid supervisor, I look to extend Jasper's focus by examining an intriguing copy of LD, that in Padua, Biblioteca del seminario vescovile MS 529. By focusing on two unusual—if brief—series of penitential canons, one at the end of the manuscript and one inserted after Book 17; I look to expand the discussion of Burchard's Italian reception by considering his monastic readers and to offer some preliminary comments about what this may tell us about law and penance in the age of the so-called Gregorian reform.

Verbreitung—Vorlagen (MGH Hilfsmittel 12; Munich 1991). For further literature and manuscripts see Kéry, *Can. Coll.* 134–48. Cf. Austin, *Shaping* 28–31.

3. On these collections, see Fowler-Magerl, *Clavis* 94, 95–97, 98, 101; Joseph Motta, ed. *Liber canonum diversorum sanctorum patrum sive collectio in CLXXXIII titulos digesta*, MIC, ser. B 7 (Vatican City 1988); Mario Fornasari, '*Collectio canonum Barberiniana*', *Apollinaris* 36 (1963) 127–41 (analysis) 214–97 (edition); and Kathleen G. Cushing, '"Intermediate" and minor collections: the case of the *Collectio canonum Barberiniana*,' in Martin Brett and Kathleen G. Cushing, eds., *Readers, Texts and Compilers in the Earlier Middle Ages: Studies in Medieval Canon Law in Honour of Linda Fowler-Magerl* (Aldershot 2009) 73–86.

4. Joseph J. Ryan, *St Peter Damiani and His Canonical Sources: A Preliminary Study in the Antecedents of the Gregorian Reform* (Toronto 1956) 13, 21, 160–62 and tables I and II at 176–85, 188–91.

5. See Roger E. Reynolds, 'Penitentials in South and Central Italian Canon Law Manuscripts of the Tenth and Eleventh Centuries,' *Early Medieval Europe* 14.1 (2006) 65–85, esp. 76–79 and literature cited there.

6. Detlev Jasper, 'Burchards Dekret in der Sicht der Gregorianer,' in *Bischof Burchard von Worms 1000–1025*, ed. Wilfried Hartmann (Mainz 2000) 167–98.

I. Padua MS 529

Padua 529 contains what is known as an Italian Order of Worms, Type B version of LD.[7] Meyer, Mordek, and Kéry dated the manuscript to the late eleventh century,[8] whilst in the recent catalogue of Paduan manuscripts, Donello et al. dated it to the first quarter of the twelfth century.[9] It is likely that the manuscript was copied at the Benedictine monastery San Benedetto di Polirone or, perhaps, in its environs. The manuscript, or possibly its two parts—it is unclear whether the last quire was part of the LD manuscript or was joined to it later—seems to have come not long afterward to Polirone as is indicated by an *ex libris* in a twelfth-century hand at fol. 160v (there is also a twelfth/thirteenth-century *ex libris* at fol. 1r). The manuscript—or at least its exemplar—reveals traces of a Ravennese connection, as is shown by Nicholas I's letter of 861 regarding the sentences against John of Ravenna (JL 2687), copied between LD 4.99 and 4.100 (fol. 56rb–57rb), and also by the second of the excommunication *formulae* (fol. 149ra–149vb), which invokes a number of patron saints associated with Ravenna.[10]

As can be seen in the Appendix, the manuscript appears at first sight to contain a typical Italian copy of LD: it has Burchard's prologue, the text of LD interrupted—as is customary in Italian copies—by the distinctive *Ordo synodalis* 5 at fol. 49ra–vb, and then includes at the (abbreviated) end of Book 20 the canons from the Council of Seligenstadt in 1023. These are followed by: the excommunication *formulae*, miscellaneous prologues, an *ordo* for the preparation of Mass, a commentary on the Paternoster, and the added series of penitential canons at 160va–b, where the text breaks off. The manuscript has considerable contemporary and later annotation (much of which seems appropriate for monastic readers), many *maniculae*, and any number of contemporary and later additions, notably the other added se-

7. This manuscript, or more properly its exemplar, seems very close to the version used by Anselm of Lucca. I am grateful to Robert Somerville for his discussions with me about Anselm's LD source, which regrettably was not Lucca, Biblioteca Capitolare Feliniana MS 124.

8. Mordek, 'Hansdschriftenforschungen' 649; Kéry, *Can. Coll.* 140.

9. *Manoscritti medievali del Veneto*, 1. *I manoscritti della Biblioteca del seminario vescovile di Padova*, ed. A. Donello et al. (*Biblioteche e archivi*, 2; Florence 1998) 89. The description of the manuscript is not entirely accurate.

10. Fol. 149ra–vb: (a) 'Ecce quam bonum et quam iocundum . . . maledictionis anathemate condempnemus.' (b) 'Maledicti sint a deo patre . . . condigname penitentiam satis fecerint' (invoking SS Vitalis, Apollinaris, Severus, etc.). In a personal communication, Sarah Hamilton has noted that these formulae are potentially quite exciting, given the received opinion that there was little use of excommunication/malediction formulae in Italy.

ries of penitential canons, which was inserted after Book 17, at fol. 108vb–109ra. The LD text itself in Padua 529 corresponds—at least in part—to what Gérard Fransen termed '*deteriores*', that is, copies of the collection marked by four lacunae; these '*deteriores*' seem to have originated in northern Italy before c. 1090, though their archetype may be even earlier.[11] Padua 529 however also omits passages that are akin to non-*deteriores* copies.[12]

Before turning to these penitential canons, however, it is important to consider the status of Polirone in the eleventh century, its library and intellectual development.

II. The Library at San Benedetto di Polirone

San Benedetto di Polirone was founded in 1007 by Count Tedald of Canossa in the Po valley south of Mantua. Tedald's death in 1012 left the monastery's further establishment to his son, Boniface, who clearly saw its augmentation as a means of extending his authority and expunging his reputation as a simonist and despoiler of Church property. Boniface actively fostered the cult of the monastery's rather obscure holy man, a gyrovague Armenian monk, Simeon, who died at Polirone in 1016 and was canonized—probably at Boniface's urging—by Benedict VIII.[13] Despite this patronage, Polirone initially remained a modest community; this is borne out by Simeon's less than stellar miracles of curing brothers choking on fish bones—often a sign of a poor monastery![14] After Boniface's assassination in 1052, Polirone came under the energetic patronage first of Beatrice and later of Matilda of Tuscany. It assumed Cluniac obedience between 27 June 1076 and 7 April 1080 but probably at the beginning of 1077, after which time a concerted effort to develop the monastery's library and scriptorium is apparent.[15]

11. Milan, Ambrosiana E 144 sup. Fransen, 'Le Décret' (1977) 8–12; 'Le Décret' (1992) 34–38; cf. Christof Rolker, *Canon Law and the Letters of Ivo of Chartres* (Cambridge Studies in Medieval Life and Thought, Fourth Series; Cambridge 2010), 45–46.

12. Fransen, 'Le Décret' (1977) 13.

13. Benedict also approved the construction of a new church in Simeon's honor: JL 4055.

14. See Paolo Golinelli, 'La vita di S. Simeone monaco,' *Studi medievali*, ser. 3, 20 (1979) 709–44 (analysis), 745–88 (edition), here: *vita* cc. 24–25, p. 779. Golinelli saw the *Life* as a work of hagiography written for canonization and dated it to before 1024, i.e. the death of Benedict VIII. John Howe, however, has argued that the text is more treacherous than it seems and has dated the *Life* to the 1050s or even later: 'The True Date of the Life and Miracles of St Symeon of Polirone,' *Studi medievali*, ser. 3, 25 (1984) 291–99.

15. See Gregory VII to Hugh of Cluny in *Italia pontificia* 7:1, ed. Paul Kehr (1923), 329 n. 5 (JL 5282); Leo Santifaller, ed. *Quellen und Forschungen zum Urkunden- und Kanzleiwesen Papst Gregors VII* (Studi e testi 190; Vatican City 1957) nos. 125–26.

A list of Polirone's holdings in the late eleventh-century manuscript Padua, Biblioteca del seminario vescovile MS 522 (fol. 171v) reveals the makings of an intriguing library under Abbot William I (1080–99). There are considerable patristic texts (a number of which can be linked to extant manuscripts) including Jerome, Ambrose, much Augustine, Cassian, Isidore, Gregory I's *Moralia*, as well as Lombard laws, etc.[16] The high quality, moreover, of the scriptorium's output from this time is shown by the impressive *Gospel Book of Matilda* (now at the Pierpont Morgan Library) and other illuminated Polirone manuscripts and in papal commissions for manuscripts from Polirone.[17] More important for the present topic, however, is the evidence of an increasing interest in canonistic texts.[18] In addition to the copy of LD (and its possibly separate end manuscript), Polirone had two copies of Pseudo-Isidore, one incomplete and the other containing extensive excerpts from Gregory I's letters, both dating from the late eleventh century.[19] The monks also possessed one of the earliest revisions of Anselm of Lucca's collection, recension A Aucta—Mantua, Biblioteca Communale MS 318 (C.II.23), discovered by Peter Landau—and as Linda Fowler-Magerl argued there is good reason to assume that the revision of the A version of the collection behind A Aucta and Anselm B was compiled at Polirone during Anselm's lifetime and perhaps even under his direction.[20] Of especial significance is the fact that MS 318 contains a number of additions that are seldom found in other canon law collections;[21] this clearly shows at the least an interest in copying canonical texts. This interest would continue in the twelfth century, as is shown in further can-

16. See the description and list in *I manoscritti della Biblioteca del seminario vescovile di Padova* 83–85. See also Corrado Corradini, Paolo Golinelli, Giuseppa Zanichelli, eds., *Catalogo dei manoscritti polironiani* 1. *Biblioteca communale di Mantova, MSS 1–100* (Storia di San Benedetto Polirone 3.1; Bologna 1998) xxxiv–xxxviii.

17. Corradini, *Catalogo dei manoscritti polironiani*, 35 and literature cited there. See also Robert H. Rough, *The Reformist Illuminations in the Gospels of Matilda, Countess of Tuscany* (The Hague 1973).

18. Giuseppe Motta, 'I codici canonistici di Polirone,' in *Sant'Anselmo, Mantova e la lotta per le investiture*, ed. Paolo Golinelli (Bologna 1987) 349–74.

19. Mantua, Biblioteca communale MS 205 (B.III.1), fol. 1r–148r: Ps. Isidore; fol. 148r–188r: Gregory I, *epistolae;* and MS 209 (B.III.5), fol. 3rb–64vb: incomplete Ps. Isidore; cf. *Catalogo dei manoscritti polironiani* 259–61; 270–71.

20. Peter Landau, 'Erweiterte Fassungen der Kanonessammlung des Anselm von Lucca aus dem 12. Jahrhundert,' in *Sant'Anselmo, Mantova e la lotta per le investiture* 323–37, here 328–30; Fowler-Magerl, *Clavis* 145–48. For this version of Anselm's collection see Giuseppe Motta, 'La redazione A "Aucta" della *Collectio Anselmi episcopi Lucensis*,' in *Studia in honorem eminentissimi cardinalis Alphonsi M. Stickler* ed. Rosalio Card. Castillo Lara (Studia et textus historiae iuris canonici 7; Rome 1992) 375–449. On the florilegium in MS 318, see Motta, 'I codici canonistici' 361–62.

21. Fowler-Magerl, *Clavis* 146.

onistic florilegia, in the monks' acquisition of a copy of the *Panormia* and a copy of Bonizo of Sutri's *Liber de vita christiana*, as well as in Mantua BC MS 266 (C.I.4) which contains thirteen canons from the Sentences on Penance later used by Gratian.[22] The monks at Polirone—perhaps galvanized by Anselm's example—had clearly become interested in canon law.

III. Penitential Canons and Additions after LD 17

At fol. 160va–b, there is a series of brief canons in a different but contemporary hand that obviously continued on now missing folios. As can be seen in the Appendix, it is something of a random list, bearing—at least to my current understanding—no block correspondence with any known extant Italian or other penitential.[23] The series begins with an excerpt from the *Constitutio Silvestri*—found only in the *Collection in 5 Books* (5L), according to Fowler-Magerl's *Clavis*—followed by an unknown, or perhaps bastardized, text that might have some relation to the 5L or the *Collection in Nine Books* (9L) of Biblioteca Apostolica Vaticana, Vat. lat. 1349; both texts address tithes, as does the third canon, which bears some resemblance to the Theodorean *Canones Gregorii*. Thereafter are explicitly penitential canons dealing: with the secrecy of the confessional (n. 4), with a sinner whose crimes are prompted by diabolic possession (n. 5), with sexual crimes, including one on bestiality (n. 7) found in the eighth-century Frankish *Paenitentiale Oxoniense II*, but in no other penitential, and also in the 9L, albeit with variants.[24] A number of other canon law collections—as noted in the Appendix—also address this topic, but these are all fundamentally different texts. The remaining canons address theft (n. 9), ritual associated with the Mass, the sacraments (nn. 10–12), and issues of ritual purity from Gregory's *Libellus Responsonium* (nn. 14–15), a text that was frequently combined with the *Capitula iudiciorum* in manuscripts.

The content of these canons is admittedly not earth-shattering, but the range of material sources is a bit more interesting; these sources include

22. *Panormia*: Mantua BC 198 (B.II.21), mid-twelfth century: *Catalogo dei manoscritti polironiani* 245–46. This is preceded by some canonistic florilegia, see Motta, 'I codici canonistici' 362–63; Bonizo: Mantua BC 439 (D.III.13), mid-twelfth century, on which see Fowler-Magerl, *Clavis* 174–76, and Motta, 'I codici canonistici' 366–71. For Mantua BC 266 and its use by Gratian, see John Wei, 'A Twelfth-century Collection of Patristic Texts on Penance,' presented at the International Medieval Congress at Leeds, July 2009. Cf. Motta, 'I codici canonistici' 355, 363–66, and Fowler-Magerl, *Clavis* 132–33. I thank John Wei for his help with references and this manuscript.

23. I am grateful to Rob Meens and Adriaan Gaastra for confirming this.

24. *Paenitentiale Oxoniense II* c. 57, ed. Raymond Kottje, *Paenitentialia minora franciae et italiae saeculi VIII–IX* (CCL 156.1; Turnhout 1994) 201. I am grateful to Adriaan Gaastra for pointing this out. The wording here seems closer to the *Oxoniense II* than to the 9L, though both have variants.

the eighth-century *Capitula iudiciorum*, various forms of Theodorean material—*iudicia Theodori*, the *Canones Gregorii*, as well as the text of the Disciple. There is also some perhaps directly accessed Cummean material, as well as three texts from the *Paenitentiale Oxoniense II*, for which no Italian copy survives. As Gaastra has shown, the penitentials composed in Italy in the tenth and eleventh centuries mainly used these sources,[25] but there is no single penitential that reproduces this exact series which could help to identify a potential formal source. The attribution of most of these canons to 'Gregorius' is intriguing and offers a potential further line of enquiry, but the texts do not depend on the Ps. Gregorian *Penitential* or completely on the *Canones Gregorii*, however much they reveal the importance of the authority of Gregory to the compiler or his exemplar. At the same time, there is no clear pattern in a specifically canon law transmission—at least there is no block series parallel—by which to identify a possible formal source. As can be seen in the Appendix, a number of the texts were widely transmitted, but their appearance in the other collections can often be explained by those collections' own formal sources; for instance, parallels with the *Atrebatensis*—often seen as a 'closed' transmission—can be explained by its own reliance on LD. That said, the parallels with the 9L and 5L are intriguing and suggest some engagement with central/southern Italian material.

When we turn, moreover, to the series of 11 canons added after Book 17, *De fornicatione* (see below, Appendix)—none of which repeats texts in Book 17 itself—we find material sources similar to those found at the end of the manuscript: *Capitula iudiciorum* and more Theodore. One text, interestingly, is only also found in the *Penitential* of Rome, Biblioteca Vallicelliana MS E62, dated as the second half of the twelfth century by Supini-Martini.[26] There are also a number of texts that I have been unable to identify. With these, however, there are yet again strong, clear parallels in the 9L and the 5L, indicating again engagement with central/southern Italian material. Indeed it should be noted that Vallicelliana E62 was probably copied at Narni, itself also the provenance of the Vatican manuscript of the 5L (Vat. lat. 1339).

25. Adriaan Gaastra, 'Penance and the Law: the penitential canons of the *Collection in Nine Books*,' *Early Medieval Europe* 14.1 (2006) 85–102 and idem, 'Between Liturgy and Canon Law: A Study of Books of Confession and Penance in Eleventh- and Twelfth-Century Italy,' PhD dissertation, University of Utrecht 2007, forthcoming from Brepols. See also Rob Meens, 'Penitentials and the practice of penance in the tenth and eleventh centuries,' *Early Medieval Europe* 14.1 (2006) 7–21.

26. Paola Supini-Martini, *Roma e l'area grafica romanesca secoli X–XII* (Alessandria 1988) 232, who thought the penitential was part of another manuscript; Gaastra has convincingly argued the opposite in his PhD dissertation, 'Between Liturgy and Canon Law,' forthcoming from Brepols.

IV. Monastic Readers, Penance, and 'Reform'

The questions remain, what was the source(s) of these two series of canons and what—if anything—do they tell us? The difficulty in tracing random lists is complicated by the fact that most additions to canon law manuscripts either dealt with issues of sacramental theology or else were penitential in nature. Although there may be a number of explanations, two seem most probable: (1) the additions were the product of a zealous researcher (or researchers) with access to a range of penitential manuscripts including something that looked like the 9L; or (the more probable, given the logistical considerations) (2) these series were derived from now lost wax tablet(s) or parchment *aide-memoire* list(s) copied elsewhere—perhaps in central/southern Italy, where there was access to some text resembling the 9L. In this scenario, such a list was either transported home by a Polirone monk or else brought to the monks' attention at Polirone by a traveling scribe, again presumably one from central/southern Italy.[27] The variants here as compared with the material sources (and even the 9L) would support such a list, copied perhaps several times over. In either case, these series clearly underline the fact that central/southern Italian material such as that found in the 5L and the 9L, which one would not normally expect to find so far north, was somehow 'leaking,' or was being deliberately moved, north. Although this is significant in itself, in conclusion, I would like to offer some preliminary comments on monastic readers of canon law and what they may tell us about law and penance in the late eleventh and early twelfth centuries.

The LD of course was especially valued in episcopal circles: it was a practical, user-friendly collection, ideally suited to episcopal administration and useful in conducting councils, as Eberhard I of Constance (d. 1046) noted in his copy of the collection.[28] Burchard's inclusion of a penitential with an ordo—Book 19 the *Corrector sive medicus*—without doubt extended the collection's practical usefulness. Hamilton has argued that it was used not so much as a priestly aid for direct pastoral care but rather as a reference work for bishops and cathedral clergy.[29] Körntgen refined this

27. The importance of logistics such as pilgrimage and travel routes as conduits for the transmission of canon law have been underlined by Linda Fowler-Magerl in 'The Collection and Transmission of Canon Law along the Northern Section of the *via francigena* in the Eleventh and Twelfth Centuries,' in Bruce C. Brasington and Kathleen G. Cushing, eds., *Bishops, Texts and the Use of Canon Law around 1100: Studies in Honour of Martin Brett* (Aldershot 2008) 129–39.

28. Meyer, 'Überlieferung' 153, n. 2.

29. Sarah Hamilton, *The Practice of Penance, 900–1050* (Woodbridge, UK, 2001) 44.

by suggesting that it had a didactic function, designed 'for those priests who became overburdened with knowledge' in the face of the formidable collection.[30]

Monasteries, however, both in Italy and elsewhere did possess copies of LD, and it is clear more broadly that monks were interested in compiling and copying canon law works, as Christof Rolker has recently shown with the 74T.[31] Monks and abbots, after all, needed canon law quite as much as bishops and other clergy for a variety of practical reasons: to defend their privileges, liberties, and exemptions in disputes with bishops and others. (For instance, a number of the additions to Mantua BC 318 involve monastic rights.)[32] Taking only the evidence from Polirone, the annotation, additions, and other signs of use in their legal manuscripts—to say nothing of the extension of their holdings in patristic texts, material on penance and theology from the late eleventh century onwards—reveal that the monks may have been reading canon law for a range of other reasons: personal study, pedagogy, ideological orientation, and perhaps other practical application. At the same time, whilst we still do not know as much as we would like about the provenance and hence actual purpose of penitentials especially in Italy in this period, a number were copied in monasteries. This must make us question why monks wanted such texts: study, reference, pastoral care? The question of monastic pastoral provision is an enormous topic that needs further investigation, though it is possible—as Gaastra has suggested—that monasteries may have acted as centers for the education of clergy not least with regard to pastoral care and penance.[33] This is regrettably not the place to address this further and it would in any event be an enormous leap from two small series of penitential texts to claims that Polirone's monks were educating clergy or even administering penance.

While historians of canon law in the era before Gratian have increasingly questioned the value of speculating about the intention of compilers and have emphasized the difference between the genesis of a collection and its reception,[34] attitudes about canon law in the age of the 'Gregori-

30. Ludger Körntgen, 'Canon Law and the Practice of Penance: Burchard of Worms' Penitential,' *Early Medieval Europe* 14.1 (2006) 103–17, here 115.

31. Christof Rolker, 'The *Collection in Seventy-four Titles*: A Monastic Canon Law Collection from Eleventh-century France,' in Brett and Cushing, eds., *Readers, Texts and Compilers* 59–72.

32. Fowler-Magerl, *Clavis* 147.

33. Adriaan Gaastra, 'Instructions for Penance and Confession' presented at the International Medieval Congress, Leeds, July 2009. See above n. 26.

34. A position most recently emphasized by Martin Brett, 'Margin and Afterthought: The *Clavis* in Action,' in Brett and Cushing, eds. *Readers, Texts and Compilers* 137–57, esp. 137–38; see also Rolker, 'The *Collection in Seventy-four Titles*' 61–62.

an' reform remain inexorably shaped by Paul Fournier. For Fournier, canon law was both an ideological program for, and a means of, a papal-oriented reform that shunted off an unsuitable pre-reform Burchard in favor of new canonical collections.[35] This model is problematic for any number of reasons, not least of all because it disregards the ongoing, and undoubtedly changing, reception of any canonical collection. Padua 529, with its additions derived from a range of penitential-legal sources, provides one further example to challenge the Fournier model. It also must make us acutely aware of the need to read around the ends of manuscripts and pay attention to what Brasington called 'notes from the edge' for evidence of a different set of readers, in this instance monastic ones.[36]

The broader relationship between penitentials and the treatment of penance in canon law collections in Italy in this period clearly needs much more work, especially in light of the still prevailing opinion that penance was a topic of little interest to 'reformers.' We clearly need both to revise this opinion as well as to extend what we mean by 'reformer.' Whilst it is important for historians to continue to speculate about the intention of compilers of canon law collections, the canonistic activity at Polirone and the unmistakably consulted Padua 529 also remind us of the need to consider both the variety and the ambitions of readers of canon law.

APPENDIX

Padua, Biblioteca del seminario vescovile, MS 529

fol. 1ra–vb	Burchard of Worms, *Epistola Brunichoni*
fol. 1vb–48vb	Burchard, *Liber Decretorum*, Books 1–3
fol. 49ra–vb	*Ordo de celebrando concilio, Ordo synodalis* 5
fol. 49vb–148ra	Burchard, LD, Books 4–20 (to c. 110)
fol. 148ra–149ra	Council of Seligenstadt, 1023, cc. 1–20
fol. 149ra–149vb	Excommunication *formulae*
fol. 149vb–152va	Miscellaneous texts including several prologues for the Sabbath, the Lord's supper, etc.; some later additions
fol. 153ra–157va	*Ordo qualiter sacerdos se preparandus ad missam agere debet*
fol. 157vb–160ra	Commentary on the Paternoster
fol. 160rb	[de aetatibus mundi]
fol. 160va	Ex dictis Leonis papae. Illud etiam dilectionem . . . ordinata esse conveniat. (later hand, unknown)

35. E.g. Paul Fournier, 'Les collections canoniques romaines à l'époque de Grégoire VII,' *Mémoires de l'academie des inscriptions et belles-lettres* 40 (1920) 271–395. Cf. Fournier–Le Bras 1.1–14.

36. Bruce C. Brasington, '"Notes from the Edge": Marginalia and Glosses in pre-Gratian Canonical Collections,' in *Bishops, Texts and the Use of Canon Law* 169–85.

There then follows at fol. 160va–b (*not* noted in the catalogue) an unnumbered series of brief canons which I number for convenience.

Text	Parallel Transmission
(1) Ex epistola Silvestri pape. Commoneo vestre consortis . . . ipso pontifice dispensante. *Constitutio Silvestri*, c. 4	5L 3.56.1–2[1]
(2) No inscription. Monemus ut decimas et provincias . . . neglexerit excommunicare. ???[2]	Cf. 9L 3.77a; 5L 3.43.2a
(3) Gregorius papa. Decimas non cogantur presbyteri . . . debeant errogare. Cf. *Iudicia Theodori* (G), *canones Gregorii*, c. 157 (diff end)	
(4) Gregorius. Caveat ante omnia sacerdos . . . et vii. annos peniteat. Cf. *Capitula Iudiciorum*, c. 35 post 3	9L 9.128[3]; 5L 4.69.02; Ans A 11.23; 13L 11.23; Bonizo 10.19; Poly. 6.20.9; 2L/8P 2.365; 7L 7.67.41; 3L 3.19.18; 9L (ASP) 9.5.17, *Casin.* 7; etc.
(5) Gregorius. Si quis a demonio vexatus . . . pro eo licet orare. Cf. *Iudicia Theodori*, (G), *canones Gregorii*, c. 152	Cf. CDP 1 2.77; CDP 2 2.318
(6) Gregorius. Si qua mulier occiderit . . . peniteat iii. annos. Cf. *Capit. Iud.*, 3.3; *Iud. Theo.* (G), cc. 105–106	
(7) Gregorius. Si quis cum quadrupedibus peccaverit . . . in deserto prohiciatur. *Paenit. Oxoniense* II, c. 57[4]	9L 9.17[5]; Cf. LD 17.33 (Ansegis 1.48 via RP 2.258); 2L/8P 8.174; Bonizo 10.41; ID 9.91, Ctp 3.16.25—in each of these the text is different.
(8) Gregorius. Si quis de quoque gradu . . . (160va/b) . . . reddat furtu(m). Unknown.	
(9) Gregorius. Si qua mulier posuerit . . . non est mulier culpanda. *Paenit. Oxoniense* II, c. 28[6]	*Casin.* 42b (diff. ending)

No further inscriptions, but red initials continue.

1. Cf. 3L 2.23.5; 9L(ASP) 4.10.4; etc.

2. The text here, which does not exactly replicate that of the 9L and the 5L (where it is given as 'Lex'), could also be a bastardization of Gregory VII, *Reg.* 6.5b, c. 9. Whichever is the case, either the scribe or the exemplar was faulty.

3. Fol. 216rb, where it is attributed 'Apostolicum.'

4. Cf. *Capit. Iud.* 7.7; Ps Gregory, *Penit.* c. 17.

5. Fol. 199ra where the inscription is 'iudicium sinodale' and the beginning is also slightly different: Si quis cum quadrupedia . . . . and there are other variants.

6. Cf. *Iud. Theo.* (G), c. 117.

Text	Parallel Transmission
(10) Omne sacrificum sordida... comburenda est. Discipulus (*Can. Theodori*, U), 1.12.6; *Excarpsus Cummeani*, c. 14.12	LD 5.50; 13L 9.102; *Coll. Barb.* 51.1; *Coll. Atrebat.* 511; *Coll. Burd.* 5.16; ID 2.59; *Coll 9 vol. Sangermanensis* 8.21, etc.
(11) Presbyter evangelium... dexterum ponat. *Iud. Theo.* (G), c. 174; Discipulus (U), 2.2.11; *Excarpsus Cummeani*, c. 14.20	
(12) Si quis super mortuum lugendo... et postea communicet. *Paenit. Oxoniense* II, c. 40	5L 3.238.02[7]
(13) Duodecim ieiunia in anno... eligit deus. Unknown.	
(14) Vir aut cum propria coniuge dormiens... ecclesiam licet introire (sic). Gregory I, *Libellus Resp.*, JE 1843	*Coll. Herovall.* 72.11; *Coll. LXXII capit.*; *Coll. Atrebat.* 321; ID 8.88b; Ctp. 3.15.51, etc.
(15) Mulier dum consuetudinem menstruam ... dum cum percipiendo ex re/MS ends. Gregory I, *Libellus Resp.*, JE 1843	*Coll. Gaddiana* 349

Penitential canons at fol. 108vb–109ra after LD Book 17, *De fornicatione*
These are in a different but contemporary hand from the Burchard text; there are two later additions as marked. Rubrics are in red ink; the canons are not numbered in the manuscript.

(1) De his qui cum deo sacrata fornicaverit. Gregorius papa. Si quis cum deo.... ad communionem reconcilietur. *Capit. Iud.* 7.2[8]
(2) De his qui cum uxore alteris fornicaverit. Gregorius papa. Si quis cum uxore... gradum accedere numquam presumat. *Capit. Iud.* 7.3
(3) De his qui cum cognata fornicaverit. Gregorius papa. Si quis cum cognata... sacerdotio priventur. Cf. *Capit. Iud.* 7.5
(4) Si cum relicta fornicaverit. [No inscription]. Si quis cum eas quampropter... in pane et aqua. Not found.[9]
(5) [Different hand and ink] [No rubric] Ex concilio niceno. Si quis voluntarie iuraverit... (108vb/109ra)... in pane et aqua. Cf. *Capit. Iud.* ante c. 15[10]
(6) [No rubric] Ex eodem (*corr.* Ex pen. Romano). Si quis in gradu pro cupiditate... mortem peniteat. Not found.

7. Where it is given as 'synodus romana.'

8. CDP 1 3.270.

9. 5L 2.63, where the rubric is more intelligible: Qui cum uxore pro deo relicta fornicaverit, 'iudicium commeani.' Not found.

10. 9L 9.67, fol. 207va, 'iudicium canonicum'; 5L 4.254, 'iudicium canonicum'; Rome, Vallicelliana T XXI, fol. 286v, 'canon.'

(7) [Different hand] [No rubric.] Ex dictis ambrosii. Tollerabilius est filatea culpa quam si culpa usurpet auctoritas. Unknown. *Followed by a brief lacuna.*
(8) [No rubric] Ex concilio libertano. Si quis sacerdos cum filia sua... femina vero similiter. Not found.[11]
(9) [No rubric] Iuditium comeani. Si quis cum filia sua spirituali... privetur honore. Not found.[12]
(10) [No rubric] Gregorius papa. Si quis episcopus fornicatus... recipiatur pristino. *Paenit. Vallicellianum E62*, c. 15
(11) [No rubric] Gregorius papa. Si quis per semetipsum... fratribus separetur. Cf. *Iud. Theodori* (D), c. 139; Cf. *Capit. Iud.* 7.9[13]

The prologue to Book 18 then follows at the bottom of fol. 109ra

Abbreviations

2L/8P	*Collection in two books/eight parts*
3L	*Collection in three books*
5L	*Collection in five books* (southern Italian)
7L	*Collection in seven books*, Vienna ÖNB 2186
9L	*Collection in nine books*, BAV, Vat. lat. 1349
9L (ASP)	*Collection in nine books*, Archivio san Pietro, C. 118
13L	*Collection in thirteen books*, BAV Vat. lat. 1361
Ans. A	Anselm of Lucca, recension A
Bonizo	Bonizo of Sutri, *Liber de vita christiana*
Capit. Iud.	*Capitula iudiciorum*
Casin.	*Collectio casinense*
CDP	*Collectio XII partium* (1 and 2)
Coll. Atrebat.	*Collectio atrebatensis*
Coll. Barb.	*Collectio canonum barberiniana*
Coll. Burd.	*Collectio burdagalensis*
Coll. Gaddiana	*Collectio Gaddiana*
Coll. Herovall.	*Collectio Herovalliana*
Coll. 9 vol. Sangermanensis	*Collectio 9 voluminorum sangermanensis*
Coll. LXXII capit.	*Collectio LXXII capitolorum* 311 (Rome, Vallicelliana T17)
Ctp	*Collectio tripartita*
ID	Ivo of Chartres, *Decretum*
LD	Burchard of Worms, *Liber decretorum*
Poly.	*Polycarpus*

11. Cf. 9L 9.42, fol. 203vb, 'sinodus'; 5L 2.63.5, no inscription.

12. 9L 9.40, fol. 203rb–va, 'iudicium synodale'; 5L 2.63.6, 'Item iudicium commeani'; *Casin.*, 199.

13. 9L 9.18e, fol. 199va; 5L 5.189a; Ans. A 11.105; 13L 11.03; *Casin.*, 67; CDP 1 8.208; CDP 2 8.199; 13L (Savigny 3) 10.103.

HERBERT SCHNEIDER

4 New Wine in Old Skins?

Remarks on the *Collectio Burdegalensis*

The biblical saying that no man should put 'new wine in old wine-skins,' for these would otherwise burst (Mt. 9:17; Mk. 2:22; Lk. 5:37), can epitomize the following reflections on the *Collectio Burdegalensis*.[1] Scholars recognized from the first that this collection from southwestern France actually combines two collections that do not entirely fit each other: the already aging, pre-Gregorian *Decretum* of Burchard of Worms[2] and a collection from the Gregorian Reform period, the *Diversorum patrum sententiae* (also called Collection in 74 Titles7, hereafter abbreviated DPS). Since Paul Fournier, the DPS has been regarded as 'le premier manuel de la réforme du XIe siècle,' as a collection giving especial prominence to the papal primacy and to the comments of ancient popes on church law.[3] In

1. A rich body of research on this legal collection has come into being in recent years: Kéry, *Can. Coll.* 215–16; Linda Fowler-Magerl, 'Fine Distinctions and their Transmission of Texts,' ZRG Kan. Abt. 83 (1997) 146–86; idem, *Clavis* 129–32; Kriston R. Rennie, 'The Collectio Burdegalensis and the Transmission of Canonical Texts to Bordeaux c. 1079,' ZRG Kan. Abt. 94 (2008) 1–20; idem, 'The *Collectio Burdegalensis*: A Poitevin Collection?' *Proceedings Esztergom* 2008 (forthcoming).

2. Cited after Migne PL 140. The literature on the *Decretum* is gathered in Kéry, *Can. Coll.* 133–55; Fowler-Magerl, *Clavis* 90. The reserve of the 'Gregorians' towards Burchard is expressly discussed by Detlev Jasper, 'Burchards Dekret in der Sicht der Gregorianer,' in *Bischof Burchard von Worms 1000–1025*, ed. Wilfried Hartmann (Quellen und Abhandlungen zur mittelrheinischen Kirchengeschichte 100; Mainz 2000) 167–98.

3. The editor, John F. Gilchrist, *Diversorum patrum sententie siue Collectio in LXXIV titulos digesta* (MIC Ser. B 1, 1973), still assumed that the collection originated in the circle of Gregory VII. More recent literature in Kéry, *Can. Coll.* 204–10, and Fowler-Magerl, *Clavis* 110, developed a new theory of origins ('Lotharingia'). Horst Fuhrmann already curtailed the reform contours of the DPS in his 'Über den Reformgeist der 74-Titel-Sammlung (Diversorum patrum sententiae),' in *Festschrift für Hermann Heimpel*, ed. by Max-Planck-Institut für Geschichte (Göttingen 1972) 1101–20: 'die Sammlung läßt nicht den rigoristischen Ernst der Reformer erkennen ...' (1120). Rudolf Schieffer, *Die Entstehung des päpstlichen Investiturverbots für den deutschen König* (MGH Schriften; Stuttgart 1982) 193–95, also has a similar assessment.

the *Burdegalensis*, this collection more or less clearly supportive of the Gregorian Reform is joined with reform texts directly connected to Gregory VII himself, appearing here possibly for the first time. One example is the decretal *Licet nova consuetudo*—not found in the papal register—where Gregory intervenes in the liturgy for the sake of reform;[4] another example comprises the ten sharply formulated reform resolutions that the papal legate Hugh (bishop of Die [1073–82], archbishop of Lyon [1082 to 1106]) imposed at the Synod of Poitiers (January 15, 1078).[5] These texts reveal the *Burdegalensis* as a most interesting subject for an investigation of how ideas of the reform period began to enter canon law and did so most likely during the lifetime of the great reform pope at a then flourishing center of canon law.[6]

To recall: the *Collectio Burdegalensis* is transmitted with gaps in seven books in MS Bordeaux, Bibliothèque municipale, ms. 11 (hereafter B); a parallel transmission is found in Würzburg, Universitätsbibliothek, ms. M.p.j.q.2 (hereafter W). Codex W contains sixteen books, revealing for the first time the true extent of this collection. In 1897 Joseph Tardif, relying on B, described this legal collection in detail and called it a 'Collection canonique poitevine' in seven books that were fragmentary, but which had

4. Uta-Renate Blumenthal and Detlev Jasper, '"*Licet nova consuetudo*"—Gregor VII. und die Liturgie,' in *Bishops, Texts and the Use of Canon Law around 1100. Essays in Honour of Martin Brett*, ed. Bruce C. Brasington and Kathleen G. Cushing (Aldershot 2008) 45–68, with proof that the decree really was issued by Gregory VII.

5. See Uta-Renate Blumenthal, 'Hugh of Die and Lyons, Primate and Papal Legate,' in *Scripturus vitam. Lateinische Biographie von der Antike bis in die Gegenwart. Festgabe für Walter Berschin zum 65. Geburtstag*, ed. Dorothea Walz (Heidelberg 2002) 487–95; Kriston R. Rennie, *The Application of Reform in Eleventh-Century France: The Conciliar Activity of Hugh, Bishop of Die (1073–82), Archbishop of Lyons (1082–1106)* (unpublished Ph.D. dissertation, King's College London, 2005). Several essays from the pen of the same author give centrality to the legatine synods of Hugh: Kriston R. Rennie, 'Reform in the Localities: The Council of Valence (May 1079),' AHC 37 (2005) 43–55; idem, 'Collaboration and Council Criteria in the Age of Reform: Legatine Councils under Gregory VII,' AHC 38 (2006) 95–118; idem, '"Uproot and Destroy, Build and Plant": Legatine Authority under Pope Gregory VII (1073–85),' JMH 33 (2007) 166–80; idem, '*Imbutus divinis dogmatibus*: Some Remarks on the Legal Training of Gregorian Legates,' RHD 85 (2007) 301–13; idem, 'Hugh of Die and the Legatine Office under Gregory VII: On the Effects of a Waning Administration,' RHE 103 (2008) 27–49; idem, 'Extending Gregory VII's 'friendship network': Social Contacts in Late Eleventh-century France,' *History* 93 (2008) 475–96; idem, 'The Council of Poitiers (1078) and Some Legal Considerations,' BMCL 27 (2008) 1–20.

6. Gabriel Le Bras, 'L'activíté canonique à Poitiers pendant la réforme grégorienne (1049–1099),' in *Mélanges offerts à René Crozet* 1, ed. Pierre Gallais—Yves-Jean Riou (Cahiers de civilisation médiéval. Supplement; Poitiers 1966) 237–239; Uta-Renate Blumenthal, 'Conciliar Canons and Manuscripts: The Implications of Their Transmission in the Eleventh Century,' *Proceedings Munich 1992*, ed. Peter Landau (MIC Ser. C 10, 1997) 357–79; Fowler-Magerl, *Clavis canonum*, 146–48; Rennie, 'Council of Poitiers,' 1f.; Rennie, 'Hugh of Die' 30f. with n. 8.

lost only one quaternio.[7] In fact, B lacks a good third of the collection. After the discovery of the new exemplar, canon law might have actually carried out a 'rebaptism' and given the collection a new name, calling it a *Collectio Wirzeburgensis* in sixteen books. But since rebaptisms are forbidden by church law, one should by all means retain the established nomenclature, especially since the Würzburg copy also originated in the southwest of today's France.[8]

A new discussion of this collection has to take stock of new studies, most of all those carried out by Kriston R. Rennie, but from a somewhat different perspective. I am not especially concerned with the questions of place of origin and of possible connections with the legate Hugh of Die. Instead, I focus on the collection itself and more precisely should like to shed light on the following three points: the exact textual relationship of the two transmissions with each other; the sources and their use; and finally, briefly, the 'contours' of the *Collectio Burdegalensis.*

1. The Textual Relationship of the Two Transmissions (B and W) to Each Other

Among the surviving sections that are common to both, instances where B preserved a more complete text are in a clear majority. At first glance, therefore, it seems as if W only abbreviated the contents of B. The most important omissions of W compared to B may be listed as follows: in book I.92, W cites the correct rubric ('Si episcopus expulsus ausus fuerit ingredi civitatem unde expulsus est') of the source (Burchard I.84), but then immediately jumps erroneously to the inscription of the next canon in Burchard ('Ex concilio Antiocheno'), simply omitting the actual text; on the next folio, W continues with 'De episcopis, qui se viventibus successores eligere desiderant. Ex concilio Antiocheno,' once again in agreement with Burchard and B.[9] The canon on 'correctio episcopi qui concubinam

7. Joseph Tardif, 'Une collection canonique poitevine,' *Nouvelle revue historique de droit français et étranger* 21 (1897) 149–216.

8. See Hans Thurn, *Die Handschriften der Universitätsbibliothek Würzburg. Fünfter Band: Bestand bis zur Säkularisierung. Erwebungen und Zugänge bis 1803* (Wiesbaden 1994) 112–14. An over-interpretation by Fowler-Magerl, *Clavis canonum* 130, and by Rennie, 'Collectio Burdegalensis and the Transmission' 5 should here be corrected. The impression that W once belonged to a Bishop Peter of Saintes (ca. 1107–11?) is based solely on the following entry on fol. 163v: 'Petrus Petrus presul Xantonensis salutat. Petrus.' Whatever this might actually mean, it does not sound like an ex libris.

9. W, fol. 15v. See Burchard I.184: 'Si episcopus expulsus ausus fuerit ingredi civitatem. Ex epist. Bonifacii papae ad episcopos Galliae.' This is followed by I.185: 'De episcopis qui, se viventibus, successores eligere desiderant. Ex concil. Antiochen. cap. 23.'

habuit' (JE 1249) is completely left out in W, including rubric, inscription, and text, while B includes the text in book I.99, following Burchard (I.195).[10] As a result, W lags behind B by two in the numbering of canons.

Book I of the *Burdegalensis* ends in B with the sequence: I.23 (in W: I.121) 'De reparatione episcoporum post lapsum. Kalixtus urbis Romę episcopus omnibus episcopis. Errant, qui putant...holocaustomatibus et sacrificiis'[11] and the *Epistula Isidori ad Massonam* on lapsed clerics.[12] In another hand on the lower margin of the page, B adds the decretal of Pseudo-Gregory I to Secundinus on the same subject of *lapsi* and positions it between the two previously mentioned canons.[13] In this B follows the formal source (DPS) more fully than W does.

Regarding the prohibition of the marriage of priests in book II, B is again more comprehensive. In c. 41 the two manuscripts still quote together the pertinent famous c. 3 of Nicaea, transmitted by Burchard II.109; followed by Burchard II.112 (in W without the rubric 'Item. De eadem re'). B continues the series with Burchard II.115. This text is left out in W. As a result, W falls behind by one in the numbering of canons in book II. The two manuscripts then again agree with each other quoting Burchard II.117 ('De incontinentibus'). In book III (B: III.91 = Burchard III.236), the canon 'Quod non liceat mortuis osculum dare' is completely left out of W, with the result that, in book III also, W counts one canon fewer than B does.[14]

In this connection it is worthwhile to consider more closely the ending of the collection in both manuscripts. Book XVI excerpts the two last

10. Tardif, 'Collection canonique' 175.

11. DPS 199 and 200 (Gilchrist 124–25) are united into one text, as may often be observed; see below the section 'Elaboration of the Sources.'

12. DPS 202 (Gilchrist 127–30). On the 'Isidorian' letter to Massona, see Roger Reynolds, 'The "Isidorian" Epistula ad Massonam on Lapsed Clerics. Notes on its Early Manuscript and Textual Transmission,' in *Grundlagen des Rechts*, ed. Richard H. Helmholz, Paul Mikat, Jörg Müller, Michael Stolleis (Paderborn 2000) 77–92.

13. DPS 199–202 (Gilchrist 124–30). The letter to Secundinus is much abridged by comparison with DPS 201.

14. Some confusions may be observed in book VI (monastic laws) of W, but they do not constitute any real omission of texts. With canons 13–17 B offers a series that copies Burchard with some omissions but in the correct order (Burchard VIII. 6, 7, 9, 21, 24). At c. 16 ('De clericis qui monachorum propositum appetunt' = Burchard VIII. 21), one might consider a derivation from DPS 312 (Gilchrist 177), but the order, rubric, as well as small textual variants confirm an origin from Burchard. In c. 13, W still agrees with B, but afterwards the manuscript continues in the first hand at first with the rubric of c. 14 ('De clericis qui se fingunt monachos esse et non sunt' = Burchard VIII. 7), corrects this rubric in a second hand to the rubric of c. 16 (... 'qui monachorum propositum appetunt' = Burchard VIII. 21), and then also inserts the text accompanying the corrected rubric. As a result the order in W becomes confused (c. 14, 15, 16, correspond to c. 16, 14, 15 in B), but with c. 17 both manuscripts again agree with each other.

books of Burchard (XIX and XX), focusing in particular on the great mirror of confession of Burchard's Corrector.[15] Manuscript B begins with what is XVI.8 of W. Here, however, notable discrepancies between the two manuscripts become apparent (see Table 4.1).

The omissions can scarcely be accidental. It is impossible that W should have 'overlooked' so many canons by chance. Rather, the omissions must reflect intention and purpose. They first turn up toward the end of the collection, whereas the earlier books (I–VII) contained in the two manuscripts are rather similar in composition. Regarding the first books, therefore, it would be incorrect to claim that W reveals a general and thorough intention to abbreviate by comparison with B. Moreover, it is noteworthy that W's citations are sometimes closer to the formal source than the citations in B are. One example of W's greater degree of faithfulness to the original is found at book I.73. The appeal of a diocesan bishop to the pope is based on DPS, declaring that the appealing bishop is not to experience any limitation of his rights during the course of the proceedings.[16] Only in W is the original decretal of Pseudo-Felix cited in full, as it is in the formal source. If this were the result of a later revision, the reviser would have had to deliberately reconstitute the abbreviated text after checking the original source. In another example, W includes a title and a *capitulatio* at the beginning of the collection; both are lacking in B.[17] The title gives an impression of great authenticity; it names the main source, Burchard of Worms, and devotes to him a historical note, drawn from the *Epistola formata* of Burchard to Bishop Walter of Speyer of the year 1012 (*Decretum* II. 227). This title has to be attributable to the redactor of the *Burdegalensis* himself, for it would surely not have occurred to a later copyist, confronted with an anonymous manuscript looking somewhat like B, that his anonymous collection was an abbreviated *Decretum* of the bishop of Worms. In this case as well, therefore, W is more original.

Evidently, the two manuscripts cannot without contradiction be reduced to a relationship of direct filiation. They might have preserved different stages of compilation; if this is correct, we ought to describe them rather as a 'work in progress' that is illustrated by both codices. One is tempted to advance the idea that both originated as 'textual stages' in one

15. W (fol. 80r–95r): book XVI.1–5 (= Burchard XIX.1–5 [with omissions]); XVI. 6 (= Burchard XIX.7), XVI.7 (= Burchard XX. 91).

16. W fol. 12v–13r: 'Quotie[n]s episcopi se a suis conprovincialibus . . . nichil erit sed viribus carebit' (= DPS, 88). In B the last sentence has been omitted.

17. See below. The *capitulatio* is reproduced (not without some errors) in Fowler-Magerl, *Clavis* 131–32.

Table 4.1

B (fol. 171r–v)	W (fol. 94v–95r)
[Texts VII.10–XVI.8 are missing]	XVI.8: De hoc, cur in hac vita sepius bonis male sit et malis bene.
Cum valde occulta sunt divina ... gehenne perducat tormenta (= Burchard XX.98)	Cum valde oculta sunt divina ... gehennę perducat tormenta (= Burchard XX.98)
Quod etiam omnes infideles resurgere debeant ad tormentum, non ad iudicium. Resurgunt vero omnes infideles sed ad ... habere conati sunt (= Burchard XX.99)	—
Quod omnes homines resurgere debeant Omnium hominum erit resurrectio ... fieri de morte (= Burchard XX.100)	—
De eadem re. Quod autem dicimus in simbolo ... reformati a mortuis iudicent[ur] (= Burchard XX.101)	—
Quod angeli apostate et impii homines post tormenta quasi expurgati suppliciis non iustorum societate donentur. Post resurrectionem et iudicium si ... et angelis suis (= Burchard XX.102)	—
Quod resurrectio fieri debeat in etate perfecte iuventutis, que non indigeat perfectione. Inchoatio pacis sanctorum est in ... disiungi sciendum est (= Burchard XX.103)	—
Quod districtus iudex ad iudicium veniens peccatores videat, ut feriat, non ut salvet.	XVI.9: Quod districtus iudex ad iudicium veniens peccatores videat, ut feriat, non ut salvet.
In iudicium quidem dominus veniens ... vitam pereuntium ignorat (= Burchard XX.104)	In iudicium quidem dominus veniens ... vitam pereuntium ignorat (= Burchard XX.104)
De gloria sanctorum post iudicium.	XVI.10: De gloria sanctorum post iudicium.
Non faciet in futuro cor ... nos ascensuri sumus (= Burchard XX.108)	Non faciet in futurum cor ... nos ascensuri sumus (= Burchard XX.108)
Quod finito iudicio incipiat esse celum novum et terra nova.	XVI.11: Quod finito iudicio incipiat esse cęlum novum et terra nova.
Ut ait beatus Augustinus. Peracto finitoque ... figura non natura (= Burchard XX.109)	Ut ait beatus Augustinus. Peracto finitoque ... figura non natura (= Burchard XX.109)
Contra eos, qui dicunt, si post factum iudicium erit conflagratio mundi, ubi tunc poterunt esse sancti, qui non contingantur flamma incendii.	
Hanc questionem beatus Augustinus dissolvit ... illesa vivere potuerunt (= Burchard XX.110)	

and the same workshop, where the same sources were assembled in accordance with a rather similar plan.[18] Under such circumstances, W itself could also be dated close to the presumed time of origin of the *Collectio Burdegalensis,* assumed to fall shortly after the date of the most recent source it contains, the legatine council of Hugh of Die on January 15, 1078.[19]

2. The Sources and Their Elaboration

Tardif attempted to provide an exact quantification of the percentages of both of the main sources of the *Burdegalensis* and proposed that four-fifths of the canons were derived from Burchard and one-fifth from the DPS.[20] He precisely inventoried the respective shares of the sources in two lists.[21] Rennie subsequently continued the analysis for parts that were still unknown to Tardif, but he catalogued only the borrowings from the DPS.[22] What the *Burdegalensis* owes to the Burchard *Decretum* in the parts transmitted by the Würzburg manuscript will not be presented in detail here.[23] An analysis confirms and strengthens the assessment that the *Burdegalensis* is basically an abbreviated Burchard *Decretum.* In any case, this is made very clear already by the title found exclusively in W (fol. 2v)[24]:

In huius codicis corpore libri sexdecim continentur secundum atitulacionem Bruchardi(!) Wormatiensis aecclesiae venerandi antistitis, qui floruit anno dominice incarnationis millesimo duodecimo ac deinceps prout ipse in quadam sua epistula testatur quę in fine secundi istius libri continetur et formata dicitur.

Thus, the redactor of the *Burdegalensis* intended to reduce the twenty books of Burchard to sixteen. He achieved this goal by simply leaving out much of the material and re-organizing much else. He cited from all the books of the *Decretum,* but to a greatly varying extent. In the first six books he remained rather faithful to the sequence and approximately also

18. See the following section.

19. This is not contradicted by the most recent entry in W that can be securely dated. On fol. 148r, Calixtus II (1119–24) is entered in the papal catalogue without regnal dates. But the list from Pope Marinus (W: *Martinus*) to Calixtus is paleographically very different from the rest of the manuscript and appears on a sewn-in single leaf (fol. 148r–v) that is meant to complement a papal catalogue that originally ended with John VIII (872–82). Undoubtedly the single leaf is more recent and was only later, after 1119, sewn into the manuscript. In B, moreover, the papal catalogue ends with John VIII.

20. Tardif, 'Collection canonique' 150.

21. See Tardif, 'Collection canonique' 151–53 ('Extraits du Décret de Burchard,' in total 307 canons) as against 155 ('Extraits de la Collection en LXXIV Titres,' in total 74 canons).

22. Rennie, 'Collection Burdegalensis and the Transmission,' 16–20. There are small departures from Tardif's groupings.

23. But see below n. 25.

24. W: fol. 2v. See also above at n. 17.

the extent of Burchard's text, but beginning with book VII he increasingly mixed his sources.[25] The desire to abbreviate evidently brought with it many problems affecting the inscriptions. When, for example, Burchard drew from one and the same source in a series of canons, he could refer to them as 'De eodem.' But the redactor of the *Burdegalensis* skipped several items in the formal source and therefore falsified some references.[26] It is possibly because of the difficulty of presenting inscriptions, rubrics, and canonical texts in the correct sequence that W omitted entire rubrics at points where he would certainly have found them in Burchard.[27] Often, the rubrics and the canons that follow no longer fit together. There are cases, therefore, where the redactor at first followed Burchard's rubric but then actually cited the legal text from the next canon.[28] The tendency to abbreviation and terseness shows itself not only in the entire layout but occasionally also within the canons taken over from the source. The redactor does not hesitate sometimes to confine himself to the legally relevant text, with the result that a search for agreements by mere comparisons of incipits is not fruitful.[29]

25. For books I–VII, 10, see the list of Burchard citations in Tardif, 'Collection canonique.' The later books cite Burchard (in parentheses) as follows: VII (Burchard VII and VIII), VIII (IX and VII), IX (X), X (XII), XI (XVII), XII (VI, XI, XIX and XX), XIII (XI and XV), XIV (X, XV and XVI), XV (XIII, XIV, XVIII and XIX), XVI (XIX and XX).

26. Examples within book VIII. In VIII.8, W cites Burchard IX.26 ('Ex concilio apud Vermeriam, cui interfuit Pipinus rex'), but under the inscription 'Ex eiusdem decretis,' which theoretically ought to relate in W to the preceding decretal of Pope Hormisdas. Burchard IX.27 ('Ex eodem concilio,' thus Verberie) is cited in VIII.9, but with the inscription 'Ex decretis cuius supra,' thus again referring to the Hormisdas decretal. Book VIII.27 cites Burchard IX.73 ('Ex conc. Triburiensi, cui interfuit Arnolfus rex, c. 46'), but under the inscription 'Ex eodem concilio,' thus resulting in a reference to a 'concilium Namnetense' etc.

27. Examples from book VIII (the Burchard passages in parentheses): VIII.10 (IX.28), VIII.11 (IX.29), VIII.12 (IX.30), VIII.15 (IX.41), VIII.16 (IX.45), VIII.17 (IX.46), VIII.18 (IX.47), VIII.19 (IX.55), VIII.20 (IX.57), VIII.21 (IX.60), VIII.23 (IX.64), VIII.28 (IX.74).

28. Two examples again from book VIII: VIII.13 'De illis, qui sponsas alienas rapuerunt' adopts the rubric of Burchard, IX.32. But the text that follows is derived from the next canon in Burchard (IX.33): 'Placuit ut hi, qui rapiunt... eam uxorem habeant.' Book VIII.22 'De illis, que nulla causa interveniente reliquerunt viros suos' adopts the rubric of Burchard, IX.62, but then transcribes the text of c. 63 with a slightly altered incipit.

29. Again examples from book VIII. Canon VIII.14 intends to clarify the status of a marriage tie in case of proven impotence and cites Burchard IX.40, under the largely correct rubric 'De his (Burchard, 'illis'), qui in matrimonio sunt (Burchard: 'iuncti sunt') et concumbere non possunt.' But in Burchard the actual legal decision is dressed in the form of a epistolary inquiry ('Quod autem interrogasti de his, qui matrimonio iuncti sunt et nubere non possunt...'), based on the material source (Hrabanus Maurus, *Paenitentiale ad Heribaldum*, c. 29 = Migne PL 110, Sup. 491 A)—with the false inscription 'Ex epistola Gregorii ad Ioannem Ravennatem episcopum.' The *Burdegalensis* is interested only in the legal content: 'Vir et mulier, si se coniunxerint... aliam acceperit separentur.' Book VIII.19 cites Burchard IX.57 and thus the case of women who, on the

Of course, the methodology of the redactor of the *Collectio Burdegalensis* could be established with complete precision only if we knew which copy of Burchard served as his exemplar.[30] Without carrying this search too far, a first hint may be given here. Book I ends with an 'Ordo, qualiter in aecclesia ab episcopo sinodus agatur.'[31] In its formulation this synodal ordo was created specifically for the *Burdegalensis*—in any case, it is transmitted only here—and combines the same main sources as the collection itself: Burchard and the DPS. However, an older synodal ordo served as its basis and can be easily identified. As far as we know, it occurs only after book III in Italian copies of Burchard's *Decretum*.[32] A further observation also seems to point to an early Italian copy of Burchard as a basis for the new compilation. It concerns a specific text that is transmitted in both manuscripts as an addition to the canonical collection: the 'Sermo in synodo dicendus, quem sanctus Leo papa composuit.'[33] This widely circulated, originally anonymous synodal address (JE 2659) was first composed in Mainz in connection with the Pontificale Romano-Germanicum; it had a far-flung circulation afterwards as a text 'extravagans.'[34] In B and W it is at-

---

return of their husbands who had been believed to be dead, preferred to remain in the more recent marriage. Again, the *Burdegalensis* is interested only in the purely legal decision that the new ties were to be dissolved ('Si autem alique mulieres ita…ecclesiastica communione priventur'), whereas Burchard supplied the entire justificatory argument of the material source (Leo I., JK 536, c. 45) without abbreviation.

30. In any case the copy had to have had Burchard's prologue or the compiler of the *Burdegalensis* would not have been able to formulate the title in W. He thus expressly admits his dependence on another canonist, just as Burchard himself does in his prologue. See Robert Somerville and Anders Winroth, '"Collecting Tidbits": Aulus Persius Flaccus and Bishop Burchard of Worms,' SG 27 (1996) 507–16.

31. B: fol. 157r–158r, W: fol. 21v–24v, is found Ordo 5D of my edition MGH Ordines de celebrando concilio (Hannover 1996) 277–84, see also the introduction pp. 41–42. To some extent, the ordo is treated like an item 'extravagans,' for it has been transcribed after an 'Explicit liber I'; but then, curiously, after the ordo another 'Explicit liber primus, incipit secundus…' follows.

32. Ordo 5, ibid. 230–57, introduction 31–37.

33. B: fol. 179r–v, W: fol. 108v–110v. Likewise outside the collection proper and preceding it in B is a further example of this synodal address (fol. 76v–77r), which will not be further taken account of here.

34. Older bibliography for this Admonitio synodalis: Robert Lawson, 'L'homelia dit de Léon IV,' *Revue d'histoire et de littérature religieuses*, n.s. 5 (1914) 117–37; Paul Willem Finsterwalder, 'Die sogenannte Homilia Leonis IV., ihre Bedeutung für Hinkmars Capitula und Reginos Inquisitio,' ZRG Kan. Abt.27 (1938) 639–64; Robert Amiet, 'Une "Admonitio Synodalis" de l'époque carolingienne. Étude critique et Édition,' *Mediaeval Studies* 16 (1964) 12–82; Peter Brommer, 'Die bischöfliche Gesetzgebung Theodulfs von Orléans,' ZRG Kan Abt. 60 (1974) 1–120; Friedrich Lotter, 'Ein kanonistisches Handbuch über die Amtspflichten des Pfarrklerus als gemeinsame Vorlage für den Sermo synodalis "Fratres presbyteri" und Reginos Werk "de synodalibus causis",' ZRG Kan. Abt. 62 (1976) 3–57; Rudolf Pokorny, 'Nochmals zur Admonitio synodalis,' ZRG Kan. Abt. 71 (1985) 20–51.

tributed to a Pope Leo. Only B retained it in the original form, with an addition which indicates that it was originally derived from a synodal ordo: 'Tunc si est synodus in estivo tempore ...'[35] The attribution to Leo and the addition are markers of the transmission of this synodal address in several Italian copies of Burchard's *Decretum*.[36]

Although many texts of the *Burdegalensis* itself, as well as material in the wider context in both B and W, hint at a transmission through Hugh of Die, Pope Gregory VII's legate in Aquitaine, one should not forget Rennie's discovery that a Burchard *Decretum* was among the items of Hugh's testamentary book legacy.[37] To be sure, we do not know anything about the appearance of this 'liber Burchardi,' but it is reasonable to think that it was a copy brought from Italy. Concerning the second main source, the DPS, Linda Fowler-Magerl completely changed the discussion surrounding the localization of this first collection of the reform period when she argued that it originated not in the papal circle in Italy but north of the Alps, in 'Lotharingia,' perhaps even in Cologne.[38] Quite apart from the question of the geographical origin of the DPS though, it is of interest here to pursue the question of how this collection was used in the *Burdegalensis*, and to begin with, to ask to what extent its texts were adopted. Tardif and now Rennie have undertaken to determine this materially.[39] Tardif partly

35. In B the addition is only found after an additional synodal address ('Audite fratres et conpresbyteri quomodo ...') on fol. 180r, but it originally certainly belonged to the end of the Admonitio 'Fratres presbyteri et sacerdotes domini': 'Tunc si est sinodus illa in estivo tempore... His omnibus rite peractis signis simul sonantibus ab episcopo vel a cantore excelsa voce incipiatur antiphona: "In viam pacis dirige nos, domine," cum psalmo.' See MGH Ordines de celebrando concilio 232 n. 3 and p. 488. Franz Pelster, 'Das Dekret Bischof Burkhards von Worms (1000–1025) in Vatikanischen Handschriften,' in *Miscellanea Giovanni Mercati 2: Letterature medioevale* (Studi e testi 122, 1946) 144, considered this 'ein Zeichen, daß in Mittelitalien die Synode im Frühsommer gehalten wurde.' The phrase was originally coined for springtime ('Tunc si est synodus illa in vernali tempore ...'), see MGH Ordines de celebrando concilio 488 (Ordo 17 Nr. 42). This synodal ordo 17 is found at the beginning of the copy of the *Decretum* written under the eyes of Burchard himself (Pal. lat. 585); but there is also an early transmission in MS Parma, Bibl. Palatina, Parm. 3777.

36. The following Italian *Decretum* manuscripts have the same form of the Admonitio synodalis: Lucca, Bibl. Cap. Feliniana, ms. 124 (11th cent. 4th quarter; fol. 193v–194r); Paris, Bibl. Nat., ms. lat. 9630 (12th cent, 1st quarter, Central Italy; fol. 257r); Rome, Bibl. Vallicelliana, A.20 (12th cent., middle; connected to book XIX of the *Decretum*); Città del Vaticano, Bibl. Apostolica Vaticana, Vat. lat. 1355 (11th cent.; fol. 310r–311v); Vat. lat. 7790 (12th cent., beginning; fol. 163r–164v); Vat. lat. 14731 (11th cent. ex.).

37. Rennie, 'Council of Poitiers' 18 n. 46.

38. Fowler-Magerl, *Clavis* 110–18, according to Detlev Jasper, this argument is "brisant... und [könnte] zur Neubewertung eines Teils der vorgratianischen Kirchenrechtssammlungen führen ..." (DA 62, 2006) 215.

39. Tardif, 'Collection canonique' 155 and Rennie, 'Collectio Burdegalensis and the Transmission,' 16–20.

contradicted himself by attributing several canons of the *Burdegalensis* to Burchard and to the DPS at the same time;[40] in most of these cases a clear decision for either one or the other is possible.[41] But Rennie's tables also need to be corrected in several instances.[42] It is sometimes difficult to decide which of the two sources the compiler followed;[43] in other cases, the readings differ so much from Burchard or the DPS that one cannot but conclude that the compiler used other sources as well, such as possibly the Pseudo-Isidorian Decretals directly, the original source for a number of texts.[44]

Although the source analysis still has to be refined, a few observations may nevertheless be offered regarding those ca. sixty-six canons from the DPS that, among about 631 canons, comprise about ten percent of the *Collectio Burdegalensis*. In contrast to his usage of Burchard's *Decretum*, the

40. Tardif declares that 27 canons were derived from the DPS for which he had formerly proposed a provenance from Burchard (I.5, 6, 37, 39, 43, 44, 61, 63, 66, 67, 70, 71, 72, 78, 79, 83, 88, 91, 123b, 124; II.5; III.21, 22, 78; IV.18; VI.12, 16).

41. As a result, in book I, cc. 37, 39, 43 und 44 must be excluded as borrowings from DPS; they are all derived from Burchard. Also I.88 ('De dampnatione episcoporum accusantium episcopum absque auctoritate apostolicę sedis') corresponds in rubric and extent to Burchard I.175, not DPS 96; likewise I.91 (= Burchard I.180, not DPS 108) and II.5 (= Burchard II.5, not DPS 146).

42. Rennie, 'Collectio Burdegalensis and the Transmission,' omitted the following borrowings from the DPS: I. 66 (= DPS 48). Likewise the decretal of Gregory I to Secundinus I. 125 (numbering of B; the decretal is missing in W) presumably is dervied from DPS 201, because the final chapters of this book are all taken from it. Book III. 24 corresponds to DPS 207; III. 78 corresponds to DPS 309 by its attribution to Pseudo-Fabian as well as by textual variants; on the other hand, the following ostensible borrowings from DPS listed by Rennie should be deleted: VII. 1 (rather Burchard VIII. 15 than DPS 248, because the rubric is incorporated into the book title and the addition 'et non ante XXV annos' is also found in Burchard); IX. 3 (Burchard X.23 because of the rubric, the inscription and the ordering of the surrounding canons), XIII.3 (Burchard XV.6 and 7 combined). The compiler could have taken the famous Two Powers decretal of Gelasius (XIV.1) from DPS 227; XIV. 2 corresponds to DPS 180.

43. In I. 83 the rubric corresponds to Burchard I. 140 ('De infamatis et dilaceratis episcopis et a civitatibus propriis pulsis'), the textual variants correspond in part to DPS 82. In XIV. 15 laymen are denied any rights with regard to church property. The rubric suggests a borrowing from Burchard XV. 35, and several textual variants ('legitur umquam adtributa facultas') point partly to DPS 260. The *Burdegalensis* also departs from both with an addition of its own: 'Rex quoque pius Theodoricus (corr. 'Theodericus') in causa Simmachi papę nichil ad se praeter reverentiam de ęcclesiasticis negociis pertinere professus est.' The origin of XIV. 38 also cannot be clearly explained: the rubric, inscription, and ordering of the surrounding canons speak for Burchard XVI. 15, the incipit on the other hand for DPS 50.

44. Burchard and the DPS are by no means the only sources for the *Burdegalensis*. Fowler-Magerl, *Clavis* 131, already drew attention to patristic texts in book IX that precede those of *Collectio IV librorum* in MS London, Brit. Libr., Arundel 173. Further, at least the following canons of the *Burdegalensis* cannot be found in the same form in Burchard and the DPS: IX. 7–12; XII. 6 and 7.14–17, 24, 25 (penitential texts); XIV. 12–14, 18, 20–23, 28, 30–32, 36; XV. 4 (an address to penitents), 11, 17, 18, 23.

compiler in general cites the DPS carefully, that is, while working eclectically, he strove to supply the canons with the correct rubric, even if they were found much further ahead within the DPS.[45] As a rule, the inscriptions were also faithfully copied, including papal names and addressees. In some cases, two canons from the DPS were not separated from each other but copied as a single canon.[46] One might assume that the textual version of the canons derived from the DPS agreed with the readings of the texts of the DPS in the *Collectio Tarraconensis,* which is transmitted attached to the *Burdegalensis* in both B and W. The two collections have at least fourteen canons in common.[47] However, there are no significant agreements, and thus it seems unlikely that the two canonical collections were derived from one and the same exemplar of the DPS. It is now time to return to the initial question: does the new canonical collection have a claim to being particularly reform-oriented?

3. The 'Contours' of the *Burdegalensis*

To begin with, the compiler essentially follows Burchard's *Decretum,* up to book V inclusively, but with a clear intention to abbreviate. The topics, therefore, also match Burchard's at first: church hierarchy, starting with the pope and passing on to the patriarchs and primates, metropolitans, bishops, priests, down to the remaining *ordines ecclesiastici.* Then follow the canons on church building and the founding of churches, tithes, canonical and apocryphal books, the sacramental law concerning baptism and the Eucharist—thus, there are all the Burchard topics, enriched with occasional chapters of the DPS. Beginning with book VI, the *Collectio Burdegalensis* departs

45. For book I, see I. 1 'De electione Romani antistitis' following c. 177 of the DPS ('Item de eadem re cap. IIII,' Gilchrist 111), but there referring to title 22 'De Romano pontificatu' (Gilchrist 110). I.5 'Ut non laici nec bigami non viduam mariti sed inreprehensibiles ordinentur episcopi,' canon 118 of the DPS, under the rubric 'Item de eadem re cap. III' (Gilchrist 77), is part of the title 'De prelatis imperitis indignis symoniacis neophitis' (Gilchrist 74). Or I. 6 'Quod nolentibus clericis vel populis nullus ordinetur episcopus,' after DPS 113 ('Item de eadem re cap. V,' Gilchrist 75), part of the same title. Examples are numerous.

46. Book I: I. 16 combines canons 165 and 166 of the DPS, in I. 121 (in B: 123) DPS 199 and 200 are combined (Gilchrist 124–25). The peculiarity of the so-called 'Swabian recension' of the DPS to dispense with the rubrics, is probably not the reason why the *Burgdegalensis* occasionally combines two canons, for the collection certainly uses rubrics elsewhere.

47. I have compared the following thirteen canons from W that are common to both collections—B relies more often on DPS. The Gilchrist numbers are given in parentheses; the canons are listed in the order of the excerpt from the *Tarraconensis*: I. 1 (1); I. 76 (96); I. 114 (167); I. 7 (111); I. 16 (165 and 166); in B the abbreviated decretal of Pseudo-Gregory to Secundinus is also relevant: (I. 124 = 201); III. 22 (205); IV. 17 (216); III. 27 (223); XIV. 1 (227); I. 122 (247); I. 118 (B: 120) (314); VI. 14 (312).

from the order provided by Burchard and conspicuously turns to monastic law under a separate title: 'Sextus liber continet de monasteriorum monachorumque libertate et eorum sancto proposito.' Book VII continues the monastic topic ('de viris ac feminis deo dicatis sacrum propositum transgredientibus, de revocatione et penitentia eorum'). Books VIII to XVI, although inspired by Burchard, no longer follow him step by step, but instead combine all sorts of canons dealing with marital and penitential law: with oaths, murder, and adultery, and respective penances, with excommunication and the judicial system, as well as rules regarding fasts and food. The collection concludes with book XVI, whose contents are mainly composed of the great penitential from Burchard's *Corrector*, combined with a few theologico-speculative canons from Burchard's *Speculator*.

The emphasis on monastic regulations could lead to the compiler's background. Indeed, scholarship has retreated from the old theory according to which the *Burdegalensis* originated in a special legal school at Poitiers. It now seems more likely that it was compiled at a monastery, possibly La Sauve Majeure at Bordeaux, an establishment that experienced a great expansion toward the end of the eleventh century in connection with the pilgrimage route to Compostella.[48] This might also explain why the special topics of the Gregorian Reform, such as simony, the purchase of offices, priests' marriage, and royal investiture, are of minor importance in the collection. The compiler even disregarded some of the respective material that Burchard supplied concerning these topics. For example, the strict prohibition of simony from the Council of Meaux-Paris (845–46) that Burchard supplied via Regino of Prüm was simply omitted.[49] Several canons of Burchard against the marriage of priests and the prohibition of the cohabitation of priests and women are included, but by no means all.[50] Out of about eleven relevant canons in Burchard, the new collection basically adopted four (W) or five (B). Even the supposed Canon of the Apostles, which could have been presented as a pièce de résistance of the primitive church against lay investiture, was passed over: 'Si quis episcopus saecularibus potestatibus usus ecclesiam per ipsas obtineat, deponatur et segregetur omnesque qui illi communicant.'[51] Burchard's book XV 'De lai-

48. Rennie, 'Collectio Burdegalensis and the Transmission' 10f. A historical note about the origins of monasticism (Antonius, Martin von Tours) in W (fol. 163r, see Thurn, *Handschriften Würzburg* 114) possibly also points to an origin of the manuscript in a monastery.

49. Burchard, *Decretum* I.21 (Migne PL 140, 555).

50. Book II. 40, 41, 42 and 44 ≑ Burchard II. 108, 109, 112 and 117. Canon 43 is missing in W, but is present in B and corresponds to Burchard II. 115.

51. Burchard III. 109. See the comments in Schieffer, *Investiturverbot* 35.

cis' most clearly details the coordination of spiritual and temporal power, but the *Burdegalensis* did not even adopt the pertinent texts under a title of their own; instead, it scattered individual canons derived from it over several books. From its perspective, what mattered in this connection were not emperors but kings.[52]

The examples mentioned were all taken from Burchard and certainly do not at all reveal a particular interest in reform. And what of the contribution of the DPS? Perhaps the *Collectio Burdegalensis* derived from it the famous decretal of Pope Gelasius I about the relationship of the Two Powers.[53] But if this is the case the compiler markedly sharpened its tone, for he lets his Gelasius end with a strongly anti-lay embellishment: 'quapropter regalis seu iudicialis potestas subdi debet praesulibus...in iudiciis saecularibus'! That temporal power should also be subordinated to the spiritual *in iudicibus saecularibus* notably intensifies the customary sense of the Gelasian decretal and cannot be read in this form in the DPS. But the revised text is not related to a specifically 'Gregorian' topic either. All in all, only the decretal 'Licet nova consuetudo' and those ten resolutions of the 1078 synod of Poitiers can be clearly attributed to the Gregorian Reform. The latter decrees also appear in three additional contemporary collections compiled in the same region.[54] They are 'the oldest prohibition of investiture that has been transmitted in its full text.'[55] The compiler of the *Burdegalensis* placed this prohibition at the end of his first book that focuses on the reconstruction of the church, but one might consider it an item 'extravagans,' as though the author was surprised by this drumbeat of the reform in the midst of his own work. He did not distribute the individual decisions systematically under corresponding rubrics or create a separate book dealing with the topic; only 'Licet nova consuetudo' is found

52. Cf. Book XIII. 1 (= Burchard XV.1). Book XIII. 4 cites Burchard XV. 8, but replaces 'imperator' with 'rex': 'Quod non liceat regibus vel cuiquam potentum aliquid agere contra divinum mandatum,' and then changes the context by adding from Burchard's c. 10 the sentence: 'Rex enim et imperator non est super legem, sed subtus' (against Burchard: 'Lex imperatorum non est supra legem, sed subtus').

53. Book XIV. 1, similarly DPS 227 (Gilchrist 142). Burchard does not include the decretal.

54. The almost contemporary collections from southwestern France also include the text: the Turin collection in seven books (D. IV. 33), the *Tarraconensis*, the collection in Thirteen Books; see above all Rennie, 'Council of Poitiers' 2f; Rennie, 'Hugh of Die' 28; Rennie, 'Collectio Burdegalensis and the Transmission' 2f. On the *Tarraconensis* see also Fowler-Magerl, 'Vier französische und spanische vorgratianische Kanonessammlungen', in *Aspekte europäischer Rechtsgeschichte. Festgabe für Helmut Coing zum 70. Geburtstag* (Ius commune. Sonderheft 17, 1983) 123–46.

55. Schieffer, *Investiturverbot*, 166. An early prohibition of investiture, which Hugh of Die imposed at a synod of Autun in 1075 at Gregory VII's behest, may be only indirectly inferred; ibid. 162–65.

at a systematically relevant place. The Synod of Poitiers is put at the disposal of users in the typical fashion of historically ordered canonical collections. The provisions are labeled as *Decretum generale.*[56] Gregory VII is not cited by name. Thus, this canonical collection, originating in the years of the accelerating reform, included and heeded revolutionary new ideas but did not actually integrate them. In this manner the 'new wine' was isolated in 'old skins,' and did not burst the skins; rather, it could ripen there unhindered.

56. As is stressed by Fowler-Magerl, *Clavis* 130, and Rennie, 'Collectio Burdegalensis and the Transmission' 2f., this label is peculiar to the *Burdegalenis.* Such a characterization of the resolutions of Poitiers in 1078 no longer lets the decrees appear as local church law ('partikulares Kirchenrecht'), as Schieffer, *Investiturverbot* 166f. suggested. Not until the Lateran synod of November 9, 1078, did Pope Gregory VII demonstrably promulgate this new law to its full extent for the entire Church, Reg. VI 5b, c. 3 (MGH Epp. sel. 2, 403).

FRANCK ROUMY

5 A New Manuscript of the *Collectio Sinemuriensis* (New York, Columbia University, Western MS 82)

An early twelfth-century manuscript, whose precise origin remains unknown, was sold at the Hotel Drouot in Paris, on Wednesday, January 28, 2004. Although the volume includes no miniatures but only a few decorated initials, the bidding reached the high sum of €46,500. The codex was acquired by a dealer that specialized in the sale of rare manuscripts, the *Les Enluminures* bookstore. Thanks to the speedy action of Robert Somerville, to whom these lines are dedicated, and to Dr. Consuelo Dutschke of the manuscript and rare book department of Columbia University Library in New York, the *Les Enluminures* bookstore sold the manuscript to Columbia, where it is housed at present under the call number Western MS 82.

The manuscript was auctioned as part of a lot including various items. Among them were several old books, but especially a sizable collection of autographs and letters of the nineteenth century, some photographs, and the watch of the famous interwar French poet Antoine de Saint-Exupéry.[1] The incongruous presence of a medieval manuscript of unidentified content in this rather heterogeneous gathering of objects gave rise to an appraisal, entrusted to the author of these lines. Thanks to the indispensable CD-Rom of Linda Fowler-Magerl that inventories the canonical collections prior to Gratian's *Decretum*,[2] it was easy to establish the nature of the text in

1. The sale, entrusted to the auctioneers Bernard Oger and Étienne Dumont, occasioned a catalogue containing a summary description of the manuscript, including several photographs: Oger et Dumont, *Livres anciens, lettres et manuscrits autographes, 28 janvier 2004* (S. l. n. d. [Paris 2003]) 7–8. One fourth of the cover contains a photo of the manuscript.

2. The analysis of the text in question was carried out using the second version of the CD-Rom: Linda Fowler-Magerl, *KanonesJ*[2] (Piesenkofen 2003). A new enlarged version, accompanied by a valuable volume presenting the analyzed collections, is now available: Linda Fowler-Magerl, *Clavis.*

the manuscript: it clearly was a copy, hitherto unknown, of the celebrated *Collectio Sinemuriensis*. Since the time allotted to the appraisal was generous, it was possible to undertake a detailed analysis of the codex,[3] whose interest for the literary history of the Semur collection is far from negligible.

The Semur collection takes its name from manuscript 13 of the Municipal Library of Semur-en-Auxois, in Burgundy.[4] Not known to Paul Fournier and Gabriel Le Bras, the collection appears to have been first identified by Paul Hinschius in manuscript 438 of the National Library in Madrid.[5] His discovery appears, however, to have remained unknown for about a century, until the importance of the collection was set out by Gérard Fransen, who was able to identify the Semur manuscript thanks to information furnished by Robert Somerville.[6] But it is to Linda Fowler-Magerl, who discovered three more manuscripts of this text (Orléans, BM, 306; Paris, BN, lat. 18221; Sélestat, BM, 13), that the collection owes its first detailed study.[7]

As has often been emphasized, the *Collectio Sinemuriensis* does not adopt either of the two classic schemas found in most canonical compilations prior to Gratian's *Decretum:* it is neither chronological nor systematic. Instead, it takes the form of the collections similar to Benedictus Levita's, which compile texts by blocks of sources, a method that seems rather characteristic of 'militant' collections, gathered with a view to reform or to the defense of ecclesiastical rights.[8] As it is, the *Sinemuriensis* is consid-

3. I should like to warmly thank M. et Mme Pascal Ract-Madoux, booksellers in Paris, who invited me to examine the manuscript and gave me all the time needed to engage in its study, in the best possible conditions.

4. For a very summary description: Cat. gén. (1887) 6.301–302.

5. Paul Hinschius, 'Über Pseudo-Isidor-Handschriften und Kanonessammlungen in spanischen Bibliotheken', ZKG 3 (1863) 139–41, gave the collection, organized in three books, a hasty but quite precise description, notably underscoring borrowings from Burchard and the presence of fragments of Ansegis of Fontenelle and Hincmar.

6. Gérard Fransen, 'Manuscrits de collections canoniques,' BMCL 6 (1976) 67–68, repr. in Gérard Fransen, *Canones et quaestiones* (Bibliotheca eruditorum 25; Goldbach 2002) 1.1.479–83.

7. Linda Fowler-Magerl, 'Vier französische und spanische vorgratianische Kanonessammlungen,' *Aspekte europäischer Rechtsgeschichte. Festgabe für Helmut Coing zum 70. Geburtstag* (Ius commune, Sonderheft 17; Frankfurt am Main 1982) 124–41. She suggested that the collection should be named *Collectio Remensis* owing to its place of composition, but returned to the former name in order to avoid possible confusions with the collection of ms. Berlin, Staatsbibl., Philipps 1743: Linda Fowler-Magerl, *Ordo iudiciorum vel ordo iudiciarius. Begriff und Literaturgattung* (Ius commune, Sonderheft 19; Frankfurt am Main 1984) 20, n. 63.

8. On this method of compilation, see the comments of Linda Fowler-Magerl, 'Vier französische und spanische vorgratianische Kanonessammlungen' 125–26, and Franck Roumy, 'Remarques sur l'œuvre canonique d'Abbon de Fleury,' in *Abbon, un abbé de l'an mil*, ed. Annie Dufour and Gillette Labory (Bibliothèque d'histoire culturelle du Moyen Âge 6; Turnhout 2008) 311–41.

ered today the oldest of the collections having brought into play the ideas of the Gregorian Reform.[9] Yet it was composed in several stages. As Linda Fowler-Magerl has shown, a first version appears to have been completed at Reims at the end of the tenth century. This first recension may have been contemporaneous with or a little later than the pontificate of John XII († 964), the last pope in the list occurring in the Semur manuscript.[10] The origin of this recension may be inferred from the inclusion of a series of privileges aiming to justify the primacy of the archepiscopal see of Reims, as well as several fragments of the works of Hincmar.[11] As to its contents, the recension contained no more than 209 canons, among them many extracts from Pseudo-Isidore and from the letters of Gregory the Great.[12]

This first version, whose numbering of canons left traces in two of the existing manuscripts (Orléans and Semur), has not survived. The oldest recension that has come down to us, a revision of the first, is now represented by two witnesses: manuscripts Paris BN, lat. 18221, and Sélestat, BM, 13, dating respectively from the beginning of the twelfth century and the end of the eleventh. The texts transmitted by these two manuscripts, which appear to have been assembled in the second quarter of the eleventh century, attest to the reception in northeast Gaul of the *Decretum* of Burchard of Worms. We know, moreover, that what may be called the oldest surviving recension of the *Collectio Sinemuriensis* was utilized by Bernold of Constance or his entourage, as is attested by the Sélestat manuscript, originating from the monastery of St. Aurelius at Hirsau.[13]

The second surviving recension of the collection, which one might say represents the 'Gregorian' recension, was till now represented by three manuscripts (Madrid, BN, 428; Orléans, BM, 306; Semur-en-Auxois, BM, 13), all of which date from the beginning of the twelfth century. The Madrid and Semur manuscripts have very similar contents, comprising 561 and 574 canons, grouped in three books. Whereas the first two books of the collection vary only in their chapter numbering—the Semur manuscript has 229 canons in book one, and book two starts at canon 190 in

9. Cf. Kéry, *Can. Coll.* 203–4.

10. Semur-en-Auxois, BM, fol. 77–78r = *Collectio Sinemuriensis* 3.105.

11. Cf. Fowler-Magerl, 'Vier französische und spanische vorgratianische Kanonessammlungen' 128–30.

12. The main texts of this first version are presented in Fowler-Magerl, *Clavis* 104–5.

13. Ian Stuart Robinson, 'Zur Arbeitweise Bernolds von Konstanz und seines Kreises. Untersuchungen zum Schlettstädter Codex 13,' DA 34 (1978) 51–122. Robinson, who did not identify the collection as such in the Sélestat manuscript, nevertheless gives a good summary of the material sources that it contains (pp. 57–58). See also Martina Stratmann, 'Zur Rezeption Hinkmars von Reims durch Burchard von Hildesheim und Bernold von Konstanz,' DA 44 (1988) 170–80.

the Madrid manuscript—the order of the third book is quite different.[14] This same order is found in the Orléans manuscript, whose chaptering also resembles that of the Madrid codex but which in addition contains an important appendix of 164 canons, a large number of which appear to be borrowed from the collection of Anselm of Lucca or that of Cardinal Deusdedit; they were used for composing version two of the *Collectio Tarraconensis*, a work regarded as a privileged witness to the diffusion of Gregory VII's reform policy.[15] Series of fragments borrowed from this second recension of the *Sinemuriensis* are found in various other Gregorian assemblages, such as the *Collectio Atrebatensis*,[16] the collection of Vallicelliana manuscript B.89,[17] the collection of Cambridge, Corpus Christi College 442,[18] or even in the Swabian Appendix of the *Collection in 74 Titles*.[19] Besides, according to Alfons Becker, Urban II very probably used the *Sinemuriensis*, which he would have come in contact with when he was archdeacon of Reims.[20] In a judicial mandate of 1091, the pope appears to have borrowed from it the concept of *ordo judiciarius* found in Hincmar's *Opusculum in 55 Chapters*, many fragments of which are in the Semur collection.[21] This second version of the *Sinemuriensis* seems to have been composed after the Reims council of 1049 and without doubt to have begun to circulate a little after 1067, as is attested by the presence of a letter of

14. Cf. Fowler-Magerl, 'Vier französische und spanische vorgratianische Kanonessammlungen' 127.

15. Fowler-Magerl, ibid. 128, and *Clavis* 108, 133–34 and 167; the fragments borrowed from the Orléans ms. form c. 151–224 of *Tarraconensis IIa*.

16. Linda Fowler-Magerl, 'Fine Distinctions and the Transmission of Texts,' ZRG Kan. 83 (1997) 130.

17. Wilfried Hartmann, 'Die Kanonessammlung der Handschrift Rom, Biblioteca Vallicelliana, B. 89,' BMCL 17 (1987) 45–64.

18. Martin Brett, 'The Collectio Lanfranci and its Competitors,' *Intellectual Life in the Middle Ages. Essays presented to Margaret Gibson*, ed. Lesley Smith and Benedicta Ward (London–Rio Grande 1992) 169.

19. Fowler-Magerl, 'Vier französische und spanische vorgratianische Kanonessammlungen' 137, and Fowler-Magerl, *Clavis* 116.

20. Alfons Becker, 'Rechtsprinzipien und Verfahrensregeln im päpstlichen Gerichtswesen zur Zeit Urbans II,' *Landesgeschichte und Reichsgeschichte. Festschrift für Aloïs Gerlich zum 70. Geburtstag*, ed. Winfried Dotzauer et al. (Geschichtliche Landeskunde 42; Stuttgart 1995) 54–55.

21. JL 5451. The expression appears in the *Collectio Sinemuriensis* 2.49 (Semur-en-Auxois, BM, 13, fol. 40–42r), in a fragment borrowed from the *Opusculum LV Capitulorum* 28, ed. Rudolf Schieffer, *Die Streitschriften Hinkmars von Reims und Hinkmars von Laon. 869–871* (MGH, Conc. 4, Suppl. 2; Hanover 2003) 266. Nevertheless, as noted by Alfons Becker himself, 'Rechtsprinzipien' 56, this text also appears in the Collection of Anselm of Lucca (3.67, ed. Friedrich Thaner [Innsbruck 1906–15, repr. Aalen 1965] 149). For the reception of Hincmar's Opusculum in the *Sinemuriensis*, see Schieffer, *Streitschriften* 123–24, and on the diffusion of the concept *ordo judiciarius*, see Fowler-Magerl, *Ordo iudiciorum* 14–27.

the citizens of Florence to Alexander II about the simoniac Peter, dated in that year.[22]

Although the *Sinemurensis*, neither chronological nor systematic, could not have been very convenient to use, it had a relatively wide circulation. This was undoubtedly due to its extent and its dogmatic contents, in particular its many provisions condemning simony. As Linda Fowler-Magerl has put it, the collection presented itself as 'ein Beispiel für eine Reform initiative aus dem höheren französischen Klerus.'[23]

As we shall see, Western MS 83 of Columbia University Library is unquestionably related to this second recension of the *Sinemuriensis*. We shall now describe it (I) before analyzing its contents (II).

I

The codex is a small parchment volume, close to in-8° format (222 × 152 mm). It consists of 119 unnumbered folios, comprising 15 quaternios. The first folio of the first gathering, as well as the last two folios of the last gathering, have disappeared. The binding, of rigid vellum, dates from the eighteenth century, and the back of the volume has the old call number 'E 91,' which reappears on the verso of the cover accompanied by the auxiliary number 1 (E 91/1), justifying the inference that there was originally a second volume. The presence of this call number leads naturally to the question of where the manuscript was housed at the end of the Ancien Régime. Unfortunately, call numbers of this kind were very often used and cannot furnish precise information on this point. The classification 'E' was, at it happens, often used in library catalogues of modern times to classify volumes concerning canon law.[24] Failing the least information about later owners of the volume, we can resort only to rather vague conjectures, based on the comments present on the flyleaf accompanying the binding. This flyleaf contains a summary of the contents of the codex, written by an eighteenth-century hand, which specifies that the volume includes a *Notitia provinciarum* as well as a collection of canons containing at its midpoint the *De*

22. *Collectio Sinemuriensis* 3.95 (Semur-en-Auxois, BM, 13, fol. 76r) = New York, Columbia, Western MS 82, 3.87 = Madrid, BN, 428, 3.86 = Orléans, BM, 306, p. 228, no. 456; the letter was transmitted by Andreas Strumensis († 1106), *Vita sancti Johannis Gualberti* 8 (PL 146.801A). See, on this point, Fowler-Magerl, 'Vier französische und spanische vorgratianische Kanonessammlungen' 130, and *Clavis* 106.

23. Fowler-Magerl, 'Vier französische und spanische vorgratianische Kanonessammlungen' 141.

24. Such is the case, for example, of the catalogue of printed books of the Royal Library in Paris, drawn up by Nicolas Clément in 1684, as well as his second catalogue, compiled in 1688. This system continued to be used into the nineteenth century, cf. Leopold Delisle's introduction to the *Catalogue général des livres imprimés de la Bibliothèque nationale* 1 (Paris 1924), especially pp. IV–V.

vita et ordinatione episcoporum of Pseudo-Ambrose, attributed to Gerbert by Mabillon, as well as an ample fragment of Hincmar of Reims's *Opusculum* in 55 chapters.[25] These quite accurate particulars bear witness to the passage of the manuscript through relatively learned hands. The fact is confirmed by another note, also in an eighteenth-century hand, in the margin of a chapter of the second book of the canonical collection contained in the codex (2.88). This note indicates that the chapter, a formula for the emancipation of a serf, comes from the formularies of Sirmond and Lindenbruch and was present in the *Decretum* of Burchard of Worms.[26] These elements justify the inference that the volume was in a relatively major ecclesiastical library under the Ancien Régime or, at the very least, in the hands of a learned community, such as for example, the congregation of Saint-Maur.

Turning now to the inside of the codex, the text is first transcribed by the same hand in two columns for the nine first folios, which contain the *Notitia provinciarum* and the capitulatio of the collection.[27] In contrast, the canons are then transcribed in long lines; the written space is 155 × 95 mm. Lined in dry point, the parchment has traces of prickings. Generally, it has 26 lines per page, and the text begins to be written above the top line. The writing dates from the first half of the twelfth century and belongs to the north of France, as was confirmed by the paleographers whom I consulted.[28] Several graphical peculiarities deserve to be underscored: besides the regular use of ę, systematically for *ęcclesia* and its derivatives, one often

25. New York, Columbia University, Western MS 82, flyleaf, verso: 'Notitia provinciarum ecclesiasticarum Galliae. Collectio canonum, quibus admiscetur post medium praefatio et libellus beati Ambrosii nomine inscriptus De vita et ordinatione episcoporum et simoniaca haeresii a Domino Johanni Mabillono restitutus Silvestro II papa et vulgatus Anaclet., etc. Circa medium habetur amplum fragmentum libri 55 capitum Hincmari, incipiens a capite 35 hujus libri, ab his scilicet verbis: "Cuicumque igitur primates provinciarum"'.

26. New York, Columbia University, Western MS 82, fol. 79r: 'Iisdem prope verbis concipitur formula 91 apud Lindenbrogium, apud Sirmondum formula 12 et apud Burchardum Lib. 2, cap. 30.' The text in question does in fact come from Burchard (*Decretum* 2.30, ed. Köln 1548, repr. Aalen 1992, fol. 37v) and belongs to a group of fragments (*Decretum* 2.27, 28 et 30, ed. cit. fol. 37rv) that he borrowed from Regino of Prüm (*Libri duo de synodalibus causis* 1.414–15, ed. Hermann Wasserschleben [Leipzig 1840, repr. Graz 1964] 187–89); its substance, though, does not exactly correspond to the Frankish formularies: cf. Hartmut Hoffmann and Rudolf Pokorny, *Das Dekret des Bischofs Burchard von Worms* (MGH, Hilfsmittel 12; Munich 1991) 182–83. The canon occasions the note (*Sinemuriensis* 2.88: 'Qui debitum sibi nexum—tempore maneat inconvulsa') derived from the Tours formulary (Sirmond), no. 12 (= Lindenbruch, no. 91), ed. Karl Zeumer, *Formulae merowingici et karolini aevi* (MGH, Leges, sect. 5; Hanover 1886) 141.20–142.9.

27. Each column is 40 mm wide, with 20 mm between the columns.

28. I should like to give special thanks for their valuable advice to Mme Marie-Françoise Damongeot and M. François Avril, curators at the Cabinet des manuscrits of the Bibliothèque nationale de France, as well as to Mme Patricia Stirnemann, researcher at the Institut de recherche et d'histoire de textes.

encounters the tironian ligature &, including at the end of certain words, and, occasionally, *qu* for *c* (for example, 1.67: *quassabitur*). The text is written in brown ink. The beginning of each of the three books has a large initial, which is about eight lines high. Each initial is formed by plant tendrils that have also been outlined in brown, while their interiors have been left unfilled to give relief to the motif, which is shaded in red. The first initial is a *C* (fol. 10), composed of twisted coils ending in acanthus leaves. The two others, a *P* (fol. 49v) and a *D* (fol. 99v) are formed of coilings ending in heads of fanciful birds vomiting tendrils. The incipit of the books, and the rubrics and headings of certain canons, have been traced in red. The rubricator appears to have had a list of titles, of which several differed from those present in the capitulatio. Whereas some of them seem to have simply been abridged or simplified, or even corrupted by a mistaken reading, others seem to have been markedly different from the start and are, besides, longer than those of the table of contents (1.33; 1.173; 1.213; 2.81; 2.89).[29]

In view, on one hand, of the decorations that have just been described and, on the other hand, of the very tidy book hand of the volume, which has no marginal annotations—except those already mentioned dating from modern times—the codex looks like a de luxe copy rather than a working one. As such, it resembles manuscript lat. 18221 of the Bibliothèque nationale, containing the oldest surviving recension of the collection, which is itself richly decorated by an English or Norman hand.[30] According to the specialists of illumination whom I consulted, the New York manuscript appears to have been decorated by northeastern French hands.[31]

This hypothesis seems confirmed by the *Notitia provinciarum* at the head of the volume. The *Notitia*, of which a transcription is supplied in Appendix II, contains certain archaisms present in most late witnesses of the text.[32] But it also has certain noteworthy variants supplying clues to

29. For the main variants see Appendix I.

30. This manuscript is listed in François Avril and Patricia Stirnemann, *Manuscrits enluminés d'origine insulaire, VIIe–XXe siècle* (Paris 1987) 27 no. 39; the volume comes from the collection of Roger de Gaignières († 1715), presented to the king of France in 1711; it belonged to a group of 120 manuscripts given to Gaignières by the abbé de Castres in 1709: cf. Léopold Delisle, *Le Cabinet des manuscrits de la Bibliothèque impériale* 1 (Paris 1868) 350.

31. We again thank Mme Stirnemann and M. Avril for their counsel here.

32. Thus: in Lugdunensis III, the references to Carhaix (*Civitas Oscismorum*) and Jublains (*Civitas Diablintum que alio nomine aliud vel Adala vocatur*) and, in Belgica II, Boulogne-sur-Mer (*Civitas Bononensium*), which did not become episcopal sees; in Germania II: Tongres (*Civitas Tungrorum id est Tungris*), the see having been transferred to Liege in the eighth century. For comparison, see the study of Roger Edward Reynolds, 'The *Notitia Galliarum*: an Unusual Bavarian Version,' *Readers, Texts and Compilers in the Earlier Middle Ages. Studies in Medieval Canon Law in Honour of Linda Fowler-Magerl*, ed. Martin Brett and Kathleen G. Cushing (Farnham-Burlington 2009) 3–14.

dating and localization. Some of these consist simply of an updating of the list of dioceses. This is the case of the addition of Nevers to Lugdunensis IV, which, in the manuscripts of the *Notitia,* begins to appear only at the beginning of the tenth century, then becomes systematic in the twelfth century.[33] But other, rarer variants are found only in a limited number of witnesses. Such is the case of Romance forms like *Magoncia,* for Mainz, or *Guarmatia* for Worms, in Germania I, or the interpolation *id est Bois,* for Teste-de-Buch in Novempopulonia, present only in three or four manuscripts.[34] The designation of Metz, in Belgica I, and of Alba, in Viennensis, are found only in two manuscripts.[35] One of these contains, besides, a unique variant for Digne, in Alpes Maritimae, whereas the other contains two specific variants, deriving from misreadings, for Port-sur-Saône, in Sequania, and Pau, in Novempopulonia.[36] Now, these manuscripts share the characteristic of having both been composed in the north of France. The first (Paris, BN, lat. 4375) dates from the first half of the twelfth century and seems to come from the east of France.[37] It contains canonical materials exclusively: two decretal collections, unknown till now, comprising 142 and 118 titles respectively—the first composed on the basis of Pseudo-Isidore, the second from the letters of Gregory the Great—followed by a collection of canons in 92 titles, which mainly follows the order of the abridgement of Burchard contained in manuscript lat. 4283; in it, the *Notitia* is set at the head, after the capitulatio, in a form similar to that of the New York manuscript.[38] The second manuscript (Paris, BN, lat. 4955) is a

33. Cf. *Notitia Galliarum,* ed. Theodor Mommsen, *Chronica minora saec. IV. V. VI. VII.,* I (MGH, Auct. Ant. 9; Berlin 1892) 589; *Notitia provinciarum et civitatum Galliae, Itineraria et alia geographica* (CCL 175; Turnhout, 1965) 390.

34. *Metropolis civitas Magontia:* mss. Paris, BN, lat. 4375 et 4955 and Leiden, Voss. 96; *Vangiorum id est Guarmatia:* mss. lat. 4375, lat. 4955, n. a. l. 2253; Chartres, BM, 193; the interpolation *id est Stratburg,* following *Civitas Argentoratensium* is again found only in mss. lat. 4375 and 4955, Saint-Gall, Stiftbibl. 397 and Leiden, Voss. 96. *Civitas Boacium id est Bois:* mss. lat. 4375, 4955 et 4909.

35. *Civitas Mediomatricorum id est Metthis;* the form *Civitas Albensium nunciauuarum,* resulting from a misreading of *nunc Vivarium:* mss. Paris, BN, lat. 4375 and 4955.

36. *Civitas Diniensium id est Dia:* mss. Paris, BN, lat. 4375; *Ortus Abbucina* (for *Portus Bucini*): lat. 4955; *Civitas Baranensium:* lat. 4955.

37. Here, I should like to thank Mme Marie-Thérèse Gousset, curator at the Cabinet des manuscrits of the Bibliothèque nationale, who kindly agreed to examine its decoration, which, according to her, shows German influence.

38. Paris, BN, lat. 4375: (1) fol. 1: Varied canons; (2) fol. 2–5: *Notitia Provinciarum;* (3) fol. 5v: Formulas of royal and archiepiscopal oaths; (4) fol. 6–33v: Decretal collection in 142 titles [after Pseudo-Isidore]; (5) fol. 34–58: Collection of letter fragments of Gregory I in 118 titles; (6) fol. 58v–60v: List of popes to John XXII; (7) fol. 60v–61v: Patristic extracts; (8) fol. 62–76: Collection of canons in 92 titles [abridgment of Burchard]; (9) fol. 76v–79v: 'Ex decreta regum Caroli, Ludovici atque Lotarii et B. legatus Rom.'; (10) fol. 79v–82: 'Ex conciliis regum quibus legatus Romane

volume composed of various pieces, basically historical in nature, extending from the tenth to the fourteenth century. The *Notitia* is on a fragment originating from western France, dating from the very end of the twelfth century or the very beginning of the thirteenth, containing the chronicle of St-Aubin d'Angers, a genealogy of French kings from Pharamond to Philip I, and the episcopal lists of the dioceses of Tours, Angers, Le Mans, and Nantes down to the end of the twelfth century.[39]

The kinship of the *Notitia* of the New York manuscript with those in the latter two codices thus confirms the northern origin of the volume. The contents of the *Collectio Sinemuriensis* that it transmits does not contradict this localization.

II

Straight off, it is apparent that the New York manuscript contains a copy of the second surviving version of the *Sinemuriensis*, the one most widely diffused. This conclusion imposes itself at once in respect to both the extent of the compilation and its physical organization. For while the first recension contained only a few more than 200 canons, the second comprises more than 550 in the witnesses that have come down to us till now.[40] The New York manuscript, which is truncated, now contains only 491 canons. It is easy, however, thanks to the capitulatio at the head of the volume, to restore the missing pieces. In its original state, the collection thus comprised 539 canons, including the 48 absent chapters once written on

---

Sedis interfuit Bonifacius' [extracts ordered in 32 titles]; (11) fol. 82v–85v: Various canons. On the abridgement of Burchard, see Fowler-Magerl, *Clavis* 203–4. The author thanks his colleague and friend Linda Fowler-Magerl for having brought this manuscript, which she found in 2004, to his attention.

39. Paris, BN, lat. 4955: fol. 96–99: Chronicle of St-Aubin d'Angers; fol. 99v–100v: *Notitia Provinciarum;* fol. 101–102: Genealogy of the kings of France; fol. 102v–103v: Episcopal lists. The text is wrongly dated to the fourteenth century by Mommsen, *Notitia Provinciarum* 569; the writing clearly belongs to the end of the twelfth or the very start of the thirteenth; besides, the first line is transcribed above the top line, which agrees with the dates of the last bishops cited in the lists: Barthélemy de Vendôme (1174–1206) for Tours (Geoffroy La Lande [† 1208] and Jean de Faye [† 1228] were added by a later hand); Jean de Bellesmains († 1181) for Poitiers; Raoul de Beaumont († 1197) for Angers; Guillaume de Passavant († 1187) for Le Mans; Robert Ier († 1184) for Nantes, followed by the comment 'Amitto vocatus s . . ,' implying that the list was ended before 1198, so that the aggregate itself of the lists could not be later than 1181.

40. The first version apparently contained 209 canons. The incomplete Paris manuscript, whose contents can also be recovered thanks to the capitulatio, must have contained 438 titles. But a large number were nevertheless additions not found in the other witnesses to the collection. The incomplete Sélestat manuscript only confirms the original form of the first version. The Semur manuscript, however, contains 574 canons, that of Madrid 561. Cf. Fowler-Magerl, 'Vier französische und spanische vorgratianische Kanonessammlungen' 126–27.

the last leaves of the manuscript, which have disappeared.[41] The original number of chapters was therefore largely the same as that of the other witnesses to the second recension of the text. The order of canons and the rubrics are also exactly like that of the Semur-en-Auxois manuscript, barring some rare exceptions. The most numerous differences concern the chapter titles; as already noted, they sometimes diverge from those of the chaptering, which, on the whole, conforms to that of the Semur manuscript. Except for these, there are only ten really different rubrics, mainly situated in books II and III.[42] The order of four canons in book I is also inverted.[43]

41. New York 3.87–134 = Sémur 3.111–158.1: 'Ut sacerdotes et levite cum suis uxoribus non coeant'; 'De peccato ad mortem et non ad mortem'; 'Utrum presbiteri et clerici post lapsum suo debeant fungi offitio'; 'Ut episcopus crimine deprehensus et presbiteri et diaconi conscii deponantur'; 'De presbiteris et diaconibus lapsis'; 'Quomodo Deus flagellet hominem'; 'De legibus sine lege et consule prolatis et quod nulli nescire leges liceat et que dampnentur a legibus et quę lex non evacuetur ab una causa et quod nullus sit judex in causa sua et quod pervasori nulla dilatio tribuatur et de ecclesiarum negotiis et de die dominico et feriis'; 'De male ordinatis'; 'Ut episcopus jure depositus perpetue inserviat penitentię'; 'De deposito et iterum ad episcopatum aspirante'; 'De eadem'; 'Quod sufficiat solis sacerdotibus confiteri peccata'; 'De eo qui contra professionem suam in aliquem erat'; 'Ut presbiter non sit post lapsum revocandus'; 'De ordinatione metropolitani'; 'De dampnatis et ministrare temptantibus'; 'Quod Arrianorum clerici non sint suscipiendi in suis officiis'; 'Quod pro remedio necessitatis repperit cessante necessitate cessare debet'; 'Quod soleat transire multum quod a multis peccatur'; 'De moderantia ęcclesiaticorum institutorum'; 'Ut universalis Ęcclesia teneat observantiam Romane Ęcclesię'; 'De observatione decretorum'; 'De eodem'; 'De instituta dandarum indutiarum'; 'De maximo cinico et ejus inordinata constitutione'; 'Ut regule sanctorum patrum proprium robur optineat'; 'Quod non liceat principibus judicare de sacerdotibus'; 'De his qui post ordinationem rei reperiuntur'; 'De eodem'; 'De eodem'; 'De episcoporum solutis juditiis'; 'De presbitero quod ante ordinationem peccaverit confesso'; 'De ecclesiasticis excommunicato communicantibus'; 'De eo qui cum dampnato clerico oraverit'; 'De episcopo extra parrochiam ordinante'; 'De episcopo absque consensu metropolitani ordinato'; 'De excommunicato ante audientiam presumente communionem'; 'De dampnatis a suo episcopo et ministrare presumentibus'; 'Qui non sint admittendi ad accusationem'; 'Qualiter ordinandus sit episcopus'; 'De his qui in opinionem heresis offenderint'; 'Ut nemo sola judicis voluntate removendus sit a suo officio'; 'Quod non sit dissimulandum a correptionibus culparum'; 'De conjurantibus vel conspirantibus vel insidias ponentibus'; 'De clericis de suorum juditio episcoporum conquerentibus'; 'Exemplar regie professionis'; 'Sacramentum judaicum [*sic*]'; 'De imitatore et auctore simoniace hereseos.'

42. New York, 1.119: 'Quod in ultima necessitate nulli deneganda sit venia et reconciliatio' for '. . . sit penitentia et reconciliatio,' in the Semur ms, *venia* was corrected to *penitentia* by a superscription in the capitulatio; 2.81: 'Quod illecebre occulorum et aurium fugiende sint sacerdotibus' for '. . . et aurium fugiende sint'; 2.82: 'Quę sint episcopis necessaria ad discendum' for 'Que sint sacerdotibus . . .'; 2.137: 'Quod decime ab omnibus christianis debeantur' for '. . . christianis debeant resposci ex debito' in Semur 2.141; 2.156: 'De judeis qui ad fidem venire volunt' for 'Quomodo accipiendi sint judei ad fidem venientes' in Semur 2.165; 3.5: 'De abolitione criminis objecti' for 'De eodem,' in Semur 3.7; 3.47.1: 'Quod male agens qui increpationem odit plus se diligit quam veritatem' for 'De errore cui non resistitur' in Semur 3.70.1; 3.48.1: 'De errore cui non resistitur' for 3.70.4 without rubric in Semur; 3.64: 'De electo episcopo non legitime' for 'De episcopo non legitime electo' in Semur 3.86; 3.122: 'De episcopo absque consensu metropolitani ordinato' for '. . . metropolitani consecrato' in Semur 3.146.

43. Canons 1.130–31 and 1.42–43.

But, apart from these minor differences, the arrangement of the text is everywhere the same. The carving out of the canons is completely similar, and it is worth noticing that, when a rubric heads several chapters in the Semur manuscript, the same holds in the New York manuscript, with only one exception.[44] In this last case, however, the organization of the canons in the Semur manuscript may explain the modification carried out by the author of the Columbia manuscript.[45] One particularly observes that the collection in both volumes, as in that of the Madrid manuscript, is divided into three books. In the Madrid copy, though, book III has a very different order of canons from that of the Semur codex, whose order is also in the Orléans manuscript, itself not divided into books. The New York manuscript faithfully follows the chapter order of that of Semur, with the breaks between books occurring at the same places; the uneven numbering results only from the elimination of certain texts and the joining of four canons in book III.[46]

The very close kinship between these two codices is confirmed when one examines the canons contained in the various witnesses of the *Sinemuriensis*. All those present in the New York manuscript are found in that of Semur, without exception. Conversely, a chapter of book III, which appears to have been simply omitted by the copyist of the Semur manuscript, though it is in its capitulatio, is also absent in the Columbia manuscript.[47]

44. Thus: 1.103.1–2; 1.102.1–4; 2.30.1–2; 2.139.1–2 (= Semur 2.143.1–2); 2.167.1–3 (= Semur 2.177.1–3); 3.52.1–2 (= Semur 3.74.1–2); 3.69.1–2 (= Semur 3.91.1–2). The sole exception concerns 3.47.1–2 and 3.48.1–2 (= Semur 3.70.1–5), where the rubric was changed ('Quod male agens qui increpationem odit plus se diligit quam veritatem'), the §1 of the canon becoming an inscription ('Gregorius in regula pastorali quod pro posse vel nosse quilibet erranti debet resistere ne forte non resistendo videatur erroris fieri participes') topping §2 ('Qui ergo vult prava agere—subditi humiliter audiunt'), after which is blended §3 ('Ambrosius in primam ad Corinthios. Si qui revelatur fuerit sedenti—vacuus gratia Dei'), whereas §4, turned into a new canon (3.48.1–2), is given a new rubric.

45. As it is, the first paragraph of the canon (3.70.1) in the Semur manuscript does not have an initial allowing the chapter to be located, whereas the second (3.70.2) has one and the third (3.70.3) is blended after it. The fourth (3.70.4) is then distinguished by an initial whereas the fifth (3.70.5) is blended into it. The general appearance could encourage a revision into two canons, each of them subdivided into two paragraphs.

46. New York 1.1–230 = Sémur 1.1–230; NY 2.1–112 = SM 2.1–112; NY 2.113–116 = SM 2.114–117; NY 2.117–134 = SM 2.119–136; NY 2.135–136 = SM 2.138–139; NY 2.137–139 = SM 2.141–143; NY 2.140 = SM 2.145; NY 2.141–142 = SM 2.147–148; NY 2.143–148 = SM 2.150–155; NY 2.149–153 = SM 2.157–161; NY 2.154–166 = SM 2.163–175; NY 2.167 = SM 2.177; NY 2.168–169 = SM 2.179–180; NY 2.170–175 = SM 2.182–187; NY 3.1–4 = SM 3.1–4; NY 3.5–11 = SM 3.7–13; NY 3.12 = SM 3.14–17; NY 3.13–15 = SM 3.18–20; NY 3.16–46 = SM 3.22–52; NY 3.47 = SM 3.70.1–3; NY 3.48 = SM 3.70.4–5; NY 3.49–78 = SM 3.71–100; NY 3.79–81 = SM 3.102–104; NY 3.82–86 = SM 3.106–110; [NY 3.87–134] = SM 3.111–158 (this last series is reconstructed from the capitulatio only, since the text of the New York ms. ends at 3.86).

47. This is 3.21 in the Semur manuscript, which should have been inserted between 3.15 and

It is naturally difficult to affirm in a definitive way that the author of the Columbia codex had the Semur manuscript as his model. But one may venture without fear of contradiction that he at least had a very close copy.

It must be noted nevertheless that a certain number of canons present in the Semur manuscript are lacking in that of New York. If one uses the chaptering to make up for the last, lost leaves of the codex by reconstructing their contents, there are 29 missing canons.[48] Certain of these gaps, isolated ones, may be explained by copyists' errors. This goes for the last chapter of book II, which picks up a canon of the Council of Chalcedon setting out a universally accepted rule, the condemnation of venal ordinations; its exclusion is very probably due to a change of book.[49] This seems to have also been the case with a chapter of book III taken from the *Epitome of Julian* specifying that goods given by a bishop to his diocese before or after his ordination have the value of an oblation; it also establishes a payment to the cathedral.[50] The absence of this text appears to result from an omission by homoeoteleuton, which, once more, argues in favor of a very probable use of the Semur manuscript by the scribe of the New York one.[51]

But most of the gaps appear to result from a deliberate wish to eliminate certain texts, chosen in a very selective way. It is difficult, though, to detect a genuine direction in these suppressions. A first group of texts clearly seems to have been excluded because of their age or their excessively local character. Many of them, from the *Decretum* of Burchard of Worms, retain the mark of this origin, and some of them could perhaps not be transposed into another context of geography and time. This may

3.16 in that of New York. The text, present only in the Sélestat manuscript, 13, fol. 185–189, contains the acts of the Roman synod of 747 judging Aldebert and Clement, transmitted by the letters of Boniface: Bonifacius, Ep. 59, ed. Michael Tangl, *Die Briefe des heiligen Bonifacius und Lullus* (MGH, Epp. sel. 1; Berlin 1916) 108–20.

48. In the Semur manuscript, they correspond to 2.113, 118, 137, 140, 144, 146, 149, 156, 162, 176, 178, 181, 188; 3.5, 21, 53–69, 101, 105.

49. *Sinemuriensis* 2.188 (Semur-en-Auxois, ms. 13, fol. 58) = Council of Chalcedon (451), c. 2 (COD[3] 87.31–88.17) = Burchardus Wormaciensis, *Decretum* 1.112, ed. fol. 16rab = C. 1 q. 1 c. 8.

50. *Sinemuriensis* 3.5 (Semur-en-Auxois, ms. 13, fol. 58v) = Ep. Jul. 115.5 (431) = *Lex romana canonice compta* 17, ed. Carlo Guido Mor (Publicationi della R. Universita di Pavia, Facolta di Giurisprudenza 13; Pavia, 1927) 45–46.

51. The preceding canon (3.4) is truncated from the words *objecti criminis;* the text takes up at once with the contents of the next canon (3.6), which begins with the words 'Si quem penituerit accusasse criminaliter ..,' which follow the terms *objecti criminis* in the preceding chapter, whose beginning is similar up to '... criminosum esse cognoverit.' In the Semur manuscript, the two similar passages are face to face, placed at exactly the same height, on the lines of the two leaves facing each other (fol. 58v, at line 26, and fol. 59r, at line 27). This layout may explain such a large omission—it amounts to 40 lines, a whole page; the copyist no doubt mistook the page after an interruption in his work.

have been the case with a formulary of letters dimissory attesting to the ordination of priests in the diocese of Worms, in connection with a new incardination in the bishopric of Speyer.[52] The same probably goes for a canon containing the ordination oath of Hincmar of Reims.[53] The same case again applies to another canon containing a catalogue of popes down to John XII († 964), probably considered obsolete.[54] Another chapter proclaimed the necessity of appealing to a synod in a written libellus, and invoked Hincmar in support; it referred to an institution with little relevance to twelfth-century France.[55]

Various texts may have gone counter to existing practices in the place where this copy of the collection was compiled. A chapter telling priests to enjoin the women of the common people in their charge to prepare the altar cloths was thus withdrawn.[56] Also set aside was a letter of Gelasius I establishing, for the benefit of a diocese, the thirty-year prescription for real estate owned by the bishop.[57] The same reason applies to a fragment, attributed to Augustine, ordering that couples should be buried together, which later passed into Gratian's *Decretum* and is known to have occasioned controversies in the classical period of canon law.[58] Yet another case of omission concerns a canon of the Fourth Council of Toledo—it too was later included in the *Decretum*—which maintained a patronage permitting the revocation of the liberty of serfs emancipated by a church when they left without authorization.[59] A chapter ordering the destruction of altars not

52. *Sinemuriensis* 2.113 (Semur-en-Auxois, ms. 13, fol. 47v) = Burchardus Wormaciensis, *Decretum* 2.227, ed. fol. 52vb–53ra.

53. *Sinemuriensis* 3.101 (Semur-en-Auxois, ms. 13, fol. 77) = Hincmar, *Professio fidei* (PL 125.1199–1200D).

54. *Sinemuriensis* 3.105 (Semur-en-Auxois, ms. 13, fol. 77–78).

55. *Sinemuriensis* 2.176 (Semur-en-Auxois, ms. 13, fol. 53) = Minutes of the Synod of Soissons (853), ed. Wilfried Hartmann, *Die Konzilien der karolingischen Teilreiche 843–859* (MGH, Conc. 3; Hanover 1984) 266.14–267.19 = Burchardus Wormaciensis, *Decretum* 2.197, ed. fol. 50vab.

56. *Sinemuriensis* 2.137 (Semur-en-Auxois, ms. 13, fol. 49) = Ansegisus, *Collectio capitularium* 1.146, ed. Gerhard Schmitz (MGH, Cap. nov. ser. 1; Hanover 1996) 511.7–8 = Burchardus Wormaciensis, *Decretum* 3.115, ed. fol. 67vb.

57. *Sinemuriensis* 2.144 (Semur-en-Auxois, ms. 13, fol. 49v) = JK 637 Gelasius, Ep. 17.2, ed. Andreas Thiel, *Epistolae Romanorum Pontificum genuinae* (Brunsbergae 1868, repr. 1974) 382 = Burchardus Wormaciensis, *Decretum* 3.149, ed. fol. 70vab = C. 16 q. 3 c. 2 §2.

58. *Sinemuriensis* 2.146 (Semur-en-Auxois, ms. 13, fol. 50) = *Collectio Hibernensis* 18.9 et 18.1c, ed. Hermann Wasserschleben, *Die irische Kanonensammlung* (Leipzig 1885, repr. Aalen 1966) 59 et 56 = Burchardus Wormaciensis, *Decretum* 3.163. ed. fol. 72rb = C. 13 q. 2 c. 3. On this text, see Antoine Bernard, *La sépulture en droit canonique du Décret de Gratien au concile de Trente*, thèse droit (Paris 1933) 91.

59. *Sinemuriensis* 3.149 (Semur-en-Auxois, ms. 13, fol. 50) = Council of Toledo IV (633), c. 71 = Burchardus Wormaciensis, *Decretum* 3.184, ed. fol. 74ra = C. 12 q. 2 c. 61.

containing bodies or relics of martyrs may also have vanished for the same reason.[60] Finally, the same explanation may apply to a series of twelve canons which contain the letter of Hincmar of Reims to archbishops Raoul of Bourges and Frotarius of Bordeaux, concerning the marriage of Stephen, count of Auvergne.[61] This famous *Epistola de nuptiis* transmitted a doctrine firmly defending the indesolubility of marriage but on condition—at least for the most part—of the consummation of the union.[62] It is well known, though, that northern French theologians in the first half of the twelfth century tried to promote a new, strongly consensualist doctrine, devoted in particular to defending the marriage of the Virgin, which would lead finally to a reintroduction of the Roman system of betrothals.[63] The desire to remove a text legitimizing practices that one was trying to combat may thus explain the disappearance of this group of canons. In view, however, of the large diffusion of this treatise of Hincmar's, of which a fragment even passed into Gratian's *Decretum*,[64] the explanation may also be that the person who ordered the volume already had a copy and so wished only—by virtue of a principle universally respected in the Middle Ages—to save on the parchment.

In closing, we are bound to observe that the elimination of other texts is difficult to explain, since they have universal validity. This goes for a fragment of a letter of Augustine, later taken into Gratian, assimilating the customs of the Church to a law and punishing those who violated them as though transgressing it.[65] It is also hard to understand the removal of an extract of Benedictus Levita, it too taken into Gratian, forbidding kings and everyone else to sell or exchange monasteries.[66] Also eliminated was

60. *Sinemuriensis* 2.156 (Semur-en-Auxois, ms. 13, fol. 50v) = *Registri Ecclesiae Carthaginensis Excerpta* 83, ed. Charles Munier, *Concilia Africae A.* 345-A. 525 (CCL 149; Turnhout 1974) 204.754–205.766 *forma minor ex* Clm 6241 = Burchardus Wormaciensis, *Decretum* 3.225, ed. fol. 80ra.

61. *Sinemuriensis* 3.53–69 (Semur-en-Auxois, ms. 13, fol. 65v–73v) = Hincmarus, Ep. 136 ed. Ernst Perels (MGH, Epp. 8; Berlin 1939) 88–107.

62. See the study of Gérard Fransen, 'La lettre d'Hincmar de Reims au sujet du mariage d'Étienne. Une relecture,' *Pascua medievalia. Studies voor Prof. Dr. J. M. De Smet* (Mediaevalia Lovaniensia 1.10; Louvain 1983) 133–36, repr. in Gérard Fransen, *Canones* 2.143–46.

63. This is the doctrine of the principal French masters, from Anselm of Laon to Peter Lombard, via William of Champeaux, Abelard, or Hugh of Saint-Victor: Cf. Jean Gaudemet, *Le mariage en Occident* (Paris 1987) 165–69.

64. C. 33 q. 1 c. 4.

65. *Sinemuriensis* 2.140 (Semur-en-Auxois, ms. 13, fol. 49v) = Augustinus, Ep. 36.1, ed. Alois Goldbacher, Vienna, 1898 (CSEL 34.2) 32.10–12 = Burchardus Wormaciensis, *Decretum* 3.126, ed. fol. 68rb = D. 11 c. 7.

66. *Sinemuriensis* 2.118 (Semur-en-Auxois, ms. 13, fol. 48) = Benedictus Levita, *Capitularia* 1.386, ed. Georg Pertz (MGH, LL 2.2; Hanover 1837) 69.12–20 = Burchardus Wormaciensis, *Decretum* 3.23, ed. fol. 58va = C. 16 q. 1 c. 40.

an African canon prescribing the obligation to baptize found children when there was no witness to prove that they had already been baptized, a text finally integrated into the *De consecratione*.[67] Still another discard was a letter of Leo I assimilating to heretics those who did not contest their error when they could, a passage which ended up in the *Liber Extra*.[68] Finally, the same goes for another text, by Gregory the Great, forbidding the episcopal ordination of someone guilty of the crime of solicitation, regardless of what his personal merits might otherwise be.[69] It is hard to discern what reasons might lie behind these five omissions.

Manuscript Western 82 of Columbia University Library is far from having yielded all its secrets. This new witness to the second recension of the *Collectio Sinemuriensis* at least sheds light on the interest of the text version transmitted by the Semur manuscript, which does now appear to have constituted an archetype, at least for a while. Failing access to an almost identical copy, the author of the volume now housed in New York very probably used it directly. The making of the New York copy also confirms the importance of the *Sinemuriensis* in the history of the Gregorian movement and its extensions, showing that it was used for a time and in places—the north of France, during the first half of the twelfth century—where other, more easily usable reform collections, such as those of Ivo of Chartres, began to circulate widely. Like every canon law collection, however, the new copy was made in response to needs proper to the institution that ordered it. That is how one may explain the removal of several texts that were considered out of place owing to their origin, date, or contents.

APPENDIX I

Variants of the titles of the *Collectio Sinemuriensis* in the manuscript of New York, Columbia University, Western MS 82

1.24: 'Ne credentis de tractionibus ante certam probationem,' for: 'Quod non sit credendum accusatoribus ante …' in the capitulatio; 1.26: 'Pessimum esse de suspitione aut exhorta confessione quemquam judicare concordat titulus III' for

67. *Sinemuriensis* 2.162 (Semur-en-Auxois, ms. 13, fol. 51) = *Registri Ecclesiae Carthaginensis Excerpta* 72, ed. Munier 201.665–202.671 *ex Dionysiana* = Burchardus Wormaciensis, *Decretum* 4.45, ed. fol. 86rb = *De cons.* D. 4 c. 111.

68. *Sinemuriensis* 2.178 (Semur-en-Auxois, ms. 13, fol. 56) = JK 412, Leo Magnus, Ep. 15 (PL 54.688B) = X 5.7.2.

69. *Sinemuriensis* 2.181 (Semur-en-Auxois, ms. 13, fol. 56v) = JE 1292, Gregorius Magnus, *Registrum* 4.20, ed. Ludo Moritz Hartmann (MGH, Epp. 2; Berlin 1891) 254.13–15).

'De eodem'; 1.29: 'Sacrilegium fornicatione gravius esse' for 'Quod sacrilegium gravius sit fornicatione'; 1.31: 'Ut accusati causa in sua provincia terminetur et ut accusato si judicem suspectum habuerit liceat appellare' for 'Ut causa accusati in sua terminetur provincia et si . . .'; 1.32: 'De incertis non judicandis' for 'De incertis non temere judicandum'; 1.33: 'Injustum judicium cujuscumque potentis metu actum' for 'Injustum judicium metu potestatis actum'; 1.43: 'Quod quidam querunt . . .' for 'Quare quidam querunt . . .'; 1.66: 'Quod accusans quemlibet ex clero et non probans jacturam infamie incurrat' for '. . . incurrat quod nullum crimen potest obici expoliatis et expulsis nisi finitis anniversariis indutis aut sex mensuim post plenariam restaurationem'; 1.102: 'Quod non sint retractanda apud Nicenam et Chaldedoniam definita' for '. . . et Chaldedoniam constituta vel definita'; 1.108: 'Qui sint admittendi . . .' for 'Qui non sint admittendi . . .'; 1.115: 'Quod liceat ancillam abicere et ingenuam ducere' for 'Quod non sit duplicatio conjugii ancillam . . .'; 1.119: 'Quod in ultima necessitate nulli deneganda sit venia et reconciliatio' for '. . . sit pęnitentia et reconciliati'; 1.136: 'Quod sublata sint possessori restituenda' for '. . . possessori sint restituenda ante litem'; 1.173: 'Ut pro qualitate audientium temperandus sit sermo doctorum' for '. . . sermo pastorum'; 1.179: 'Quod non sit vera absolutio . . .' for 'Quando sit vera absolutio . . .'; 1.193: 'Ordinandi presbiteri de legitima etate' for 'De legitima etate ordinandi presbiteri'; 1.209: 'Captivos redimendos de rebus ecclesiasticis' for 'Quod capitivi redimendi sint de rebus . . .'; 1.213: 'De episcopo qualiter agat erga suos clericos' for 'Qualiter episcopus agendum erga . . .'; 1.214: 'Modus accusationis episcoporum' for 'Quod sit modus . . .'; 1.215: 'Nihil pretii accipiendum propter sepulchra, nihil petendum, nihil exigendum pro corpore in ecclesia sepeliendo' for 'Ut nihil pretii recipiatur pro sepulchra, nil petatur pro corpore sepeliendo in ecclesia'; 1.216: 'Quod antichristus sabbatum et diem faciet custodiri' for 'Quod antichristus faciet sabbatum et diem dominicum custodiri feriatos'; 1.217: 'De judeis a suis sollempnitatibus non prohibendis' for 'Quod judei a suis . . . non sunt prohibendi'; 1.220: 'Qualiter absens judicari vel dampnari possit' for 'Qualiter absens accusari vel . . .'; 1.228: 'Quod resecandum sit quicquid scripturarum auctoritate non continetur consuetudine universalis Ęcclesię' for '. . . non continetur vel non roboratur consuetudine universalis Ęcclesię'; 2.29: 'De clericis alienas res conducentibus' for 'De clericis aliena predia lucraque turpia ac secularia negotia conducentibus'; 2.36: 'De defendentibus peccantes et consentientibus' for '. . . et de eis consentientibus'; 2.42: 'Quod magnis et parvulis dandum sit sacramentum' for '. . . sit sacramentum dominice mense'; 2.48: 'Unde serventur in ęcclesia quędam quę non sunt scripta et alia quod ad metropolitanum pertineat totius sollicitudo provincie et quod sit privilegium Nicene sinodi' for '. . . scripta et quod non omnia quę in conciliis dicta sint attendenda sed quę communi consensu sunt definite et quod ad metropolitanum . . .'; 2.49: 'Quod episcopi quanticumque meriti subdi debeant suo primati inter se habentibus et quod duo sint judiciarii ordines et quod unum peremptorium sic damnet contumacem ut tria edicta et quod sine scripto sententia judicis non valeat' for '. . . primati et ubi debeat agitari acusatoris causa et acusati et quando liceat appellare vel non et de clericis causam vel contentionem inter se . . .'; 2.52: 'Quod suffraganeus episcopus non possit ligare vel solvere quem metropolitanus juste ligavit' for '. . . ligavit vel solvit, quem vero provincialis id est suffraganeus injuste ligavit vel solvit metropolitanus solvere vel ligare potest et decreta ...'; 2.89: 'De servorum ordinatione' for 'De servis ordinatis'; 2.109: 'De eo qui ...' for 'De illo qui ...'; 2.117 (= ms. Semur 2.119): lacks the rubric 'De pictura ecclesiarum' present in the capitulatio; 2.126 (= SM 2.128): 'Ut nullus ...', for 'Quod nullus ...'; 2.132 (= SM 2.134): 'Cur altaris sacrificium non in serico vel tincto panno sed tantum lineo celebratum sit' for '... sed lineo consecrandum si'; 2.140 (= SM 2.145): 'In ecclesia non gravibus peccatis quod prosit sepeliri' for 'Quod prosit sepeliri in ecclesia non depressit gravibus peccatis'; 2.142 (= SM 2.148): 'Quod tantum remedium ...' for 'Quod tantum venie remedium ...'; 2.169 (= SM 2.180): 'Quod nullus per simoniam ordinandus reprobandus' for '... ordinandus et qui sit ad ordinem admittendus et qui reprobandus'; 2.175 (= SM 2.187): 'Quot et quante sint species arrogantium' for '... arrogantium et quod esse mites [sic] episcopos oporteat et quid sit non percussorem esse episcopum et quod prelatio et honores esse habentibus ipsis et quod nullus clericus vel suo nomine vel alieno exerceat fenus'; 3.3: 'De rebus ad venerabilia loca pertinentibus non alienandis' for '... non alienandis et de interpretationibus nominum'; 3.10 (= SM 3.12): 'Quod nulla misericordia est habenda erga simoniacos in servanda dignitate' for 'Quod nulla misericordia erga simoniacos est habenda in servanda dignitate et de his qui gratis sunt ordinati a simoniacis et qui in posterum ordinabuntur scienter ab hujusmodi et ne quis scienter audiat missam concubinam habentis et de ipsis habentibus palam concubinas et de clericis per laici manum ęcclesias habentibus et ne presbiter duas ęcclesias optineat et de oblationibus mortuorum et vivorum et ne quis ordinetur in ęcclesia vel promoveatur per pecuniam et ne laicus repente promoveatur ad gradum ęcclesiasticum'; 3.11 (= SM 3.13): 'Qui sint eligendi ad divina officia et de his qui ...' for '... officia et quid agendum his ...'; 3.41 (= SM 3.47): 'Quid agendum sit de fure deprehenso' for '... de fure et latrone deprehenso'; 3.60 (SM 3.82): 'Quod non castus et luxuriosus episcopus subditorum vitam corrigere non possit' for '... episcopus non possit subditorum vitam corrigere'; 3.64 (= SM 3.86): 'Utrum oporteat oblationem accipere a presbitero habente uxorem' for 'Utrum oblationem accipere oporteat ...'

APPENDIX II

Notitia Provinciarum

(*ex codice manuscripto bibliothecae universitatis Columbiae Novi Eboraci, Western MS 82*)

[*Provincia Lugdunensis Prima deest*]

[Fol. 1ra]
[Provincia Lugdunensis Secunda]
Metropolis civitas Rotomagensium. Civitas Bajocasium. Civitas Abrincatium. Civitas Ebroicorum. Civitas Salarum id est Saisorum. Civitas Luxoviorum. Civitas Constantia.
[*Rouen, Bayeux, Avranches, Évreux, Séez, Lisieux, Coutances*]

Provincia Lugdunensis Tertia habet civitates numero VIIII.
Metropolis civitas Turonorum. Civitas Cenomannorum. Civitas Redonum. Civitas Andecavorum. Civitas Nannetum. Civitas Coriosoperitum. Civitas Venetum.

Civitas Oscismorum. Civitas Diablintum quę alio nomine aliud vel Adala vocatur.
[*Tours, Le Mans, Rennes, Angers, Nantes, Corseul, Vannes, Carhaix, Jublains*]

Provincia Lugdunensis Quarta habet civitates numero VIII.
Metropolis civitas Senonum. Civitas Carnotum. Civitas Autisiodorum. Civitas Trecassium. Civitas Aurelianorum. Civitas Parisiorum. Civitas Meldorum. Civitas Nivernensium.
[*Sens, Chartres, Auxerre, Troyes, Orléans, Paris, Meaux, Nevers*]

[Fol. 1rb]
Provincia Belgica Prima habet civitates IIII.
Metropolis civitas Treverorum. Civitas Mediomatricorum id est Metthis. Civitas Leucorum id est Tullo. Civitas Veredimensium.
[*Trier, Metz, Toul, Verdun*]

Provincia Belgica Secunda habet civitates XII.
Metropolis civitas Remorum. Civitas Suessionum. Civitas Catalaunorum. Civitas Veramandorum. Civitas Atrabatrum. Civitas Camaracensium. Civitas Tornacensium. Civitas Silvanectum. Civitas Bellovagorum. Civitas Aribanensium (*sic*). Civitas Morinorum id est Ponticum. Civitas Bononensium.
[*Reims, Soissons, Châlons-en-Champagne, Vermand, Arras, Cambrai, Tournai, Senlis, Beauvais, Thérouanne, Boulogne-sur-Mer*]

Provincia Germania Prima habet civitates IIII.
Metropolis civitas Magoncia. Civitas Argentoratensium id est Stratburg. Civitas Nemetum id est Spira. Civitas [fol. 1va] Vangiorum id est Guarmatia.
[*Mainz, Strasbourg, Speyer, Worms*]

Provincia Germania Secunda habet civitates duas.
Metropolis civitas Agripinensium id est Colonia. Civitas Tungrorum id est Tungris.
[*Köln, Tongres*]

Provincia maxima Sequanorum habet civitates X.
Metropolis civitas Vesontiensium. Civitas Equestrium. Civitas Elviciorum id est Avendicum. Civitas Nundunum.[a] Civitas Basilea. Castrum Vindonense. Castrum Ebredunense. Castrum Argentamense. Castrum Rauracense. Ortus Abbuccina.
[*Besançon, Nyon, Avenches, Basel, Windisch, Yverdon, Horburg, Augst, Port-sur-Saône*]

Provincia Alpium Gratarum et Peninarum habet civitates II.
Civitas Centronium id est Tarentasia. Civitas Vallensium id est Octodorius.
[*Moutiers, Martigny*]

Provincia Viennensis habet civitates XIIII.
Metropolis civitas Viennensium. Civitas Gennavensium. Civitas Gratianopolitana. Civitas Albensium nunciauuarum. Civitas Detensium. Civitas [fol. 1rb] Valentianorum. Civitas Tricastrinorum. Civitas Vasionensium. Civitas Arausicorum. Civitas Cabellicorum. Civitas Avennicorum. Civitas Arelatensium. Civitas

a. *Civitas Nundunum nihil aliud est quam 'Nyon', qua antea ut Civitas Equestrium jam designata est.*

Carpentoratensium nunc Vindausca. Civitas Massiliensium.
[*Vienne, Genève, Grenoble, Alba, Die, Valence, Saint-Paul-Trois-Châteaux, Vaison, Orange, Cavaillon, Avignon, Arles, Carpentras, Marseille*]

Provincia Aquitanica Prima habet civitates VIII.
Metropolis civitas Biturigum. Civitas Arvernorum. Civitas Rotenorum. Civitas Albigensium. Civitas Cadurcorum. Civitas Lemovicum. Civitas Gabalum. Civitas Vallavorum.
[*Bourges, Clermont-Ferrand, Rodez, Albi, Cahors, Limoges, Javols, Le Puy*]

Provincia Aquitanica Secunda habet civitates VI.
Metropolis civitas Burdegalensium. Civitas Agennensium. Civitas Engolismensium. Civitas Sanctonum. Civitas Pictavorum. Civitas Petrogoricum.
[*Bordeaux, Agen, Angoulême, Saintes, Poitiers, Périgueux*]

Provincia Novempopulana habet civitates XII.
Metropolis civitas Ausciorum. Civitas Aquensium. Civitas Lac[fol. 2ra]toracium. Civitas Convenarum. Civitas Consuranorum. Civitas Boacium <id est Bois>. Civitas Baranensium <id est Banama>. Civitas Aturensium. Civitas Vasatica. Civitas Tussa ubi castrum Bigorra. Civitas Ellorensium. Civitas Elosaticum.
[*Auch, Dax, Lectoure, Comminges, Couserans, Bayonne, La Teste-de-Buch (?), Aire, Bazas, Tarbes, Bigorre, Oloron, Eauze*]

Provincia Narbonensis Prima habet civitates VIII.
Metropolis civitas Narbonensium. Civitas Tolosacium. Civitas Beternensium. Civitas Agatensium. Civitas Neumasensium. Civitas Magalonensium. Civitas Lutenensium. Castrum Utiense.
[*Narbonne, Toulouse, Béziers, Agde, Nîmes, Maguelonne, Lodeve, Uzès*]

Provincia Narbonensis Secunda habet civitates VII.
Metropolis civitas Aquensium. Civitas Abtensium. Civitas Regensium. Civitas Forojulensis. Civitas Vapensentium. Civitas Segesteriorum. Civitas Antipolitana.
[*Aix-en-Provence, Apt, Riez, Fréjus, Gap, Sisteron, Antibes*]

Provincia Alpium Maritimarum habet civitates VIII [fol. 2rb].
Metropolis civitas Ebredimensium. Civitas Diniensium <id est Dia>. Civitas Rigomagensium. Civitas Sollinensium. Civitas Saniciensium <id est Sanesio>. Civitas Glannatena. Civitas Celemensium. Civitas Unisiciensium <id est Vencio>. Explicit.
[*Embrun, Digne, Barcelonnette, Castellane, Senez, Glandève, Cimiez, Vence*]

ROGER E. REYNOLDS

6 The Influence of the Eastern Patristic Fathers on the Canonical Collections of South Italy in the Eleventh and Early Twelfth Centuries

In the spring of 1967, while I was working at the Vatican Library on my doctoral thesis as a Harvard Sheldon Traveling Fellow, I received a message from Robert Somerville, then a graduate student preparing his doctoral thesis at Yale. Professor Stephan Kuttner had asked him to contact me, and so we first met at the convent of the Piccole Suore della Sacra Famiglia, across from the Vatican Museum, where my family and I were staying. Thereafter Bob, as I came to know him, and I worked together at the Vatican Library and then in that summer at the Bibliothèque Nationale in Paris, where we spent long lunch hours talking shop in the park across from the library. All of this was the beginning of a close friendship, both academic and personal, that has flourished and endured over the years. The enormous debt of academic help and information I owe Bob is only partially reflected in the multiple acknowledgments to him in my articles and books. Beyond this, he has always been there for assistance and encouragement in the problems and joys of my life. One of our most recent meetings was to have been at the XIII International Congress of Medieval Canon Law in Esztergom in 2008, where he was the chairman of the session in which I was to deliver a paper. Fate would have it, however, that I spent those days in a hospital in Toronto and that because of the time constraints of that session Bob was not able to read the paper I had prepared and sent him. Since that paper was not part of the 'Proceedings' of the Congress, which are traditionally published, I offer it here in honor of the chairman of that session, my dear friend and colleague, Bob Somerville.

Research for this article has been partially supported by the Social Sciences and Humanities Research Council of Canada for the program Monumenta Liturgica Beneventana.

By way of introduction I should explain why a paper on the eastern patristic fathers should come from one who is not a specialist in eastern patristic studies. As is well known, the Pontifical Institute of Mediaeval Studies in Toronto, which is my base, was founded by the renowned Étienne Gilson and by the fathers of the Congregation of St. Basil. Over the years the majority of professors at the Institute were Basilian priests, and they continued to be in the vast majority when I arrived in 1976. Naturally when I came I asked them an oft-put question, 'How are the Basilian fathers connected with the great eastern father, Basil of Caesarea?' The simple and surprising answer, they told me, is that after the French Revolution, when the congregation was founded in Anonay, France, the local parish church was named after that eastern father and the priests of the congregation simply adopted his name.

More than a century after their founding, as the 1600th anniversary of the great eastern father's death approached, the Congregation of St. Basil wanted to celebrate it by sponsoring a major international conference on St. Basil in Toronto. That is, they wanted to solidify in belated fashion their connection with St. Basil, perhaps in much the same way that the compilers of the Pseudo-Isidorian Decretals cloaked their work under the name of Isidore of Seville. Hence, to organize the conference, the Basilians in Toronto took on at the Institute a young scholar specializing in the works of St. Basil, Paul Fedwick. He did a magnificent job of inviting major international specialists on Basil from the world over and of planning a multivolume work with the proceedings of the conference.[1] But what would be the role of the Basilian professors themselves at the Institute in this conference—beyond paying for it? They must have anguished in private over this a great deal. So a plan was hatched to, as they have often said, 'ask Reynolds to help us out.'[2] Hence, as the youngest and most vulnerable member of the Institute, I was targeted to give a paper. My first answer was a firm negative. I was not a Basil specialist, my Greek had long ago lapsed, and I

1. See P. J. Fedwick, ed., *Basil of Caesarea: Christian, Humanist, Ascetic: A Sixteen-Hundredth Anniversary Symposium* (Toronto 1981).

2. The results of other of these 'bail-outs' written when the Basilians were uneasy about writing on certain topics can be seen in my articles 'The Pagan Side of Christmas,' *Graduate: University of Toronto Alumni* 7.2 (Nov./Dec. 1979) 6–9 and 'Sarcophagi of the Roman Empire,' *Ladders to Heaven: Art Treasures from Lands of the Bible: A Catalogue of Some of the Objects in the Collection Presented by Dr. Elie Borowski to the Lands of the Bible Archaeology Foundation and Displayed in the Exhibition 'Ladders to Heaven: Our Judeo-Christian Heritage 5000 B.C.–A.D. 500' Held at the Royal Ontario Museum June 23–October 28, 1979*, ed. O. W. Muscarella (Toronto 1981) 296 + pls. 277–80; translated as 'Sarkophage des römischen Imperiums,' *Archäologie zur Bibel: Kunstschätze aus den biblischen Ländern* (Mainz 1981) 315–16.

had not read any of Basil's work since my nearly forgotten days as a graduate student working under Fr. Georges Florovsky. I did not want to embarrass myself or the Institute before the distinguished scholars invited to attend the conference. But then I remembered—I had come across canons attributed to St. Basil in a number of western canon law collections I had studied, especially those from southern Italy. Hence, I delighted my Basilian colleagues by telling them I would manfully fill the Basilian void and deliver a paper on Basil in the early medieval Latin canonical collections. This I did, and one can read the results of the research of the lone professor from the Institute in the volumes of the proceedings of the Basil conference.[3]

In doing research for that paper I went through microfilm of all of the south Italian canon law collections I knew at the time[4] and was startled to discover how many canons were attributed to the eastern fathers, and I have mentioned this in passing in many articles I have written since. The XIII International Congress of Medieval Canon Law, whose theme was the canonistic relations of East and West, thus led me to extend that paper on Basil by examining the presence of the texts attributed to yet more eastern patristic fathers in the south Italian canonical collections of the eleventh and early twelfth centuries. This task has been made immensely simpler than it was in the 1970s through the use of the *Clavis canonum* of Linda Fowler-Magerl[5]—clearly reflected in the results and footnotes below—but as she and I both know, the manuscripts (or microfilm thereof) must be checked and rechecked, since in the manuscripts the presence of canons attributed to one father can be hidden within texts of another.[6]

Collections of canon law compiled during the early Middle Ages in the West are well known for their paucity of canons drawn from the fathers. Unlike the Greek collections—one thinks especially of the Nomocanon, which fairly bristles with such texts—the western collections are made up largely of the decisions of councils and papal decrees. Fifty years ago Charles Munier, in a widely acclaimed Strasbourg thesis, investigat-

3. 'Basil and the Early Medieval Latin Canonical Collections,' in *Basil of Caesarea: Christian, Humanist, Ascetic* 513–32.

4. For more now see my article 'The South-Italian Canon Law Collection in Five Books and its Derivatives: New Evidence on its Origins, Diffusion, and Use,' *Mediaeval Studies* 52 (1990) 278–95.

5. Linda Fowler-Magerl, *Clavis*.

6. This accounts for some of the discrepancies in our accounts of the presence of the texts in the manuscripts. See, e.g., below, n. 29 with Vall. Tom. XVIII, fol. 89v: 'Basilius interrogat, Si is qui consentit,' not listed in Fowler-Magerl, *Clavis* under *Hibernensis beta*.

ed the use of patristic texts in the major collections down to Gratian and found that patristic texts formed only a small proportion of the total legal statements.[7] Of these the overwhelming majority, as one might expect, was from the western doctors: Augustine, Ambrose, Gregory, Jerome, and Isidore. Only occasionally were the eastern fathers used. Out of 3846 patristic texts Munier found in ten published collections, the major eastern fathers, Basil, John Chrysostom, and Gregory Nazianzus, contributed only 95, or 2.47 percent.

Given his monumental task of sifting through and identifying patristic texts scattered through thousands of canons in the collections, Professor Munier limited his research largely to the collections printed in his time: the *Collectio hibernensis*, Pseudo-Isidore, Regino, Burchard, Anselm of Lucca, Deusdedit, Ivo's *Panormia* and *Decretum*, and Gratian. But if one goes to the manuscripts of early medieval western collections, especially those from southern Italy, an unexpected number of canons attributed to the eastern patristic fathers can be found, enough to show that their role in the formation of western canon law was not quite as insignificant as a hasty look at the collections might seem to indicate.

That texts from the eastern fathers should be found in southern Italian collections of canon law should come as no surprise to anyone acquainted with the south Italian region in the eleventh and twelfth centuries. Monasteries such as Montecassino had close ties with Mount Athos and the Byzantine world.[8] Greek texts and manuscripts were common in the south.[9] Large communities of Greek-speaking people were common there, Greek monasticism flourished in the south under such individuals at St. Nilus, and in the liturgies of both Greek- and Latin-speaking peoples, elements of the Greek liturgies could be found. For example, in some instances a Greek text was transliterated into Latin characters in manuscripts to be used on several of the most significant feasts in the liturgical rite of Benevento,[10] and I have published a transliterated Greek text in Beneventan script with the Liturgy of St. John Chrysostom.[11] This scribe, knowing both Latin and

7. Charles Munier, *Les sources patristiques du droit de l'Église du VIIIe au XIIIe siècle* (Strasbourg 1957).

8. Tommaso Leccisotti, *Monte Cassino*, ed. and trans. Armano O. Citarella (Monte Cassino 1987) 48–50 and 53; and Mariano Dell'Omo, *Montecassino, Un'abbazia nella storia* (Biblioteca della Miscellanea Cassinese 6; Montecassino 1999) 35 and 45 for bibliography on this.

9. See my article 'The Greek Liturgy of St. John Chrysostom in Beneventan Script: An Early Manuscript Fragment,' *Mediaeval Studies* 52 (1990) 296–302 + 2 pls.

10. Forrest Kelly, *The Beneventan Chant* (Cambridge 1989) 203–18.

11. See my article 'The Greek Liturgy of St. John Chrysostom in Beneventan Script.'

Greek, was probably writing the text for a Latin-speaking priest who could not read Greek characters but who had to serve a Greek-speaking community using the Liturgy of St. John Chrysostom. That a Latin-speaking priest might offer the Eucharist according to the Greek rite rather than the Roman or Beneventan might seem extraordinary, until it is remembered that in southern Italy there were frequent liturgical interchanges by Greek and Latin communities, and that prior to the schism of 1054 between the Greek and Latin churches this probably would not have been considered unusual or uncanonical in southern Italy. We do know of occasional services at Montecassino on a portable altar being celebrated in Latin and Greek in the tower of St. Benedict, and if it was a Greek Mass, there might simply have been a Greek translation of the Latin rite such as is found in later manuscripts.[12] But it is not beyond the realm of possibility that at Montecassino and elsewhere, the Greek liturgy celebrated in these occasional joint services might have been that of St. John Chrysostom as found in our unusual manuscript.

Turning now to the canon law collections one must begin with a limitation and a caveat. The contribution of the eastern fathers in the texts of the patristic councils—e.g. Nicea, Constantinople, Ephesus, Chalcedon, etc.—was extremely important in the West, as canons from these ecumenical councils were included in the canonical collections both historically and topically arranged. But here, except in a few limited cases, we will limit ourselves to the patristic fathers themselves rather than as they appear in these conciliar texts. In looking to the texts attributed to the eastern fathers themselves the compilers of the collections—both those compiled in southern Italy and transalpine collections, which might be used in southern Italy—often used what we now consider pseudo-texts. For example, Basil's works in the collections are often Pseudo-Basilian texts. Further, the attributions to the eastern fathers are at times incorrect, and the texts themselves actually belong to another father, even a western father. Moreover, a text attributed to an eastern father in one of our south Italian collections may not be attributed to the same father—or even to any father at all—in another related south Italian collection. And finally, the compilers often did not always distinguish between eastern fathers of the same name. For example, 'John' can be styled as John Chrysostom, John of Constantinople, or even John Chrysostom of Constantinople. Despite all

12. On this see my article 'St. Peter, Liturgy of,' *Dictionary of the Middle Ages* 10 (New York 1988) 620–21.

of these difficulties, the texts attributed to the eastern fathers in the south Italian collections, be they correct or not, will be listed here, since the canonical compilers most likely considered them to be genuine texts of the father cited.

Canonistic scholars are familiar with the distinct types of arrangements of canonical collections, the major ones being the historical or chronologically arranged collections and the systematically or topically arranged collections. Since the historically arranged collections are made up largely of councils and the decrees of popes, it seems unlikely that the works of the eastern patristic fathers would be found in them. But occasionally the historically arranged collections supplement the conciliar and papal canons with miscellaneous canons from other sources. And here occasionally one can find texts attributed to the eastern fathers. Such is the case with the *Collectio Hadriana aucta* found in the south Italian codex Vat. lat. 5845, which was copied in Beneventan script in the tenth century by monks from Montecassino who had taken temporary refuge in Capua.[13] The text is from Basil's *De spiritu sancto* as used in the *Gesta Ephesena*.[14] Another text, attributed to Basil but actually taken from Rufinus's translation of Origen's *Peri archon*, is included in one of Pope Leo I's letters, Epistle 165, which made its way into a number of early canonical collections, including the Pseudo-Isidorian Decretals, one of whose manuscripts is the famous eleventh-century manuscript Montecassino 1 copied in Beneventan script.[15] Another text attributed to Basil, said to be from his *Contra Eunomium*, was embedded in a florilegium associated with the canons of the Second Council of Seville and as a result found its way into our eleventh-century Montecassino manuscript of the Pseudo-Isidorian Decretals.[16] A text of John Chrysostom also made its way into this manuscript of the Pseudo-Isidorian Decretals embedded in the decretals of Pope Hormisdas.[17]

13. E. A. Loew (later Lowe), *The Beneventan Script: A History of the South Italian Minuscule* (1st ed. Oxford 1914; 2nd ed. prepared and enlarged by Virginia Brown, 2 vols., Sussidi Eruditi 33–34, Rome 1980) 54.

14. '[xv] Basilii sanctissimi episcopi Caesariae Cappadocie Primae. Neque tantum caelum et terra...inpassibilitatem donaret.'

15. 'xiiii. Item sancti Basilii episcopi Cappadocis. Cum ergo quaedam in Christo...inlusa imaginibus aestimentur.'

16. 'Sanctus quoque Basilius in quarto libro contra Eunomium ita scribit: Quid est: dominus creavit me et ante omnes...ut utramque naturam in una persona ostenderet.' Cf. Paul Hinschius, ed., *Decretales Pseudo-Isidorianae et Capitula Anglilramni* (Leipzig 1863: hereafter Hinschius) 443; and PL 130.607.

17. '*Libellus fidei Joannis Constantinopolitani episcopi directus ad sanctum Hormisdam papam, in quo anathematizat Nestorii et Eutichetis et reliquorum haereticorum blasphemias.* Redditis mihi

Turning to the systematically arranged collections with texts of the eastern patristic fathers, the *Collectio canonum hibernensis*,[18] compiled in the late seventh or early eighth century,[19] takes pride of place in the number and variety of these texts. The so-called A or Alpha recension of the *Hibernensis* contains fifty texts attributed to Origen, fifteen attributed to Gregory Nazianzus, eleven to the *Vita monachorum*, three to Basil, and one each to John Chrysostom, and Abraham Philosophus.[20] But it is in the B or Beta recension of the *Hibernensis*, found in the south Italian eleventh-century codex written in Beneventan and Romanesca scripts, Rome, Biblioteca Vallicelliana, Tom. XVIII,[21] that this number increases. For Origen alone there are seventy-one canons, of which twenty-nine are additional texts. From the *Vita monachorum* there are seven additional texts. For Basil there are four additional texts from his *Asceticon*, and for Gregory Nazianzus there are three additional texts. Beyond these there are texts from John Chrysostom, Dionysius Exiguus, and Eusebius Emisenus.[22] Since the Vallicelliana manuscript is from the south of Italy, one might think that these

litteris vestrae sanctitatis in Christo... Ora pro nobis, sanctissime et beatissime frater. Data mense Martio, die XXVIII, indictione XI, consulibus Domino Justino imperatore Augusto et Heradio IV CC. aera DC.' PL 130.1038–40; and Hinschius 688f.

18. On this collection see my article 'Collectio Hibernensis,' in The *History of Western Canon Law to* 1140, ed. Wilfried Hartmann and Kenneth Pennington (Washington, D.C forthcoming). Since the article was submitted to the editors in 1993, revisions will be necessary to take account of research since that time, especially the new edition being prepared for the Royal Irish Academy by Roy Flechner.

19. On the date of the collection see my article 'Penitentials and Penitential Materials in South Italy in the Tenth and Eleventh Century,' *Early Medieval Europe* 14 (2006) 65–84.

20. See Appendix 1.

21. On the Beneventan features of this manuscript see my article 'Odilo and the *Treuga Dei* in Southern Italy: A Beneventan Manuscript Fragment,' *Mediaeval Studies* 46 (1984) 450–62 + 1 pl., esp. 454, n. 25. The only other south Italian codex containing the B or Beta version is Montecassino MS 297, (s.XIin), but the text breaks off after a quire on p. 248 (*De elimosina*). This break was noted even in the Middle Ages, since a medieval scribe has entered the word 'actenus' in the table of contents on p. 206 next to the book entitled *De elimosina*. Where the missing folios went is unknown. At present, the manuscript is in rather poor condition with folios and quires either loose or about to fall out of the binding. Parts of the manuscript, especially the *De temporum ratione* of Bede (pp. 138–203), the *Hibernensis* (pp. 204–48), and the *Breviarium* of Festus (pp. 249–64) were probably written at Montecassino, since the flesh-side folios have rubbing of the writing characteristic of eleventh-century codices written at the abbey. As to how the *Collectio canonum hibernensis* reached Italy and especially southern Italy, see my 'Collectio Hibernensis,' *History of Medieval Canon Law*. That the *Hibernensis* was known and used in the tenth century in southern Italy is seen in the manuscripts, Montecassino 384, 439 and Vatican Archivio di San Pietro H-58, on which see my 'A Monastic Florilegium from the *Collectio Canonum Hibernensis* at Montecassino,' *Revue Bénédictine* 114 (2004) 92–111; and 'Excerpta from the *Collectio hibernensis* in three Vatican manuscripts,' BMCL 5 (1975) 1–9.

22. See Appendix 2.

additional texts of the eastern fathers came from direct contact with the easterners there, but the texts also appear in the much earlier Breton manuscript of the *Hibernensis*, Oxford, Bodl., Hatton 42 (saec. IX^1 and med: Bischoff; saec. IX^2: Bieler; saec. IX–X: Ker; Brittany, later at Worcester), which also has a text not appearing in the Vallicelliana manuscript. Found also in Rome, Biblioteca Vallicelliana, Tom. XVIII in the tract *De transmigratione episcoporum* is a canon from the *Chronica Greca*.[23]

Moving to other continental collections that contain texts from eastern fathers found in manuscripts in southern Italy, one of the Basil texts in the *Hibernensis* appears in an early tenth-century florilegial codex from Montecassino, MS 384, with patristic and canonistic texts.[24] One would expect to find texts from the *Rule of St. Basil* in the famous *Collectio Vetus Gallica* codex in Beneventan script, Montecassino 372, made for monks there.[25] While these canons appear in northern manuscripts of the *Vetus Gallica*, they are strangely lacking in the Montecassino codex.[26]

Since at least the nineteenth century it has been widely recognized that the penitential collections functioned as one of the chief vehicles for the transmission of the texts of the eastern fathers and their ideas in the West. For our purposes a convenient distinction can be made between penitentials that specifically cite the eastern fathers and those that simply reflect their works. In both cases the compilers of the penitentials seem to have known the fathers' penitential discipline from Greek, or perhaps Syriac, sources.

Surprisingly, the whole of the preface to the Irish *Paenitentiale Cummeani* is ascribed to Basil and is found in a south Italian manuscript written in Beneventan script in the eleventh century, the *Collection in Nine Books* of Vat. lat. 1349.

The *Collectio Quadripartita*, a great canon law/penitential compiled in the late ninth century in northern France, was copied in the eleventh century in the Montecassino manuscript 541 and in the ninth-century Rheims manuscript[27] Vatican, BAV, lat. 1347, which was annotated and supplement-

23. See Appendix 3.

24. Montecassino, MS 384, p. 89: 'Basilius. Omnis sermo qui non proficit ad ... christi otiosus est.' On this codex see my article 'A South Italian Liturgico-Canonical Mass Commentary,' *Mediaeval Studies* 50 (1988) 646.

25. On this manuscript and its contents see my article 'Further Evidence for the Influence of the *Collectio canonum hibernensis* in Southern Italy: An Early Eleventh-Century Canonistic Florilegium at Montecassino (Cod. 372),' *Peritia* 19 (2005) 1–17.

26. On this see my article 'A Beneventan Monastic Excerptum from the *Collectio Vetus Gallica*,' *Revue Bénédictine* 102 (1992) 298–308.

27. Loew, *The Beneventan Script* 2.89.

ed in Montecassino in the eleventh century.[28] In both of these manuscripts only L. IV or a portion thereof is present,[29] leading some scholars to speculate that this book was independent of the first three books of the *Quadripartitus*.[30] The four books of the *Quadripartitus* as found north of the Alps have many canons attributed to Basil, Gregory Nazianzus, John Chrysostom, Macarius, Pachomius, Apollonius, and others,[31] but L. IV has twenty-one of Basil, one of Pachomius, and one of Apollonius.[32]

A florilegial manuscript, London BL Addit. 16413, written in the late tenth or early eleventh century in the south of Italy, contains a number of northern penitentials,[33] and inserted among these are texts attributed to our eastern fathers: Origen, John Chrysostom, and Basil.[34]

By the early eleventh century there were two flourishing traditions of Basil and other eastern fathers, one in the south Italian canonical manuscript, the *Collectio hibernensis* in Vallicelliana, Tom. XVIII and the other in the *Quadripartita* of the Montecassino manuscripts, 541 and Vat. lat. 1347. The texts of the eastern fathers were soon transmitted into the Beneventan-script *Collection in Nine Books* of Vat. lat. 1349 and the *Collection in Five Books* of Montecassino 125 and the Romanesca-script manuscripts of the latter, Vat. lat. 1339 and Rome, Bibl. Vall. B-11. In the *Collection in Nine Books* there are fifty-two canons of Origen, sixteen of Gregory Nazianzus, six canons of Basil, one of John Chrysostom, one of the *Chronica Greca*, one from Apollonius, two from Serapion, and eight from the *Vita monachorum*.[35] In the *Collection in Five Books* there are seven canons attributed to Basil, twelve to Gregory Nazianzus, sixteen to John Chrysostom, thirty-two to Origen, one to the *Chronica Greca*, one to Dionysius Exiguus, one to Eusebius of Caesarea, one to Serapion, one to the *Vita Macharii*, and three to the *Vita monachorum*.[36] In the *Collection in Nine Books* and in the *Collection of Five Books*, most of the canons of the eastern fathers can be found in the Beta version of the *Collectio canonum hibernensis*. But sev-

28. Ibid. 2.145.

29. Franz Kerff, *Der Quadripartitus: Ein Handbuch der karolingischen Kirchenreform* (Quellen und Forschungen zum Recht im Mittelalter, ed. Raymund Kottje and Hubert Mordek; Sigmaringen 1982) 19 and 29.

30. Ibid. 41.

31. Ibid. 85–102.

32. See Appendix 4.

33. On this manuscript, see Loew, *The Beneventan Script* 2.51. For a partial description of the contents, see Letha Mahadevan, 'Überlieferung und Verbreitung des Bussbuchs "Capitula Iudiciorum",' ZRG Kan. Abt. 72 (1986) 24–28.

34. See Appendix 5.

35. See Appendix 6.

36. See Appendix 7.

eral cannot, suggesting that a somewhat different or modified recension of the Beta version, which contains the vast majority of the canons of the eastern fathers, was circulating in southern Italy. The two collections, in *Nine Books* and in *Five Books*, also shared canons from penitentials perhaps inspired by Basil's *Canonical Epistles* in which penitential periods of fifteen years are prescribed, a favorite period in the works of Basil. That Greek sources were being used in some form in the collections is likely because the *Collection in Five Books* also contains an extract from the *Vita Basilii* of Amphilochius (the story of the conversion of a Jew) in a recension quite unlike the only known Latin versions of the Amphilochian *Vita* listed by the Bollandists.[37]

In comparing the use of the texts attributed to eastern fathers in the *Collection in Nine Books* and in the *Collection in Five Books*, it is clear that the vast majority derive from the south Italian form of the *Collectio canonum hibernensis*. Beyond that there are smaller differences. The *Collection in Nine Books* has single canons attributed to Apollonius and John Chrysostom, the latter appearing in the *Collectio Britannica* attributed to Pope Hadrian. The *Collection in Five Books* has a number of canons attributed to John Chrysostom appearing in none of our other south Italian collections, suggesting a source independent of the *Collectio canonum hibernensis*. The *Collection in Five Books* has single canons attributed to Serapion, the *Vita Basilii*, and *Vita Macharii*. For the canons attributed to Gregory Nazianzus, Origen, and the *Vita monachorum*, the *Collection in Nine Books* has far more than the *Collection in Five Books*.

The *Collection in Five Books* in one of its three manuscripts, Vat. lat. 1339, written perhaps at Farfa, is also of interest for the famous 'author portraits' in the quire preceding the collection itself. As well as portrayals of six ecumenical councils in the East it has portraits of Gregory Nazianzus and John Chrysostom.[38] Strangely, there is no portrait of Basil, who has seven canons in the collection itself. It is worth noting here that in the portraits of all of the canonistic authors, including Gregory Nazianzus and John Chrysostom, there is no trace of eastern or Byzantine vestments or

37. Vat. lat. 1339, fol. 138v [3.171.2], Fornasari 3.220.2: 'Vita Basilii archiepiscopi. Item de eodem. Quidam hebreus venit in sanctam ecclesiam... nostrum Iesum Christum.'

38. On these see my article 'Rites and Signs of Conciliar Decisions in the Early Middle Ages,' *Segni e Riti nella Chiesa Altomedievale occidentale, XXXIII Settimane di Studio del Centro Italiano di Studi sull'Alto Medioevo, Spoleto, 11–17 Aprile 1985* (Spoleto 1987) 216–19; and Richard F. Gyug, 'The List of Authorities in the Illustrations of the Collection in Five Books (MS Vat. Lat. 1339),' in *Ritual, Law and Text: Essays in Honor of Roger E. Reynolds*, ed. Kathleen Cushing and Richard F. Gyug (Aldershot 2004) 241–54.

dress, although Christopher Walter has said there is an eastern model behind some of the depictions.[39] It is also noteworthy that although Origen is represented by thirty-two canons in the collection, his portrait does not appear, perhaps because he was regarded as a heretic and portrayed in the manuscript under discussion here as one of the fallen heretics condemned at the Second Ecumenical Council at Constantinople.[40]

During the course of the eleventh and early twelfth centuries, the tradition of the *Collection in Five Books* with its texts of the eastern fathers worked a significant influence on a number of minor southern Italian collections and its derivatives. At times the canons of the eastern fathers in these derivatives come from the south Italian tradition, at other times from the newly introduced collections from the north, such as Burchard's collection. For example, the *Collection of Vat. lat. 4977*, written in Romanesca script, was noted by Paul Fournier long ago, but he missed its four Basil canons, two of John Chrysostom, four of Origen, two of Gregory Nazianzus, and one of Eusebius Emisenus.[41] Less well known are several other collections with texts of the eastern fathers: the *Collection of Vatican, Arch. San Pietro H-58* (containing two Basil texts and one of Gregory Nazianzus),[42] the *Collection of Rieti* (with three Basil texts, two of Origen, one of the *Vita sanctorum*, one of the *Vita monachorum*, and one of John Chrysostom),[43] the *Collection of Vallicelliana Tom. XXI* (with one text of Origen),[44] the *Collectio Toletana*[45] (with one text of Basil and seven attributed to John of Constantinople),[46] the *Collectio Angelica*[47] (with thirteen texts attributed to John of Constantinople, nine to Origen, five to Gregory Nazianzus, and three to Basil),[48] the *Collectio canonum Casinensis* (with one canon at-

39. Christopher Walter, *L'iconographie des conciles dans la tradition byzantine* (Paris 1970) 66f.

40. See my article 'Rites and Signs of Conciliar Decisions in the Early Middle Ages,' fig. 12.

41. See Appendix 8.

42. See Appendix 9.

43. See Appendix 10.

44. Rome, Bibl. Vallicelliana, Tom. XXI, fol. 288r: 'Origenes. Alii frustra iurant nec seipsos adiuvant . . . videatur quam implore.' See my article 'The South-Italian *Collection in Five Books* and its Derivatives: The *Collection of Vallicelliana Tome XXI*,' *Proceedings of the Eighth International Congress of Medieval Canon Law: San Diego, University of California at La Jolla, 21–27 August 1988*, ed. S. Chodorow (MIC Ser. C 9; Vatican 1991) 77–92.

45. On this collection see Douglas Adamson and Roger E. Reynolds, eds., *The Collectio Toletana: A Canon Law Derivative of the South-Italian Collection in Five Books; An Implicit Edition with Introductory Study* (Monumenta Liturgica Beneventana 5, Studies and Texts 159; Toronto 2008).

46. See Appendix 11.

47. On this collection see my article 'The Collectio Angelica: A Canon Law Derivative of the South Italian Collection in Five Books,' in *Bishops, Texts and the Use of Canon Law around 1100: Essays in Honour of Martin Brett*, ed. Bruce Brasington and Kathleen Cushing (Ashgate 2008) 7–28.

48. See Appendix 12.

tributed to John Chrysostom and one canon attributed to Origen in the *Collection in Nine Books* and the *Collection in Five Books* but not in this collection),[49] and the Farfa *Liber multiloquiorum* (with two Basil texts,[50] three of John Chrysostom, one of Gregory Nazianzus, one attributed to Dionysius the Areopogite, one to the *Vita sanctorum*, and two to Eusebius).[51] Of special interest in this last collection is the first Basil text listed below from a Greek *Vita Basilii* like the one Combefis edited in which the ages of the world are described.[52] Two other collections contain derivatives of the south Italian *Collection in Five Books* with texts attributed to the eastern fathers, the *Collectio Barberiniana* and the *Collection of Vat. lat. 3830*, both written in north central Italy about the middle of the eleventh century. The first has one canon attributed to 'Ex dictis Iohanni Alexandrini episcopi,'[53] and a second to Gregory Nazianzus.[54] This latter canon is also found in the *Collection of Vat. lat. 3830*.[55] This same text appeared much earlier but in a different form in the *Collectio canonum hibernensis* Alpha and Beta, in the first attributed simply to Gregory and in the second to Gregory Nazianzus. In the *Collection in Nine Books* and in the *Collection in Five Books* the attribution is to Gregorius Nanzanzenus.

Perhaps the most important systematic collection compiled in the early eleventh century was Burchard's *Decretum*. Of its many texts, nine

49. Montecassino 216, pp. 68–69 [CVII]: 'Iohannes Chrisostomus, Theodori et Commeani. Si quis uxorem suam invenerit adulteratam . . . ad imparia iudicantur'; p. 210 [CCCLVII]: 'Si accepisti commendatum observa ne perdideris . . . perdideris reddes neglegentiam.' On these see my *The Collectio canonum Casinensis duodecimi saeculi (Codex terscriptus): A Derivative of the South-Italian Collection in Five Books; An Implicit Edition with Introductory Study* (Monumenta Liturgica Beneventana 3, Studies and Texts 127; Toronto 2001) 54, 105.

50. Vat. lat. 4317, fol. 171v–172r. 32: 'De etatibus mundi in Vita sancti Basilii. Basilius. A primo plasto homine cui nomen . . . ducenti nonaginta septem. Item Basilius. In prima vero die . . . quadrupedia et reptilia'; fol. 197v: 'Basilius. Si quis sacerdos palam . . . peregrinando finiat.' On this collection see my article 'The Isidorian *Epistula ad Leudefredum*: An Early Medieval Epitome of the Clerical Duties,' *Mediaeval Studies* 41 (1979) 306f.

51. See Appendix 13.

52. Cf. *Acta Sanctorum* 23.420B.

53. Vat. Barb. lat. 538, fol. 16v–17r: 'Item ex dictis Iohannis Alexandrini episcope. Nullatenus aliquando hereticorum communione immo coinquinatione . . . huiusmodi oratoriis applicetis.'

54. Vat. Barb. lat. 538, fol. 21v: 'Gregorius Nazianzenus. De medicina penitentie illius qui donum dei studet pretio mercari. Nam de eo qui donum dei . . . is communicet iudicamus.' On the influence of *The Collection in Five Books* or its derivates on the *Collectio Barberiniana*, see Fowler-Magerl, *Clavis* 96.

55. Vat. lat. 3830, fol. 24v: 'Gregorius Nazanzenus. De medicina penitentie qui donum dei studet pretio mercari. Nam de eo qui donum dei . . . is communicet iudicamus.' On the relationship of the *Collection in Five Books* or its derivatives and the *Collection of Vat. lat. 3830*, see Fowler-Magerl, *Clavis* 98 and my article 'The *Collectio Angelica*: A Derivative of the South Italian *Collection in Five Books*' 13f.

are attributed to Basil, seven to John of Constantinople, one to Eusebius of Caesarea, and two to Origen.[56] Most of these came from the northern tenth-century *Libri duo synodalibus* of Regino of Prüm, a few from the *Collectio hibernensis*, and one block, 19.44–48, from unknown previous collections.[57] By the eleventh century, Burchard's *Decretum* was known and used in southern Italy. Written in Beneventan script are three manuscripts, Montecassino 45 and Vat. lat. 14731, both of the eleventh century, and Vat. lat. 4981 of the thirteenth century.[58] Also Montecassino 44, written in Romanesca, has glosses in Beneventan script.[59]

This paper began by noting the contacts and close relations of western and eastern Christians in southern Italy in the eleventh and twelfth centuries, and noted that it could be expected that the western canonistic compilers would use texts from the eastern fathers. One might also expect that they took these directly from eastern sources. For the northern collections copied and used in southern Italy, such as the *Quadripartitus* and Burchard, this was clearly not the case. But what of such collections compiled in southern Italy, such as the *Collection in Nine Books* or *Collection in Five Books* and its derivatives? In our survey we have seen that this may be true in a very few cases. The vast remainder of the eastern fathers' canons, however, were taken, strangely, from northern sources, especially the *Collectio canonum hibernensis*. Thus, it is to the earlier Irish collections that the south Italian compilers owe their vast majority of texts from the eastern fathers, not to their eastern Christian neighbors.

APPENDIX 1

Hermann Wasserschleben, *Die irische Kanonensammlung* (2nd ed. Leipzig 1885; repr. Aalen 1966: hereafter Wasserschleben) 1.17e: 'Origines. Quid vobis videtur mutare gubernatoris nostri…minima non credimus'; 13.1: 'Origines. De nomine elemosine. Elemosina hebraice dei mei opus latine…divinum opus indicat'; 15.1: 'Origenes ait. De quattuor modis quibus vivi adiuvant mortuos. Anime defunctorum quattuor modis solvuntur aut…aut ieiunio cognatorum'; 16.5a: 'Origenes. De eo quod non usque quaque abnuenda testificatio. Non ita arrogantia caveatur ut veritas…ut veritas relinquatur'; 16.11b: 'In annalibus Origenis. Quando iacob aperuit puteos patris sui…quantum et quot'; 17.9a: 'Origenes. De oblatione monachi nihil proficiente sine abbatis permissu. Omnis monachus sine abbate et

56. See Appendix 14.

57. On this see Hartmut Hoffmann and Rudolf Pokorny, *Das Dekret des Bischofs Burchard von Worms: Textstufen, Frühe Verbreitung, Vorlagen* (MGH Hilfsmittel 12; Munich 1991) 173–244.

58. Loew, *The Beneventan Script* 2.61, 151, and 157.

59. On this see my *Collectio canonum Casinensis duodecim saeculi* 6, n. 25.

aliquando...permiserit pauca commendat'; 18.5: 'Origenes ait. De eo quod sors mittenda est inter ecclesiam et sepulcrum patrum. Si unusquisque secularis voluerit dividat sors...in honorem patrum'; 21.5b: 'Origenes. Omnis iudex indiget tribus hoc est...bonorum sobrietate morum'; 25.16c: 'Orosius. (Origenes elsewhere). Boni pastoris est pecus tondere non...tondere non deglobere'; 26.2c: 'Origines. De multis duos eligere nostrum est...prevaricatus est iudas'; 27.23a: 'Origenes ait. De ecclesia defendente dignos et indignos. Columba avis simplex que alienos pullos...ecclesia debet fieri'; 29.4a: 'Origenes. De notatione veritatis animantium in furto reddendo. In bove ideo quinque redduntur quia...utroque sexu ponitur'; 30.1b: 'Origenes dicit. Qui iurat non reddat quia innocens...quia innocens est'; 30.2b: 'Origines. Si accepisti commendatum observa ne pereat...propter neglegentiam tuam'; 30.5a: 'Origenis. De commendatis per furtum raptis ab ecclesia catholica non reddendis. Si ad id depositum requiritur ut...alicuius non accipiat'; 30.5b: 'Item Origenes. Omnis locus refugii non debet ledere...ab ullo ledi'; 31.6b: 'Inde Origenis. Si patriarcha sciret eos bene facere...eris et reliqua'; 31.15c: 'Origenes. Patrem et matrem honora ut tibi...cum inhonoras parentes'; 32.13: 'Originis in libro de heredibus ait. De divisione hereditatis in tres partes. Pater moriens det tertiam partem filiis...filios et pauperes'; 32.17b: 'Origenes in annalibus hebreorum. Iacob moriens partem dedit filie sue...mansit post virum'; 32.19a: 'Origenes dicit. De eo quod femine dividunt hereditatem non tamen principalem. Raab meretrix in ierícho hereditatem consecuta...hereditatem consecuta est'; 33.03c: 'Origenes. Qui querit debitum ab inope exactor...aliene rei efficitur'; 33.12f: 'Origenes. Accomoda fratri tuo et accipe quod...nihil superfluum queras'; 35.2c: 'Origenes. Omnis audax iuramenti mendacii proximus est...mendacii proximus est'; 35.5e: 'Origenes. Alii frustra iurant nec seipsos adiuvant...videantur quam implere'; 35.6c: 'Origenes. Prohibenda multa iuratio sed post iurandum...iuravit nec solvit'; 36.7b: 'Origenes. Quicumque sua propria in alienitate reliquerit...non facile retrahet'; 37.4e: 'Origenes. Quidam assumpta ecclesia dei et rebus...quam principes nomino'; 37.17: 'Origenes. De excommunicatione contradicentis principi. Qui fastu superbie domino suo contradixerit...sit aut abiciendus'; 37.20d: 'Origenes. Tria in ordinatione necessaria sunt consensus...petrus ordinavit clementem'; 38.2b: 'Origenes. Si tabule et pelles et ministri...et doctores ecclesie'; 38.4g: 'Origenes. Doctor docens et non implens similis...non dans virtutem'; 38.15b: 'Origenes. Si doctor erraverit et in suo...nemo potest emendare'; 40.02b: 'Origenes. Si paradisus adam excommunicatum eiecit quantomagis...eiecit quantomagis ecclesia'; 41.01b: 'Origenis in annalibus hebreorum ait. Moises commendavit hereditatem iethro sacerdoti madian...suam iohanni commendavit'; 41.05b: 'Origenes. Omnis habere propria princeps debet quibus...filios si habuerit'; 41.07a: 'Origenes. Omnis monachus sine abbate et aliquando...permiserit pauca commendat'; 42.2: 'Origenes. De tribus quibus ecclesia non debet uti. Tria debet ecclesia dona iniquorum non...innocentis non accipietis'; 42.4f: 'Origenes. Sicut ovis tunicam suam dimittit tondenti...celestia non possidebit'; 46.20: 'Origenes. De eo quod mulier debet sequi virum suum ad vota cristiana confugientem. Discant mulieres exemplis patriarcharum sequi viros...suum videt deo'; 47.8e: 'Origenes. Quod oculis concupiscentibus mundum conspicimus oculis...oculis flentibus penitemus'; 48.1d: 'Origenes ait. Notandum quomodo argentee et auree et...constituuntur et fulciuntur'; 49.10: 'Origenes ait. De resurrectione transmutatorum martirum. Alii putant eos in loco cineris ... in ea flantem'; 50.1a: 'Origenes ait. De eo quod multi homines dei in deserto sepulti sunt ut ab angelis frequentarentur et a malis vitarentur. Moises homo dei in monte phasga ... a malis vitaretur'; 50.2b: 'Origenes ait. Non tantum scimus vivos a deo ... visitari et adiuvari'; 54.11a: 'Origenes. De esu suium licito. Suis immunda prius nunc consecrata per ... imperium in pena'; 59.4a: 'Origenes. De ductore qui non implet animi effectum. Omnis qui ducit alienos si affectum ... reatum omnium sumpsit'; 61.3a: 'Origenes. De inimico proprio non maledicendo sed inimico dei et ecclesie. Non maledico inimicum meum sed inimicum ... compatiuntur omnia membra'; 66.7: 'Origenes. De consilio a pluribus perquirendo. Interroga plures sed non a pluribus ... viventes usque eorum'; 67.3: 'Origenes. De eo quod iudicem oporteat tria observare, probare sine discrimine, iudicare sine mora, verum non tacere. Omnis iudex debet mendacium destruere fallacem ... eo non querere.'

Wasserschleben 2.13a: 'Gregorius Nazanzenus. De indignis mercantibus sacerdotium et de vendentibus donum dei. Quicumque hoc donum studet donatione mercari ... in profundo descendat'; 21.1a: 'Gregorius Nazianzenus. De personis dignis ad iudicandum. In omnibus causis ecclesiasticis tres persone ... maxime conscientiam suam'; 21.01b: 'Gregorius Nazianzenus. In negotiis secularibus rex et senex ... ne temere iudicaverint'; 21.28: 'Gregorius Nazianzenus. De laicis non iudicantibus presente episcopo vel scriba vel contemptibili. Si episcopus vel scriba presentes sint ... episcopis laici disputent'; 25.07: 'Gregorius Nazianzenus. De brevi regno iusto meliore longo iniquo. Multo melius est pauci temporis legitimum ... possessiones cum iniustitia'; 28.12b: 'Gregorius Nazianzenus ait. Duo in ecclesia cavenda ne solverit ... quod non alligandum'; 32.02b: 'Gregorius Nazianzenus. Benedictio patrum domos filiorum confirmat ... domos filiorum confirmat'; 32.21a: 'Gregorius Nazianzenus. De ministris egrotantium hereditatem consequentibus. Qui nutrit infirmos hereditatem eorum consequatur ... possidete hereditatem meam'; 37.04a: 'Gregorius Nazanzenus. De malis principibus increpandis. Timeo hoc quod video canes affectare ... perdere quam conservare'; 37.24c: 'Gregorius Nazianzenus. Quidam desiderio honoris inflati defunctis episcopis ... magisterii non formidant'; 37.25a: 'Gregorius Nazianzenus. De eo quod indigni sunt principatu ecclesie qui non bene regunt domos suas. Qui nec regiminis in se rationem ... tuos quam me'; 37.25b: 'Item. Noverat indigne agere filios suos et ... non corripuit eos'; 37.25c: 'Item. Quicumque domui sue bene preesse nescit ... potest habere regimina'; 37.26: 'Gregorius Nazianzenus. De eo quod non genus nec locus sed mores edificent principes. Nos qui presumus non ex locorum ... sed fidei puritate'; 38.04a: 'Gregorius Nazanzenus ait. De eo quod doctores debent implere quod docent. Mundari prius oportet et sic alios ... dominum accedere facere.'

Wasserschleben 15.4b: 'Item in Vita monachorum. Quidam episcopus ministrum inobedientem habuit qui ... et solvit ministrum'; 16.11a: 'In Vita monachorum egipti, Ovius eps ait. De eo quod non facile firmatur testimonium super mortuum. Omnis qui testificatur super mortuum addat ... ille diminutus est'; 17.10: 'In Vita monachorum. De oblatione degentis sub censu non proficiente. Quidam rusticus vas eneum sacerdoti in ... ne propria amittam'; 17.11a: 'In Vita monachorum. De oblatione puerorum mutanda si in malum, si in catholicum non mutanda. Duos filios artifices legimus quorum pater...deo dedit relinquere'; 18.07b: 'In Vita monachorum. Quidam clericus in aliena ecclesia moriens...nec dimittendus vacuus'; 41.07b: 'In Vita monachorum. Quidam monachus cuidam fratri casulam commendavit...dixit sume hoc'; 42.16b: 'In Vita monachorum. Quidam episcopus ait de quodam alumno...in quantum desertor'; 50.02c: 'In Vita monachorum. Legimus quosdam martires in desertis sepultos...eorum himnos cantare'; 53.02e: 'In Vita monachorum. Quidam ieiunavit ad dominum ut prohiberet...devastarent messem heremite'; 55.03b: 'In Vita monachorum. Quidam puer male usus febre correptus...meritum etatem adiuvat'; 56.02c: 'In Vita monachorum. Quidam latrones causa predandi venerunt ad...et penitentiam egerunt.'

Wasserschleben 12.14: 'Basilius dicit. De eo quod non ad unam mensuram ieiunandum omnibus. Modus et qualitas temperabitur cibi nec...aliqua diversitatis existit'; 21.11b: 'Basilius. Cum dominus aliquando dicit nolite iudicare...de hoc iudicare'; 31.16f: 'Basilius. Nam et parentes nostros quasi propria...sepultura illis debetur.'

Wasserschleben 31.07b: 'Iohannes metrópolitanus. David post adulterium homicidiumque egit penitentiam...tui accipiam illud.'

Wasserschleben 65.03: 'Abraham philosophus ait. De tribus partibus anime. Tres partes anime sunt rationabilis irascibilis...noxia terrenaque generabit.'

APPENDIX 2

Vall. Tom. XVIII, fol. 67r: 'Origenis. Iudas scarioth de gradu suo cecidit...iterum non invenit'; fol. 72v: 'Origenis. Satis age cum tibi proficit et...prece sanctorum solveris'; fol. 74r: 'Origenis in veritate hebraice. Quando moises terram amor reorum divisit...firmaverit terminum suum'; fol. 75r: 'Origenis. Hi quattuor cibi significant quattuor oblationes...christianis et monachis'; fol. 75v: 'Origenis. Omnis monachus si absens sit abba...commutetur ab abbate' (inc. Hatton 42: 'Omnis monachus sine abbate vel aliquando'); fol. 75v: 'Originis. Parvuli quoquemodo voverint votum deo...prevaricationis pena teneantur'; fol. 82r: 'Origenis. Omnis iudex debet mendacium disputare fallacem...excecant oculos sapientium'; fol. 85r: 'Origenis. Boni pastoris est pecus tondere non...tondere non deglobere'; fol. 85r–v: 'Origenis. Ipse autem tiberius plurima imperii sui...pecus non deglobere'; fol. 88v: 'In annalibus. Quidam gentilis in navi periclitatis fertur...vitam meruisse narrator'; fol. 92r: 'Origenis (ait). De notatione varietatis que est inter vetus et novum in furto reddendo. Notandum quod hec varietas prestet in...substantiam domus sue'; fol. 92v: 'Origenis item. Si illi iudicaverint duplum restituat dominus...cur prius iurat'; fol. 94r: 'In annalibus hebreorum. De iniquitate filiorum patres non contaminante si correxerint (corripuerint). Noe corripuit cham quantum potuit et...dona largitus est'; fol. 94v–95r: 'Item Origenis. Designat amonium semper viridem et dare...nocet et urit'; fol. 97r: 'Item in annalibus. Pars que venit in partem tribus...non reversa est'; fol. 98r–v: 'Origenis item. Iugurta mican ipse aumularum regi adoptivus...victum africa expulit'; fol. 104r: 'Origenis in annalibus. Noe divisit orbem terre filiis suis…suis antequam moreretur'; fol. 104v: 'Origenis. Quid vobis videtur commutare gubernatoris nostri…minima non credimus'; fol. 106r: 'Origenis. Omnis princeps propria habere debet quibus…ecclesie sibi serventur'; fol. 110r–v: 'De excommunicanda mensam malorum. Christus antequam pateretur triduo non comedit…participatione mense Saul' (not attributed to Origen in Vall. Tom. XVIII, but only in Vat. Lat 1349); fol. 110v: 'Origenis in annalibus. Ezechias excommunicavit nuntios babilonis dominus a…orationem et reliqua'; fol. 125r: 'Origenis in annalibus. De loco penitentie et orationis. In tabernaculo david penitentiam agebat hinc…ad templum oravit'; fol. 127r: 'Origenis. De eo quod non minus reliquie in deserto posite frequentantur a deo et ab angelis. Non tantum scimus vivos a deo…visitari et adiuvari' (exp. Hatton 42: 'iuvari'); fol. 127v: 'Originis. Duo abusiva iudicari comam nutrientem et…ei dati sunt'; fol. 130r: 'Origenis in annalibus. Infans quidam in templo positus erat…sine culpa parentum'; fol. 131r: 'Origenis. Cum homo iste peccaverit suam substantiam…ut iudicium retraharis'; fol. 131r: 'Origenis in omeliis de vaccarufa dicitur. Peccatum humanum non sustinet pecus si…pecus si auferet'; fol. 131r: 'Item Origenis. Quantum ad omnes usus apta sunt…tantum libera sunt'; fol. 131v: 'Origenis. Omnis qui ducit alienos si affectum…reatum omnium sumpsit'; fol. 133r: 'Origenis. De homine non habente quod reddat proximi nisi pacem. Homo cui dimisit dominus omnia peccata…nisi pacis signa'.

Vall. Tom. XVIII, fol. 70v: 'In Vita monachorum. De ieiunio pro mortuis. Quidam episcopus ministerium alicuius episcopi in…dominus suscitavit eum'; fol. 74r: 'In vita monachorum. Quidam monachum moriens suum habitaculum suo…firmavit et accepit'; fol. 112r: 'In Vita monachorum. De degente sub censu nihil commendante. Quidam rusticus vas eneum sacerdoti in…ne propria amittam'; fol. 114r: 'In Vita monachorum. Alius episcopus ait de alumno sui…in quantum discessor'; fol. 128r: 'In Vita monachorum. Quidam parvam messem nutriens bestie devoraverit…prohiberet et prohibuit'; fol. 130r: 'In Vita monachorum. Ubi vel que ecclesia dei illic…enulum allectum suum'; fol. 133r: 'Inde in vita monachorum. Quidam vitam penitentis agens in monasterio…quem defraudavit reddidit'.

Vall. Tom. XVIII, fol. 65v: 'Basilius. De voce moderanda clerici (clericorum). Vocis mensuram definivit audiendi modus si…quod est mutabile'; fol. 68v: 'Basilius. De ieiunio ut non sit in propria voluntate. Ieiunii mensura non debet eximius cuiuscumque…unam habuisse signantur'; fol. 89v: 'Basilius interrogat. Si is qui consentit…Adam aequievit Eve'; fol. 135r: 'Basilius. Omnis sermo qui non proficit ad…est et reliqua'.

Vall. Tom. XVIII, fol. 105r: 'Gregorius Nazonzenus. Timeo autem quod canes affectare…. affectare officium pastorale'; fol. 105r: 'Gregorius Nazonzenus. Tacui non semper tacebo habetis me…redime tuam benedictionem'; fol. 106r: 'Gregorius Nazonzenus hoc dicens. Ab hoc enim altario non quislibet…esse deputet pedes'.

Vall. Tom. XVIII, fol. 94v: 'Iohannes metropolitanus. David post adulterium homicidiumque egit penitentiam…tua accipiam illud'; fol. 136v: 'Iohannes metropolitanus. De eo quod nec satis homine boni nec satis mali habebunt compensationem in die iudicii. Erit enim ibi sine dubio compensatio...confinio gehenne revocabunt'.

Vall. Tom. XVIII, fol. 60v: 'Item. Dionisius exiguus. Et si quis episcopus aut presbiter... et presbiteris dirigantur'; fol. 61v: 'Item. Dionisius exiguus et Laurentius auctoritates (auctores) grecorum peritissimi de eadem causa dicunt. Episcopo non licet alienam parochiam rapere...maxima supplicatione proficiat'; fol. 61v: 'Dionisius exiguus. De eo quod eunuchi episcopatum accipiant. Eunuchus si per insidias hominum factus...dei conditionis inimicus.'

Vall. Tom. XVIII, fol. 135v: 'Iusebius. De sabbato et quinta feria. Silvester statuit sabbato ieiunandum et quintam...potest non querit.'

APPENDIX 3

Hatton 42, fol. 14v: 'Origenis. Iudas scarioth de gradu suo cecidit...iterum non invenit'; fol. 23v: 'Origenis. Satis age cum tibi proficit et...prece sanctorum solveris'; fol. 26r: 'Origenis in veritate hebraice. Quando moises terram amor reorum divisit...firmaverit terminum suum'; fol. 27v: 'Origenis. Hi quattuor cibi significant quattuor oblationes...christianis et monachis'; fol. 28v: 'Origenis. Omnis monachus sine abbate vel aliquando...commutetur ab abbate'; fol 28v: 'Originis. Parvuli quoquemodo voverint votum deo...prevaricationis pena teneantur'; fol. 40r: 'Origenis. Omnis iudex debet mendacium disputare fallacem...excecant oculos sapientium'; fol. 45v: 'Origenis. Boni pastoris est pecus tondere non...tondere non deglobere'; fol. 45v: 'Origenis. Ipse autem tiberius plurima imperii sui...pecus non deglobere'; fol. 50v: 'In annalibus. Quidam gentilis in navi periclitatis fertur...vitam meruisse narrator'; fol. 56v: 'Origenis (ait). De notatione varietatis que est inter vetus et novum in furto reddendo. Notandum quid hanc...substantiam domus sue'; fol. 57r: 'Origenis item. Si illi iudicaverint duplum restituat dominus...cur prius iurat'; fol. 59v: 'In annalibus hebreorum. De iniquitate filiorum patres non contaminante si correxerint (corripuerint). Noe corripuit cham quantum potuit et...dona largitus est'; fol. 60r: 'Item Origenis. Designat canimonium semper viridem et dare...nocet et urit'; fol. 64r: 'Item in annalibus. Pars que venit in partem tribus...non reversa est'; fol. 65v: 'Origenis item. Igitur iugurta.mican ipse aumularum regi adoptivus...victum africa expulit'; fol. 75r: 'Origenis in annalibus. Noe divisit orbem terre filiis suis...suis antequam moreretur'; fol. 75v–76r: 'Origenis. Quid vobis videtur commutare gubernatoris nostri...minima non credimus'; fol. 78v: 'Origenis. Omnis princeps propria habere debet quibus...ecclesie sibi reserventur'; fol. 85v: 'De excommunicanda mensam malorum. Christus antequam pateretur triduo non comedit...participatione mense Saul' (not attributed to Origen in Hatton 42, but only in Vat. Lat 1349); fol. 85v: 'Origenis in annalibus. Ezechias excommunicavit nuntios babilonis dominus a...orationem et reliqua'; fol. 110v: 'Origenis in annalibus. De loco penitentie et orationis. In tabernaculum David penitentiam agebat hinc...deprecabantur tres pueri.ad templum oravit'; fol. 113v: 'Origenis. De eo quod non minus reliquie in deserto posite frequentantur a deo et ab angelis. Non tantum scimus vivos a deo...visitari et iuvari'; fol. 115r: 'Originis. Duo abusiva iudicari comam nutrientem et...ei dati sunt'; fol. 119r: 'Origenis in annalibus. Infans quidam in templo positus erat... sine culpa parentum'; fol. 120v: 'Origenis. Cum homo iste peccaverit suam substantiam... ut iudicium retraharis'; fol. 121r: 'Origenis in omeliis de vaccarufa dicitur. Peccatum humanum non sustinet pecus si... pecus si auferet'; fol. 121r: 'Origenis. Quantum ad omnes usus apta sunt... tantum libera sunt'; fol. 121r: 'Origen ait Omnis qui ducit alienos... reatum omnium sumpsit'; fol. 124r: 'Origenis. De homine non habente quod reddat proximi nisi pacem. Homo cui dominus dimisit omnia peccata... nisi pacis signa'; fol. 12v: 'Basilius. De voce moderanda clerici (clericorum). Vocis mensuram definivit audiendi modus si... quod est mutabile'; fol. 17r: 'Basilius. De ieiunio ut non sit in propria voluntate. Ieiunii mensura non debet eximius cuiuscumque... unam habuisse signantur'; fol. 52v: 'Basilius interrogat. Si is qui consentit... Adam aequievit Eve'; fol. 129r: 'Basilius. Omnis sermo qui non proficit ad... est et reliqua'; fol. 20r: 'In Vita monachorum. De ieiunio pro mortuis. Quidam episcopus ministerium alicuius episcopi in... dominus suscitavit eum'; fol. 26r: 'In Vita monachorum. Quidam monachum moriens suum habitaculum suo... firmavit et accepit'; fol. 88r: 'In Vita monachorum. De degente sub censu nihil commendante. Quidam rusticus vas eneum sacerdoti in... ne propria amittam'; fol. 91v: 'In Vita monachorum. Alius episcopus ait de alumno sui... in tantum discessor'; fol. 115v: 'In Vita monachorum. Quidam parvam messem nutriens bestie devoraverit... prohiberet et prohibuit'; fol. 119r: 'In Vita monachorum. Ubi vel que ecclesia dei illic... enulum allectum suum'; fol. 123v–124r: 'Inde in Vita monachorum. Quidam vitam penitentis agens in monasterio... quem defraudavit reddidit'; fol. 76v: 'Gregorius Nazonzenus. Timeo autem quod canes affectare.... affectare officium pastorale'; fol. 77r: 'Gregorius Nazonzenus. Tacui non semper tacebo habetis me... redime tuam benedictionem'; fol. 78v: 'Gregorius Nazonzenus hoc dicens. Ab hoc enim altario non quislibet... esse deputet pedes'; fol. 59v: 'Iohannes metropolitanus. David post adulterium homicidiumque egit penitentiam... tua accipiam illud'; fol. 129v–130r: 'Iohannes metropolitanus. De eo quod nec satis homine boni nec satis mali habebunt compensationem in die iudicii. Erit enim ibi sine dubio compensatio... confinio gehenne revocabunt'; fol. 4r: 'Item Dionisius exiguus. Et si quis episcopus aut presbiter... et presbiteris dirigantur'; fol. 6r: 'Item Dionisius exiguus et Laurentius auctoritates (auctores) grecorum peritissimi de eadem causa dicunt. Episcopis non licet alienam parochiam rapere... maxima supplicatione proficiat'; fol. 6r: 'Dionisius exiguus. De eo quod eunuchi episcopatum accipiant. Eunuchus si per insidias hominum factus... dei conditionis inimicus'; fol. 129r: 'Iusebius. De sabbato et quinta feria. Silvester statuit sabbato ieiunandum et quintam... diei copulandus.'

Hatton 42, fol. 65r: 'Origenis. De eo quod filie dividunt hereditatem non tamen principalem. Raab meretrix in iericho hereditatem patris... fratribus suis fuerit'.

Vall. Tom. XVIII, fol. 144r: 'Item unde supra ex Chronica greca. Imperante igitur romanorum secundo anno arthemio... germanum sanctissimum archiepiscopum'.

APPENDIX 4

Vat. lat. 1347, fol. 79v [4.2]: 'Timorem quidem docet...calicem domini percipit' (attributed to Basil); fol. 152r [4.19]: 'Hoc sit in iudicio positum...facit differentium poenae' (attributed to Basil); fol. 152r [4.24]: 'Poenitentem ex corde...ovem meam quam perdideram' (attributed to Basil); fol. 152v [4.25]: 'Affectum illum in se recipiat...sicut Zacheus fecit' (attributed to Basil); fol. 152v [4.26]: 'Erga eum qui pro peccato...tradidimus vobis' (attributed to Basil); fol. 153r [4.32]: 'Si quis semel notatus...cura similes adhibetur' (attributed to Basil); fol. 153v [4.42]: 'Id [sic] omnimodis observari...non est qui erigat eum' (attributed to Basil); fol. 154r [4.49]: 'Non oportet eum qui...brevis sermocinatio facienda' (not attributed to Basil, cf. Kerff, *Quadripartitus* 94 and Fowler-Magerl, *Clavis* QU04.049); fol. 159r [4.109]: 'Si quis preventus...in irritum revocetur' (attributed to Basil); fol. 162r [4.152]: 'Apostolus dicit Omnia facite...et opus eius abiciatur' (attributed to Basil); fol. 162r [4.153]: 'Si quis murmurans extiterit...sacerdotis iudicio paeniteat' (attributed to Basil); fol. 162r [4.157]: 'Si quis detrahit...detraxit Moysi poeniteat' (attributed to Basil); fol. 162r. [4.158]: 'Si quis detraxerit eo qui peest...quae detraxit Moysi poeniteat' (not attributed to Basil, cf. Kerff, *Quadripartitus* 97 and Fowler-Magerl, *Clavis* QU04.158); fol. 162v [IV.161]: 'Si quis videtur contentiosus esse...notetur usque corrigatur' (not attributed to Basil, cf. Kerff, *Quadripartitus* 97 and Fowler-Magerl, *Clavis* QU04.161); fol. 166r [4.210]: 'Si is qui praeest...evangelizavimus vobis anathema sit' (attributed to Basil); fol. 166r [4.211]: 'Si quis prohibit nos facere...qui diligunt Deum' (attributed to Basil); fol. 166r [4.212]: 'Is qui praeest si praeter voluntate...aut sacrilegus habeatur' (attributed to Basil); fol. 167r [4.221]: 'Firma autem tunc erit...deputari ac perfecta' (attributed to Basil); fol 167r [4.225]: 'Oportet tamen infantes...excludatur hominum pessimorum' (attributed to Basil); fol. 168v [4.240]: 'Qui consentit peccantibus...culpabilem iudicandum' (attributed to Basil); fol. 169r [4.251]: 'Qui alterius consentit peccato...consentit contrahat poenam' (attributed to Basil).

Vat. lat. 1347, fol. 162r [4.156]: 'Si quis promptus facilisque...fraterno consortio peniteat' (no attribution, cf. Kerff, *Quadripartitus* 96 and Fowler-Magerl, *Clavis* QU04.156).

Vat. lat. 1347, fol. 173v [4.296]: 'Ex dictis sancti Apollonii. De ieiunio quarte et sexte ferie. Ieiunia sane legitima idest quarta et...cum crucifigentibus crucifigere' (cf. Kerff, *Quadripartitus* 100 and Fowler-Magerl, *Clavis* QU04.296).

APPENDIX 5

Fol. 36r: 'Origenis. De consolatione defunctorum. Anime defunctorum quattuor modis solvantur...elymosynis aut ieiunio cognatorum.'

(Incorrectly attributed to John Chrysostom) fol. 49r–52v: 'Johannes Crissostomus. De eadem re. Exsufflatur igitur exorcizatur ut fuga...ignominia desentor antiquus'; 'Johannes Crissostomus. Accidit et iam cathecuminus benedictum sal...suavitatem perveniat'; 'Johannes Crissostomus. De tacto narium. Cum vero tanguntur nares eorum...mandatisque perdurent'; 'Johannes Crissostomus. De peccatoris unctionem. De in pectus eorum oleo consecrationis...Christi mandata sectantur'; 'Johannes Crissostomus. Cunctis vero renati de albis bestibus...in futura figuravit ecclesiae'; 'Idem Johannes. Utuntur igitur albis vestibus ut quorum...gloriae proferat indumentum'; 'Johannes. De crismate unctione. Inplete enim baptismate caput nostrum crismate...Christi nomine censeatur.'

Fol. 16v–17v: 'Increpatio sancti Basilii ad sacerdotem. Attende tibi et cave officium quam accepisti...qui obediunt tibi per Jesum Christum dominum nostrum'; fol. 126r–129v: 'Incipit de doctrina vel ammonitionis beati Basilii archiepiscopus. Audi filii ammonitionem patris tui et inclina...in nobis requirescere cupit'.

APPENDIX 6

Vat. lat. 1349, fol. 9v [1.8g]: 'Origenes. Quidam assumptam ecclesiam dei et rebus...quam principes nomino'; fol. 17r [1.62b]: 'Origenes in annalibus. Noe divisit orbem terre filiis suis...suis antequam moreretur'; fol. 17v [1.65d]: 'Origenes. Tria in ordinatione necessaria sunt consensus...petrus ordinavit clementem'; fol. 17v [1.66c]: 'Origenes. Quid vobis videtur commutare gubernatoris nostri...minima non credimus'; fol. 49v [2.124]: 'Origenes. De excommunicatione contradicentis principi. Qui fastu superbie domino suo contradixerit...sit et abiciendus'; fol. 50r [2.128b]: 'Origenes. Si tabule et pelles et ministri...digni sunt honore'; fol. 50r [2.129c]: 'Origenes. Doctor docens et non implens similis...non dans virtutem'; fol. 51r [2.134b]: 'Origenes. Si doctor erraverit et in suo...nemo potest emendare'; fol. 69r [2.256c]: 'Origenes. Iudas scarioth de gradu suo cecidit...iterum non invenit'; fol. 87r [3.76c]: 'Origenes. Hi quattuor cibi significant quattuor oblationes...christianis et monachis'; fol. 89r [3.88.2a]: 'Origenes. De eo quod mittenda sors inter ecclesiam et sepulcrum patris. Si unusquisque secularis voluerit dividat sors...in honore patrum'; fol. 90r–v [3.93]: 'Origines. De cura pro mortuis, de quattuor modis quibus adiuvantur mortui. Anime defunctorum quattuor modis solvuntur aut...aut ieiunium cognatorum'; fol. 91v [3.99e]: 'Origenes. Satis age cum tibi proficit et...aut precessorum solveris'; fol. 119v [6.1.3]: 'Origines. De tribus quibus debet ecclesia non uti. Tria ecclesia debet custodire dona iniquorum...innocentis non accipietis'; fol. 119v [6.5b]: 'Origines. Sicut ovis tunicam suam dimittit tondenti...celestia non possidebit'; fol. 123r [6.4.3c]: 'Origenes. Si paradisus excommunicatum adam eiecit...quantomagis ecclesia dei'; fol. 123r [6.4.4b]: 'Origenes. Ezechias excommunicavit nuntios babilonis dominus a...cum veste sordida'; fol. 125v [6.6.6b]: 'Origines. Omnis iudex tribus indiget hoc est...bonorum sobrietate morum'; fol. 128r [6.6.30c]: 'Origenes. Omnis iudex debet mendacium disputare fallacem...excecant oculos sapientium'; fol. 128r [6.7.1d]: 'Origenes in annalibus hebreorum. Moises commendavit hereditatem iethro sacerdoti madian...et firmatum est'; fol. 129v [6.9.4c]: 'Origenes. Qui querit debitum ab inope exactor...aliene rei efficitur'; fol. 133r [6.12.16c]: 'Boni pastoris est pecus tondere non...tondere non deglobere'; fol. 134r [6.14.8a]: 'In annalibus hebreorum. De iniquitate filiorum patres non criminante si correxerint. Noe corripuit cham quantum potuit et...dona largitus est'; fol. 134v [6.14.8b]: 'Inde Origenis. Si patriarcha scisset eos bene facere...sequentem consilia iuvenum'; fol. 135r [6.14.15h]:

'Origenes. Patrem et matrem honora ut tibi...cum parentes inhonoras'; fol. 136r [6.15.9a]: 'Origenes. De divisione hereditatis in tres partes. Pater moriens dat tertiam partem filiis...dividat inter pauperes'; fol. 136v [6.15.13a]: 'Origenes. De eo quod filie dividunt hereditatem non principalem. Raab meretrix in iericho hereditatem patris...fratribus suis fuerit'; fol. 137r [6.16.5]: 'Origenes. De homine non habente quod reddat proximo nisi pacem. Homo cui dimisit dominus omnia peccata...nisi pacis signa'; fol. 137v [6.17.1g]: 'Origenes. Cum homo iste peccaverit sua substantiam...ad iudicium retraharis'; fol. 137v [6.17.2d]: 'Origenes. Peccatum humanum non sustinet pecus si...pecus si auferet'; fol. 137v [6.17.2e]: 'Item Origenes. Quantum ad homines usus apta sunt...tantum libera sunt'; fol. 138r [6.19.02a]: 'Origenes. De ductore accipiente reatum licet animi effectum non habuerit. Omnis qui ducit alienos si possit...reatum omnium sumpsit'; fol. 139r [6.20.8b]: 'In novo testamento Origenis. Suis immunda prius erat non consecrata...per stragem porcorum'; fol. 140v [6.24.4a]: 'Origenes. De inimico proprio non maledicendo sed inimico dei et ecclesie. Non maledico inimicum meum sed inimicum...omnia membra compatiuntur'; fol. 141v [6.25.5c]: 'Origenes. Hoc de scriptura sensit'; fol. 141v [6.25.5f]: 'In annalibus hebreorum demonstretur. In tempore Ozie a duodecim tribus...armario offerre deberent'; fol. 159r [7.97]: 'Origenes ait. De eo quod mulier debet sequi virum suum ad vota christiana confugientem. Discant mulieres exemplis patriarcharum sequi viros...suum videat deo'; fol. 165v [7.138]: 'Origenes. De notatione varietatis animantium in furto reddentium. In bovem ideo quinque redduntur quia...sunt hec reddat'; fol. 166r [7.140]: 'Origenes. De notatione varietatis inter veterem et novum et furtum reddendum. Notandum quod hec varietas prestet in...substantiam domus sue'; fol. 167r [7.147.1b]: 'Origenes. Item. Si illi iudicaverint duplum restituat dominus...cur prius iurat'; fol. 167r [7.148b]: 'Origenes. Si accepisti commendatum observa ne perdideris...perdideris reddes neglegentiam'; fol. 168r [7.152a]: 'Origenes. De commendatis per furtim raptis ab ecclesia catholica non reddendis. Si ad id depositum accipitur ut...alicuius non accipiat'; fol. 168v [7.155c]: 'Origenes. Omnis audax iuramenti mendacio proximus est...mendacio proximus est'; fol. 169r [7.158d]: 'Origines. Alii frustra iurant nec seipsos adiuvant...videatur quam implere'; fol. 169r [7.159g]: 'Origenes enim ait. Prohibenda multa iuratio sed post iurandum...quam irrita facienda'; fol. 173v [7.196]: 'Origenes. Incipit de elemosina, imprimis de nomine elemosine. Elemosina hebraice dei mei opus latine...sed voca pauperes'; fol. 178v [8.14e]: 'Origines. Quod oculis concupiscentibus mundum conspicimus oculis...oculis flentibus peniteamus'; fol. 183v [8.53a]: 'Origenes in annalibus. De loco penitentie et orationis. In tabernaculo David penitentiam agebat huic...ad templum orabat'; fol. 212v [9.105b]: 'Origines. Si paradisus excommunicatum adam eiecit...quantomagis ecclesia dei'; fol. 212v [9.106.1f]: 'Origenes. Christus antequam pateretur triduo non comedit...cum veste sordida'; fol. 217r [9.131.2c]: 'Origines. Scito precipueris aut deo oblationibus aut...aut precessorum solveris'; fol. 217r [9.131.3a]: 'Origenes. De quattuor modis quibus adiuvantur anime defunctorum. Anime defunctorum quattuor modis solvuntur aut...aut ieiunium cognatorum.'

Vat. lat. 1349, fol. 9v [1.8a]: 'Gregorius Nazongenus. De malis principibus potius increpandi quam ordinandi. Timeo quod video canes affectare officium...perdere quam conservare'; fol. 10r [1.10b]: 'Gregorius Naziongenus. Timeo hoc quod video canes affectare...affectare officium pastorale'; fol. 10r [1.11c]: 'Gregorius Nazionzenus. Quidam desiderio honoris inflati defunctis episcopis...magistri non formidant'; fol. 10r [1.11d]: 'Item. Nec recipiendos qui non digna conversatione...abluunt crimen amissum'; fol. 10r [1.12a]: 'Gregorius Nazionzenus. De eo quod indigni sint principatu ecclesie qui non bene regunt domos suas. Qui nec regiminis in se rationem...potest habere regimina'; fol. 10r [1.12b]: 'Item. Noverat indigne agere filios suos et...non corripuit eos'; fol. 10r [1.12c]: 'Item. Quicumque domui sue bene preesse nescit...potest habere regimina'; fol. 10r [1.13c]: 'Gregorius Nazionzenus cap 303. Tacui non semper tacebo habetis me...redime tuam benedictionem'; fol. 10v [1.16]: 'Gregorius Nazionzenus. De eo quod non genus nec locus sed mores edificant principem. Nos qui presumus non ex locorum...sed fidei puritate'; fol. 32r [1.184]: 'Gregorius Nazionzenus. De mercantibus sacerdotium et vendentibus donum dei. Nam quicumque hoc donum studet donatione...dei pretio mercari'; fol. 50r [2.129a]: 'Gregorius Nazionzenus. Doctores debent implere quod docent. Mundari se prius oportet et sic...ad dominum facere'; fol. 125r–v [6.6.2b]: 'Gregorius Nazanzenus. In omnibus causis ecclesiasticis tres persone...maxime conscientiam suam'; fol. 127v [6.6.26]: 'Gregorius Nazionzenus. De laicis non iudicantibus presente episcopo vel scriba vel sancti. Si episcopus aut scriba presentes sint...malum ex vobis'; fol. 133r [6.12.17]: 'Gregorius Nazionzenus. De brevi regno iusto melius est longo iniquo. Multo melius est paucitatem temporis legitimum...possessiones cum iniustitia'; fol. 136v [6.15.14a]: 'Gregorius Nazionzenus. De ministris egrotantium hereditatem consequentibus. Qui nutrit infirmos hereditatem eorum consequatur...et visitastis me'; fol. 144r [7.17b]: 'Gregorius Nazionzenus. Duo in ecclesia cavenda ne solverit...non est alligandum.'

Vat. lat. 1349, fol. 126r [6.6.12c]: 'Basilius. Cum dominus aliquando dicit nolite iudicare...de hoc iudicare'; fol. 135r [6.14.16f]: 'Basilius. Nam et parentes nostros quasi propria...sepultura ei debetur'; fol. 140v [6.23.4d]: 'Basilius. Omnis sermo qui non proficit ad...christi otiosus est'; fol. 171v [7.186]: 'Basilius. De ieiunio ut non sit in propria voluntate. Ieiunii mensura non debet eximius cumque...unam habuisse signantur'; fol. 172va [7.192.6]: 'Basilius. De eo quod si advena mensurat ieiunanda est omnibus. Modus et qualitas temperabitur cibi nec...aliqua diversitatis existit'; fol. 193r–v [9.1]: 'De remediis penitentie expositis sancti Basilii inquisitione acumiani longii. Imprimis de remediis vulnerum. De remediis vulnerum secundum priorum patrum...coercere se debet.'

Vat. lat. 1349, fol. 114r [5.66.2]: 'Beatus Iohannes Archiepiscopus Constantinopolitanus qui et Chrisostomus ubi parabolas seminis exposuit sic ait. Item de imaginibus propter deum venerandis. Indumentum imperiale si iniuriaveris nonne eamque...imperator unicum imaginem.'

Vat. lat. 1349, fol. 71v–72r [2.265]: 'Ex Cronica grece. De reconciliatione episcoporum. Pari modo et Iohannes Chrisostomus a...et quale oportere.'

Vat. lat. 1349, fol. 141r [6.25.3c]: 'Apollonius. Solus in illicitis non cadit qui...licitis caute restringit.'

Vat. lat. 1349, fol. 202v [9.37.2]: 'Capitula Serapionis. De fornicatione. Fornicationis genera sunt tria primum quod...una deterret exclusio'; fol. 224r–v [9.152.2]: 'Serapionis abbatis. De octo vitiis principalibus unde supra Sunt octo vitia principalia que humanum ... et corporis acquiruntur.'

Vat. lat. 1349, fol. 87v [3.78]: 'In Vita monachorum. De oblatione degentis sub censu non proficiente. Quidam rusticus vas eneum sacerdoti in ... ne propria amittam'; fol. 91v–92r [3.100d]: 'In Vitas monachorum. Quidam monachum moriens suum habitaculum suo ... firmavit et accepit'; fol. 120r [6.1.10d]: 'In Vitas monachorum. Quidam episcopus ait de columno sui ... in quantum discessor'; fol. 128v [6.7.5a]: 'In Vita monachorum. De degente sub censu nihil commendante. Quidam rusticus vas eneum sacerdoti in ... ne propria amittam'; fol. 137r [6.16.1f]: 'Inde in Vitas monachorum. Quidam vitam penitentis agens in monasterio ... que defraudavit reddidit'; fol. 137v [6.18.2e]: 'In Vita monachorum. Quidam parvam messem enutriens bestie devoraverint ... prohiberet et prohibuit'; fol. 140r [6.22.2c]: 'In Vitas monachorum. Quidam latrones causa predandis in quodam ... penitentiam reversi sunt'; fol. 173v [7.195.5]: 'In Vita monachorum. De ieiunio pro mortuis. Quidam episcopus ministerium alicuius episcopi in ... dominus suscitavit eum.'

APPENDIX 7

Vat. lat. 1339, fol. 55r [1.133c], *Collectio canonum in v libris (lib. i–iii)*, ed. M. Fornasari (CCCM 6; Turnhout 1970: hereafter Fornasari) 1.220.3: 'Basilius. Cum dominus aliquando dicit nolite iudicare ... de hoc iudicare'; Vat. lat. 1339, fol. 142v [3.188d], Fornasari 3.242.4: 'Basilius. Omnis sermo qui non proficit ad ... christi otiosus est'; Vat. lat. 1339, fol. 144r [3.201.1b], Fornasari 3.254b: 'Basilius eps. Item. Scire debemus quia rationem reddituri sumus ... opus dei neglegenter'; Vat. lat. 1339, fol. 181r [4.69.3], Montecassino 125, p. 207 [4.41]: 'Basilius eps. Si quis sacerdos palam fecerit et ... eos peregrinando finiat'; Vat. lat. 1339, fol. 200r [4.176c], Montecassino 125, p. 227 [4.105]: 'Basilius. Nam et parentes nostros quasi propria ... eis detur honor'; Vat. lat. 1339, fol. 215r [4.271b]: 'Basilius dicit. Plurimi namque homines per vinum maximam ... de celo delere' (cf. Montecassino 125, p. 245 [4.15]: 'Salomon dicit. Luxuriosa res est vinam et tumulavosa ebrietas ... vino nolite bibendo immoderane nomina vestra de celo delere'); Vat. lat. 1339, fol. 227r [4.348], Montecassino 125, p. 358 [4.141]: 'Basilius. De temperatis cibis. Modus et qualitas temperabitur cibi nec ... aliqua diversitatis existit.'

Vat. lat. 1339, fol. 23r [1.17.1c], Fornasari 1.31.2: 'Gregorius Nanzanzenus. Timeo quod video canes affectare officium ... perdere quam conservare'; Vat. lat. 1339, fol. 23r–v [1.17.2d], Fornasari 1.32.3: 'Gregorius Nanzanzenus. Timeo hoc quod video canem affectare ... potest habere regimina'; Vat. lat. 1339, fol. 24v–25r [1.24.2b], Fornasari 1.42.2: 'Gregorius Nanzanzenus. Item. Nec recipiendos qui non digna conversatione ... abluunt admissum peccatum'; Vat. lat. 1339, fol. 33r [1.40.3], Fornasari 1.71: 'Gregorius Nanzanzenus. De mercantibus sacerdotium. Nam quicumque hoc donum dei studet ... dei pretio mercari'; Vat. lat. 1339, fol. 38v [1.56.2b], Fornasari 1.106.(2): 'De talibus dicit Gregorius Nanzanzenus. Timeo quod canes affectant officium pastorale ... pastoralibus preparaverint disciplinis'; Vat. lat. 1339, fol. 49v [1.113], Fornasari 1.188: 'Gregorius Nanzanzenus. De medicina penitentie qui donum dei student pretio mercari. Nam de eo qui donum dei ... is communicet iudicamus'; Vat. lat. 1339, fol. 128r [3.116a], Fornasari 3.156.1: 'Gregorius Nazanzenus. De eo quod debent doctores implere quod docent. Mundari se prius oportet et sic... a domino facere'; Vat. lat. 1339, fol. 151v–152r [3.245.2b], Fornasari 3.314.1: 'De talibus dicit Gregorius Nanzanzenus. Timeo quod video canes affectare officium... et non corripientes'; Vat. lat. 1339, fol. 181v–182r [4.70.2b]: 'De talibus dicit Gregorius Nanzanzenus. Timeo quod canes affectant officium pastorale... vivos et mortuos'; Vat. lat. 1339, fol. 183v [4.76.2]: 'Item Gregorius Nanzanzenus. Sciendum vero est quia pretium redemptionis... que sequuntur plurima'; Vat. lat. 1339, fol. 185r [4.86b]: 'Gregorius Nanzanzenus. Duo in ecclesia cavenda sunt nec... non est alligandum'; Vat. lat. 1339, fol. 185r [4.86c]: 'Item. Si defendis reos cave ne aliis... ne aliis noceas'; Montecassino 125, p. 227 [4.104]: 'Gregorius (Nazianzenus) Benedictio patrum domos filiorum confirmat' (cf. Wasserschleben 32.2).

Vat. lat. 1339, fol. 289va [5.149]: 'Iohannes Constantinopolus episcopus atque alii eruditissimi viri providentes conciliorum canones decretaliumque pontificum de coniugibus adulterinis iudicium ediderunt. Imprimis de coniugatis fornicariis. Si quis vir habens uxorem forsitan... virum et uxorem'; Vat. lat. 1339, fol. 290v–291r [5.155.2]: 'Iudicium Iohannis Constantinopolitani. Vir si voluntarie preter causam fornicationis... mulieribus sicut viris'; Vat. lat. 1339, fol. 291r [5.156]: 'Iohannes Constantinopolitanus eps. De his qui consentiunt coniugibus suis fornicari. Si quis quod illecebrosissimum et turpius... et luctu penitere' (cf. Montecassino 125, p. 308 [5.79]); Vat. lat. 1339, fol. 291r–v [5.158]: 'Iohannes Constantinopolitanus eps. De his qui coniugibus suis se dividunt et alteris nubunt. In multorum conciliis decretisque pontificum comperimus... emendationem ita arbitretur'; Vat. lat. 1339, fol. 291v–292r [5.160]: 'Iohannes Constantinopolitanus eps. De his qui coniugati sunt si dimissas ducunt. Si quis quod est mercatum incestuosissimum... simul et emendationem'; Vat. lat. 1339, fol. 292r [5.161]: 'Iohannes Constantinopolitanus eps. De his qui non sunt coniugati si dimissas ducunt. Scriptum est in evangelio secundum lucam... uxore sua nupserit'; Vat. lat. 1339, fol. 292v [5.163]: 'Iohannes Constantinopolitanus eps. De ipsis fornicantibus dimissis. Scriptum est quia meretrix et que... ignorantis ita peniteat'; Montecassino 125, p. 307 [5.75(3)]: 'Iohannes Constantinopolitanus episcopus. Similiter Theod. et Commen. De coniugibus si adulterate invente sunt. Si quis uxorem suam invenerit adulteratam et deincips placuit... invenerit adulterum non ad imparia iudicatur'; 'Iohannes Constantinopolitanus. De his qui consentiunt coniugibus suis fornicari'; Montecassino 125, p. 308 [5.79.2]: 'Iohannes Constantinopolitanus. De ius qua coniugibus suis se dividunt et alteri nuberunt. In multorum conciliis decretisque pontificum comperimus scriptum si qua quod deterius... conversationem simul et emendatione ita arbitretur'; Montecassino 125, p. 309 [5.81]: 'Iohannes Constantinopolitanus. De his qui coniugationis si dimissas ducunt. Si quis quodam est mercatum incestuosissimum preter fornicationem uxorem suam dimisererit dimissam... nisi tantum post urgeatur obitum ortis. Si mulier commercio si virum suum preter fornicationem dimiserit et dimissum preter... et quantitatem criminis et conversationes simul et emendationem'; Montecassino 125, p. 309 [5.82]: 'Iohannis Constantinopolitanus. De his qui non se coniugati si dimissas ducunt. Scriptum est in evangelio secundum Lucam, Qui dimissa a viro ducunt mechatur. Si qui non habens uxorem et dimissa a viro absque causa... superiora sententia sequatur nisi tantum ut xii. an. penit. Similiter mulier non habens virum, si dimisso viro ab uxores sine fornicatione...superiora sententia sequater nisi tantum ut x. an. penit. Si quis non habens uxorem preter fornicationis causam abiectam a viro vivente viro duxerit...circa compunctionem et conversationem et emendationem. Si quis inscius dimissam a viro vivente viro suo duxerit.... ab uxore vivente uxore sua nupserit. De non fornicationibus dimissis. Expos. ut sup. Scriptum est mulier enim alligata est quamdiu vir eius vivit ergo consequenter...adulteros fieri si illa alterius nupserit et ille alteram duxerit. (Augustinus, *De adult. coniug.*, lib. 2, cap. 9) Ut supra. Si qua mulier fornicans dimissa a viro et si post illam alia duxerit,...et ille vivente uxore sua aliam ducunt non habentem virum.'

Vat. lat. 1339, fol. 23r [1.17.1h], Fornasari 1.31.7: 'Origenes. Quidam assumptam ecclesiam dei et rebus...quam principes nomino'; Vat. lat. 1339, fol. 46r [1.94e], Fornasari 1.157.5: 'Origenes. Quid vobis videtur commutare gubernatoris nostri...minima non credimus'; Vat. lat. 1339, fol. 54v [1.131.1b], Fornasari 1.217.2: 'Origenes. Item. Omnis iudex tribus indiget hoc est...bonorum sobrietate morum'; Vat. lat. 1339, fol. 56v [1.140c], Fornasari 1.233.3: 'Origenes. Item. Boni pastoris est pecus tondere non...tondere non deglobere'; Vat. lat. 1339, fol. 86v [2.76c], Fornasari 2.93.3: 'Origenes. Item. Iudas scarioth de gradu suo cecidit...iterum non invenit'; Vat. lat. 1339, fol. 124v [3.91.2b], Fornasari 3.128.4: 'Origenes. Item. Qui fastu superbie domino suo contradixerit...ecclesia est abiciendus'; Vat. lat. 1339, fol. 125v–126r [3.99c], Fornasari 3.137.3: 'Origenes. Item. Tria ecclesia debet custodire dona iniquorum...innocentis non accipies'; Vat. lat. 1339, fol. 126r [3.100b], Fornasari 3.138.2: 'Origenes. Sicut ovis tunicam suam dimittit tondenti...celestia non possidebit'; Vat. lat. 1339, fol. 128r [3.116c], Fornasari 3.156.3: 'Origenes. Item. Doctor docens et non implens similis...non dans virtutem'; Vat. lat. 1339, fol. 129r–v [3.130b], Fornasari 3.170.2: 'Origenes. Item. Si doctor erraverit et in suo...nemo potest emendare'; Vat. lat. 1339, fol. 148r [3.227d], Fornasari 3.292.4: 'Origenes. Si paradisus excommunicatum adam eiecit...quantomagis ecclesia dei'; Vat. lat. 1339, fol. 148r–v [3.228a], Fornasari 3.293.1: 'De evitanda mensa malorum. Christus antequam pateretur triduo non comedit...cum veste sordida' (not attributed to Origen in Vat. lat. 1339 or *Collectio canonum hibernensis* Beta, but in Vat. lat. 1349 9.106f); Vat. lat. 1339, fol. 156r [3.246.2a], Fornasari 3.319.2: 'Origenes. Item inde. Anime defunctorum quattuor modis solvuntur oblationibus...elemosinis ieiunio cognatorum'; Vat. lat. 1339, fol. 159v [3.263], Fornasari 3.340: 'Origines. De ductore malitie accipiente reatum licet animi affectum non habuerit. Omnis qui ducit alienos si affectum...reatum omnium sumpsit'; Vat. lat. 1339, fol. 166r [4.6d]: 'Origines. Quod oculis concupiscentibus mundum conspicimus oculis...oculis flentibus peniteamus'; fol. 199ra [4.170a]: 'In annalibus hebreorum. De iniquitate filiorum patres non contaminante si firmiter correxerint. Noe corripuit cham quantum potuit et...dona largitus est'; fol. 199r [4.170b]: 'Inde Origenes. Si patriarcha scisset eos bene facere...sequentem consilia iuvenum'; fol. 200r [4.175g]: 'Origenes. Patrem et matrem honora ut tibi...cum parentes inhonoras'; fol. 202r [4.191]: 'Origenes. De notatione varietatis animantium in furto reddentium. In bovem ideo quinque redduntur quia...sunt hec reddat'; fol. 202v [4.193]: 'Origenes. De mutatione varietatis inter veterem et novum et furtum reddendum. Notandum quod hec varietas prestet in...substantiam domus sue'; fol. 203r [4.195b]:

'Origenes. Si illi iudicaverit duplum restituat dominus... ut duplum reddatur'; fol. 203r [4.196b]: 'Origenes. Si accepisti commendatum observa ne perdideris... perdideris reddes neglegentiam'; fol. 203v [4.198b]: 'Origenes. Si ad id depositum accipitur ut... alicuius non accipiat'; fol. 206v [4.227b]: 'Origenes. Vir iurans audaciter quodcumque boni fecerit... super eum manebit'; fol. 207r [4.228d]: 'Origenes. Alii frustra iurant nec seipsos adiuvant... videatur quam implere'; fol. 207v [4.229d]: 'Origenes. Prohibenda multa iuratio sed post iurandum... quam irrita facienda'; fol. 216v [4.285d]: 'Origenes. Qui querit debitum ab inope exactor... aliene rei efficitur'; fol. 221r [4.310f]: 'Origenes. Acommoda fratri tuo et accipe quod... nihil superfluum queras'; fol. 234r [4.381]: 'Origenes. De nomine elemosine. Elemosina hebraice dei mei opus latine... sed voca pauperes' (in Montecassino 125, p. 367 [4.203] attributed to 'Grig'); Vat. lat. 1339, fol. 243r [4.431a]: 'Origenes. De inimico proprio non maledicendo sed dei. Non maledico inimicum meum sed inimicum... omnia membra compatiuntur'; fol. 295r–v [5.171]: 'Origenes. De eo quod mulier debet sequi virum suum ad vota christiana confugientem. Discant mulieres exemplis patriarcharum sequi viros... suum videat deo.'

Vat. lat. 1339, fol. 89r [2.86], Fornarsi 2.104: 'Ex Cronica greca. De reconciliatione episcoporum. Pari modo et Iohannes Chrisostomus a... multa que sequuntur.'

Vat. lat. 1339, fol. 65v–66r [Prologus]: 'Incipit prologus Dyonisii episcopi conciliorum, domino venerando, domino patri Stephano archiepiscopo Dyonisius eps in domino salutem. Quamvis carissime frater noster Laurentius assidua... aliquod attulisse videamur.'

Vat. lat. 1339, fol. 203r [4.197a]: 'Eusebius Coesariensis in Hystoria ecclesiastica, Spiridion Cyprius eps. De vivente querente depositum ab herede mortui. Vir unus ex prophetis filiam habuit... repertam tradidit reposcenti.'

Vat. lat. 1339, fol. 246r–v [4.443.1c]: 'Serapionis abbatis. Item unde supra de octo vitiis principalibus. Sunt octo principalia vitia que humanum... et corporis acquiruntur.'

Vat. lat. 1339, fol. 80r–v [2.47], Fornasari 2.60: 'Iudicium Macharii Alexandrini. De sacerdote qui in fornicatione pollutus est non debet misteria domini violare. Quidam multas sententias de Machario Alexandrino... ad propria remeavit.'

Vat. lat. 1339, fol. 122r–v [3.76a], Fornasari 3.104.1: 'In Vita monachorum. De oblatione puerorum mutanda si in malum, non mutanda si in catholicum. Duos filios artificis legimus quorum pater... deo dedit relinquere'; Vat. lat. 1339, fol. 160r [3.266d], Fornasari 3.343.4: 'In Vita monachorum. Item. Quidam parvam messem enutriens bestie devoraverunt... prohibe bestias tuas'; Vat. lat. 1339, fol. 227v [4.352]: 'In Vita monachorum. De elemosina pro mortuis. Quidam episcopus ministrum alicuius episcopi in... dominus suscitavit eum.'

APPENDIX 8

Fol. 44v: 'Basilius eps. Scire debemus quia rationem reddituri sumus... opus dei neglegenter'; fol. 47v: 'Basilius. Si quis sacerdos palam fecerit et... eos peregrinando finiat'; fol. 52v: 'Basilius interrogat, Si is qui consentit...Adam aequievit Eve'; fol. 69v: 'Ex dictis Basilii eps. Qui consentit peccantibus et defendit alium...iudicandum et excommunicandum.'

Fol. 1v: 'Iohannes Chrisostomus ait super Mattheum cap. viiii. Sicut crudelis et iniquus...celat crimen uxoris'; fol. 57r: 'Iohannes Chrisostomus. Age penitentiam quamdiu poteris agere cum...et gemitum perspicis.'

Fol. 43v: 'Origenis. Tria ecclesia debet custodire dona iniquorum...innocentis non accipietis'; fol. 48r: 'Origenis. De illis qui accipiunt regimine ecclesiarum et cunctos fastu superbie parvipendunt. Quidam assumpta ecclesia et rebus divinis...quam principes nominantur'; fol. 54r: 'Origenes ereticus et multi phylosophorum dixerunt. Animas hominis semel et una hora...Isidorus ita ait'; fol. 54r: 'Origenus. Anime defunctorum quattuor modis solvuntur oblationibus...elemosinis ieiunio cognatorum'; fol. 54r: 'Origenes ereticus et multi phylosophorum dixerunt Animas hominis semel et una hora...Isidorus ita ait.'

Fol. 32v–33r: 'Gregorius Naziancenus. Qui donum dei pretio mercatur nulla...est antichristus est'; fol. 38r: 'Gregorius Nantianzenus: Timeo quod video canes affectare officium...perdere quam conservare.'

Fol. 61v: 'Eusebius. Is quis penitentiam petens dum sacerdos...obsequis ei sumministrat.'

APPENDIX 9

Fol. 52v: 'Basilius. Vocis mensuram diffinit...quod est notabile.' On fol. 148v there is a reference to Basil: 'Basilius episcopus Cesariensis clarus Cappadocie babetur [sic] qui multa continentiae et ingenii bona uno superbiae malo perdidit.' On these texts see my 'Basil and the early medieval Canon Law Collections' 528, n. 68.

Fol. 58r–59v: 'De eo quod debet doctorem inplere quod docet. Gregorius Nazianzenus. Mundari se prius oportet et sic alios sapientes...sic alios accendi a Domino facere.'

APPENDIX 10

Fol. 36v: 'Basilius. Nam et parentes nostros...sepultura di debetur'; fol. 42r: 'Basilius. Plurimi namque homines...vestra di celo Dei'; fol. 73r: 'Basilius. Si quis sacerdos palam...peregrinando finiat.'

Fol. 13r: 'Origenus. Anime defunctorum quattuor modis solvuntur oblationibus...elemosinis ieiunio cognatorum'; fol. 55r: 'Origines. Si accepisti commendatum observa ne perdideris...perdideris reddes neglegentiam.'

Fol. 30v: 'In Vita sanctorum. Ieiunia sane legitima idest quarta et...cum crucifigentibus crucifigere.'

Fol. 30v: 'In Vitas monachorum. Quidam episcopus ministrum alicuius episcopi in...dominus suscitavit eum.'

Fol. 31v: 'Iohannes Chrysostomus. Deinde etsi erramus modicam penitentiam imponentes... et grandia facientem.'

APPENDIX 11

Collectio Toletana, canon 336: 'Basilius episcopus. Si quis sacerdos palam fecerit et secretum penitentie usurpaverit... in cunctum populum deponatur et diebus vite sue inter eos peregrinando finiat.'

Collectio Toletana, canon 86: 'Iohannes Constantinopolitanus episcopus atque alii eruditissimi viri prudentes conciliorum canonum decretaliumque pontificum de coniugibus adulter(in)is iudiciu(m) ediderunt. Imprimis de coniugatis fornicariis. Si quis habens uxorem forsitan si cum muliere, et ipsae tamen vacans... virum par forma pudicitiae et continentiae inter virum et uxorem'; canon 88: 'De coniugibus. Si adulterati hi inventi sunt. Iohannes Constantinopolitanus episcopus. Similiter Theodorus et Comeanus. Si quis uxorem suam invenerit adulteratam... si invenerit adulterum non ad imperia iudicatur'; canon 90: 'Iohannes Constantinopolitanus episcopus. Vir si voluntariae preter causa(m) fornicationis uxorem dimiserit suam nec tamen duxerit aliam, unde si illa forte ex hac occasione... viris ex hac causa sicut muliaeribus'; canon 91: 'De his qui consentiunt coniugibus suis fornicari. Iohannes Constantinopolitanus. Si quis quod inlecebrosissimum turpeve (est) uxorem suam ab alio... omnibus diebus vitae suae arbitrio periti sacerdotis cum flaetu et luctu penitere'; canon 92: 'De his qui coniugibus suis se dividunt et alteris nubunt. Iohannes Constantinopolitanus. In multorum conciliis decretisque pontificum comperimus scriptum. Si quis quod deterius est suam uxorem preter fornicationem reliquerit... si vel e xii. annis vel minus circa compunctionem simul et emendationem ita arbitraetur'; canon 93: 'De his qui coniugati sunt si dimissas ducunt. Iohannes Constantinopolitanus. Si quis quod est mercatum incestuosum preter fornicationem uxorem suam... iusta qualitatem et quantitatem criminis et conversationem simul et aemendationem'; canon 94: 'De non fornicantibus dimissis. Expositum ut supra. Si que mulier non fornicans dimissa a viro et post illam aliam duxerit... alii nupserit forsitan et vivente uxorae sua aliam ducit non habentem virum.'

APPENDIX 12

P. 129: 'Commonitio Iohanis Grisostomi. Quotiens igitur quis nostrum dederit consilium... cum emendatione confessi'; p. 129: 'Quotiens dederimus consilium peccatori quantum debeat... suis peccatis agere' (no attribution); p. 130: 'Quotienscumque videt sacerdos aliquem ad penitentiam... et celorum regnum' (no attribution); p. 137: 'Iohannes Crisostomus. Nemo enim hoc scire debet... nulla scientia custodit'; p. 149: 'Ex decretis Iohanni Constantinopoli episcopi atque alii eruditissimi viri providentes conciliorum canones decretaliumque pontificum de coniugibus adulterinis iudicium ediderunt. Imprimis de coniugatis fornicariis. Si quis vir habens uxorem forsitan... virum et uxorem'; p. 150: 'Iohannes Constantinopolitanus episcopus similiter Theodorus et Commenus. Si quis uxorem suam invenerit adulteratam et deincips placuit... invenerit adulterum non ad imparia iudicatur'; p. 151: 'Iohannes Constantinopolitanus episcopus. Vir si voluntariae preter causam fornicationis uxorem dimiserit suam nec tamen duxerit aliam, unde si illa forte ex hac occasione... viris ex hac causa sicut mulieribus aut reconcilientem aut in imparia permaneant'; p. 151: 'Iohannes Constantinopolitanus Si qua femina conscio marito fuerit... finem percipere communionem'; p. 152: 'Iohannes Constantinoplitanus. Hoc in exordio Genesios scriptum... volumus nolumus sustinenda'; p. 153: 'Iohannes Constantinopolitanus. Scriptum est in evangelio secundum Lucam, Qui dimissa a viro ducunt mechatur. Si qui non habens uxorem et dimissa a viro absque causa... superiora sententia sequatur nisi tantum ut xii. an. penit. Similiter mulier non habens virum, si dimisso viro ab uxores sine fornicatione... superiora sentientia sequater nisi tantum ut x. an. penit. Si quis non habens uxorem preter fornicationis causam abiectam a viro vivente viro duxerit... circa compunctionem et conversationem et emendationem. Si quis inscius dimissam a viro vivente viro suo duxerit.... ab uxore vivente uxore sua nupserit'; p. 154: 'Si qua mulier fornicans dimissa a viro et si post illam alia duxerit,... et ille vivente uxore sua aliam ducunt non habentem virum' (no attribution); p. 154: 'Scriptum est quia meretrix et que... ignorantis ita peniteat' (no attribution); p. 193: 'Iohannes quoque Grisostomus a duobus synodis orthodoxis episcoporum fuit indicatus... sanguine redimere venit.'

P. 15: 'Origenes. Iudas scarioth de gradu suo cecidit... iterum non invenit'; p. 43: 'Origenes. Qui fastu superbie domino suo contradixerit... sit et abiciendus'; p. 80: 'Origenes. In bovem ideo quinque redduntur quia... sunt hec reddat'; p. 80: 'Origenes. Si accepisti commendatum observa ne perdideris... perdideris neglegentiam reddes'; p. 86: 'Origenes. Alii frustra iurant nec seipsos adiuvant... videatur quam implere iuramentum'; p. 95: 'Origenes. Commoda fratri tuo et accipe quod... nichil superfluum queras'; p. 114: 'Origenes. Si paradysus excommunicatum adam eiecit... quantomagis ecclesia dei'; p. 116: 'Origenes. Anime defunctorum quattuor modis solvuntur oblationibus... elemosinis ieiunio cognatorum'; p. 118: 'Origenes. Satis age cum tibi proficit et... prece sanctorum solveris'.

P. 44: 'Gregorius Nazanzenus. Valet interdum conversis pro salute anime... aspectu mentis opponitur'; p. 116: 'Gregorius Nazanzenus. Timeo quod video canes affectare officium pastorale maxime cum nichil... preparaverint discipline'; p. 138: 'Gregorius Nazonzenus. Timeo autem quod canes affectare.... affectare officium pastorale maxime cum hichil in semetipsis pastoralis disciplina preparaverunt'; p. 146: 'Gregorius Nanzanzenus. Sciendum vero est quia pretium redemptionis... que sequuntur plurima'; p. 148: 'Gregorius Nazanzenus. Quod laboras vidis positione operum domini. Quod scis virum humana cogitatone meditatur.'

P. 56: 'Basilius. Omnis sermo qui non proficit ad... christi otiosus est'; p. 108: 'Basilius eps. Scire debemus quia rationem reddituri sumus... opus dei neglegenter'; p. 137: 'Basilius eps inquit, Si quis sacerdos palam fecerit et... eos peregrinando finiat'.

APPENDIX 13

Fol. 117v: 'Iohannes Grisostomus. De latrine. Latro de cruce vindemiat inmortalitatem...tibi hodie mecum etis in parasyso'; fol. 160r–v: 'Iohannes Chrisostomus a duobus synodis episcoporum ordodoxis fuit...in Antiochia patriarcha'; fol. 197v: 'Iohannes Crisostomus. lviii. De alterius. Nolite suscipere ante omnes eamque occulte...nulla scientian custodit.'

Gregorius Nazianzenus. De medicina penitentie qui donum Dei studet. Nam de eo quod donum Dei...his communicet iudicamux.'

Fol. 178r–179v: 'xl. De duobus infidelibus. Sanctus Dionysius Ariopagita. Divinam visionem sancti cuisusdam...dicta sunt.'

Fol. 179v–180v: 'In Vita sanctorum. Dicebat quidam senex qui etiam dignus...ut per patientiam laborent invenire Deum.'

Fol. 192r: 'l. De Petro apostolo. Item Eusebius. Beatus Petrus cum vidisset...tam perfecta fuit affectio beatorum'; fol. 192r–v: 'Item Eusebius. Prius enim quam Romanorum...per Moysen fuerat tradita.'

APPENDIX 14

Vat. Pal. lat. 585/586, fol. 160r [2.228]: 'Ex dictis Basilii. De illo qui fugam fratris celaverit. Si quis eum qui districtionem ecclesiasticam...ille valeat revocari'; fol. 197r–v [3.127]: 'Ex dictis Basilii cap. 27. Item de consuetudinibus ecclesiasticis observandis. Ecclesiasticarum institutionum quasdam scripturis quasdam vero...quam publicata scripto'; fol. 309r [8.9]: 'Ex dictis Basilii. Ut monacho sine conscientia sui abbatis votum vovere non liceat. Monacho non licet votum vovere sine...voverit frangendum erit'; fol. 11v–12r [9.45]: 'Ex dictis Basilii epi. De coniugatis qui secularia relinquere desiderant. Si quis vult coniugatus converti ad...voluntate castitatis consensum'; fol. 50r [10.67]: 'Ex dictis Basilii epi. De illis qui detrahunt suis prioribus. Si quis detraxerit qui ei preest...detraxit moisi peniteat'; fol. 67r [11.46]: 'Ex dictis Basilii epi. De illis qui defendunt delinquentes. Qui consentit peccantibus et defendit alium...iudicandum et excommunicandum'; fol. 130v–131r [17.35]: 'Ex dictis Basilii. De clericis vel monachis si fuerint masculorum insectatores. Clericus vel monachus adolescentium vel parvulorum...deinceps iuvenibus coniungendus'; fol. 196v [19.39]: 'Ex dictis Basilii epi. Ut penitentem ex corde magna exhilaratione sacerdotes suscipere debeant. Penitentem ex corde ita oportet suscipi...meam quam perdideram'; fol. 212r [19.79]: 'Ex dictis Basilii epi. De eadem re. Qui sub gradu peccat debet excommunicari...venire difficile est.' There are also four additional texts of Basil or Pseudo-Basil not attributed to him in Burchard, 10.52, 10.54, 10.59, and 19.64, on which see my article 'Basil in the Early Medieval Latin Canonical Collections' 528f.

Vat. Pal. lat. 585/586, fol. 282r [7.19]: 'Epistola Iohannis Constantinopolitani epi ad Felicem epm. Sicilie Quid sanctus Gregorius Augustino Anglorum predicatori propter teneritatem nove fidei permiserit. Gregorius papa requisitus ab Augustino Anglorum...licenter sibi iungantur'; fol. 282r–283r [7.20]: 'Item idem. Iohannes dicit. Quod sanctus Gregorius hoc Anglorum genti specialiter, non generaliter permiserit. Verum post multum temporis a felice... temporaliter permisisse cognoscant'; fol. 201r–203r [19.44]: 'Excerptum de libro Iohannis Constantinopolitani ad Theodorum cap 59. Quod anima multis gentis nobilior sit deflenda et multis urbis pretiosior, quodque non sit desperandum de venia. Quis dabit capiti meo aquam et... se reparare festinet'; fol. 203r–v [19.45]: 'Item Iohannes Constantinopolitanus de lapsu bacharii ad eundem Theodorum cap 60. Quod nullus a consolatione vulnerati fratris se subtrahere debeat. Ubi est misericordia christiane religionis quam... sacri communione ministerii'; fol. 203v–204r [19.46]: 'Ex epistola Iohannis Constantinopolitani ad Theodorum. De eadem re. Unde vides quia sic peccati contagione... a domino consequetur'; fol. 204r [19.47]: 'Ex epistola eiusdem Iohannis Constantinopolitani ad Theodorum. De eadem re. Evangelicus sermo dixit si peccaverit in... fame turpis emittat'; fol. 204r–v [19.48]: 'Ex epistola item Iohannis Constantinopolitani ad Theodorum. De eadem re. Qualiter rogo de misericordia domini possumus... neque misericordiam consecutum.'

Vat. Pal. lat. 585/586, fol. 90r [13.26]: 'Eusebius in Ecclesiastica historia dicit. De quodam alcibiade qui sibi grave iugum ieiunii imposuerat. Alcibiades quidam erat ex numero eorum... idem spiritus persuadebat.'

Vat. Pal. lat. 585/586, fol. 26v–27r [1.13]: 'Origenes dicit. De illis qui accipiunt regimina ecclesiarum et cunctos fastu superbie parvipendunt. Quidam assumpta ecclesia et rebus divinis... quam principes nominantur'; fol. 217v [19.112]: 'Ex dictis Origenis. Quot modis anime defunctorum solvi debeant. Anime defunctorum quattuor modis solvuntur aut... aut ieiunio cognatorum.'

BRUCE C. BRASINGTON

7 *Differentia est*

A Twelfth-Century *Summula* on Anathema and Excommunication

Introduction

Professor Somerville has analyzed some of the most challenging sources of medieval canon law. His studies of the canons of Claremont and papal decretals to Scotland are but two examples of this willingness to confront vast, complicated textual traditions. Equally, however, he has devoted considerable attention to the briefest of works, for example, prefaces to canonical collections, an enterprise in which this author was privileged to participate. The following study, offered in admiration to a master of canonistic texts both great and small, offers a similar miniature as it considers a twelfth-century *summula* on anathema and excommunication. Preserved in MS Cambridge, UL Add. 3321.1, this *summula* occupys three-quarters of the first folio in this composite manuscript. It has escaped scholarly attention since the notes made by F. W. Maitland when it was acquired in 1895.[1] Written by a French scribe in often faint brown ink,

Originally presented at the 2009 Leeds International Mediaeval Congress. I thank Cambridge University Library for allowing me to examine this manuscript. Dr. Brett helped me with the transcription of the text. I am also grateful to the Stephan Kuttner Institute of Medieval Canon Law, and the Forschungstelle für vergleichende Ordensgeschichte (Eichstätt) for allowing me to use their resources. Finally, I thank the inter-library loan department of the WTAMU Library.

1. Cambridge, UL Add. 4432, augmented by the description made by Ms. Jane Ringrose, which is available in the Manuscripts Room. A microfilm is also at the Stephan Kuttner Institute of Medieval Canon Law in Munich. The longest work in this composite manuscript is the *Distinctiones Cantabrigenses*, an early commentary on Gratian briefly described by Stephan Kuttner, *Repertorium der Kanonistik. Prodromus corpus glossarum* (Studi e Testi 71; Rome 1937) 213–14. See also the entry at http://faculty.cua.edu/pennington/1140d-h.htm accessed on 7 November 2011, dating it to the 1160s.

it is hard to read, particularly at the right margin. UV light is occasionally necessary; unfortunately, even this cannot uncover the name of the monastery written by an early-modern hand and subsequently erased.

The *summula*'s theme was of considerable interest to a twelfth-century audience. Conceptions of anathema and excommunication were changing.[2] Anathema remained true to its New Testatment origins. It orignated as a curse relying on the charisma and power of the individual who declared it. Increasingly, excommunication was being defined and applied by legal process.[3] Here, the formulation of excommunication *latae sententiae* was particularly important.[4] Elizabeth Vodola has argued that Gratian was uncomfortable with this, for *latae sententiae* meant that excommunication took effect immediately upon the criminal act, not after legal process.[5] He distinguished between excommunication, which barred the

2. Among many works, Walter Doskocil, *Der Bann in der Urkirche. Eine rechtsgeschichtliche Untersuchung* (Munich 1958) 59–68 on 1 Corinthians 5 and, more recently, Elisabeth Vodola, *Excommunication in the Middle Ages* (Berkeley and Los Angeles 1986) 2–10. Noting the important change introduced by private penance and a 'tempering' introduced in the Carolingian period, Peter Browe, 'Die Kommunion in der gallikanischen Kirche der Merowinger- und Karolingerzeit,' in idem., *Die Eucharistie im Mittelalter. Liturgiehistorische Forschungen in kulturwissenschaftlicher Absicht*, ed. Hubertus Lutterbach and Thomas Flammer (Münster-Hamburg-London 2003) 431–58; also Roger Reynolds, 'Rites of Separation and Reconciliation in the Early Middle Ages,' in *Segni e riti nella chiesa altomedievale occidentale* (Settimane di Studio; Spoleto 1987) 1.405–33; Sarah Hamilton, *The Practice of Penance, c. 900–c. 1050* (Woodbridge, UK, 2001); Lotte Kéry, *Gottesfurcht und irdische Strafe. Der Beitrag des mittelalterlichen Kirchenrechts zur Entstehung des öffentlichen Strafrechts* (Konflikt, Verbrechen, Sanktion in der Gesellschaft Alteuropas 10; Cologne 2006) esp. part 1.

3. Richard Helmholz, 'Excommunication as a Legal Sanction: The Attitudes of Medieval Canonists,' ZRG Kan. Abt. 99 (1982) 204–21. There are wider theological and ecclesiological dimensions to this 'separation' of anathema and excommunication. It recalls the sharp distinction occuring in the twelfth century between the Church as a mystical body, theologically defined, and an organization defined by law. See Rudolf Sohm, *Das Altkatholische Kirchenrecht* (Leipzig 1918). Among many critical responses, Stephan Kuttner, 'Reflections on Law and Gospel in the History of the Church,' in *Liber amicorum Monsieur Onclin*, ed. Jean Lindemans and H. Demeester (Louvain 1976) 199–209.

4. Richard Helmholz, 'Si quis suadente' C. 17 q. 4 c. 29. 'Theory and Practice,' in *Proceedings Cambridge 1988*, 425–38. In general, see also Josephus Zeliauskas, *De Excommunicatione vitiata apud Glossatores (1140–1235)* (Zurich 1967), and Francisco Javier Egas Eguez, *La excomunion en Graciano y en los decretistas de la escuela de Bolonia* (Universidad de Navarra 1990).

5. Vodola, *Excommunication*, 28–30, esp. at 29 n. 4, on C. 11 q. 3 dpc. 24 §1. Excommunication bars one from the Eucharist, while anathema, from society; §3 notes that anathema would include separation from the Eucharist as well. See also Zeliauskas, *De Excommunicatione*, 62, 70–72 and 122–123*, citing the *Summa Lipsiensis* on C. 3 q. 4 dpc. 11: Notandum. Que sit differentia inter excommunicationem et anathematizationem et alia, que ad presens spectant negotium sufficienter infra xi. q. iii. dicemus. Hic tamen in summa dicatur breviter quia excommunicatio est extra communionem ecclesie expulsio vel a perceptione corporis et sanguinis domini prohibitio. Excommunicatur quis quandoque apud deum et ecclesiam ut cum aliquis iuste ob delictum suum nominatus est ab ecclesia; quandoque excommunicatur quis apud ecclesiam tantum ut cum iuste notatus est ab ecclesia quando ecclesia decepta sententiam tulit. Excommunicationis autem

sinner from the sacraments, and anathema, utter exclusion from the Body of Christ, both in heaven and on earth, which took place only after a formal judgment.[6] The papacy, however, never parted with *latae sententiae*, and the decretists and decretalists followed. By the late twelfth century, canonists began to differentiate 'minor' and 'major' excommunication. The former entailed exclusion from the sacraments that could be resolved through penance.[7] The latter, enhanced by the declaration of anathema, was reserved for the contumacious.[8] It should be noted that the *summula* does not treat any of these points. There is no evidence of *latae sententiae*, nor effort to distinguish 'major' from 'minor.' These suggest, though cannot prove, a date of composition earlier rather than later in the century.

The *summula* begins by quoting 1 Cor. 5:5: 'Hand such a man over to Satan, to be destroyed as far as natural life is concerned, so that on the Day of the Lord his spirit might be saved'.[9] This highlights the gravity of anathema, a penalty that should never be imposed for a trivial reason, the point of the next authority, canon 56 from the Council of Meaux (845), taken, undoubtedly, from Gratian's *Decretum*.[10] While many early decretists commented on this text,[11] the *summula* does not dwell on it.

---

sententia duplex est: alia que dicitur simplex excommunicatio, alia que dicitur anathematizatio. Hec maior appellatur quando scil. quis separatur a communione fidelium ut hic dicitur …

6. Vodola, *Exommunication*, 29.

7. Ibid., 38.

8. Ibid., 45.

9. There are various citations of the passage from 1 Corinthians in the *Decretum*, for example C. 24 q. 1 dpc. 4, on a decretal of Alexander II asserting that one excommunicated person cannot excommunicate another. See also Artur Landgraf, 'Sünde und Trennung von der Kirche in der Frühscholastik,' *Scholastik* 5 (1930) 210–47 at 217.

10. C. 11 q. 3 c. 41: Nemo episcoporum quemlibet sine certa et manifesta peccati causa communione privet ecclesiastica. Sub anathemate autem sine conscientia archiepiscopi, aut coepiscoporum nullum presumat ponere, nisi unde canonica docet auctoritas, quia anathemate eterna est mortis dampnatio, et non nisi pro mortali debet imponi crimine, et illis qui aliter non poterint corrigi. C. 11 q. 3 c. 42 (Rubric): Pro parvis et levibus causis nullus communione privetur.

11. For example, a gloss by a Master Wilhelmus, at 'nullum praesumat': Quatuor faciunt ut quod licite potest fieri non fiat sine consensu alterius: scandali uitatio ut supra di. lxiii c Principali (c. 15). Iuris communio ut supra q. ii. c. Precarie (c. 4), cautele respectus ut infra xvii q. iiii c. Nullus res (c. 39), presumptionis exclusio ut hic. Nam episcopi presumebant excommunicare sine causa, cited by Rudolf Weigand, *Die Glossen zum Dekret Gratians. Studien zu den frühen Glossen und Glossenkompositionen* (Studia Gratiana 25–26; Rome 1991) 2.640. Compare also the *Summa Simonis*: Usque 'quia anathema eterne mortis dampnatio est,' idest anathematizati qui non resipiscunt in eternum, deinceps non iudicabuntur. Nam de talibus dicitur: 'iam iudicati sunt.' Cum uero anathematizati resipiscunt, ipsa uindicta est eis medicinalis non mortalis, ut supra C ii q. i. Multi et C. xxiiii q. iii. Corripiantur. Usque 'et qui aliter non poterunt corrigi.' Hinc collige nullum excommunicandum nisi cum in contumacie morbum proslierit,' accessed at http://www.unifr.ch/cdc/summa_simonis_2baende/summa_simonis_BAND_I.14.10.2007.pdf accessed on on 7 November 2011. Additional examples include a gloss to Vat. lat. 2494, fol. 128ra, supra ii. q. i. Nemo (c. 11). Neminem excommunicari, nisi pro mortali peccato et qui aliter cogi vel corrgi non potest. *J*, cited

The next authority cited by our author, John VIII's decretal concerning the wayward wife of Count Boso, also attracted decretist attention.[12] Paucapalea focused on how anathema excluded one from communion and entrance into the church. While excommunication also punished, it was intended to lead the sinner to penance and eventual restoration to communion.[13] Subsequent decretists expanded this view, commenting in particular on the 'fraternal society' from which the anathematized was barred.[14] Some also emphasized the difference between anathema and excommunication, leading to the distinction between 'major' and 'minor' noted above.[15] In general, the trend was toward listing and explaining the process of excommunication.[16]

by Zeliauskas, *De Excommunicatione*, 135*. Perhaps this was Johannes Faventinus. On contumacy, see the *Summa Lipsiensis*: Maiore sive maxima que anathema dicitur percellitur quis ob evidentem contumaciam ut infra. e. q. Certum (c. 43), Nemo (c. 41), cited by Zeliauskas, *De Excommunicatione*, 124*; also Stephan Kuttner, *Die Kanonistische Schuldlehre von Gratian bis auf die Dekretalen Gregors IX. Systematisch auf Grund der handschriftlichen Quellen dargestellt*, (Studi e Testi 64; Rome 1935) 34–35; and Alfons Gommenginger, 'Bedeutet die Exkommunikation Verlust der Kirchenmitgliedschaft?' *Zeitschrift für katholische Theologie* 73 (1951) 1–71 at 42.

12. C. 3 q. 4 c. 12: Aliud est excommunicatio, aliud anathematizatio. Hengiltrudam uxorem Bosonis noueris non solum excommunicatione, que a fraterna societate separat, sed etiam anathemate, quod ab ipso corpore Christi (quod est ecclesia) recidit, crebro percussam. dpc. 12: Unde datur intelligi, quod anathematizati intelligendi sunt non simpliciter a fraterna societate omnino separati, sed a corpore Christi (quod est ecclesia).

13. *Die Summa des Paucapalea über das Decretum Gratiani*, ed. Johann Friederich von Schulte (Giessen 1890) 65: Engeltrudam, ad v. 'a fraterna societate separat': ut est ingresus ecclesiae et collocutio fidelium et convictus eorum. ad v. 'sed etiam anathemate,' etc. Et sciendum, quod sententiae notatio tripliciter intelligitur. Separatur enim quis a communione corporis et sanguinis Christi et a liminibus ecclesiae vel teste conscientia tantum, veluti cum aliquis, conscientia propria redgarguente, a communione corporis et sanguinis Christi cessat, vel sententia ecclesiastica, sicut publice penitentes, qui a communione corporis et sanguinis Christi, non a consortio fidelium et a corpore et sanguine domini. Compare also the gloss in Vat. lat. 2494, fol. 99vb, cited by Zeliauskas, *De Excommunicatione*, 135*: fraterna societate: id est, a perceptione corporis Christi; *a corpore Christi*: id est, a communione fidelium, qui sunt ecclesia. The *Summa Lipsiensis* was equally terse: Engeltrudam, ad v. 'que a fraterna societate'; i. sacramentis ecclesie, in quibus fratres dicuntur, scil. a communione corporis et sanguinis domini; 'ipso corpore Christi,' scil. a communione fidelium, cited by Zeliauskas, *De Excommunicatione*, 123*.

14. Interestingly, *Summa Tractaturus Magister*, cited by Zeliauskas, *De Excommunicatione*, 103*, compared the body of Christ to a collection of canons: 'Engeltrudam,' ad v. 'a fraterna societas': i. a sacramentis, in quibus attenditur fraterna societas; ab ipso corpore Christi: i. a communione fidelium qui sunt corpus Christi sicut collectio legum vel canonum unum corpus.

15. For example, the *Summa De iure canonico tractaturus*, cited by Zeliauskas, *De Excommunicatione*, 116*: Engeltrudem:... caute exponas cap., quia superficies sonat excommunicationem esse anathema et viceversa; 'excommunicationi,' i. minori, scil. que separat a fraterna societate, i. a sacramentis per que fratres efficimur et coheredes Christi et in corpus ipsius consociamur; 'anathema': que a corpore quod est ecclesia, i. a communione fidelium, faciunt ecclesiam que est corpus Christi ut de cons. di. ii. Dupliciter (c.49). See also the careful distinctions made by a *summula* in Bamberg, Staatsbibl. Can. 39, fol. 120v, which discusses 'simplex' excommunication and 'multiplex' anathema.

16. For Huggucio, Zeliauskas, *De Excommunicatione*, 67–68*: Eod., c. 12: Engeltrudam, ad v. 'a

Instead of considering procedure, our *summula* pursues theological and ecclesiological questions. By distinguishing the corporal and spiritual aspects of membership in the Body of Christ, it was contributing to an ancient discourse that showed no signs of diminishing in the twelfth century.[17] What excommunication and anathema meant, for both those excluded from the Body of Christ and those who remained in communion, invited just the sort of careful distinctions on which early scholasticism thrived.[18] Our author draws parallels between physical and spiritual membership in the Church and the visible and invisible qualities of the Eucharist, which itself had sparked considerable debate for more than a century.[19]

While it comes as no surprise that the *summula* judges the spirit superior to the flesh, it is interesting how the merely corporal taking of the Eucharist is denigrated by the citation of a text attributed here to Augustine: *melius...assumitur mente quam atteritur dente.* While it is found in no authentically Augustinian work, we do hear echoes in other sources. In his commentary on the Gospel of John, John Scotus Eriugena had explained that only faith enabled an intellectual understanding of the spiritual sacrifice in communion, an eating with the mind, not with the teeth.[20] Hugh of

fraterna societate': i. a communicatione sacramentorum, in qua omnes fratres dicuntur ut xi. q. iii Ad mensam (c. 24) ad v. 'corpore Christi quod est ecclesia': i. a consortio et communione fidelium. Hac eadem differentia poterit colligi infra. iiii q. i. cii. et C. v q. ii. Presenti. et infra e.q. proxima. Accusatoribus. See also his gloss at C 4 q. 3 dpc. 11, Zeliauskas, *De Excommunicatione*, 67*: Notandum: quia fecerat mentionem de anathemate, ostendit, differentiam inter excommunicationem et anathematizationem et dicit quod excommunicatio non separat hominem nisi a communione sacramentorum et non a consortio fidelium, unde et dicitur excommunicatio, i.e., a sacramentorum communione separatio vel explusio. Anathema separat a communione sacramentorum et a consortio fidelium. Unde et anathema interpretatur separatio ut xxiiii q. iii Certum. Set sepe excommunicatio pontitur pro anathemate et anathema pro excommunicatione ut de cons. di. i. Nemo per ignorantiam (c. 40). Compare also *Summa De multiplici iuris divisione*, cited by Zeliauskas, *De Excommunicatione*, 53–54.

17. In the context of excommunication, Landgraf, 'Sünde und Trennung,' 223–24. Compare also John de Beleth's *Summa de ecclesiasticis officiis*, ed. H. Douteil (CCCM 41–41; Turnhout 1976) 103.2–6: Ad primum intelligendum sciendum est, quod ecclesia alia corporalis, alia spiritualis. Corporalis domus est, in qua diuinum celebratur officium, spiritualis est fidelium conuocatio. Sicut enim ecclesia corporalis ex lapidibus de diuersis locis congregratis construitur, ita ecclesia spiritualis ex diuersis hominibus conuocatur.

18. On the theological and legal debates, Nicholas Häring, 'The Interaction between Canon Law and Sacramental Theology in the Twelfth Century,' *Proceedings Toronto* 1976, 483–94.

19. Hugh of St. Victor, *De sacramentis christianae fidei* 2.8.7 (PL 176.466C): Nam cum unum sit sacramentum, tria ibi discreta proponuntur: species videlicet visibilis, et veritas corporis, et virtus gratiae spiritualis. Aliud est enim visibilis species quae visibiliter cernitur; aliud est veritas corporis et sanguinis quae sub visibili specie invisibiliter creditur, atque aliud gratia spiritualis quae cum corpore et sanguine invisibiliter et spiritualiter percipitur. See also in the same treatise, *De cognitione rerum visibilium*, PL 176.271AB.

20. *Commentarius in S. Evangelium super Johannem*, PL 122.311B: Nam et nos, qui post per-

St. Victor noted Eriugena's argument as well.[21] Given the widespread reception of Hugh's works, it is conceivable that our author borrowed, and modified, the text, though this does not explain the attribution to Augustine.

The *summula* views the earthly Church as a mixture of both good and bad, just and unjust.[22] To illustrate this, the author continues the comparison with the Eucharist. While all may be partaking, we cannot see who really belongs to the Christian communion; similarly, we cannot perceive the spiritual grace lying under, and communicated by, the Eucharistic bread. This helps us to understand anathema, which the author finds in 1 John 2:19.[23] While the anathematized seemed to have left the Church, in fact, they had never belonged. Like reprobates at Mass taking the Eucharist, their physical presence and action had not been authentic. For only the invisible, spiritual, counted. The point is then explained further by a citation attributed to Jerome on Matthew 26:21.[24] The phrase *nomine non numine,* with variants, was used by various authors, thus making it difficult to isolate a formal source.[25] However, I have found only one other example of the phrase being used in describing communion. It appears in Peter the Chanter's *Verbum Abbreviatum,* a work that should be more or less contemporary with our text.[26]

actam ejus incarnationem et passionem et resurrectionem in eum credimus, ejusque mysteria, quantum nobis conceditur, intelligimus, et spiritualiter eum immolamus, et intellectualiter mente non dente, comedimus. Compare a later author, Odo Tornacensis, *Expositio in canonem missae,* PL 160.1065C.

21. Hugh of St. Victor, *Commentarium in hierarchiam coelestem dionysii areopagitae,* PL 175.952B, echoing his argument in the *De sacramentis.*

22. This was commonly expressed in contemporary treatises on excommunication through the biblical image of the wheat and chaff, on which see Landgraf, 'Sünde und Trennung,' 238–39; MS Bamberg, Can. 14, fol. 155v, gloss on *De Pen.* 1.70: '... quandoque large sumitur, ut grana vel paleam compectatur.'

23. Ex nobis prodierunt, sed non erant ex nobis, nam si fuissent ex nobis, permansissent nobiscum, sed ut manifestaretur quoniam illi omnes non sunt ex nobis.

24. Pseudo-Hieronymous, *Expositio Euangelii secundum Marcum,* ed. Michael Cahill (CCL 82; Turnhout 1997) 60.14. On twelfth-century interest in Jerome's works, see Constant Mews, 'Un lecteur de Jérôme au xiie siècle: Pierre Abélard,' in *Jérôme entre l'occident et l'orient. XVIe centenaire du départ de saint Jérôme de Rome et de son installation à Bethléem,* ed. Yves-Marie Duval (Paris 1988) 429–44; also Giesela Muschiol, 'Hoc dixit Ieronimus: Monastische Tradition und Normierung im 12. Jahrhundert,' in *Normieren, Tradieren, Inszenieren. Das Christentum als Buchreligion,* ed. Andreas Holzem (Darmstadt 2004) 109–26.

25. Landgraf, 'Sünde und Trennung,' 237–38. See also the *Glossa ordinaria on the Psalter, Prologus,* in *Biblia Latina cum glossa ordinaria,* (1992) 2.458, cf. E. Ann Matter, 'The Church Fathers and the Glossa Ordinaria,' in *The Reception of the Church Fathers in the West,* ed. Irena Backus (Leiden 1997) 1.83–112 at 94 n. 41, also *Bernard of Clairvaux, Sententiae,* ed. Jean Leclercq and Henri M. Rochais (*Bernardi opera* 6.2, Rome: Editiones Cistercienses 1972) 199.4 and Petrus Lombardus, *Collectanea in omnes Pauli apostoli Epistulas,* PL 192.53A, on 2 Corinthians 7.1.

26. Petrus Cantor, *Summa quae dicitur verbum abbreviatum,* ed. M. Boutry (CCCM 196;

The passage from Matthew, *unum ex uobis me traditurus est*, was, from a canonistic perspective, an unusual choice to illustrate anathema or excommunication.[27] Jesus' curse had never named Judas. The anathema was tacit. As for illustrating excommunication, Judas also judged and executed himself, thus preventing any sort of process against himself. (His suicide, of course, was a mortal sin, which itself merited damnation.)[28] Neither Jesus nor the apostles sentenced or banished him. To gain a better understanding of what our author may have had in mind, we can turn to C. 2 q. 1 c. 6, a text attributed to Augustine.[29] There is no *dictum* to give us an idea of what Gratian thought, but, presumably, this text would interest a reader concerned about excommunication *latae sententiae*. Jesus had tolerated His betrayer and not cast him out. However, though no one else knew, Judas had already been damned. Such hidden judgments were part of a divine omniscence beyond human understanding.

This text in Gratian apparently elicited little decretist commentary. Commentators focused instead on the introduction to the *quaestio*, which distinguished between occult and manifest crimes,[30] and whether, once a crime became known, one could be excommunicated without accusation. Discussion on this point was influenced by *latae sententiae*.[31] Rufinus likely

Turnhout 2004) 1.25.26:...set intuendum quod Dominus acetum noluit bibere, ita 'nec tales sibi incorporat,' etsi sacramentaliter Eucharistiam sumant, qui de Ecclesia sunt nomine sed non numine.

27. On the twelfth-century debate over what effect, if any, Judas's own taking of the Eucharist from Christ had, see Marcia Colish, *Peter Lombard*, 2 vols. (Leiden 1994) 2.562–63 and n. 63, citing Rolandus's *Sententiae*, which argued that while he indeed took Christ's body and blood there was no benefit and, instead, he found damnation. See also 571–72 discussing how the Lombard argued that not even a notorious criminal should be denied the Eucharist, for even Judas received it. Only the publicly excommunicated should be denied.

28. On late-medieval reflections on whether Judas might have, at the last moment, attempted to free himself and not commit suicide, see Norbert Schnitzler, 'Judas' Death: Some Remarks Concerning the Iconography of Suicide in the Middle Ages,' *The Medieval History Journal* 3 (2000) 103–18 at 111, and 114–16 on Judas's suicide. As Schnitzler notes, medieval iconography introduced a gallows to replace the tree from which Judas had hanged himself. This innovation, along with others, marked an increasingly 'judicial' rendering of the suicide.

29. C. 2 q. 1 c. 6: *Multi per tolerantiam sustinendi sunt, quamvis sententia divini iudicii sint condempnati*. Item Augustinus. Unus ex uobis me traditurus est. Bene dixit: ex uobis, et non: ex nobis. Ex uobis enim est, a quibus per iudiciariam potestatem confessus aut conuictus exclusus non est. A me uero, qui nullis indigeo argumentis, et omnia certissime noui, separatus et diuisus est. Tale est, ac si diceret: Etsi ego per occulti iudicii sententiam eum dampnatum habeo, uos tamen adhuc illum per tollerantiam sustinete. It appears in the *Collection in Three Books*, 2.33.60, Gratian's probable source, as well as in an 'additional' text in a manuscripts of the Pseudo-Ivonian *Panormia* (Rome, Biblioteca Casanatense 335, 4.116A), on which see http://project.knowledgeforge.net/ivo/panormia/conspectus_1p3.pdf accessed on 22 June 2009.

30. Kuttner, *Kanonistische Schuldlehre*, 20 on the maxim 'ecclesia de occultis non iudicat.'

31. For example, *Die Summa Magistri Rolandi*, ed. Friedrich Thaner (Innsbruck 1874) 16: C. 2

referred to actual experience in the courtroom, when the accused revealed a hidden crime.[32] The *Summa Parisiensis* followed this line, but also echoed 1 Corinthians 5: 'If the act is so manifest that it is impossible to deny, as with the adulterer, the Apostle handed the matter (*opem*) over to Satan, since the man was openly (*publice*) living with his stepmother, then deposition is able to be done without trial.'[33]

The structure of the *summula* here is similar to Gratian's text. Just as the Pseudo-Augustinian text notes what Jesus did not say, the *summula*, citing 1 Cor. 6:17, comments that 'He did not say "one body" but rather "one spirit".'[34] It then illustrates the converse of Gratian's text and applies it to the status of the excommunicate. One could be separated physically from contact and communion with the faithful and yet remain, spiritually, in the body of Christ.

The *summula* concludes that excommunication separates one from the corporal participation in the sacrament, while anathema utterly cuts him off from the Church and Christ. This conclusion is not unusual.[35] Simon

---

q. 1, *Quod autem nullus*: In hac causa viii formantur quaestiones. Qu. 1. Primo queritur, an in manifestis iudiciarius ordo sit requirendus. Ad haec notandum, quod crimium quedam sunt manifesta iudici et non aliis …

32. *Die Summa Rufini zum Decretum Gratiani*, ed. J.F. von Schulte (Giessen 1892) 238: *Quod autem nullus*: criminum quedam sunt occulta, quedam manifesta. Que autem manifesta sunt, alia sunt manifesta iudici et non aliis, alia aliis et non iudici, alia iudici et aliis. Sed cum hoc est, aliquando reus, qui commisit crimen semel, postea infitiatur; aliquando ipsa evidentia rei adeo crimen publicat, ut illud nullo pacto diffiteri valeat, sicut fornicator ille Corinthius, qui publice novercam suam apud se impudice tenebat—et ideo Paulus excommunicavit cum nullo accusante. Tunc crimen non solum manifestum, sed etiam dicitur esse notorium. Quando ergo crimen est occultum, nisi reus sponte in iudicio confiteatur, condemnandus non est …

33. *The Summa Parisiensis on the Decretum Gratiani*, ed. Terence P. McLaughlin (Toronto 1952), 101: Si ita sit manifestum opere quod negare non possit, ut de adultero, opem tradidit Satanae Apostolus quia publice habebat novercam suam, tunc sine ordine iudicii potest fieri depositio.

34. Qui adhaeret deo unus spiritus est cum eo.

35. *Summa Parisiensis*, C. 3 q. 4 c. 6, 119: Illud. Differt inter excommunicatum et anathematizatum. Nam excommunicatus dicitur pro separatione privata a sacramento corporis domini *sive precipiatur abstinere sive ipse sibi conscius abstineat. Dicitur etiam excommunicatus.* See also the *Summula de excommunicatione*, Vat. Pal. Lat. 678 fol. 83ra–va, cited by Zeliauskas, *De Excommunicatione*, 87–88* at 87*:… Differunt anathema et excommunicatio quia anathema est a deo separatio ut infra xxiii. q. iii Certum est (c.9). Item anathema est eterne mortis dampnatio ut xi. q. iii. Nemo episcoporum (c.41). Item ab excommunicatione proceditur ad anathema ut infra. v. q. ii. Presenti (c.2) et xxiiii. q. iii. Quisquis (c.22) et cap. de proscriptione (?) Excommunicatio vero a fraterna societate separat ut infra iii. q. iiii. Engeltrudam vel ab ingressu ecclesie ut colligitur infra. v.q. ii. Presenti (c.2). Item excommunicatio temporalis potest esse ut infra. di. lxxxviiii. Decenter omnibus (c.6), cum contra altera perpetua. Verumtamen indifferentibus nominibus uusi inveniuntur auctores sicquidem nomine excommunicationis quandoque censetur anathema ut illud: Cum excommunicato nec orare nec loqui licet, etc. ut infra xi. q. iii. Item nomine anathematis excommunicatio significari invenitur. infra. p. ult. q. i (?) et xii (=xi?) q. Iii.

of Bisignano even uses similar language.[36] The *summula* also brings excommunication under the power of the keys. Perhaps C. 24 q. 1 c. 6, in a *quaestio* treating a bishop lapsed into heresy, may be echoed here.[37] When reading this text, some decretists, not suprisingly, focused on papal power.[38] Others read it within an argument prohibiting a heretical priest from condemning someone.[39] Huguccio, however, would engage the canon in a way closer to the *summula's* focus on the visible Church as a mixture of good and bad.[40] To Huguccio, God uses the Church as it is. Some of the 'bad' are priests; some of these have, so far, not been discovered and expelled. Neverthless, the power of the keys, like the Sacrament, is not effected by the quality of the priest. However, mere exercise of this power—like the taking of the Eucharist or being 'numbered' in the Church—did not mean that sin goes unnoticed by God. Priest or layman, all is done for the 'good.'

Conclusion

The *summula* admonishes the Church which, after all, is a community of sinners, to be humble. It stresses the limitations of human perception. The disciples had seen Judas—who had taken communion with them—but had never known who he really was or what he was doing.[41] To our author, nothing had changed, and his audience, from judge to layman, ought

36. *Summa Simonis*: *Engeltrudem* usque *que a fraterna societate*, id est a corpore christi vel Domini per quod fratres sumus. Usque *a corpore*, id est a communione fidelium qui sunt corpus christi spirituale, at http://www.unifr.ch/cdc/summa_simonis_2baende/summa_simonis_BAND_I.14.10.2007.pdf., accessed on 7 November 2011.

37. C. 24 q. 1 c. 6: In persona Petri ecclesia ligandi et soluendi potestatem accepit. Item Augustinus super Iohannem. Quodcumque ligaueris super terram, erit ligatum et in celo. Si Petro hoc tantum dictum est, non hoc facit ecclesia. Si autem et in ecclesia fit, (utique que in terra ligantur et in celo, et que soluuntur in terra soluta sunt et in celo, quia, cum excommunicat ecclesia, in celo ligatur excommunicatus; cum reconciliat ecclesia, in celo soluitur reconciliatus.), si hoc ergo in ecclesia fit, Petrus, quando claues accepit, ecclesiam sanctam significavit. Si in Petri persona significati sunt in ecclesia boni, in Iudae persona significati sunt in ecclesia mali.

38. For example, *Summa Simonis*, 386–87, http://www.unifr.ch/cdc/summa_simonis_2baende/summa_simonis_BAND_I.14.10.2007.pdf. accessed on 7 November 2011.

39. Rolandus, *Summa*, 98–99, and the *Summa* 'Sicut vetus testamentum,' on which see Titus Lenherr, *Exkommunikations- und Depositionsgewalt der Häretiker bei Gratian und den Dekretisten bis zur Glossa Ordinaria des Johannes* (St. Ottilien 1987) 266–67.

40. Lenherr, *Exkommunikations- und Depositionsgewalt*, 297:...omnibus enim catholicis, siue bonis siue malis, sacerdotibus, dum tollerantur ab ecclesia conuenit, saltem ex officio suo, soluere et ligare, quia ecclesia in persona Petri hanc potestatem recepit, et donec non separatur sacerdos ab ecclesia hanc potestatem exercere potest, ut xxuiii q i manet Quodcumque. Potest tamen dici, quod et de malis adhuc ab ecclesia tolleratis intelligitur sicut littera precedens uidetur uelle, quia, etsi per ministerium malorum sicut per bonorum deus peccata dimittit, illud tamen non est dictum nisi bonis et propter bonos.

41. A point discussed by Colish, *Peter Lombard*, 571–72.

to bear that in mind. Canon law, however, was imperfect and, even at its best, could never entirely comprehend the mystical body of Christ.[42] Only God truly saw, and judged, things as they actually were.

More than nine centuries ago, a text attributed to Pope Urban II pondered, like the *summula*, the Christian's relation to the law. As Professor Somerville noted in his careful study of this document, *Duae sunt*, it declared, 'Indeed, the law is the Spirit of God, and those who are motivated by the Spirit of God are led by the law of God.'[43] Our author would have agreed. Canon law was more, far more, than the constitution of the Church. It was the instrument of salvation.[44] Its sole purpose, even in excommunication, was to restore the sinner to communion, both corporeal and spiritual. This was a message of hope.[45] That we see only the law in excommunication, and not its Gospel of hope, is one measure of how the centuries have changed our perception. For his part, this author is not certain that our vision has improved.

EDITION

Ex monasterio <<>>[1] Commentario <<>>

+Anathema uero que *in interitum carnis.*[2]

Differentia est inter excommunicationem et anathema et grauioris pene est uinculum anathematis quam excommunicationis. Est ergo excommunicatio a communione priuacio qua iuxta apostolum quis *traditur sathane*[3] ut ab eo fornicarius *in interitum carnis est et spiritus* iuxta eundem apostolum non solum ab eiusdem ecclesie set corporis christi unitate scilicet et deo separatur. Unde in fine prime epistole ad corinthos, *si quis non amat dominum nostrum iesum christum sit anath-*

42. Landgraf, 'Sünde und Trennung,' 233–34. On unjust excommunication not separating the victim from the mystical Body of Christ, see the *Distinctio* 'Eorum qui communicantur' preserved in Paris, BN lat. 16540, fol. 113v: Apud ecclesia et non apud deum excommunicatus est? Qui iniuste nulla subsistente causa sententiam excommunicationis accepit.

43. Robert Somerville, 'Canon Law, Inspired Law, and Papal Authority,' *Neti'ot LeDavid. Jubilee Volume for David Weiss Halivini* (Jerusalem 2004) 119–34 at 122, with allusion to Romans 8.14. The translation is Professor Somerville's.

44. Gabriel LeBras, 'Le droit classique de l'Église au service de l'homme,' in *Congrès de droit canonique médiéval*, ed. Stephan Kuttner, Henri Wagon, Gérard Fransen (Louvain: 1959) 104–10 at 105: 'La finalité du droit canonique n'est point l'organisation constitutionnelle et administrative de l'Église: elle est le salut éternel de chaque homme ...'

45. There is ample biblical commentary, for example on 1 Thess. 4.13, where Christians are contrasted with those 'who have no hope.' See, for example, Hugh of St. Victor, *Quaestiones*, PL 175.588A.

1. *err.*

2. Cf. 1 Cor 5.5, also C 11 q. 3 c. 21.

3. 1 Cor. 5.5, also cf. C 11 q. 3 c. 21.

ema marantha[4] quod sancti exponunt anathema separatus a deo marantha donec ueniat dominus uel in aduentum domini. Hoc exemplo patet quid sit anathema et quod non ex leui causa sit anathematizandum. Utrumque quorum probatur ex concilio meldensi. Ait enim *nemo episcoporum quemlibet sine certa et manifesta peccati causa communione priuet ecclesiastica. Sub anathemate autem sine conscientia archiepiscopi aut coepiscoporum episcopus nullus ponat*[5] *nisi unde canonica docet auctoritas quia anathema eterna est dampnatio mortis et nonnisi pro mortali debet imponi crimine et illi qui aliter non potest corrigi.*[6] Iohannis octauus engeltrudem uxorem bosonis[7] etc. § Sacramentum christi et ecclesie participatio siue communio alia corporalis alia spiritualis. Corporalis est que boni et mali, iusti et reprobi uisibili actu countuntur ut uisibilis baptisma susceptio et participatio corporis et sanguinis christi. Spiritualis est que inuisibiliter cum effectu inuisibili<<s>> gratie suscipiuntur, unde dominus *spiritus est qui uiuificat.*[8] Spiritualis uidelicet sacramentorum suscept<<i>>o : caro autem nichil prodest usus scilicet set solus eorundem usus corporalis. Unde Augustinus de corpore christi *melius inquid assumitur mente quam atteritur dente.*[9] Propter primum dictum est *ex nobis exierunt* propter secundum set *ex nobis non erant,*[10] unde ieron.[11] propter primum de iude super illum locum *unus ex uobis me traditurus est.*[12] *Unus* inquid *numero non merito nomine non numine.*[13] Sacramentorum participatione non caritatis unione corporali igitur communicatur in fraterna societate spiritualiter non nisi in corporis christi *quod est ecclesia*[14] unitate. Corpus enim christi *quod est ecclesia*[15] non corporalis societas set spiritualis unitas operatur uidelicet unius fidei et dilectionis *que membra eiusdem corporis inuicem coniuguntur et capiti.*[16] Unde apostolus *Qui adheret deo*[17] non inquid unum corpus set unus spiritus est sicut ergo in ecclesia quis esse potest per fraternam societatem ut iudas ante manifestam repulsionem et non esse membrum christi sic extra ecclesiam seperatus a fraterna societate corporaliter et manere in unitate corporis christi. Excommunicatio enim[18] separat a fraterna societate sublata corporali participatione sacramentorum anathema uero ab unitate corporis christi recidit[19] spiritualem eorundem sacramentorum auferens participationem; super utrumque enim ecclesia in petro potestatem accepit ubi ei a domino dictum est *quecumque ligaueris etc.*[20]

4. 1 Cor. 16.22.
5. ponat *omac*
6. C. 11 q. 3 c. 41.
7. C. 3 q. 4 c. 12.
8. 1 Ioh. 6.63.
9. *Non inveni.*
10. 1 Ioh. 2.18.
11. Pseudo-Hieronymous, *Expositio Euangelii secundum Marcum*, ed. Michael Cahill (CSSL 82, Brepols: Turnhout 1997) 60.48.
12. Mt. 26.21.
13. *Glossa ordinaria on the Psalter, Prologus*, in: *Biblia Latina cum glossa ordinaria*, (1992) 2.458, cf. E. Ann Matter, 'The Church Fathers and the Glossa Ordinaria,' in *The Reception of the Church Fathers in the West*, 2 vols., ed. Irena Backus (Leiden: Brill 1997) 1.83–112 at 94 n. 41.
14. C. 3 q. 4 c. 12, dpc. 12.
15. C. 3 q. 4 c. 12, dpc. 12.
16. Cf. 1 Cor. 12.12.
17. 1 Cor. 6.17.
18. *add supra ln.*
19. que a fraterna—recidit, cf. C. 3 q. 4 c. 12.
20. Mt. 16:18–19, cf. C. 24 q. 1 c. 6.

ANNA TRUMBORE JONES

8 ⊰ The Power of an Absent Pope

Privileges, Forgery, and Papal Authority in Aquitaine, 877–1050

In 930, Frotier II entered his fourth decade as bishop of Poitiers. Possibly in a bid to close his long episcopate in a fitting manner, or possibly—as some scholars have argued—in an attempt to settle a dispute with the local comital house, Frotier set out over the next few years to reconstruct the monastery of Saint-Cyprien, which lay on the banks of the river Clain on the outskirts of the city.[1] This was a long process involving multiple steps. Frotier rebuilt the structures of the house.[2] He endowed it with land and income both from his own holdings and from those of the cathedral of Saint-Pierre in Poitiers.[3] He expanded the dedication of the monastery from the local saint, Cyprien, to include the more widely revered Virgin

This essay has deep roots in my dissertation research, done under the direction of Robert Somerville. It is indicative both of his formidable learning and of his generosity that he was willing to oversee a dissertation whose subject fell outside his own era of focus. His unyielding demand for precision and rigor in his students' work is responsible for much of the worth that that dissertation—and subsequent pieces based on it—may possess. The process of producing it, meanwhile, was eased immeasurably by his perceptive nature, his humor, and his myriad kindnesses. I am forever grateful. I thank Mary Harvey Doyno and John S. Ott for their comments on previous drafts of this essay. Any errors that remain are mine alone.

1. Alfred Richard, *Histoire des comtes du Poitou, 778–1204*, 2 vols. (Paris 1903) 1.72 and 1.83–84. Evidence for a dispute between Frotier and the count of Poitou, Ebles Manzer, is found in a charter from Saint-Cyprien that states that Frotier was restored to the bishopric after Ebles's death: Louis Rédet, ed., *Cartulaire de l'abbaye de Saint-Cyprien de Poitiers, Archives historiques du Poitou* 3 (1874) [hereafter *Saint-Cyprien*] 126, p. 90. I have argued elsewhere that this restoration took place at some point in 934, thus tightening the likely date range for the restoration of Saint-Cyprien from 931–36 to 934–36: Anna Trumbore Jones, 'Lay Magnates, Religious Houses, and the Role of the Bishop in Aquitaine (877–1050),' in *The Bishop Reformed: Studies of Episcopal Power and Culture in the Central Middle Ages*, ed. John S. Ott and Anna Trumbore Jones (Aldershot 2007) 21–39 at 25–26.

2. *Saint-Cyprien* 1, pp. 1–2; 3, pp. 4–5; and 183, p. 117.

3. *Saint-Cyprien* 3–4, pp. 4–7; 65, pp. 58–60; 118, p. 87; 183–84, pp. 117–19; 232, pp. 150–51.

Mary and Martin of Tours. Fittingly, he brought in Martin's successor, Archbishop Téotelon of Tours, to consecrate the new house and confirm its possessions.[4] Frotier enlisted local powerful men to stand as witnesses to Saint-Cyprien's new status. And finally, he forged, or had forged, a papal privilege purporting to come from Pope John XI, which would later open the monastery's cartulary.[5]

It was an inelegant document. The modern editor remarks on the informal language of the privilege, its inconsistency with papal *formulae* of the time, and the jarring mention of Roman consuls; even a less well-trained eye spots immediately the lack of the usual ringing intitulation invoking *Johannes episcopus, servus servorum Dei* and its replacement with the more homely *Ego Johannes papa*. Both the existence of this document as part of Frotier's restoration program and its unusual form raise a number of questions. Had Frotier attempted to acquire a genuine papal privilege and when rebuffed turned to forgery, or did he not bother to petition the pope? When the document's author set about creating the false privilege, why did he not try to approximate more closely the form of a genuine decree? More broadly, what did a papal privilege—and the papacy itself—mean for a bishop and monastery in tenth-century Aquitaine? At the time of Frotier's actions at Saint-Cyprien, popes had not been seen in person in France for more than fifty years and would not reappear for more than a century. In the absence of the pope himself, what power did his office, his name, his documents wield?

Most general accounts of the history of the medieval papacy describe the era from the late ninth to the mid-eleventh century as a low point in papal status and authority. After a period of cooperation with the Carolingian dynasty, and the relatively high level of papal activity in the Frankish territories that stemmed from that relationship,[6] the long tenth century saw a serious retreat of the papacy's influence outside Italy.[7] The papal of-

4. *Saint-Cyprien* 3, pp. 4–5.

5. *Saint-Cyprien* 1, pp. 1–2; JL 3592. A modern critical edition is found in Harald Zimmermann, ed., *Papsturkunden 896–1046*, 3 vols. (Österreichische Akademie der Wissenschaften, Denkschriften 174, 177, and 198; Vienna 1985–89) 63, pp. 105–6. The cartulary manuscript is Paris, BN lat. 10122; the privilege is on fol. 1.

6. For examples of papal letters to Aquitanian bishops in the Carolingian period, see the letter of Leo IV to Ebroin of Poitiers, in MGH Epp. 5.606, and a letter of Nicholas I to Frotier of Bordeaux, in MGH Epp. 6.662–63. By the 'long tenth century' I mean the years from ca. 877 to ca. 1050.

7. Harald Zimmermann makes the point that while certain popes of this period, particularly Sylvester II, have been praised, and while historians have attempted to take a more measured view of the tenth-century papacy as a whole, the fact remains that this period saw less contact between the popes and the rest of Europe: 'Die Beziehungen Roms zu Frankreich im Saeculum obscurum,'

fice in this period functioned as a prize passed back and forth in struggles between Roman political factions. Certain individual popes were the instigators or (sometimes *and*) the victims of plots and assassinations.[8] The one bright spot in this rather grim scholarly picture of papal authority in tenth-century Europe was papal grants of privileges exempting monasteries from the control of their local bishops.[9] Indeed, scholarship on papal authority in these years, particularly in France, has focused primarily on this aspect of papal activity. This is due in large part to the groundbreaking work of Jean-François Lemarignier, who argued that the papacy's privileges for French monasteries were crucial in creating the foundation for the later successes of the eleventh-century papal reform movement.[10] Focusing in particular on the cases of Cluny and Fleury, Lemarignier described a mutually beneficial relationship between popes and monasteries. The popes benefited when monasteries sought help from Rome to escape the authority of their bishops, thus extending the papacy's prestige and practical influence and laying the groundwork for more ambitious future claims along these lines. Monasteries, meanwhile, used these papal privileges to achieve their desired exemption from episcopal authority, which they sought as a result of political conditions in the former Carolingian Empire. Lemarignier asserted that as the kings of west Francia lost the ability to control appointments to episcopal sees, which devolved into 'playthings of political opponents,' bishops became, on average, less worthy and their attention to monasteries less beneficent, forcing those communities to turn to Rome for help.[11]

Lemarignier's argument, although it remains influential, has been modified from a number of different perspectives.[12] First, the profoundly

---

in *L'Église de France et la papauté (Xe–XIIIe siècle)*, ed. Rolf Grosse (Bonn 1993) 33–47 at 46–47; see also bibliography in n. 45.

8. Rosamond McKitterick, 'The Church,' in *The New Cambridge Medieval History*, vol. 3: *900–1024*, ed. Timothy Reuter (Cambridge 1999) 130–62 at 137–42; Walter Ullmann, *A Short History of the Papacy in the Middle Ages* (London 1972) 115.

9. Ullmann, *Short History* 126. For a more recent survey of the history of papal privileges, see Barbara H. Rosenwein, *Negotiating Space: Power, Restraint, and Privileges of Immunity in Early Medieval Europe* (Ithaca, NY 1999) 4–5 and n. 5, 67, 106–9, 171–72. For an examination of the relationship of the papacy and the monastery of Luxeuil, which had a long history of turning to the popes for exemptions from diocesan control, see Gerard Moyse, 'Luxeuil et la papauté jusqu'au XIe siècle,' in *L'Église de France et la papauté*, ed. Grosse 179–96.

10. Most notably, see Jean-François Lemarignier, 'L'exemption monastique et les origines de la réforme Grégorienne,' in *À Cluny: Congrès scientifique* (Dijon 1951) 288–340.

11. Lemarignier, 'Structures monastiques et structures politiques dans la France de la fin du Xe et des débuts du XIe siècle,' in *Il monachesimo nell'alto Medioevo e la formazione della civiltà occidentale, Settimane* 4 (Spoleto 1957) 357–400.

12. For an example of a work deeply influenced by Lemarignier's arguments, see Ludwig

negative assessment of a chaotic late Carolingian and early Capetian era—and of its rapacious bishops—has been refined.[13] Second, some historians, such as Gerd Tellenbach, have become wary of describing the granting of these monastic privileges as a coherent prestige-building policy on the part of the papacy, both because the initiative often came from the monasteries rather than the popes and because the popes were rarely in conflict with bishops in this period.[14] Third, Lemarignier's argument centers around the cases of Cluny and particularly Fleury under its zealous abbot, Abbo, who believed—despite both legal tradition and contemporary practice to the contrary—that a diocesan bishop need have no meaningful role at a monastery in his diocese.[15] Given that Lemarignier's model is built so much upon Abbo's writings and their radical ecclesiology, it seems less widely applicable to other communities and regions. Barbara Rosenwein and Thomas Head, for example, have noted that even to lump Cluny and Fleury together as monasteries seeking papal privileges is problematic, as they used their privileges very differently: Cluny's relationship with its local bishop was generally amicable, whereas Fleury under Abbo fought tooth and nail to limit the power of its diocesan, Arnulf of Orléans.[16] Other authors have underlined the great variety that existed in the relationships between monasteries, bishops, and the papacy in the tenth and early eleventh centuries, both between and within regions; Abbo of Fleury did not speak for France, or even for the Loire region.[17]

Given all these challenges to the received narrative of papal involve-

---

Falkenstein, *La papauté et les abbayes françaises aux XIe et XIIe siècles: Exemption et protection apostolique* (Bibliothèque de l'École des Hautes Études 336; Paris 1997) esp. at 5–7, 36–56.

13. For an overview of this new vision of the era and its prelates, see Timothy Reuter, 'Introduction,' in *The New Cambridge Medieval History*, vol. 3, ed. Reuter 1–24; Ott and Jones, 'Introduction,' in *The Bishop Reformed*, ed. Ott and Jones, 6–12.

14. Gerd Tellenbach, *The Church in Western Europe from the Tenth to the Early Twelfth Century*, trans. Timothy Reuter (Cambridge 1993) 65–74.

15. On Abbo's ecclesiology, see Marco Mostert, 'L'abbé, l'évêque et le pape: L'image de l'évêque idéal dans les oeuvres d'Abbon de Fleury,' in *Religion et culture autour de l'an mil: Royaume capétien et Lotharingie. Actes du colloque Hugues Capet 987–1987: La France de l'an mil*, ed. Dominique Iogna-Prat and Jean-Charles Picard (Paris 1990) 39–45; Thomas Head, *Hagiography and the Cult of Saints: The Diocese of Orléans, 800–1200* (Cambridge 1990) 238–39, 245–50; Jones, 'Discovering the Aquitanian Church in the Corpus of Ademar of Chabannes,' *The Haskins Society Journal* 19 (2007) 82–98.

16. Barbara H. Rosenwein, Thomas Head, and Sharon Farmer, 'Monks and Their Enemies: A Comparative Approach,' *Speculum* 66 (1991) 764–96 at 766–68.

17. Jean-Hervé Foulon, *Église et réforme au Moyen Âge: Papauté, milieux réformateurs et ecclésiologie dans les Pays de la Loire au tournant des XIe–XIIe siècles* (Bibliothèque du Moyen Âge 27; Brussels 2008) 50–56. Falkenstein acknowledges this variety (*La papauté et les abbayes* 48–49), although his narrative of the period remains fundamentally informed by Lemarignier's vision.

ment in France in this period, the time seems ripe for more in-depth consideration of papal influence in particular regional churches.[18] In this essay I will examine the surviving papal documents and references to papal activity in the region of Aquitaine, from the death of Charles the Bald in 877—and the concomitant end of effective royal rule in the southwest of France—to the advent of Pope Leo IX and the rise of a new articulation of the appropriate exercise of papal power in 1049.[19] I do not limit myself to genuine and forged papal decrees, but also include as evidence mentions of papal authority and activity in charters and narrative sources. In line with the recent scholarship I summarized above, I shall argue that Lemarignier's vision of the papacy and religious houses united against a hostile episcopate does not hold for Aquitaine. It is true that the general framework of papal activity in Aquitaine feels familiar, in that the popes were more involved in the region in the late Carolingian era and the mid-eleventh century, with a lull in between. On closer inspection, however, the picture becomes more complex: monasteries *and* bishops throughout the period valued and sought (or created) papal support in specific circumstances, but the popes did not have the ability to assert their will without local invitation. An understanding of the importance of the papacy in Aquitaine in this period must therefore be grounded first in the circumstances of any given house or diocese, rather than in a general model of papal history that risks shading into teleology as it anticipates developments in the late eleventh century.

The documents from tenth-century Aquitaine relating to the papacy are striking, first of all, for their paucity: for a period of roughly one hundred and seventy-five years, documents concerning the papacy—including both full texts and passing mentions in written sources—number in the low dozens. Indeed, true to the common understanding of papal authority as anemic in this period, there are many moments in the documents in which the lack of reference to Roman authority or papal power is

18. Certain French regional studies that are focused on ecclesiastical history devote space to relations between local churches and the papacy in the tenth and early eleventh centuries, but that space is often surprisingly limited. Examples include Elisabeth Magnou-Nortier, *La société laïque et l'Église dans la province ecclésiastique de Narbonne (zone cispyrénéenne) de la fin du VIIIe à la fin du XIe siècle* (Publications de l'Université de Toulouse–Le Mirail A20; Toulouse 1974) 374–75; Foulon, *Église et réforme* 50–61; Michel Aubrun, *L'ancien diocèse de Limoges des origines au milieu du XIe siècle* (Publication de l'Institut d'Études du Massif Central 21; Clermont-Ferrand 1981) 167–68.

19. For the purposes of this paper, 'Aquitaine' refers to the six dioceses of Angoulême, Bordeaux, Limoges, Périgueux, Poitiers, and Saintes, which correspond roughly to the region ruled by the dukes of Aquitaine once that title passed to the comital house of Poitou in the mid-tenth century.

conspicuous. For example, the cathedrals of both Poitiers and Angoulême were dedicated to Saint Peter, and the charters from those dioceses contain frequent references to 'the see of Blessed Peter, prince of the apostles' and similar formulations.[20] And yet the charters from this period, whether mentioning the see of Peter or invoking the protection of that saint, do not ruminate on consequent connections to the papacy brought on by their shared saintly patron.[21] The documents leave little doubt that when Aquitanian bishops thought of the successors of Peter, or the power of the keys, they thought first of themselves, and only later (if at all) of the popes.[22] Bishop Radulf of Périgueux (ca. 1000–ca. 1013) emphasized his role as a successor of Peter in a charter for the house of Saint-Astier from 1013, in which he argued that those who threatened the rebuilt community would 'be anathematized by authority of the holy and indivisible Trinity and of Saint Peter, prince of the apostles, in whom and through whom the power of binding and loosing was given to us, although unworthy ...'[23] Elsewhere, in a striking juxtaposition, Hilduin of Limoges (990–1014) invoked his own power as the vicar of Peter before making passing mention of the authority of Pope Sylvester II in attempting to dissuade those who would threaten his cathedral of Saint-Étienne.[24]

Chronologically, the evidence for papal activity and authority that survives from tenth-century Aquitaine falls into three main groups of roughly similar size. At the outset, there is a cluster of documents from

20. See, for example, André Debord, ed., *Cartulaire de l'abbaye de Saint-Amant-de-Boixe* (Poitiers 1982) 4, pp. 95–96. The cathedral of Angoulême is relatively well-documented, due to the survival of the cartulary: Jean Nanglard, ed., *Cartulaire de l'église d'Angoulême* (Angoulême 1900); documents 5, 6, 29, 43, 46, 50–51, 55, and 118 are examples of these references. For the cathedral of Poitiers, one document survives from the period: Archives départementales de la Vienne, pièces restaurées no. 35.

21. Even in a case such as a charter for Saint-Pierre d'Anzême (ca. 1031–33) that placed that monastery under the protection of Saint Peter's in Rome, the connection of their shared dedication was not elaborated upon; this may, of course, be a function of limited space or document conventions, but it is notable nonetheless. Jacques de Font-Réaulx, ed., 'Saint-Pierre d'Anzême et les origines de son prieuré,' *Mémoires de la Société des sciences naturelles et archéologiques de la Creuse* 23 (1925) 139–56 at 151–52.

22. Jean-Hervé Foulon argues that this is the case for the Loire region, succinctly laying out the tradition of debate on this point, notably in the writing of Fulbert of Chartres: *Église et réforme* 50–61.

23. Paris, BN Collection Périgord, vol. 12 (microfilm 14680), fol. 206v–208: 'Si qui vero hoc nostrum praeceptum ausi temerario praesumpserint ex auctoritate sanctae et individuae trinitatis sanctique petri apostolorum principis in quem et per quem quamvis indignis nobis potestas data est ligandi atque solvendi, sint anathematizati ...'

24. Jacques de Font-Réaulx, ed., 'Cartulaire de Saint-Étienne de Limoges,' *Bulletin de la Société archéologique et historique du Limousin* 69 (1922) 189, pp. 181–82.

late Carolingian popes in the 870s; most of these come from Pope John VIII (r. 872–82), who was, not coincidentally, the last pope to visit France for more than 150 years.[25] Another cluster occurs at the end of the period, from 1024 into the 1040s. The remaining documents are spread across the century and a quarter from 900 to 1024. The papacy appears in sources from a range of genres, including a few genuine papal decrees, false privileges and letters like that regarding Frotier's renovation of Saint-Cyprien, and mentions in charters and in narrative sources, such as the chronicle of Ademar of Chabannes.[26] The papal activity recorded in this evidence falls into two main categories: documents in which popes served as judges or final courts of appeal, and those in which popes granted (or were claimed to grant) privileges for religious communities.

The first, and less numerous, category of documents involves the popes as judges, pronouncing sentences or receiving appeals in their court in Rome. At the outset of this period, Pope John VIII addressed two letters (one considered genuine and one false) to Bishop Anselm of Limoges (869–98). The genuine letter concerns the case of a layman named Stephen who had baptized his dying son. Anselm had judged Stephen harshly, insisting that he live apart from his wife, and Stephen had appealed this decision to the papal court. John writes to Anselm in gentle reproof, acknowledging that the bishop had acted from good motives—'blazing with the zeal of rectitude'—but reversing his decision nonetheless. The pope reminded Anselm that a man and wife are joined by God and should not be separated, certainly not for attempting to save a dying child.[27] Elsewhere, in a document he issued to protect the goods of the church of Poitiers, John demanded that certain cases concerning church property be brought be-

25. On John VIII: Fred E. Engreen, 'Pope John the Eighth and the Arabs,' *Speculum* 20 (1945) 318–30 at 324–26. John's trip to France was a failed attempt to rally the king and princes to aid him against Arab power in Italy, but while there he issued numerous decrees for religious houses. It is difficult to assess the relative importance of John's large number of documents for French monasteries. On the one hand, his visit to France may mean that he was spurred to issue more privileges than other popes of the period. On the other hand, John's is the only papal register to survive between those of Gregory I and Gregory VII; it may be, therefore, that his colleagues issued many more privileges than we know of, and John's activity looms larger because of the vagaries of source survival. On John's register, see Engreen 318, n. 3, and Dietrich Lohrmann, *Das Register Papst Johann VIII. (872–882)* (Tübingen 1968).

26. Ademar of Chabannes, *Ademari Cabannensis Chronicon*, ed. Pascale Bourgain, Richard Landes, and Georges Pon, CCCM 129 (Turnhout 1999).

27. JE 3258; *Iohannes VIII papae epistolae*, ed. Erich Caspar, MGH Epp. 7.156. For the document believed to be false, which contains a more generalized meditation on the role of a judge, see JE 3026; *Iohannes VIII papae epistolae dubiae*, ed. Erich Caspar, MGH Epp. 7.331–32; J. von Pflugk-Harttung, *Acta pontificum Romanorum inedita*, 3 vols. (Graz 1958) 2.37.

fore him.[28] The impression gleaned from this very small number of documents is that in the Carolingian era, or at least under John VIII, the popes were assertive in Aquitaine, whether in relatively minor matters such as overturning a judgment concerning an individual of no particular status, or on issues of broader concern, such as overseeing the restoration of church estates. The fact that John's is the only surviving papal register from this period, however, makes it difficult to know how far to generalize from his example.[29]

This trend of papal judicial assertiveness would not continue: in the tenth and early eleventh centuries papal judgments did not arrive frequently in Aquitaine, and the initiative generally seems to have been on the side of the individuals seeking judgment rather than the popes. In one case, a bishop, Grimoard of Angoulême (991–1018), who had been imprisoned by Viscount Guy of Limoges as part of a dispute over possession of a monastery, brought his complaint against Guy to Pope Sylvester II in Rome. Apparently Guy at least temporarily acquiesced to the pope's judgment in the case, which was harsh: for the crime of imprisoning a bishop, Guy was to be torn apart by wild horses. However, the two antagonists came to an agreement and left Rome before the sentence was carried out.[30] This incident was part of a wider dispute between powerful families in Aquitaine, and it is not clear why Grimoard went to Rome to complain of his treatment rather than to the duke or another, more immediate, authority.[31] It is possible that, in the midst of a feud that had encompassed a number of powerful families, Grimoard sought an outsider, looking for something resembling impartiality. Or he may have felt that at the papal court the story of a wronged bishop might get a more sympathetic hearing than it would in Aquitaine, where the full range of his political activity, and that of his family, was known. It is impossible to be certain.[32]

Indeed, it is this question of what circumstances prompted appeals to

28. JE 3181; *Iohannes VIII papae epistolae*, MGH Epp. 7.93–94.

29. See above, n. 25.

30. Ademar of Chabannes, *Chronicon* 3.36, pp. 158–59; the same incident (with some key details missing) was mentioned in the twelfth-century *Historia pontificum et comitum Engolismensium*, ed. Jacques Boussard (Paris 1957) 15–16.

31. For the context of the dispute, see Thomas Head, 'The Development of the Peace of God in Aquitaine (970–1005),' *Speculum* 74 (1999) 656–86 at 678–79; Pierre Riché, 'Les églises de Francie occidentale et de Lotharingie à l'époque de Sylvestre II,' in *L'Église de France et la papauté*, ed. Grosse 48–53 at 51–52.

32. Dominique Barthélemy, *L'an mil et la paix de Dieu: La France chrétienne et féodale, 980–1060* (Paris 1999) 301–2; in a felicitous phrase, Barthélemy describes Rome as 'cette ville lointaine où l'on va raconter les choses à sa façon ...'

the papacy or papal intervention that looms over the intermittent cases of papal judicial action in Aquitaine in this period. Why, for example, did Pope Benedict IX excommunicate Count Aldebert III of the March and the others responsible for burning the collegiate church at Lesterps around 1040? While it was certainly a tragic incident, in which—according to a charter issued by Aldebert's daughter—1700 people were killed, it was neither the first nor the last church to be attacked in Aquitaine in this period, so why did this incident inspire papal reaction?[33] Furthermore, how much real effect did a papal judgment have? Reaction seems mixed: on the one hand, Bishop Grimoard and Viscount Guy reconciled despite the pope's harsh sentence and left Rome; on the other hand, Aldebert gave a major donation in order to reconcile himself to both his bishop and the pope and to have the excommunication lifted. Elsewhere, the pope seems to be invoked in passing, as a rhetorical flourish, rather than with any real interaction in mind. For example, when Ademar of Chabannes discussed the election and consecration of Bishop Jordan of Limoges (1023/4–1050/1), he emphasized that Limoges's metropolitan, the archbishop of Bourges, had been excluded from the process due to the simoniacal election of the current tenant of that office, Gauzlin. When Jordan finally did submit to Gauzlin, doing barefoot penance in Bourges with a large number of his clergy, Ademar portrays this as an act of courtesy on Jordan's part, arguing that Jordan could have purged himself of his sins before the pope at Rome, but nevertheless chose to do penance before the archbishop in order to rectify the relationship.[34]

Despite these lingering questions concerning the impetus for papal judgments and their impact, an intriguing paradox emerges in these documents: the initiative for interactions between the papacy and local figures or communities occasionally came from the papacy itself, particularly at the very beginning and very end of our period, but more often lay with the recipient of the papal judgment. The papacy, it seems, had little ability (particularly in the heart of this period) to assert its will where it was not wanted. And yet, at the same time, the papacy was not simply ignored or forgotten: papal authority was seen as useful to powerful men and women in Aquitaine at certain key moments. This pattern recurs in the more abundant evidence concerning privileges given by the papacy to religious houses.

Such evidence often follows expected models of interaction among the

33. Gustave Babinet de Rencogne, ed., 'Charte d'Almodis, comtesse de la Marche,' *Bulletin de la Société archéologique et historique de la Charente* 3rd ser., 4 (1862) 409–14.

34. Ademar of Chabannes, *Chronicon* 3.57, p. 179.

papacy and the powerful men of the region. The letters and privileges of the late Carolingian popes John VIII and Marinus, for example, tend to emphasize royal power and cooperation with bishops in their attempts to protect religious houses. In 878, while staying at Troyes, John VIII issued a pair of related documents: the first went to the bishops of western France (including those of Poitiers and Limoges), calling on them to help reassemble the properties of Saint-Maurice of Tours, which, as John had been informed by the archbishop of that city, had been carried away by overzealous laymen.[35] The second document was sent to Bishop Hecfrid of Poitiers (ca. 878–900) and gave the bishop the authority to reassemble the properties of his cathedral, which had been laid waste.[36] Pope Marinus, meanwhile, issued a privilege for the monastery of Solignac, in which he emphasized the efforts of previous Frankish kings to patronize the house, as well as the role of its founder, the holy bishop Eligius of Noyon.[37] Though Marinus's privilege did limit the right of both kings and bishops to demand hospitality, it did not particularly target them as enemies of the house and it also warned abbots and other clergy and laypeople against diminishing the community's properties. Most of these documents also seem concerned with what they portray as an atmosphere of disorder in France at the time; Marinus's privilege discusses the 'infidels devastating Christendom.' This may refer to Viking incursions and/or the internal conflicts that both allowed for and followed from those incursions.[38] Either way, these documents repeatedly invoke a very Carolingian alliance between king, bishops, and popes to ensure church welfare.

The only papal privilege from this period that differs somewhat from this pattern is that issued by John VIII in September of 878 for the monastery of Charroux in Poitou, in which he confirmed the rights of the monastery and granted it independence from a number of powers who might interfere there, including kings, priests, and counts.[39] John then turned to the bishops of Poitiers in particular, forbidding them to perform mass at

35. JE 3145; *Iohannes VIII papae epistolae*, MGH Epp. 7.88; PL 126.801.

36. JE 3181; *Iohannes VIII papae epistolae*, MGH Epp. 7.93–94; PL 126.796–97.

37. JL 3388; PL 126.967–68.

38. For an overview of the question of damage caused to religious houses in the region by Viking attacks, see Jones, 'Pitying the Desolation of Such a Place: Rebuilding Religious Houses and Constructing Memory in Aquitaine in the Wake of the Viking Incursions,' *Viator* 37 (2006) 85–102.

39. JE 3187; Pierre de Monsabert, ed., *Chartes et documents pour servir à l'histoire de l'abbaye de Charroux, Archives historiques du Poitou* 39 (1910) 67–70. On the legendary dossier of Charroux in which this and the later privilege based on it appear, see Amy Remensnyder, *Remembering Kings Past: Monastic Foundation Legends in Medieval Southern France* (Ithaca, NY 1995) 257–59.

the house, to demand hospitality during tours of the diocese, or to take up residence in order to hold a council or for the purpose of overseeing the lifestyle of the house. The reason given for these prohibitions is that the peace of the monastery would be disturbed by the worldly hubbub that accompanied a bishop wherever he went. Nor could the bishops excommunicate the house, which was placed under apostolic protection. This particular privilege targets the bishop's authority at a religious house more directly than do the others from the same few years, and the king is not invoked in any substantive way. It is worth noting that the form of this privilege, unlike the others, would be reused almost a hundred years later (about which more below).

After relatively few documents from the long period from 885 to the 1020s, there is another cluster of texts from the other end of our period. One of the latest documents is a 1036 privilege from Benedict IX for Sainte-Croix in Bordeaux and its daughter house of Notre-Dame de Soulac that is by far the most aggressive of the Aquitanian documents in its limitation of episcopal power. Benedict does not limit himself to the well-worn path of forbidding bishops to interfere in abbatial elections, act against the privilege, or demand hospitality from the abbeys. He goes further, attacking the key episcopal powers of excommunication and consecration.[40] Benedict declares that any person who has been excommunicated and flees to Notre-Dame de Soulac shall be absolved from the excommunication; he gives the right of excommunication to the abbot of Sainte-Croix and the monks of the houses; and he orders that the church of Sainte-Croix cannot be excommunicated by any person. Benedict thus vitiates, from a number of angles, the carefully guarded episcopal right to bind and loose. Furthermore, he offers the monks of the two houses more than one opportunity to bypass the power of their ordinary in matters of consecration: should the archbishop of Bordeaux disapprove of an abbot chosen by the monks of Sainte-Croix, the popes would anoint the abbot, and the monks in both houses could choose whatever bishop they wished to consecrate their sanctuary vessels. By going further than other documents in limiting episcopal power and proposing papal authority in its place, by not including bishops in the protection of the monastery, and by its pointed tone, this document seems to herald a new era in the relationship between the papacy and monasteries.

40. JL 4108; Zimmermann, *Papsturkunden* 602, pp. 1133–35. An older edition is found in A. Ducaunnès-Duval and L. Drouyn, eds., *Cartulaire de l'abbaye de Sainte-Croix de Bordeaux* (Bordeaux 1892) 85, pp. 115–17.

Thus in its broad outlines the general narrative of papal history seems to be reflected in Aquitanian privileges: in the early period we have a cluster of documents representing a Carolingian-style alliance between bishops, royalty, and the papacy to protect monasteries; there are relatively few cases from the tenth century as the papacy reached the nadir of its influence; and then the popes become more active and ambitious in the mid-eleventh century. In the nature of broad outlines, however, this picture misses important nuance. This is brought home immediately in the case of Benedict IX, author of the aggressive privilege for Sainte-Croix and Soulac. Despite his stance on monastic independence from episcopal power (at least in this case), in other aspects Benedict does not fit the model of a proto-Gregorian. In fact, he was one of the popes whose rivalry for the papal throne prompted the intervention of the Emperor Henry III, leading eventually to the election of Leo IX.[41] I want to spend the remainder of this essay focusing on two themes that further complicate the picture of papal-episcopal-monastic relations found in papal privileges issued for Aquitaine from the late ninth to the mid-eleventh centuries: the involvement of bishops in acquiring and enforcing privileges, and the sustained importance of the idea—if not the reality—of papal authority.

One of the most striking features of privileges and exemptions granted to monasteries in Aquitaine in this period is that bishops were almost always involved in limiting their own power at these communities.[42] This point highlights key flaws in any model that posits a rivalry between the papacy and monasteries on the one hand and bishops on the other: first, in many privileges the stated threat to the house was not bishops but laypeople; second, the bishops often commissioned or supported the privileges for houses in their dioceses.[43] For example, when Pope Benedict VII issued a privilege for Charroux in the late tenth century, he took as his model the 878 privilege of John VIII discussed above, which limited the bishop's right to claim hospitality and perform ceremonies at the monastery.[44] How did Charroux's diocesan, Gilbert of Poitiers (975–1023/4),

41. Tellenbach, *The Church in Western Europe* 141–42.

42. The episcopal exemption was always issued by bishops and limited their own power: Rosenwein, *Negotiating Space* 32–36. It is worth noting, however, that bishops also supported or even commissioned papal privileges for religious houses in their dioceses.

43. For an example of a papal privilege aimed squarely at Aquitanian laymen in this period, see John XIX's document for Saint-Jean d'Angély: JL 4097; Zimmermann, *Papsturkunden* 597, pp. 1124–26.

44. JL 3815; Zimmermann, *Papsturkunden* 238, pp. 473–74; Monsabert, ed., *Chartes et documents pour servir à l'histoire de l'abbaye de Charroux* 70–72.

react to this curbing of his authority? The available evidence suggests that he offered little resistance: the main divergence between the 878 document and that of Benedict VII is that the latter was addressed to Gilbert himself rather than to the abbot of Charroux. It seems likely that Benedict did this either because he trusted the bishop to carry out the restrictions enclosed or because he recognized that the bishop had the authority and ability to enforce the provisions of the decree.

Even more striking evidence of a bishop working to facilitate privileges comes in a constellation of documents surrounding the foundation of the church of Notre-Dame at Lusignan around 1025.[45] The founder, the castellan Hugh of Lusignan, established the new church within sight of his castle and took various steps to endow and protect it. He requested that the pope support the foundation 'by a document of [his] sacred authority,' and John XIX responded by ordering that the church of Lusignan be 'removed from all domination except that of the monastery of Nouaillé, to such an extent that it is not compelled to pay anything to the church of Poitiers, in whose diocese it lies, and nothing to the bishop who presides over them.'[46] What is notable, however, regarding this limitation of episcopal power is that it was not done in opposition to the bishop. Rather, we find Isembert I of Poitiers (1023/4–1047) involved at all stages in the creation of special status for Lusignan. Pope John acknowledged that Isembert had requested that the privilege be issued, and that the bishop was consulted throughout the process. Isembert's support for the privilege is then underlined in two other documents concerning Lusignan. Isembert and Duke William the Great of Aquitaine gave permission for the house of canons of Saint-Hilaire in Poitiers to exchange land with Notre-Dame de Lusignan, which allowed a property that lay at the foot of the castle to pass into the hands of the new church.[47] Furthermore, King Robert the Pious of France, while at Tours in 1025, responded to a request made by Duke William and Bishop Isembert to mobilize royal authority in protection of property donated to the church.[48]

45. JL 4073; Zimmermann dates the papal privilege for Lusignan to 1024–32 (the papacy of John XIX): Zimmermann, *Papsturkunden* 555, pp. 1048–49. The royal privilege for the church, from King Robert the Pious, carries the date of 1025, however, and another document that refers to the endowment of the new church is dated to March 1025: Pierre de Monsabert, ed., *Chartes de l'abbaye de Nouaillé de 678 à 1200, Archives historiques du Poitou* 49 (1936) 104, pp. 172–74; 106, pp. 176–77.

46. Zimmermann, *Papsturkunden* 555, p. 1049: 'petitionibus tuis condescendimus monasteriumque idem ab omnium dominatione excepto Nobiliacensis ecclesie sustollimus, in tantum, ut nec Pictavensi ecclesie, in cuius parrochia est, vel episcopo, qui eidem in tempore prefuerit, aliquod reddere cogatur ... constituimus.'

47. Monsabert, ed., *Nouaillé* 104, pp. 172–74.

48. Monsabert, ed., *Nouaillé* 106, pp. 176–77.

All of this indicates that, rather than understanding the papal privilege as a blow struck against an unwilling bishop in the course of a struggle with a monastery and its papal allies, we must rather look to other, local, contexts for the reasons such privileges were issued and supported by bishops. In this case, the foundation, endowment, and protection of the monastery at Lusignan is but one moment in the ongoing negotiation between William the Great of Aquitaine and his allies (including Bishop Isembert) and Hugh of Lusignan, a conflict recorded at length in the famous *Conventum* issued by Hugh to enumerate his grievances against his lord.[49] Although the *Conventum* was drafted in the 1020s (scholars differ as to the exact date), at roughly the same time as the church was being built, it does not mention Notre-Dame de Lusignan. It is likely, however, that William and Isembert's support for the church represents an attempt at rapprochement in the up-and-down relationship between Hugh and William.[50]

This situation underlines the fact that the relations between the papacy, bishops, and monasteries cannot be explained without taking into account—or even privileging—local circumstances. Furthermore, the examples of both Gilbert at Charroux and Isembert at Lusignan show that bishops were not uniformly hostile to the limitation of their own powers at monasteries. In Aquitaine at least, it seems that they were often willing to cooperate when asked, or even initiated the creation of a papal privilege. In a final example of such activity, Bishop Hildegar of Limoges (976/7–990) consulted with the canons of his cathedral and with local nobles to establish that the monastery of Uzerche could be excommunicated only in the context of a synod—that is, not by an individual bishop—and that its abbot should be consecrated by the pope and thus be relatively independent of episcopal power, as was the abbot of the nearby monastery of Saint-Martial.[51] Hildegar's family ties may have driven him to grant this exemption for Uzerche:

49. For a critical edition, see George T. Beech, Yves Chauvin, and Georges Pon, eds., *Le Conventum (vers 1030): Un précurseur des premières épopées* (Geneva 1995). On the document and the relations between Hugh and William, see Barthélemy, *L'an mil* 339–54; idem, 'Autour d'un récit de pactes (*Conventum Hugonis*): La seigneurie châtelaine et le féodalisme, en France au XIe siècle,' in *Il feudalismo nell'alto Medioevo, Settimane* 47 (Spoleto 2000) 447–95; George T. Beech, 'The Lord/Dependant (Vassal) Relationship: A Case Study from Aquitaine c. 1030,' *Journal of Medieval History* 24 (1998) 1–30; Susan Reynolds, *Fiefs and Vassals: The Medieval Evidence Reinterpreted* (Oxford 1994) 125–26; Stephen D. White, 'Politics of Fidelity: Hugh of Lusignan and William of Aquitaine,' in *Georges Duby: L'écriture de l'histoire*, ed. Claudie Duhamel-Amado and Guy Lobrichon (Brussels 1996) 223–30.

50. White, 'Politics of Fidelity' 229–30; I also argue this in *Noble Lord, Good Shepherd: Episcopal Power and Piety in Aquitaine, 877–1050* (Leiden 2009) 176–77. Different interpretations of the document are found in Barthélemy, *L'an mil* 342, and Sidney Painter, 'The Lords of Lusignan in the Eleventh and Twelfth Centuries,' *Speculum* 32 (1957) 27–47 at 32–33.

51. Jean-Baptiste Champeval, ed., *Cartulaire de l'abbaye d'Uzerche* (Paris and Tulle 1901) 40,

the viscomital family of Limoges, of which he was a member, had a history of patronizing the monastery.[52] But whether bishops acted out of political dictates, as did Isembert at Lusignan, or family pressure, as did Hildegar at Uzerche, or other (or combined) factors, the fact remains that careful examination of the evidence reveals that local and individual concerns dictated episcopal relations with monasteries, rather than any broad principle.

All the above has refocused attention on local events, and on the power of bishops in helping solicit or grant privileges, rather than on papal power. It would be a mistake, however, to allow a commendable effort to re-ground the solicitation of privileges in local contexts to lead us to lose sight of the importance of the papacy in tenth-century Aquitaine. For the papacy was important, even in this period, when the real efficacy of papal authority was minimal. The fact that the initiative for contact with the papacy usually came from local monasteries, bishops, or patrons illustrates on the one hand that the papacy probably did not have the prestige and authority to interfere where it was not wanted, but also that the idea of the papacy still carried weight, at least among certain monasteries, advocates, and bishops. Some lay patrons of monasteries, for example, seem to have had a penchant for involving the papacy with the houses they founded. The most dramatic such case in Aquitaine is that of Emma of Blois, who became duchess of Aquitaine upon her marriage to Duke William IV Iron-Arm. Emma founded major monasteries both in her natal region at Bourgueil-en-Vallée near the Loire and in her adopted home of Aquitaine at Maillezais. And in both cases Emma, along with other advocates for the houses, pushed for papal recognition and protection.[53] In another such example, Wardradus, a nobleman from the Saintonge and apparently a frequent visitor to Rome, was inspired to build his monastery at Bassac by directions he received from Pope Benedict VIII while in the city. Wardradus then returned years later, in 1017, with his task completed, to request a document of protection for the new community.[54]

pp. 73–75 at 75. The exact status of Saint-Martial is difficult to pin down. The chronicler Bernard Itier refers in an opaque passage to a privilege from Pope John: Bernard Itier, *Chronique*, ed. and trans. Jean-Loup Lemaître (Paris 1998) 11. The extravagant claims for Saint-Martial made in the forgeries of Ademar of Chabannes have also obscured the issue—see below, notes 58–62.

52. See, for example, Champeval, ed., *Cartulaire de l'abbaye d'Uzerche* 31, pp. 60–65; 47, pp. 79–82; 61, pp. 110–11; 134, pp. 154–55; 174, pp. 162–63; 354, p. 208; 444, pp. 251–52; 462, pp. 258–62.

53. For Bourgueil: JL 3940; Zimmermann, *Papsturkunden* 407, pp. 774–77. For Maillezais, where Emma encouraged her son Duke William V to seek papal recognition for the house, see Georges Pon and Yves Chauvin, eds., *La fondation de l'abbaye de Maillezais: Récit du moine Pierre* (La-Roche-sur-Yon 2001) 144–45, 199–206.

54. Zimmermann, *Papsturkunden* 519, pp. 986–87; text in GC volume 2, instrumenta cols. 472–73.

The papacy could, therefore, feature in real documents requested by Aquitanians to support their efforts to establish religious houses. But as we saw at the opening of this essay, the papacy also figures in Aquitanian forgeries; that is, even when the papacy was not actually involved, pious and canny Aquitanians sometimes sought to invoke the idea of the papacy. The forged papal privilege for Saint-Cyprien claims that Frotier sent legates to the pope, asking that he confirm the status of the newly rebuilt monastery.[55] The pope responded by stipulating that the monks should be left to serve God without being troubled by anyone, and that no one could claim any obedience from them, except for a limited number of prayers for private individuals and for 'the congregation of Saint Peter'—presumably the cathedral of Poitiers. We do not know the circumstances in which this charter came to be. Perhaps Frotier sent legates to the pope requesting a privilege, and, receiving a negative response or no response, decided to manufacture the desired document. Or perhaps he did not even send a request, believing that while the document itself was valuable, it did not need to be genuine, because any aid for Saint-Cyprien was more likely to come from the existence of the charter rather than from any direct intervention from Rome.[56] That he bothered to have the document created, however it occurred, suggests that having a sign of papal approval—genuine or false—was valuable in Aquitaine in the 930s. It is clear from other charters that Aquitanian religious houses used documents to defend their properties and rights in court cases, and Frotier may have thought that a papal privilege would provide such protection for Saint-Cyprien.[57] The fact that the privilege's author took few pains to make it resemble a genuine papal decree suggests relatively little concern for discovery of the falsehood. Unlike certain other papal privileges (genuine and forged) for Poitevin monasteries, such as that of John XIX for Lusignan or Benedict VII for Charroux, this document did not specifically curtail the rights of bishops over Saint-Cyprien, although presumably bishops were included in the general prohibition against imposing obligations on the monastery.

A final and dramatic example of the forged invocation of papal authority comes in the substantial dossier created by Ademar of Chabannes to assert the apostolicity of the local patron saint of Limoges, Martial. Ademar's campaign of forgery, begun in the wake of his spectacular failure to

55. Zimmermann, *Papsturkunden* 63, pp. 105–6.

56. It is also possible that this privilege was created at a later time, when a relationship with the papacy might yield more concrete results. Zimmermann and others, however, have been convinced that the forgery does indeed date to the reign of Frotier II.

57. See, for example, *Saint-Cyprien* 184, pp. 118–19.

convince his contemporaries of Martial's exalted status, sought instead to persuade future generations.[58] To this end, Ademar composed a voluminous dossier of documents, including a *procès-verbal* of the Council of Limoges 1031, a series of sermons, and an exchange of letters between Bishop Jordan of Limoges and successive popes Benedict VIII and John XIX.[59] The first letter purported to show Jordan writing to Benedict to argue for the lesser status of Martial as a confessor.[60] The second saw John XIX responding to Jordan and asserting in ringing tones the apostolicity of the saint.[61] Scholars have concluded that the papacy probably had no actual involvement whatsoever in these events, but these forgeries from the 1030s make the same point as Frotier's from the 930s: in certain situations, Aquitanians thought it beneficial to be able to wield signs of papal approval for a community or a cause. And indeed, in Ademar's case, the papal documents did help his position: the success of the campaign for Martial's apostolicity was taken for granted until late nineteenth- and twentieth-century scholars uncovered the truth about Ademar's machinations.[62]

In conclusion, the evidence from Aquitaine supports the scholarly challenges to the neatness of Jean-François Lemarignier's model of papal relations with bishops and monasteries in Europe from the late ninth to the mid-eleventh century. In southwestern France the papacy was not consistently in alliance with monasteries against a hostile episcopate. Rather, founders, abbots, patrons, and bishops thought it advisable on occasion—often spurred by local circumstances—to involve the papacy in the protection of a house. Bishops in particular often consented to the limitation of their own power at such communities. It was rare that the papacy imposed its will in the region without solicitation by one of these parties. And yet, despite what later popes might see as a regrettable lack of power, the idea of the papacy and the desire to harness its prestige and authority for a particular community or cause were still strong.

58. Richard Landes, *Relics, Apocalypse, and the Deceits of History: Ademar of Chabannes, 989–1034* (Cambridge, MA 1995) 3–7, followed by detailed analysis in chapters 11–13.

59. The council proceedings are printed in Mansi 19.507–48. Both the account of the council and Ademar's sermons are found in BN lat. 2469. For a description of the manuscript, see Daniel Callahan, 'The Sermons of Adémar of Chabannes and the Cult of St. Martial of Limoges,' RB 86 (1976) 251–95 at 263–64; see also Michael Frassetto, 'The Art of Forgery: The Sermons of Ademar of Chabannes and the Cult of St. Martial of Limoges,' *Comitatus* 26 (1995) 11–26.

60. Jean Becquet, ed., *Actes des évêques de Limoges des origines à 1197* (Documents, études et répertoires publiés par l'Institut de recherche et d'histoire des textes 56; Paris 1999) 13, pp. 39–42.

61. Zimmermann, *Papsturkunden* 591, pp. 1114–17.

62. On the scholarly discovery of Ademar's forgery, see Landes, *Relics, Apocalypse* 14–16; Jones, 'Discovering the Aquitanian Church' 84 n. 10 and 86.

Given the papacy's relative lack of effective authority in this period, what gave it this continued appeal? Why did Frotier II of Poitiers and other clergy forge papal privileges or refer to papal authority? This is a difficult question to answer, given the relative scarcity of sources. It is possible that Aquitanians wished to be associated with a successor of Peter, although they more often seemed inclined to see a local bishop in that role. Any bishop could pronounce excommunication, so they did not need to turn to the popes to invoke that punishment, although papal anathema may have been thought to carry special weight. Tenth-century clergy and others may have hearkened back to an idealized Carolingian past, when the papacy had special connections with the Frankish lands; if this is the case, however, they expressed it only obliquely, as when they adopted the form of Carolingian-era privileges. In the end, perhaps the best hypothesis is that the papacy offered authority that was on the one hand real and useful and on the other comfortably distant; an Aquitanian house or bishop could invoke papal authority against their enemies but was unlikely to find it interfering when it was not wanted.

PETER LANDAU

9 The Origin of Civil Procedure

Treatises in Durham during the Twelfth Century

The twelfth century was a period of revival of jurisprudence in Italy for the two fields of Roman law and Canon law, later labeled as *Jus commune*. Mainly fostered by contemporary canonists, this revival soon spread to other parts of Europe outside Italy, so to southern and northern France, to some parts of Germany as for example Cologne, and also to England. The Anglo-Norman realm of King Henry II had a remarkable number of canonists among its leading figures and is outstanding for its activity in collecting papal decretals after 1150, thus preserving one of the most precious heritages of sources in legal history from the Middle Ages.[1]

Anglo-Norman canonists wrote numerous glosses to the *Decretum Gratiani* and composed some remarkable commentaries or *summae* on the *Decretum*. The most important is the *Summa Lipsiensis*, preserved by manuscripts in Leipzig and Rouen, written around 1186 by a man with the strange name or nickname Rodoicus Modicipassus, who later on taught in Bologna and died as *praecentor* in the French episcopal city of Sens around 1204.[2]

Rodoicus was not only a leader among the canonists, probably even the most original English scholar in that field during the Middle Ages—he was also the author of a famous *ordo iudiciarius* with the incipit *Olim edebatur*

1. Cf. the fundamental study by Stephan Kuttner and Eleanor Rathbone, 'Anglo-Norman Canonists of the twelfth century,' *Traditio* 7 (1949/51), 279–358—also in Stephan Kuttner, *Gratian and the Schools of Law 1140–1234* (London 1983). No. VIII. For the School of Cologne cf. now Peter Landau, 'Die Kölner Kanonistik des 12. Jahrhunderts' (Kölner Rechtsgeschichtliche Vorträge H. 1, Badenweiler 2008).

2. For Rodoicus Modicipassus cf. Peter Landau, 'Rodoicus Modicipassus—Verfasser der Summa Lipsiensis?' ZRG Kan. Abt. 92 (2006), 340–54. Edition of the *Summa Lipsiensis* (D. 1–100) by Rudolf Weigand, Peter Landau, and Waltraud Kozur, *Summa « Omnis qui iuste iudicat » sive Lipsiensis*, T. I (MIC, Ser. A, vol. 7, Città del Vaticano 2007).

dating from around 1180. It is one of the earliest textbooks on civil procedure written for the use of canonists.[3]

Procedural law had never been a special field for studies in Roman antiquity, because procedure was interwoven with substantive law in that legal system as well as in the literature of Roman jurists preserved by the *Digest*. But the specific circumstances of ecclesiastical courts in the twelfth century, when old customs in procedure were replaced by new institutions taken over from Roman law, required sufficient information concerning those rules from reliable textbooks that could be used without a comprehensive study of the *Corpus Iuris Civilis*. These early textbooks were mainly written for the practice of ecclesiastical judges, not for lectures in classrooms. Thus it is not surprising that the earliest treatises in that field were not written in Bologna, but rather in other centers of legal learning in Europe.

It is true, nonetheless, that Bulgarus, the leader among the famous four doctors of Bologna, wrote a treatise on rules of procedure around 1130. However, he wrote it as a letter to Chancellor Aimeric of the Roman curia, not for his students.[4] Bulgarus's letter was later taken over in some compendia of Roman law, but it cannot be called an *ordo iudiciorum* in the strict sense of the word. The first textbook of Roman procedural law written for the classroom in Bologna was the *Ordo iudiciarius* by Ricardus Anglicus, the famous English canonist from Lincoln, who taught at Bologna after 1190.[5] This fact was known to Johannes Andreae when he composed a short history of procedural literature one and a half century later in 1346.[6]

Before 1190 we have only *ordines iudiciorum*, dealing exclusively with Roman law, and *ordines iudiciarii*, dealing mainly with Canon law and also with Roman law, all of which were written outside Italy.[7] Research

3. Rodoicus as author of the *ordo* "Olim" was discovered by André Gouron, 'Qui a écrit l'ordo "Olim edebatur"?' *Initium* 8 (2003), 65–84, repr. in André Gouron, *Pionniers du droit occidental au Moyen Age* (Aldershot 2006), no. XIII; for manuscripts and editions of "*Olim edebatur*" cf. Linda Fowler-Magerl, *Ordo iudiciorum vel ordo iudiciarius* (Ius commune. Sonderhefte 19, Frankfurt/Main 1984) 73–80.

4. For manuscripts and editions of Bulgarus's letter see Linda Fowler-Magerl, *Ordo iudiciorum*, 35–40. Fowler-Magerl is pointing out that Bulgarus did not create a new type of legal literature, but wrote a letter called by him the *preludia* of a Summa (p. 38).

5. For manuscripts and editions of the *ordo Editio sine scriptis* by Ricardus Anglicus see Linda Fowler-Magerl, *Ordo iudiciorum*, 114–19. For the Ordines of the twelfth century cf. now also Peter Landau, 'Die Anfänge der Prozessrechtswissenschaft in der Kanonistik des 12. Jahrhunderts,' in Orazio Condorelli, Franck Roumy, and Matthias Schmoeckel, eds., *Der Einfluss der Kanonistik auf die europäische Rechtskultur*, vol. 1: Zivil- und Zivilprozessrecht (Norm und Struktur 37/1, Köln etc. 2009), 7–23; here p. 19 for Ricardus Anglicus.

6. The text of Johannes Andreae was printed by Friedrich Carl von Savigny, *Geschichte des römischen Rechts im Mittelalter*, vol. 3 (2nd ed. Heidelberg 1850, repr. Darmstadt 1956), 635–39.

7. A survey of these Ordines is given in my article 'Die Anfänge der Prozessrechtswissenschaft.'

in those ordines can now be based on the essential *Repertorium* of Linda Fowler-Magerl[8] and the remarkable discoveries of André Gouron.[9] In a recent paper I presented at a conference in the Villa Vigoni in 2008 I could enumerate eight *ordines* written in the Anglo-Norman school, seven composed by other authors in France—among them three from Provence—and four originating in Germany, altogether a remarkable production of nineteen *ordines* during approximately thirty years.[10] The oldest German *ordo* is the *Rhetorica ecclesiastica*,[11] a textbook from Hildesheim from around 1161, probably written by Bertram of Metz, the most important author of the Cologne school of canon law around 1170.[12] The earliest English *ordo* seems to be the famous *Ulpianus de edendo*, an *ordo* discovered in the late eighteenth century, and immediately vividly discussed because it was assumed by some scholars that it might have been written in antiquity by Ulpian himself.[13]

Legal historians of the nineteenth century soon found out that *Ulpianus de edendo* had its origin in the twelfth century. Several editions were published—the last and best by Gustav Hänel, the great scholar in Leipzig, in 1838.[14] This edition is somewhat rare in public libraries and has been studied in detail only by a small number of scholars in the last two centuries. *Ulpianus de edendo* is known today from 15 manuscripts—the *ordo* is mentioned also in some medieval library catalogues. The manuscripts we have are found in England, Belgium, France, Germany, and Switzerland.[15] The distribution of manuscripts makes an origin in England or Northern France rather probable. The *ordo* has a systematic division in titles influenced by the *Codex Iustinianus*. In the title *De plus petitionibus* we read: *Plus autem*

8. Fowler-Magerl, *Ordines iudiciorum* and idem, *Ordines iudiciarii and Libelli de Ordine iudiciorum* (Typologie des Sources du Moyen Age occidental, Fasc. 63, A-III.1, Turnhout 1994).

9. Cf. Gouron, 'Olim edebatur,' and idem, 'L'entourage de Louis VII face aux droits savants: Giraud de Bourges et son ordo,' *Bibliothèque de l'École des Chartes* 146 (1988) 5–29; repr. in Gouron, *Droit et coutume en France au XIIe et XIIIe siècles* (Aldershot 1993), no. XII. André Gouron, 'Une école de canonistes anglais à Paris: maître Walter et ses disciples (vers 1170),' *Journal des Savants* (2000), 47–72; repr. in idem, *Pionniers*, no. VI.

10. Cf. my article, 'Die Anfänge der Prozessrechtswissenschaft.'

11. For the "Rhetorica ecclesiastica" cf. Fowler-Magerl, *Ordo iudiciorum*, 45–56; also Peter Landau, 'Die *"Rhetorica ecclesiastica"*—Deutschlands erstes juristisches Lehrbuch im Mittelalter,' in *Summe-Glosse-Kommentar*, ed. F. Theisen and W. E. Voss (Osnabrücker Schriften zur Rechtsgeschichte 2.1, Osnabrück 2000), 125–39.

12. Landau, 'Kölner Kanonistik,' especially 17–18 and 26–29.

13. The first discussion on the origin of *Ulpianus de edendo* can be found in G. Hugo, *Civilistisches Magazin* 1 (1790).

14. Gustav Hänel, ed., *Incerti auctoris ordo iudiciorum* (Leipzig 1838).

15. List of the manuscripts Fowler-Magerl, *Ordo iudiciorum*, 65–66.

IIII modis petitur ... loco, si hic petat quis, quod Parisius solvi debet.[16] Thus it is a *plus petitio* to have a debt paid in Paris—Paris must be a remote city for the author. This fact nearly excludes an origin of the *ordo* in Northern France. England is much more probable as the country of its composition.

When could the *ordo* have been written? A text from it was quoted by the *Summa Parisiensis* on Gratian in 1168[17]—it therefore must be earlier than that year. On the other hand, the author is familiar with the existence of the *Decretum Gratiani*. In his section *De appellationibus* he writes: 'Quandocumque quis et quoties voluerit appellare, poterit in decimum diem per eam, quae obtinet Decretorum sanctionem.'[18] This very general citation points to a period when the *Decretum* was already known, but not yet studied in detail or used as a handbook. We can assume that this slight knowledge of Gratian could be expected in England during the fifties of the twelfth century.

In the literature dealing with *Ulpianus de edendo* we find hints of connections between the *ordo* and the famous *Liber Pauperum* of Vacarius.[19] But any conjecture regarding a connection is almost negated by modern research on Vacarius. This pioneer of Roman law in England wrote his major work after 1170—he might have been influenced by *Ulpianus de edendo,* but the *ordo* did not depend on the *Liber Pauperum.*[20]

At the moment one may suppose that the *ordo* was written in England between 1150 and 1160. Is there any possibility that we might learn more about the *ordo* and its origin? In manuscript Harley 2355 of the British Library we find a supplement to *Ulpianus de edendo*—some formulae with the incipit *Nunc primo nobis adversarius* on fol. 8v–9v of the codex. These formulae are connected to the *ordo* without any separation. They were edited first by C. T. Cooper in the first complete edition of *Ulpianus de edendo* and later also by Hänel under the title *Accessio ex Codice Harleiano.*[21] The formulae are also found in a manuscript at Evreux in Normandy,[22]

16. Hänel, *Incerti auctoris,* 20.

17. Cf. Fowler-Magerl, *Ordo iudiciorum,* 67. Fowler-Magerl indicates as date: probably before 1160.

18. Hänel, *Incerti auctoris,* p. 51. The ordo refers to C. 2, q. 6, c. 28.

19. Fowler-Magerl, *Ordo iudiciorum,* 67 sees connections between *Ulpianus de edendo* and the activity of Vacarius in England.

20. For Vacarius and the date of his *Liber Pauperum* cf. now Peter Landau, 'The Origins of Legal Science in England in the Twelfth Century; Lincoln, Oxford and the Career of Vacarius,' in *Readers, Texts and Compilers in the Earlier Middle Ages, Studies in Medieval Canon Law in Honour of Linda Fowler-Magerl,* ed. Martin Brett and Kathleen G. Cushing (Aldershot 2009), 165–82.

21. Hänel, *Incerti auctoris,* 54–56.

22. Fowler-Magerl, *Ordo iudiciorum,* 156.

but there without any connection to *Ulpianus de edendo*. The final formula with the title *Coram summo iudice*, which I will discuss in this paper, is not included in the Evreux manuscript or other manuscripts of *Ulpianus de edendo*—the Harley manuscript is its exclusive source.

The text of *Coram summo iudice* refers to a specific lawsuit regarding a royal chapel that was at the disposal of King David of Scotland. King David had conferred a dignity together with a portion of the chapel to the lord of the advocate in this lawsuit—this lord (*dominus meus*) is obviously the plaintiff. The lord, who had been in possession of the chapel for some time, had lost it by the intervention of an archdeacon of the same diocese (*archidiaconus noster*) who had expelled the plaintiff from the chapel with the help of money. The archdeacon is called a contemptor of law, a possessor in bad faith, and a simonist. The former possessor claims to have been confirmed in his rights to the chapel by papal authority. The bad archdeacon had acted according to the formula without any regard of the *ordo iudiciarius* and defied not only the lord of the advocate, but also the pope and the universal church. The advocate claims justice for his lord from a higher judge, who is himself subject to an even higher authority, who could ask for a response by him as an inferior judge. King David of Scotland, who had been responsible for giving a portion of the chapel to the plaintiff, had died in the meantime.[23] The entire formula *Coram summo iudice* seems to refer to a real lawsuit. Who are the persons involved in it, when did it happen and in which diocese?

There can be no doubt that we are dealing with an ecclesiastical lawsuit; the *summus iudex* must be a bishop subordinated to the pope. As *summus iudex* the judge cannot be an ordinary bishop, but should be rather a

23. Hänel, *Incerti auctoris*, 56: Coram summo iudice. Tutela publici iuris ad id in medio sita est, ut iustis possessoribus iura eorum immutilata conserventur. Sollicitudinis ergo vestrae curam respicit providere religiose et sancte, ut nemini ius suum detrahatur, quia vos publici iuris tutorem creavit ecclesia. Archidiaconus quidam noster contemptor legis et iuris publici dominum meum, pro quo necessitatem standi suscepi, a quadam dignitate, quam de manu *dd.* regis, inclitae recordationis et divae memoriae, gerendam susceperat, mediantibus sordibus pecuniarum expulit et portionem capellae domini regis, in cuius persona dominus meus solenniter et canonice creatus est, mediantibus pecuniis sibi usurpavit illicite contra ordinem iudiciarium et citra omnem causae disceptationem et eam possidet tamquam malae fidei possessor et praedo simonialis. Hanc praedictam portionem possedit dominus meus sub apostolica confirmatione et sub pia domini papae munificentia. Archidiaconus vero noster piis privilegiis domini papae et sacris annotationibus illius pecuniarum sordibus obviavit. Protestantur vero leges et iura, sacrilegii instar esse divinis sub aliquibus administrationibus obviare beneficiis. Hanc iniuriam irrogavit archidiaconus noster summo pontifici et domino meo et universae ecclesiae. Expetit ergo dominus meus, pro quo verba facio, ut ei super his exhibeatis iustitiam. Et scitote, quod opportunius erat vobis in foro vestro libera frui potestate iudicandi, quam alibi subire necessitatem respondendi.

papal legate. The plaintiff, who got the chapel and a certain dignity from the king, could have been a bishop himself, because the adversary is called *archidiaconus noster,* our archdeacon. The advocate seems to be a man trained in canon law. The royal chapel is under the authority of the king of Scotland, so the lawsuit might have happened in Scotland. If it is connected to the composition of *Ulpianus de edendo,* we could find in our treatise the first testimony of Scottish jurisprudence in history.

Did the lawsuit happen in the diocese of St. Andrews or perhaps in Glasgow? Could the plaintiff even have been Walter de Bidun, chancellor for the kings of Scotland between 1150 and 1161? Is it possible that the archdeacon was a cleric named Ingram, who was archdeacon of Glasgow before he became chancellor of Scotland in 1162?[24] But we also have to consider the possibility that our lawsuit did not occur in Scotland at all, but rather in some part of northern England belonging to Scotland during the reign of King David. The county of Northumberland with the episcopal city of Durham had been transferred in 1139 by King Stephen of England to King David of Scotland for David's son Henry. Malcolm IV then had to cede Northumberland to England again in 1157.[25]

Under the circumstances we have to take into account that our lawsuit may have occurred in the diocese of Durham some time after King David's death. Durham is well known as an early center of canonistic learning with at least three glossed manuscripts of the *Decretum* dating to the twelfth century;[26] not to be forgotten is a comprehensive decretal collection that was analyzed by Walther Holtzmann and published by Christopher and Mary Cheney in 1979.[27] It would not be surprising to find in Durham a canonist who as early as the fifties had some knowledge of the *ordo iudiciarius.*

24. Cf. G. W. S. Barrow, *The Acts of Malcolm IV King of Scots 1153–1165* (Edinburgh 1960) 28–29. I have to thank Martin Brett (Cambridge) for his kind assistance.

25. Cf. Barrow, s.v. 'Northumberland,' Lex.MA 6 (1993) 1255.

26. Description of those manuscripts by Rudolf Weigand in his *Die Glossen zum Dekret Gratians. Teil III und IV* (Studia Gratiana 26, Rome 1991), 731–36. The manuscripts are: Durham Cathedral Library C.II.1., C.III.1., and C. IV.1.

27. Cf. for the *Collectio Dunelmensis prima* (MS Durham, Cathedral Library C.III.1) Walther Holtzmann and C. R. and M. G. Cheney, *Studies in the Collections of Twelfth-Century Decretals* (MIC, Ser.B., vol. 3, Città del Vaticano 1979), 75–99. Cf. also Charles Duggan, 'A Durham Canonical Manuscript of the Late Twelfth Century,' *Studies in Church History* 2 (1965), 179–85; repr. in idem, *Canon Law in Medieval England* (London 1982), no. VI. The collection of the decretals from the twelfth century is preceded in this manuscript by extracts from Burchard's *Decretum* and by a mixture of patristic excerpts, conciliar canons, and early papal decretals. The whole collection seems to have been assembled in northern England, probably as an addition to an exemplar with an appendix to Gratian brought from Italy. (Hereafter, WH = Walther Holtzmann)

In 1153 Hugh Puiset from the family of the counts of Blois became bishop of Durham and stayed there until his death in 1195.[28] He was experienced in canon law and received at least 13 decretals from the popes after 1160.[29] He had been archdeacon of Winchester before he came to Durham, encountering in the beginning much opposition in his new diocese. In the beginning of Hugh's pontificate the diocese had two archdeacons, one archdeacon for Durham and another one for Northumberland.[30] A struggle between Bishop Hugh and one of his archdeacons can be imagined between 1155 and 1160, and it is conceivable that Bishop Hugh brought the lawsuit to Archbishop Roger of York for decision as papal legate.

We know nothing about the outcome of this lawsuit, but I am inclined to locate it in the diocese of Durham, because I doubt that canonistic learning already existed either at St. Andrews or in Glasgow shortly after the death of King David. It may be impossible to conjecture who might have been the advocate who framed the formula *Coram summo iudice*. Being no specialist in British medieval ecclesiastical history I can only offer a tentative guess. During the years 1154 to 1158/59 a certain Absalon was prior of Durham cathedral.[31] According to the sources he was educated abroad, perhaps in France or even in Italy. Absalon could have had an education that would enable him to use the terminology of *ordo iudiciarius*. Might he even have written an *ordo iudiciarius* himself?

I return to *Ulpianus de edendo*. The formula connected to our *ordo* points to a legal center in northern England that was under Scottish domi-

28. For the life and career of Hugo Puiset cf. F. V. Scammell, *Hugh du Puiset, bishop of Durham* (Cambridge 1956); also John Hudson, s.v. 'Puiset, Hughes du,' Lex.MA 7 (1995) 322.

29. The decretals sent to Hugo Puiset are (1) WH 33 = Sang. 2.1.15, ed. H. Singer, 'Neue Beiträge über die Dekretalensammlungen vor und nach Bernhard von Pavia,' *Sitzungsberichte*. Ak. Wien 171/1 (1913), 132–133; (2) WH 38 = Font.2.4, ed. Walther Holtzmann, Papsturkunden in England 3 (Abh. Göttingen, Dritte Folge. 33, Göttingen 1952), 385 (no. 252); (3) WH 83 = Sang. 3.15.8, ed. Singer, 170–171.; (4) WH 130 = Font.2.7., ed. Holtzmann, *Papsturkunden* 3, p. 298 (no. 156); (5) WH 207 (JL 13868) = Sang.5.10.23, ed. Singer p. 204s.; (6) WH 404 = Bridl. 152, ed. Stanley Chodorow and Charles Duggan, *Decretales ineditae saeculi XII* (MIC, Ser. B, vol. 4, Città del Vaticano 1979), 130–31. (no. 76); (7) WH 508 (JL 17620) = X 3.20.23; (8) WH 618 (JL 11836) = Sang.3.18.8, ed. P.L.200, p. 703; (9) WH 748 = Claustr. 150, ed. F. Schönsteiner, *Die Collectio Claustroneoburgensis*, Jahrbuch des Stiftes Klosterneuburg II (Wien etc. 1909), 70s; (10) WH 762= 1 Abr. App. 20, ed. Singer, p. 397, n. 39; (11) WH 823 (JL 13869) = 1 Comp.1.9.5; (12) WH 846 (JL 14365) = X 2.22.4; (13) WH 999 (JL 13870) = X 2.28.15. [Holtzmann, Unpublished Register of Papal decretals of the Twelfth Century, http://www.Irz.de/~SKIMCL/index_e.htm]

30. The system of two archdeacons existed at least until 1158—cf. H. S. Offler, 'The Early Archdeacons in the Diocese of Durham,' *Transactions of the Architectural and Archaeological Society of Durham and Northumberland* 10 (1962), 182–207; also in idem, *North of the Tees* (Aldershot 1996), no. III.

31. Cf. Scammell (n. 28), 70.

nation for some time. I could find only the town of St. Cuthbert, Durham, as such a center. If the *ordo* had any connection to Prior Absalon, it must have been written before 1159, perhaps between 1157, when Durham had come back to England, and 1159. During these years Gratian's *Decretum* might have reached northern England without having been studied in detail. These years, therefore, are the most plausible period for what is most likely the first treatise on legal procedure in European history. *Ulpianus de edendo* is also a precious testimony to the ingenuity of English canonists in the twelfh century.

I want to give at least one example of this ingenuity at the end of this paper. Legal historians know that appeal according to Roman law could be lodged only after a sentence. But during the twelfth century canon law developed the type of appeals to the pope preceding a sentence, with the possibility to consult beforehand the highest judge of the universal church. Many decretals in this period are consultation decretals written during ongoing lawsuits. I refer for these facts to a recent paper by Anne Duggan in the volume dedicated to Martin Brett.[32] In the *ordo Ulpianus de edendo* we read: 'Solent autem plerumque iudices haesitare super sententia promulganda, et causam ad maiorem iudicem, si quid inopinatum emerserit, referre. Quod si fecerint, consultationem vel relationem fecisse dicentur, quae una species est appellationis.'[33]

The author of *Ulpianus de edendo*, whoever he was, gave us the first definition of *appellatio ante sententiam*, appeal before the sentence, indeed a juristic discovery.

32. Anne L. Duggan, '*De consultationibus*: The Role of Episcopal Consultation in the Shaping of Canon Law in the Twelfth Century,' in *Bishops, Texts and the Use of Canon Law around 1100. Essays in Honour of Martin Brett*, ed. Bruce C. Brasington and Kathleen G. Cushing (Aldershot 2008), 191–240.

33. Hänel, *Incerti auctoris*, 49.

PART TWO ⟡ RELIGION

CHARLES R. SHRADER

10 The Surviving Manuscripts of the Eucharistic Treatises of Heriger of Lobbes

994. Florebant hoc tempore in scientia litterarum in Lothgaringia Herigerus abbas Lobiensis, Adelboldus episcopus Vultrajectensis; in Francia Fulbertus episcopus Carnotensis, Abbo abbas Floriacensis....[1]

Thus did Sigebert of Gembloux include Abbot Heriger of Lobbes among the great scholars of the late tenth century. Heriger's reputation was fully merited by his important contributions in such varied fields as history, hagiography, mathematics, chronology, and hymnology. He also wrote two separate but related treatises on the Eucharist, both of which support a realist interpretation of the sacrament. No fewer than fifteen medieval manuscripts containing either or both of the two treatises survive and bear witness to the spread of Abbot Heriger's ideas as far as England and the Alps.

Heriger of Lobbes (940–1007)

Heriger was born at Moerbeke in eastern Flanders shortly after 940 and entered the Benedictine monastery of St. Peter at Lobbes on the Sambre River around 955.[2] He rose to become head of the monastic school at Lobbes under Abbot Folquin (965–990) and formed a number of students who later became important men. By 980, his excellence as a teacher and scholar brought him to the notice of the famous Bishop Notker of Liège (972–1008). The bishop and the monk became such close literary collabo-

1. Sigebert of Gembloux, *Chronicon*, MGH SS 4.353.

2. HLF 7.194, and Godefroid Kurth, 'Heriger,' *Biographie nationale de Belgique*, 9 (Bruxelles 1886–1887) 245.

rators that it is now difficult to determine the authorship of several works on which they apparently combined their efforts.[3]

In addition to scholarly collaboration, Heriger was also charged with important missions of confidence concerning the administration of Notker's diocese and involving political matters, both in Lotharingia and in Italy, connected with Notker's role as an important official of the Ottonian empire.[4] Notker also involved Heriger in the revival of the cathedral school at Liège, and no small part of the prestige that the school achieved must be attributed to Heriger's learning and organizational ability. Among his most famous pupils were Burchard, bishop of Worms and a renowned canonist; Adalbold, bishop of Utrecht; the abbot and canonist Olbert of Gembloux; the bishop and canonist Wazo of Liège; Hugo, abbot of Lobbes; and the reformer and abbot Theodoric of St. Hubert.[5]

At the death of Abbot Folquin in 990, Heriger became abbot of Lobbes. He extended the claustrum walls, constructed a chapel in honor of St. Benedict and an altar for St. Thomas, and enriched the abbey's store of ornaments, of which he also made an inventory.[6] He died at Liège on 31 October 1007 and was buried at Lobbes, where he was later revered as a saint and where miracles were said to have occurred at the site of his tomb.[7]

Despite the burden of his numerous duties as confidant of Bishop Notker, *scholasticus* at Liège, and abbot of Lobbes, Heriger produced a large number of works on a wide range of subjects. Among the writings that can definitively be assigned to his authorship are a history of the bishops of Liège, two treatises on mathematics and two on chronology, several hagiographical pieces, and a number of hymns and anthems.[8]

3. Kurth, 'Heriger' 246.

4. Continuator of the *Gesta abbatum Lobbiensium*, MGH SS 21.309.

5. Cora Elizabeth Lutz, *Schoolmasters of the Tenth Century* (Hamden 1977) 101.

6. Continuator of the *Gesta abbatum Lobbiensium*, MGH SS 21.309.

7. Ibid.; *Annales Laubienses et Leodiensium*, MGH SS 4.181; and Kurth, 'Heriger' 246.

8. The *Gesta episcoporum Tungrensium et Leodiensium* has been edited by Rudolf Koepke in MGH SS 7.134–94, and the *Regulae de numerorum abaci rationibus* and the *Ratio numerorum abaci secundum Herigerum* by Nikolai Bubnov in *Gerberti postea Silvestri II papas opera mathematica (972–1003)* (Berlin 1899) 208–25. For the chronological works, see A. Cordoliani, 'Abbon de Fleury, Hériger de Lobbes, et Gerland de Besançon sur l'ère de l'Incarnation de Denys le Petit,' RHE 44 (1949) 471–72. The *Epistola ad quondam Hugonem monachum* is edited in PL 139.1129–36. Heriger's other chronological work, the *Dialogus de dissonantia ecclesiae de adventu Domini*, is lost. For Heriger's hagiographical works, see nos. 335, 1184, 2251, 3733, 4331, 4700–4706, 7115–16, and 8046 in *Bibliotheca hagiographica Latina antiquae et mediae aetatis*, ed. Socii Bollandiani (2 vols. Bruxelles 1898–1911). Heriger's musical works have also been lost.

Heriger's Treatises on the Eucharist

Heriger also composed two works on the question of the Real Presence in the Eucharist, both of which support a realist interpretation of the sacrament against the symbolism of earlier writers such as Paschasius Radbertus and the extreme views of the little-known Stercoranist heretics, who held that it was absurd to believe that the actual Body of Christ should be ingested, digested, and expelled in such crude fashion.[9] Heriger's treatises are important witnesses to the continued vitality of Eucharistic controversy in the tenth century and mark the transition in the orthodox position from one of symbolism in the ninth century to that of realism in the eleventh.[10] Heriger's Eucharistic treatises continued to be copied long after his death and thus a brief description of the fifteen extant codices containing his compilations on the Eucharist, and a discussion of their origins and physical transmission, may be of value to understanding the spread of Eucharistic realism and opposition to the Stercoranist heresy during the eleventh and twelfth centuries.

The *Exaggeratio plurimorum auctorum de corpore et sanguine Domini*, a relatively short compilation of extracts from the writings of the Church Fathers, was apparently the first of Heriger's Eucharistic treatises to be composed. Both Sigebert of Gembloux and the Continuator of the *Gesta abbatum Lobbiensium* attest that Heriger wrote such a treatise.[11] Indeed, item no. 116 in the 1049 catalogue of the library of St. Peter at Lobbes is 'Heriger abbatis exaggeratio plurimorum auctorum de corpore et sanguine domini vol. I Ratranni de corpore et sanguine domini ad Karolum regem lib. I. Eiusdem de predestinatione dei ad eundem lib. II.'[12]

Usually identified as 'Omelia Eusebii de corpore et sanguine Domini,' the *Exaggeratio* indeed begins with a passage from Eusebius's *Omelia de corpore et sanguine Domini*: 'Magnitudo celestium beneficiorum angustiae ...', and ends with a passage from the eighteenth sermon on Psalm 118 of St. Ambrose: '... qui vitam dat huic mundo.' The work, which remains unedited, has been attributed to Paschasius Radbertus by Jan N. Bakhuizen Van den

9. Charles R. Shrader, 'The False Attribution of an Eucharistic Tract to Gerbert of Aurillac,' *Mediaeval Studies* 35 (1973) 178–204, and Joseph Lebon, 'Sur la doctrine eucharistique d'Hériger de Lobbes,' *Studia Mediaevalia in Honor of R. J. Martin* (Bruges 1948), 61–84.

10. Ernst Dümmler, 'Zum Heriger von Lobbes,' NA 26 (1901), 755–59.

11. Sigebert of Gembloux, *De scriptoribus ecclesiasticis*, c. 127, PL 160.578, and the Continuator of the *Gesta abbatum Lobbiensium*, MGH SS 21.309.

12. Henri Omont, 'Catalogue des manuscripts de l'abbaye de Lobbes,' *Révue des Bibliothèques* 1 (1891) 11. This book is now Gent, Rijksuniv. 909.

Brink, primarily on the basis of Bernard Bischoff's dating of Gent, Rijksuniv. 909, as being of the first half of s. X.[13] However, Bischoff appears to address only the two Ratramnus texts, which were written in s. IX, and I am thus unconvinced by Bakhuizen Van den Brink's arguments, particularly in view of the convincing arguments for Heriger's authorship put forward by Dümmler, Morin, and Lebon.[14] In any event, nothing would have precluded Heriger from including in the *Exaggeratio* the text of *auctoritates* used earlier by Paschasius Radbertus. Therefore, I retain the traditional attribution of the work to Heriger pending more conclusive evidence to the contrary.

The *Dicta Herigeri abbatis de corpore et sanguine Domini* is a more extensive collection of patristic *auctoritates* in favor of Eucharistic realism, and appears to have been compiled subsequent to the *Exaggeratio* and with the earlier work at hand.[15] The *Dicta*, which begins 'Sicut ante nos dixit quidem sapiens ...' and ends 'Liquet igitur non obnoxium secessui esse,' was first published as an anonymous work by Louis Cellot in 1655.[16] It was later erroneously attributed to Gerbert of Aurillac (Pope Sylvester II) by Bernard Pez.[17] The *Dicta* is somewhat more sophisticated than the *Exaggeratio*, displaying both greater depth of analysis and an innovative use of the dialectic as well as of *auctoritates*.[18]

The Surviving Manuscripts

The *Exaggeratio* today survives in eight manuscripts and the *Dicta* in twelve. Five books contain both texts. The two Heriger texts are most commonly found with other works concerning the Eucharist, notably works of St. Augustine, St. Ambrose, Ratramnus of Corbie, Paschasius Radbertus, Gottschalk of Orbais, Ratherius of Lobbes, and the *Responsio cuiusdam de corpore et sanguine Domini*. Heriger's two treatises are also frequently included in collections of materials bearing on the twelfth-century Eucharistic controversy, including works of Berengar of Tours, Lanfranc of Bec, and Hildebert of Lavardin, among many others. It would thus seem that

13. Ratramnus of Corbie, *De corpore et sanguine domini*, ed. Jan N. Bakhuizen Van den Brink (2nd ed. Amsterdam 1954) 10, and Bernard Bischoff, 'Hadoard und die Klassikerhandschriften aus Corbie,' *Mittelalterliche Studien* 1 (1966) 57.

14. See Dümmler, 'Zum Heriger von Lobbes' 758 and *passim;* Dom Germain Morin, 'Les *Dicta* d'Hériger sur l'Eucharistie,' RB 24 (1908) 1–18; and Lebon, 'Sur la doctrine eucharistique d'Hériger de Lobbes' 62 and *passim.*

15. The edition of the *Dicta Herigeri* prepared by Bernard Pez, *Thesaurus anecdotorum novissimus*, 1, pt. 2 (Augsburg 1721) is reproduced in PL 139.179–88.

16. Louis Cellot, *Historia Gottescalci praedestinatiani* (Paris 1655) 541.

17. Pez, *Thesaurus anecdotorum novissimus*, 1, pt. 2, 133.

18. Josef Geiselmann, *Die Eucharistielehre der Vorscholastik* (Paderborn 1926) 277.

readers valued Heriger's collections of *auctoritates* as useful guides to understanding the proper realist view of the Eucharist and as shields against the increasingly disfavored symbolist view and dangerous heresies such as Stercoranism.

It may be beyond both the available evidence and my limited linguistic skills to construct an accurate *stemma* of the extant Heriger Eucharistic manuscripts. However, the manuscripts themselves offer some important clues as to the probable relationships, and it is thus possible to make some tentative suggestions. There appear to be five main groupings of the surviving manuscripts. I have identified them as Groups A through E.

Group A consists of three books, all of which contain both the *Exaggeratio* and the work of Ratramnus of Corbie entitled *De corpore et sanguine Domini*. The *Exaggeratio* is found complete and alone in two of the manuscripts, and the other contains a truncated version. The earliest copy is now Gent, Bibliotheek van de Rijksuniversiteit, MS 909, a composite manuscript on vellum of 110 folios in quarto format bound in stamped brown calf. Part A (fols. 1–15v) has usually been dated to s. X ex.–XI in. and was written by a single Caroline minuscule hand in single columns with 26–29 lines per page. It contains the *Exaggeratio*, without title, on fols. 1–15. This may well be Heriger's original or a direct copy of it. Indeed, the marginal notes against Ratramnus found on fols. 36v and 41v are thought to be in Heriger's own hand.[19] Part B (fols. 16–56v) contains Ratramnus's *De corpore et sanguine Domini*, and Part C (fols. 57–110v) contains the same author's *De predestinatione Dei*. Parts B and C are said by Bakhuizen Van den Brink to have been written by distinctly different hands at Corbie, ca. 840–80.[20]

The three texts appear to have been bound together before 1049 when the book was listed as no. 116 in a catalogue of Lobbes manuscripts.[21] It also bears on fol. 110v the s. XII inscription: *Liber sancti Petri Lobbiensis ecclesiae*. The book survived several disastrous fires at Lobbes and the destruction of the abbey by French Revolutionary forces in 1794. Some time after 1794, it came into the possession of a former Lobbes monk, M. Lengrand. It was subsequently purchased at the Bataille-Lengrand sale in Bruxelles in April 1836 by M. Vergauwen of Ghent and then passed to the University Library in 1884.

Heidelberg University Salemitanus MS IX,20 appears to be closely related to Gent 909. It is a composite book of six parts written in s. XI and

19. Dummler, 'Zum Heriger von Lobbes' 756.

20. Ratramnus, *De corpore et sanguine domini*, ed. Bakhuizen Van den Brink, 2–14 (MS 'L').

21. Omont, 'Catalogue des manuscripts de l'abbaye de Lobbes' 11.

s. XIV and bound in s. XV white leather over wood. It has 134 vellum folios in quarto format and contains writings in both Latin and German. Items 1–18 of Heriger's *Exaggeratio,* identified here as 'Eusebius de corpore et sanguine Domini et alia' and copied in two columns of 28 lines per page in a s. XIV gothica textualis hand, begin in Part B (fol. 2) 'Magnitudo celestium …' and end in the middle of the second column of fol. 14 at '… et cum benedictione complecti que sitque horto tu… .' The remainder of the *Exaggeratio* [Items 19–23] was copied in Part C, fols. 15–17v, in two columns of 28–35 lines per page by a neat Caroline minuscule hand of s. XI ex. Items 1–18 (fols. 2–14) were probably written to replace folios damaged or lost before the various portions were bound together in s. XV. The two Ratramnus texts are found here in Part C (fols. 17v–58v) in the same s. XI hand as the *Exaggeratio* portion.[22] The remainder of the present codex (Parts D–F, fols. 59–134v) was once a separate book written in s. XI ex. and contains various works of Berno of Reichenau, mystical interpretations of Holy Scripture, a piece that begins 'Missus est angelus Gabriel,' and the *Musica Enchiriadis* of Hoger of Werden.

There is reason to believe that Parts C–F, including the s. XI ex. Heriger portion and the Ratramnus texts, were copied in the cathedral school at Constance, perhaps from the Lobbes manuscript (now Gent 909), which is the only other book known to contain Heriger's *Exaggeratio* and the two Ratramnus texts together.[23] The book was once in the library of the Cistercian monastery of Sankt Maria in Salemweiler on the Aach River in Baden (founded in 1134 and suppressed in 1802) and later in the collection of the classicist Claude de Saumaise (†1653) before being purchased by the Universitätsbibliothek in 1826.

The final member of Group A is Auxerre, Bibliothèque Municipale, MS 25, a s. XII book of 102 vellum folios in small quarto format bound in calf.[24] It was written in single columns with 18 lines per page and has rubrics and rustic capitals for titles. The manuscript contains a miscellaneous collection of prayers, homilies, etc., some of which are attributed to St. Augustine and Florus of Lyons; Ratramnus's *De corpore et sanguine Domini;* and a truncated version of the *Exaggeratio.* The work of Ratramnus begins on fol. 32 but ends abruptly at the end of chapter 52 on

22. Ratramnus, *De corpore et sanguine domini,* ed. Bakhuizen Van den Brink, 11–15 (MS 'S').

23. The attribution to the cathedral school at Constance was made by Johanne Autenrieth, *Die Domschule von Konstanz zur Zeit des Investiturstreits* (Stuttgart 1956) 98.

24. This book is dated, incorrectly I believe, as s. X in France, Ministère de l'Éducation Nationale, *Catalogue Général des manuscrits des bibliothèques publiques de France. Départements* (Paris 1887) VI.16.

fol. 47.[25] It is followed immediately on fol. 47 by a version of Heriger's *Exaggeratio* that begins in item 6 ('Item alibi. Venisti ad altare ...') and continues through the end of the work on fol. 59. The codex is thought to have once been at the Cistercian monastery of Pontigny, and it came to the Bibliothèque de la Ville d'Auxerre after 1796.

Group B also consists of three manuscripts, all of which contain both the *Dicta* and the *Exaggeratio* plus the *Responsio cuiusdam de corpore et sanguine Domini*, the work of an as yet unidentified s. X author directed against the Stercoranists and used by Heriger in composing the *Dicta*. The oldest of the books of Group B is Liège, Bibliothèque du Grand Séminaire, MS 6.F.30 bis, written and decorated at the monastery of SS. Pierre et Exupère de Gembloux (OSB; devastated by the Calvinists in 1598; burnt in 1678 and 1712; suppressed in 1796), an establishment near to and closely connected with Lobbes, under Abbot Olbert (1012–48). It is a book of 164 vellum folios in octavo format written in single columns of 27–32 lines per page by several late Caroline minuscule hands and has the characteristic orange-red Gembloux rubrics and initials. The manuscript contains works of St. Augustine, Pseudo-Augustine, Pseudo-Origen, Quodvultdeus, Caesarius of Arles, and the Venerable Bede; these are followed on fols. 138v–152 by Heriger's *Exaggeratio*, which is in turn followed by the *Dicta* on fols. 152v–161v without title. The Heriger portions are in a different hand with a different ruling and 27 lines per page. Immediately following the *Dicta* on fols. 162–164v is the *Responsio cuiusdam*.

MS 6.F.30 bis was still at the abbey of SS. Pierre et Exupère in s. XIII. It then passed to the Croisiers (Canons Regular of the Order of the Holy Cross) in Liège and thence, before 1904, to the library of the Grand Séminaire. On fol. 1 is the inscription *Libri sumus sancta ritilius* [St. Rutilius Namanatianus?] *in Leodio*.[26]

The second member of Group B, Bruxelles, Bibliothèque Royale Albert Ier, MS 5576–5604, contains a large collection of treatises and excerpts on theological matters, most of which deal with the Eucharist.[27] It is a s. XI composite manuscript of 213 vellum folios in octavo format bound in old brown calf and was written by several transitional minuscule hands. Part A[1] (fols. 1–47v) was written in s. XI ex. and contains principally works of

25. Ratramnus, *De corpore et sanguine domini*, ed. Bakhuizen Van den Brink, 15–20 (MS 'P').

26. Thus far I have been unable to identify such a religious establishment in the diocese of Liège or elsewhere.

27. The contents are listed in J. Van Den Gheyn et al., *Catalogue des manuscrits de la Bibliothèque Royale de Belgique* (9 vols. Bruxelles 1901–9) 1.194–99, no. 364. See also Hubert Silvestre, *Les manuscrits de Bede à la Bibliothèque Royale de Bruxelles* (Leopoldville 1959) 11.

St. Ambrose. Part A^2 (fols. 48–132 *bis*) was written in single columns of 26 lines per page at the end of s. XI and also has the characteristic orange-red rubrics and initials of Gembloux. Heriger's *Exaggeratio* on fols. 95–113 is followed by the *Responsio cuiusdam* (fols. 113–115), the *Dicta cuiusdam sapientis* [Gottschalk of Orbais] *de corpore et sanguine Domini adversus Ratbertum* (fols. 115–120v), and a work entitled simply *De corpore et sanguine Domini* that begins 'Aliud specialiter corpus Domini ...' (fols. 120v–121). The *Dicta Herigeri* (fols. 121–129v) is immediately followed by Ratherius's *Confessio de corpore et sanguine Domini* (fols. 129v–131) and Haymo of Halberstadt, *Expositione in epistola sancti Pauli* (fols. 131–132). Part B (fols. 133–213v) was written in s. XII in. (ca. 1120) and contains works of Rhabanus Maurus, Berengar of Tours, Adelman of Liège, Guarner of Resbach (Abbot of St. Vincent Martyr), Hildebert of Tours, Lanfranc of Bec, Theodore of Verdun, Pope Gregory VII, Sigebert of Gembloux, and Ivo of Chartres.

This book and Liège, Grand Seminaire, MS 6.F.30 bis, may have been copied from a common exemplar at SS. Pierre et Exupère de Gembloux. MS 5576–5604 was written at Gembloux in s. XI, and a s. XV note on fol. 1v identifies the book as belonging to the abbey of SS. Pierre et Exupère. At the top of fol. 133 is the name *Magister Iohannes Beleth*, possibly a reference to Jean Beleth, a s. XII liturgist and theologian perhaps of English origin who was active at Tiron ca. 1182 and wrote a *Summa de ecclesiasticis* ca. 1160–64. The book also bears the stamp of the Bibliothèque de Bourgogne (fols. 1 and 213v) and the Bibliothèque Royale de Belgique (fol. av).

The final member of Group B is Bruxelles, Bibliothèque Royale Albert Ier, MS II.1121, written at the beginning of s. XIII in Flanders, perhaps near Liège, and once at the abbey of Ste. Marie d'Aulne (OSB until 1144, then Augustinian canons until 1147, and O. Cist. thereafter), a dependency of the see of Liège on the Sambre River.[28] It may well have been copied from Bruxelles, MS 5576–5604.

MS II.1121 consists of 170 vellum folios in folio format and was written in two columns of 35 lines per page in a primitive gothica textualis hand of s. XIII in. Once again the *Responsio cuiusdam* (fols. 164–165) follows the *Exaggeratio* (less the two excerpts from St. Ambrose at the end, fols. 156–164) and the *Confessio* of Ratherius and the *Expositione in Epistola sancti Pauli* of Haymo (fols. 168v–170) follow the *Dicta* (here entitled the *Compilatio*, fols. 165–168v).

An inscription on fol. 170v identifies this book as having once been

28. Van Den Gheyn, *Catalogue des manuscrits* 2.120–21, no. 1082. See also Silvestre, *Les manuscrits de Bede* 11 and 13.

a possession of the Cistercian house of Ste. Marie d'Aulne, where it was seen as late as March 1632.[29] It was later in the collection of Sir Thomas Phillipps at Cheltenham (no. 4689) and was acquired by the Bibliothèque Royale de Belgique in 1888.

Group C consists of three manuscripts all written in England in s. XII and all containing both the *Dicta* and the *Exaggeratio* or parts thereof. The earliest of the three, Salisbury Cathedral, MS 61, appears have been written at Salisbury in early s. XII, probably before 1125, for the most part by the scribe identified by Neil Ker as 'D1.'[30] It consists of 52 vellum folios in folio format written by four or more Caroline minuscule hands tending toward primitive gothic.[31] Part A (fols. 1–10v) contains various works of St. Augustine. Part B (fols. 11–20v) was written by a hand perhaps a bit earlier than that of Part A and also contains various works of St. Augustine. Part C (fols. 21–30v) was written by a more rounded early gothica textualis hand and contains St. Augustine, *Liber de natura boni adversus Manicheos*. Part D (fols. 31–52v) was written in single columns of 40–42 lines per page. The *Dicta* is found on fols. 31–34v without title and is followed on fols. 35–41v by the *Exaggeratio*. The Heriger works are followed by an unidentified tract on the Eucharist that begins 'Sacerdos qui sanctam corpus et sanguinem Christi presumis ...' and Arnobius Catholicus and Serapion, *De Deo trino et uno* (fols. 42–52v).

The second member of Group C is Cambridge, Sidney Sussex College, MS 51 (Δ.3.6), a four-part composite manuscript of 102 vellum folios in octavo format bound in modern brown stamped leather and written in several small s. XII gothica textualis hands.[32] Part A (fols. 1–16v) was perhaps written in part at the cathedral priory of St. Cuthbert at Durham and contains Hildebert of Lemans's *De expositione misse* and some verses on the Eucharist and other religious topics. Part B (fols. 17–26v) was written in single columns of 26 lines per page and contains Heriger's *Dicta* but not the *Exaggeratio* or the other Eucharistic texts usually found with the works of Heriger. Part C (fols. 27–45v) contains medical recipes, and Part D (fols. 47–102v) contains a gloss on the Psalter.

29. Antoon Sander, *Bibliotheca Belgica manuscripta*, 2 (Lille 1644) 241.

30. Neil R. Ker, ed., *Medieval Libraries of Great Britain: A List of Surviving Books* (2nd ed. London 1964) 173. Salisbury 61 is listed as no. 112 in the catalogue of Salisbury books composed by Patrick Young in 1622/3.

31. E. M. Thompson and S. M. Lakin, *A Catalogue of the Library of the Cathedral Church of Salisbury* (London 1880) 14.

32. M. R. James, *A Descriptive Catalogue of the Manuscripts in the Library of Sidney Sussex College, Cambridge* (Cambridge 1895) 36–37.

Part A is listed in the s. XII Durham catalogue and in the subsequent catalogues of 1391 ('S') and 1416 ('P').[33] An owner's inscription on fol. 1, dated 1591, is repeated on fol. 47 and identifies the entire book as the property at that time of Archdeacon John Pilkington, the brother of James Pilkington (Bishop of Durham, 1561–76).

The third Group C book is now New Haven, Yale University, Beinecke Library, MS 181, written in England in the second half of s. XII.[34] It consists of 23 vellum folios in small quarto format written in single columns of 33 lines per page by several early gothica textualis hands. The *Exaggeratio* appears on fols. 1–16v and is followed immediately by the *Dicta* on fols. 16v–23v. A different, perhaps French, hand has added on fol. 23v a processional antiphon with neumes that begins 'Quam pulcra es et quam decore....'

MS 181 once belonged to John Stacye of Handworth, Yorkshire (†1658) and other members of the Stacye family in s. XVII and to Martin Bretland (Mayor of Chesterfield, Derbyshire, 1608–9) and other members of the Bretland family also in s. XVII. The name *Tobias* appears on fol. 7 (s. XVII), and the book subsequently belonged to Francis Sitwell of Eckington, Yorkshire, reputedly the world's largest manufacturer of iron nails in s. XVII. It later fell into the hands of the infamous Guglielmo Libri in s. XIX before being owned by Thomas B. Strong, Vice Chancellor of Oxford and later Lord Bishop of Oxford at the end of s. XIX. It passed to Frederick Fox Bartrop, ca. 1937, and thence to H. P. Kraus. It was purchased from Kraus by Thomas E. Marston in 1947 and was subsequently presented to Yale University by Marston in 1951.

Group D consists of just two books, both written at the Benedictine abbey of Sankt Maria in Göttweig, Austria. The earliest is Göttweig, Stiftsbibliothek, MS 54 (58), a composite manuscript of 87 vellum folios in folio format bound in whitened vellum over boards. Part A (fol. 1r–v) is ruled for music and contains musical notation in a s. XV gothica textualis hand. Part B (fols. 2–27) was written in a s. XII transitional minuscule hand in single columns of 37 lines per page. Heriger's *Dicta*, here wrongly attributed to Gerbert of Aurillac (Pope Sylvester II), appears on fols. 16–21v.

33. *Catalogi veteres librorum ecclesiae cathedralis Dunelmensis* (London 1838) 4, 24, and 104. See also Ker, *Medieval Libraries of Great Britain* 62.

34. Barbara A. Shailor, *Catalogue of Medieval and Renaissance Manuscripts in the Beinecke Rare Book and Manuscript Library, Yale University* (Binghamton 1984) I.244–47. Shailor includes both Heriger texts as parts of an anonymous catena of Eucharistic texts and thus wrongly identifies the *Exaggeratio* as Eusebius's *Omelia de corpore et sanguine Domini* and the *Dicta* as the *De corpore et sanguine Domini* of Gerbert of Aurillac (Pope Sylvester II).

The *Dicta* is preceded by Rhabanus Maurus, *Liber contra eos qui repugnant institutes beati patris Benedicti;* Cuthbert, *Obitus S. Bedae venerabilis;* and Origen, *Lamentum,* and is followed by Ratramnus's *De corpore et sanguine Domini.* Part C (fols. 28–87v) consists of 59 folios written in two s. XII transitional minuscule hands and contains some of John Cassian's *Collationes patrum.*

According to V. Werl, the compiler of the 1844 Göttweig catalogue, Part B was written by two Göttweig scribes in early s. XII.[35] As I discussed in a 1973 article in *Mediaeval Studies,* Heriger's text was perhaps first brought to Göttweig in connection with an outbreak of Stercoranism at the end of s. XI, the attribution to Gerbert being made by the s. XII scribes to enhance the authority of the text.[36]

The second book of Group D is today Göttweig, Stiftsbibliothek, MS 285 (312), an exact copy of MS 54 (58) made in s. XV at Göttweig and consisting of 219 paper folios in folio format written in two columns of 37–40 lines per page by two gothica textualis hands of s. XV. It also contains the *Stella clericorum,* Richard Maidstone's *Sermones,* William of Pagula's *Regula de vita de rectura secularium sacerdotum,* the *Gesta Romanorum,* the *Sigillum beatae Mariae,* Honorious of Autun's *Hexameron,* and Ratramnus's *De corpore et sanguine Domini* as well as various sermons, Richard of Saint-Victor's *Commentarius super quosdam Psalmos et quasdam sententias scripturarum,* Thomas Cobham's *Sermones de poenitentia,* and John Cassian's *Collationes patrum,* and other works.

The final group, Group E, consists of four manuscripts, all containing the *Dicta* (or fragments of it) and all apparently written in France. The oldest of the Group E books is now Paris, Bibliothèque Nationale, MS Latin 2987, probably written in France in s. XI–XII.[37] It consists of 126 vellum folios in small quarto format bound in brown marbled calf and was written in single columns of 20–25 lines per page by at least three distinct transitional minuscule hands. The book contains several works of St. Augustine and Paulus Orosius as well as the *Dicta* on fols. 92–104.

A s. XII–XIII note on fol. 126 connects MS Latin 2987 with one Jocenus of Beauvais, perhaps the owner who on two occasions used it as se-

35. I am indebted to the Hill Monastic Manuscript Library, St. John's University, Collegeville, Minnesota, for providing in 1970 a xerographic copy of this manuscript and of pages 186–88 of the 1844 handwritten Göttweig catalogue by V. Werl ('Manuscripten-Catalog der Stifts-Bibliothek zu Gottweig,' vol. 1). See Werl's note on fol. 1 of the manuscript.

36. Shrader, 'The False Attribution of an Eucharistic Tract to Gerbert of Aurillac.'

37. France, Bibliothèque Nationale, *Catalogue général des manuscrits latins* (Paris 1952) III.371.

curity for a loan of 12 *sous Parisis* from a Jewish banker. It was later in the library of the Cordeliers (OFM) in Paris and passed temporarily to Pierre de Souvions, chaplain of Jean Cholet (Cardinal of Ste. Cécile, 1291–92). De Souvions ordered it returned to the Cordeliers in his will, and the book eventually came to the Bibliothèque Nationale by way of the library of Cardinal Jules Mazarin (†1661) and the Bibliotheca Regius (no. 4587).

The second member of Group E is Aberdeen, University Library, Marischal College, MS 61, a book of 102 vellum folios written in single columns of ca. 15 lines per page by several hands in early s. XII (in part after 1143).[38] It contains a large, miscellaneous collection of texts on religious matters, most of which are concerned with the Eucharist. A portion of the *Dicta*, here identified as *Johannes Scottus contro eos qui corpus domini asserunt secessum pati*, appears in confused form on fols. 81–86v, and the excerpts from the writings of Basil, Gregory the Great, Fulgentius, Eusebius, Cyril, and Hilary that appear on fols. 44v–48 were also apparently copied from the *Dicta*. Among the other Eucharistic pieces found in this manuscript are works of Lanfranc of Bec and of his disciple, Guitmond of Aversa, and the Eucharistic confessions of their opponent, Berengar of Tours.

Marischal Coll. 61 is probably of continental (French?) origin, but it was in England at least by early s. XVIII. An inscription on the second flyleaf refers to 'Honest Tom' Martin (†1771), a lawyer, antiquarian, and book collector from Palgrave in Suffolk whose manuscripts were sold in London in April 1773 and May 1774. The book was a gift to Marischal College by Dr. Samuel Guise (†1811), once a surgeon in the Bombay Army and a well-known collector of Arabic and oriental manuscripts who received an LL.D. degree from Marischal College in February 1809.

The third Group E manuscript is today Bibliothèque Nationale, MS Latin 2083, a composite manuscript of two parts, both of s. XIII, bound in red morocco stamped with the arms of Jean Baptiste Colbert (†1683).[39] Part A (fols. 1–102v) consists of 101 vellum folios written in two columns of 60 lines per page by two very neat gothica textualis hands. Part B (fols. 103–132v) was also written in two columns of 60 lines per page by a gothica textualis hand slightly later than those in Part A. MS Latin 2083 contains a defective copying of the *Dicta* on fols. 33–36, here identified as *Tractatus quidam Augustini de corpore Christi*, which ends 'in pluribus eius ne fueris vel curiosus,' words not part of the *Dicta*. The book also contains several

38. M. R. James, *A Catalogue of the Medieval Manuscripts in the University Library Aberdeen* (Cambridge 1932) 52–53.

39. France, Bibliothèque Nationale, *Catalogue général des manuscrits latins* (Paris 1940) II.311–12.

works of Augustine, Pseudo-Augustine, Hugh of St. Victor, Cyprian, Ausonius, and Paul of Aquilia. It was once in the collection of Jean Baptiste Colbert (no. 426) and was then sold to King Louis XV (*Regius* 3380^{5}c), probably with the rest of the Colbert library in 1732.

The final book of Group E is now Bibliothèque Nationale, MS Latin 2982, a s. XV codex consisting of 170 paper folios in quarto format bound in red pebbled leather.[40] The book has two parts, both written in single columns of 28–39 lines per page in the same gothica cursive hand. Part A (fols. 1–112v) contains various works of St. Augustine. Part B contains on fols. 112v–126 the *Dicta,* here identified as *De sacramento eucharistie ex dictis sanctorum. Contra errores circa istud sacramentum,* followed by an unidentified text, perhaps an extract from Boethius.

MS Latin 2982 once belonged to Jean Budé, secretary to Louis XI and Charles VIII and audiencier of France (†1502), whose autograph *ex-libris* dated 25 April 1447 appears on fol. 169. It was later in the collections of Jacques-Auguste de Thou († 1617), of Jean Baptiste Colbert (no. 3840), and of the Bibliotheca Regius (*Regius* 4551^{3}).

Attested Copies

Two other manuscripts are reported to contain vestiges of the *Exaggeratio.* A version of the *Exaggeratio* similar to that found in Auxerre 25 may be found in Dublin, Trinity Coll. 236, a book thought to have been copied in s. XVII or s. XVIII from a manuscript (perhaps MS no. 785) from the collection of Jacques Auguste de Thou.[41] I have not yet seen Dublin, Trinity Coll. 236 and thus cannot confirm the presence of a Heriger text. Two short excerpts from the *Exaggeratio,* item 2 (St. Hilary, *De trinitate libri duodecim,* VIII) and item 8 (St. Ambrose, *De sacramentis libri sex,* VI.1) also appear with Pachasius Radbertus's *De corpore et sanguine Domini* in Oxford, Keble Coll. 22, a book written at Salisbury Cathedral in the last quarter of s. XI.[42]

In the eighteenth century, Casimir Oudin noted two other manuscripts containing the *Dicta Herigeri.*[43] One was in the possession of the canons regular of St. Martin at Louvain and the other was at the Cister-

40. France, Bibliothèque Nationale, *Catalogue général des manuscrits latins* (Paris 1952) III.363–64.

41. Cf. Paris, BN lat. 2982, which contains, however, the *Dicta,* not the *Exaggeratio.*

42. M. B. Parkes, *The Medieval Manuscripts of Keble College, Oxford* (London 1979) 69–70. Salisbury 161, written between 1089 and 1125, contains both the *Dicta* and the *Exaggeratio* and was perhaps the exemplar for Keble Coll. 22.

43. Casimir Oudin, *Commentarius de scriptoribus ecclesiasticis,* 2 (Leipzig 1722) 486.

cian house of Signy in the diocese of Reims. I have not yet been able to link positively either of the two books cited by Oudin with extant manuscripts. There are no obvious clues to the whereabouts of the book from St. Martin's in Louvain. There was, however, a copy of the *Dicta* listed in the s. XVI catalogue of books at the abbey of Signy (O. Cist.; in the diocese of Reims; founded 1135). Most of the Signy books are now preserved in the Bibliothèque Municipale at Charleville-Mézières, and the Signy book in question may be either Charleville-Mézières, BM, MS 172, written in s. XII (ca. 1140–1174), or Charleville-Mézières, BM, MS 202, written in s. XII ex. and bearing the Signy *ex-libris*. Both manuscripts have 138 folios and contain works on the Eucharist. MS 172 contains a work identified only as *Liber de corpore et sanguine Dominis* that is probably Alger of Liège's *De sacramento corporis et sanguinis Domini*, but may be Heriger's *Dicta*. MS 202 contains an extensive collection of the various works of St. Augustine as well as a work identified as *Liber beati Pachasii de corpore de sanguine Domini*, which may in fact be the *Dicta Herigeri* mistaken for the work of Paschasius Radbertus. I have not yet seen the manuscripts, either *in situ* or on microfilm, and inquiries directed to the library have yet to produce results.

Conclusion

Further study is required before definitive relationships among the various manuscripts of Heriger's Eucharistic writings can be established. At this point, only a few general observations can be made. The temporal range of the extant manuscripts is from s. X ex.–s. XI in. (one manuscript) to s. XV (two manuscripts). The rest are of s. XI (one MSS), s. XI ex.–s. XII in. (three manuscripts), s. XII (five manuscripts), s. XIII (two manuscripts), or s. XI + XIV (one manuscript) production. The geographical focus of the earlier manuscripts with respect to origin is, as might be expected, the area around Liège in Flanders. Many of the extant manuscripts were written or owned by religious establishments near to or closely connected with Heriger's own abbey of Lobbes, but the early copying of the *Exaggeratio* at Constance and the dissemination of the *Dicta* to Austria and England suggests that interest in Heriger's realist and anti-Stercoranist compilations was not restricted solely to the author's homeland. Heriger's works seem to have been especially popular in Cistercian houses (three occurrences) and in cathedral libraries (three occurrences), perhaps as an aid to interrogations for orthodoxy.

The dating and distribution of the extant manuscripts of Heriger's two Eucharistic compilations suggest that not only was interest in the question of Eucharistic realism maintained in s. XI and XII, but that Heriger's works, although for the most part compilations of *auctoritates,* were still considered of sufficient value on the question as to merit reproduction and extended distribution. Written in a period long considered to have been rather barren of original, or even imitative, thought on the Eucharist, Heriger's compositions reinforced the shift from symbolism to realism that brought Berengar of Tours to grief in the eleventh century. Continued opposition to the Stercoranist heresy and the need to defend the newly-accepted realist orthodoxy against articulate supporters of the old symbolist position thus made both the *Exaggeratio* and the *Dicta* useful long after their composition and may explain the appearance of Heriger's work in such diverse locations as Salisbury Cathedral and the abbey of Göttweig as well as in the neighborhood of Lobbes itself.

APPENDIX

Handlist of Manuscripts

1. **Aberdeen,** University Library, Marischal College, MS 161. XII (after 1143); *Dicta* (excerpts), (fols. 44v–48 and 81–86v). Perhaps written in France.

2. **Auxerre,** Bibliothèque Municipale, MS 25. XII; *Exaggeratio* (excerpts), (fols. 47–59). Perhaps once at the abbey of Pontigny (O. Cist.).

3. **Bruxelles,** Bibliothèque Royale Albert Ier, MS 5576–5604. XI ex. (Heriger) + XII in.; *Exaggeratio* (fols. 95–113) and *Dicta* (fols. 121–129v). Written at the abbey of SS. Pierre et Exupère de Gembloux (OSB).

4. **Bruxelles,** Bibliothèque Royale Albert Ier, MS II.1121. XIII in.; *Exaggeratio* (fols. 156–164) and *Dicta* (fols. 165–168v). Perhaps written near Liège and once found at the abbey of Ste. Marie d'Aulne (O. Cist.).

5. **Cambridge,** Sidney Sussex College, MS 51. XII; *Dicta* (fols. 17–26v). Written in part at the cathedral priory of St. Cuthbert at Durham.

6. **Ghent,** Bibliotheek van de Rijksuniversiteit, MS 909. IX (840–888) (Parts B and C) + X ex.–XI in. (Part A = Heriger); *Exaggeratio* (fols. 1–15). Parts B and C were written at St. Pierre de Corbie, ca. 840–888, and Part A was perhaps written at Lobbes in Heriger's time. The marginal notes on fol. 36v are thought to be in the hand of Heriger himself.

7. **Göttweig,** Stiftsbibliothek, MS 54 [58]. XII (Heriger) + XV; *Dicta* (fols. 16–21v). Written at the abbey of Sankt Maria in Göttweig.

8. **Göttweig,** Stiftsbibliothek, MS 285 [312]. XV; *Dicta* (fols. 73v–78). Copied at the abbey of Sankt Maria in Göttweig from Göttweig 54 [58].

9. **Heidelberg,** Universitätsbibliothek, Salemitanus MS IX, 20. XI ex.–XV (Heri-

ger = XI ex. + XIV); *Exaggeratio* (fols. 2–17v). Written in part at the Domschule in Constance, Part A perhaps having been copied from Gent 909.

10. **Liège**, Bibliothèque du Grande Seminaire, MS 6.F.30 bis. XI; *Exaggeratio* (fols. 138v–152) and *Dicta* (fols. 152v–161). Written at the abbey of SS. Pierre et Exupère de Gembloux (OSB).

11. **New Haven**, Yale University, Beinecke Library, MS 181. XII^2; *Exaggeratio* (fols. 1–16v) and *Dicta* (fols. 16v–23v). Written in England.

12. **Paris**, Bibliothèque Nationale, MS Latin 2083. XIII; *Dicta* (fols. 33–36). Perhaps written in France.

13. **Paris**, Bibliothèque Nationale, MS Latin 2982. XV; *Dicta* (fols. 112v–126). Perhaps written in France.

14. **Paris**, Bibliothèque Nationale, MS Latin 2987. XI–XII; *Dicta* (fols. 92–104). Perhaps written in France.

15. **Salisbury**, Cathedral Library, MS 61. XI ex.–XII in. (1089–1125); *Dicta* (fols. 31–34v) and *Exaggeratio* (fols. 35–41v). Written at Salisbury Cathedral.

MARTIN BRETT

11 The *De corpore et sanguine Domini* of Ernulf of Canterbury

Robert Somerville's magisterial series of studies on the church councils of the eleventh and twelfth centuries has led him to touch on almost every one of the great issues of the time. Of these, few generated more passionate debate than the Eucharistic controversy provoked by the teachings of Berengar of Tours.[1] The text below is only marginal to the issue, but deserves attention as an unusual and early example of that reflection on custom, reason and authority which became so dominant a theme in the period.

It was written by Ernulf, born in northern France in 1039/40. After early study at Bec under Lanfranc, he took the monastic habit at the abbey of St. Simphorien at Beauvais, and played an active part in the schools just as Ivo, abbot of St. Quentin by 1069, and later bishop of Chartres, was establishing his reputation at Beauvais as one of the leading masters of northern France. Some time before 1077 Ernulf became dissatisfied with the life of his house and consulted Anselm at Bec before moving to Canterbury where Lanfranc had become archbishop in 1070. In the cathedral

I am particularly grateful to Professor Isabella Gualandri, whose expertise in Latin has provided many corrections and helpful suggestions on the text, though she has no responsibility for the outcome.

1. The modern literature is extensive, and includes Robert Somerville, 'The case against Berengar of Tours—a new text,' *Studi Gregoriani* 9 (1972) 55–75, repr. in his *Papacy, Councils and Canon Law in the 11th–12th Centuries* (Variorum CS 312; Aldershot 1990) no. I. See recently: Jean de Montclos, *Lanfranc et Berenger: La controverse eucharistique du XIe siècle* (Spicilegium sacrum Lovaniense, Études et documents 37; Leuven 1971); Gary Macy, *The Theologies of the Eucharist in the Early Scholastic Period: A Study of the Salvific Function of the Sacrament according to the Theologians c. 1080–c. 1220* (Oxford 1984); *Auctoritas und Ratio: Studien zu Berengar von Tours* ed. Peter Ganz, R. B. C. Huygens, and Friedrich Niewöhner (Wolfenbütteler Mittelalter Studien 2; Wiesbaden 1990); *Pratiques de l'eucharistie dans les Églises d'Orient et d'Occident (Antiquité et Moyen Âge)*, ed. Nicole Bériou, Béatrice Caseau, and Dominique Rigaux (Études Augustiniennes Moyen-Âge et Temps Modernes 45–46; Paris 2009) esp. 1.371–420; 2.843–77.

community he enjoyed a high reputation as a teacher of grammar, but clearly had much wider talents, for he became prior of the house around 1096 soon after the arrival of Anselm as the new archbishop, and went on to become abbot of Peterborough in 1107, and bishop of Rochester in 1114. He died early in 1124, the last survivor of the generation of monks trained for high office under Lanfranc.[2]

Two substantial letters on law and theology survive in his name. The first, *De incestis coniugibus* of 1090 x 1097, was written to Bishop Walkelin of Winchester in response to a question on the legitimacy of the dissolving of marriages under certain conditions in the light of Christ's apparently absolute prohibition. This was analysed in detail by Peter Cramer, who showed that both its sources and its method of argument were in many respects much closer to the patterns of thought of Ivo of Chartres than to those of Lanfranc; he suggested that this might well be explained by Ernulf's experience in the schools of Beauvais.[3] The second, printed below, responds to five questions, four on the Eucharist and one on biblical exegesis, put to him by a certain Lambert, a distant correspondent whom Ernulf had never met. While the sources deployed in the letter suggest a close acquaintance with the *Collectio Lanfranci*, the archbishop's own abbreviation of Pseudo-Isidore, much of the argument is distinctive.[4] Ernulf shares with Lanfranc (and with Ivo) a resolutely realist understanding of Christ's presence in the sacrament, but addresses different problems, and in a different manner, than Lanfranc did in his *De corpore et sanguine*.[5]

2. David Knowles, Christopher N. L. Brooke, and Vera C. M. London, *The Heads of Religious Houses, England and Wales. 1, 940–1216* (2nd ed. Cambridge 2001) 33, 60 and authorities cited there; S. *Anselmi Cantuariensis archiepiscopi opera omnia*, ed. Franciscus S. Schmitt (Edinburgh 1946–61) 3 Epp. 38, 64, 74. Since Anselm says in Ep. 38 that he had not seen Ernulf since he took the monastic habit, and saw no prospect of doing so, the appearance of 'Hernolfus episcopus' immediately after Anselm himself in the list of Bec monks printed in André Porée, *Histoire de l'abbaye du Bec* (Evreux 1901) 1.629 cannot be taken as evidence that he was a monk there; the entry more probably refers to Ernost, the first post-Conquest bishop of Rochester, a monk of Bec who is not otherwise accounted for in the list (*English Episcopal acta.* Rochester 1076–1234, ed. Margaret Blount and Martin Brett, forthcoming). See too Peter Cramer in *Oxford Dictionary of National Biography* (Oxford 2005) 18.511–12. On Ivo at Beauvais see MGH SS 15.1140–41; Christof Rolker, *Canon Law and the Letters of Ivo of Chartres* (Cambridge 2010), 6-9.

3. Peter Cramer, 'Ernulf of Rochester and Early Anglo-Norman Canon Law,' JEH 40 (1989) 483–510, discussing the text reprinted from D'Achery in PL 163.1457–74. D'Achery used Paris BN lat. 2446, noted below; a second and perhaps earlier copy from Rochester is Brussels, Bibl. royale 8794–99 (Cat. 1403) fols. 2–13, and a third (damaged) one, also of s. xii, from Peterborough, is London, Lambeth Palace 191 fols. 232–236.

4. Ernulf treats his sources with some freedom, but all his citations of pseudo-Isidorean texts are also found in the *Collectio Lanfranci*, and there is no significant overlap with e.g. the *Decretum* of Burchard, which was an important source in his *De incestis coniugibus*. See the notes to the text below.

5. Ludwig Ott, *Untersuchungen zur theologischen Briefliteratur der Frühscholastik: unter beson-*

The date of the letter largely depends on the identification of Lambert, its recipient. In one of the four surviving copies the rubric has him as abbot, and the cataloguer of a lost Peterborough copy, or the book he was describing, identified him as the abbot of St. Bertin, who took office in 1095 after a long period of monastic training. However, in a second copy of around the same date the addressee is simply a clerk, while the others have nothing. It seems most unlikely that this letter was written to an abbot. Ernulf had been gently rebuked by Anselm earlier for arrogance, and his other letter to the great prelate Walkelin certainly addresses him with notable freedom. Nevertheless, here there is not a word of that conventional deference which one might expect of a monk, or even prior, of Christ Church when addressing the head of a famous house; rather he is firmly instructed, and even sometimes rebuked for treating the sacrament as an occasion for mere sophistry. It is possible that Lambert was described as abbot only by anticipation, as Ernulf was styled bishop. If so, the work might be dated no later than 1095. If this is some other Lambert, the name is frequent in Flanders and northern France, if rarer elsewhere, and there are innumerable possible candidates. Whoever it was seems familiar with the debates in the schools of his day—his fourth question is related generically to a number of the *Sententiae* associated with Laon around this time. On that basis the letter can only be dated very approximately, probably between 1080 and 1107, and perhaps to the 1090s, given the similarity in the form of argument between it and the *De incestis coniugibus*.

Space precludes any discussion of the relation between the letter and the writings of that multitude of authors who also treated some of the issues raised by Lambert, though a few cross-references to other contemporaries are found in the notes. One issue, though, does deserve rather more attention. In the first, longest and most developed of Ernulf's answers he defends the *hodierna ecclesie consuetudo* and *cotidianus usus* of administering the bread of the Eucharist dipped in the wine, intinction, rather than the two elements separately.[6] This practice is first clearly attested in some Cluniac customaries from the tenth century on, and is defended, at least for the laity, on the same argument of convenience by John

derer Berücksichtigung des Viktorinerkreises (Beiträge zur Geschichte der Philosophie und Theologie des Mittelalters NF 34; Münster 1937) provides some context to Ernulf's tract; see esp. 13–14, 28–29, 36. Peter J. Cramer, 'Ernulf of Rochester and the Problem of Remembrance', *Anselm Studies* 2 (1988) 144–63, esp. 147–53, is the most extended modern treatment.

6. For an extended and still valuable discussion see E. Dublanchy in DThC 3.552–72 esp. 560, and Josef Jungmann, *Missarum sollemnia*, here cited from the translation by Francis A. Brunner, *The Mass of the Roman Rite: Its Origins and Development* (London 1959) 2.384, 387n.

of Avranches in his *De officiis ecclesiasticis* of 1060x1067.[7] It was, however, widely denounced. Cardinal Humbert had used a similar practice in the Eastern Churches as evidence of their departure from orthodox principles in 1053/4; it was attacked energetically by Bernold of Constance in his *Micrologus*, was formally condemned in a widespread version of the canons of the Council of Clermont in 1095, and rather later at Cluny by Pope Gelasius II, and (probably) Hildebert of le Mans.[8] It seems at least as if Lanfranc himself did not suppose that it would always be followed when he wrote:[9]

Sumitur quidem caro per se, et sanguis per se non sine certi misterii ratione.

Although Ernulf writes, then, as if the custom he was defending was the established norm of the Church at large, it is clear that this was far from the case; indeed, at one point he expressly recognises that this was so.[10] The issue continued to be debated in the Church throughout the twelfth century. While many agreed with Ernulf that the case of Judas at the Last Supper did not constitute a decisive objection, most continued to advocate communion in both kinds on other grounds until the Fourth Lateran Council of 1215 transformed the terms of the debate.

Edition

Manuscripts

O = Oxford, Bodleian Library Bodley 569 (s. xii^{1}/^{4}, at St. Albans by s. xii/xiii), fols. 92v–101r; preceded by Lanfranc and Guitmund, *De corpore*

7. *Corpus consuetudinum monasticarum*, ed. Kassius Hallinger (Sieberg 1963–83) esp. 7(2).91, 303; 7(3).172, 316 and n; *The Sacramentary of Ratoldus*, ed. Nicholas Orchard (Henry Bradshaw Society 116; Woodbridge 2005) 244, from late-tenth-century Corbie, has the priests and deacons communicating in both kinds, but the subdeacons by intinction; *Le* De officiis ecclesiasticis *de Jean d'Avranches, archevêque de Rouen (1067–1079)*, ed. René Delamare (Paris 1923) 15: 'Non autem intincto pane, sed iuxta diffinitionem Toletani concilii [*apparently an error for Braga, cf. below n. 16*] seorsum corpore, seorsum sanguine, sacerdos communicet, excepto populo, qui intincto pane, non auctoritate, sed summa necessitate timoris sanguinis Christi effusionis, permittitur communicare'; compare the observation printed in Odon Lottin, *Psychologie et morale aux XIIe et XIIIe siècles* (Louvain 1942–60) 5.55 (no. 62) from the *Liber Pancrisis*: 'Ut pueris solet tantum vinum dare, rusticis propter frequentiam populi panis; divisim tamen dari consuetum est.'

8. Humbert, *Adversus Graecorum calumnias* (PL 143.951); Robert Somerville, *The Councils of Urban II. 1. Decreta Claromontensia* (AHC Supplementum 1; Amsterdam 1972), 80, 96, 109, 112, 116; JL 6624; Hildebert, Ep. II. 15 (PL 171.223): 'attendas judicialem esse pertinaciam, consuetudinem praeferre veritati.'

9. *Lanfranco. El cuerpo y la sangre del Señor* c. 5, the text of the 2004 Catania edition by Concetto Martello with translation and notes by Manuel Aroztegi Esnaola (Studia theologica Matritensia 14; Madrid 2009) 78 (and compare 70). See, however, the Corbie text cited in n. 7 above, where communion in both kinds is received by the priests and deacons, if not by all communicants.

10. See p. 173.

et sanguine Domini, and Anselm, *De incarnatione Verbi*. Written in long lines, ruled in dry point. Ernulf's tract begins immediately after the end of Anselm's. The end of fol. 101r is blank. A later hand has added on fols 101v–102r part of S. *Anselmi opera* 5 Ep. 417.[11]

P = Paris BN lat. 2446 [ex Bigot, Reg. 4070] fols. 187v–193, ending on the last leaf. There is a leaf missing after fol. 189. It is preceded by Ernulf's *De incestis coniugibus*. Fols. 1–177r contain Angelomo of Luxeuil, *Ennarrationes* (*PL* 115.247–552). The hand is Norman, and perhaps rather earlier than the mid-twelfth century. There were copies of Angelomo's commentary at Fécamp, le Bec, Mont St. Michel and perhaps St. Evroul in the twelfth century, and at St. Ouen in the fourteenth century.[12]

R = London, BL Royal 7 C viii fols. 100ra–106va (s. xii); tentatively attributed to Gloucester.[13] It is preceded by Paschasius Radbertus, *De corpore et sanguine Domini* and his letter to Fredugard, by Lanfranc and Guitmund, and some lesser extracts. Much of this, though not the tract of Ernulf, is also found in Oxford, Trinity College 51, which also may have some connection with Gloucester. It is an eccentricity of the scribe that an initial 'i' is often written superscript.

L = Lyon, BM 617, s. xv fols. 71v–73, incomplete, ending at 'periculum ingruerit, gentiles' (below p. 173). A paper MS in an Italian binding, containing the letters of Leo I with several additions. The text is mildly idiosyncratic. The marginal heading shows that the compiler of the book was specially interested in Ernulf's argument against communion in both kinds, though he had clearly misunderstood it. He abandoned his transcript about the point where the tract moves to other matters.

Lost: The fourteenth-century library list of Peterborough Abbey lists as j. in its item 14:[14] 'Quedam soluciones Ernulphi episcopi Rofensis ad quasdam questiones Lamberti abbatis sancti Bertini.'

The mid-twelfth-century catalogue of le Bec included as item 82 a volume containing letters of Lanfranc, Fulbert of Chartres, Hildebert of le Mans, 'in eodem liber Ernulfi de incestis coniugiis. Item .iiii. questiones

11. Rodney M. Thomson, *Manuscripts from St. Albans Abbey 1066–1235* (Woodbridge 1982) 1.102–3 no. 43.

12. Geneviève Nortier, *Les bibliothèques médiévales des abbayes bénédictines de Normandie* (Paris 1971) 'Liste des oeuvres' s.n. Angelomus.

13. Rodney M. Thomson, 'Books and Learning at Gloucester Abbey in the Twelfth and Thirteenth Centuries,' in *Books and Collectors 1200–1700. Essays Presented to Andrew Watson*, ed. James P. Carley and Colin G. C. Tite (London 1997) 3–26 at 21.

14. *Corpus of British Medieval Library Catalogues 8. Peterborough Abbey*, ed. Karsten Friis-Jensen and James M. W. Willoughby (London 2001) 60.

diuine scripture solute ab eo.'[15] Much of this appears distributed between BAV Reg. lat. 278 and 285, though the Ernulf texts are not now there. The second entry is probably an inaccurate description of this tract.

The only edition, lacking the passage missing in its exemplar, is that of Luc d'Achery, *Veterum aliquot scriptorum qui in Galliae bibliothecis, maxime Benedictinorum, latuerant* (Paris 1667) 2.431–44 (= D) from P, his 'MS Bibliothecae Bigotianae' (*Elenchus*, preface, unnumbered), reprinted with minor errors in *Spicilegium sive collectio veterum aliquot scriptorum qui in Galliae bibliothecis delituerant*, rev. ed. Ludovicus-Franciscus-Joseph de la Barre (Paris 1723) 3.470–474.[16]

The text below is based on O, with the punctuation slightly modernized. D is noted only where it departs from P.

Tractatus Arnulfi monachi de corpore et sanguine Domini ad Lambertum abbatem[a]

Venerabili ac gremio caritatis uenerabiliter confouendo Lamberto, frater Ernulfus[b] in sanctorum felicitate consortium felicitatis ęternę.

Faciem uestram in carne nunquam uidi, quam ut uiderem terrarum intercapedo non concessit. Per ea uero quę de moribus uestris, de humilitate, benignitate, affabilitate, cęterisque animę uestrę ornamentis[c] latore litterarum uestrarum referente cognoui, noticiam uestri certius in animo meo teneo impressam quam si presens presentem his incognitis aspiciam. Ita fit[d] ut animi uestri egregie compositioni ea nectar dilectionis [93r] qualitate, quę nescit amico recte petita denegare, largitur propria, uindicat[e] aliena. Cuius rei dilectione uestra condigna postulante, experientia uestra meam possibilitatem seruata ordinis integritate inueniet efficacem. Ante biennium, ni fallor, quamdam scedulam, quam ad me uestra beatitudo direxerat, suscepi, preferentem conscriptas questiones quinque, nonnullas habentes pauca uerba, sed tegentes mysteria immensa. Cuius portitor se

15. Henri Omont in *Cat. gén.* 2 (1888) 385–98. See too *The Letters of Lanfranc, Archbishop of Canterbury*, ed. Helen Clover and Margaret Gibson (Oxford Medieval Texts; 1979) 21.

16. There is an unpublished transcription from O in Kendall F. Downs, 'Ernulf of Rochester: A Preliminary Examination' (West Texas A&M MA thesis; 1994).

a. Tract.—abb. O *in alternating lines in green and red;* Tractus Arnulfi monachi de corpore et sanguine Domini ad Lambertum clericum R; Optima epistola contra communicantem [?] populum sub utraque specie *in mg.* L; *no heading* P

b. Ernulfus OP; Ernulphus R; Arnulfus L

c. ornatis L

d. fuit L

e. uind- ORL; uend- P

obsequio uestro aiebat postulare, quatinus ad interrogata responderem, et quod ibi tenebrosum claudebatur, nonnullorum tarditatem fallens, aliquo splendore uestirem. Per idem tempus graui egritudine correptus diutissime lecto decubui, ea languoris uehementia fatigatus, ut pre doloris impatientia pene membris omnibus[f] exstiterim dissolutus. Hęc iccirco posuerim[g] ne petitioni dignationis uestrę uidear parere noluisse, dum tanto tempore sit dilatum, quod ante tantum temporis fuerat postulatum. Proinde sedato aliqua ex parte languore diuturno, de uestris inquisitionibus quam petieratis sententiam fero, ponens mea, supererogans aliena.

[I]

Prima ergo posita est percunctatio de sacramento altaris; ita proposita, ut queratur cur hodierna ęcclesię consuetudo alio et pene contrario ritu censeat porrigi corpus dominicum, quam a Domino in cena discipulis suis fuerit distributum. Id enim cotidianus ęcclesię pretendit usus, ut tribuatur hostia sanguine intincta, cum a Domino prius[a] corpus, deinde sanguis[b] porrectus fuisse memoretur. Quem etiam ęcclesię morem[c] ex decretis Iulii papę nitimini improbare, quibus idem papa dominicum commendat ordinem, et apostolica confidentia ęcclesiasticam arguit dispositionem, [93v] adiciens intinctam panis buccellam Dominum proditori suo contulisse, et ex ea mentis eius impuritatem prodidisse.[17] De cuius dubietatis ambiguitate quod intelligimus, quod a nostris doctoribus accepimus, edicere parati sumus.

Redemptor[d] noster ueniens in mundum, quia[e] propter hominum salutem inter homines apparuit, quęque reparationi infirmitatis humanę commoda seu necessaria fore preuidit, sicut oportere uidit in sapientia sua, ita ab hominibus fieri et esse uoluit in ecclesia sua. Hęc eis cum quibus conuersari dignatus est, uerbo uel exemplo insinuauit, que facienda[f]

17. JK † 203, which is properly C. Braga III c. 1, as it appears in the *Collectio Lanfranci* (Coll. Lanf., cited from Cambridge, Trinity College MS B.16.44) p. 393, *Decretales Pseudoisidorianae* ed. Paul Hinschius (Leipzig 1863, henceforward H.) 434a. The attribution to Pope Julius is first reported in Burchard of Worms, *Decretum* (BD, from PL 140.537–1066) 5.1, and reappears widely after that, as e.g. in Ivo of Chartres, *Decretum* (ID, from PL 161.59–1022) 2.11, and more briefly as 2.85. Bernold of Constance also cites an unspecified 'Ordo Romanus' in *Micrologus* c. 19 in PL 151.989; Michel Andrieu, *Les Ordines Romani du haut Moyen Âge* (Spicilegium sacrum Lovaniense Études et documents 12; Louvain 1965) describes no such copy.

f. memb. omn. ORL; omn. memb. P
g. posui L
a. *ss* O
b. sanguis PR(*p.c.*)L; sanguinis O
c. eccl. mor. ORL; mor. eccl. P
d. Redemptor PRL; Redeptor O
e. *corr. fr.* qua O
f. -da PL; -do OR

erant docens,[g] certum quo[h] facienda[i] erant modum prefigere omittens.[18] Hinc esse uidetur quod ait, Hoc facite in meam commemorationem. Non ait, hoc modo facite. Et,[j] Ite baptizate omnes gentes in nomine Patris, et Filii, et Spiritus sancti.[19] Non ait, hoc modo baptizate. Non ait, Semel mergite, aut[k] tertio mergite. Non ait, scrutinium facite, crisma sacrate.[l] Qua in re insinuasse uidetur que precepta sunt non fieri non licere; pro ratione uero necessitatis uel honestatis alio et alio modo fieri licere. Vnde nonnulla Christianę religionis instituta eum in ęcclesię nascentis inicio suę modum originis accepere,[m] quem in progressu[n] eiusdem crescentis propter quasdam rationabiles causas non diu tenuere. Id beati Augustini responsiones ad Ianuarium euidenter ostendunt, de eo ipso de quo agitur sacramento[o] hęc dicentes,[20] 'Sacramentum corporis et sanguinis Domini apparet discipulos non accepisse ieiunos. Ex hoc placuit Spiritui sancto[p] ut in honorem tanti sacramenti in os Christiani prius Dominicum corpus intraret, quam cęteri cibi. Nam ideo per uniuersum orbem mos iste seruatur.' Idipsum ex [94r] sancti Ieronimi scriptis potest approbari, in expositione epistole Pauli ad Titum ita loquentis,[21] 'Antequam diaboli instinctu studia in religione fierent, et diceretur in populis, Ego sum Pauli, ego Apollo, ego autem Cephę, communi consilio presbiterorum ęcclesię gubernabantur. Postquam uero unusquisque eos quos baptizauerat suos esse putabat non Christi, toto orbe decretum est ut unus de presbiteris electus superponatur cęteris, ad quem omnis cura ęcclesię pertineret, et scismatum semina tollerentur.'[q] Quibus documentis redditur manifestum,[r] aliquos ęcclesię ritus alio modo cepisse, et alio modo per eius incrementa cucurrisse. Vbi patet atestantibus scripturis sacramenta altaris, quę ieiuni modo accipimus, discipulos Domini cenatos accepisse. Patet etiam quod sumimus de mensa lapidea ac sacrata illos de mensa sumpsisse lignea non secundum morem ęcclesię sacrata, aut fortasse nulla. Ibi panes cotidianos comederunt, de genimine uitis biberunt. Nos in forma nummi panem accipimus, uinum aqua mixtum potamus.[22] Neminem ergo dubitare licet, tanti ritum

18. For a vigorous assertion of the counter view see Durand of Troarn in PL 149.1381.

19. 1 Cor. 11:24; Matt. 28:19.

20. Ep. 54.6.8 (CSEL 34/2.166–67).

21. In cap. 1 'Et constituas' (PL 26.562).

22. Compare Honorius, *Gemma animae* c. 35 (PL 172.555, and 564–65) 'in modum denarii'; Jungmann, *Missarum sollemnia* 2.36.

g. dicens L
h. quo PL; quod O; quid R
i. -da PL; -do OR
j. Eciam L
k. *ss* P
l. *p.c.* O
m. *obsc. corr.* R
n. -su OPL; -sus R
o. *p.c.* P
p. Sp. san. ORL; san. Sp. P
q. tollentur L
r. man. red. D

sacramenti[s] multis ac longe diuersis modis in presentis ęcclesia temporis celebrari, quos in primordio non accepit.

Qui ergo quęrit cur non accipiantur exemplo dominico singulatim, quę de altari sumuntur noua consuetudine simul mixta, simili ratione quęrere potest, cur non sumantur[t] simili loco, aut de simili[u] mensa, uel in simili forma, aut cur etiam aliud sumatur, uidelicet aqua, quę[v] a Domino non legitur in cena esse porrecta.[w] Si uero ea necessariis causis intelligit rationabiliter esse[x] parta ac reperta,[23] nouerit et[y] ea de quibus quęritur, et cur aliter[z] fiant quam a Domino facta sunt[aa] inquiritur, ratione non inferiori esse comparata. [94v] Porro cur miratur[bb] quispiam quod sacramenta porriguntur simul mixta? Nonne indesinenter in dominici corporis et sanguinis consecratione diuiso corpore in tres partes, una a sacerdote, uidelicet quę ab ipso sumenda est, in calice reseruatur, sanguini admiscetur, sanguine infunditur, cum sanguine sumitur? Quis sacerdotem peccare dicat, dum in cotidiano tanti mysterii officio carnem cum sanguinis suscipit admixtione? Si ergo bonum est sumere hostiam[cc] sanguine infusam, malum erit porrigere hostiam sanguine intinctam? Quod qui malum non esse agnouerit, desinet mirari, cum ratione factum esse cognouerit. Arguitur iste mos ex eo quod[dd] buccellę intincte a Domino traditori suo porrectę similitudinem uidetur habere. Id si diligenter inspiciatur, nichil dignum reprehensione continere uidebitur. Si enim exteriora pensentur, nemo dicet iustum hominem edere non debere panem intinctum in sua cena, quia id proditor manducauit Iudas in Dominica cena. Aut nemo ideo non dabit osculum pacis, quia Iudas osculo dedit signum proditionis. Simili modo quid nobis obstat accipere corpus Domini Dominico sanguine intinctum, licet Iudas acceperit buccellam de manu Domini dominico uino[ee] intinctam? Si autem interiora cogitemus, propter aliud ille, propter aliud nos. Ille in suę signum nequitię, in signum doli et proditionis quam mente gerebat, de manu Domini buccellam intinctam intinctus fraude suscepit, nos carnem Domini intinguimus[ff] in sanguine Domini, non ut designe-

23. Cf. Augustine, *De Trinitate* 9.9 (CCL 50.305).

s. -menti *ss* O

t. in *add.* PL, *om.* OR

u. de sim.] dissimili L

v. quam L

w. porrectam L. R² *mg. add*: Paschasius dicit, Post consecrationem non nisi sanguis bibitur.

x. nec. causis intelligit rationabiliter esse parta] ORP; racionabilibus et necessariis causis intelligit esse parata L

y. etiam L

z. aliter PRL; alter O

aa. sint L

bb. miretur L

cc. in *add.* R, *om.* OPL

dd. quod ex eo *a.c.* P

ee. uino PRL; uinu O

ff. -gimus L

mus maliciam esse in cordibus nostris, sed ne accipientes siue porrigentes peccemus[gg] non habita forte competenti cautela in labiis et in[hh] manibus nostris.[24] Euenit enim frequenter ut barbati et prolixos habentes granos, [95r] dum poculum inter epulas sumunt, prius[ii] liquore pilos inficiant quam ori liquorem[jj] infundant. Hi[kk] si accesserint ad altare liquorem sanctum bibituri, quomodo periculum deuitare[ll] poterunt inter[mm] accipiendum, quomodo uterque, accipiens uidelicet ac porrigens, effugient grande peccatum?[25] Preterea si inberbes et sine granis,[nn] aut mulieres, ad sumendam communionem sanctam conueniant,[oo] quis sacerdotum poterit tam prouide ministrare, tam caute calicem Domini distribuere ut multis eum singulatim diuidat, diuidens sic in ora eorum fundat ut infundens nihil effundat? Sepe enim dum sibi soli calicem infundere disponit, neglegentia aut[pp] imprudentia facienti[qq] effusionis[rr] periculum incurrit. Quanto facilius in multitudine posito sacerdoti, multis diuersarum formarum ministranti, contingere potest unde grauiter offendat, unde doleat, unde eum[ss] asperam penitentiam agere oporteat?

Ne ergo polluamus sanguinem nostrę redemptionis, ne tamquam impietatis manibus effundamus poculum humanę salutis, a religiosis[tt] uiris prouide actum est ut dominici[uu] portiuncula corporis non sicca, sicut Dominum[vv] egisse nouimus, porrigatur sed Domini infusa sanguine fidelibus tribuatur. Quo pacto euenit, ut secundum Saluatoris preceptum eius carnem edat, sanguinem bibat, periculum euadat, qui[ww] in tanta re offendere oppido formidat. Id enim solidum edimus, id liquidum bibimus, quod simul separatimue ore sumptum per guttur traicimus. In qua distributione nemo ut dictum est formidare debet quod buccella panis intincta proditori Domini a Domino similiter est porrecta. Non enim ea operatio congruam habet similitudinem, quę causę habet dissimilitudinem. Vnde

24. Compare Abelard, *Sic et non* Qu. 118, ed. Blanche B. Boyer and Richard McKeon (Chicago/London 1977) 411–12, and *Magistri Petri Lombardi sententiae in IV libris distinctae* D. xi c 6(1) (Spicilegium Bonaventurianum 4–5; Rome 1971, 1981) 2.303–4.

25. Above n. 7.

gg. caremus *add. ss* L
hh. in ORL; *om.* P
ii. eius *add.* L
jj. *p.c.* O
kk. Hi ORL; Ii P
ll. uitare L
mm. contra L
nn. *An erasure follows in* O; *a later hand adds* uiri
oo. *corr. fr.* -ent O
pp. vel L
qq. -enti OR; -ente PR^{2}L
rr. in fusionis L
ss. eum LD; eam O; cum P; *om.* R (*?rightly*)
tt. -osis OPL; -onis R
uu. dominici PRL; *om.* O
vv. Iesum L
ww. qui ORL; quem P

Iulii papę decreta quamquam rationabi[95v]liter data fuere,[xx] apud aliquos modernos hac in parte quieuere, ęcclesię preualuit consuetudo, quę pondere rationis antecellit eminentiore. Nec mirum, rationabilem usum tantis actum[yy] necessariis causis Iulii decretis anteponi cum legamus, et ipsis cotidianis actionibus frequentari uideamus, ceterorum instituta pontificum propter similes aut inferioris ut uidetur generis causas discretiore prudentia esse[zz] mutata. Thelesphorus papa in decretis suis missarum officia qua hora celebranda sint, his uerbis absoluit: 'Nocte sancta Natiuitatis Domini missas celebrent. Reliquis temporibus missarum celebrationes ante horam diei terciam minime sunt celebrandę, quia eadem hora et Dominus crucifixus, et super apostolos Spiritus sanctus descendisse legitur.'[26] Quod[aaa] cuius decretum quam pauci seruauere,[bbb] quam multi abiecere, testatur ipsa[ccc] ęcclesiastici frequentia seruitii, testatur[ddd] pro fidelibus uiuis[eee] ac defunctis sacerdotalis oratio et dominici corporis ac[fff] sanguinis cotidiana immolatio; testatur nec non pro se ac suis siue id fieri petens seu presentiam suam exhibens popularis multitudo. Intellexerunt enim satius esse, multis horis multas fieri oblationes, quam usque ad horam terciam pluribus omissis paucarum oblationum fieri dilationes. Similiter Victor papa in decretis suis docet baptismum faciendum esse in Pascha, sic dicens, 'Eodem tempore, id est Paschę, baptismus celebrandus est[ggg] catholicus.[hhh] Si tamen mortis periculum ingruerit, gentiles[iii] ad fidem uenientes quocumque loco uel tempore baptizentur.'[27] Quod etiam Papa Siricius decretali assertione corroborat sic dicens:[28] 'Baptismi priuilegium apud nos et apud omnes ęcclesias dominicum specialiter[jjj] cum Pentecoste,[kkk] Pascha defendit. Quibus tamen in qualibet necessitate opus fuerit, omni uolumus celeri[96r]tate succurri.'[lll] Id uero ęcclesia Dei longe aliter custodit,

26. A catena from JK † 34, H. 110–11 (Coll. Lanf. p. 29). BD 3.20, ID 3.65 have slightly less.

27. JK † 74, H. 128 (Coll. Lanf. p. 34) abbreviated toward end.

28. A catena from JK 255, H. 520b–21a (Coll. Lanf. pp. 85–86). BD 4.3, ID 1.198 have less.

xx. fuere ORL; perfuere P

yy. actum R; actam OP (P *obsc. corr.*)L; auctum R²

zz. *obscure addn in* L

aaa. *om.* L

bbb. seruauere O²PR; seruare OL

ccc. ipsa ORL; *om.* P

ddd. ipsa *add.* P¹, *om.* OPRL

eee. *ss* O

fff. et L

ggg. cel. est ORL; est cel. P

hhh. -cus OP; -cis RL

iii. L *breaks off, leaving two blank lines before the next passage.*

jjj. dom. spec. OPR²; Domini conspecialiter R

kkk. -ste OR; -sten P

lll. P *fol. 189v ends* celeritate, *and resumes on fol. 190 below.* D *supplies* succurri, *but is otherwise as* P. OR *continue.*

adeo ut huius decreti seruatores non seruantibus comparati breuissimo uideantur numero comprehendi. Aiunt enim tutius esse, et gratius in oculis Dei, si ei qui possunt quamdiu possunt, sani uel infirmi, nascantur de Spiritu Dei, quam subitanea morte pressi mergantur in profundum ęternę damnationis. Preterea[a] Gregorius maior, audito quod presbyteri pueros in fronte signarent baptizandos quos episcopi in eodem loco signaturi erant baptizatos, in registro suo tale contra excessum tantum canonicum mandatum dedit: 'Episcopi baptizatos infantes signare in frontibus bis crismate non presumant, sed presbyteri baptizandos tangant in pectore, ut episcopi postmodum tangere debeant in fronte.'[29] Super qua iussione presbyteris[b] indignatis, scandalizatis, et in eius odium grauiter concitatis, ob mitigandam eorum tristiciam in epistola Ianuario episcopo missa prudenti consilio quę de tanta re prouidenter decreuerat ita permutauit, 'Peruenit ad nos quosdam scandalizatos fuisse quod presbyteros crismate tangere eos qui baptizandi sunt prohibuimus. Et nos quidem secundum usum ueterem ęcclesię nostrę fecimus. Sed si omnino hac re aliqui contristantur, ubi episcopi desunt, ut presbyteri et in frontibus baptizandos crismate tangere debeant concedimus.'[30] Qui ergo audit et legit[c] mutationes huiusmodi pro talibus causis esse factas, mirari non debet[d] Iulii papę assertiones predictis rationibus esse mutatas. Sancti patres quod faciendum erat, quod ratio postulabat pro seruanda religione Christiana, si humana fragilitas admitteret, debere fieri decreuerunt, sed imminentes humanę infirmitatis plurime necessitates plurima aliter atque aliis modis fieri compulerunt. Et rationis ac sapientię fuit quod ab eis iubebatur, nec ratione carebat, [96v] quod cogente necessitate ab ecclesia concorditer mutabatur. Illud bonum quia pro Deo, pro salute institutum, istud non inferioris glorię, quia ne pereat homo, ne salus amittatur, uidetur esse preparatum. Valuit illud suo tempore inter obseruare ualentes, ualeat istud nostro tempore inter infirmos et periculum formidantes. Quamquam de negotio presenti alia ratio satis accommoda questioni uideatur posse reddi. Sicut enim altissimo constat Dominum Iesum Christum consilio discipulis suis sua sacramenta tribuisse, ita Christianę menti probabile est non inaniter sed ratione excellentissima eadem eisdem separatim distribuisse. Intelligunt enim fideles Christi, Christum Dominum hac distinctione significare uoluisse quod non uno uerum duobus modis passurus esset pro humana salute, dum et

29. JE 1281, Reg. 4.9 (CCL 140.226).
30. JE 1298, Reg. 4.26 (CCL 140.245–46).

a. Preterea O; Propterea R
b. -b- *ss* R
c. et legit R; legi O
d. non debet *in mg.* O

carne ligno crucis esset affigendus et cruore proprio perfudendus. Quibus modis filios ęternę salutis ad compatiendum maluit inuitare, uolens socios fieri suę passionis quos participes futuros esse nouerat suę retributionis. Vnde dicit scriptura: 'Sicut Christus animam suam pro nobis posuit, ita et nos debemus pro fratribus nostris animas ponere.'[31] Et alio loco: 'Si compatimur, et congaudebimus. Si sustinemus et conregnabimus.'[e] Passionem ergo crucis Christi imitantur ii qui mortificationem carnis in corpore suo circumferentes carnem suam crucifigunt cum uitiis et concupiscentiis. Effusionem autem sanguinis Christi illi merentur imitari qui mundi huius principem contemnentes pro nomine et testimonio Filii Dei[f] gaudebundi occumbunt.[32] In quibus utrisque illud sacrę scripturę eloquium cernitur esse congrue adimpletum: 'Ad mensam magnam sedisti, scito quoniam talia te oportet preparare.' De quo uersiculo expositores [97r] sic loquuntur:[33] 'Quę est hęc mensa nisi de qua accipimus corpus Christi? Et quid est, talia te oportet[g] preparare nisi talia te oportet[h] imitari?' Hac ergo causa quę dicta est, uidelicet ut electi Dei heredes fierent in regno Christi et Dei, Christus Dominus non sola predicatione, uerum passionis exhibitione, uolens ad compatiendum premonere, quos in regno Patris dignatus est hereditare. Primus uoluit prius ligno configi, deinde lancea latus eius perforante sanguine suo perfundi, ut eos alterutro martyrii genere instrueret mundum superare, diabolum expugnare et per angustias carnis regnum cęleste intrare. Quod etiam uerbo docuerat, dicens:[34] 'Per multas passiones oportet uos introire in regnum Dei.' Commoda ergo ratione significanti mysterio placuit Saluatori nostro discipulos suos prius pascere carne sua, deinde potare sanguine suo,[i] ut ipse[j] sue passionis misterio per predicta martyrii genera ad uitam migrandum esse insinuaret, signans etiam per certamen[k] legitimum neminem posse coronari, qui non uno horum studuerit corporaliter seu spiritualiter crucifigi.

31. 1 John 3:16, here as cited in Augustine, *Enarrationes in Psalmos* Ps. 51 c. 9 (CCL 39.629).

32. 'Gaudebundus' is a very rare word; in view of Ernulf's known expertise in grammar (*S. Anselmi opera* 3 Ep. 64) it is tempting to suppose he found it in Virgilius Maro Grammaticus, Ep. V: *Opera omnia* ed. Bengt Löfstedt (Bibliotheca scriptorum Graecorum et Romanorum Teubneriana; Munich 2003) 87.

33. Ecclesiasticus 31:12 as cited and expounded in Augustine Sermo 31 (PL 38.193), here slightly modified.

34. Acts 14:21.

e. conreg. O; congaudebimus R
f. *p.c.* O
g. *p.c.* O
h. *p.c.* O
i. P *resumes*
j. ipse O[2]R; ipso OP
k. -men OP; -mina R

[II]

Secunda quęstione percunctatum est, cur quarta pars hostię in calice ponitur. De qua ita respondemus: Non est nostrę consuetudinis ut quarta pars hostię in calice dimitti debeat,[a] sed tercia. Alicui fortassis quarta iccirco mitti uidetur quod hostia per medium secta; medietatis quasi medietas in calice ponitur, quę quia ad totius hostię quantitatem ceu quadrans est; quarta ideo esse uidetur. Sed nouerit dilectio uestra quia non attendimus quanta quęque pars sit in toto, sed quota sit de toto. Sufficit enim in diuisione [97v] hostię ternarium numerum consummare,[b] non quę parcium maior quęue minor sit attendere. Vnde nonnulle ęcclesię illum habent usum ut hostiam non per medium diuidant sed eam trium equalitate partium comminuant. Cur autem in tres determinate[c] diuidatur[d] ex decretis Anacleti papę probabiliter conicitur. In eisdem nanque legitur quia:[35] 'Episcopus sacrificans[e] Deo in solennioribus diebus septem aut quinque aut tres diaconos et subdiaconos, et reliquos ministros secum habeat.' Et paulo post: 'Peracta consecratione omnes communicent, qui noluerunt[f] ęcclesiasticis carere liminibus.' Inde ęcclesiastica inoleuit consuetudo ut episcopo aut presbytero sacrificante et[g] diacono ac subdiacono cooperante, eiusdem obsequii nemo, aut raro quisquam a sancte communionis excipiatur participatione. Quia ergo his ipsis[h] tribus Dominici altaris seruitoribus commissa sunt Dominica sacramenta, quibus scriptura communicare iubet, statutum est ut archanę recordationis hostia in tres partes[i] diuidatur, quę diuise a singulis seruitoribus singulę suscipiantur, quarum una sacerdos in calice securius sibi reseruata,[j] ceteras in patena ministris, si presentes fuerint, porrigendas custodit. Eis absentibus sicut agit[k] quod erant acturi, ita accipit quod erant accepturi. Nec tamen uacat a misterio, quod numero Trinitatis illa solet fieri diuisio. Corpus enim Domini, quod in altari conficitur, sacramentum est eius corporis, quod est ęcclesia. Quę quia in tribus electorum ordinibus consummatur, prepositis, continentibus et coniugatis,[l] recte corpus Domini tripertito diuiditur, quod electis omnibus signum est unitatis, signum concordię et pacis, et causa ęternę

35. JK † 2, H. 70 (Coll. Lanf. p. 20), slightly modified. BD 7.71, 77 (omitted in ID) have less.

a. in calicem dim. deb. OR; dim. deb. in calice P
b. cumsummare O
c. *corr. fr.* -ante O
d. diuididatur O
e. sacrificans O(*p.c.*)R; sacrificaturus P
f. -unt OR; -int P
g. *ss* O
h. his ipsis O; ipsis P; his ex ipsis R
i. *corr. fr.* panes O
j. reseruata OP(*p.c.*)R[2]; seruata R
k. *corr. fr.* ait O
l. *corr. fr.* contug- O

salutis. Hi sunt illi ordines, in quorum[m] figura Ezechiel propheta se tres liberatos uiros legitur audisse, [98r] Noe scilicet, Danielem[n] et Iob.[36] Noe quippe qui rector archę extitit inter undas prepositorum ordinem signat, Daniel pro sua excellenti abstinentia a mundanis delectationibus continentium uitam figurat. Sanctus Iob figuram gerit sanctorum coniugum de acceptis bonis ministrantium Deo[o] in operibus bonis.[37]

Dicunt non improbandę auctoritatis uiri, iccirco trifariam tanti fieri sacramenti diuisionem ut ipso numero presentia Trinitatis ęternę adesse cognoscatur, cuius de modica creatura tantam fieri operationem credimus et miramur. Videtur etiam nonnullis summe pericię uiris hanc iccirco inter sacra missarum solennia dominici corporis triformiter fieri diuisionem, quatenus illo partium numero solenniter recolatur, qualiter ipsa eadem[p] carnis substantia in figura humani corporis a uerbo Dei assumpta, sub trina uarietate hominibus propter homines fuerit exhibita.[q] Mortalibus enim oculis mortalis apparuit, in sepulcro mortuus iacuit, immortalis surrexit.[38] Quibus contractę infirmitatis quasi medelis, clementię placuit diuinę desperantes animos stoliditatis humanę ad fidem erudire, ad amorem accendere, ad uenturę spem resurrectionis[r] attollere.

[III]

Tertio loco tercia sequitur quęstio. Haec ita proponitur. In perceptione eucharistię corpus Domini aut ex toto sumitur aut ex parte. Si uero ex toto sumitur ore fidelium, et integer Christus in partes non scinditur, quemadmodum certum tenemus, quomodo tunc uel quare separatim sanguis sine corpore sumitur? Duas in una proponitis quęstiones; uidelicet quare et quomodo separatim sanguis sumitur. Hęc uero, quare sumitur, nulla responsione indigere uidetur. Puto enim a me sufficienter [98v] absolu-

36. Ezech. 14:14.

37. Cf. Gregory the Great, *Moralia in Iob* 1.14 (CCL 143.34).

38. The Trinitarian symbolism seems obvious, but it is not clear which expositors Ernulf has in mind here; the threefold aspect of Christ's life in the Church was often employed in this context, though in varying ways: Amalarius, *Liber officialis* 3.35 in *Amalarii episcopi opera liturgica omnia* ed. J.M. Hanssens (Studi e Testi 138–40; 1948–50) 2.367–368, followed slightly later by Alger of Liège, *De sacramentis corporis et sanguinis dominici* 1.19 (PL 180.795), *Panormia* 1.140 (PL 161.1076), and by Honorius in his *Gemma animae* 1.63–64 (PL 172.563–64, and cf. 795) among others. See Henri de Lubac, *Corpus mysticum: l'eucharistie et l'église au Moyen Âge: Étude historique* (2nd ed. Paris 1949) 298–339, citing Ernulf at 301.

m. quorum OP; quarum R
n. -lim *p.c.* O
o. min. Deo OR; Deo min. P
p. eadem ipsa *a.c.* O
q. *corr. fr.* Ex hab- O
r. –ionis PR; -ioni O

tum esse, quare sumitur corpus Domini sine sanguinis admixtione, puto absolutionis perspicuitatem diligenter attendenti sufficere debere. Quia ergo in manifestę rei uestigatione ineptum est superfluę laborare, omittimus de ea ulterius loqui, fautores[a] dominici ordinis nequaquam arguentes, ęcclesiasticę uero disciplinę cautelam minus prouidis commendantes. Altera uero quęstio quę dicit, Quomodo sumitur sanguis separatim sine corpore, non magna discussione uidetur egere. Si enim eam paulo attencius aspiciatis, facili explicatione se ipsam prodit uobis. Quia enim omnem corpoream substantiam constat corpus esse, sanguinem Domini corpus esse manifestum est, remota omni ambiguitate. Sed cum Dominus passionis suę sacramenta commendaret, dicens,[39] 'Hoc est corpus meum,' et item, 'Hic est calix sanguinis mei,' corpus a sanguine distinxit, corpus proprie intelligens quod solidum erat, quod cruci affigendum erat, per sanguinem assignans quod erat liquidum, quod erat effundendum, in utroque passionis suę qualitatem prefigurans. Et nos quotiens de corpore et sanguine Domini loquimur in eadem significatione nomina ipsa memoramus. Domini ergo corpus quamquam in sacramentorum uelamine sumatur ex toto sicut uidemini asseuerare, separatim tamen et sanguis sine corpore et corpus percipitur sine sanguine, dum et liquor sine soliditate, et soliditas consumitur sine liquore. Nec repugnare uidetur si totus sanguis separatim sumatur sine corpore, quem totum credimus sumi cum corpore, cum et totum ab uno, totum a multis corpus dominicum percipi certissime teneatis. Quomodo autem totum ab isto, totum ab illo sumitur, separatim uero sumitur ab isto et ab illo, ita cum totum corpus accipitur per se, et totus sanguis per se, separatim et sanguis sine corpore et corpus [99r] sumitur sine sanguine. De quęstione uero tanti sacramenti modestius, ut opinor, esset colloquendo dicere quod dici opus habet, quam discutiendo scribere quod periculosum iudicium habet; ne forte quod perspicuum est inutiliter exponatur, aut quod obscurum est incaute relinquatur; seu ambiguo uerbo dum scriptor non aduertit, auditor offendatur. Familiari enim colloquio commodius ostenderetur[b] et quantum dici debet et quantum credi oportet, et quod dici siue credi catholica fides abhorret.

[IV]

In quarta quęstione sic quęritur: Si integer Christus sumitur, utrum solum corpus sine anima an etiam anima cum corpore sumitur? Cuius generis

39. Matt. 26:26.

a. faut- OR; fact- P

b. -eretur OP; -etur R

percunctationes ab iis[a] frequenter proponi solent qui appetunt sapientes uideri, quos magis delectat philosophicis disputationibus elate inseruire quam ęcclesiasticis disciplinis et sacris auctoritatibus humiliter ac[b] fideliter[c] obedire. Hi timentibus Deum, et fide potius quam ratione probantibus corpus Christi sanguinemque esse quod sumitur de altari, decipulas[d] huiusmodi obtendere solent. Corpus Christi quod sumitur de altari aut est animatum aut est inanimatum; si est animatum, cur non ex se mouetur? Si uero inanimatum, quomodo est illud quod resurrexit[e] a mortuis, et uiuit in secula seculorum? Itemque sic aiunt: Corpus Domini aut est corruptibile, aut est incorruptibile. Si est incorruptibile, quomodo frangitur, minuitur, inueteratur? Si autem est corruptibile, qualiter uerum est ueram resurrectionem illud accepisse, uere incorruptelę particeps esse? Has, ut dictum est, nodosas disputationes[f] illi obicere moliuntur quos amor humanę laudis, quos fauor fatigat popularis, qui gaudent imperitis scrupulosarum parare laqueos questionum, quibus sacrarum non [99v] sufficit robur et auctoritas scripturarum, quibus cordi est, potius sequi rationem sapientię secularis quę stulta facta est a sapientia Dei, quam fidei ueritatem quę inscrutabilia penetrat, et rationis inpotentiam pertransiens ascendit usque ad ipsum nutum[g] Dei. At iustus ex fide uiuens, humiliter sapiens, non sensum suum preferendo sed Domini sui mandata reuerenter amplectendo, omnia credit quę Spiritus sanctus credenda esse precepit, non quęrens quomodo hoc uel illud esse[h] possit, sed ad omnia diuinitus imperata quę legit uel audit, ut pote mitis et humilis corde, humillime adquiescit. Hęc idcirco dixerim, ut quę fide sola[i] intuenda sunt in quęstionem non adducatis, quia non est utilę animę Christianę insolitis disputationibus discutere misteria redemptionis nostrę. Quoniam de sua salutę dubitare uidetur qui de mysteriis salutis quęstiones facere cognoscitur. Scriptum quippe est, Qui dubitat, non credit.

Cęterum quo argumento, quaue disputandi subtilitate queat quis approbare, panem et uinum corpus sanguinemque fieri Christi[j] per[k] uerba Christi? Tamen quia omnipotens ueritas locuta est, ita dicens,[40] 'Hoc est corpus meum' et, 'Hic est sanguis meus,' neminem dubitare licet ita uerum esse ut scriptura docet; tum quia ueritas mentiri non potest, tum quia om-

40. Matt. 26:26.

a. iis OR; his P
b. *corr. fr.* et P
c. -irer O
d. *corr. fr.* desc- R
e. resurr- OR; surr- P
f. -nes *ss* P
g. P *obsc. corr.*
h. *ss* O
i. fide sola OR; sola fide P
j. *ss* P
k. per PR; pro O

nipotens non facere hoc non potest. Porro si rationis acumine comprehendi non potest utrum panis et uinum per consecrationem fiant corpus et sanguis, nemo disputandi arte fretus uestigare debet quomodo sit corpus, aut quale sit corpus, uel quomodo sit sanguis, uel qualis sanguis. Cum enim secreta cęlestia nequeat quis ratione scrutari, ineptus sit si, quamuis quod de ipsis legitur fide teneat, quod non legitur, uidelicet quam pulchra, aut quomodo sint disposita, ratione inquirere seu discutere presumat. Qui enim de qua[100r]cumque re an sit ignorat,[l] frustra de ea qualis sit, aut quomodo se habeat, interrogat. Ita huiusmodi sacramenta cum quid sint nemo ratione apprehendere queat, qualia sint superflua curiositate indagare curat. Id sane mysterii genus iccirco mysterium fidei uocatur, quia eius secreta sola capit fides, quę ratio assequi non potest. De quo nimirum ita scriptum est:[41] 'Si quid residuum fuerit, igni comburetur.' Eius profecto secreta abscondita sunt in thesauris sapientię cęlestis, quę inde furari sacrilegium est,[m] presertim sic prohibente Spiritu Dei,[42] 'Altiora te ne quesieris.' Et illud, 'Ne transgrediaris terminos patrum[n] tuorum.' Vnde id sacrilegii perpetrare cauendo quod fidei solius archano custoditur, disputationis acumine discutere deuito. Nichil enim pro arbitrio intelligentię meę[o] ponere uolo, sed id solum quod ex scripturis autenticis uel probatorum sententia doctorum collectum est proferre intento.[p] Aut certe si dicendum sit quid aliud, uel quare aliud quęri[q] debet de carnę nostrę redemptionis quam quod omnipotens ueritas allegauit? Quę ubi inter cenandum carnem suam discipulis edendam protulit, dicens, Hoc est corpus meum, de qualitatibus tacuit, mutationem substantię esse factam insinuauit.[r] Quid ergo? Nonne sicut dixit facere potuit? Nonne potuit mutare panem in substanciam carnis sine assumptione qualitatum ipsius carnis? Quid omnipotens facere non potuit? Credimus et certum tenemus, substantiam panis uerborum uirtute mutatam esse[s] in substantiam dominicę carnis. Certissime tamen scimus, et sensibus corporeis comprobamus qualitates panis immobiliter permanere, cuius substanciam quia caro facta est credimus non manere. Visu enim candorem, gustu contrectamus panis saporem, [100v] ceterasque eisdem ceterisue sensibus qualitates[t] panis ita iudicamus, ut panis cuius substancia deest, qualitatem nullam deesse[u] uideamus, carnis cui-

41. Exod. 12:10.
42. Eccl. 3:2, Prov. 22:28.

l. ignorat PR; *om, with erasure* O
m. fur. sac. est O; sac. est. fur. P; fur. est sac. R
n. *corr. fr.* parum O
o. int. mee OR; mee int. P
p. intento OR; intendo P
q. queri OR; *om.* P
r. *corr. fr.* insinuarit R
s. mut. esse OR; esse mut. P
t. -ta- *ss* O
u. *p.c.* O

us[v] substancia adest,[w] qualitatem nullam adesse sentiamus. Cum ergo manentibus panis qualitatibus non miremur panis abesse substantiam, sed integritate fidei in substanciam carnis credamus eam esse,[x] non mutatis eius qualitatibus permutatam, quid mirum si presente carnis substancia, qualitates carnis sicut non uidentur[y] adesse, ita dicantur abesse? Quo pacto quod sacratur quamuis[z] concedatur esse Christi caro, non tamen recte quęritur mortalis, mortua, siue immortalis existat; sicut non recte fideles a fidelibus querimus an hostia sacrata, cum qualitates panis aspiciamus, panis existat. Sicut enim, ut dictum est, translata panis substancia qualitates eius uidentur non esse translatę, ita admissa carnis substancia, qualitates eius non sentiuntur esse admissę. Sed ad me redeo, mei excessus presumptionem castigo, malens cum simplicibus[aa] simpliciter credere, quam simplicitati[bb] columbę amarus existere.

[V]

Quinto loco uestra uenerabilis diligentia uersiculum de propheta Iohel sumptum digerit, percunctans uidelicet quid intelligere uoluerit[a] propheta, cum[b] dicit:[43] 'Quis scit si conuertatur, et ignoscat Deus, et relinquat post se benedictionem?' Huius lucubraciunculam de beati Ieronimi commentariolo super duodecim prophetarum expositionem composito decerpere potuistis, si forte librum apud uos habuistis.[44] Quod quia liber idem nobiscum est, et ego possem, nisi breuitatem eius sufficere uobis non posse dubitarem. Dicam itaque quod sentio; iudicet qui uult; capiat qui potest. Propheta suos auditores, Domini contemptores, hortatur ad penitentiam, dicens:[45] 'Conuertimini ad Dominum Deum uestrum.' Et quasi quis quęreret, Qua spe conuertemur? Id est, unde possumus sperare nos ueniam consecuturos,[c] subiungit dicens,[46] 'Quia benignus et misericors est, patiens, [101r] et multum misericors, prestabilis super maliciam.' Quo

43. Ioel 2:14.

44. Hieronimus in Ioelem 2.12–14 (CCL 76.182–83), thoroughly reworked. The second volume of a copy of Jerome's commentary on the minor prophets from Christ Church, Canterbury survives as Cambridge, Trinity College B.3.5 (James no. 84), identified among the early scribal work of Eadmer by Michael Gullick, 'The Scribal Work of Eadmer of Canterbury to 1109,' *Archaeologia Cantiana* 118 (1998) 173–89 at 179–80 as written before 1086.

45. Ioel 2:13.

46. Ibid.

v. cuius OR; *om.* P

w. *corr. fr.* ad. sub. P²

x. esse OR; adesse P

y. -etur *a.c.* O

z. *p.c.* O

aa. cum simplicibus OP; cum simpliciter O²; simpliciter R

bb. -te *a.c.* O

a. uoluerit OR; uoluit P

b. *ss* R²

c. -uros P; -ures O; -oros R

posito equipollenter interrogatiuam pro enuntiatiua oratione subinfert, sic[d] dicens: Quis scit si conuertatur? Hoc est, forsitan conuertetur; ac si diceret, Quia Deus misericors est, si conuertamini a prauis operibus, forsitan et ipse conuertetur ab ea sententia quam merentur peccata uestra. Scriptum est enim,[47] 'Mutat Deus sentenciam, consilium nunquam.' Quomodo autem conuertatur, mutetque sententiam, exponit dum dicit: 'Et ignoscat, et relinquat[e] post se benedictionem,' id est, et peccata remittat, et remissis peccatis gratiam tribuat. Quod uero dicit relinquat post se, id est sequentibus se, est sicut illud:[48] 'Pacem meam do uobis, pacem relinquo uobis.' Quod expositor sic dicit:[49] 'Sequentibus relinquo, peruenientibus do.' Quod ibi dicitur sequentibus, est id ipsum quod hic dictum est, post se. Relinquit igitur benedictionem, id est pacem siue gratiam post se, id est sequentibus se; iis scilicet qui uolunt facere uoluntatem Dei, non quęrunt ut Deus faciat uoluntatem suam. Quamuis et eundem uersiculum sed apertius positum in prophetia Ionę ualeamus inuenire, sic:[50] 'Quis scit si conuertatur, et ignoscat Deus, et reuertatur a furore irę suę et non peribimus?'

Explicit tractatus Arnulfi monachi de corpore et sanguine Domini ad Lambetum[f]

47. Gregory I, *Moralia in Iob* 16.10 (CCL 143A.806): 'Deus etsi plerumque mutat sententiam, consilium nunquam.' Cf. Barbara Faes de Mottoni, 'Profezia e consilium: "Deus mutat sententiam, non consilium",' *Consilium. teorie e pratiche del consigliare nella cultura medievale*, ed. Carla Casagrande, Chiara Crisciani, Silvana Vecchio (Firenze 2004) 57–76.

48. John 14:27.

49. Gregory I, *Homiliae in evangelia*, hom. 30 (CCL 141.259).

50. Jonah 3:9.

d. *repeated and canc.* O

e. et rel. *in mg.* O

f. Expl.—Lambetum *in red capitals, O only*

PART THREE ⇜ POLITICS

ALISON I. BEACH

12 Imagining *Libertas*

Keeping the Bishop at Bay in the Twelfth-Century Chronicle of Petershausen

On 27 August 1134, 'with great joy and exaltation, with hymns and praises,' the monks of Petershausen, accompanied by Bishop Ulrich II (1127–38) of Constance, monks from seven other monasteries, and a great crowd of clerics and lay people, carried the relics of their community's founder, Bishop Gebhard II (979–95), into the newly restored monastery church.[1] In preparation for the translation, Abbot Conrad (1127–64) had opened Gebhard's tomb in the presence of the bishop and discovered the holy body,

1. Anno a condito monasterio centesimo quinquagesimo secundo advenit Oudalricus episcopus et ex monasteriis patres septem invitati a Counrado abbate iam sepe dicti monasterii. Sed et turba clericorum et monachorum aliorumque fidelium affuit non modica, et cum immani gaudio et exultatione, cum ymnis et laudibus honorifice transtulerunt ossa et cineres beati confessoris Christi atque pontificis Gebehardi de loco prioris sepulchri et in sarchofago posita ambitum monasterii lustraverunt et postea cum magno honore in novo tumulo condiderunt. *Casus Monasterii Petrishusensis. Die Chronik des Klosters Petershausen*, ed. and trans. Otto Feger (Schwäbische Chroniken der Stauferzeit 3; Lindau and Constance 1956) 208–11 (hereafter cited as CP). For an earlier printed edition of the Chronicle of Petershausen, see MGH Scriptores 20 (Hannover 1868) 21–682. All of the Latin quotations from the Chronicle in this article are from Feger's 1956 edition. On the history of Petershausen, see Ilse J. Miscoll-Reckert, *Kloster Petershausen als Bischöflich-Konstanzisches Eigenkloster. Studien über das Verhältnis zu Bischof, Adel und Reform vom 10. bis 12. Jahrhundert'* (Konstanzer Geschichts- und Rechtsquellen 18. Neue Folge der Konstanzer Stadtrechtsquellen; Sigmaringen 1973); Arno Borst, *Mönche am Bodensee 610–1525* (Darmstadt 1985) 136–54; Manfred Krebs, 'Quellenstudien zur Geschichte des Klosters Petershausen', *Zeitschrift für die Geschichte des Oberrheins* 48 (1935) 463–543; Sibylle Appuhn-Radtke and Annelis Schwarzmann, eds., *1000 Jahre Petershausen. Beiträge zu Kunst und Geschichte der Benediktinerabtei Petershausen in Konstanz* (Constance 1983); *St. Gebhard und sein Kloster Petershausen. Festschrift zur 1000. Wiederkehr der Inthronisation des Bischofs Gebhard II. von Konstanz*, ed. Kath. Pfarrgemeinde St. Gebhard, Konstanz (Constance 1979). On the manuscripts that survive from Petershausen, placed in the context of the history of the monastery, see Wilfrid Werner, *Die mittelalterlichen nichtliturgischen Handschriften des Zisterzienserklosters Salem* (Wiesbaden 2000) lviii–lxv, 254–59.

'more precious than any costly treasure,' lying in decaying burial garments that clung to the bones and threatened to disintegrate at the slightest touch. Only a part of Gebhard's alb and his bright yellow stole remained intact.[2] The condition of the body itself was also precarious; the depth of the crypt, combined with its proximity to the Rhine, brought perennial problems with seepage and dampness, and the body had begun to decay. The monks laid Gebhard's body out to dry in the open air to prevent further deterioration.[3]

This celebration marked the culmination of an extensive program of restoration and expansion of a number of the monastery's buildings. Although only 152 years old, Petershausen's church had been constructed on a weak foundation on soft, swampy land. The walls had cracked on all sides, and storms and wind over the years had worn the western pediment down to bare stone, leaving this face of the basilica 'black, monstrous, and ugly.'[4] Alarmed by the condition of the building and fearing its collapse, Hugo, a canon of the cathedral, urged Conrad to take action. Masons repaired the cracks and holes in the west wall, and Wernher, a glassmaker who served the monastery, replaced the original window with a new, larger one, and added two smaller windows above it. The frescoes that decorated the interior wall, already disfigured by age and neglect and further damaged in the course of the repairs, were covered over with fresh plaster.[5] With the restoration of the church and the translation of its founder's relics, the decay of both basilica and saintly body was halted.

For the anonymous monk of Petershausen who recorded these events, the reverse of the physical decline of the monastery and the rescue of the disintegrating body of its founder constituted a metaphor for reform. His chronicle, begun at the very end of a long period of reform initiated in 1086 by the former Hirsau monk, Bishop Gebhard III (1084–1110), now survives in a single copy, University of Heidelberg, Codex Salemitani IX 42a (folios 34r–98v).[6] The reference in book one to Abbot Conrad provides a *terminus post quem* of 1127 for the start of the project.[7] The preface and first four books comprise both original narrative and a variety of sources gathered from existing charters, papal privileges, and other historical chronicles.[8] After 1138, however, the entries take on a different quality,

2. 2 CP 5.3.

3. CP 5.7.

4. CP 5.1.

5. CP 5.1.

6. A copy of the complete manuscript is available online through the University of Heidelberg's digital manuscript project: http://digi.ub.uni-heidelberg.de/diglit/salIX42a.'

7. CP 1.22.

8. CP 2.26–47 draws heavily on the account of the Investiture Conflict from the Chronicles of Berthold of Zwiefalten and Bernold of St. Blasius. See Feger, *Chronik*, 106–7, nn. 26 and 27.

with shorter, more sporadic entries, generally dated by year, that are less carefully written. These entries are also distinguished by the varying color of their ink, which alternates between black and brown.[9] This change from historical retrospection to reportage is also reflected in the physical structure of the manuscript; the first six quires comprise regular gatherings of four bifolia. Quire 7, in which the author begins to record 'current' events, around 1139, however, was made from two single folios and two bifolia (I + I + II). The section of the chronicle, then, that reports 'current' events begins in c. 1139 and continues down to 1156, after which a series of less-skilled author-compilers continued the work with varying degrees of detail and regularity until 1249.

Central to the retrospective section of the work, compiled and written between c. 1127 and 1138 and recounting the history of the monastery from the time of the founder's ancestors through the translation of his relics in 1134, is the chronicler's claim that liberty—and especially freedom from the depredations of unscrupulous bishops—was a fundamental right of Petershausen's monks from the start. This theme emerges already in the first book, when the author emphasizes the care that Gebhard II took to establish the monastery's *libertas;* the monks, the chronicler insisted, owed 'no service, no tribute, no tax, no legation, and no performance of any other service, either to the Roman pope or emperor, or to the bishop of Constance or any other person of power or office, but to God alone.'[10] He also included in the text the papal privilege that Gebhard II had obtained from Pope John XV (985–96) in 989, which clearly grants to the monks the right of the free election of the abbot and explicitly limits the role of the bishop to blessing and confirming their choice. Included in this letter is a creative twelfth-century interpolation that grants the monks the right to appoint their own advocates.[11] As Ilse Miscoll-Reckert stressed in her 1973 study of Petershausen, however, Bishop Gebhard III worked to reform the monastery within the framework of the proprietary church system. Petershausen remained an episcopal *Eigenkloster,* a community over which the bishops of Constance

9. Compare, for example, folio 42v (http://digi.ub.uni-heidelberg.de/diglit/salIX42a/0098) and folio 87r (http://digi.ub.uni-heidelberg.de/diglit/salIX42a/0187).

10. CP 1.37: De Libertate Monasterii. Nullum sane servitium, neque tributum, neque vectigal, neque legationem, neque alicuius omnino ministerii functionem tam Romano pontifici quam imperatori, sed neque episcopo Constantiensi, nec alicui persone, cuiuscumque potestatis sit aut dignitatis, de hoc monasterio beatus Gebehardus impendere constituit, nisi soli Deo.

11. CP 1.27. Miscoll-Reckert and others have argued convincingly that such concern electing advocates is an anachronism in the context of a tenth-century papal monastic privilege. For a discussion of the 'modernization' of this letter as a reflection of the agenda of Petershausen's twelfth-century monks, see Miscoll-Reckert, *Kloster Petershausen* 62–65, 214–16.

exercised proprietary rights, and there is no evidence that the monks made any sustained effort to establish 'liberty' from their episcopal proprietor, or to exercise their right to the free election of abbots, until after 1127.

This insistence upon monastic liberty stems clearly from troubles with Bishop Ulrich I (1111–27) when the drawbacks of dependence became dramatically apparent. This dependence had worked in the monastery's favor when bishops took seriously the spiritual and material interests of the monastery. Gebhard III, for example, like his namesake, Gebhard II, had taken a special interest in Petershausen and worked hard to protect its interests. He initiated the reform of 'his' community, and tended to make decisions that had a positive impact on its welfare. During the episcopacy of his successor, Ulrich I, however, the monks saw their relationship with the bishop decline, and their rights and material welfare erode. First, Ulrich I's pro-imperial stance in the investiture conflict set him apart from his predecessor. He was chosen to serve as bishop and invested with his episcopal staff by King Henry V (1105–25). This, and his continued association with Henry, caused Pope Paschal II (1099–1118) to refuse to recognize him as legitimate bishop of Constance, and his consecration came only after Paschal's death. Ulrich I's attitude toward Petershausen, which was clearly allied with Rome, ranged from pre-occupied disinterest to blatant hostility.[12] By the 1120s, the bishop's relationship with the monastery had become openly antagonistic. In 1120, he terminated Petershausen's oversight of Wagenhausen, a small community (cell) founded by the monks of All Saints, Schaffhausen, a Hirsau Benedictine monastery on the Rhine, not far from Constance. In the course of an earlier dispute with a disgruntled donor, Gebhard III had placed Wagenhausen under Petershausen's jurisdiction, even going so far as leading a group of 'capable' monks to the monastery himself. But the monks of Schaffhausen had continued to dispute Gebhard's assignment of oversight of Wagenhausen to Petershausen. Ulrich settled the matter, at least temporarily, by freeing Wagenhausen from Petershausen's oversight.[13] 'Although all religious and worldly affairs there appeared to be in good order,' the chronicler complains, 'Bishop Ulrich,

12. Although Gebhard III had died in November of 1110, the news of the resulting vacancy in the See of Constance did not reach Rome until some time between February and April of 1111. The messenger thus arrived at some point during the two months in which King Henry V held Pope Paschal II prisoner in the course of the ongoing struggle over lay investiture. See *Germania Sacra* 42,1:2 (Berlin and New York 2003) 266–268. On this phase of the struggle between Henry and Paschal, see Uta-Renate Blumenthal, *The Investiture Controversy: Church and Monarchy from the Ninth to the Twelfth Century* (Philadelphia 1988) 169–70.

13. See Miscoll-Reckert, *Kloster Petershausen* 179–182 and *Germania Sacra* 42,1:1, pp. 270–80. The question of the oversight of Wagenhausen was still a disputed matter between 1127 and 1134. See

believing that he could make it all better in short order, dismissed us and appointed a certain Udo as abbot and supported him as well as he could.[14] This same Udo, the chronicler notes, would later be deposed for bad behavior by Ulrich's successor. Ulrich also orchestrated the resignation of the abbot of Neresheim, who had come from Petershausen, and repopulated the monastery with monks from Zwiefalten.[15] As both Schaffhausen and Zwiefalten were Benedictine communities associated with the Hirsau reform, the bishop's actions suggest hostility toward Petershausen in particular, rather than toward Benedictines or to the reformers more generally.

But Ulrich I's apparent lack of affection for Petershausen may also reflect his own spiritual tendencies. As a traditional contemplative community, turned away from the world in an era marked by strong and growing interest in new forms of religious life that engaged with the world beyond the monastery, Petershausen may have seemed outmoded to the bishop, who showed a clear preference for Augustinian canons. He himself seems to have been a regular canon at Marbach in Alsace before he became bishop, and is said to have worn the clothing of an Augustinian canon throughout his episcopacy. He actively promoted the life of regular canons in the diocese of Constance and beyond, demonstrating a particular fondness for the community of St. Märgen in the Black Forest. One of his pet projects was promoting the canonization in 1123 of his tenth-century predecessor, Bishop Conrad I (934–75).[16] In 1125, the bishop received permission from Henry V to revive a defunct hospice—known as 'Crucelin' for the relic of the True Cross it claimed to house—originally founded in the tenth century by Conrad I. In that same year, Pope Honorius II confirmed this new community, which was to be governed by the Rule of Saint Augustine, and granted the canons the right to free election of a prior. Ulrich I located the new com-

---

CP 4.20: Per hec tempora Waginhusensis cella curam et regimen a nostro monasterio habuit, sed ex contentione Scafhusensium impedita *usque in hodiernum* parum profecit (emphasis mine).

14. CP 4.20: Sed cum satis ordinate tunc temporis divina et humana ibi haberentur, Oudalricus episcopus, credens se citius quiddam magni patraturum, dimist nos et Utonem quendam abbatem ibi fecit eumque in quibus potuit adiuvit.

15. Ulrich's parents, Hartmann of Dillingen and Adelheid of Kiburg, had founded Neresheim in 1095 as an Augustinian community in the diocese of Augsburg. Twenty years later, however, after returning from crusade, Hartmann asked Abbot Theodorich to convert Neresheim into a Benedictine community, and he placed it under Petershausen's authority. See Miscoll-Reckert, *Kloster Petershausen* 174–76; for the Peterhausen chronicler's account of the monastery's dealings with Neresheim, see CP 3.38 and 3.40.

16. On the episcopacy of Conrad I, see Helmut Maurer, 'Bischof Konrad von Konstanz in seiner ottonischen Umwelt,' in *Der Heilige Konrad, Bischof von Konstanz. Studien aus Anlass der tausendsten Wiederkehr seines Todesjahres: 975–1975*, ed. Helmut Maurer, Wolfgang Müller and Hugo Ott (Freiburg [Breisgau], Basel, and Vienna 1975) 41–55.

munity, called Kreuzlingen, a second episcopal *Eigenkloster*, just outside the gates of the city at the church of Saints Ulrich and Afra.[17] He linked his new saint to his new religious community by establishing an annual procession of relics between church and hospice on the feast of St. Conrad (26 November).[18] The appearance of this new community represented competition for Petershausen, not only for support of the bishop, but also for liturgical importance within the religious landscape of the diocese of Constance, and potentially for new recruits and donations from among the area's laity.

It isn't hard to read a certain degree of satisfaction in the words of the Petershausen chronicler when he describes the terrible illness that killed the bishop during one of his frequent absences from the city to visit his beloved St. Märgen: Ulrich's eyes popped out of his head, and he suffered a most excruciating death. 'He would have been exceedingly well-suited to the office of priest,' the chronicler comments, 'had he not been so very cantankerous'.[19]

With the arrival of a new bishop, Ulrich II (1127–38), the monks must have been hoping for better things, for this new Ulrich was a Benedictine of the old school. His elevation to the episcopacy offered Petershausen the opportunity to regain some of the strength it had lost over the course of sixteen years under Ulrich I. Perhaps emboldened by the arrival of both a new bishop and a new abbot, the chronicler began to create a text that might function as a form of protection against future problems with unwanted episcopal interference. One of his strategies was to highlight, sometimes with imaginative embellishment, situations that exemplify both proper and improper episcopal behavior. He imagines Gebhard II, for example, as a kind of superhero who detects and avenges the trickery of dishonest painters, and returns from beyond the grave to rescue the chronicler's own nephew from a head-down fall into the crypt fountain.[20] He was a 'good bishop' who secured the physical, legal, and economic foundations of the monastery. His successor, Lambert (995–1018), on the other hand, provides material for a cautionary tale. When Emperor Henry II (973–1024) established the diocese of Bamberg, he demanded contributions from existing German bishoprics to equip the new church, and Lambert appropriated precious

17. See Anton Hopp, 'Das Hospiz des hl. Konrad und die Gründung des Chorherrenstiftes St. Ulrich und Afra zu Konstanz,' *Schriften des Vereins für Geschichte des Bodensees und seiner Umgebung* 107 (1989) 97–105.

18. See *Germania Sacra* 42,1:2: pp. 273–78.

19. CP 4.25: Post menses quatuor Oudalricus episcopus apud cellam sancte Marie in Brisgouwe, quorum etiam habitu enituerat, regio morbo depressus et violenter oculis de capite eiectis laborioso fine defunctus est, vir officio pontificali valde idoneus, si animo non fuisset adeo acerrimus.

20. CP 1.23 and CP 3.15.

liturgical objects to comply: 'Thus it was,' comments the chronicler, 'that Lambert took away by force from the monastery that Gebhard had built many of the treasures that Gebhard had given to God and to Saint Gregory, in order to satisfy the will of the emperor'.[21] After devoting a entire chapter to a detailed list of the items that were taken—and claiming that some of the monks had defied the bishop by removing and hiding some particularly precious gold ornaments from a stole and matching hand towel—he went on to describe, with evident delight in the detail, the descent of God's wrath upon Lambert for his crimes against the monastery.[22] Like Ulrich I, Lambert came to a horrible end: the bishop's body began to team with lice (*pediculi*). Even after his servants vigorously scrubbed him down, both in the Rhine and in a bath, the insects continued to emerge, pouring out of his ears and one of his joints 'like a swarm of bees or ants from an ant hill until finally, under these abominable torments, he breathed his last.'[23] This detailed account of the bishop's last hours appears to emerge entirely from the author's imagination; contemporary sources that mention Lambert's death in 1018 make no reference to such a hideous end.[24] The chronicler was making a point: the monastery of Petershausen was *not* powerless against the depredations of unscrupulous bishops.

Another vivid anecdote details a confrontation between Abbot Meginrad (1079–80) and Bishop Otto of Lierheim (1071–80), an imperial supporter in the investiture controversy, and a figure with whom Petershausen's monks would have had little sympathy in the wake of their troubles with Ulrich I. Like Ulrich and Lambert, Otto put politics ahead of the welfare of the monastery:

> When Meginrad had been abbot for a short while, the bishop of Constance, because he needed to provide service to the king, began rudely to demand provision from the aforementioned abbot, saying that he was entitled by law to an armored horse from the monastery.

Clearly, Otto had overstepped, creating a conflict that the monks could not afford to lose if they were to retain their liberty. The abbot's opposition to the bishop was dramatic:

21. CP 2.3: Unde factum est, ut idem Lampertus ex monasterio, quod beatus Gebehardus construxerat, multa de thesauro, quem ipse iam dictus Gebehardus Deo et beato Gregorio donaverat, per vim subtraheret, ut imperatoris voluntati satisfaceret.

22. CP 2.4.

23. CP 2.5. Plerumque enim a famulis tam in Rheno quam in balneis lavabatur, ut imminens passio aliquantulum mitigaretur, sed in ipsa aqua ex ipso quasi exanima apum tam de auribus quam de singulis artubus sicut formice de acervo prodibant, quousque sub hoc fedo tormento spiritum exalavit.

24. Feger, *Chronik* 90, note 5.1.

When Meginrad vehemently objected, saying that by law they owed nothing at all to him, and the bishop obstinately continued to insist that it be given, [Meginrad] threw his abbot's crosier from him saying that he would certainly never agree to anything that would allow the holy see to take away his liberty through violence.

"'And,' he continued, "since I am unable to oppose you, it is better that I renounce my abbacy." Thus he renounced the abbacy and the bishop got nothing from them.'[25] Although Meginrad was later restored to office, the bishop encroached again, entering the monastery uninvited to celebrate the Mass.[26] Meginrad was ready once again to defend Petershausen's liberty. This time he threw his pastoral staff down on the altar in protest and walked out.[27] While the chronicler later names Meginrad among the community's deposed abbots, this account of his confrontation with the bishop clearly culminates with a rather impressive abdication.[28]

The scribe stressed the importance of entire episode with a nota mark extending down the right margin of the page, drawing the eye of the reader to the passage. 'That the abbot dealt with the bishop in such a spirited manner is only half of the story,' commented Arno Borst in his account of this episode in the chronicle. 'The other side is the enthusiasm with which the monk recounted it, almost a century after Meginrad.'[29] A defiant abbot, willing to stand up twice to a bishop who had overstepped his authority, was a compelling image for a monk of Petershausen at the end of the 1120s.

The task of keeping the bishop at bay was more difficult when there were allegations of spiritual laxity or decline within a monastery. St. Benedict himself had mandated direct intervention in cases in which, 'a whole community should conspire to elect a man who goes along with its own evil ways.'[30] In such cases, the bishop or any other witness to the difficul-

25. CP 2.15: Cumque Meginradus abbas vehementer reluctaret dicens, nihil ei omnino exinde ex iure deberi, et episcopus pertinaciter insisteret, ut daretur, ille abiecit virgam regiminis a se dicens, numquam se prorsus velle consentire, ut sacer locus libertatem suam per violentiam cogatur ammitere.

26. On Pope Gregory V's 998 prohibition against bishops or priests performing ordinations or celebrating Mass at Cluny without an invitation from the abbot, see Blumenthal, *Investituture Controversy* 17–18.

27. CP 2.15: Attamen postea sedi sue restitutus, cum iterum quadam die episcopus sine ipsius rogatu missam in eodem monasterio vellet cantare, baculum pastoralem super altare proiecit et recessit. For a discussion of this episode as evidence for the practice of self-investiture of Petershausen's abbots, see Miscoll-Reckert, *Kloster Petershausen* 195–204.

28. CP 4.27: Arnoldus, Meginradus et Liutoldus depositi.

29. 'Daß der Abt so temperamentvoll mit dem Bischof umging, ist die eine Hälfte der Geschichte. Die andere ist die Begeisterung, mit der die Mönche noch fast ein Jahrhundert lang von Meinrad erzählten.' Borst, *Mönche am Bodensee*, p. 139.

30. RSB 64.3–5: Quod si etiam omnis congregatio vitiis suis—quod quidem absit—consen-

ties was obliged to intervene: 'They must block the success of this wicked conspiracy, and set a worthy steward in charge of God's own house.' Even more, then, a proprietary bishop would have had a right, and even an obligation, to intervene in such cases of spiritual emergency. This was the course that Bishop Gebhard III pursued in 1086 when he appealed directly to William, the reforming abbot of Hirsau, to send a team of his own monks to Petershausen. As a monk of the reform era himself and a supporter of the reforming ideas emanating from Hirsau, the chronicler had to concede the need for benign and appropriate intervention. 'Since at the monastery of St. Gregory, which is called Petershausen, the vigor of regular life was already lacking and growing ever worse,' he writes, 'when Gebhard III received the episcopal see of Constance by apostolic authority, he—lamenting that a monastery of his church was neglecting the Divine Office—appealed to the venerable abbot William of Hirsau to send monks from his monastery to Petershausen, through whom monastic order might be revived'.[31] Dramatic action was needed to reverse this alleged decline. The bishop also took the dramatic step of deposing the sitting abbot, Liutold, to make way for a new abbot from Hirsau.

While this step may have been necessary for the success of the reform, it was, particularly looking back from the perspective of c. 1128, also dangerous ground. The chronicler was careful to show the monks, even in the midst of the upheaval of the reform, retaining some measure of control over the choice of abbot. Among the new arrivals from Hirsau, the chronicler explains, 'was a certain Otto, intended to be their abbot if, after a short trial period, they found his life and habits pleasing.' But the monks were apparently in no mood to be compliant:

> When within a short time they judged Otto, the leader who had been assigned to them, to be reprehensible, they immediately sent him back and requested, with the support of Bishop Gebhard, the appointment of another worthy to rule them.

While there is no suggestion of any election, the chronicler does show the monks exercising some agency in the selection of their new abbot. William complied with their request for a different choice, sending his own prior

---

tientem personam pari consilio elegerit, et vitia ipsa aliquatenus in notitia episcopi ad cuius diocesim pertinet locus ipse... prohibeant pravorum praevalere consensum....

31. CP 3.1: Cum apud monasterium sancti Gregorii pape, quod dicitur Domus Petri, vigor regularis vite iam iamque deficeret et nec proficue esset nec deesset, et Gebehardus tertius pontificalem sedem ex apostolica auctoritate apud Constantiensem ecclesiam obtineret, dolens, in monasterio ecclesia sue contiguo defectum divini ministerii excrevisse, interpellavit venerabilem Willhelmum Hirsaugiensem abbatem, ut de suo monasterio regulares viros ad Petrishusam dirigeret, per quos monasticus ordo inibi revivisceret.

Theodorich, the son of Count Kuno of Wülfingen in Thurgau (d. 1092), who was 'trained in the highest degree in all secular and monastic learning and suitable for this command.'[32] The monks accepted Theoderich, who would serve as abbot from 1086 to 1116.[33]

In 1103, Gebhard III was forced by supporters of the emperor to flee Constance, and his place was taken by anti-bishop Arnold of Heiligenberg (1092–1112). The bishop-usurper immediately began to overstep the boundaries between the monastery and the diocese. 'He began,' the chronicler complains, 'to assign benefices [from the monastery] to his men, which the bishops were at no time allowed to do.'[34] While Abbot Theodorich was forced into exile, taking refuge with twelve of his monks at the Hirsau-affiliated monastery of Wessobrunn in Bavaria, the monks who remained designated Werner of Epfindorf as abbot. But Werner was no disciplinarian, and under his direction the measures that the reformers had put in place to insure close adherence to the Rule were forgotten. The monks, the chronicler reports, began to live lives of laxity, and before long the monastery lay in near ruin:[35]

> But after Werner with his followers and Arnold with his, brought the condition of the monastery to one of extreme destitution and helplessness, he set aside the name of abbot and went to Theodorich in Bavaria and submitted himself to him. Theodorich received him kindly and restored the office of the altar to him, against the will of Bishop Gebhard. But he did not remain long *in the horn of the sinner*.

In ending his account of the incident with this unusual phrase, the chronicler points his readers to 1 Maccabees 2, which tells the story of the defiance of Mathathias and his five sons in the face of Antiochus, who had sacked Jerusalem and profaned the temple. 'The holy places are come into the hands

32. CP 3.3: . . . cum Ottonem sibi designatum magistrum in brevi reprehensibilem in quibusdam deprehendissent, protinus eum ad suos remiserunt et alium, qui eis preesse dignus esset, favente Gebehardo episcopo destinari petierunt. Quapropter Willihelmus abbas optimo consilio usus, misit venerabilem valde virum Theodericum, omni seculari et monastica eruditione adprime imbutum et huic regimini satis idoneum.

33. CP 3:1–2.

34. CP 3.34: Recedente igitur Theoderico de Domo Petri hi qui tunc remanserant constituerunt Wernherum quendam de Epfindorf natum sibi in abbatem et obliti regularis discipline quam didicerant, remissius agere ceperunt. Arnolfus quoque intrusus episcopus beneficia inde suis concedere cepit, quod nulli umquam episcopurum facere licuit.

35. 1 Maccabees 2:48 reads, 'and they yielded not to the horn of the sinner.' CP 3.34: Postquam autem Wernherus cum suis fautoribus et Arnolfus cum suis res monasterii ad ultimam penuriam et inopiam perduxerunt, ipse relicto abbatis nomine ad Theodericum se in Baioariam contulit eique se subiecit, quique eum benigne suscepit eique officium altaris invito episcopo Gebehardo restituit. Sed no diu permansit cornu peccatoris.

of strangers: her temple is become as a man without honor' (1 Maccabees 2:8), just like Constance and Petershausen. And perhaps resonating even more directly with Petershausen's situation: 'All her ornaments are taken away. *She that was free is made a slave*' (1 Maccabees 2:11). When many of the Jews began to consent to the commandments of the king, Mathathias and his sons—like Theodorich and his twelve monks—fled the city and gathered around them like-minded resistors.[36] 'And they recovered the law out of the hands of the nations, and out of the hands of the kings: and they yielded not to the horn to the sinner' (1 Maccabees 2:48).

It is only with the post-Hirsau reform abbots that the chronicler starts to describe abbatial elections. Transitions between abbots were often particularly delicate moments in the life of a monastery. A bishop or other 'outsider' might try to intervene, either appointing an abbot from within the community or from another house, meddling in the election carried out by the monks, or deposing an abbot for political or other reasons. To emphasize the importance of electing an abbot from among the community's own monks, the chronicler refers his readers to the Book of Acts: 'The general election of the father,' he asserts, 'was prefigured in the beatific community of the early Christians,' when they gathered to choose a replacement from among their own number for Judas (Acts 1:21–22).[37] This is a significant, and perhaps surprising point given that no abbot until Bertolf (1116–27) seems to have been either elected or selected from among Petershausen's own monks.[38]

The first abbatial election after the reform would have been an important test case for Petershausen, and the chronicler is careful to show that

36. 'And Mathathias cried out in the city with a loud voice, saying: Every one that hath zeal for the law, and maintaineth the testament, let him follow me. So he, and his sons fled into the mountains, and left all that they had in the city' (1 Maccabees 2:27–28). Around the refugees gathered the Assideans, 'the stoutest of Israel, every one that had a good will for the law' (1 Maccabees 2:42).

37. CP Preface. 10: In hac quoque discipulorum Christi tam felici commanentia etiam generalis electio patris premonstrata est. Nam Petrus surgens in medio fratrum dixit: Viri fratres, oportet ex his viris, qui nobiscum sunt congregati in omni tempore …

38. The chronicler tells us little of Petershausen's first abbots. He reports (CP 2.2) that Gebhard II appointed the monastery's first abbot, Periger, a monk from the monastery of Einsiedeln, a Benedictine community with strong ties to Gebhard's family, to serve as Petershausen's first abbot. This connection was extended and intensified through the subsequent appointment of five monks of Einsiedeln as abbot. There is no evidence that any of these abbots was elected; on the contrary, the chronicler states that Siegfried was 'constituted' (CP 2.8: abbas constitutus est), not elected (CP 4.24: electus est), which is the language he uses later to describe the post-reform abbots selected by the monks from within their own ranks. He also reports that Abbot Arnold was deposed (CP 2.14: deponitur), probably by the bishop in 1064, which would have been during the episcopacy of Rumold of Bonstetten, but this information is not given.

the monks were, in fact, empowered by the canons and the bishop to elect their own abbot:

After the death of the venerable Father Theodorich was made known, the canons of Constance gathered and went to the monastery of Petershausen and into the chapter of the brothers and read both the letter about the death of the abbot and the exhortation of Bishop Ulrich, the elected bishop, in which the brothers were exhorted to elect an abbot. The canons judged that this election could be carried out at their own discretion, and exhorted them to do it immediately.[39]

Emphasizing the gravity of the decision, the senior monks of the monastery objected 'modestly and humbly' that such a decision could not be rushed and that 'with careful deliberation, through prayers to God, the brothers ought to deliberate among themselves and to consider prudently whom they should choose for this, so that they might entrust their soul and body to him, and also the business of the monastery and the monastery itself.' 'Nobody,' the chronicler states emphatically, 'was to be present at the election except he who desired to be subject to the one elected.'[40] Although this demand for total autonomy in the election did not sit well with the canons, the monks prevailed:[41]

When the canons argued that they ought to be present for the election, the entire congregation began with one voice to contradict them, and they forced them to leave. After they discussed the matter among themselves, they elected Bertolf, a venerable old man who had served at that same monastery in the office of prior, and nobody from outside the community was present at the election.

While the monks had won, choosing Bertolf (1116–27) through a free and unsupervised election, the events that followed illustrate the sometimes-delicate balance that the monks needed to maintain with their bishop. Abbots who were properly elected in the presence of only the voting monks were not, of course, necessarily good abbots, and though the monks asserted that they should be left in total independence to select an abbot, they had to concede, at least on occasion, the need for help in deposing one. Bertolf was already an old man when the monks elected him in 1116,

39. CP 4.1: Pervulgato obitu venerandi patris Theoderici, congregati sunt canonici Constantienses et venerunt ad monasterium Domus Petri et intraverunt capitulum fratrum, atque perlectis literis tam de obitu abbatis quam etiam de exhortatione Oudalrici electi episcopi, qua hortabatur fratres ad eligendum abbatem, existimabant canonici, quod eorum arbitrio electio futura esset, quam et statim perfici hortabantur.

40. CP 4.1: Tunc seniores modeste et humiliter respondebant, non posse hoc ita prepropere peragi negotium, sed moroso consilio per orationes ad Deum fratres inter se deliberare et prudenter pertractari oportere, quem ad hoc assumant, ut ei animam et corpus suum resque monasterii atque ipsum locum [committerent], nec aliquem huic dicebant electioni debere interesse, nisi qui etiam electo velit subesse.

41. CP 4.1: Cumque canonici contenderent, interesse se electioni debere, omnis simul congregatio cepit uno ore contradicere, et fecerunt eos abire. Deinde habito inter se consilio elegerunt Bertholfum venerabilem senem, qui iam diu in eodem monasterio prioris fungebatur officio, nullusque omnino alienus huic interfuit electioni.

and his age and deteriorating mental state caused him to neglect more and more the most basic needs of the monastery. By 1127 the material and spiritual life of the monastery had reached a breaking point. A small contingent of senior monks began to meet secretly with Bishop Ulrich I to solicit his aid in getting Bertolf to step down.[42] The 'eloquent and clever bishop' was quite willing to help and ultimately effective in his efforts, as Bertolf agreed to abdicate and live out his life as a regular monk. The process of the abbot's abdication, however, offered the bishop the opportunity to press his advantage. On the day on which Bertolf was to step down, the bishop appeared at the monastery together with Abbot Ulrich of Zwiefalten and announced the news of Bertolf's decision to the monks gathered in their chapter house.[43] The next step in the process was not clear, however, and the assembled men began to argue about the proper protocol for the abbot's transition out of office. One group demanded that it was enough that Bertolf had stated his intention to abdicate; another asserted that he must go forward to the altar and renounce his office there. Clearly, the bishop saw this as an opportunity to assert his authority, if only through the symbolism of the control of the abbots' staff. 'This is not necessary,' he argued. 'He should return the staff of his office to me.'[44] But some of the monks clearly saw what the bishop was up to, and they 'cried out loudly saying that he was in no way entitled to this'.[45] But the chronicler then shows Bertolf taking the lead, walking up to the altar and placing his abbatial staff on it, and settling the matter succinctly: 'Behold what I have by God's and your grace I put aside, and I absolve you all from obedience to me.'[46] This stage in the process of transferring abbatial authority thus remained clearly in the hands of the monks.

The election of Bertolf's successor followed immediately in the monks' chapter house. Here the chronicler outlines a model election process, not-

42. CP 4.23: Anno ab incarnatione Domini 1127, cum iam Bertholfus abbas senio gravaretur, moribus quoque ita insolesceret, ut nec ipse faceret, nec aliis permitteret necessaria loci providere, et iam iamque omnia simul in defectione viderentur, quidam de senioribus ceperunt cum Oudalrico episcopo clam agere, ut Bertolfo persuaderet, quatenus abbatia se abdicaret et alium pro se ordinari permitteret, ipse vero reliquum vite sue tempus privatus requiesceret …

43. CP 4.23: Et quoniam episcopus eloquens erat et versutus, persuasit eum, quamvis diu reluctaret. Die ergo statuta advenit Oudalricus episcopus et Oudalricus Zwivildensis abbas, et consilio diu habito venerunt ad capitulum et nuntiaverunt multitudini.

44. CP 4.23: Cumque ille libens consentiret, ut privatus viveret, dixerunt quidam, ut ibidem rem conficeret, alii autem dicerent, ad altare eum debere peregere et ibidem se abdicare, episcopus ait: Non est, inquit, necesse, virgam mihi regiminis reddat.

45. CP 4.23: Tunc omnes reclamaverunt dicentes, hoc nullatenus ad eum pertinere.

46. CP 4.23: Ergo accessit ad altare et virgam deposuit desuper dicens: Ecce quod Dei et vestri gratia habui depono et omnes vos a mei obedientia absolvo.

ing clearly the absence and non-intervention of the bishop. 'The bishop rightly absented himself,' the chronicler notes, 'and by free choice the entire congregation selected Conrad.'[47] Conrad, who was not a monk of Petershausen but a long-term guest at the monastery, had departed with the other outsiders before the election. As a model of humility, Conrad had no desire to serve as abbot, and the monks had to track him down and forcibly return him to the monastery, where 'although exclaiming and objecting,' he was, 'at length overcome and installed in his office.'[48]

With the canonization of their founder and the translation of his relics to their freshly restored and expanded church, the monks of Petershausen answered their rivals at Kreutzlingen: now they, too, had their own saint, their own festive procession, and a bishop on their side. They also had in hand the beginnings of an historical chronicle that promised a measure of protection from the kind of interference that had given them so much trouble during the difficult years under Bishop Ulrich I; in the chronicle's imagined past, those who interfered with the liberty of the monastery came to a bad end through divine intercession and abbatial elections proceeded according to a biblical and legal plan. The monks could not know, however, that still more trouble was in store: just twenty-five years later, a catastrophic fire would destroy the entire monastery:[49]

> In the year of the Lord 1159, in the 177th year after the founding of the monastery, in the 7th indiction, on the second day of the month of June, on Tuesday of the holy week of Pentecost, when the Holy Spirit came down upon the disciples of Christ in fire, not consuming but illuminating, so also a fire descended upon us, but just as we deserved—consuming and devouring, casting down walls and shattering unyielding stones.

When townspeople, and even some of the monks, rushed into the smoldering ruins to grab what treasure they might find, there would be no protection—either episcopal or supernatural—for the monastery.

47. CP 4.24: Deinde iterum conventus ad capitulum rediit. Episcopus vero secessit, et libera electione omnis congregatio Counradum elegit.

48. CP 4.24: Electione autem peracta, requisitus et inventus, clamans et multum reluctans violenter adductus et tandem laboriose devictus sedi est impositus.

49. CP 5.43: Actum anno ab incarnatione Domini millesimo centesimo quinquagesimo nono, a primitus condito ipso monasterio centesimo septuagesimo septimo, indictione septima, die secunda mensis Iunii, hoc est 4. non. Iunii, feria tertia sacratissime ebdomade pentecostes, quando Spiritus sanctus super discipulos Christi venit in igne, non tamen consumens sed illuminans, super nos autem, ut meriti fueramus, venit ignis consumens et devorans, muros deiciens et duros lapides comminuens.

DETLEV JASPER

13 The Deposition and Excommunication of Emperors and Kings

A Collection of Historical Examples from the Investiture Conflict

January of the year 1076 began and ended dramatically. On New Year's Day, the envoys of King Henry IV returning from Rome handed over to the ruler in Goslar a missive from Gregory VII, in which the pope demanded from Henry strict obedience towards the church in all things.[1] The letter, written in the most reproachful and irritated tone, was complemented by the orally transmitted demands of the pope: the king must renounce continued relations with the excommunicated councilors, as well as further intervention in the episcopal nominations at Milan, Fermo, and Spoleto. Gregory threatened him with excommunication and deposition as king if he did not comply.[2] Henry IV, who, after his victory over the rebellious Saxons, considered himself at the high point of his power, responded to the papal ultimatum with his own attack. With all haste, an imperial diet was summoned to Worms for January 24, Septuagesima Sunday; with two archbishops and twenty-four bishops, it brought together a large part of the imperial episcopate. As a result of the assembly, the bishops renounced obedience to Gregory VII and affirmed their resolve to no longer regard him as their pope in the future.[3] The decision of the

1. Register Gregory VII 3.10 (MGH Epp.sel. 2.263–67).

2. Cf. Gregory VII, *Epistolae Vagantes*, ed. H. E. J. Cowdrey, *The Epistolae Vagantes of Pope Gregory VII* (Oxford 1972) no. 14, p. 38. The Lenten Synod should be taken as the *terminus ante* for binding promises, as results from a combination of the letters in the register of Gregory VII: 3.5; 3.10 and *Epistolae vagantes* 14 regarding the dispatch and stay of the envoys of Henry IV.

3. Letter of renunciation of the German bishops to Gregory VII, ed. Carl Erdmann, *Die Briefe Heinrichs IV.* (MGH Deutsches Mittelalter 1; Stuttgart 1937) Anhang A, 65–68; on the reproaches raised against Gregory VII, see Werner Goez, 'Zur Erhebung und ersten Absetzung Papst Gregors VII,' RQ 63 (1968) 122–44.

bishops was complemented by letters of Henry IV to Gregory VII and to the Romans, in which Henry commanded the pope to renounce his office and called upon the clergy and people of Rome to chase Gregory VII from his office, if necessary by force, and to accept a new pope.[4] The emissaries would have to bring these documents to Rome within three weeks if they were to be presented to the Roman Lenten synod called for February 14, 1076, for discussion. On their way, the royal envoys assured themselves of the support of many northern Italian bishops, who, on about February 5, assembled at a synod in Piacenza on account of the consecration of Tedald of Milan: they too committed themselves by an oath not to recognize Gregory VII as pope henceforth.[5] Gregory had not anticipated this defection of large parts of the German and Italian episcopate, but his reaction to it was prompt and hard. Archbishop Siegfried of Mainz, as initiator of the Worms assembly, and the bishops who had freely signed its decision, were excommunicated, that is, suspended from their offices and excluded from the Eucharist. Those bishops who had taken this step only under pressure had until August 1, 1076, to justify their action in Rome. The Lombard bishops also met with excommunications. After that, Henry IV was deposed as king, his subjects were absolved of their oaths of fidelity, and the king was excluded from the church community as a disobedient Christian. This final act took the form of a solemn prayer to the prince of the apostles in order to dramatize its special gravity.[6] The measures announced in Rome reached the German court at Easter 1076 in Utrecht. They led to a public condemnation of Gregory VII during the Easter mass on March 27, 1076, and to the preparation of the further steps against Pope Gregory VII

4. *Briefe Heinrichs IV.*, nos. 10 and 11, 12–15; a version of the letter of Gregory VII altered for purposes of propaganda, which appeared in the course of 1076 and was widely circulated in Germany, is found in Ep. 12, pp. 15–17; see the fundamental works of Carl Erdmann, 'Die Anfänge der staatlichen Propaganda im Investiturstreit,' Historische Zeitschrift 154 (1936) 491–512 and Ian S. Robinson, *Authority and Resistance in the Investiture Contest: The Polemical Literature of the Late Eleventh Century* (Manchester 1978) 60–62.

5. On the Synod of Piacenza, see Claudia Zey, 'Die Synode von Piacenza und die Konsekration Tedalds zum Erzbischof von Mailand im Februar 1076,' QF 76 (1996) 496–505, who points out in this connection that the Piacenza synod was not prompted by the Assembly of Worms; and Rudolf Hiestand, 'Planung—Improvisation—Zufall. Politisches Handeln im 11. Jahrhundert oder noch einmal Piacenza 1076,' in *Von Sacerdotium und Regnum. Geistliche und weltliche Gewalt im frühen und hohen Mittelalter. Festschrift für Egon Boshof zum 65. Geburtstag*, ed. Franz-Rainer Erkens and Hartmut Wolff (Cologne 2002) 361–79, who conjectures that the synod was initiated from Goslar by the German court in 1075. The question whether summonses were sent from Germany or were a result of a Milan initiative cannot be definitely answered. It certainly seems to me as though the activities of the Milanese could not have taken place without the knowledge and agreement of the German court.

6. Register Gregory VII, 3.12a. p. 268–71.

that had been agreed upon at Worms; but these came to nothing, owing to the rapid collapse of the royal camp.[7]

The events of the first half of 1076 deeply stirred contemporaries.[8] The exclusion of a ruler from the church, his deposition as king, and the dissolution of the bond of fidelity between ruler and subject were unprecedented. They required explanation.[9] Particularly among the partisans of Gregory VII historical precedents for royal depositions were sought, so as to deprive the events at the Lenten synod of 1076 of their singularity. This was most likely the time when the collection of source materials about ruler depositions originated that is the subject of the following pages. The text has long been known. In 1897, Ernst Dümmler included it in the *Libelli de lite*. He conjectured that Bernold of Konstanz was the author, since some parallels existed with Bernold's polemical *Apologeticae rationes* of 1086.[10] In the decades since Dümmler's publication, additional witnesses to the collection of examples have incidentally turned up. This paper will attempt to summarize and delineate its transmission. In this context the presumed place of origin of the collection, its sources, and the intensity and duration of its reception will also be investigated.

The collection of examples in the *Libelli de lite* is based on a manuscript of the Munich State Library Clm 3853 and was first published by Victor Krause in 1894.[11] The manuscript was written in south Germany in the second half of the tenth century and was probably in the possession of the Cathedral Library of Augsburg since the mid-eleventh century. It contains

7. The events of spring 1076 have often been narrated and discussed so that a reference to a few works may suffice. See Wolfram von den Steinen, *Canossa. Heinrich IV. und die Kirche* (Munich 1957) 49–61; Christian Schneider, *Prophetisches Sacerdotium und heilsgeschichtliches Regnum im Dialog 1073–1077. Zur Geschichte Gregors VII. und Heinrichs IV.* (Münstersche Mittelalter-Schriften 9; Munich 1972) 146–201; Tilmann Struve, 'Gregor VII. und Heinrich IV. Stationen einer Auseinandersetzung,' *Studi Gregoriani* 14 (1991) 29–39; Wilfried Hartmann, *Der Investiturstreit* (Enzyklopädie deutscher Geschichte 21; 3d ed. Munich 2007) 23–24; H. E. J. Cowdrey, *Pope Gregory VII 1073–1085* (Oxford 1998) 129–50; Uta-Renate Blumenthal, *Gregor VII. Papst zwischen Canosssa und Kirchenreform* (Darmstadt 2001) 178–80; Werner Goez, *Kirchenreform und Investiturstreit* (Stuttgart 2000) 119–30; Ian S. Robinson, *Henry IV of Germany, 1056–1106* (Cambridge 1999) 143–52; Gerd Althoff, *Heinrich IV.* (Darmstadt 2006) 133–45; Stefan Weinfurter, *Canossa. Die Entzauberung der Welt* (Munich 2006) 119–34.

8. See for instance Bishop Gebhard of Salzburg in his letter to Hermann of Metz, MGH Ldl 1.278–79 c. 33–34, which influenced Hugh of Flavigny's *Chronicon* 2, MGH SS 8 p. 431.9–14.

9. See Gregory VII's letter to his supporters in Germany, *Epistolae vagantes* 14; cf. in this context Schneider, *Sacerdotium* 139–45.

10. Included in MGH Ldl 3.601–2 as an appendix to an anonymous polemic, which Dümmler (p. 599) also attributes to the authorship of Bernold of Konstanz, without producing convincing proof.

11. Viktor Krause, 'Die Münchener Handschriften 3851. 3853 mit einer Compilation von 181 Wormser Schlüssen,' NA 19 (1894) 125–26.

an 'extensive compendium of early medieval ecclesiastical and temporal law.'[12] The first canonical section contains mainly penitentials, genuine and supposed canons of the Council of Worms (868), and a small canonical collection in 77 chapters. At its end, a scribe inserted the examples of royal depositions on the remaining blank space at the end of the quire on fol. 158v. It is not certain whether this addition still dates to the eleventh century or only to the twelfth.[13]

In order to convey an idea of the contents, I shall briefly set out the historical exempla of the series as they appear in the text. The first witness adduced is Pope Felix II (355–58), who is supposed to have classed the Emperor Constantius II among heretics. The excommunications of the Merovingian king Charibert by Bishop Germanus of Paris, dated to the year 563, and of King Lothar II by Pope Nicolas I in 866 on account of his marriage to Waldrada follow. The fourth case mentioned is the ruler-penance of the Emperor Louis the Pious under the date 834. As a last example we are referred to the deposition of the Merovingian king Childeric III and his committal to a monastery, *'auctoritate Stephani papae'*, and the anointing of Pepin the Younger by Boniface.[14] It has long been known and repeatedly emphasized that the examples given here do not correspond to historical facts.[15]

12. The manuscript has been described in detail by Hubert Mordek, *Bibliotheca capitularium regum Francorum manuscripta. Überlieferung und Traditionszusammenhang der fränkischen Herrschererlasse* (MGH Hilfsmittel 15; Munich 1995) 287–305 with a complete indication of earlier literature. The quote is found on p. 288. Hartmut Hoffmann, *Schreibschulen des 10. und 11. Jahrhunderts im Südwesten des Deutschen Reichs* (MGH Schriften 53; Hanover 2004) 1.32–33, palaeographically identified the hands involved.

13. According to Hoffmann, *Schreibschulen* 33, the same copyist inserted chapter 2.184 from the Decretum of Burchard of Worms on fol. 315r of the codex. Mordek, *Bibliotheca* 303, dates this addition to the twelfth century, whereas Hoffmann considers the writer to have worked 'towards the end of the eleventh century.'

14. See MGH Ldl 3.601.23–30.

15. See Carl Mirbt, *Die Publizistik im Zeitalter Gregors VII* (Leipzig 1894) 163–70, who, after examining the listed exempla (p. 168), reaches the conclusion that, of all the cases, only 'the excommunication of Charibert by Germanus of Paris can rank as a certain historical fact.' See also the references in Hans-Werner Goetz, 'Geschichte als Argument. Historische Beweisführung und Geschichtsbewusstsein in den Streitschriften des Investiturstreits,' Historische Zeitschrift 245 (1987) 37–49; idem, 'Fälschung und Verfälschung der Vergangenheit. Zum Geschichtsbild der Streitschriften des Investiturstreits', in *Fälschungen im Mittelalter* 1 (MGH Schriften 33, 1; Hanover 1988) 167–78; idem, 'Tradition und Geschichte im Denken Gregors VII.', in *Historiographia mediaevalis. Festschrift für Franz-Josef Schmale zum 65. Geburtstag*, ed. Dieter Berg and Hans-Werner Goetz (Darmstadt 1988) 142–46. For particular issues see Werner Affeldt, 'Königserhebung Pippins und Unlösbarkeit des Eides im Liber de unitate ecclesiae conservanda,' DA 25 (1969) 313–46, and Rudolf Schieffer, 'Von Mailand nach Canossa. Ein Beitrag zur Geschichte der christlichen Herrscherbuße von Theodosius d. Gr. bis zu Heinrich IV,' DA 28 (1972) 359–69.

These cases listed are followed by three more texts. It is not clear whether they belong to the original contents of the collection or were added later. They prescribe unconditional obedience to the canons and papal decretals and say that one must heed God more than men. As corroboration of the correctness of this last principle the fate of Emperor Julian the Apostate is mentioned. Whereas the pagan emperor ended his life wretchedly in Persia,Valentinian became ruler of the empire because he held fast to Christianity.[16] The first two sentences stem from canonical sources. Via the *Collectio Vetus Gallica* and a branch of the *False Decretals*, the section from the letter of Gregory the Great to the Gallic bishops (Reg. 9,218) cited here reached the *Collection in 74 Titles* and was especially favored by Bernold of Konstanz among the citations in his early writings of 1074 and 1076.[17] The next decree, attributed to Pope Hadrian I, paraphrases chapter 20bis of the *Capitula Angilramni*. It is found as c. 307 in the *Collection in 74 Titles* and, with a slightly altered text, as c. 329 in the appendix to the collection. It is found often in collections of the Reform period and is also among the texts particularly prized by Bernold of Konstanz.[18]

Both Krause and Dümmler overlooked that Max Sdralek had already published the catalogue in 1890 from manuscript Göttweig, Stiftsbibliothek 53 (56), and commented on it.[19] The Göttweig codex, written in the

16. See MGH Ldl 3.601.31–602.8. Cf. Paulus Diaconus, *Historia Romana* 11.1.4 ed. Hans Droysen (MGH SS rer. Germ. 49; Berlin 1878) 90, or also the chronicles of Hermann of Reichenau ad a. 363 (MGH SS 5; Hanover 1844) 79. This example is cited by Bonizo of Sutri, *Liber ad amicum* 1 (MGH Ldl 1.374.38–41).

17. On the transmission of the letter of Gregory I, Reg. 9.218 (MGH, Epp. 2.205–210), see Detlev Jasper and Horst Fuhrmann, *Papal Letters in the Early Middle Ages* (Washington 2001) 74–75; in the *Collection in 74 Titles* the applicable section (MGH Epp. 2.209.30–210.5) forms c. 131 (ed. John Gilchrist, *Diversorum patrum sententie sive Collectio in LXXIV titulos digesta* 88–89). In his exchange of letters with the priest Alboin, Bernold of Konstanz often cites the dictum of Gregory the Great; see MGH Ldl 2 p. 8.25–31; p. 13. 8–9; p. 21. 21–27. The citation from Gregory's letter in Bernold's first letter to Alboin is particularly instructive, for it agrees in extent and inscription with the excerpt that Bernold inserted in his own hand in Codex Sankt Gallen 676, p. 181.

18. See the edition of Karl-Georg Schon, *Die Capitula Angilramni. Eine prozessrechtliche Fälschung Pseudoisidors* (MGH Studien und Texte 39; Hanover 2006) 166, with reference to later collections; further such references are found in Fowler-Magerl, *Clavis*, under the incipit 'Generali decreto constituimus.' Fowler-Magerl, 59–60, has pointed to the change of text and sense of c. 20bis by the author of DPS in c. 307. Bernold of Konstanz cites this canon in his early work on the sources of church law (MGH Fontes iuris Germanici antiqui 15; Hanover 2000, p. 171.10–11) and includes it as c. 329 in his appendix to DPS.

19. Max Sdralek, *Die Streitschriften Altmanns von Passau und Wezilos von Mainz* (Paderborn 1890). The catalogue, however, was of secondary interest to Sdralek, for the focus of his extensive study was his completely failed attempt to prove that Bernhard of Hildesheim's *Liber canonum contra Heinricum IV*, transmitted by the Göttweig manuscript, was the work of Bishop Altmann of Passau; see the refutation of Sdralek's argument by Friedrich Thaner, 'Zu zwei Streitschriften

twelfth century, brought together a canonical collection composed both of excerpts from the *False Decretals* in the most expanded version (C-version) and of excerpts from the register of Gregory the Great, the Lorch forgeries, and the polemical treatise of Bernard of Hildesheim against Henry IV.[20] As in the Augsburg transmission, the collection of examples here is also among the supplements to the canonical collection. It begins with the preface and four decrees of the Roman Lenten synod of Gregory VII of 1080 (fol. 127); the *Capitulum Angilramni* 20bis attributed to Hadrian I, here in its complete wording and in the form of c. 307 of the *Collection in 74 Titles;* and the famous chapter *'De depositione regum'* which concludes the Swabian appendix to the *Collection in 74 Titles* as c. 330.[21] These items are followed by our collection of historical examples (fol. 128r); excerpts from papal letters and the church fathers, partly coinciding with texts in the *Libellus de vitanda excommunicatorum communione* from the circle of Bernold of Konstanz; and finally the forgery on the pastoral care of monks attributed to Pope Boniface IV (fol. 128f.).[22]

A comparison of the Göttweig collection of examples with that of the Munich manuscript reveals greater expansiveness in the Göttweig catalogue and a different ordering of the individual cases. The reason for the

des 11. Jahrhunderts,' NA 16 (1891) 529–40. Sdralek printed the collection of examples under the title 'Die Zusätze zu der collectio canonum des codex Gottwicensis' on pp. 173–75; it is reprinted without commentary in the supplements of MGH, Ldl 3.738.

20. See the description of the codex by Vinzenz Werl, *Manuscripten-Catalog der Stifts-Bibliothek zu Göttweig* (Handwritten, Göttweig 1843) 1.169–82; Johann Friedrich von Schulte, *Die Rechtshandschriften der Stiftsbibliotheken von Göttweig Ord .S. Bened.* Sb. Akad. Wien 57 (1867) 561–69; Sdralek, *Streitschriften* 64–66; Uta-Renate Blumenthal, *The Early Councils of Pope Paschal II 1100–1110* (P.I.M.S. Studies and Texts 43; Toronto 1978) 89–90; John Gilchrist, 'The Influence of the Monastic Forgeries attributed to Pope Gregory I (JE † 1951) and Boniface IV (JE † 1996),' in *Fälschungen im Mittelalter* 2 (MGH Schriften 33.2; Hanover 1988) 270.

21. This reception of the Roman canons of 1080 is missing in John Gilchrist's 'The Reception of Pope Gregory VII into the Canon Law (1073–1141),' ZRG Kan. Abt. 59 (1973) 80, and ZRG Kan. Abt. 66 (1980) 227. The use of c. 330 of DPS is apparent from the given inscription: 'Ex decretis sancti Gregorii pape primi.' On Gregory VII's intensified interpretation of Gregory the Great's penalty formula, see Horst Fuhrmann, 'Papst Gregor VII. und das Kirchenrecht; Zum Problem des Dictatus Papae,' *Studi Gregoriani* 13 (1989) 137–39. One should note that here c. 307 and 330 of the *Collection in 74 Titles* are combined, although c. 20bis of the *Capitula Angilramni* directly precedes c. 330 in the expanded *Collection in 74 Titles.* Was the Swabian appendix to DPS perhaps still in development when these chapters of the collection were added? See also below n. 44.

22. *Libellus de vitanda excommunicatorum communione,* ed. Ernst Dümmler, MGH Ldl 3.599–601. In the Göttweig manuscript the texts found on pp. 599.37–600.9 and p. 600.23–25 were included. Further partial transmissions of the polemic are transmitted in MSS Stuttgart, Württembergische Landesbibliothek, Cod. theol. fol. 206 fol. 40 and Cod. theol. fol. 225 fol. 84 formerly of Zwiefalten; see Wilfried Hartmann, 'Eine unbekannte Überlieferung der falschen Investiturprivilegien,' DA 24 (1968) 499f., and Claudia Märtl, *Die falschen Investiturprivilegien* (MGH Fontes iuris Germanici antiqui 13; Hanover 1986) 108–9.

rearrangement is probably not an attempt by the reviser of the example collection to present a correct chronological succession of the examples of condemnation. The Göttweig catalogue begins with the excommunication of King Charibert (563), continues with the condemnation of Emperor Constans II and his bishops by Pope Martin I (ca. 650), linking it with the deposition of the Merovingian Childeric III reported by chronicles under the year 752 and the supposed excommunication of Lothar II dated to 867. Regarding the remaining three cases, one has the impression that the compiler augmented his catalogue with additional material that he acquired later, specifically the condemnation of Emperor Constantius II by Pope Felix II (358), the ruler-penance of Louis the Pious (833), and the ecclesiastical penance of Theodosius the Great (390). The Augsburg example collection is built on the same pattern: the first three instances stand in a correct chronological succession, and the church penance of Louis the Pious in 833 and the deposition of Childeric III in 751 are mentioned afterwards. The Göttweig codex moreover adds the alleged excommunication of the Byzantine emperor Constans II by Martin I and the ecclesiastical penance of Theodosius as two further examples of measures against emperors, which, however, acquired a very contrasting resonance in the polemical literature. Whereas the actions of Pope Martin I and the Roman synod of 649 against the Monothelite patriarch of Constantinople and the Typos of Emperor Constans II found almost no echo in the literature of the Investiture Controversy, the exclusion of Theodosius from the Eucharist was turned into an excommunication by Gregory VII after 1076 and became a model case of the excommunication of rulers.[23] It is a noteworthy feature of the Göttweig catalogue that it frequently indicates the source of its information—not a standard practice at that time—creating the appearance of greater weightiness for its evidence.[24] To be sure, the sources cited do not always state what has been asserted in the notice. The report that Pope Martin I along with the Lateran Council of 649 excommunicated Emperor Constans II and his adherents is attributed to the *Liber Pontificalis* and the *Historia Romana*, but these works only mention a condemnation of the Monophysite patriarch of Constantinople.[25] With

23. On the rare presence of Pope Martin I in the Ldl, who is often confused there with the author of the *Capitula* of Martin of Braga, see the indices of the Ldl 1–3. Gregory VII first mentioned the ecclesiastic penance of Theodosius in his letter of August 1076 to Bishop Hermann of Metz. It subsequently became a topic of debate: see the detailed discussion in Schieffer, 'Von Mailand nach Canossa' 359–69.

24. See Goetz, 'Geschichte als Argument' 58–69.

25. See *Vita Martini* 3 in *Liber Pontificalis*, ed. Louis Duchesne 1 (Paris 1886) 337: 'Et condem-

a little fantasy it is perhaps possible to detect in an hitherto unpublished version of the Reichenau *Kaiserchronik* the condemnation of the emperor, which declares '*Constantinus filius Constantini filii Heraclii regit annos XXVIII. Hic a supradicto Paulo [the patriarch of Constantinople] deceptus hereticus efficiatur, exposuitque tipum adversus catholicam fidem.... Unde a Martino papa et CV episcopis sub anathemate damnati sunt supradicti episcopi.*'[26] One should be cautious, though, about attributing the intention of a deliberate falsification to the author of the catalogue.[27]

A third transmission of the collection of examples is found in Codex 8 of the Library of the University of Freiburg. The manuscript, which was written in the region of the Lake of Konstanz in the second half of the ninth century, contains the *Collectio Dionysio-Hadriana*, preceded by the *Notitia provinciarum Galliae* and opinions on matters of marriage law (fol. 1–4); these are followed by a few liturgical instructions and excerpts from the *Liber Pontificalis*.[28] The manuscript belonged to the Cathedral Library in Konstanz and was extensively glossed by Bernold of Konstanz and an Anonymous early in the 1070s.[29] On the inside of the front cover of the

naverunt [the bishops of the Lateran synod] Cyrum Alexandrinum, Sergium, Pyrrum et Paulum patriarchas Constantinopolitanos, qui novitates contra inmaculatam fidem praesumpserunt innectere.' This report of the *Liber Pontificalis* is followed by the chronicles of Hermann of Reichenau and Bernold of Konstanz ad a. 649 and 650 (MGH SS 5.94 and 415).

26. Reichenauer Kaiserchronik in the transmission of MS Sarnen, Bibliothek des Kollegiums, Cod. membr. 10 fol. 27r/v.

27. The report of the excommunication of Lothar cannot have been derived from the *Chronicle* of Regino, which the catalogue of the Göttweig manuscript names as source, because it is not included in the chronicle. The report does appear in the chronicles of Hermann of Reichenau and of Bernold of Konstanz at 867 (MGH SS 5.106 and 420). The remaining text of the notice, however, was clearly taken over from Regino's *Chronicle* at a. 869 (MGH SS rer. Germ. 50.97–98): 'qui [Lothar II] cum Romae de illatis se criminibus excusare vellet, sibique hoc iudicium praeponeretur, ut si innocens esset, fiducialiter ad communionem accederet, accessit temerarius et de manu apostolici iudicium sibi suisque complicibus sumpsit. Nam non multo post ipse suique fautores subita morte perierunt, tantaque clades hanc praesumptionem divinitus subsecuta est, ut in eiusdem Lotharii regno tota virtus ac nobilitas non peste, sed quasi hostili gladio simul deleta videretur' (MGH Ldl 3.738; Sdralek, *Streitschriften* 174). It is noteworthy that Bernold of Konstanz entered the words from 'si innocens–videretur' as a later marginal note to the year 868 in the autograph of his chronicle. Perhaps it was based on this or a related manuscript.

28. See Johanne Autenrieth, *Die Domschule von Konstanz zur Zeit des Investiturstreits* (Forschungen zur Kirchen- und Geistesgeschichte N. F. 3; Stuttgart 1956) 68–75; Walter Hagenmaier, *Die lateinischen mittelalterlichen Handschriften der Universitätsbibliothek Freiburg im Breisgau (Hs. 1–230)* (Kataloge der Universitätsbibliothek Freiburg im Breisgau 1.1; Wiesbaden 1974) 10–12, both with further literature.

29. See Autenrieth, *Domschule* 69–73, 121–33, where the glosses are edited and their use in Bernold's writings are commented on; on their date see Ian S. Robinson, 'Zur Arbeitsweise Bernolds von Konstanz und seines Kreises. Untersuchungen zum Schlettstädter Codex 13,' DA 34 (1978) 98–99.

codex, an 'unknown but certainly Konstanz hand of the ending eleventh century' entered examples of depositions and excommunications of rulers under the heading *'De eo quod et regi est contradicendum, si ipse est contrarius statutis catholic(orum patrum).'*[30] Except for minor variants, these examples coincide with the Augsburg copy, even in the texts that follow the Augsburg example collection.[31] To this the writer attached a further text that, with reference to the first letter of Pseudo-Clement and the fate of King Saül, extols unconditional obedience to papal commands.[32] But this text presumably has no connection to our collection of examples.

This tradition was copied again in Codex Stuttgart, Württembergische Landesbibliothek HB VI 107. The manuscript originated at the end of the eleventh century in southwest Germany, possibly in Konstanz. As the main work, it contains the *Collection in 74 Titles,* along with the so-called Swabian appendix of Bernold of Konstanz, the canons of the first four ecumenical councils, the *Epitome Hadriani* (found only in connection with the enlarged *Collection in 74 Titles*), the *Ordines Romani,* and the penitentials of Hrabanus Maurus and Halitgar of Cambrai. To this main body of texts are added small collections on the topic *'de ecclesiis'* and *'de illicitis coniunctionibus',* many excerpts from the *Decretum* of Burchard of Worms, and the writings *'De damnatione scismaticorum'* and the *Apologeticus,* both by Bernold of Konstanz.[33] The inclusion of the collection of examples in this manuscript is curious. At the lower third of fol. 58v, the copyist ended his work with the collection *'de ecclesiis'* in the middle of an excerpt from Augustine's Sermo 350. The scribe added the two missing lines, and then continued on fol. 59r with the next chapter of the collection. He entered the ruler exempla on the blank space on fol. 58v, but ran out of space for the last two exempla. He therefore omitted the date of the next-to-last notice, on the ruler-penance of Louis the Pious, and noted only with *'Per Stephanum papam Hildericus detonsus deponitur'* the absolute minimum on the deposition of the last Merovingian.

30. This is pointed out by Autenrieth, *Domschule* 74–75, the quotation is found on p. 74.

31. See pp. 202–03.

32. Printed in Autenrieth, *Domschule* 74–75. In his letters to Hermann of Metz in 1076 and 1081, Gregory VII justified the right to depose Henry IV with reference to Pseudo-Clement c. 18 (Hinschius 36); see Reg. Gregory VII 4.2 p. 294. 8–11 and 8.21 p. 551.8–15.

33. For the manuscript see Autenrieth, *Domschule* 106–115; idem, 'Bernold von Konstanz und die erweiterte 74-Titel-Sammlung', DA 14 (1958) 375–94; idem, *Die Handschriften der ehemaligen Hofbibliothek Stuttgart* 3: *Codices iuridici et politici. Patres* (Die Handschriften der Württembergischen Landesbibliothek Stuttgart 2.3; Wiesbaden 1963) 100–105; Gilchrist, *Collectio* LV–LVII; Raymund Kottje, *Die Bussbücher Halitgars von Cambrai und des Hrabanus Maurus: Ihre Überlieferung und ihre Quellen* (Beiträge zur Geschichte und Quellenkunde des Mittelalters 8; Sigmaringen 1980) 61–62.

Codex Sankt Gallen, Stiftsbibliothek 676, is closely related in contents to the Stuttgart manuscript; it contains the last of the collection of examples presented here.[34] The manuscript belongs together with the Stuttgart Codex and with Codex Engelberg, Stiftsbibliothek 52, written in St. Blasien or Einsiedeln, to a group of canonistic handbooks that are closely connected to Bernold of Konstanz and the circle of south German partisans of Gregory VII.[35] All three manuscripts were written in the last decades of the eleventh century and they mostly contain the same canonistic works and materials.

The Sangallensis unites various manuscripts in one volume, so that one should, to begin with, briefly examine its contents. A first part (pp. 1–173) transmits the penitentials of Hrabanus Maurus and Halitgar of Cambrai, excerpts from the *Decretum* of Burchard of Worms, the *Adnotationes I* and *II* on the Councils, the *Epitome Hadriani*, and, as a main component, the *Collection in 74 Titles* augmented by the Swabian appendix. On p. 98 it seamlessly attaches title 1 *'De primatu Romanae aecclesiae'* to the *Epitome Hadriani* and ends on p. 158 with the famous deposition decree (title 89 c. 330) attributed to Gregory the Great but transformed by Gregory VII. With as little transition as at the beginning, there follow the Pseudo-Gelasian decree *'De libris recipiendis et non recipiendis'* (JK † 700) and the small collections *'De ecclesiis'* and *'De illicitis coniunctionibus,'* which break off, incomplete, on p. 173. From the appearance of the leaf, this page might, after loss of a leaf, have formed the end of the manuscript. On a single and a double leaf, the *capitulatio* missing at the beginning of the collection, and the special heading of the enlarged *Collection in 74 Titles* are entered. On the very damaged p. 180 starts a new collection ending on p. 195. Whereas the previous, mostly double columned leaves were largely written in 34

34. For the manuscript see Johanne Autenrieth, 'Bernold von Konstanz und der Codex Sangallensis 676,' in Festschrift Friedrich Baethgen (Typewritten, Munich 1950) 1–17; Gilchrist, *Collectio* LII–LIII with additional literature; Robinson, 'Arbeitsweise Bernolds von Konstanz,' 55, 119; Doris Stöckly—Detlev Jasper, *Bernold von Konstanz, De excommunicatis vitandis, de reconciliatione lapsorum et de fontibus iuris ecclesiastici* (*Libellus* X) (MGH Fontes iuris Germanici antiqui 15; Hanover 2000) 54–55, 58–60.

35. That the three manuscripts are not directly dependent on each other was shown by Kottje, *Bussbücher* 134–139, on the basis of the penitentials. Also connected is Codex Sélestat, Bibliothèque humaniste 13, originating in Hirsau, containing in its first section among other items Bernold's treatises *De prohibenda sacerdotum intontinentia* (MGH Ldl 2.7–26), his *Apologeticus* (MGH Ldl 2.59–88), as well as the third letter from *De damnatione scismaticorum* (MGH Ldl 2 pp. 49.32–58.33), and in a second part the Collectio Sinemuriensis. The manuscript was analyzed by Robinson, 'Arbeitsweise Bernolds von Konstanz,' 51–122, and classed among the literary products of the Bernold-circle. See also idem, 'Bernold von Konstanz und der gregorianische Reformkreis um Bischof Gebhard II,' *Freiburger Diözesan-Archiv* 109 (1989) 170ff.

lines, this collection has 27 long lines per page. The new collection begins with the letter of Wido of Arezzo against simony attributed to Pope Paschal (MGH Ldl 1.5–7) and Bernold's autograph note that the letter was by Wido of Arezzo; it also includes excerpts from conciliar canons and papal letters, particularly letters of Gregory the Great, emphasizing topics of the reform period (*'contra symoniacum heresim'*, p. 184; *'de incontinentia clericorum'*, pp. 187, 189).[36] On pp. 196 to 213 a fragment of a canonical collection is found that has not yet been adequately studied but occasionally shows proximity to the Italian Collection in Two Books. Perhaps it originated in Italy, as is suggested by the 1074 letter of Gregory VII to Matilda of Tuscany, only here transmitted in full.[37] An extensive excerpt from the *Libri II de synodalibus causis* of Regino of Prüm begins on p. 214. The excerpt has not yet been analyzed. Canons are mostly given in abbreviated form and occasionally commented on; the text ends on p. 254.[38] The conclusion of the collection consists of the *Admonitio synodalis* and several canons that stem in part from the *Collectio de raptoribus*. On pp. 259–61, chapters 326 and 327 of the Swabian appendix to the *74-Title Collection* are copied because they are missing on p. 158 of the actual collection. Owing to the loss of a leaf, the manuscript breaks off in the middle of the fourth paragraph of c. 327. These complements to the *Collection in 74 Titles* suggest that this section of the manuscript and its first part to p. 173 (178) from the beginning constituted a single manuscript.

A special feature of this codex is the fact that Bernold of Konstanz filled it with numerous marginal notes, glosses, and rubrics and often supplied the missing inscriptions of canons from other collections. The most instructive part in this connection is the quire covering pp. 180–95, where, on pp. 181–82 and 191–93, Bernold inserted autograph excerpts from pa-

36. Beginning with p. 187, the old pagination is incorrect, because the person who wrote the page numbers entered 167 instead of 187, certainly because of inattention, and continued the numbers from that figure; the numbers given in the present text are limited to the new pagination except when noted otherwise.

37. The incomplete letter is preserved in Reg. Gregory VII 1.47 pp. 71–73. The conclusion was edited by Johanne Autenrieth, 'Der bisher unbekannte Schluß des Briefes Gregors VII. an Mathilde von Tuscien vom 16. Februar 1074 (Reg. I, 47),' DA 13 (1957) 534. She used it and c. 6 of the Roman Lenten Council of 1080 to date the manuscript (p. 203). Since the collection is not a genuine part of the St. Gall codex, it cannot supply a basis for its date, as Autenrieth had proposed (pp. 536–37).

38. See the editions of Friedrich G. A. Wasserschleben, *Reginonis abbatis Prumiensis libri duo de synodalibus causis* (Leipzig 1840), and Wilfried Hartmann, *Das Sendhandbuch des Regino von Prüm* (Freiherr-vom-Stein-Gedächtnisausgabe 42; Darmstadt 2004), as well as the study of Wilfried Hartmann, *Kirche und Kirchenrecht um 900. Die Bedeutung der spätkarolingischen Zeit für Tradition und Innovation im kirchlichen Recht* (MGH Schriften 58; Hanover 2008) 301–3.

pal letters and councils on the topic of incontinent priests and the punishment of *'violatores canonum.'* Between pp. 187 and 188 of this collection a half leaf is inserted presenting the historical precedents for the deposition and excommunication of rulers.[39] The insert has no connection to the adjoining text, for p. 188 connects seamlessly to p. 187[40] and the content of the leaf does not fit the context. On p. 187a (old numbering p. 168) the table of contents of Amalarius of Metz's *Ecloge de ordine Romano* is entered, and the upper third of p. 187b (old numbering p. 169) contains a section of chapter 19 of Walafrid Strabo's treatise *De exordiis,* rejecting the blessing of the Easter Lamb.[41] Another hand then filled in the rest of the free space with our collection of examples. It is impossible to decide whether this leaf belonged to this section of the collection from the start or was only added later. The handwriting suggests that the insert was written towards the end of the eleventh century.

On the whole, the Sangallensis agrees with the Göttweig transmission. This holds for the succession of examples as well as their content. The Göttweig text is sometimes fuller, especially in its notice of the marriage problem of King Lothar II, which was enriched by information from Regino's *Chronicle,* or in its report of the ecclesiastical penance of Emperor Theodosius, where the adapter relied on Eusebius's *Ecclesiastical History* and Cassiodorus's *Historia ecclesiastica* as he tells us.[42] In contrast to the Göttweig catalogue, the St. Gall list adds a final, contemporary case. It apparently was quickly recognized as grossly false information and never appeared in the debates of the Investiture Controversy. According to this case, King Peter of Hungary was excommunicated by Pope Leo IX, driven from his kingdom, and died after blinding. To be sure, it is true that King Peter was driven out in 1046 by his rival Andrew, was blinded, and died of his wounds in this year or in 1047, but Leo IX became pope only in 1049. A confusion occurred with the events of 1052, when Emperor Henry III besieged King Andrew of

39. In the new pagination of the manuscript (see n. 36 above) the half leaf was numbered p. 187a and p. 187b.

40. On p. 187, under the title *'De incontinentia clericorum',* c. 46 from the second letter of Pseudo-Clement (JK † 11) is quoted: '(Ad) dominica ministeria tales eligantur, qui ante ordinationem coniuges suas nove [p. 188]rint' etc. (Hinschius p. 48).

41. See *Amalarii episcopi opera liturgica,* ed. I. M. Hanssens (Vatican City 1950) 3.229–31, and Walafrid Strabo, *De exordiis et incrementis quarundam in observationibus ecclesiasticis rerum* c. 19, ed. Victor Krause (MGH Capit. 2; Berlin 1897) 491.37–492.6.

42. See Eusebius, *Die Kirchengeschichte in der Übersetzung des Rufinus* 11.18, ed. Theodor Mommsen (Die griechischen christlichen Schriftsteller der ersten drei Jahrhunderte 2.2; Leipzig 1908) 1022–23 and Cassiodorus, *Historia ecclesiastica tripartita* 9.30, ed. Walter Jakobs—Rudolf Hanslik (CSEL 71; Vienna 1952) 540–46; cf. Adolf Lippold, *Theodosius der Große und seine Zeit* (Stuttgart 1968) 33–38, and Schieffer, 'Von Mailand' 334–39.

Hungary in Pressburg (Bratislava) and, based on the mediation of Pope Leo IX and promises of the Hungarian king, raised the siege after a few months. When Andrew did not keep to his undertakings, Leo IX threatened him with excommunication. In their chronicles, Hermann of Reichenau and Bernold relate the events at length in this manner; the author of the catalogue must have drawn his misunderstood information from them.[43] The catalogue is followed by chapter 20bis of the *Capitula Angilramni* attributed to Hadrian I, which is found in the *Collection in 74 Titles* and again as c. 329 in the appendix to the collection composed by Bernold of Konstanz. Although the text agrees in general with c. 307 of the DPS, a few readings may be noted that then reappear in c. 329 of the Appendix.[44]

On the basis of their script, the five catalogues of ruler depositions should be dated to the end of the eleventh or—as in the Göttweig catalogue—to the twelfth century. To conclude one should ask whether there are signs of the use of these sources. The most extensive utilization of our catalogue was made by Berthold of Reichenau in his chronicle for the year 1077. In an excursus justifying the deposition of Henry IV and stating the duties and responsibilities of kingship, Berthold disputes the notion of several incorrigibles that no one may pass judgment on kings. Berthold shows the incorrectness of this opinion by seven cases of ruler-excommunications and depositions. The rulers named are: Emperor Constans II (641–68), Emperor Constantius II (337–61), the Merovingian kings Charibert I (561–67) and Childeric III (743–51), the Carolingians Lothar II (855–69) and Louis the Pious (814–40), and Emperor Theodosius the Great (379–95).[45] All these exempla are given in the St. Gall and Göttweig catalogues; Berthold's texts stands closer to the St. Gall transmission.[46] It is impos-

43. For background see Ernst Steindorff, *Jahrbücher des Deutschen Reichs unter Heinrich III.* (Leipzig 1881) 2.179–82, and Bálint Hóman, *Geschichte des ungarischen Mittelalters* (Berlin 1940) 1.243–68.

44. The indication 'XXIIIo' in the codex must be a mistake for XVIII. With c. 307 the readings 'Dominum' (c. 329: 'Deum') and 'crediderit' (c. 329: 'violaverit') agree; at c. 329 the readings 'Romanorum presulum' (c. 307: 'Romanorum pontificum') and 'permiserit violari' (c. 307: 'permiserit violandum') belong together; see the edition of Gilchrist, *Collectio* 175 and 195–96. In his *Chronicle* at a. 1076, Berthold of Reichenau cites Sentences c. 307 in the form of the Sangallensis, see Robinson, *Chroniken* (at n. 45) 244.22–245.4.

45. Berthold von Reichenau, *Chronik* ad a. 1077, ed. Ian S. Robinson, *Die Chroniken Bertholds von Reichenau und Bernolds von Konstanz 1054–1100* (MGH SS rer. Germ. N.S. 14; Hanover 2003) 281.15–283.11; see esp. his introduction to the edition, pp. 74–75.

46. See Berthold, *Chronik* ad a. 1077 p. 283.2–7: 'Qui (Lothar II) cum Rome *se de illatis* criminibus excusare vellet, sibique hoc iudicium *iniungeretur*, ut si innocens esset, fiducialiter ad communionem accederet, accessit temerarius et de manu *domini* apostolici iudicium sibi sumpsit. Nam non multo post *ipse et omnes fautores eius* subita morte perierunt.' The St. Gall codex transmits this text word-for-word, whereas one finds in the Göttweig manuscript: 'Qui (Lothar II) cum

sible to determine definitely the difficult question of when Berthold began the revision of the first form of his chronicle—after 1073, according to the painstaking research of Robinson—and whether he worked at his text later than 1080. The unusually extensive reports of the annals from 1075 onward, heavily based on information from Reichenau, must have been written close to the events.[47] This implies that the collection of historical examples of ruler depositions was already available before 1080. It was also used in the next decade, as could be illustrated by reference to a number of authors, but the necessary extensive source studies cannot be pursued here. They include Bernold of Konstanz's treatises *Apologeticus rationes* and *De solutione iuramentorum*; the *Liber ad Gebehardum* of Manegold of Lautenbach, who was close to the south German adherents of Gregory VII; or Bernhard of Hildesheim, closely associated with them as well, in his *Liber canonum contra Heinricum quartum*.[48] In these years, the debate was focussed primarily on the supposed condemnation of Emperor Arcadius by Pope Innocent I, the deposition of the last Merovingian, Childeric III, and the ecclesiastical penance of Theodosius the Great, which Gregory VII had markedly emphasized as a historical precedent, especially in his widely circulated letter of 1081 to Bishop Hermann of Metz.[49]

If, in closing, we look again at the five manuscript witnesses of the catalogue, it appears that there are two strands of transmission, with the Freiburg, Stuttgart, and Munich codices on one side and St. Gall and Göttweig on the other. Presumably, the catalogue of St. Gall/Göttweig, augmented by two examples, was based on an exemplar of the Freiburg/Munich tradition; among these the catalogue from Göttweig may rank as the most elaborated copy and thus as the latest representative of this

Rome *de illatis se* criminibus excusare vellet, sibique hoc iudicium *praeponeretur*, ut si innocens esset, fiducialiter ad communionem accederet, accessit temerarius et de manu apostolici iudicium sibi *suisque complicibus* sumpsit. Nam non multo post *ipse suique fautores* subita morte perierunt.' The manuscript then continues, utilizing the chronicle of Regino of Prüm: 'tantaque clades hanc praesumptionem divinitus subsecuta est, ut in eiusdem Lotharii regno tota virtus ac nobilitas non peste, sed quasi hostili gladio simul deleta videretur, ut cronica Reginonis abbatis testantur'; see MGH Ldl 3.738.19–21.

47. See Robinson, *Chroniken Bertholds* 44–67, and more briefly *Eleventh-Century Germany: The Swabian Chronicles*, selected sources translated and annotated with an introduction by Ian S. Robinson (Manchester 2008) 20–41.

48. See Bernold of Konstanz, *Apologeticae rationes* (MGH Ldl 2 p.97.18–30); *De solutione iuramentorum* (MGH Ldl 2 p.148.12–24); Manegold von Lautenbach, *Liber ad Gebehardum* c. 29 (MGH Ldl 1 pp.362.22–363.7); Bernhard of Hildesheim, *Liber canonum contra Heinricum IV* c. 25 (MGH Ldl 1.495–98); see in general Goetz, 'Geschichte als Argument' 37–49.

49. Gregory VII, Reg. 8.21 p. 554.1–3 and 11–15; Goetz, 'Tradition und Geschichte' 142–46; Stefan Beulertz, 'Gregor VII. als 'Publizist': Zur Wirkung des Schreibens Reg. VIII, 21,' AHP 32 (1994) 7–29.

series of examples. The manuscripts from Freiburg, Stuttgart, and St. Gall stem from the circle of Bernold of Konstanz; the Göttweig manuscript very likely belongs to this group as well. Since all the additions of the Göttweig manuscript—such as on fol. 86 the canons of Paschal II's Council of Troyes (1107), which are found between excerpts from the letters of Leo I and of his successor Hilary, or the text of leaves 127 to 129 analyzed above—are all written in a twelfth-century hand, the codex must have reached Göttweig as a copy. In 1094, the house of Augustinian canons founded by Altmann of Passau became a Benedictine monastery adhering to the reforms of St. Blasien, as Bernhold reports in great detail and with interest in his chronicle.[50] One result of the change was a close relationship with the south German reformers. If the dates given above for the composition of the Chronicle of Berthold of Reichenau are correct, then the collection of examples must have originated in connection with the first deposition of Henry IV. The possibility that it came from the pen of Bernold of Konstanz, as scholars have believed, cannot be excluded, but convincing proof of this argument has not been found.

APPENDIX

The Deposition and Excommunication of Emperors and Kings

Saint Gall, Stiftsbibliothek 676, p. 187b (old numbering p. 169; pasted in leaf)
Last Quarter of the Eleventh Century

Anno dominicae incarnationis DLXIIIo Haribertus[1] rex a sancto Germano[2] Parisiorum episcopo excommunicatus est pro libi(dine) sua et ita excommunicatus descendit ad inferna.

Paulus[3] Constantinopolitanus episcopus Constanti[4] augusto cui(dam) heresi suę favere persuasit. Unde sanctus Martinus[5] papa anno dominicae incarnationis DCL eundem episcopum et praedictuṃ imperatorem et omnes eius sectatores in Romana synodo[6] excommunicavit.

Auctoritate Stephani[7] papae, de(po)sito ac detonso immo in monasterium misso Hilderico[8] rege, electus est Pipinus[9] rex Francorum et a sancto Bonefacio[10] ad regnum consecratus.

50. Bernold, *Chronik* (MGH SS rer. Germ. N.S. 14) 513.14–514.8.
1. Charibert I, king of the Franks (561–67).
2. Germanus, bishop of Paris († 576).
3. Paul, patriarch of Constantinople (641–53).
4. Constans II, Byzantine emperor (641–68).
5. Pope Martin I (649–55).
6. Lateran Synod of 649.
7. Pope Stephen II (752–57).
8. Childeric III, king of the Franks (743–51).
9. Pippin the Younger, king of the Franks (751–68).
10. Boniface, bishop and archbishop of Mainz (722–54).

Anno dominicae incarnationis DCCCLXoVII. Nicolaus[11] papa excommunicavit Lothar(ium)[12] regem Francorum, eo quod repudiata legitima uxore sua Waldradam[13] concubinam habere praesumpserit, qui cum Romę se de illatis criminibus excusare vellet et sibi hoc iudicium iniungeretur, ut si innocens e(sset), fiducialiter ad communionem accederet, accessit temerarius et de manu domni apostolici iudicium sibi sumpsit. Nam non multo post ipse et omnes fautores eius subita morte perierunt.

Felix[14] papa in ordine XXXV(III) Constantium[15] imperatorem inter hereticos reputandum esse declaravit.

Anno dominicae incarnationis DCCCXXXIIIIo Lodowicus[16] imperator armis depositis ad agendam penitentiam iudicio episcoporum includitur.

Theodosius[17] imperator a sancto Ambrosio[18] ab introitu aecclesiae repulsus ob homicidium commissum ad penitentiam agendam VI mensibus Mediolani includitur.

Petrus[19] rex Ungariorum a sancto Leone[20] papa excommunicatus a sede regni depulsus et excecatus moritur.

Beatus papa Adrianus in decretis suis kapitulo XXIIIo[21] Generali decreto statuimus, ut execrandum anathema fiat et velut praevaricator katholicę fidei semper apud Dominum reus existat, quicumque regum seu episcoporum vel potentum deinceps Romanorum praesulum decretorum censuram in quocumque crediderit vel permiserit violari.

11. Pope Nicholas I (858–67).
12. Lothar II, king (855–69).
13. Waldrada, Frankish queen († after 869).
14. Pope Felix II (355–58).
15. Constantius II, Roman emperor (337–61).
16. Louis the Pious, emperor (813–40).
17. Theodosius the Great, Roman emperor (379–95).
18. Ambrose, bishop of Milan (374–97).
19. Peter Orseolo, king of Hungary (1038–41; 1044–46).
20. Pope Leo IX (1049–54).
21. See above n. 44.

EDWARD PETERS

14 Another Canonist Heard From

Gervase of Tilbury's *Kaiserspiegel* for Otto IV

Between 1211 and 1214, Gervase of Tilbury, the widely travelled English polymath, jurist, collector of *mirabilia*, and marshal of the imperial *aula* at Arles, found himself in a three-sided dilemma. One side was Innocent III, a pope whom Gervase perhaps knew, but in any case greatly admired and respected. Another was Gervase's loyalty to his patron, the recently excommunicated and therefore deposed Emperor Otto IV (r. 1209–11), to whom Gervase may have been distantly related through the Plantagenets and who had appointed Gervase marshal of the kingdom of Arles in 1209. The third was Gervase's more professional interest as a canonist about the relations between papal and imperial powers, a subject recently heightened for political thinkers and jurists by the long dispute between Frederick Barbarossa and Alexander III (the outcome of which Gervase had personally witnessed at Venice in 1177). The political consequences of the sudden death of Henry VI in September 1197 and the subsequent decade-long *Thronstreit* between Philip of Swabia and Otto of Brunswick constituted another difficulty, as did the dispute between Innocent III and Otto in 1210–11.

Gervase's dilemma may be traced through parts of his vast *Otia imperialia* (or *Solacium imperatoris*), which Gervase dedicated to Otto IV in 1215 to amuse and instruct Otto's imperial (or post-imperial) leisure.[1] The *Otia*

Earlier versions of this essay were given as talks at the International Medieval Conference at Leeds in 2006 and the New College Conference in Sarasota in 2008. I am grateful for the comments of several participants and others, particularly Armin Wolf, Jonathan Shepard, and James Blythe. It is an honor to offer this study as a tribute to my friend of nearly half a century, Bob Somerville. May he consider it very minimal *Otia academica* or a *Solacium Roberti!*

1. Gervase of Tilbury, *Otia Imperialia: Recreation for an Emperor*, ed. and trans. S. E. Banks and J. W. Binns (Oxford 2002), hereafter cited as *Otia*. All translations are from Banks and Binns.

is generally known for the articulated moral geography and history found in the second of its three sections, *decisio* II (sometimes too readily dismissed as merely potted Peter Comestor and Orosius) and the *mirabilia* of the known and unknown world in *decisio* III. This last part of his work was often detached and excerpted from the rest of the *Otia*, translated into European vernaculars and studied, usually as high-end folklore and wonder-literature in the manner of Walter Map and Gerald of Wales. Many of the events in Gervase's life and some of his interests in *mirabilia* are reflected in the distorting, fun-house mirror of Umberto Eco's *Baudolino*.

But Gervase also provided a substantial amount of direct and often quite specific advice to Otto IV on how (and how not) to be an emperor, advice that is irregularly distributed throughout his vast work and appears in different and sometimes surprising places, often without warning, in one instance (III. 103) as a personal letter to Otto directly from God (to which I will return at the end of this essay)! Some of that advice is the conventional Christian morality of the genre of *Fürstenspiegel*, but more of it is also sharp and Otto- (and early thirteenth-century empire/papacy-) specific, probably written and added to the earlier parts of the *Otia* in the crucial years 1211–14. Gervase was only briefly and indifferently considered by Wilhelm Berges in his classic 1938 study of *Fürstenspiegeln*. But Gervase clearly and explicitly addressed a particular emperor in particular circumstances, not just any imperial ruler, and particularly the nature of the western empire and that emperor's relations with the pope.[2] So I will consider some of his advice, cagily wrapped in a recreation, as a *Kaiserspiegel*, a mirror for a particular emperor in particular circumstances.

Gervase (b. ca. 1160) had long associated with and entertained the powerful.[3] Long ago, he states in the preface, he had made a *Liber facetiarum* (most likely a book of courtly conduct) for Henry the Young King (d. 1183; the work is now lost), and he then planned another, 'in recognition of his kindness' (*Otia*, Preface).[4] Gervase's description of that second book

2. Wilhelm Berges, *Die Fürstenspiegel des hohen und späten Mittelalters* (Leipzig 1938) 105.

3. On Gervase's life, *Otia*, xxv–xxxviii, and Armin Wolf, 'Gervasius von Tilbury und die Welfen. Zugleich Bemerkungen zur Ebsdorfer Weltkarte,' in Bernd Schneidmüller, ed., *Die Welfen und ihr Braunschweiger Hof* (Wiesbaden 1995) 417–38, and idem, 'Albert oder Gervasius? Spät oder früh? Kritische Bemerkungen zu dem Buch von Jürgen Wilke über die Ebsdorfer Weltkarte,' *Niedersächisches Jahrbuch* 76 (2004) 285–318.

4. On the genre, John Gillingham, 'From *Civilitas* to Civility: Codes of Manners in Medieval and Early Modern England,' TRHS, 6th Series 12 (2002) 267–89. On the role of the game of chess in one instance, Olivia Remie Constable, 'Chess and Courtly Culture in Medieval Castile: The *Libro de ajedrez* of Alfonso X el Sabio,' *Speculum* 82 (2007) 301–47. Henry the Young King was long remembered as a chivalric hero; e.g., *The Novellino, or, One Hundred Ancient Tales*, ed. and trans.

for Henry in his Preface is virtually that of most of the present *Otia*. Much of the *Otia* thus reflects Gervase's collection of materials assembled over a quarter century, but some of it, including some *mirabilia* and the troublesome material in the preface and elsewhere in the *Otia* dealing with papal-imperial relations, must date from the early years of the thirteenth century, although it is not always presented or dated clearly. Otherwise, Gervase is often quite specific on names, dates, and places, and it may be possible to offer a provisional chronology for some of his advice.[5]

Gervase led a much-travelled life, from England to Venice, Bologna, Naples, Nola, Palermo, and Arles, where he seems to have arrived in or just after 1191.[6] Along the way, Gervase became admirably learned in many subjects, including canon law, in which he earned a doctorate—and which he briefly taught—at Bologna sometime in the 1180s. He also knew other kinds of law, including Roman law and local law in the Arelate and probably the *Libri Feudorum*, and he seems regularly to have served in various legal capacities in Arles.[7] Besides being an accomplished mirabilist, Gervase was also a competent and versatile jurist.

His connection to Otto IV, made or renewed at Otto's imperial coronation in Rome in 1209, probably on the basis of his Plantagenet connections, landed him an appointment as marshal of the imperial *aula* of Arles and the imperial confirmation of his possession of a *palatium* by right of his wife around 1210. He was related by marriage to the archbishop of Arles, Imbert d'Aiguières (abp. 1191–1202) and served as a legal expert in several different capacities, including those of judge and arbiter. At Arles, Gervase

Joseph P. Consoli (New York 1997) xix, xx, and Carol Lansing, *The Florentine Magnates* (Princeton 1991) 158–59.

5. E.g. his noting the murder of Philip of Swabia in 1208 in II.19 and his detailed description of the coronation of Otto in 1209 in III, Praef. In a discussion of how to calculate the indiction in II.15 Gervase picks the year 1211, probably the year in which he was writing that section. Nowhere does Gervase mention Bouvines. The only study of the topic of this paper is that by Karl Schnith, 'Otto IV und Gervasius von Tilbury,' HJb 82 (1963) 50–69, whose emphasis is different from that of this essay and is very useful on Gervase's thought about the eastern and western empires and on the distortion of Otto's character by Staufer polemicists.

6. I assume that he left Palermo after the departure of Richard I and Richard's sister, Johanna of Sicily, from Messina to Cyprus and the Holy Land in that year, following the death of Johanna's husband and Gervase's patron William II in 1189. He certainly visited Naples in 1190. There seems to be no explanation as to why he chose Arles, unless he was already in contact with Archbishop Imbert d'Aiguières.

7. In *Otia* I.19 Gervase discusses rulings by Lothar III and Frederick Barbarossa in 1136 and 1154 regarding the inalienability of fiefs without permission of the lord from whom the fief is held. Susan Reynolds, *Fiefs and Vassals: The Medieval Evidence Reinterpreted* (Oxford 1994) 215–30, 483–86. On Roman law in Gervase, *Otia* I. 19, II.10–11. Further on Gervase's legal activities, *Otia*, xxx–xxxv.

met and spoke with Pedro II and Alfonso II of Aragon. He is last recorded as marshal in 1221 and last as residing in Arles in 1222. His subsequent career is a matter of considerably interesting dispute, since a number of scholars have asserted that he went on to Ebsdorf, where he designed the great Ebsdorf *Weltkarte* on the basis of the geography in the *Otia*.[8] Gervase was an extremely well-informed geographer, one of the best in twelfth- and early thirteenth-century Europe.

He dedicated the *Otia* to Otto IV a year or less after the defeat at Bouvines, when the unhappy former emperor may perforce have had rather more *otium* than usual. The *Otia* reflects a vast reading and thinking program on Gervase's part.[9] Geography, history, and *mirabilia* indeed abound, but *mirabilia* could also serve as a kind of moral and geographical mnemonic, and *decisiones* II and III may be a bit more functional in this way than has often been thought.[10] *Recreations*, or *solacium*, perhaps—that's how one got the attention and time of an emperor, but the genre often offered shrewd legal advice besides.[11]

A final preparatory note on Gervase. Of his orthodox Latin Christian bonafides there can be no doubt. The recently discovered *Commentary on the Lord's Prayer* and other lost devotional works confidently attributed to him are hardly necessary to establish it.[12] He thought that the Albigensian Crusade, for example, was a Very Good Thing.[13] Gervase's perspective, however, was not that of a cleric with pastoral, magisterial, or disciplinary responsibilities, nor that of a chronicler, nor always that of a professional canonist, but rather that of an extremely learned and devout professional layman and royal servant who had travelled up and down in the world and had formed firm opinions regarding both religious truths and proper rulership. He displays very little sympathy for those who contest their authoritative character.

8. See the literature cited in Wolf, 'Albert oder Gervasius,' above, n. 2.

9. I have taken all biographical information from the admirable Introduction to the *Otia*, xxv–xcv, Wolf, arts. cit., and from Bernd Ulrich Hucker, *Kaiser Otto IV* (MGH Schriften; Hannover 1990), esp. 407–9, and idem, *Otto IV, der wiederentdeckte Kaiser* (Frankfurt-Leipzig 2003). For further material, see my article 'The Lady Vanishes: Gervase of Tilbury on Heresy and Wonders,' in *Mind Matters: Studies of Medieval and Early Modern Intellectual History in Honour of Marcia Colish*, ed. Cary J. Nederman, Nancy Van Deusen, and E. Ann Matter (Turnhout 2009), 171–90. On the topic of this paper, *Otia*, xlviii–lv, with bibliography.

10. As it often is in Gerald of Wales. See the discussion in my essay 'The Desire to Know the Secrets of the World,' *Journal of the History of Ideas* (2001) 593–610.

11. The standard biography is now Hucker, *Otto IV. Der wiederentdeckte Kaiser*. For Gervase, pp. 200–201, 326–27, 386–87, 502–8.

12. *Otia*, xcii–xcv, II.16, and 902–23.

13. *Otia*, III.103. Mark Gregory Pegg, *A Most Holy War: The Albigensian Crusade and the Battle for Christendom* (New York 2008) 5, 14, 146–47, 152.

Gervase devotes virtually the entire Preface (probably, but not certainly, written in 1214–15—and quite distinct from the dedicatory material proper) to a treatise called the *Collatio sacerdocii et regni* concerning the proper relationship between spiritual and temporal authority. He begins with a paraphrase, not a direct quotation, of the first sentence of the famous letter of Gelasius I to the Emperor Anastasius of 494, probably known to him from its inclusion in Gratian's *Decretum* as D.96 c.10, *Duo sunt*. By the turn of the thirteenth century, as Robert L. Benson clearly demonstrated, the original text of Gelasius, which had focused on priestly orders, had been reinterpreted in several different ways, including both a dualist and a hierarchical interpretation that had the emperor receiving his authority from the pope.[14] Here Gervase emerges as a firm, if respectful, dualist: he breaks off paraphrasing after the first sentence, but he adds a series of tightly compressed, distinctly spiritual functions for *sacerdotium* (read pope) and *regnum* (read emperor):

> The priest prays, the king commands. The priest forgives sins, the king punishes transgressions. The priest binds and looses souls, the king tortures and kills bodies. Each is the executor of divine law, giving to each what is due him, coercing the wicked and rewarding the good.

For Gervase the two realms directed by *sacerdotium* and *regnum* are those of the soul and the body, and legitimate authority over each is given directly by God. Even though rulership arose from 'divine sufferance, not divine ordinance' and 'the chronological precedence of kingship [over priesthood] is that of age, not dignity,' as is the chronological precedence of body over soul, *regnum* is nevertheless conferred directly by God with liturgical, but not constitutive clerical cooperation—anointing. There follows a complex analysis of the anointing of priest and king—on the head and shoulder respectively—and detailed analysis of their spheres of responsibility and of the history of rulership, supported by a wide variety of scriptural references.

14. Robert L. Benson, 'The Gelasian Doctrine: Uses and Transformations,' in *La notion d'autorité au Moyen Age: Islam, Byzance, Occident*, George Makdisi, Dominique Sourdel, Janine Sourdel-Thomine, eds. (Paris 1982) 13–44. For the later period, Robert Folz, 'Translation de l'Empire et Déposition de l'empereur dans la vision des canonistes et des papes (1140–1245),' in *Deus qui mutat tempora: Menschen und Institutionen im Wandel des Mittelalters. Festschrift für Alfons Becker*, Ernst-Dieter Hehl, Hubertus Seibert, Franz Staab, eds. (Sigmaringen 1987), 321–34; James A. Watt, 'Spiritual and Temporal Powers,' ch. 14 of J. H. Burns, ed., *The Cambridge History of Medieval Political Thought* (Cambridge 1988) 367–423, and Kenneth Pennington, *The Prince and the Law* (Berkeley–Los Angeles 1993) 8–75. Johannes Fried has recently argued for a similar series of reinterpretations of the Donation of Constantine: Donation of Constantine *and* Constitutum Constantini: *The Misinterpretation of a Fiction and Its Original Meaning* (Berlin–New York 2007).

Gervase rereads the Donation of Constantine (D. 96 cc. 13–14) in such a way as to deny that Constantine had conferred any form of empire on the pope—'he did not wish the name (*nomen*) of empire or the imperial power itself (*imperium*) to pass to Sylvester'—rather reserving them for himself and his successors at Constantinople, only *potestas* over the western regions as well as the crown and other insignia being given to Sylvester, until Charlemagne 'withdrew from the authority of the Greeks, on the advice of Pope Gregory the Younger [*sic*].' Gervase then turns to a compact reiteration of his earlier assertion:

God is the author of the empire, and the emperor is the author of the papal triumph. The pope is, after Christ, the head of souls, the emperor is, after God, the lord of bodies, or rather through God, by whom the right of the king was established.

And on, from Christ to Melchizedech, to Peter and to the papal plenitude of power over spiritual matters and the clergy (but not the laity) and the instability of earthly institutions, but not their dependence upon any sacerdotal office or gift.[15]

Although most of Gervase's citations in the *Collatio* are scriptural, he clearly stands in a canonist political dualist tradition that runs from Damasus, Stephen of Tournai, Huguccio, Ricardus Anglicus, and Alanus Anglicus to Johannes Teutonicus and is opposed to the hierocratic views of Laurentius Hispanus, Innocent III, Hostiensis, and Innocent IV. Banks and Binns suggest that Gervase's material in the preface may derive from an unknown canonist text, but one can just as readily assert that the arguments are those of *Magister Gervasius Tilleberiensis Anglicus* himself, shaped between 1209 and 1215 to address the particular case of Otto IV. One wonders under whom Gervase had studied at Bologna—perhaps Huguccio, or Ricardus, a fellow Englishman who also had a second career in a different kind of law in England.[16]

15. On *plenitudo potestatis*, Robert L. Benson, '*Plenitudo potestatis*: Evolution of a Formula from Gregory IV to Gratian,' SG 14 (1967) 193–218; William D. McCready, 'Papal *Plenitudo Potestatis* and the Source of Temporal Authority in Later Medieval Papal Hierocratic Theory,' *Speculum* 48 (1973) 654–74; Pennington, *The Prince and the Law*, ch. 1. On Gervase's treatment of the Donation of Constantine in the Preface, Gerhard Laehr, *Die Konstantinische Schenkung in der abendländischen Literatur des Mittelalters bis zur Mitte des 14. Jahrhunderts* (Berlin 1926) 76–78. On Gervase and the Donation, Fried, *Donation of Constantine*, 21, 42, and for Walter von der Vogelweide's criticism of the Donation, Fried, 7–8.

16. Robert C. Figueira, 'Ricardus de Mores at Common Law—The Second Career of an Anglo-Norman Canonist,' in Lothar Kolmer and Peter Segl, eds., *Regensburg Bayern und Europa. Festschrift für Kurt Reindel zu seinem 70. Geburtstag* (Regensburg 1995) 281–99. Further on papal power, Robert C. Figueira, 'Papal Reserved Powers—Some Decretist Texts,' in Richard H. Helmholz,

Gervase discusses the general moral qualities desirable in any ruler and illustrates them in his portraits of earlier princes, notably those of Charlemagne, Henry the Young King, and Richard I, in II.16 and II.21, but his focus is on the nobility of Otto's descent (for all his emphasis on the virtues of elective rulership, Gervase nevertheless expects the most noble candidate to be the *electus*), the importance of imperially neglected Arles, and Otto's problems with Innocent III.[17] Gervase is most interesting when he turns to Otto's own circumstances between 1198 and 1214.[18]

Gervase's discussion of papal and imperial authority and their sources is laid out very carefully and not always clearly along the lines of contemporary papal ideas and imagery: the Donation of Constantine, the idea of *translatio imperii*, and the two swords (in an unusual way in I.16, identifying them with the 'turning sword' of Genesis 3:24, which punished both soul and body; the ecclesiastical sword of the pope was used exclusively for penitential and pastoral purposes, but sometimes with temporal consequences).[19]

In *decisio* II.16 Gervase returns to the Donation of Constantine, as he had indicated he would in the Preface. Citing Constantine's construction

---

Paul Mikat, Jörg Müller, and Michael Stolleis, eds., *Grundlagen des Rechts. Festschrift für Peter Landau zum 65. Geburtstag* (Paderborn 2000) 477–90. Schnith, 'Otto IV und Gervasius von Tilbury,' 65, suggests that Huguccio was Gervase's teacher.

17. In 1207 it appears that Otto was offered the kingdom of Arles if he would give way to Philip of Swabia in the electoral struggle. *Otia*, Intro., p. xxxii, and Friedrich Kempf, S.J., 'Innocenz III und der deutsche Thronstreit,' AHP 23 (1985) 63–91 at 83. After Philip's murder in 1208 the offer became moot. According to the unknown German author of an account of the Fourth Lateran Council, a number of Otto's supporters presented intricate arguments for his restoration, and some present thought that Innocent III had begun to swing toward Otto; Stephan Kuttner and Antonio García y García, 'A New Eyewitness Account of the Fourth Lateran Council,' *Traditio* 20 (1964) 115–78, esp. 126–27, 147–53. Gervase was not Otto's only defender. As Schnith points out, Otto had the firm support of Richard I of England and later of John. On the deposition, Anton Haidacher, 'Über den Zeitpunkt der Excommunication Ottos IV durch Papst Innocenz III,' *Römische Historische Mitteilungen* 3 (1960) 132–85. Frederick II had been crowned at Aachen in July 1215, four months before IV Lateran convened.

18. In his discussion of how to calculate the indiction in II.15, Gervase seems to use as a calculating date the current year in which he was writing, 1211. But the *Otia* makes no mention of Bouvines (27 July 1214) and may well have been completed before the battle took place. An exception may depend on how one reads Gervase's mention of Otto's 'cares' in III.85. In III.103 Gervase refers to the second imperial year, that is, 1211. Of course much of the *Otia* had been assembled by Gervase over the preceding twenty-five years, since he had begun it as his second book for Henry the Young King, most likely sometime in the very early 1180s. As I read it Gervase seems to add material either as separate chapters, mostly in III, or in continuations, insertions, or additions to existing chapters, as in II.

19. The reference seems to be an early instance of what later became something of a canonist commonplace: James A. Brundage, *The Medieval Origins of the Legal Profession: Canonists, Civilians, and Courts* (Chicago and London 2008) 476.

of Constantinople as the new Rome and the seat of continuing imperial authority, Gervase observes simply, 'Thus the old Rome, bereft of the honor of the imperial crown, passed, along with the imperial insignia, to Sylvester, exchanging empire for pontificate, and dominion for Greek rule.' The diminution of old Rome, the independence from the pope of the emperor at Constantinople, the political peculiarity of the papal position in the West, and the pope's retention of the imperial insignia are themes that Gervase reiterates. In II.16 Gervase also states that Charlemagne fought on behalf of the Roman state, 'and ultimately, at the end of his life, assumed the title of emperor,' with no mention of papal action at all, let alone a *translatio imperii*. Gervase instead turns to the vexing problem of Rome:

> Rome no longer deserves her accustomed title of capital of the world, but can only be said to be a shadow of the former capital... while she claims to have two lords, she falls between the pontificate and the empire, and shuts one out while she despises the other. In a word, the most convincing indication of the demise of the Roman empire is that it has changed from an empire into a pontificate.

Gervase is kinder about Rome elsewhere, as in his set piece in II.8.[20]

In II. 18, his short history of the Frankish kingdom, Gervase returns to the confusion caused by the Donation of Constantine. Here, Charlemagne accepts from Leo (III) and 'the whole Roman people' the imperial *nomen* and *imperium*, which he received from Leo with consecration. After that, 'the authority of the Greeks passed away in the West, and the title of emperor was restored to certain parts of western Europe'.[21] But Gervase is not finished. The coronation of Charlemagne created a great confusion, since there were now two people holding the same title, made more confusing by the fact that the authority of the emperor at Constantinople derives from God alone, 'but on the other hand, the pope claims that the authority over the west derives from the Roman see alone.' The pope alone bears the imperial insignia, 'and the Roman emperor holds the imperial title while bearing the common insignia of other kings.' The pope rules Rome, the emperor is said to be the servant of the pope, and he is designated the executor of the apostles in temporal affairs, while the pope is vicar of Christ and the successor of the apostles. 'See what an unhappy state Rome has been reduced to ...'

20. Rather like the description of London in *Otia* II.17.

21. Although at the time Gervase was probably writing this passage there was a Latin emperor on the throne in Constantinople and had been since 1204, the fact does not seem to have troubled Gervase's concept of the Greek emperor's deriving his authority directly from God. For the election and coronation of Baldwin I, see Jonathan Phillips, *The Fourth Crusade and the Sack of Constantinople* (London 2004) xi–xii, 270–77.

In this situation, Rome itself 'may be said to serve two lords, one wearing the crown, the other holding the power,' but in fact she scorns both, playing one off against the other, degenerate and stiff-necked. But worse: the emperor is elected by the princes of Alemannia, 'but the pope confirms the election and consecrates the emperor.' This observation surely refers to the debates over Innocent III's *Deliberatio* of 1200 or the decretal *Venerabilem* of 1202. 'The emperor's title proclaims his authority, while his consecration belies that authority: for he does not actually receive the imperial insignia, which the pope retains as having been conferred only on him, and [the emperor] is consecrated only at the small altar on the right-hand side of St. Peter's.'[22] The emperor in Constantinople (one assumes indifferently Greek or Latin) is not hampered in this way.

Gervase then raises a series of risky questions, especially for an otherwise extremely respectful papalist, and he notes, 'were it not that I should seem to be setting my mouth against heaven' (Ps. 72 [73]:9) it would be possible to lodge a complaint against Leo III. Did Leo even have the authority to crown an Augustus in the first place? Further, either the empire has no right to relinquish Rome even by an emperor's gift, or even if it did, the pope had no right to give another the title (*nomen*) of Augustus, since he did not hold the title himself, especially when doing so was contrary to the interests of the emperor at Constantinople, who had given Leo's predecessor his authority. These queries sound like those of the canon law schoolroom. The very next sentence addresses Otto directly. In Otto, God seems to have re-established the fullness of the old imperial dignity (*plenitudo veteris imperialis dignitatis*), since Otto comes from an old and devout imperial family, has been elected twice (in 1198 and 1208—in all, there seem to have been seven imperial elections between 1198 and 1212, depending on what and how one counts), and has been confirmed by the pope. His enemies have all been laid low, and Otto will surely acquire the monarchy of Constantinople because of his wife's right of inheritance—the death of Beatrice in 1212 provides a *terminus ante quem* for this statement.[23] Gervase

22. Gervase's repeated point about the emperor's lack of the imperial insignia is puzzling, since Otto IV was certainly crowned in imperial fashion, although in a new *ordo* written by Innocent III—an extremely able stage-manager, as witness the Fourth Lateran Council. On the ceremony, Hucker, *Wiederentedeckte Kaiser* 183–96, Eduard Eichmann, *Kaiserkrönung im Abendland*, Vol. I (Würzburg 1942) 266–279, and below, n. 20. I leave aside here the problem of the crown and other insignia. See below, n. 26.

23. Otto was married to Beatrice, daughter of Philip of Swabia and the Byzantine princess Irene-Maria, daughter of Isaac Angelos and sister of Alexius III, in 1212, although Beatrice died shortly after the wedding. They had been betrothed in 1209, and that year looks like a plausible date for this passage, or at least a *terminus post quem*. 1210 would see rather more disasters for Otto,

advises Otto to be grateful to Innocent III, who has crowned him, since he will receive an even greater new *imperium*, this one with full imperial authority and regalia; i.e., that of Constantinople. Such high and fanciful hopes became improbable from the papal perspective after 1210 and impossible after Beatrice's death in 1212.

No pope, not even Gregory VII, had ever laid out a view of the relations between papacy and empire more elaborately argued than Innocent III, and no pope had ever done so in so tight a time-frame.[24] Five months after his coronation in July 1198, Innocent received the first of the communications from a group of electors (*ad quos de iure spectat electio*) that, with other communications on the topic and his initially cautious responses, inspired the creation of the first special papal register, the *Regestum Innocentii III papae super negotio romani imperii*.[25] Around the same time (ca. 1200) there appeared Innocent's remarkable *Deliberatio* on the three candidates for the imperial office, Frederick II, Philip of Swabia, and Otto of Brunswick.[26] Besides assessing the qualities of each candidate, Innocent here also explicitly laid down several academically argued general principles: the empire is related to the papacy *principaliter* (because of the papal *translatio imperii* from the Greeks by Leo III) and *finaliter* (because the pope promotes to empire by the *approbatio* and the laying-on of hands); the pope does so according to law, seemliness, and expediency; the electors have acted inappropriately; and their own role was very nearly usurped by Henry VI's wicked *Erbreichsplan* of 1195/6 (of which Gervase also strongly disapproved).

Two years later, several of the electors' protests over the actions of the papal legate, the bishop of Palestrina, in condemning Philip of Swabia and favoring Otto elicited the decretal *Venerabilem*, which contained several additional and quite novel principles:[27] neither the bishop of Palestrina nor the pope is an imperial *elector* or a *cognitor* of imperial elections; the papal translation of the empire included the translation of the rights of the electors; the pope, who was to crown and consecrate the emperor, had

---

although Gervase seems to have remained optimistic. There seems to have been some hope for Otto's restoration even at the Fourth Lateran Council.

24. Still fundamental is Friedrich Kempf, S.J., *Papsttum und Kaisertum bei Innocenz III. Die Geistigen und rechtlichen Grundlagen seiner Thronstreitspolitik*, Miscellanea Historiae Pontificiae vol. 19 (Rome 1954), as well as Kempf's 'Innocenz III und der deutsche Thronstreit.'

25. Ed. Friedrich Kempf, Miscellanea Historiae Pontificiae 12 (Rome 1947), hereafter RNI followed by document number.

26. RNI 29. The *Deliberatio* is an interesting document, since it was presented orally by Innocent III to a secret consistory, which suggests that it might be considered as a kind of Consilium.

27. RNI 62; X 1.6.34.

the obligation to examine him for his suitability for the office, lest electoral folly or self-interest elect an unsuitable *rex;* the bishop of Palestrina had in fact been an evangelical *denuntiator* (a legitimate legal accuser who would later figure importantly in Innocent's reforms of canon law criminal procedure). As a number of scholars have pointed out, there was absolutely no precedent or evidence for Innocent's assertion of the papal origins of the electoral office. Although there had existed both a form of *scrutinium/approbatio* for candidates for clerical office and for emperors, it had largely been a pure formality in the case of emperors.[28] Innocent here elevates it to a profound instrumental responsibility (and a source of authority) on the part of the pope, although he does not say when or where it was to take place—certainly not at the coronation ceremony itself, not after the effort, risk, and expense of the *Römerzug*. Ironically, this possibility in the case of a papal election became an argument against papal election only by cardinals on the part of several later conciliarists.

Finally, there was the coronation of Otto IV, in Rome on Sunday, 4 October 1209, according to the *ordo* created for that occasion by Innocent III himself, which Schramm and Eichmann call *Ordo* D and Elze *Kaiserkronung Ordo* XVIII.[29] And Gervase was present, as he reminds Otto. He witnessed Otto kissing the pope's foot, offering him gold, and repeating the oath to protect and defend the pope and the Roman church, their possessions, honors, and laws to the best of his ability. After several prayers, the king moves to the side chapel of St. Maurice, where he is anointed on the arm and shoulder by the bishop of Ostia. The company then moves to the high altar of St. Peter, where the pope says the *Missa pro imperatore,* at which the emperor serves as a deacon. After the Epistle and Gradual the pope crowns the emperor with a clerical miter and then the imperial miter and presents

28. Eichmann, *Die Kaiserkronung im Abendland,* I, 57. Dagmar Unverhau, *Approbatio-Reprobatio. Studien zur päpstlichen Mitspracherecht bei Kaiserkrönung und Königswahl vom Investiturstreit bis zum ersten Prozess Johanns XXII gegen Ludwig IV* (Lübeck 1973); Jürgen Miethke, art., 'Approbatio der deutschen Königswahl,' in *Lexikon fur theologie und Kirche,* 3rd ed., ed. Walter Kasper und Konrad Baumgartner, vol. I (Leipzig 1993) cols. 888–91.

29. For Otto IV, Latin text and full discussion in Eichmann, *Kaiserkrönung im Abendland,* vol. I, 253–95. Better and fuller text in Reinhard Elze, *Die Ordines für die Weihe und Krönung des Kaisers und der Kaiserin* (Hannover 1960) 69–87. Cf. Reinhard Elze, 'Eine Kaiserkronug um 1200,' repr. in Elze, *Päpste-Kaiser-Könige und die mittelalterliche Herrschaftssymbolik,* ed. Bernhard Schimmelpfennig and Ludwig Schmugge (Aldershot–Burlington VT 1982) # V. Innocent III wrote his own version of the imperial coronation *ordo* of 1209, emphasizing the status of the emperor as *vicarius papae.* It is not known how much *ordo*-history Gervase knew, since the only Roman imperial coronation in his lifetime until 1209 was that of Henry VI, in Rome in 1191, which he did not witness, although he certainly had great access to the papal archives in Rome in 1209, which he used for other material in the *Otia.*

him with the sword, scepter, and orb. This is followed by the *laudes regiae*. Liturgically as well as in Innocent's letters, the pope is the *Vicarius Christi* and the emperor *Vicarius Papae*. The liturgy is what Gervase saw in 1209. I think that he was confused about the *regalia*—he had probably never witnessed a coronation of any kind before and may thus have mistaken the imperial *regalia* of 1209 for ordinary royal *regalia*.[30]

Hence the advice in *decisio* II.19. Show yourself innocent to Innocent, give way in a small thing (Sicily and South Italy) to him who conferred the whole of your power upon you:

> The empire, to be sure, is not yours, but Christ's, not yours, but Peter's. It has not come to you from yourself, but from the vicar of Christ and the successor of Peter.

And Otto, like all men, emperors or not, will leave it all behind when he dies. Public opinion (here indicated as being in favor of Innocent in the matter of the Sicilian kingdom) should overcome any overscrupulous imperial conscience about the imperial oath prohibiting the alienation of imperial territory—*dilapidatio imperii*. Other matters of conscience should be confessed to the pope, who 'is judge over you and for you: he who is himself subject to no mortal judge.' Constantine granted authority over the West to Peter:

> By the pope's gift, not her own, Rome regained the title of empire in the time of Charlemagne. By the pope's gift, the imperial sovereignty [*imperium*] is now due to the king of the Germans, not the king of the Franks. Nor is the sovereignty [*imperium*] granted to whomever Germany chooses, but to whomever the pope has decreed it should be granted.

Thus Gervase on the unique and historically produced constitutional dilemma of the western empire. He is rephrasing and exaggerating the bold claims of *Venerabilem*, advising Otto simply to accept Innocent's claims only in the small case of Sicily, and hence only tactical and practical legal advice for Otto. Gervase goes on:

> Now the pope will either be good to you as the arbiter of your common cause, or not so good, not to say bad. If he is good, you will gain by his just judgment, if you have a just cause; if he is not so good, by making him the judge in his own case you will unburden yourself of the danger of ill-repute, and you will lay on him the burden of justice.

30. Folz, too, thinks that Gervase was confused about the regalia: Robert Folz, *The Concept of Empire in Western Europe from the Fifth to the Fourteenth Century*, trans. Sheila Ann Ogilvie (London 1969) 199–201, although I think that he otherwise makes Gervase less of a dualist than I think he was in regard to Innocent.

'Not to say bad'—and a final piece of lawyer's advice, the canonist commonplace prohibiting a judge from deciding in his own case.[31]

Otia III.35 contains a direct address to Innocent III in the context of Gervase's account of the Theban Legion. The chapter had begun with a substantial discussion of the necessity of a ruler's obeying spiritual precepts which may be erroneous. Gervase then turns to a pope's prohibition of an imperial command, with an examination of the qualifications and circumstances. Gervase then simply states;

If therefore, [the emperor's] commands constitute a lawful exercise of his imperial authority, I shall, I say, obey, not a sacrilegious ruler, but a sacred law, not an emperor, but the imperial authority; so too I obey not a bad bishop, but the see, not a prelate, but the Church, not the pope, but Peter, not a human being, but God, whose mission he performs, according to C. 2 q. 6 c. 6: 'Accusatio.'

Evidently writing no earlier than 1211, after Otto's excommunication by Innocent, Gervase warns Innocent:

Take heed, therefore, Your Holiness, when you command me not to obey my earthly ruler. I gladly render obedience to you, as the guardian of my soul, in what belongs to God; but I shall also obey my earthly ruler in what touches the lawful exercise of his authority. I shall keep faith with the empire, to which I have pledged myself in the person of the emperor. I shall keep my faith with God, to whom I pledged myself at baptism.

Gervase remained a respectful dualist, but a dualist nonetheless.

Two final points. In *Otia* III.103, Gervase tells Otto that he has received information directly from God concerning the ways in which Otto is and is not pleasing to Him. Gervase has put this information into a letter which he is sending via a reliable messenger. There is no evidence that Otto received it, and the letter has not survived. Second and last: as Banks and Binns emphasize, Gervase exerted considerable, indeed extraordinary, control over several manuscripts containing various recensions of the *Otia*. And yet from none of these did he excise the early dualism and skepticism about the Donation of Constantine and the *translatio imperii*. It was probably safer to say so among instructional and diverting *mirabilia* out in the Arelate, and expressed in a truly formidable and ambivalent rhetoric than it would have been in either Rome or Bologna—whether in a classroom or in the formal text of an *Apparatus*.

31. In III.103, Gervase tells the story of the count of Toulouse's repentance before the abbot of Bonnevaux, repentance inspired by the abbot's emphasis on communion among Christians and the terrors of excommunication. The *exemplum* may have been directed at Otto and may reflect Gervase's genuine anguish at the emperor's moral dilemma after 1210.

GILES CONSTABLE

15 Charter Evidence for Pope Urban II's Preaching of the First Crusade

Most of the scholars who have studied Urban II's call to the crusade at the council of Clermont in November 1095 and his subsequent preaching of the crusade have relied on the narrative accounts, which were written by the anonymous author of the *Gesta francorum et aliorum Hierosolymitanorum*, Peter Tudebode, Raymond of Aguilers, Fulcher of Chartres, Robert (the Monk) of Rheims, Guibert of Nogent, Baldric of Bourgeuil, William of Malmesbury, and Orderic Vitalis.[1] The relations among the works of these writers are debated, but there is general agreement that they were written at the beginning of the twelfth century, after the crusade, and that they were influenced by its outcome.[2] Some of them, furthermore, were

1. See in particular the influential article by Dana C. Munro, 'The Speech of Pope Urban II. at Clermont, 1095,' *American Historical Review* 11 (1906) 231–42, which is cited by almost all students of the subject. Among recent accounts see Frederic Duncalf, 'The Councils of Piacenza and Clermont,' in *A History of the Crusades*, 1: *The First Hundred Years*, ed. Marshall W. Baldwin (Madison-London 1969) 238–42; Herbert E. J. Cowdrey, 'Pope Urban II's Preaching of the First Crusade,' *History* 55 (1970) 177–88; Robert Somerville, 'The Council of Clermont and the First Crusade,' SG 20 (1976) 325–37, repr. in idem, *Papacy, Councils and Canon Law in the 11th–12th Centuries* (Variorum Collected Studies 312; Aldershot 1990); Hans E. Mayer, *The Crusades*, trans. John Gillingham (2nd ed. Oxford 1988) 8–11; Penny J. Cole, *The Preaching of the Crusades to the Holy Land, 1095–1270* (Cambridge, MA 1991) 2–5; Jean Flori, *La première croisade* (Brussels 1992) 27–34; Thomas Asbridge, *The First Crusade: A New History* (Oxford 2004) 31–39 (with a brief bibliography in n. 28 on p. 348); Christopher Tyerman, *God's War: A New History of the Crusades* (London 2006) 63–72.

2. According to Louise and Jonathan Riley-Smith, *The Crusades: Idea and Reality, 1095–1274* (Documents of Medieval History 4; London 1981) 40, 'All the reports of Urban's address at the end of the Council of Clermont were written after the success of the crusade, and the words put into the pope's mouth reflected these subsequent events.' See also August C. Krey, 'Urban's Crusade—Success or Failure,' *American Historical Review* 53 (1947–48) 236, and Asbridge, *First Crusade* 32, who said that all the accounts of Urban's address were written after the crusade and 'must, therefore, be read with a healthy dose of suspicion in mind.'

written with propagandistic aims in favor of one or another of the crusader leaders.[3]

A few scholars have also taken into account some of the charters issued by crusaders (mostly to raise money for their journeys) in the period immediately or very soon after the council,[4] but those charters which explicitly refer to Urban and his preaching of the crusade have not, to the best of my knowledge, been studied as a group. They were written by men who may have heard Urban speak or at least heard reports of his preaching and were certainly not influenced by subsequent events. Probably the earliest, from Marcigny-sur-Loire, is dated 'in the year that pope Urban II came into Aquitaine,' which may be either 1095 or 1096;[5] another, from the monastery of St-Pierre-de-la-Cour at Le Mans, was issued 16–17 February 1096;[6] and a grant by count Robert of Flanders can be dated before September or October 1096, that is, less than a year after the council.[7] A charter from Sauxillanges was issued 'not long after' ('non longo post tempore') Urban delivered his 'exhorting decree' (*exhortans decretum*), which probably refers to the council.[8] To these can be added a pancharte from St-Aubin at Angers dated 20 March 1098 and confirming, among other grants, a charter issued before that date and, therefore, close to the date of the council.[9]

These documents differ in what they say about Urban. According to the Marcigny charter, he 'inspired the army of Christians to repress the ferocity of the eastern pagans' ('Christianorum exercitum movit at [*for* ad?]

3. See Jean Flori, 'De l'anonyme normand à Tudebode et aux *Gesta Francorum*. L'impact de la propagande de Bohémond sur la critique textuelle des sources de la première croisade,' *Revue d'Histoire Ecclésiastique* 102 (2007) 217–46.

4. Notably Cowdrey, 'Urban II's Preaching' 182–87 (where he cited seven charters, three for Cluny, and one each for St Victor at Marseilles, St-Père at Chartres, St-Chaffre du Monastier, and Marcigny-sur-Loire); Jonathan Riley-Smith, 'The Idea of Crusading in the Charters of Early Crusaders, 1095–1102,' *Le concile de Clermont de 1095 et l'appel à la croisade. Actes du Colloque Universitaire International de Clermont-Ferrand (23–25 juin 1995)* (Collection de l'Ecole français de Rome 236; Rome 1997) 155–66, who cited most of the charters discussed here, but in a different context.

5. Jean Richard, *Le cartulaire de Marcigny-sur-Loire (1045–1144). Essai de reconstitution d'un manuscrit disparu* (Analecta burgundica; Dijon 1957) 89, no. 119.

6. *Cartulaire du chapitre royal de Saint-Pierre-de-la-Cour du Mans*, ed. Menjot d'Elbenne and L.-J. Denis (Archives historiques du Maine 4; Le Mans 1903–7) 15, no. 11.

7. Fernand Vercauteren, *Actes des comtes de Flandre, 1071–1128* (Commission royal d'histoire. Recueil des actes des princes belges; Brussels 1938) 63, no. 20.

8. Henry Doniol, 'Cartulaire de Sauxillanges,' *Mémoires de l'Académie des sciences, belles-lettres et arts de Clermont-Ferrand* 34 (N.S. 3; 1861) 966–67, no. 697.

9. *Cartulaire de l'abbaye de Saint-Aubin d'Angers*, ed. Bertrand de Broussillon and Eugène Lelong (Société d'agriculture, sciences et arts d'Angers. Documents historiques sur l'Anjou 1–3; Paris 1903) 1.407, no. 354.

comprimendam feritatem orientalium paganorum'). The St-Pierre-de-la-Cour charter described the restoration of some property to the monastery 'when pope Urban preached the way to Jerusalem and came to these parts for the sake of this preaching' ('dum Urbanus papa predicaret uiam Jerusalem, et causa illius predicationis ad istas partes uenisset'). In the arenga to a grant to the church of St Peter at Lille, Robert of Flanders expressed his hope to win salvation by grants to the poor and the intervention of the saints and then said of himself:

> I therefore at the instigation of the divine admonition, promulgated by the authority of the apostolic see, [am] about to go to Jerusalem to free the church of God that has long been oppressed by barbaric peoples, in order that almighty God may give effect to the exercise of my labor by which the blessed honor of His name may be spread and the gift of the coin that never fails [that is, salvation] may be granted to me. (Ego igitur, instinctu diuinę admonitionis, auctoritate apostolicę sedis promulgato, iturus Jherusolimam, ad liberandam Dei ęcclesiam diu a feris nationibus conculcatam, ut Deus omnipotens exercitio mei laboris effectum preberet, quo et honor nominis ejus sanctificatus dilateretur, et michi indeficientis denarii donatiuum restitueretur.)

The grant to St-Aubin, more briefly, was made 'when pope Urban first moved the world to go to Jerusalem' ('quando Urbanus papa primum commouit orbem ire Jerusalem').

The charter from Sauxillanges is more problematical owing both to its lack of a date and to the possible corruption of the text, at least in the printed edition.[10] There is no reason to question the substance of its contents, however, which, after describing a grant to Sauxillanges by the bishop of Clermont, went on to say:

> Furthermore, not long after the time when the barbarian persecution rose up to destroy the liberty of the eastern church, an exhorting decree was issued by the supreme pontiff that the entire strength and faith of the western peoples should hasten to assist the destroyed religion. (Preterea, non longo post tempore, cum ad libertatem orientalis. [sic] Ecclesiae deuastandam barbarica persecutio inhorresceret, exhortans decretum a summo pontifice, processit ut omnis occidentalium nationum uirtus ac fides in auxilium destructe religionis festinaret.)

A father and son, the charter continued, made a grant to Sauxillanges in return for the remission of their sins, the right to be buried at Sauxillanges, and a mule worth two hundred shillings. There is no certainty that they went on the crusade, but the references to the plight of the eastern church and the pope's exhorting decree and the grant of a mule worth two hundred shillings strongly suggest that they planned to join the expedition.

10. Mayer, *Crusades* 10–11, said that it 'unmistakably' referred to the first crusade, but Riley-Smith, 'Idea of Crusading' 156, n. 10, said that it 'looks like a forgery.'

Among the several points that stand out in these documents, the most striking is the emphasis on 'the ferocity of the eastern pagans' (Marcigny), 'the oppression of barbaric peoples' (Robert of Flanders), and 'the barbarian persecution' (Sauxillanges). The need to free the eastern church was also stressed in the Robert of Flanders and Sauxillanges charters. They all refer to the inspiration, preaching, or decree of the pope, and the St-Pierre-de-la-Cour, Robert of Flanders, and St-Aubin charters stress Urban's summons to take the way or to go to Jerusalem, to which there is no reference in the Marcigny or Sauxillanges charters. Robert of Flanders referred to his own salvation and to the spread of 'the honor of the name of God,' and the father and son in the Sauxillanges charter made a grant 'in remission of their sins' and in order to be freed from the punishment of hell by the intercession of the monks, but there is no evidence that this was connected with the crusade or formed part of the pope's message. Together the charters suggest that Urban emphasized the themes of going to Jerusalem and of assisting the eastern church, though whether by this he meant the Byzantine church in particular or the eastern churches in general is uncertain. There is no reference in the charters to the Greeks, but the oppression and persecution by the barbarians and pagans suggest he had in mind the eastern Christians in Muslim lands.

The evidence of these charters therefore supports the view that the goals of going to Jerusalem and helping the Christians in the east were linked from the beginning of the crusade, rather than the view that Jerusalem was added later to the original goal of freeing the eastern churches or of reuniting the Greek and Latin churches.[11] The second canon of the council of Clermont referred to the remission of penance assured to anyone who out of devotion and not for the sake of honor or money 'will have gone to Jerusalem to free the church of God' ('ad liberandam ecclesiam Dei Hierusalem profectus fuerit').[12] Urban himself, in his letter written in late December 1095 to the people of Flanders—which count Robert may have heard or seen—spoke of freeing the eastern churches ('ad liberationem

11. On the question of the relative priority of the goals of the first crusade, which was posed by Carl Erdmann, see the works cited in n. 1, in most (but not all) of which the liberation of the eastern churches and reconquest of Jerusalem are presented as 'two interlocking goals' (as Asbridge, *First Crusade* 33, put it) from the inception of the crusade. According to Bernard McGinn, '*Iter Sancti Sepulchri*: The Piety of the First Crusaders,' in *The Walter Prescott Webb Memorial Lectures: Essays in Medieval Civilization*, ed. Bede Lackner and Kenneth R. Philip (Austin-London 1978) 44, 'It is difficult to believe that Urban did not give central attention to the liberation of Jerusalem.'

12. Robert Somerville, *The Councils of Urban II*, 1: *Decreta Claromontensia* (AHC Suppl. 1; Amsterdam 1972) 74; see also 124, n. 14.

orientalium ecclesiarum') without referring to Jerusalem,[13] but on 7 October 1096 he wrote to the monks of Vallombrosa saying he had heard that some of them wanted to go with the soldiers who 'are going to Jerusalem for the sake of freeing Christianity' ('qui Ierusalem liberandę christianitatis gratia tendunt').[14] This appears to have been the message that spread in France and the Low Countries and was associated, according to the charters cited here, with the name of Urban.

13. Heinrich Hagenmeyer, *Die Kreuzzugsbriefe aus den Jahren 1088–1100* (Innsbruck 1901) 136, no. II, trans. in Riley-Smith, *Crusades* 38–39. See Mayer, *Crusades* 10.

14. Wilhelm Wiederhold, 'Papsturkunden in Florenz,' Nachrichten Göttingen 1901, p. 313, repr. in Paul Fridolin Kehr, *Papsturkunden in Italien* (Acta Romanorum pontificum 1–6; Vatican City 1977) 3.216.

KENNETH PENNINGTON

16 Roman Law at the Papal Curia in the Early Twelfth Century

More than thirty years ago, Robert Somerville wrote an essay that dealt with one of the many puzzles facing scholars when they confront Gratian's *Decretum*.[1] He pointed out that although Gratian included many canons from the Second Lateran Council in the last version of his *Decretum*, he did not include canon nine, *Prava autem consuetudo*. He wondered why. The canon's content was strange. Pope Innocent II had promulgated a prohibition forbidding monks and canons regular to study Roman law. The canon also barred them from representing litigants in lawsuits as *patroni*.[2] It declared that those monks who used their glorious voices to participate in the clamor of the courtroom neglected their liturgical songs and prayer because of greed. Instead, they argued cases using a thicket of legal citations that resulted in confusing the just with the unjust and divine law with impiety. This conciliar admonishment was hardly a positive view of an advocate's job, whether a monk, canon regular, or neither.[3]

There are two features of the canon that merit attention. First, Inno-

1. Robert Somerville, 'Pope Innocent II and the Study of Roman Law,' *Revue des Études islamiques* 44 (1976) 105–14, reprinted in *Papacy, Councils and Canon Law in the 11th–12th Centuries* (Variorum Collected Studies 312; Aldershot 1990).

2. *Decrees of the Ecumenical Councils*, 1: *Nicaea I–Lateran V*, ed. Norman P. Tanner (2 volumes; London-Washington, D.C. 1990) 198–99 at 198: 'Prava autem consuetudo prout accepimus et detestabilis inolevit quoniam monachi et regulares canonici post susceptum habitum et professionem factam spreta beatorum magistrorum Benedicti et Augustini regula leges temporales et medicinam gratia lucri temporalis addiscunt. Avaritiae namque flammis accensi se patronos causarum faciunt. Et cum psalmodiae et hymnis vacare debeant gloriosae vocis confisi munimine allegationum suarum varietate iustum et iniustum fas nefasque confundunt.'

3. Criticism of lawyers was a common theme in medieval writings; see James A. Brundage, *The Medieval Origins of the Legal Profession: Canonists, Civilians, and Courts* (Chicago-London 2008) 125, 215–17.

cent had issued it at least three times earlier in his pontificate, almost word for word. He had promulgated it at a council that he held at Clermont in 1130, at Reims in 1131, and at Pisa in 1135. In 1139 he included the canon in the legislation of the Second Lateran Council.[4] Secondly, forbidding monks to study Roman law must have been an important 'reform' item on Innocent's agenda. The Council underlined its displeasure with lawyer-monks by citing a constitution of the Roman Emperor Justin from Justinian's *Codex*. The emperor had declared that it was absurd and shameful for clerics (not just monks) to want to become learned experts in the law courts.[5] The wording of Justin's statute incorporated into the conciliar canon was almost exactly the same as the wording in the *Codex;* the only difference between the text of the conciliar canon and that of the *Codex* was that Justin's decree stipulated a penalty of 50 pounds of gold for violating the canon's strictures. Innocent did not. The juxtaposition of a prohibition against studying Roman law snuggled up against an authoritative text of Roman law in a papal conciliar decree gave Somerville pause—as it should have. We are still struggling to understand the complex relationship between the rediscovery of Roman law, the emergence of ecclesiastical jurisprudence, and the papacy's and the canonists' attitudes towards the use and study of Roman law.

Besides the explicit citation of Justin's statute there is another tacit citation to Roman law in the canon. The source for the canon's elegant rhetorical flourish that described the voices of monk-lawyers in the courtroom, *gloriosae vocis confisi munimine,* was either an anonymous homilist's sermon on the Resurrection that Migne included, wrongly, among the sermons of Peter Damian or another constitution in Justinian's *Codex,* issued by the emperors Leo and Anthemius. Undoubtedly, the homilist took his praise of lawyers from the *Codex*.[6] Whoever drafted the text of the conciliar canon transformed these very positive views of a lawyer's work in the

4. Somerville, 'Pope Innocent II' 106; the canon also appeared among the decrees of Reims 1131 and Pisa 1135. Atria Larson has noted that the early twelfth-century papacy issued identical or similar canons at councils fairly regularly; see her essay 'Early Stages of Gratian's *Decretum* and the Second Lateran Council: A Reconsideration,' BMCL 27 (2007) 21–56 at 37–39.

5. *Decrees of the Ecumenical Councils* 198 'Attestantur vero imperiales constitutiones absurdum immo et opprobrium esse clericis si peritos se velint disceptationum esse forensium. Huiusmodi temeratores graviter feriendos apostolica auctoritate decernimus.' Cod. 1.3.40: 'Absurdum etenim clericis est, immo etiam opprobrium, si peritos se velint disceptationum esse forensium: feriendis temeratoribus huius sanctionis poena quinquaginta librarum auri.'

6. Most likely, however, the person who drafted the conciliar canon took the phrase from the sermon because 'gloriosae vocis confisi munimine' in the sermon and in the papal conciliar canon is placed before the description of the lawyer's work, both good and bad, reversing the order of the *Codex*.

courtroom into a dark picture of a lawyer's being the sower of confusion in the courtroom. The homilist had written:[7]

This is a public act, and it is the duty of advocates to trust in the muniment[8] of their glorious voices to correct errors and to heal disturbances. They do not do less for the human race than those who defend their country with shields and armor.

There is some irony that the metaphor used to praise lawyers' courtroom gravity in the *Codex* and the sermon was employed in a diatribe against the practice of law in the conciliar canon.[9]

Gratian and the canonists rejected *Prava autem consuetudo*. It never entered the collections of canon law. However, Leo's, Anthemius's, and the homilist's praise of advocates lived on in the literature for centuries.[10] Lawyers continued to find comfort in the virtue of their calling when they read the *Codex*, and the writer of the sermon must have been well known, at least to John of Salisbury. John quoted him without attribution in his *Policraticus*, a book that circulated widely in the medieval and early modern periods.[11]

7. PL 144.563: 'Si consulamus adjutorium [*male* auditorium] jurisperitorum, primum capituli propositi verbum sic describitur: postulare est desiderium suum, vel amici sui in jure apud eum, qui jurisdictioni praeest, exponere, vel alterius desiderio contradicere. Actus iste publicus est, et est officium advocatorum, qui gloriosae vocis confisi munimine, lapsa erigunt, fatigata reparant, nec minus provident humano generi quam si clypeis et thoracibus sese patriamque defendant.' On Damian's Sermons see the excellent essay by Kennerly M. Woody, 'Peter Damian, St,' DMA 9.508–9. Woody lists all the spurious sermons in Migne.

8. The Latin word 'munimen' generally meant defense, protection, or fortification. In early medieval legal texts it was used to describe the evidentiary materials put forward in court cases by advocates to defend the rights of their clients. Pseudo-Damian has this meaning of the word in mind when he thinks about the purpose of the advocate's voice in the courtroom. There is no word in English that captures this meaning. Perhaps in this context 'munimen' should be rendered 'force and weight.'

9. Cod. 2.7.14: 'Imperatores Leo, Anthemius. Advocati, qui dirimunt ambigua fata causarum suaeque defensionis viribus in rebus saepe publicis ac privatis lapsa erigunt, fatigata reparant, non minus provident humano generi, quam si proeliis atque vulneribus patriam parentesque salvarent. Nec enim solos nostro imperio militare credimus illos, qui gladiis clupeis et thoracibus nituntur, sed etiam advocatos: militant namque causarum patroni, qui gloriosae vocis confisi munimine laborantium spem vitam et posteros defendunt.' Dated 469. See Brundage, *Legal Profession* 605 sub numero 2.7.14.

10. A version of the canon was inserted, evidently, into a manuscript of Ivo of Chartres' *Panormia*, and printed by Migne, PL 161.1342, but with no indication of the council to which it belonged.

11. John of Salisbury, *Policraticus: Of the Frivolities of Courtiers and the Footprints of Philosophers*, ed. and trans. Cary Nederman (Cambridge Texts in the History of Political Thought; Cambridge–New York 1990) Book 6, chapter 1, p. 104, who does not quite capture the meaning of the passage. The Latin text reads: 'sed et patroni causarum, qui gloriosae vocis confisi munimine, lapsa erigunt, fatigata reparant; nec minus provident humano generi, quam si laborantium vitam,

These facts about *Prava autem consuetudo* lead to a few basic questions that lie at the center of this essay: How receptive were ecclesiastical judges, advocates, and compilers of canonical collections to the use of Roman law in the early twelfth century?[12] When did the papacy begin to use Roman law in its curial court and in its legislation as an authoritative norm? I have already treated these two questions in previous essays using secular and ecclesiastical evidence.[13] In this essay I want to review the scholarship on these questions and examine a case heard at the papal court during the pontificate of Innocent's predecessor, Honorius II, in detail. In his essay Somerville attempted to provide a context for understanding *Prava autem consuetudo*'s prohibition of studying Roman law and for Gratian's rejection of the canon. The goal in this essay is to continue to explore how Roman law developed as a tool of analysis in the courtrooms of the early twelfth century and to provide further evidence for its use in the papal curia. I must confess at the beginning that the evidence that I will present in this essay makes it easier for us to understand why Gratian rejected the canon but even more difficult to know why Pope Innocent II promulgated *Prava autem consuetudo* repeatedly during his pontificate.

The Use of Roman Law in the Courts

Julius Ficker was the first to attempt a survey of Roman law in ecclesiastical and secular courts.[14] He published 531 court cases that he excavated from manuscripts in European archives and from printed sources. The earliest document dated to 776 and the last to 1474. The breadth and richness of his source collection has not yet been superseded. His insights

spem, posterosque, armorum praesidio ab hostibus tuerentur.' Because of the order of the phrases, John must have used the sermon and not the *Codex*.

12. Most recently see Anders Winroth, *The Making of Gratian's Decretum* (Cambridge Studies in Medieval Life and Thought, 4th Series, 49; Cambridge 2000) 146–74 and 'Neither Slave nor Free: Theology and Law in Gratian's Thoughts on the Definition of Marriage and Unfree Persons,' in *Medieval Church Law and the Origins of the Western Legal Tradition: A Tribute to Kenneth Pennington*, ed. Wolfgang P. Müller and Mary E. Sommar (Washington, D.C. 2006) 97–109. See also the two recent essays by Somerville's former Ph.D. students in *Bishops, Texts and the Use of Canon Law around 1100: Essays in Honour of Martin Brett*, ed. Bruce Brasington and Kathleen Cushing (Church, Faith and Culture in the Medieval West; Aldershot-Burlington 2007): Greta Austin, 'Secular Law in the *Collectio duodecim partium* and Burchard's *Decretum*' 29–44, and Anders Winroth, 'Roman Law in Gratian and the *Panormia*' 183–90.

13. Kenneth Pennington, 'The Birth of the Ius commune: King Roger II's Legislation,' RIDC 17 (2006) 1–40, and 'The "Big Bang": Roman Law in the Early Twelfth-Century,' RIDC 18 (2007) 43–70.

14. *Forschungen zur Reichs- und Rechtsgeschichte Italiens* (4 vols. Innsbruck 1868–74, reprinted Aalen 1961).

into legal practice in European courts over seven centuries are still worth reading.

More recently Antonio Padoa Schioppa surveyed the use of Roman law in the eleventh and twelfth centuries, basing his study on four of Ficker's cases.[15] Justinian's *Codex, Digest,* and the *Institutes* were cited in these court cases that chronologically extend from 1060 to 1107. As Padoa Schioppa points out, the case from 1107 in Rome reached a new stage for the role of juridical learning in legal practice.[16] The advocates in the case explicitly or tacitly cited Roman law texts almost a dozen times in the minutes of the proceedings.

Padoa Schioppa noted that Roman law did not always win the day in these early cases. Its standing was not yet preeminent. In a dispute held before two delegated judges of the Countess Matilda of Canossa in 1098 between the monastery of San Prospero in Reggio Emilia and certain laymen *de Vallibus,* the monks were told that they must submit themselves to a trial by battle. The monastery's advocate displayed royal charters and cited Justinian's *Institutes* and *Codex* in which gifts from the imperial home were always considered secure. He also put forward many other *optimae allegationes.* To no avail. The monks were told to prepare for the ordeal. The trial by battle was a disaster. The laymen's champion threw down a woman's glove on the monks' champion's head maliciously and contrary to all the rules of proper behavior. Laymen intervened in the fight and attacked the monks and their champions. Matilda's judges were at a loss and decided that a decision could not be rendered.[17] Although customary norms trumped Roman law on this occasion, the ordeal as a mode of proof was fast disappearing in Italy. The *ordo iudiciarius* was quickly taking its place, particularly in ecclesiastical courts. We have a number of papal letters in the mid-twelfth century that objected to clerics being subjected to procedures other than those dictated by the *ordo iudiciarius.*[18]

It should not surprise us that ecclesiastical courts would use Roman law. Popes began to insert Roman law texts into their decretals in the

15. Ficker, *Forschungen* vol. 4, no. 67, pp. 91–93, no. 73, pp. 99–100, no. 91, pp. 135–36, and no. 92, pp. 136–38. Ficker discussed Roman law in his cases in volume three, pp. 298–305. Antonio Padoa Schioppa, 'Il ruolo della cultura giuridica in alcuni atti giudiziari italiani dei secoli XI e XII,' *Nuova rivista storica* 64 (1980) 265–89.

16. Padoa Schioppa, 'Il ruolo' 276.

17. Ibid. 274–75; Ficker, *Forschungen* 135–36.

18. See my discussion in *The Prince and the Law 1200–1600: Sovereignty and Rights in the Western Legal Tradition* (Berkeley–Los Angeles 1993) 136–42 and a few more examples in my essay 'Due Process, Community, and the Prince in the Evolution of the *Ordo iudiciarius*,' RIDC 9 (1998) 9–47 at 14–17.

1120s. The earliest example I know of is a letter of Pope Calixtus II in 1123 in which the pope (or his curial staff) cited a constitution of the Emperor Constantine to justify the rights of people to make wills.[19] The papal use of Roman law as an authoritative norm is not a remarkable or unusual fact for the early twelfth century.[20] Secular law and Roman law were rife in canonical collections before Gratian. Churchmen were never reluctant to bring secular law to bear on ecclesiastical legal problems in both ecclesiastical and secular courts. A very rough piece of evidence to justify this statement can be gleaned from Linda Fowler-Magerl's *Clavis canonum*. She has listed secular and Roman laws under one rubric in her list of chapters—and her list contains many repeated canons present in many collections—but the numbers are still significant: by her count there are 3967 secular legal texts in pre-Gratian collections.[21] Consequently, although the evidence is sparse from the ninth to the beginning of the twelfth century, we should not be surprised that advocates in ecclesiastical courts cited and used Roman law and other pieces of secular legislation.

Chris Wickham took a different route from Ficker's in his recent study of twelfth-century central Italian court practices.[22] Although his study is based on substantial unpublished and published archival materials, Wickham printed only small swatches of text in his notes and no complete texts. Consequently, although Wickham developed a number of theses about how the courts of central Italy used Roman law (or more significantly, did not use Roman law or canon law in their decisions) during the twelfth century, because he presents so few texts to justify his generalizations one may wonder whether he has provided enough evidence to justify his conclusions.[23]

Wickham argues that there were differences among the various urban centers in their use of Roman law in their judicial proceedings. However, his conclusions are based upon evidence that is *ex silentio*: when a court decision did not cite Roman or canon law, then he concludes that legal

19. JL 7075a, July 10, 1123, *Bullaire du pape Calixte II 1119–1124*, ed. Ulysse Robert (2 vols. Paris 1891) 2.214[410]: 'Sic enim et magnus ille Constantinus imperator legum suarum promulgatione constituit dicens: "Nihil est quod magis hominibus debeatur, quam supremae voluntatis, postquam iam aliud velle non possunt, liber sit stilus et licitum quod iterum non redit arbitrium".' The text is Cod. 1.2.1.

20. For the intensive use of Roman law in the legislation of King Roger II (ca. 1140) in Sicily, see my essays 'The Normans in Palermo: King Roger II's Legislation,' *The Haskins Society Journal* 18 (2006) 140–67, and 'Birth of the Ius commune.'

21. A search done electronically with *Clavis*.

22. Chris Wickham, *Courts and Conflict in Twelfth-Century Tuscany* (Oxford 2003).

23. Ibid. 171–72, 235–38, and passim.

norms were not used by the judges when they decided cases. His methodology is flawed because court decisions, whether ecclesiastical or secular, only rarely cited the legal texts upon which the judges or arbiters based their judgments in the first half of the twelfth century and almost never in the second half. Unlike modern American or English court decisions, in which courts cite precedents supporting their holdings, medieval secular and ecclesiastical decisions did so only rarely.

Furthermore, Wickham discounts almost completely the influence that the twelfth-century jurists had on court procedure. I would argue that the jurists employed Roman law with the intention to shape the theory and the practice of procedure in secular and ecclesiastical courts during the first half of the twelfth century. Wickham disagrees.[24] He thinks that some courts ignore legal norms altogether and that Roman law was just an abstract science, 'as divorced from practical knowledge as any Parisian theological treatise'.[25] He argues that, as late as the end of the twelfth century, in many cases judges decided disputes on the facts of the case and common sense rather than on the law.[26] Particularly startling is his assertion that 'texts dealing with practical forensic issues' (i.e. the *ordo iudiciarius*) were rare in Italy.[27] A glance at Linda Fowler-Magerl's list of procedural treatises produced during the twelfth century would have quickly disabused him of that idea.[28] Jurists began to write procedural treatises in the second half of the eleventh century. This genre became very important in the twelfth century. When the papal chancellor Haimeric asked the

24. See my essays 'Birth of the Ius commune' and 'Big Bang.'

25. Wickham, *Courts and Conflict* 4.

26. Ibid. 236–37; also 91, 100, 172, and passim.

27. For a rather polemical discussion of the thesis that the study of law was divorced from 'practical forensic issues' in the medieval period, see my essay 'Learned Law, Droit Savant, Gelehrtes Recht: The Tyranny of a Concept,' RIDC 5 (1994) 197–209 and *Syracuse Journal of International Law and Commerce* 20 (1994) 205–15 and the many books and essays of Manlio Bellomo, beginning with, most conveniently, *The Common Legal Past of Europe, 1000–1800* (Washington, D.C. 1995).

28. Linda Fowler-Magerl, *Ordo iudiciorum vel ordo iudiciarius: Begriff und Literaturgattung* (Ius commune, Texte und Monographien, 19; Repertorien zur Frühzeit der gelehrten Rechte; Frankfurt am Main 1984) and her *Ordines iudiciarii and Libelli de ordine iudiciorum (From the Middle of the Twelfth to the End of the Fifteenth Century)* (Typologie des sources du moyen âge occidental 63; Turnhout 1994). Bruce Brasington, '*Crimina que episcopis inpingere dicis*: The Contribution of the *Collectio Polycarpus* to an Early *Ordo iudiciorum*', in *Readers, Texts, and Compilers in the Earlier Middle Ages: Studies in Medieval Canon Law in Honour of Linda Fowler-Magerl*, ed. Martin Brett and Kathleen Cushing (Church, Faith and Culture in the Medieval West; Farnham-Burlington 2009) has edited and analyzed a short treatise on witnesses produced in Italy mid-twelfth century, which is one example of many such treatises that were written by the canonists and the civilians. The jurist's citation of a canon from the *Polycarpus* instead of from Gratian is a good piece of evidence that it was written at a time when Gratian's *Decretum* had not yet swept the field.

leading teacher of Roman law in Bologna, Bulgarus, for a treatise on procedure in the 1130s, he did so for practical reasons, not because of intellectual curiosity.[29] Wickham does not seem to know about this very important early text. Although many of these treatises are lost, many manuscripts have survived. The canonists quickly followed in Bulgarus's footsteps and wrote many procedural tracts. As he expanded his *Decretum* in the 1130s, Gratian emphasized procedure, often using Roman law to establish procedural principles in his first *causae*.

We would have a much better idea about how advocates used Roman law in the courtroom if we had the minutes of the proceedings. These courtroom minutes would have preserved the advocates' arguments in court. Padoa Schioppa's conclusions about why these *memorie* have not survived are still valid.[30] He noted that 'we should not be surprised by the fact that these documents (memorie) [containing the arguments of the parties] redacted by one of the parties or by their command are quite rare.'[31] The victorious party might find the oral and written arguments useful in the future only if the decision had not definitively settled the dispute.[32] For most court decisions litigants were probably satisfied to keep a copy of the final judgment in their archives and not the minutes.

We do have some rare examples of court cases in which the arguments of the advocates are recorded. The case that I will discuss below is a splendid example. We have another window into the clamor of the courtroom and clash of litigants in the courtroom in the first half of the twelfth century that has been too often overlooked. In *Causa* 13 of his *Decretum*, which may have been drafted as early as the 1120s, Gratian constructed an elaborate courtroom scene in which the advocates put forward arguments that were replete with biblical, literary, and legal allegations.[33] Whether Gratian's courtroom scene reflects an actual case or not, his real or imagined description of the testy and acrimonious exchanges between the litigants is undoubtedly typical of advocates' rhetorical maneuverings and arguments in the first half of the twelfth century.[34]

29. On the date of Bulgarus's treatise, see my essay 'Big Bang' 48–52.

30. Padoa Schioppa, 'Il ruolo' 284–89, where he outlines the various reasons why court decisions do not contain the allegations of legal norms.

31. Ibid. 284.

32. Ibid. 285.

33. Melodie Harris Eichbauer, 'St. Gall Stiftsbibliothek 673 and the Early Redactions of Gratian's *Decretum*,' BMCL 27 (2007) 105–39 at 117–23, has argued that *Causa* 13 may represent one of the first causae that Gratian drafted.

34. See Frederick S. Paxton, 'Gratian's Thirteenth Case and the Composition of the *Decretum*,' in *Proceedings of the Eleventh International Congress of Medieval Canon Law, Catania, 30 July–6*

Siena v. Arezzo 1125

An early and unusual example of a papal document that included legal arguments of the advocates is a decision of Pope Honorius II in 1125. The bishops of Siena and Arezzo had been litigating over 18 parishes located within the diocese of Siena for years. Since the judgment granted possession to the Aretines but left open questions of *proprietates* (rights of ownership) that the Sienese might claim over the parishes, the pope, probably at the request of one of the litigants, committed the arguments and the decision to writing (*carta et atramentum*, i.e. parchment and ink).[35] Honorius's letter was first published by Pflugk-Harttung. The pope wrote to Bishop Guido of Arezzo to document the decision that the papal judges rendered in his favor against Bishop Gualfredus of Siena. At issue were 18 parishes over which both bishops claimed jurisdiction. The report of the case is very unusual because the letter contains the arguments of the advocates and the decision of the six judges who heard the case—i.e. the minutes of the proceedings. The tone of the letter was set by the arenga. It declared that the unity of religion and a love of justice demanded that the commands of the law should be obeyed: to live honestly and to give each person their due. Those sentiments and language were taken directly out of Justinian's *Institutes* or *Digest*.[36]

The trial had begun under Pope Calixtus II before Christmas. The pope became ill and died. Although the new pope and his cardinals tried to find a compromise, they had no success. Honorius postponed the proceedings.[37] The delay gave the two bishops time to send learned lawyers (*legis periti*) and advocates to the Lateran for the trial. The Aretines opened

---

August 2000, ed. Manlio Bellomo and Orazio Condorelli (MIC, Ser. C, 12; Città del Vaticano 2006) 119–37. A translation of the case may be found at: http://faculty.cua.edu/pennington/GratianCausa19English/Causa13FirstPage.html.

35. Julius von Pflugk-Harttung, *Acta pontificum romanorum inedita, 2: Urkunden der Päpste vom Jahre c. 97 bis zum Jahre 1197* (Stuttgart 1884) 252–57 at 252: 'Ne igitur controversia, inter Senensem et Aretinum episcopos de decem et octo plebibus orta, recolendi obumbretur desuetudine, ad presentium et posterorum clariorem evidentiam rei geste ordinem carte et atramento duximus committendum.'

36. Dig. 1.1.10 and Institutes 1.1.3. See my essay 'Big Bang' 50–51 for the same Roman law citation in letters of Pope Innocent II dated to 1133–36 and 1137 (JL 7696 and JL 7864).

37. Pflugk-Harttung, *Acta* 253: 'Cumque protraheretur inter vos per dies aliquot altercatio et nos una cum fratribus nostris, episcopis et cardinalibus, ad pacem inter vos et concordiam componendam summopere studium preberemus, interveniente ipsius domni nostri obitu et, me in curam et administrationem sedis apostolice, disponente divina gratia, evocato, maiori, ut in talibus fieri assolet, sollicitudine occupati, negotium hoc usque ad mediam quadragesimam subsequentem distulimus.'

their arguments with a dossier of papal and secular documents that supported their claims. They produced documents from Liutprand, the Lombard king (712–44), Pope Stephen (768–72), Charlemagne, and Pope Victor (1055–57 or 1086–87). These documents proved, they alleged, that the parishes were established through the preaching of St. Donatus of Arezzo. The dispute arose because, at an unspecified time, a judge named Godobertus, who had been killed by the Aretines, gave the Sienese the cause to take possession of these churches that were located within the diocese of Siena. The document stated that rights to the parishes were investigated during the reign of King Liutprand when the testimony of 70 clerics and honest laymen was gathered.[38] This testimony evidently confirmed the Aretine claim that the parishes had been long in their possession.[39]

The advocates for the Sienese countered with their own dossier of materials. They claimed to have charters from Pope Leo IV (847–55) and the Emperor Louis; however, they did not produce them. They did produce a letter of Pope Nicolas II (1058–61) that they read in the papal curia. Nicolas had decreed in a synod that the pope had invested the bishop of Siena with the 18 disputed parishes until the next synod, when the claims of the Aretines could be considered. They claimed that Arnaldus of Arezzo refused to attend the hearing. The advocates then recited a charter, confirming their investiture of the 18 churches, which had been issued by Pope Calixtus II.[40]

38. It was an old tradition in canonical norms that 70 or 72 witnesses constituted a proof in serious ecclesiastical matters; see C.2 q.4 c.2 and c.3 (from Pseudo-Isidore and Pope Leo IV), which were transmitted through a number of canonical collections.

39. Pflugk-Harttung, *Acta* 253: 'tu frater Guido, Aretine episcope, allegasti, parrochiam illam a beato Donato per predicationis fuisse offitium acquisitam, et a tuis predecessoribus per longa tempora quiete possessam, sed a Senensibus occasione mortis Godoberti iudicis, qui ab Aretinis occisus est, occupatam fuisse et, quia sita erat in Senensi territorio, vendicatam. Retulisti etiam, qualiter postmodum iussu Liuprandi regis ab Ambrosio, dispensatore domus sue, causa fuerit inquisita, et per septuaginta presbiteros et honestos laicos eiusdem parrochie antiquissima possessio fuerit iurata, et ab episcopis Tuscie atque a Liuprando rege in vico sancti Genesii honeste fuerit decisa, a papa Stephano firmata et a Karolo imperatore legaliter in Senensi civitate sopita. Insuper Aretinam muniebas ecclesiam decisione Victoris pape, qui in eadem parrochia inquisitionis causa per octo dies moratus est et Senensibus perpetuum silentium de eadem lite imposuit, Leonis, quoque Romani pontificis, Adriani, Paschalis, Stephani, Alexandri et Paschalis qui omnia privilegia eiusdem Aretine ecclesie confirmaverunt munimentis, preceptis etiam et confirmationibus imperatorum Karoli magni, Lodoici, Lotharii, Ottonis, Berengarii, Chonradi et Heinrici easdem plebes pertinere Aretine ecclesie affirmasti.'

40. Ibid.: 'Contra vero Senensis episcopus affirmavit, easdem decem et octo plebes iuris esse Senensis ecclesie, et scriptum Leonis quarti pape ac Lodoici imperatoris se dixit habere. Nikolai quoque secundi pape scriptum in medium protulit, in quo continebatur, Senensem episcopum fuisse in sinodo ab ipso papa de illis decem et octo ecclesiis, salva querela episcopi Aretini, usque

Both sides then turned to legal texts to support their case. The Aretines cited three imperial constitutions. The first declared that the emperor could not revoke his judgment or the sentences of his predecessors.[41] With a maxim that still remains valid today, the second affirmed that judicial decisions must be preserved: *Rebus iudicatis standum est.* Cicero used the phrase in his speech defending Aulus Cluentius, it migrated into an imperial Roman statute, and two thousand years later, it still retains its place among the maxims of law.[42] The Aretines cited a third constitution that rescripts cannot be admitted in a matter that has been decided by a court.[43] The Aretine argument was simple and straightforward: what had been decided in the eighth and ninth centuries could not be undone.

The Sienese countered with Roman law texts that supported their contention that they had rights to the parishes, held possession of them, and had been violently dispossessed by the Aretines. When they were dispossessed is not clear. These Roman norms, however, destroyed the Aretine case. The Sienese cited a statute of the emperors Valerius and Arcadius (389) that if people seized a person's property before a judgment of the court had been rendered, they would lose all title claims as well as possession of the property.[44] The second citation was from Book 48 of the

ad aliam synodum investitum, eo quod Arnaldus Aretinus, vocatus ad synodum, venire comtempsit, et scriptum investitionis a predecessore nostro, sancte memorie Calixto secundo papa, factum fecit coram fratribus recitari.'

41. Ibid.: 'Imperator Gordianus augustus Secundo: neque suam neque decessoris sui sententiam quemquam posse revocare in dubium non venit.' Cod. 7.50.1: 'Imperator Gordianus. Neque suam neque decessoris sui sententiam quemquam posse revocare in dubium non venit: nec necesse esse ab eiusmodi decreto interponere provocationem explorati iuris est.' Pflugk-Harttung misunderstood some of these citations. I have silently corrected his text.

42. Ibid.: 'Imperator Antoninus Augustus Stellatorio. Rebus iudicatis standum est.' Cod. 7.52.1: 'Imperator Antoninus. Rebus quidem iudicatis standum est. Sed si probare poteris eum cui condemnatus es id quod furto amisisse videbatur recepisse, adversus iudicati agentem doli exceptione opposita tueri te poteris.' See also Dig. 38.2.12.3: 'Si quis, cum esset exheredatus, pronuntiatus vel perperam sit exheredatus non esse, non repellitur: rebus enim iudicatis standum est.' See *The Speech of Cicero for Aulus Cluentius*, ed. William Ramsey (Glasgow 1858) 41, and *Lateinische Fachausdrücke im Recht*, ed. Rolf Lieberwirth (Heidelberg 1986) 50.

43. Ibid.: 'Imperator Constantinus ad Proculum: Impetrata rescripta non placet admitti, si decise semel causae fuerint iudiciali sentientia, quam provocatio nulla suspendit.' Cod. 7.50.3: 'Imperator Constantinus. Impetrata rescripta non placet admitti, si decisae semel causae fuerint iudiciali sententia, quam provocatio nulla suspendit: sed eos, qui tale rescriptum meruerint, etiam limine iudiciorum expelli.'

44. Ibid.: 'Imperatores Valerius et Archadius augusti et Thaeodorus ad Mesianum: Si quis in tantam furoris pervenerit audaciam, ut possessiones rerum apud fiscum vel apud homines quoslibet constitutarum ante eventum iudicialis arbitrii violenter invaserit, dominus quidem constitutus possessionem quidem, quam abstulit, restituat possessori et dominum eiusdem rei amittat.' Cod. 8.4.7: 'Imperatores Valentinianus, Theodosius, Arcadius. Si quis in tantam furoris pervenit

Digest. The third part of the *Digest* (*Digestum novum*) had been circulating in Italy since ca. 1100 and was now brought to bear on an issue before the papal curia.[45] The reference was very vague, but the citation to the text of the *Digest* was exact. The passage contained an elegant definition of force (*vis*). The emperor declared, 'do you think that force is only defined by the wounding of men? Force is whenever someone seeks what is owed to him outside the courtroom.'[46]

The assessors who were assisting the judges in the courtroom became frustrated by the arguments of both parties. The advocates for the parties, they noted, first put forward arguments about possession and then about rights, which led only to confusion in the courtroom. Both parties were ordered to stick to the issue of possession.[47] Assessors were officials in the courts of Rome who gave non-binding legal advice to the judges.[48] This papal letter is the earliest documented use of an assessor in the papal curia. It is further evidence of the influence of Roman law on curial practices in the early twelfth century.

The bishop of Siena immediately broke with courtroom decorum and shouted that he wanted the judgment of Pope Calixtus put into effect: ten parishes that had been invested and eight more should be.[49] Bishop Guido countered with two sophisticated arguments based on Roman law, but, if we accept the evidence of Honorius's letter, did not cite any specific texts. First, he pointed out that Pope Nicolas's legate had only invested two parishes *corporaliter*. This fact is known through the testimony of the Sienese

audaciam, ut possessionem rerum apud fiscum vel apud homines quoslibet constitutarum ante eventum iudicialis arbitrii violenter invaserit, dominus quidem constitutus possessionem quam abstulit restituat possessori et dominium eiusdem rei amittat.'

45. Wolfgang P. Müller, 'The Recovery of Justinian's Digest,' BMCL 20 (1990) 1–29 at 7.

46. Pflugk-Harttung, *Acta* 253: 'Pretor ait: extat edictum divi Marci in hec verba: optimum est ut si quas putas te habere petitiones, actionibus experiaris. Cesar dixit: "tu vim putas esse solum, si homines vulnerentur? vis est et tunc, quotiens quis id, quod deberi sibi putat, non per iudices reposcit." Dig. 48.7.7. 'Callistratus 5 de cogn. Creditores si adversus debitores suos agant, per iudicem id, quod deberi sibi putant, reposcere debent: alioquin si in rem debitoris sui intraverint id nullo concedente, divus Marcus decrevit ius crediti eos non habere. verba decreti haec sunt. "optimum est, ut, si quas putas te habere petitiones, actionibus experiaris: interim ille in possessione debet morari, tu petitor es." et cum Marcianus diceret: "vim nullam feci." Caesar dixit: "tu vim putas esse solum, si homines vulnerentur? vis est et tunc, quotiens quis id, quod deberi sibi putat, non per iudicem reposcit."

47. Ibid.: 'Ceterum advocatis alternatim, nunc de possessione ad proprietatem, nunc de proprietate ad possessionem confusum transitum facientibus, ab assessoribus imperatum est, ut de possessione inter se disceptarent.'

48. Cod. 1.51 and 1.52. Dig. 1.22.

49. Pflugk-Harttung, *Acta* 253: 'Senensis igitur episcopus se de decem tantum plebibus investitum et de octo esse investiendum et clarissimi viri, domni pape Calixti sententiam effectui mancipandam, protinus acclamavit.'

witnesses. Second, since the parishes were not in his possession, the bishop cannot ask for their restitution. A legitimate restitution can only be one in which the prior legal state is restored.[50] Roman law defined lawful possession as one that had been bestowed *corporaliter* or *possessio in corpore*. This type of possession was not ownership (*proprietas*, which can mean ownership or more commonly right to property).[51] The Aretine bishop made an excellent legal point: the only restitution that is legitimate, is restitution to an earlier legal status.[52]

The Sienese advocates were quick to employ arguments that used the norms taken from the Roman law of possession: since Pope Nicolas's nuncio had granted possession of two of the parishes, he had granted them all.[53] Their advocates probably cited or had in mind a passage from the *Digest* that the Aretines would quickly demonstrate could not be used to support their argument.[54]

The Aretine closing arguments were detailed, Roman, and brutal. They began with two citations to the *Digestum novum*. Possession cannot be gained with only the intent to possess if the intent is not preceded by 'natural possession' (*naturalis possessio*).[55] Natural possession was the simple possession or holding of property without ownership. It was, however, a necessary prelude to claiming possession.[56] In one of the few errors they made in their citations, Aretine advocates made the same point with a second text from the *Digest*.[57]

50. Ibid.: 253–54: 'Contra tu frater, Aretine episcope, respondisti, papam Nycolaum non investivisse per legatum suum corporaliter Senensem episcopum, nisi de duabus plebibus tantum, et hoc te per relatum tibi iuramentum testium Senensium cognovisse, atque ob hoc eum illam restitutionem non debere petere asserebas eo quod non fuerit destitutus. Est enim restitutio prioris status redintegratio legitima.'

51. E.g. Dig. 41.2.3 and Cod. 7.32, especially 7.32.10. See Mary G. Cheney, '*Possessio/proprietas* in ecclesiastical Courts in mid-12th-century England,' in *Law and Government in Medieval England and Normandy: Essays in Honour of Sir James Holt*, ed. G. Garnett and J. Hudson (Cambridge 1994) 245–54.

52. Dig. 4.1.

53. Pflugk-Harttung, *Acta* 254: 'Ex adverso Senenses dicebant, se a nuntio Nicolai pape fuisse de duabus plebibus et per illas de omnibus aliis investitos.'

54. Dig. 41.2.3.1.

55. Pflugk-Harttung, *Acta* 254: 'Neritius et Proculus: Solo animo non posse nos acquirere possessionem, si non antecedat naturalis possessio.' Dig. 41.2.3.3: 'Paulus 54 ad ed. Neratius et Proculus et solo animo non posse nos adquirere possessionem, si non antecedat naturalis possession.'

56. Scholars have disputed the meaning of *possessio naturalis;* see W. W. Buckland, *A Text-Book of Roman Law from Augustus to Justinian* (2nd edition; Cambridge 1932) 197.

57. Pflugk-Harttung, Acta 254: 'Celsus: Possessio nisi naturaliter comprehensa ad nos non pertinent.' Dig. 41.2.23 pr.: 'Iavolenus 1 epist. Cum heredes instituti sumus, adita hereditate omnia quidem iura ad nos transeunt, possessio tamen nisi naturaliter comprehensa ad nos non pertinet.' Gratian analyzes possession with similar arguments about the principles that governed posses-

The Sienese attempted a counter offensive with two more citations from the *Digest*. They cited an excerpt from the Roman jurisconsult Paul that bodily possession and touch was not necessary for possession.[58] To justify their claim that investiture of two parishes extended to the other sixteen, they turned to another text of Paul's that, at first glance, seems to support their case: One must not have to enter every part of a property in order to claim possession of the entire estate.[59] The Aretines, however, pointed out that Paul's text described taking possession of a contiguous piece of property, not scattered parcels.[60]

The court then recessed for an unspecified time. When it reconvened, the Aretines petitioned the court that, after having given a security deposit, they should have the parishes returned to them. They cited a statute of Justinian supporting their contention:[61]

> If, anyone, however, should possess property, not by force, but through a judicial decision, if perchance the prior absent possessor who having been summoned does not respond, the possessor, like others who possess property, shall be permitted, within a year, to take the said property if he presents himself, and offers security for the conduct of the case and promises to obey the decision of the court.

---

sion in C.3 q.1 d.p.c.2 and referred to the same sections of the *Digest;* see my discussion in 'Big Bang' 53–56.

58. Ibid.: 'Paulus: non est enim corpore et tactu necesse apprehendere possessionem, sed etiam oculis et affectu.' Dig. 41.2.1.21: 'Paulus 54 ad ed. Si iusserim venditorem procuratori rem tradere, cum ea in praesentia sit, videri mihi traditam Priscus ait, idemque esse, si nummos debitorem iusserim alii dare. non est enim corpore et tactu necesse adprehendere possessionem, sed etiam oculis et affectu argumento esse eas res, quae propter magnitudinem ponderis moveri non possunt, ut columnas, nam pro traditis eas haberi, si in re praesenti consenserint: et vina tradita videri, cum claves cellae vinariae emptori traditae fuerint.'

59. Ibid.: 'Idem: non oportet omnes glebas fundi circumambulare, sed sufficit quandam partem eius fundi introire.' Dig. 41.2.3.1: 'Paulus 54 ad ed. Et apiscimur possessionem corpore et animo, neque per se animo aut per se corpore. quod autem diximus et corpore et animo adquirere nos debere possessionem, non utique ita accipiendum est, ut qui fundum possidere velit, omnes glebas circumambulet: sed sufficit quamlibet partem eius fundi introire, dum mente et cogitatione hac sit, uti totum fundum usque ad terminum velit possidere.'

60. Ibid.: 'quod Aretini non de discretis, sed de continuis fundis dictum fuisse, firmabant.'

61. Ibid.: 'Imperator Iustinianus augustus Menne prefecto pretorio: si quis non per vim sed per sententiam iudicis eam rem detinuit, ea tamen occasione, quod absens prior possessor et ad litem vocatus minime respondit, licebit ei ad similitudinem ceterorum, qui rei dominium habent, intra annum se offerenti cautionemque suscipiende litis danti eandem rem recipere superque ea cognitionalia subire certamina.' Cod. 7.39.8.3: 'Imperator Justinianus. Sed et si quis non per vim, sed sententia iudicis eam detinuit, ea tamen occasione, quod absens prior possessor et ad litem vocatus minime respondit, licebit ei ad similitudinem ceterorum, qui rei dominium habent, intra annum se offerenti cautionemque suscipiendae litis danti eandem rem recipere superque ea cognitionalia subire certamina' (528 A.D.). This text is not a model of clarity. Parts of my translation are interpretations.

The Sienese jumped on the Aretine allegation and repeated an argument they had made earlier. Arnaldus, the bishop of Arezzo, was contumacious, did not give security, and did not appear in court as Pope Nicolas had ordered.[62] This time, however, the Aretines were prepared with a final and clinching argument from Justinian's *Codex* from a letter that Justinian wrote to Pope John II. Comparing the bishop's relationship to his church in Arezzo to a procurator or servant or other representatives of the owner of property, Justinian had declared that if the representative had acted with negligence or with fraud, this malfeasance would not injure the property rights of the owner.[63]

That concluded the judicial debate. The curial judges asked each party if it had new evidence to present and then examined the arguments and allegations that the parties had put forward. After having the litigants take an oath of calumny by swearing on the Gospels, the judges rendered their decision.[64] There were six judges, who were led by Ferrucius, Primicerius of the judges of the Lateran Palace.[65] With the consent of the other judges, Ferrucius first dealt with the issue of possession. The decision was a triumph for the Aretines. Gualfredus, the bishop of Siena, was ordered to restore possession of sixteen parishes to Guido, bishop of Arezzo and his church. If the other two parishes were in Sienese possession, Gualfredus was to guarantee that the Aretines would be able to take possession of them.[66] However, the triumph of the Aretines was not complete. In order

62. Ibid.: 'Contra Senenses, Arnaldum, Aretinum episcopum, infra annum nec venisse, nec cautionem optulisse dixerunt.'

63. Ibid.: 'Imperator Iustinus (sic) augustus Iohanni pape: sive servus sive procurator vel colonus vel inquilinus vel quispiam alius, per quem licentia est nobis possidere, corporaliter nactam possessionem cuiuscumque rei eam derelinquerit vel alii prodiderit, desidia forte vel dolo, ut locus aperiatur alii eandem possessionem detinere, nihil penitus domino preiudicium generetur, ne ex aliena malignitate alienum damnum emergat.' Cod. 7.32.12: 'Imperator Justinianus. Ex libris Sabinianis quaestionem in divinas nostri numinis aures relatam tollentes definimus, ut sive servus sive procurator vel colonus vel inquilinus vel quispiam alius, per quem licentia est nobis possidere, corporaliter nactam possessionem cuiuscumque rei eam derelinquerit vel alii prodiderit, desidia forte vel dolo, ut locus aperiatur alii eandem possessionem detinere, nihil penitus domino praeiudicium generetur, ne ex aliena malignitate alienum damnum emergat' (531–32 A.D.).

64. Ibid.: 'Indagatis ergo utriusque partis allegationibus et advocatis, si quid novi possent addere, diligentius inquisitis, iudices nostri, prius utrinque tactis sacrosanctis evangeliis, de calumpnia hanc in scriptis communi assensu protulerat sententiam.' On the oath of calumny see Brundage, *Legal Profession* 28–29, 182, 286, 293–94, 433–34.

65. Primicerius was the highest official in the late antique Roman court system and was a title adopted by the Roman papal tribunal.

66. Pflugk-Harttung, *Acta* 254: 'Ego Ferrucius, primicerius iudicum sacri Lateranensis palatii, consensu iudicum, scilicet Benedicti, dativi iudicis, et Guittonis, primi defensoris iudicis, et Ildicii Tiburtini et advocatorum Nykolai et Seniorilis iubeo, Gualfredum, Senensem episcopum, restitutionem facere sedecim plebium Guidoni Aretino episcopo sueque ecclesie, de duabus quoque

that the church of Arezzo did not escape judgment on the issue of rights to the parishes, Bishop Guido of Arezzo was ordered to give security immediately that he would submit to the court on the matter of property rights.[67] Ferrucius's judgment was incorporated into Honorius's letter. For his part, Honorius then declared that he, with the counsel of his cardinals and bishops, confirmed Ferrucius's sentence. The decretal letter was endorsed by Haimeric, a friend of the Roman jurist Bulgarus, from whom he had received the *ordo iudiciarius* that I mentioned earlier.

The relationship between the Pope Honorius, the Chancellor Haimeric, and Bulgarus has generated much speculation. All three have been associated with the city of Bologna. Some scholars have even placed Honorius and Haimeric in the same Bolognese church, where they were thought to be canons regular.[68] Others have doubted that one or the other was a canon regular.[69] Perhaps, an exact location is not necessary. All three may have had roots in Emilia-Romagna. Haimeric must have had a connection of some kind with the teaching of Roman law in Bologna to have become friends with Bulgarus.[70] What cannot be doubted is the sophisticated use of Roman law in the papal curia by 1125, the year in which this case between Arezzo and Siena was decided.

Scholars have differed over what the evidence provided by this case proves. Hermann Kantorowicz observed that the trial demonstrated that Haimeric had learned 'sufficient Roman law to decide an intricate cause with its help.'[71] Anders Winroth objected that the case proved very little about Haimeric's legal learning. The case did demonstrate that there was

---

idem iubeo, si Senensis ecclesia eas possidet, sin autem, do ecclesie Aretine et eius episcopo securum in eas possidendi ingressum.'

67. Ibid.: 'De quibus omnibus plebibus ventilatum est iudicium ante presentiam domni Honorii secundi pape et totius curie, salva Senensis ecclesie proprietatis questione. Et ad hoc, ut Aretinus episcopus non effugiat iudicium de proprietate, iubeo eum facere cautionem ad presens Senensi episcopo de suscipiendo iudicio proprietatis.' The case did drag on. Pope Innocent II was still dealing with the dispute at the end of his pontificate. See Paul F. Kehr, *Italia Pontificia* (Berlin 1908) 3.203.

68. See the discussion of Ian S. Robinson, *The Papacy 1073–1198: Continuity and Innovation* (Cambridge Medieval Textbooks; Cambridge 1990) 68 and 215–16.

69. Werner Maleczek, 'Das Kardinalskollegium unter Innocenz II. und Anaklet II,' AHP 19 (1981) 33.

70. Colin Morris, *The Papal Monarchy: The Western Church from 1050 to 1250* (Oxford History of the Christian Church; Oxford 1989) 183, asserts that Haimeric was a Frenchman. If that were true, that fact would make his connection with Bologna and Roman law problematic. Morris, however, offers no evidence for his assertion.

71. Hermann Kantorwicz with William Warwick Buckland, *Studies in the Glossators of the Roman Law: Newly Discovered Writings of the Twelfth Century*, ed. Peter Weimar (Cambridge 1938, reprinted Aalen 1969) 71.

a 'greater currency of Roman law in Italy at this time.' Winroth concluded, however, that it did not provide evidence for Bulgarus's knowledge of Roman law, since none of the citations in the case appear in the tract that Bulgarus sent to Haimeric.[72] Winroth is right that the case proves nothing about Haimeric's learning and Bulgarus's knowledge of Roman law in 1125, but his observation that the eleven Roman law citations in the case do not appear in Bulgarus's tract on procedure is beside the point. Bulgarus's tract dealt with issues of procedure, not with problems of possession and property. There would have been no reason for Bulgarus to cite these texts in his tract. However, I have argued that, even if Bulgarus's influence cannot be detected in Honorius's decretal, not more than eight years to ten years later a papal decretal of Innocent II did cite Bulgarus's tract.[73]

All this leads to the question: what does the evidence in this papal letter prove? Three major conclusions can be drawn from the document. First, the advocates for both Siena and Arezzo had very good training and knowledge of Roman law. Their use of the *Digest* is particularly impressive. Whoever the assessor was who took the minutes of the trial and whoever drafted the decretal also knew Roman law. The reference to Justinian's *Institutes* at the beginning of the decretal set the tone for the entire text. The references to possession *corporaliter* and the legitimate restitution of prior possession demonstrate that the assessor knew Roman legal principles. Second, the judges did not decide this case on the basis of fact but according to Roman legal principles. The advocates did not make their arguments to a panel of semi-literate judges who knew no Roman law. Although the judges did have the assistance of assessors who knew Roman law—this fact is underlined by the decretal's evidence that it was the assessors who ordered the parties to restrict themselves to issues of possession and not mix property rights with possession—the judges, perhaps with the assessors' help, rendered a decision that conformed more or less to the principles of Roman law that were presented in the courtroom. There are a few facts that we would like to know to understand the legal situation completely, e.g. how long had the Sienese held the parishes and which parishes had they held; what exactly was the Aretine claim to possess them. However, the decision was congruent with the principles of law and with the facts as they were presented in the decretal. The third conclusion is perhaps the most important. By 1125 advocates, assessors in the papal curia, and perhaps even papal judges, had extensive training in Roman law.

72. Winroth, *The Making of Gratian's Decretum* 161–62.

73. Pennington, 'The Big Bang' 49–52.

The arguments of the advocates were subtle and demonstrated significant knowledge of Roman law. They could have gotten that training only in a law school. One does not find one's way around in the *Digest* or the *Codex* with home schooling. The only place we know that Roman law was taught in the first half of the twelfth century was Bologna. Consequently, the *Studium* at Bologna must have been flourishing before 1125.

In fact advocates were studying Roman law long before 1125. Another document printed by Ficker and analyzed by Padoa Schioppa offers evidence of advocates constructing sophisticated arguments about property disputes using Roman law during the pontificate of Pope Pascal II.[74] In a hearing before Primicerius Ferrucius, who would preside over the 1125 case that we have just discussed, the two litigants cited the *Codex,* and, most likely although not with certainty, the *Institutes* and *Digest* for a total of a half dozen citations to Roman law.[75] The document is not, however, a judgment of the court but only the arguments put forward by each side. In form it is only the minutes of a court hearing and not the resolution of the dispute. In other words, it is the same type of document that we have in the first section of Honorius's decretal of 1125. One could speculate that the document might later have been included in a decision rendered in the papal curia and then sent out as a papal decretal under Pascal's name, but there is no evidence for that conjecture.

There are other questions that Honorius's decretal of 1125 raises. Its form is unique. I know of no other papal decretal from this period or later that includes so much of the argumentation that preceded the decision. Later decretals will consist of the arenga, a short description of the case, and the judgment of the court. The arguments of the advocates or the authorities upon which the judges rendered their decision are included only in extremely abbreviated form. Two copies of the letter are in the Cathedral Chapter Library in Arezzo. One copy contains the decision without the argumentation of the advocates. The other copy contains the entire text that I have discussed and that Pflugk-Harttung printed.[76] The complete text, however, is without doubt a product of the Roman curia and not an *ex parte* draft of a member of the Aretine episcopal household. Did the papal chancery offer litigants minutes of the court proceedings? If the chancery did, it was a practice that seems to have quickly fallen into abeyance.

74. Ficker, *Forschungen* 4.136–38 and Padoa Schioppa, 'Il ruolo' 276–78.

75. Institutes 4.6. pr., Cod. 7.39.3, Cod. 7.39.8.1, Cod. 2.14.1.3, Dig. 44.7.51, Dig. 4.3.7.8, Dig. 50.17.112. The citations to the Institutes and the Digest are verbal but not explicit. Consequently, they are probable but not certain.

76. Pflugk-Harttung, *Acta* 255, has a very brief description of both texts.

Chris Wickham has argued that the style of citing Roman law such as is found in this decretal and in other texts, without the citations to titles of the *Digest* and the *Codex* as is common in later glosses and commentaries, is evidence of another school of law outside Bologna with another system of citation.[77] This mode of citation is not tied to schools but to genres and to a time in which a system of citation had not yet been established. Gratian sometimes used exactly the same method of citation in his *Decretum* when he cited Roman law texts in his dicta.[78] In the canonistic literature of the period, papal letters and the Church Fathers are often cited with only their names as well.

Finally, to return to the question about *Prava autem consuetudo* that Robert Somerville asked thirty years ago that I discussed at the beginning of this essay. Does this papal decretal, describing the dispute between Siena and Arezzo, so laden with sophisticated arguments of Roman law, in a courtroom presided over by Chancellor Haimeric, who would continue to be chancellor when *Prava autem consuetudo* was promulgated and repromulgated at the beginning, middle, and end of Pope Innocent II's pontificate, offer any clues as to why Gratian and the canonists completely rejected the conciliar canon? The most obvious clue is a fact supported by Honorius's decretal: Roman law was an indispensible tool in ecclesiastical courts by the 1120s. During the 1130s when Gratian added most of his texts of Roman law to his *Decretum,* he added Roman law not because he was interested in the jurisprudence of Roman law as an antiquarian, but because it was an essential tool in the canonical courts.[79] We may speculate endlessly about why Innocent II attempted to forbid monks and canons regular from studying Roman law and who else in the curia supported his campaign. On that point, I have no suggestions that would go beyond what Somerville wrote in his essay.[80]

77. Wickham, *Courts and Conflict* 119. The anonymous author of the text printed by Hermann Fitting, *Questiones de iuris subtilitatibus des Irnerius* (Berlin 1894, reprinted Berlin 1977), used the same method of citation. Also, as Padoa Schioppa, 'Il ruolo' 278 n. 63, speculates, this mode of citation might be a style of the Roman curia.

78. See e.g. C.2 q.6 d.p.c.27 and c.28.

79. See the analysis of José Miguel Viejo-Ximémez, 'El Derecho Romano "Nuevo" en el Decreto de Graciano,' ZRG Kan. Abt. 88 (2002) 1–19. Viejo-Ximémez notes (p. 1) that Gratian included 259 fragments from Justinian's codification: 107 from the *Digest,* 122 from the *Codex,* and 30 texts from the *authenticae* added to the margins of the *Codex.*

80. Robinson's discussion of the importance of canons regular and monks in the eleventh- and early twelfth-century papal curia, *The Papacy* 210–23, could lead one to speculate in two different ways about the significance of banning monks and canons regular from the courtroom: (1) The tawdry business of the law courts sullied their religious vocation (as described in *Prava autem consuetudo*). This program of 'reform' was rejected by the canonists and later popes. (2) It simply

What this decretal letter of Honorius II demonstrates is that Roman law brought clarity and precision into the courtroom, not, as *Prava autem consuetudo* contended, confusion and impiety. Pope Innocent II, Haimeric, and the judges in the Roman curia must have known that was true. So, all of Robert Somerville's questions about *Prava autem consuetudo* can still not be answered. They remain, however, excellent—which is characteristic of all his scholarship: sound, cautious, and anchored in the texts.

---

seems contrary to reason that Innocent and the curia would want to hinder these clerics from making significant contributions to their monasteries and cathedral chapters. Therefore, unless we uncover some new evidence, there is no answer that can explain their motives. Robinson notes that of the 19 popes between 1073 and 1198, eleven were monks or canons regular and that they were very important in the papal curia.

CHARLES DONAHUE JR.

17 Thoughts on Diocesan Statutes

England and France, 1200–1500

As is well known, local councils and synods proliferated in the thirteenth century. They generated, among other things, a large body of conciliar canons and synodal statutes, some of which have been given modern editions.[1] The recent general history of medieval canon law in the classical period, however, does not deal with them.[2] I have neither the space nor the competence to offer a general account here. What I would like to do, however, is to take one particular form of synodal statute, sometimes called the *liber synodalis,* make some suggestions as to what became of that form in the fourteenth and fifteenth centuries, and offer some examples of how conciliar canons and synodal statutes were used in the later Middle Ages. It seemed fitting to dedicate the effort to a scholar who has done so much to enhance our understanding of councils in a slightly earlier period and who was a fellow member of Stephan Kuttner's seminar at Yale in 1964–65.

On 16 April 1287, Peter Quinil, bishop of Exeter, held a diocesan synod, which promulgated fifty-six statutes, to which was attached a *summula,* a sort of 'Reader's Digest' version of a manual for confessors.[3] The statutes,

1. E.g., *Councils and Synods II: A.D. 1205–1313,* ed. F. M. Powicke and C. R. Cheney, 2 vols. (Oxford 1964); *Les statuts synodaux français du xiiie siècle,* ed. Odette Pontal and Joseph Avril, 5 vols. (Paris 1983–2001); *Synodicon hispanum,* gen. ed. Antonio García y García, 8 vols. (Madrid 1981–2007); *Concilia Poloniae; źródła i studia krytyczne,* ed. Jakub Sawicki, 12 vols. to date (Warsaw 1945–).

2. *The History of Medieval Canon Law in the Classical Period, 1140–1234: From Gratian to the Decretals of Pope Gregory IX,* ed. Wilfried Hartmann and Kenneth Pennington (Washington, DC 2008).

3. *Councils and Synods II,* 2.982–1077. For Quinil (also, and apparently mistakenly, referred to as 'Quivil'), see most recently N. Orme, in *Oxford Dictionary of National Biography* [ODNB] (Oxford 2004), s.n. In common with the modern literature, I refer to gatherings of the clergy at the diocesan level as 'synods' and those at the provincial and higher levels as 'councils.' The 'legislative'

now known as 'Exeter II,' are quite elaborate, occupying seventy-eight pages in the modern edition, with the *summula* giving us twenty-three more. There is little in the statutes that is new as a matter of substance, though the rhetoric is more elaborate than most. The contents of the statutes have much in common with other thirteenth-century statutes in the western part of England, and they belong to a family of statutes that Professor Cheney has shown are derived from Worcester III (1240). The more immediate ancestor of the 1287 statutes seems to have been statutes promulgated for the diocese of Wells probably around 1258. The author of the 1287 statutes, perhaps Quinil himself, seems also to have used Winchester III (1262 X 1265), another member of the family, and other English statutes and canons that are outside of the family.[4] His rewriting, however, was quite comprehensive. In marked contrast to other English synodal statutes of this period, there are relatively few verbal borrowings from other statutes and canons.

Exeter II is quite well organized. This is not the case with many synodal statutes and conciliar canons of the period, even those promulgated at the highest level (e.g., Lateran IV). The surviving manuscripts of Exeter II all have rubrics, and it seems clear that the rubrics go back the original exemplar. Not only that, but Exeter II, its ancestor Wells, and its sibling or cousin Winchester III all show a distinct form of organization of the individual statutes into a coherent whole.[5]

This form of organization can be seen most clearly if we organize the rubrics of Exeter II into tabular form and assign to each group of statutes a general title (which, admittedly, is in most cases not there):

De sacramentis	cc. 1–8
De ecclesiis	cc. 9–16
De clericis	cc. 17–30
De iudiciis	cc. 31–46
Miscellanea	cc. 47–56

products of the former are 'statutes,' of the latter are 'canons,' though it is not clear that these distinctions were observed by contemporaries. I have also tried to finesse the question whether these legislative products are to be regarded as the work of the synod or council, in fact or in law, or of the prelate who convoked the synod or council and who promulgated his legislation there. At least until the conciliar movement, the canonists tended toward the latter view, and that seems to have been Peter's view ('a sacramentis sumat tractatus noster synodalis exordium'; Exeter II, proem.), but that view may not have been shared by all the participants.

4. For the details, see *Councils and Synods II*, 2.982–84, and the apparatus to Exeter II.

5. This pattern of organization goes back to Worcester III, but it was not consistently followed in those statutes.

That the scheme is a conscious one can be seen most clearly in the first chapters of the first and third 'titles': *De sacramentis* begins with a chapter 'De sacramentis in genere,' and then proceeds to chapters on each of the seven sacraments. *De clericis* begins with a general chapter 'De vita et honestate clericorum'[6] and then proceeds to various things that clerics should do (e.g., celebrate the office night and day [c. 21]) and (mostly) should not do (e.g., keep concubines [c. 18], alienate church goods [c. 26]). The title *De ecclesiis* begins with construction and repair of churches, chapels and oratories (c. 9), and then proceeds to dedications (cc. 10–11) and to various other provisions mostly concerning the physical arrangements and décor of churches and cemeteries. The shift to procedure is a bit awkward, beginning as it does with rural chapters (c. 31), but it quickly becomes apparent that the section deals with ecclesiastical procedure in general. Three chapters in the middle of this section (cc. 36–38) might have been placed in the section *De clericis*, but the focus of the first might be thought of as being on the priest as judge; the focus of the second is clearly on the procedure for admitting those ordained elsewhere, and of the third is on the responsibility of superiors to see to it that simony does not take place. Even the title *Miscellanea* is not so miscellaneous as it might at first seem. It contains three chapters on practices and people who might be a danger to the faith (cc. 47–49), and three on death (cc. 50–52), the last (on mortuaries) forming a nice bridge to two on ecclesiastical revenues (cc. 53–54). Chapters directed at the laity are notable by their absence. Even the one that looks from the rubric as if it is directed to the laity (c. 22) turns out upon more careful examination to be directed to the clergy who are to instruct the laity to perform their Sunday obligations.

The overall pattern of organization of these statutes is of some interest. It is clearly not the pattern of the five books of decretals (*iudex, iudicium, clerus, conubia, crimen*), a pattern that must have been burned on the mind of anyone who knew anything about canon law in the late thirteenth century. The only coincidence is placing the title *de clericis* in the middle. It is even further away from the persons-things-actions (*de personis, de rebus, de actionibus*) pattern of Justinian's *Institutes,* though it shares with it the feature of putting procedure at the end. The pattern of organization of Exeter II seems to be derived from that of some French synodal statutes of roughly the same period. We will pursue that suggestion after we consider what happened to Exeter II and like compilations in England.

Exeter II is clearly a subcategory of the general category of conciliar

6. Cf. X 3.1.

canons and synodal statutes. Bishop Peter calls it a *tractatus synodalis.*[7] Other documents refer to such compilations as the *libellus synodalis* or the *quaternus synodalis.*[8] Priests of the diocese, or at least the archdeacons, were supposed to have a copy. They were to be brought to the synod for correction.[9] Evidence exists that copies of Exeter II were examined at visitations in the fourteenth century, and the fact that manuscripts of it date from the fifteenth century suggests that the practice was continued.[10]

'Correction' can, of course, mean either making a text conform to an exemplar or bringing it up to date with new material. As a general matter, it would seem that the former was what was done in England after the thirteenth century. This is a dangerous statement to make, because our knowledge of English synodalia and conciliar canons after 1313 is dependent on the eighteenth-century edition of David Wilkins.[11] It was a remarkable work for its time, but Powicke and Cheney's edition of the thirteenth-century statutes and canons shows that Wilkins, by modern standards, is quite deficient.[12] There is not even a comprehensive survey of the manuscripts of fourteenth- and fifteenth-century English synodalia and conciliar canons, much less an edition of them. As mentioned before, however, the fact that manuscripts of Exeter II were still being produced in the fifteenth century suggests that Quinil's statutes were the last produced for Exeter diocese before the Reformation, and a relatively systematic search in Wilkins reveals few English dioceses that reformed their statutes in those centuries.

The exceptions reported by Wilkins prove the rule. Wilkins has a collection of synodal statutes that he attributes to Henry Woodlock, bishop of Winchester, 1305–16, and that he dates to 1308.[13] They are, in fact, the statutes of John Gervais, bishop of Winchester, 1262–68, and can confidently be dated between the years 1262 and 1265.[14] Probably shortly after Cheney's ending date of 1313, Richard Kellaw, bishop of Durham, 1311–16,

7. Exeter II, proem.

8. C. R. Cheney, *English Synodalia of the Thirteenth Century*, 2d ed. (Oxford 1968), 45–48.

9. Ibid.

10. *Councils and Synods II*, 2.1059 n. 1, 983.

11. *Concilia Magnae Britanniae et Hiberniae*, ed. David Wilkins, 4 vols. (London 1737).

12. The dangers of relying on Wilkins are substantial. I spent a day while preparing this paper analyzing the statutes that Wilkins attributes to Simon Langham during the brief period when he was bishop of Ely, 1362–66 (Wilkins, *Concilia*, 3.59–61). They are, in fact, the statutes of Robert Grosseteste, bishop of Lincoln, 1235–53, and probably date from around 1240. *Councils and Synods II*, 1.265–78; cf. Cheney, *English Synodalia*, 110–41, 147–48.

13. Wilkins, *Concilia*, 2.293–308.

14. *Councils and Synods II*, 1.700–723. They are, in fact, the 'Winchester III,' referred to above.

promulgated a set of diocesan synodal statutes.[15] Cheney knew these statutes, apparently agreed with Wilkins's attribution, but also, apparently and ultimately, disagreed with Wilkins's dating (1312). They are derived from other thirteenth-century statutes and their date can be attributed to the fact that the Northern Province was a bit 'behind the curve.'[16] Ralph of Shrewsbury, bishop of Bath and Wells, 1329–63, has an apparently well-deserved reputation as a pastoral bishop in an era not know for them.[17] He did promulgate a constitution in 1342, making up for a deficiency in the synodal statutes of his predecessor, William of Bitton I, 1248–64, by listing the feasts that should be observed in the diocese as days of rest.[18] Otherwise, he, in effect, republished Bitton's statutes.[19] The constitutions that Wilkins ascribes to William Heyworth, bishop of Coventry and Lichfield, 1420–47, and to his later successor Reginald Boulers, 1453–59, deal exclusively with attempts to reform abuses in Lichfield Cathedral.[20]

Provincial collections of canons continued. Wilkins gives us collections of canons from provincial councils held by the archbishops of Canterbury: Walter Reynolds (1322), Simon Meopham (1328), John Stratford (1342), and Thomas Arundel (1408).[21] Although there are isolated constitutions promulgated by archbishops later on in the fifteenth century, Arundel's would seem to be the last collection of conciliar canons promulgated before the Reformation.

What use was made of the collections of diocesan statutes? The question is easier to ask than it is to answer. As noted, references to reading of the statutes in synod and correction of copies abound, at least for the thirteenth and fourteenth centuries. Manuscript copies of these statutes

15. Wilkins, *Concilia*, 2.416–419.

16. Cheney, *English Synodalia*, 21–22; *Councils and Synods II*, 627, 817. The set of statutes that Wilkins (2.495–497) ascribes to Kelaw's successor, Lewis de Beaumont, 1316–33, concern the consistory and are not general diocesan synodal statutes.

17. ODNB s.n.

18. Wilkins, *Concilia*, 2.711; cf. *Councils and Synods II*, 1.586–626.

19. Technically, Ralph did not republish the statutes; rather, he looked into the question whether William's statutes were properly published and determined that they were. Wilkins, *Concilia*, 2.711. The other set of statutes of Ralph's that Wilkins prints (Wilkins, *Concilia*, 2.736–38) (1347) are specific to the lesser clergy of Wells Cathedral. Wilkins derives all three from Ralph's register, and the printed edition of the register notes their presence there and refers to Wilkins's edition. *The Register of Ralph of Shrewsbury, Bishop of Bath and Wells, 1329–1363*, ed. Thomas Scott Holmes, 2 vols. (Somerset Record Society 9–10, 1896), 2.457 (nos. 1691, 1693), 2.537 (no. 1968).

20. Wilkins, *Concilia*, 3.504–7 (1428), 571–72 (1454).

21. Wilkins, *Concilia*, 2.512–14, 552–54, 696–710 (2 sets); 3.314–19. Convenient editions of these may be found in the Appendix to William Lyndwood, *Provinciale* (Oxford 1679, repr. 1968), 39–40, 41–43, 43–54, 64–68.

continued to be made in the fifteenth century. A number of records of both episcopal and archidiaconal visitations survive, and evidence of specific enforcement of the diocesan statutes may exist in them, but so far as I am aware, no one has gone through these records systematically with this question in mind.[22] Those statutes that were directed to the behavior of individuals may have been enforced informally at ruridecanal chapters, in informal enforcement proceedings by parish clergy, and in the confessional. Evidence that this happened would be hard to find. There is one more place where we might find enforcement of these statutes: the public courts of the church, be they episcopal or archidiaconal.

Let us focus, for a moment, on the diocese of Ely, where we have a remarkable register of proceedings in the consistory court of the bishop, dating from the years 1374 to 1382, known in the literature as the 'Ely Act Book.'[23] The synodal statutes of Ely diocese have a somewhat checkered history, and no one seems to have undertaken an organized revision of them in the manner of Exeter II. Cheney detected three recensions in the four known manuscripts, the first largely based on the statutes of Robert Grosseteste of Lincoln in 1239, with a couple of additions, and the last incorporating provisions from Ottobuono's legatine council of London of 1268.[24] While Cheney's evidence for placing the final recension before 1276 is not overwhelming, there is no reason to doubt that the final version that we have of these statutes was in existence before the end of the thirteenth century. It survives in two manuscripts, one of which is known as the *Vetus liber archidiaconi Eliensis,* where the copy of the statutes is in an early fourteenth-century hand, and in a similar collection of material for the use of the official of Ely, where the basic copy of the statutes is in a fourteenth-century hand that has not been dated more precisely.[25]

There can be little doubt that the diocesan synod was an institution that was alive and well in the diocese of Ely in the fourteenth century.[26] There are numerous references to it in the Ely Act Book. The manuscript of the official that contains the statutes also contains the rubrics for hold-

22. Much such material is listed unsystematically in *The Records of the Medieval Ecclesiastical Courts. II: England,* ed. Charles Donahue (Comparative Studies in Continental and Anglo-American Legal History 7, Berlin 1994); e.g., pp. 103–4, 112–14, 154–57, 160, 164–65, 167, 205.

23. Cambridge University Library, Ely Diocesan Registry MS. D2/1 [CUL EDR D2/1]. See Charles Donahue, *Law, Marriage, and Society in the Later Middle Ages* (New York 2007), 218, with references. Marcia Stentz is editing the Ely manuscript for the Ames Foundation.

24. *Councils and Synods II,* 1.515–16.

25. *Councils and Synods II,* 1.515.

26. See D. M. Owen, 'Synods in the Diocese of Ely in the Latter Middle Ages and the Sixteenth Century,' *Studies in Church History,* 3 (1966) 217–22.

ing the synod. The statutes were known; they may even have been read in the synod, but is there any evidence that they were being applied in the official's or the archdeacon's court?

The answer to this question would seem to be 'no.' Court registers do not, as a rule, contain many references to the formal law. The Ely Act Book contains more than most. In particular, there are specific references to the constitutions of Clement V on summary procedure, the provincial constitution that formed the basis of actions for defamation, and the provincial statute of John Stratford on clandestine marriage (of which more shortly).[27] But nowhere in the Ely Act Book is there a reference to the diocesan statutes.

The argument that the Ely diocesan statutes were not being applied by the courts rests on more than an absence of citation. The Ely diocesan statutes contain a provision on clandestine marriage[28] that would have been noticeable in the Act Book if it were being applied, even if was not cited. In common with Bishop Grosseteste's statutes and many others, the Ely statutes contain a general condemnation of clandestine marriage: *Clandestina quoque matrimonia districtius in ecclesiis solempniter inhibeantur, quolibet genere clandestini matrimonii.*[29] Similar provisions may be found in virtually all the English diocesan statutes.[30] The authority for them is the well-known canon *Cum inhibitio* of Lateran IV,[31] although English legislation on the topic may be found even before that council. After the portion of the statutes derived from Grossteste's statutes, the Ely legislator added two more provisions on clandestine marriage. The first repeats the provision of *Cum inhibitio* that clergy who participate in clandestine marriages shall be suspended from office for three years.[32] The second applies to the laity:[33]

27. E.g., CUL EDR D2/1, fol. 139r, 140v, 150v.

28. As is well known, the definition of 'clandestine marriage' was quite problematical, ranging all the way from a marriage in which no one except the couple were present to one that was quite public, but lacked one or more of the usual solemnities, such as promulgation of banns or the blessing of the parish priest.

29. Ely (1239 X 1256), c. 25, in *Councils and Synods II*, 1.520: "Clandestine marriages should be very strictly forbidden in churches, whatever sort of clandestine marriage."

30. See Michael Sheehan, 'Marriage and Family in English Conciliar and Synodal Legislation,' in *Essays in Honour of Anton Charles Pegis*, ed. J. Reginald O'Donnell (Toronto 1974), 205–14, repr. in Michael Sheehan, *Marriage, Family, and Law in Medieval Europe*, ed. James K. Farge (Toronto 1996), 77–86.

31. Lateran IV (1215) c. 51 (= X 4.3.3).

32. Ely (1239 X 1256), c. 32, in *Councils and Synods II*, 1.521.

33. Ely (1239 X 1256), c. 33, in *Councils and Synods II*, 1.521–22: "Parish priests shall also forbid their parishioners frequently and publicly under pain of excommunication, and the parishioners present shall explain this to their dependants (*familiis*), that they ought not presume to contract

Inhibeant eciam presbiteri parochiales frequenter et puplice parochianis suis sub pena excommunicacionis, et parochiani presentes suis famulis hoc exponant, ut sine presbiterorum presencia et bannorum edicione matrimonia sive sponsalia contrahere non presumant. Alioquin sciant se principales persone, priusquam ad docendum de iure suo admittantur, publice fustigacioni subdendos, et alios qui consensum vel auctoritatem prestiterunt eadem pena feriendos.

The injunction to parish priests that they tell their flock frequently about the prohibition of clandestine marriage is quite common, as is the threat of excommunication if they do not do so. (I must confess, however, that I have never seen the threat applied.) The threatened penalty for those who marry or contract *sponsalia* not in the presence of a priest and without publication of banns is, however, unusual; it may be unique. They are to undergo a public whipping 'before they are admitted to instruct about their right.' This is a somewhat difficult phrase, but I think its meaning is reasonably clear. Participants in a clandestine marriage are to be whipped before they will be allowed to show that they have married clandestinely and are therefore entitled to be regarded as married.

Cum inhibitio prescribed that marriages were not to take place until the banns had been proclaimed. It did not, however, change the basic rule that marriages made by the consent of the parties without solemnity or ceremony, without the presence of a priest or the publication of banns, were, nonetheless, valid marriages. Penalties were laid down for the clergy who participated in clandestine marriages, but what was to be done with the laity who formed such marriages was left to the local churches to decide. As we will see, the French church, as a general matter, provided that participants in clandestine marriages would be automatically excommunicated. No English legislation went that far. But the Ely legislator did prescribe a public whipping for such people as a condition of their marriage being made public.

This statute was not being enforced by the official of Ely in the years 1374 to 1382. There are 93 cases in the register, some begun as instance cases, some begun as office cases, in which a marriage is sought to be enforced. In virtually all of these cases one or more of the marriages at stake are clandestine, in the sense that they were entered into without the promulgation of banns. In none of them is there any indication that the parties alleging the marriage were whipped before they were allowed to allege the mar-

marriages or espousals without the presence of priests and the solemnity of banns. Otherwise, the principal persons should know that before they are admitted to instruct about their right, they are to undergo a public whipping, and others who gave consent or authorization are to suffer the same penalty."

riage. Indeed, there is no indication that any of the parties to a clandestine marriage were punished for the clandestine marriage alone.[34]

The only parties to a marriage who were punished were those who were determined to have violated John Stratford's constitution *Humana concupiscentia* of 1342.[35] A fair reading of that canon suggests that it provides that those who, knowing of an impediment (or having a reasonable suspicion of one) nonetheless have their marriages solemnized, are automatically excommunicated. That is not, however, the way in which the Ely court read it, and the register gives us the court's argument for its rather strange interpretation:[36]

[C]um in generali concilio proinde sit statutum ut cum matrimonia sint contrahenda in ecclesiis per presbyteros publice propona[n]tur competenti termino prefinito ut infra illum qui voluerit et valuerit legitimum impedimentum opponat. Et ipsi presbyteri nichilominus investigent utrum aliquod impedimentum obsistat. Cum autem apparuerit probabilis coniectura contra copulam contrahendam, contractus interdicatur expresse donec quid fieri debeat super eo manifestis constiterit documentis. [Q]uodque omnis et singuli matrimonia inter se contrahentes et ea solempnizàri facientes impedimenta legitima scientes aut suspicionem habentes verisimilem eorundem, huiusque matrimoniorum solempnisacioni interessentes maioris excommunicacionis sentencia a constitucione provinciali in proximo articulo superius recitata[37] fuerint et sint ipso facto dampnaliter involuti.

The problem with this explanation is that the first three sentences quote *Cum inhibitio*, while the last describes, more loosely, Stratford's constitution. The two constitutions are clearly related. What is not clear is that Stratford and his council intended that sanction of automatic excommunication to apply to those who married during the pendency of the investigation or even in violation of the inhibition described in *Cum inhibitio*. That is, however, the way in which the Ely court interpreted it. Parties

34. Donahue, *Law, Marriage, and Society*, 230–31, 279–80.

35. Wilkins, *Concilia*, 2.707.

36. CUL EDR D2/1, fol. 108v: "The general council has accordingly established that when marriages are to be contracted, they shall be announced by the priest in the churches, with an adequate term fixed beforehand within which whoever wishes and is able to may adduce a lawful impediment in opposition to the marriage. The priests themselves shall also investigate whether any impediment stands in the way [of the proposed marriage]. When there appears a credible reason against the proposed union, the contract shall be expressly forbidden until there has been established by clear documents what should be done about it. Any and every person who contracts marriage with another, has it solemnized, or is present at the solemnization of such a marriage who knows of a lawful impediment or has a reasonable (*verisimilem*) suspicion thereof shall, and does, incur a sentence of major excommunication in accordance with the provincial constitution."

37. *superius recitata*—probably reference to the citation of *Humana concupiscentia* in the previous entry.

were cited and punished for violations of *Humana concupiscentia* if they married during the pendency of a case before the court, even if it later turned out that the marriage was valid, but they were not cited or punished for violations of *Humana concupiscentia* if they entered into an invalid marriage, so long as a case about it was not pending. In at least some of these cases we strongly suspect that the parties were aware of the invalidity or, at least, had a reasonable suspicion of it.[38]

The evidence of the Ely Act Book thus suggests that, by the last quarter of the fourteenth century, diocesan statutes were no longer being applied in the episcopal consistory courts. Provincial constitutions were being applied, but the interpretation of them was, to say the least, free. As a general matter, the type of organized diocesan statutes that we find in Exeter II seems to have disappeared. If they were made in the thirteenth century, they continued to be copied, but so far as we know no diocese which, like Ely, had a disorganized set of statutes sought to organize them, and the development of the *genre* of synodal statutes with continual revision and updating that is so evident in the thirteenth century seems to have stopped.

The situation seems to have been quite different in France. The idea, as we noted earlier, of having a collection of synodal statutes with some sort of organization seems to be French in origin. The first set of such statutes of which I am aware are those of Eudes of Sully, bishop of Paris from 1197 to 1208. The organization is primitive; the rubrics vary from manuscript to manuscript, but the basic form of organization is clear: The first part deals with the sacraments (48 provisions all told in the modern edition), sacrament by sacrament, the second with *communia precepta,* a miscellaneous collection of provisions (23 provisions in all the modern editions). These statutes are bracketed on both sides with provisions about the holding of the synod itself.[39]

Eudes's statutes had a wide circulation. Echoes of them are found in statutes throughout France in the thirteenth century, and they had a considerable influence in England.[40] It seems likely that the basic scheme of organization that we find in Exeter II—and, in particular, the feature of beginning with the sacraments—finds its origin in the statutes of Eudes.

As in England, so too in France, the making of synodal statutes was widespread in the thirteenth century. The modern edition now runs to

38. Details in Donahue, *Law, Marriage, and Society,* 281–85.

39. *Les statuts synodaux français du xiiie siècle I,* ed. Odette Pontal (Paris 1971), 52–93.

40. The influence in France may be traced in the various volumes of *Les statuts synodaux français du xiiie siècle;* for England see references gathered under 'Paris, bishop of' in Cheney, *English Synodalia,* 163.

five volumes.[41] What is clear in the case of France, as does not seem to be the case in England, is that the process of updating and then redacting these statutes in a comprehensive form continued in France in the fourteenth and fifteenth centuries, as it does not seem to have continued in England. To judge from the massive collection of manuscripts and early printed books recorded in the *Répertoire des statuts synodaux*,[42] this process continued in France throughout the *ancien régime*.

Let us take the province of Reims as an example. There is a fine modern edition by Joseph Avril of the thirteenth-century diocesan statutes from the province, with surviving examples from the dioceses of Arras, Cambrai, Noyon, Soissons, and Tournai.[43] There is also a nineteenth-century edition, issued in the name of Archbishop Thomas Cardinal Gousset, of the statutes from the entire province, four volumes in quarto that attempt to cover the entire period from Saint Rémi at the end of the fifth century to the end of the Revolution in 1801.[44] The material for the later Middle Ages and early modern periods is drawn from the best printed texts that were available in the 1840s: *Gallia christiana*, Martène et Durand, etc. Some of the attributions are probably wrong, and the texts printed could almost certainly be improved by careful work with the manuscripts, but for our purposes they will suffice.

By the end of the thirteenth century, as already suggested, each of the dioceses of Arras, Cambrai, Noyon, Soissons, and Tournai had a synodal statute-book, a quite comprehensive collection of synodal statutes, beginning with the sacraments, and proceeding to other issues in a reasonably well-organized fashion. Gousset gives us similar collections for the dioceses of Reims (c. 1330) and Amiens (c. 1454), substantial additions to or revisions of those of Arras, Cambrai, Soissons, and Tournai, and a collection of 'one-off' statutes of Châlons-sur-Marne (now Châlons-en-Champagne) (1393).[45] The *Répertoire* lists an incunabulum edition of the

41. Although the volumes are shorter than the two volumes of *Councils and Synods II*, they make no attempt, as does *Councils and Synods II*, to record every council that was held in the century but simply edit the statutes of those councils and synods for which manuscripts survive. Altogether the quantity of surviving thirteenth-century statutory material for France is at least as great as that for England and probably greater.

42. Ed. André Artonne, Louis Guzard, et Odette Pontal (Documents, Études et Répertoires publiés par l'Institut de Recherche et d'Histoire des Textes 8, Paris 1963).

43. *Les statuts synodaux français du xiiie siècle. IV: Les statuts synodaux de l'ancienne province de Reims (Cambrai, Arras, Noyon, Soissons et Tournai)*, ed. Joseph Avril (Collection de documents inédits sur l'histoire de France, sér. in 8°, 23, Paris 1988).

44. *Les actes de la province écclésiastique de Reims*, ed. Thomas Gousset, 4 vols. (Reims 1842–44).

45. *Actes de Reims*, 2.534–75, 2.685–726, 2.604–5, 2.487–512, 2.624–38, 2.682–83, 2.749–71, 2.614–17.

statutes of Thérouanne in 1495, two early sixteenth-century editions of those from Senlis, one for Beauvais from 1531, but none for Laon until 1667.[46] Despite the absence of direct evidence for Laon, it seems likely that all of the dioceses in the province had a synodal statute book by the end of the Middle Ages, and that most, if not all, of them had a fairly substantial book arranged according to some methodical plan.

The plan varied from diocese to diocese. None of them seems to be quite so well organized as Exeter II, but one can discern in almost all of them the basic pattern of Exeter II. The sacraments come first; there will be a section *de vita et honestate clericorum;* there will be sections on church buildings, the liturgy, and procedure, though these will appear in no fixed order. Furthest away from the basic pattern are the statutes said to be of Simon de Bucy for the diocese of Soissons (1403). Even here the order of the material is approximately the same as that of the other statutes of the province, but there are no rubrics. It is, rather, divided into *precepta* about each topic followed by *consilia.*[47] Avril offers quite powerful evidence for dating this material to the thirteenth century, though the manuscript could date from de Bucy's time.[48]

We thus have two substantial differences about diocesan synodal statutes in France in the later Middle Ages, as contrasted with those in England: they continued to be made, and they continued to be organized in a pattern specific to such statutes. That the English were still taking local ecclesiastical legislation seriously in the later Middle Ages is indicated by the massive commentary on the provincial constitutions of Canterbury province by William Lyndwood.[49] The differences are these: Lyndwood focuses on statutes at the provincial level (including, as has been shown, raising some diocesan statutes to the level of provincial because of the misattributions in later manuscripts),[50] and Lyndwood organizes his discussion according to the titles of the books of papal decretals (*iudex, iudicium, clerus, conubia, crimen*).

Not only were the French continuing to issue such statutes, they were also enforcing them, in some cases quite harshly. We turn here to the diocese of Cambrai, where we have, as we do in the case of Ely, substantial survivals of records of the ecclesiastical courts, in this case sentence books

46. *Répertoire,* 431, 414–15, 121, 266.

47. *Actes de Reims,* 2.624–38.

48. *Statuts synodaux français IV,* 281–87.

49. William Lyndwood, *Provinciale seu Constitutiones Angliae* (Oxford: H. Hall, 1679; repr. Farnborough 1968).

50. See C. R. Cheney, 'William Lyndwood's Provinciale,' *The Jurist,* 21 (1961) 405–34.

from the officiality at Cambrai and from the co-equal officiality at Brussels from the mid-fifteenth century.[51]

Much of the marriage litigation at Cambrai, particularly the office cases, involves violations of local legislation. The distinctive approach of the area to the regulation of *sponsalia* is already to be seen in the synodal statutes of Guiard de Laon, bishop of Cambrai, 1238–48, which can be dated with some confidence to the years between 1238 and 1240:[52]

> [89] Prohibeant presbiteri subditis suis ne dent sibi fidem mutuo de contrahendo matrimonio, nisi coram presbitero alterius eorum qui volunt contrahere et in publico coram hominibus; et si inter se fidem dederint, non valebit.
>
> [90] Precipimus ut nullus sacerdos audeat sine licentia episcopi edicta vel bannos celebrare, nec matrimonium inter eos solempnizare, quamvis etiam veleint post primam fidem iterum coram presbiterum affidare. Si autem sacerdos contra preceptum istud inter aliquos matrimonium celebrare presumpserit, eo ipso se sciat esse suspensum.
>
> [91] Excommunicentur et denuntientur excommunicati qui clandestinas nuptias contrahunt, et sacerdos qui celebrat huiusmodi nuptias necnon denuntietur excommunicatus. Quicumque clericus vel laicus vel mulier aliquas personas modo predicto coniungere presumpserint, denuntientur etiam excommunicati.
>
> [92] Excommunicentur et denuntientur excommunicati qui post affidationem clandestinam carnaliter se congnoscunt. Quicumque clandestinis nuptiis coram sacerdote vel alio celebratis interfuerint, nisi infra quindecim dies episcopo vel eius officiali revelaverint, excommunicamus eos.

51. Details, including specific references to the cases, may be found in Donahue, *Law, Marriage, and Society*, chs. 8–9. Cambrai was, of course, not in France in the Middle Ages, and most of its extensive diocese is now in Belgium, and much of that in a part of Belgium that does not now and never has spoken French. The diocese was, however, in the province of Reims and can be regarded for our purposes as 'French.'

52. *Statuts synodaux français IV*, 45–47: "[89] Priests shall prohibit their subjects (*subditis*) from giving faith of contracting marriage mutually except before the priest of either of them who wish [so] to contract and in public before the people, and if they give faith between themselves it shall not be valid. [90] We command that no priest should, without the license of the bishop, dare to celebrate banns or edicts or solemnize marriage between them [i.e., those who violate c. 89] even if they should wish to affiance themselves again. If, moreover, a priest presumes to celebrate marriage between anyone against this precept, let him know that by that very act he is suspended. [91] Let them be excommunicated and denounced as excommunicate those who contract clandestine marriages, and let the priest who celebrates this sort of marriage also be denounced as excommunicate. Whoever, clerk, layman or woman, presume to join any persons in this manner, let them also be denounced as excommunicate. [92] Let them be excommunicate and denounced as excommunicate those who after clandestine affiancing know each other carnally. Whoever are present at clandestine marriages celebrated before a priest or another, we excommunicate them unless they reveal [this] to the bishop or his official within 15 days. [93] We excommunicate [those] who give faith, or take it, or give a gift or take it for concealing impediments to marriage. Let this excommunication be often announced by every priest in [their] parishes."

[93] Excommunicamus qui fidem dederint vel acceperint et donum acceperint vel dederint pro impedimentis celandis matrimonii. Excommunicatio ista [publicetur *supplied by ed.*] sepe a singulis sacerdotibus in parochiis.

After a paraphrase of the canon *Cum inhibitio* of the Fourth Lateran Council, the statutes continue:[53]

[96] Si quis alicui dederit fidem de matrimonio contrahendo per verba de futuro et ante carnalem copulam fidem mutuo velint remittere, non fiat huiusmodi quitatio nisi per episcopum vel eius officialem.

French statutes on the topic of clandestine marriage were strict.[54] Such marriages frequently subjected the parties to automatic excommunication. What is different about the Cambrai statutes is that they also insist that *sponsalia de futuro* be public. In the thirteenth century, they do not excommunicate those who contract *sponsalia de futuro* privately, but they do excommunicate those who, having contracted them, then form a marriage by subsequent intercourse. The control over *sponsalia de futuro* is exercised in a different way (cc. 89–90). First, private *sponsalia de futuro* are prohibited; indeed they are said to be invalid. Second, the parish priest may not proclaim the banns or solemnize the marriage of those who have so contracted without license from the bishop. This may not be a direct violation of Alexander III's decretal *Quod nobis ex tua parte*, but it is certainly in a different spirit.[55]

Further emendation to these canons followed in the compilation of synodal statutes made in 1287–88 and again in the early years of the fourteenth century. In particular, what we labeled canons 89–90 in the quotation was amended to read as follows:[56]

[65] [80] Inhibeant presbyteri parrochiales subditis suis ne sponsalia contrahant seu dent fidem de matrimonio inter eos pariter contrahendo nisi coram

53. *Statuts synodaux français IV*, 47: "[96] If anyone gives faith to another to contract marriage by words of the future tense, and before sexual intercourse they mutually wish to remit the faith, such quittance should not be done except by the bishop or his official."

54. Donahue, *Law, Marriage, and Society*, 33.

55. X 4.3.2.

56. *Statuts synodaux français IV*, 118, 160: "[65] [80] Parish priests shall prohibit their subjects (*subditis*) from contracting *sponsalia* or giving faith of contracting marriage to each other (*fidem de matrimonio inter eos pariter contrahendo*), except, at a minimum, before the priest of one of those who wishes to contract (*nisi coram presbytero alterius saltem contrahere volentium*), and this should be in a public place, a church, for example, or a cemetery or a chapel and before many other trustworthy people. And if they otherwise contract *sponsalia*, unless they repeat them within eight days before any of the above priests, the priest should not proceed to the proclamation of the banns or the solemnization of them without our special license [i.e., of the bishop] or that of our official. And anyone who presumes to do this [knowingly] shall know himself suspended by this very fact."

presbytero alterius saltem contrahere volentium, et hoc in loco publico: ecclesia videlicet cymeterio vel capella et coram pluribus fidedignis, et si aliter contraxerint sponsalia, nisi infra triduum [octo dies *in the 14th century version*] ea reiterent coram altero de presbyteris antedictis, non procedat presbyter ulterius ad bannorum publicationem, vel matrimonii sollempnisationem, sine nostra vel officialis nostri licentia speciali, et qui hoc (scienter)[57] facere presumpserit ipso facto se noverit esse suspensum.

This is, in many ways, better legislation. The sanction for not so contracting is changed from invalidity of the *sponsalia* (something that was probably not within the power of the bishop or the synod to do) to the requirement that a special license be obtained from the bishop or his official (on which occasion, presumably, a penance could be imposed) in order to proceed with the proclamation of the banns and the solemnization. Perhaps more important and by way of concession to the fact that medieval people, like modern, normally first found out whether someone was willing to marry them in a private setting, clandestine *sponsalia de futuro* were not forbidden. Rather, the couple were enjoined to publicize them within a week after they were made. This period of a week remained a feature of the Cambrai legislation throughout the Middle Ages and was being enforced in the mid-fifteenth-century sentences.

Cambrai was certainly not unique in these provisions. Similar provisions can be found in statutes of Tournai from the beginning of the fourteenth century, and in statutes of Liège of 1288.[58] The cases from Châlons-sur-Marne reported by Beatrice Gottlieb certainly suggest that similar provisions were in effect there.[59] But not every diocese in the region seems to have adopted these provisions. For example, the statutes of Soissons, already discussed, classified as a *consilium* and not a *preceptum* the following provision: *Prohibeant sacerdotes frequenter laicis sub excommunicatione, ne dent fidem sibi de contrahendo, nisi sacerdote praesente, et pluribus aliis, et si fecerint eo absente, non faciat edicta seu banna.*[60] This probably refers to *sponsalia de futuro*, but the reference to excommunication is vague. It might have

57. *scienter*—in *Actes de Reims*, 452, but not in *Statuts synodaux français IV*, 160.

58. *Statuts synodaux français IV*, 331–33 (Tournai); 45–47 nn. 148, 150, 152, 154, 158, 160 (references to Liège).

59. Beatrice Gottlieb, *Getting Married in Pre-Reformation Europe*, Ph.D. diss., Columbia University (Ann Arbor, MI 1974).

60. Soissons (1403), c. 50, in *Actes de Reims*, 2.631 (= Soissons [end 13th century] c. 53, in *Statuts synodaux français IV*, 297): "Let priests frequently prohibit lay people, under excommunication, from giving faith to each other of contracting [marriage] unless a priest is present, and many others, and if they do so in his absence, let him [the priest] not make edicts or banns." The discussion of this statute in Donahue, *Law, Marriage, and Society*, 389, needs revision in the light of what we say here and above about the date of these statutes.

been necessary to impose the sentence rather than the parties' incurring it automatically (technically an *excommuncatio ferendae sententiae* rather than *latae sententiae*). The fact that the whole statute is called a *consilium* suggests that it is considerably less binding than the Cambrai statutes.[61] Around 1454, if we can rely on the Gousset's edition, the bishop of Amiens adopted a collection of synodal statutes that said nothing about the celebration of *sponsalia de futuro*, excommunicated those who contracted *per verba de presenti* clandestinely, but then repeated the injunction of *Quod nobis ex tua parte* that those who wish to publicize such marriages be received by the church and blessed.[62]

The Cambrai courts also regularly fined couples for failure to solemnize their marriages after *sponsalia* had been entered into, and the fines mention a period 'fixed by law.' That the failure to solemnize *sponsalia* (unless they were remitted before the bishop or his official) would be an offense is clearly implied in the legislation, but no fixed period for solemnization is laid down. I have been unable to find such legislation, though I have no doubt that it existed. Because I have been unable to find the legislation, I do not know what the period was, as it is never given in the sentences. It may have been forty days, because that is the period mentioned in a number of the sentences where the couple are ordered to solemnize. It could have been as short as a month from the time of solemnization of the *sponsalia*, because that would have given ample time for the three successive proclamations of the banns on Sundays or feast days called for in *Cum inhibitio*.[63] Clearly, however, this legislation was designed to turn marriage promises into solemnized marriages quickly.

There is another Cambrai statute of relevance to the cases, which appears first in this form in the Cambrai collection of 1287–88 and carries over into that of the early fourteenth century:[64]

61. By contrast, clandestine marriages seem to be punished with automatic excommunication. Soissons (1403), c. 55, in *Actes de Reims*, 2.632 (= c. 58 in *Statuts synodaux français IV* 298); cf. Soissons (1403), c. 48, in *Actes de Reims*, 2.631 (= c. 51 in *Statuts synodaux français IV*, 297

62. X 4.3.2; Statutes of Jean Avantage (c. 1454), c. 5.10, in *Actes de Reims*, 2.712. I strongly doubt that this provision was new in 1454. *Quod nobis ex tua parte* was directed to the bishop of Beauvais, right next door, as it were, to Amiens.

63. A possible source of such a requirement is found in the statutes of 1287–88, which, it would seem, relieve the couple who consummate private or public espousals from the penalty of excommunication if they solemnize their marriage within thirty days thereafter. *Statuts synodaux français IV*, 118 (c. 66). But this provision was not carried over into the legislation of the early fourteenth century. *Statuts synodaux français IV*, 160 (c. 81).

64. *Statuts synodaux français IV*, 119: "[71] [83] Item, we excommunicate all those who propose false impediments against marriages, or who knowingly conceal the truth, out of affection, [superior] order or favor, or for any other reason, and will that priests frequently denounce them

[71] [83] Item excommunicamus omnes qui contra matrimonia falsa impedimenta proposuerint, vel vera celaverint scienter, amore, precepto vel favore, vel alia quacumque de causa, et volumus eos excommunicatos propter hoc frequenter a presbyteris nuntiari. Quod si nemo bannorum proclamationi se opposuerit, et loci presbyter verisimliem aut veram contra matrimonium habeat coniecturam, nobis aut officio nostro Cameracensi inconsultis super hoc, ad solempnisationem matrimonii non procedat, et si contra hoc fecerit, pena pro clandestinis nuptiis imposita teneatur.

The general thrust of this statute is clearly designed to encourage the raising of objections, but it could be used to penalize those who raise objections that turn out not to be provable, particularly since the *scienter* requirement does not have to be taken as applying to 'those who propose false impediments.' This statute may be the authority for a penalty that we find quite often in the cases, imposed for 'frivolous opposition' to a marriage.

Two relevant additions to the basic statutes of Cambrai are recorded in the fourteenth century. In one (c. 1310), the statute complains that *propter simplicitatem quorumdam presbyterorum,* couples who wish to contract *de futuro* are being given the form to contract *de presenti.* It recommends for *de futuro* contracts the form *Petre, vis promittere per fidem tuam quod Bertham quae hic est, accipies in uxorem, si impedimentum canonicum non obsistat.*[65] In the other (1313), a synod imposed *ipso facto* excommunication on those who separated themselves without judgment of the church.[66] This statute was being applied in the fifteenth-century cases.

Obviously, we are dealing here with a substantial difference between England and France in the attitude toward clandestine engagements and marriages. Possible reasons for that difference have been discussed at some length elsewhere.[67] Our concern here is with diocesan statutes and their enforcement, clandestine marriage simply providing the occasion for the comparison. I have considerable confidence that what we have said here about the difference in types of statutes and their durability can be generalized. I am less confident that what I say about their enforcement in the courts can be generalized, because the focus of my work has been on mar-

---

as excommunicate for this reason. Even if no one offers opposition at the proclamation of the banns, but the priest has a probable or true suspicion (*versimilem aut veram coniecturam*) against the marriage, he should not proceed to solemnize the marriage without consulting with us or our official of Cambrai about this. If he does to the contrary, he will be held to the penalty for [performing a] clandestine marriage."

65. *Actes de Reims,* 2.492–93: "Peter, do you wish to promise by your faith that you will take Bertha, who is here, to wife, if no canonical impediment stands in the way."

66. *Actes de Reims,* 2.502.

67. Donahue, *Law, Marriage, and Society,* 598–622.

riage. But let us assume that it can be. What might these differences mean?

Two possible explanations for these differences come to mind. As is well known, English secular private law in the Middle Ages did not rely particularly heavily on statutes. After the flurry of statute-making associated with Edward I at the end of the thirteenth century, the common law of England developed largely through judicial decisions. The development of the diocesan synodal statute in the late thirteenth century corresponds fairly nicely to what was happening on the secular side, and the relative neglect of the form in the fourteenth and fifteenth centuries does too. The situation in France was more complicated. There was relatively little royal legislation, particularly about matters of private law, until the sixteenth century. There was, however, beginning in the thirteenth century, considerable effort to write down in a reasonably comprehensive form the customs of particular areas. The *ordonnance* of Montil-les-Tours of 1453 called for the homologation of all the customs of the customary regions. Those homologations were ultimately made, although most of the redactions date from the sixteenth century. The analogy of the French synodal statute book to local 'codifications' of custom (*coutumiers*) is not perfect, but they do share in common an attempt to put down in a reasonably coherent form all the relevant material, and the geographical areas involved are roughly similar in scope. The legislative element in the diocesan statutes is stronger, but the form that they take is comparable to that of the *coutumiers*.

The other explanation would focus on the different types of independence that the churches in the two areas sought, and ultimately achieved. Here, the danger of anachronism is substantial. Ultimately, and not too far from our ending date, the English church broke from the papacy and became the Anglican church. The French church did not break totally from the papacy but it became the Gallican church. In both developments the respective kings played a considerable role. But if we look below the level of the king-pope relationship and focus instead on the structure of the two churches, it is striking that the diocese seems to play an increasingly unimportant role after the thirteenth century in England, while the province, and, in particular, the southern province under the leadership of the archbishop of Canterbury, remained important. The province of Reims does not drop out of the picture entirely in France. The basic proposition, for example, that those who married clandestinely were to be excommunicated, continued to be stated at the provincial level.[68] But no one wrote

68. E.g., Compiègne (1304) c. 1, in *Actes de Reims*, 2.477–78.

a *Provinciale* for Reims, or for any other French province of which I am aware. Provincial statutes existed for the province of Reims, but they pale in comparison with the diocesan ones. Despite the fact that we can organize the statutes into regions and show how statutes from one diocese were sometimes adopted wholesale in another, the fact is that the synodal statute-book was a diocesan book that was, it would seem, enforced in the diocesan courts. The Anglican historians who saw the church of England in Lyndwood's *Provinciale* saw something that was not there, but one can see how they saw it.[69] Thomas Gousset in his effort to show the independence of the province of Reims also saw something that was not there, but the documents he printed certainly do suggest a group of prelates operating independently, at least in some respects, of both king and pope.

When the reform came, as it did in different ways in both countries, it was implemented in different ways. The diocesan synodal statute was a principal vehicle for reform in France; in England it was not. Reforming bishops and reforming priests there certainly were in England, as there were in France. But formal, written law, to the extent that it was used, was parliamentary law in England, not ecclesiastical, and certainly not diocesan. To the extent that this generalization is true (a statement of one who has no business making such generalizations), we can see why this might have been the case from what we can see in the two areas in the later Middle Ages.

69. See F. W. Maitland, 'Canon Law in England: I. William Lyndwood,' *English Historical Review* (1896) 446–78, repr. in idem, *Roman Canon Law in the Church of England* (London 1898) 1–50, who is at pains to point out that it was not there.

JAMES A. BRUNDAGE

18 The Medieval Battle of the Faculties

Theologians v. Canonists

Universities recognizably similar to their modern descendants (complete with scheduled lectures that began and ended at the sound of bells and statutes that governed the mode of their presentation, as well as deans, committees, examinations, and academic degrees) first began to appear in western Europe during the decades immediately following 1200. The earliest were those at Bologna and Paris. Others soon emerged at Oxford and Cambridge, and subsequently at Montpellier, Orléans, Toulouse, Salamanca, Padua, and Naples, as well as in a host of other cities.[1]

Shortly after their initial establishment, teachers at most universities began to separate into specialized subgroups, usually called faculties, whose members lectured on one of the four major disciplines taught in medieval universities: liberal arts, theology, law, or medicine.[2] The devel-

It seems appropriate to focus this tribute to Robert Somerville on the relationship between canon law and theology, in view of his long-standing interest in the ways that medieval canon lawyers regarded themselves and their discipline.

1. Hastings Rashdall, *The Universities of Europe in the Middle Ages*, 2nd ed., rev. F. M. Powicke and Alan B. Emden, 3 vols. (London 1936), despite its age remains a basic introduction to medieval university history. Among briefer but more recent treatments see Alan B. Cobban, *The Medieval Universities: Their Development and Organization* (London 1975); Olaf Pedersen, *The First Universities: Studium generale and the Origins of University Education in Europe*, trans. Richard North (Cambridge 1997); Jacques Verger, 'Patterns,' in *A History of the University in Europe*, vol. 1, *Universities in the Middle Ages*, ed. Hilde de Ridder-Symoens (Cambridge 1992) 35–74 at 47–60, and with special reference to law teaching, Helmut Coing, 'Die juristische Fakultät und ihr Lehrprogramm,' in *Handbuch der Quellen und Literatur der neueren europäischen Privatrechtsgeschichte*, ed. Helmut Coing (Munich 1973), vol. 1 *Mittelalter (1100–1500): Die gelehrten Rechte und die Gesetzgebung* 39–128.

2. Ancient writers used the term *facultas* to describe a person's ability and skill in some subject, while medieval writers by extension used it to denote the subject itself. By the early thirteenth century it was also used to describe a corporate body specializing in a particular discipline

opment of autonomous faculties, each with its own rules concerning curriculum, examinations, and degree requirements, fostered and institutionalized rigid boundaries between disciplines. Their members also sought to exclude what they regarded as marginal topics from the curriculum—arts faculties, for example, typically omitted vernacular literatures from their lecture schedules; medical faculties refused to teach surgery; and law faculties showed no appetite for teaching customary law.[3]

The aggregation of teachers into faculties also led to turf battles, at times remarkably fierce, between these bodies. Medieval scholars commonly regarded their own discipline as more important than its competitors—something not unknown among their more recent successors.[4] Faculties struggled against one another to attract students, no doubt in part because student fees provided them with income, and also for prestige, which not only helped to bring in additional students, but furnished teachers with psychological satisfaction as well.

Herbert Grundmann (1902–70) maintained that medieval universities came into being 'neither from national nor ecclesiastical initiative, nor from social or economic developments, but from *amor sciendi*... in its origin and essence it was directed toward independent thinking, research, and teaching.'[5] Since the 1960s, however, scholars have increasingly ques-

---

within a university; Bernard Geyer, 'Facultas theologica: Eine bedeutungsgeschichtliche Untersuchung,' ZKG 85 (1964) 133–45 at 134–37; Jacques Verger, '*Nova et vetera* dans le vocabulaire des premiers statuts et privilèges universitaires français,' in his *Universités françaises au moyen âge* (Education and Society in the Middle Ages and Renaissance [hereafter ESMAR], vol. 7; Leiden 1995), 37–52 at 45, and 'The First French Universities and the Institutionalization of Learning: Faculties, Curricula, Degrees,' in *Learning Institutionalized: Teaching in the Medieval University*, ed. John van Engen (Notre Dame Conferences in Medieval Studies, no. IX; Notre Dame 2000), 5–19 at 9; James A. Brundage. *Medieval Origins of the Legal Profession: Canonists, Civilians, and Courts* (Chicago 2008) 244–48. *Facultas* in the corporate sense was used more often by medieval writers north of the Alps than by Italian writers; Alfonso Maierù, *University Training in Medieval Europe*, ed. and trans. Darleen N. Pryds (ESMAR. 3; Leiden 1994) 72–82.

3. Verger, 'First French Universities' 10; Yves M. J. Congar, 'Un témoinage des désacords entre canonistes et théologiens,' in *Études d'histoire du droit canonique dédiées à Gabriel Le Bras*, 2 vols. (Paris 1965) 2:861–84 at 862; John van Engen, 'From Practical Theology to Divine Law: The Work and Mind of Medieval Canonists,' in MIC Ser. C 10 (1997) 873–96 at 877.

4. G. H. M. Posthumus Meyjes, 'Exponents of Sovereignty: Canonists as Seen by Theologians in the Late Middle Ages,' in *The Church and Sovereignty, c. 590–1918: Essays in Honour of Michael Wilks*, ed. Diana Wood (SCH, Subsidia 9; Oxford 1991) 299–312 at 300; Jürgen Miethke, 'Kanonistik, Ecclesiologie und politische Theorie: Die Rolle des Kirchenrechts in der politischen Theorie des Spätmittelalters,' in MIC Ser. C 10 (1997) 1023–51 at 1023.

5. Herbert Grundmann, 'Vom Ursprung der Universität im Mittelalter,' *Sb. Akad. Leipzig* 103 (1957) 3–66 at 65; repr. in his *Ausgewählte Aufsätze*, pt. 3 (MGH Schriften 25; Stuttgart 1978) 292–342. I have adopted the translation from David L. Sheffler, *Schools and Schooling in Late Medieval Germany: Regensburg, 1250–1500* (ESMAR 33; Leiden 2008) 7.

tioned, and many have rejected, Grundmann's belief that universities arose solely from a disinterested love of learning.[6] They note, among other things, how medieval theologians, along with preachers, poets, and satirists, deplored the numbers of students who flocked to what they called the lucrative sciences, especially law faculties, and in lesser numbers to faculties of medicine. Where historians have been able to reconstruct the size and configuration of medieval student bodies, moreover, the figures tend to bear out contemporary complaints.[7]

Prestige in medieval universities was greatly bolstered if members of a faculty could plausibly claim that the subject they taught formed an integral part of God's plan for the world. Subjects classified as lucrative or profane were relegated to the lower levels in the hierarchy of disciplines.[8] Theology, sometimes called 'the queen of the sciences,' was the most obvious beneficiary of this belief.[9] And theologians reaped at least symbolic benefit from this, since medieval universities invariably awarded them precedence in academic processions. They also secured priority over other university teachers in royal ceremonies as well.[10]

Although people professed to hold theology in high esteem, when it came to worldly matters, such as numbers of students, income, and preferment to high positions in church and state, theologians fared less well than

6. Peter Classen, 'Die hohen Schulen und die Gesellschaft im 12. Jahrhundert,' *Archiv für Kulturgeschichte* 48 (1966) 156–80 at 158–73; Cobban, *Medieval Universities* 165, 236; Sheffler, *Schools and Schooling* 7–8; Brundage, *Medieval Origins* 466–77.

7. Thus, e.g., T. H. Aston, 'Oxford's Medieval Alumni,' *Past & Present* 74 (1977) 3–40 at 11; T. H. Aston, G. D. Duncan, and T. A. R. Evans, 'The Medieval Alumni of the University of Cambridge,' *Past & Present* 86 (1980) 9–86 at 62; Christoph Fuchs, *Dives, Pauper, Nobilis, Magister, Frater. Clericus: Sozialgeschichtliche Untersuchungen über Heidelberger Universitätsbesucher des Spätmittelalters* (1386–1450) (ESMAR 5; Leiden 1995) 20; Jacques Verger, 'Le recrutement géographique des universités françaises au début du XVe siècle d'après les Suppliques de 1403', *Mélanges d'archéologie et d'histoire* 82 (1970) 855–902 at 873, repr. in his *Universités françaises au moyen âge* 122–73; Brundage, *Medieval Origins* 267–68. Only enrollments in the arts faculty commonly exceeded those in the law faculties, but it was not unusual for arts students to go on to study law.

8. Patrick Gilli, *La noblesse du droit: Débats et controverses sur la culture juridique et le rôle des juristes dans l'Italie médiévale (XIIe–XVe siècles)* (Paris 2003) 156–57; Verger, 'Patterns' 42.

9. But seldom by medieval authors; Bernard McGinn, *'Regina quondam'*, *Speculum* 83 (2008) 817–39 at 817–19.

10. Simone da Borsano, *Lectura Clementinarum*, proem., pt. 1, in Domenico Maffei, 'Dottori e studenti nel pensiero di Simone da Borsano,' SG 15 (1972) 229–50 at 243; Andreas Bonellus de Barulo, *Commentarii in tres libros Codicis* to Cod. 12.3.1 and 5.1 (Venice 1601; repr. Bologna 1975) 261, 264; Inès Kaufmann and Matthias Schwaibold, 'Doctor dicitur fulgere: Zum Tractatus de doctoribus des Petrus Lenauderius,' *Rechtshistorisches Journal* 5 (1986) 274–89 at 278–79; Gabriel Le Bras, 'Velut splendor firmamenti: Le docteur dans le droit de l'église médiévale,' in *Mélanges offerts à Étienne Gilson de l'Académie Française* (Toronto and Paris 1959), 371–88 at 379–80; Ingrid Baumgärtner, '"De privilegiis doctorum": Über Gelehrtenstand und Doktorwürde im späten Mittelalter', HJb 106 (1986) 298–332 at 308 n. 34 and 309; Verger, 'First French Universities' 11.

lawyers, something that teachers and students alike were keenly aware of.[11] 'The schools of the legists draw a hundred or two hundred students,' declared the Dominican preacher John Bromyard († ca. 1352), 'while the schools of the theologians have perhaps just five.'[12] Dante (1265–1321), too, along with many others, lamented that students were deserting theology in order to study law.[13]

Theology professors bitterly complained that the root of their difficulty in competing with lawyers was student greed. Law flourished, they asserted, because students spurned the spiritual and intellectual profit they could draw from the study of theology and chose instead to pursue the filthy lucre to be gained from law.[14] In the words of one anonymous twelfth-century poet:

> Galen gives you wealth and so does Justinian's law;
> From these you gather grain, from the others only straw
> ...
> Socrates and Plato produce a scanty yield;
> I'll go for the money with assets as my shield:
> An abundant harvest demands a fertile field.[15]

Other critics were even more biting. Advocates at the Roman curia were 'enemies of the truth,' wrote Walter of Châtillon (ca. 1135–1202/3). Lawyers are even more perfidious than whores, according to Mattheolus (fl. ca. 1290); Philippe de Mézières (1327–1405) opined that they grew fat from defending the wicked.[16]

11. R. W. Southern, *Scholastic Humanism and the Unification of Europe*, 2 vols. (Oxford 1995–2001) 1:8.

12. John Bromyard, *Summa predicantium omnibus diuini eloquii propagatoribus usui accomadatissima*, s.v. 'Advocatus' §30 (Nürnberg 1518), fol. 16va; elsewhere in his *Summa*, s.v. 'Scientia', fol. 346vb, Bromyard declared that where masters in other disciplines had 100 students, theologians could expect only 20.

13. Dante, *Paradiso* 9.133–35, in *Tuttle le opere*, ed. Frederico Chiappelli (Milan 1965) 276; similarly Gautier de Coinci, 'Vie de Seinte Léocad,' lines 1131–46 in Étienne Barbazan, *Fabliaux et contes des poètes françois*, 2nd ed. rev. Dominique Martin Méon, 4 vols. in 2 (Paris 1808; repr. Geneva 1976) 1:270–346; Rainer Haussherr, 'Eine Warnung vor dem Studium von zivilem und kanonischem Recht in der Bible moralisée,' *Frühmittelalterliche Studien* 9 (1975) 390–407 at 390–93, among others.

14. Master Maurice of St. Victor, *Sermo communis* 4.3 in *Galteri a Sancto Victore et quorundam aliorum sermones ineditos triginta sex*, ed. Jean Châtillon (CCCM 30; Turnhout 1975) 218.

15. Stephan Kuttner, 'Dat Galienus opes et sanctio Iustiniana,' in *Linguistic and Literary Studies in Honor of Helmut A. Hatzfeld*, ed. Alessandro S. Crisafulli (Washington 1964) 237–46 at 243; repr. in his *History of Ideas and Doctrines of Canon Law in the Middle Ages*, 2nd ed. (Aldershot 1992), no. X. The translation of the first distich is by Beryl Smalley, *The Becket Conflict and the Schools: A Study of Intellectuals in Politics in the Twelfth Century* (Oxford 1973) 19; the translation of the other stanza is my own.

16. Walter of Châtillon, 'Propter Sion non tacebo,' verse 9, in *Moralisch-satirische Gedichte*

Even lawyers sometimes admitted that, although the study of law was demanding and intellectually stimulating, it might not be good for the soul. John of Salisbury (†1180), who spent much of his career advising Archbishop Theobald of Canterbury (1138–61) on appellate litigation, asked rhetorically 'Who ever arose contrite from the study of the laws or even the canons?'[17]

Placentinus (†1192), to be sure, maintained that the study of law fostered good morals, but felt bound to admit that while true philosophers should disdain money,[18] lawyers generally aimed for ample incomes.[19] The Franciscan Roger Bacon († ca. 1291) lamented that shrewd jurists were more highly valued, even at the papal curia, than clever theologians; Bromyard noted that lawyers, unlike theologians, dressed in elegant clothes and rode on fine horses. 'This,' he concluded, 'is why almost everyone wishes to study money-spinning law and families and friends send their sons and grandsons to law school.'[20]

To be sure, we have no reason to believe that theologians were necessarily purer of heart or less opportunistic than lawyers in seeking to advance their careers and increase their incomes.[21] They were bitterly aware that law professors profited from the greater numbers of students who frequented their lectures and, in universities whose professors received salaries in addition to student fees, payments to law professors were invariably greater (often two or three times larger) than those to members of other faculties.[22] It seems likely that the disparity theologians saw when

Walters von Châtillon, ed. Karl Strecker (Heidelberg 1929) 22; *Les lamentations de Matheolus et le livre de leesce*, lines 4579–84, ed. Anton Gérard van Hamel, 2 vols. (Bibliothèque de l'École des Hautes Études, fasc. 95–96; Paris 1892) 1:283; Philippe de Mézières, *Le songe du vieil pelerin* 1.51, ed. G. W. Coopland, 2 vols. (Cambridge 1969) 1:330; see further James A. Brundage, 'Vultures, Whores, and Hypocrites: Images of Lawyers in Medieval Literature,' *Roman Legal Tradition* 1 (2002) 56–103.

17. *The Letters of John of Salisbury*, no. 144, ed. W. J. Millor, H. E. Butler, and C. N. L. Brooke, 2 vols. (Nelson's/Oxford Medieval Texts; Edinburgh; Oxford 1955–79) 2:32; cf. Peter of Blois, *Epistolae* 140, in his *Opera omnia*, ed. J. A. Giles, 4 vols. (Oxford 1847) 2:36–41. On John of Salisbury as a lawyer, see C. N. L. Brooke, 'John of Salisbury and His World,' in *The World of John of Salisbury*, ed. Michael Wilks (SCH, Subsidia 3; Oxford 1994) 1–20 at 7, and Max Kerner, 'Römisches und Kirchliches Recht im *Policraticus*', in the same volume 365–79.

18. According to Papinian at Dig. 50.5.8.4.

19. Placentinus, *Sermo de legibus* in Hermann Kantorowicz, 'The Poetical Sermon of a Medieval Jurist: Placentinus and His 'Sermo de legibus,' *Journal of the Warburg Institute* 2 (1938) 22–41, repr. in his *Rechtshistorische Schriften*, ed. Helmut Coing and Gerhard Immel (Karlsruhe 1970) 111–35 at 132–33, lines 168–74.

20. Erich Genzmer, 'Kleriker als Berufsjuristen im späten Mittelalter,' in *Études . . . Gabriel Le Bras* 2:1207–36 at 1216–17, 1219–20; Bromyard, *Summa predicantium*, s.v. 'Advocatus' §30, fol. 16va.

21. William J. Courtenay, *Schools and Scholars in Fourteenth-Century England* (Princeton 1987) 37.

22. Thus, e.g., Jonathan Davies, *Florence and Its University during the Early Renaissance*

they compared their relatively meager compensation with that of their colleagues in law faculties can account for the amply documented resentment and jealousy that they felt.[23]

But economic inequality was hardly the sole factor that aroused hostility between lawyers and theologians. Theologians directed their ire especially at canon law, which prior to the second half of the twelfth century had traditionally been regarded as a branch of theology. Canon law and theology inevitably overlapped with one another, particularly where moral problems were at issue—marriage and sexual behavior had both canonical and theological dimensions, for example, as did holy orders, the obligations of monks and nuns, and clerical discipline generally.[24] Canon law was to a great extent theology in practice.[25] Even Gratian (fl. ca. 1140), whose *Decretum* provided the foundation of the classical canon law taught in thirteenth-century universities, seems to have been at least as much a theologian as a lawyer.[26] The preface to the anonymous *Summa 'Antiquitate et tempore,'* (written in the 1170s). for example, declared:

> It is clear that this book [the *Decretum Gratiani*] contains a kind of summary of the content of all theology, and one fully acquainted with this book cannot lack knowledge of the entirety of the 'sacred page.'[27]

(ESMAR 8; Leiden 1998) 34; Carlo Guido Mor, *Storia dell'Università di Modena* (Modena 1952) 46–47; Dante Zanetti, 'À l'université de Pavie au XVe siècle: Les salaires des professeurs,' *Annales: Économies, sociétés, civilisations* 17 (1962) 421–33 at 424; *Cartulario de la Universidad de Salamanca (1218–1600)*, no. 23, ed. V. B. de Heredia, 6 vols. (Salamanca 1970–73) 1:604–6; Rashdall, *Universities* 1:240, 2:71; Jacques Verger, 'Teachers,' in *History of the University in Europe* 144–68 at 151–54.

23. Van Engen, 'From Practical Theology to Divine Law' 877–78; Jacques P. Krynen, 'Les légistes "idiots politiques": Sur l'hostilité des théologiens à l'égard des juristes en France, au temps de Charles V,' in *Théologie et droit dans la science politique de l'État moderne* (Rome 1991) 171–198 at 171–172.

24. Courtenay, *Schools and Scholars* 38–39.

25. Van Engen, 'From Practical Theology to Divine Law,' 876, 895–96; R. James Long, '"Utrum iurista vel theologus plus proficiat ad regimen ecclesie": A Quaestio Disputata of Francis Caraccioli, Edition and Study,' *Mediaeval Studies* 30 (1968) 134–62 at 160–61.

26. Ennio Cortese, 'Théologie, droit canonique, et droit romain: Aux origines du droit savant (XIe–XIIe s.),' *Comptes rendus Paris Académie des Inscriptions et Belles-Lettres* (2002), no. 1, 57–74 at 65. Gratian included something on the order of 1300 biblical texts in his *Decretum*, while his work shared more than 300 of the texts that appear in Abelard's *Sic et non;* Richard H. Helmholz, 'The Bible in the Service of the Canon Law,' *Chicago-Kent Law Review* 70 (1995) 1557–1581 at 1561; Alain Boureau, 'Droit et théologie au XIIIe siècle,' *Annales: Économies, sociétés, civilisations* 47 (1992) 1113–1125 at 1115. On Gratian and his work see especially Anders Winroth, *The Making of Gratian's Decretum* (Cambridge Studies in Medieval Life and Thought, 4th ser. 49; Cambridge 2000).

27. The text appears in QL 1:249; an English translation also appears in *Prefaces to Canon Law Books in Latin Christianity: Selected Translations, 500–1245*, ed. Robert Somerville and Bruce C. Brasington (New Haven 1998) 202–212 at 211.

Beginning with the decretists writing in the 1150s, the two disciplines gradually began to diverge from one another.[28] Already Stephen of Tournai (1135–1203), writing between 1166 and 1168, reckoned that theologians and canon lawyers showed different interests and distinct viewpoints even when, as often happened, they dealt with the same texts.[29] Rufinus (fl. 1150–91), however, was more cautious. Canonists, he thought, needed to be careful and highly selective when they adopted ideas and doctrines from Roman law and other pagan sources. Borrowing from secular sources was in his view fraught with danger and should be avoided where possible.[30]

Despite Rufinus's reservations, canonists from the time of Huguccio (†1210) onward began to draw ever more heavily from civilian ideas and techniques when they interpreted and applied canonistic texts.[31] At the same time, the pace of legal change accelerated during the decades following the appearance of Gratian's work as new papal decretals became the dominant source of current law. This gradually whittled away the common ground between canonists and theologians.[32] Early in the thirteenth century Johannes Teutonicus (†1245) found it difficult to decide whether canon law ought to be classified as theology or law, and accordingly he posed a question to be disputed in the schools:

A certain man had books on theology, canon law, and civil law. At his death he made a will in which he left his theology books to the church of St. Stephen and his law books to the church of St. Proclus. He said nothing about any others. It may be asked, therefore, to which [church] the canon law books should go?[33]

28. Ennio Cortese, *Il diritto nella storia medievale*, 2 vols. (Rome 1995) 2:198.

29. Stephen of Tournai, *Die Summa über das Decretum Gratiani, praef.*, ed. Johann Friedrich von Schulte (Giessen 1891; repr. Aalen 1965) 1; an English translation appears in *Prefaces to Canon Law Books* 194. On the date of Stephen's *Summa* see Herbert Kalb, *Studien zur Summa Stephans von Tournai: Ein Beitrag zur kanonistischen Wissenschaftsgeschichte des späten 12. Jahrhunderts* (Forschungen zur Rechts- und Kulturgeschichte 12; Innsbruck 1983) 108–112.

30. Rufinus, *Summa decretorum* to D. 1 c. 7 v. *terra marique capiuntur*, D. 37 d.p.c. 7 v. *hinc etiam filius ille*, and C. 16 q. 3 pr., ed. Heinrich Singer (Paderborn 1902; repr. Aalen 1963) 9, 88, 358–59; Herbert Kalb, 'Bemerkungen zum Verhältnis von Theologie und Kanonistik am Beispiel Rufins und Stephans von Tournai', ZRG Kan. Abt. 72 (1986) 338–348 at 344–346; van Engen, 'From Practical Theology to Divine Law' 874.

31. Gabriel Le Bras, 'L'Église médiévale au service du droit romain,' RHD 44 (1966) 193–209 at 197–99.

32. Brundage, *Medieval Origins* 114–17; Jean Gaudemet, 'Théologie et droit canonique: Les leçons de l'histoire,' RDC 39 (1989) 3–13 at 9, also repr. with original pagination in his *Doctrine canonique médiévale* (Aldershot 1994), no. I.

33. Johannes Teutonicus, *Quaestiones Clostroneoburgenses* in Klosterneuburg, Stiftsbibliothek, MS 656, fol. 42r, quoted in Pierre Legendre, 'La droit romain, modèle et langage: De la signification de l'Utrumque Ius,' in *Études... Gabriel Le Bras* 2:913–30 at 918 n. 14. This *quaestio* also appears in Gérard Fransen, 'À propos des Questions de Jean le Teutonique,' BMCL 13 (1983) 39–47 at 47.

Around the middle of the century—certainly after the appearance of the revised version of Johannes's *Glossa ordinaria* on the *Decretum* prepared not long after 1234 by Bartholomaeus Brixiensis (fl. 1234–58)—a list of issues on which canonists differed from theologians was in circulation.[34] By the close of the thirteenth century the issue had been resolved. Guido de Baysio (†1313), among others, maintained that canon law and theology were two distinct and separate disciplines.[35]

During the second half of the twelfth century, canonists began to adopt a decidedly legalistic approach to moral problems. They focused sharply upon the legal issues that a situation presented, in isolation from moral considerations. Lawyers confined themselves to deciding what was lawful in a particular situation, and left it to theologians to puzzle out what was right and just. As the two disciplines became more and more estranged intellectually and methodologically, theologians became increasingly disparaging of lawyers, especially canonists.[36] Parisian theologians may well have had a hand in persuading Pope Honorius III (1216–27) to ban the teaching of Roman law at Paris in 1219, a move that not only seriously diminished the size of the law faculty there, but also gravely handicapped Parisian students of canon law as well.[37] Albertus Magnus (ca. 1200–1280), for example, advised his students to beware of the opinions of canonists, because 'They certainly say many erroneous things ... since they are men unversed in the sacred Scriptures.' Likewise his best-known student, Thomas Aquinas (1224–74), considered it 'unsuitable and foolish' for professors of theology to cite juristic glosses as authorities.[38] Nicholas of Lyra (ca. 1270–1349) lamented what he called the canonists' 'perverse interpretations' of

34. Congar, 'Un témoinage des désaccords,' supplemented by Rudolf Weigand, 'Ein Zeugnis für de Lehrunterscheide zwischen Kanonisten und Theologen aus dem 13. Jahrhundert,' RDC 24 (1974) 63–71.

35. Guido de Baysio, *Rosarium decretorum* to D. 38 c. 1 v. *sacras* (Venice 1481), fol. 54ra; cf. his *Lectura super Sexto decretalium* to VI 3.24.2 v. *Ad quovis* (Pavia 1511; unpaginated).

36. Herbert Kalb, 'Überlegungen zur Entstehung der Kanonistik als Rechtswissenschaft—Einege Aspekte,' ÖA KR 41 (1992) 1–28 at 26–27 and 'Juristischer und theologischer Diskurs und die Entstehung der Kanonistik als Rechtswissenschaft,' *Österreichisches Archiv für Recht und Religion* 47 (2000) 1–33 at 9.

37. Stephan Kuttner, 'Papst Honorius III. und das Studium des Zivilrechts,' in *Festschrift für Martin Wolff: Beiträge zum Zivilrecht und internationalen Privatrecht* 79–101, ed. Ernst von Caemmerer (Tübingen 1952; repr. in Kuttner's *Gratian and the Schools of Law* (London 1983), no. X with *Retractationes* at 43–47; Brundage, *Medieval Origins* 231–33.

38. Albertus Magnus, *De sacramento Eucharistiae* 3.3.1, and Thomas Aquinas, *Contra pestiferam doctrinam retrahentes homines a religionis ingressu* 13, both quoted in Michele Maccarrone, 'Teologia e diritto canonico nella *Monarchia* III, 3,' RSCI 5 (1951) 7–42 at 19 and 22; cf. also Aquinas, *Summa theologiae* 2–2 q. 88 a 11 *conclusio*, as well as Kalb, 'Juristischer und theologischer Diskurs' 3–4, and Miethke, 'Kanonistik, Ekklesiologie und politische Theorie' 1023–25.

the Scriptures and added that their lame explanations clouded the real issues.[39] Johannes de Legnano (ca. 1320–83) reported in his *Somnium* that in his day Paris theologians rudely referred to canonists as asses.[40]

Around the middle of the thirteenth century, Hostiensis (ca. 1200–1271) fired back at the criticisms that theologians had begun to level against canon law and canon lawyers. In the preface to his *Summa* (sometimes called the *Golden Summa,* completed about 1253) Hostiensis analyzed the relationship between canon law, Roman civil law, and theology. Theology, he declared, centers upon spiritual, one might even say angelic, matters; civil law deals with the mundane needs of mankind; canon law, though, is concerned with all of humanity, because it encompasses both the spiritual and corporeal concerns of people. One might, he continued, compare the three disciplines to the means of land travel common in his day: horses, donkeys, and mules. Thus theology is an equine science, and civil law could be called an asinine science. Canon law, however, is a mulish science because, just as mules result from crossing horses with donkeys, so canon law draws from both theology and civil law.[41] Hostiensis later varied the metaphor in his *Lectura* on the *Liber Extra,* which he was still working on at the time of his death. There he compared the disciplines to parts of the human body. Theology, he wrote, is the head, civil law the feet, and canon law the hands, because theologians produce ideas, civilians support the body, while canonists perform the work that needs to be done in the church. Canon law, Hostiensis concluded, was the noblest of all fields of learning. Jesus, he argued, as true God and true man united in his own person the human and the divine. Similarly canon law united theology with civil law, and accordingly, 'just as a composite nature is worthier and greater than all others, therefore so is our science, because the same conclusion is to be

39. Nicholas of Lyra, *Postilla* to Luke 11:52, v. *vae vobis legisperitis,* in *Biblia cum glossa ordinaria et expositione Lyre litterali et morali, necnon additionibus et replicis,* 6 vols. (Basel 1501–02), 5, fol. 156vb.

40. Vatican City, Biblioteca Apostolica Vaticana, MS Vat. lat. 2639, fol. 253ra, quoted by Helmut G. Walther, '*Canonica sapiencia* und *civilis sciencia*: Die Nutzung des aristotelischen Wissenschaftsbegriffs durch den Kanonisten Johannes von Legnano (1320–1383) im Kampf der Diziplinen,' in *Scientia und Ars im Hoch- und Spätmittelalter,* ed. Ingrid Craemer-Ruegenburg and Albert Speer (Miscellanea medievalia, 22; Berlin 1994) 863–76 at 869; G. W. Coopland, 'An Unpublished Work of John of Legnano: The "Somnium" of 1372,' *Nuova studi medievali* 2 (1925) 65–88 at 73.

41. Hostiensis, *Summa, una cum summariis et adnotationibus Nicolai Superantii, proem.* §§ 11–12 (Lyon 1537; repr. Aalen 1962), fol. 2vb–3ra; Knut Wolfgang Nörr, 'Der Kanonist und sein Werk im Selbstverständnis zweier mittelalterlicher Juristen: Eine Exegese der Proemien des Hostiensis und Durandi,' in *Ex ipsis rerum documentis: Beiträge zur Mediävistik, Festschrift für Harald Zimmermann zum 65. Geburtstag,* ed. Klaus Herbers, Hans Hennig Kortüm, and Carlos Servatius (Sigmaringen 1991) 373–80 at 376. On Hostiensis see also Kenneth Pennington, 'Henricus de Segusio (Hostiensis),' in his *Popes, Canonists and Texts, 1150–1550* (Aldershot 1993) no. XVI.

reached concerning similar things.'[42] Canon law is a more perfect field of learning than theology, he added, and therefore the opinions of canonists carried greater weight than those of theologians on issues where they differed.[43] He described canon law, therefore, as 'the science of sciences' and even went so far as to claim that it was divine.[44]

Hostiensis was not the only canonist to lash back at the theologians. In 1290 Cardinal Benedetto Caetani (later Pope Boniface VIII), a curial canonist since his youth, upbraided the theology faculty of the University of Paris for its temerity in attempting to settle the controversy raging over the mendicant orders. 'You have done a stupid thing,' he wrote, 'in trying to make doctrine out of your discipline. You sit in your professorial chairs and think that Christ is ruled by your reasoning.... Not so, my brethren, not so!'[45] Henry of Cremona (†1312) asserted that the canons were just as much inspired by the Holy Spirit as were the Scriptures. He added that those who maintained otherwise were guilty of blasphemy. Likewise Johannes de Legnano equated canon law with divine wisdom, for it, too, guides people toward happiness, both in this life and the next.[46] Johannes Andreae (†1348) further maintained in his *Questiones mercuriales* that one of the basic functions of canon law was to set people on the path that leads to salvation. He declared that since Christ himself was the founder of canon law, canonists were at least equal in dignity to theologians.[47]

Theologians, not surprisingly, rejected these claims. Theology, according to Jean Gerson (1363–1429), provided canon law with the structure within which its rules must be framed, and hence canon law was subordinate to theology.[48] A striking number of theologians, especially those who had studied at Paris, questioned the ability of men trained in law to rule the church adequately. Humbert de Romans (ca. 1194–1277), the Master General of the Dominican Order, in his *De eruditione praedicatorum*, written around 1240, roughly the same time that Hostiensis was completing the first draft of his *Summa*, concluded that theologians were better equipped than canon-

42. Hostiensis, *In quinque decretalium libri commentaria* [= *Lectura*], to X 1.1.1 §19 and 1.14.14 §6, 6 vols. in 2 (Venice 1581; repr. Turin 1965), fol. 5vb and 110ra–rb; van Engen, 'From Practical Theology to Divine Law' 878.

43. Hostiensis, *Lectura* to X 4.17.13 §23 v. *inter portas*, fol. 39rb–va.

44. Hostiensis, *Summa, proem.* §11, fol. 2vb–3ra, and *Lectura* to X 1.14.14 §§2 and 5, fol. 110ra.

45. Quoted in Long, '"Utrum iurista vel theologus"' 140 n. 7.

46. Johannes de Legnano, *Somnium*, in Vat. lat. 2639, fol. 266rb, quoted in G. M. Donovan and Maurice H. Keen, 'The "Somnium" of John of Legnano,' *Traditio* 37 (1981) 325–45 at 340–41.

47. Johannes Andreae, *Questiones mercuriales*, reg. 2 and *Novellae* to X 1.2.1, both quoted by Gilli, *La noblesse du droit* 138–39, 150.

48. Posthumus Meyjes, 'Exponents of Sovereignty' 308–9.

ists to govern the church.[49] John Peckham, later archbishop of Canterbury (1279–92), participated in a disputation at Paris about 1269 on the question 'Whether theology is more necessary than other sciences for a prelate of the church?' Although he did not specify law as the alternative to theology, in fact Peckham said nothing about men trained in liberal arts or medicine and aimed his negative argument entirely against lawyers.[50] A few years later Nicolà Malombra († ca. 1281–85) wrote a similar *quaestio.*[51] Sometime between 1290 and 1297, still another Paris theologian, Godfrey of Fontaines († after 1306) discussed the question 'Whether a good jurist might better rule the church than a theologian?' Like Nicolà Malombra, Godfrey of Fontaines based his argument on a distinction between the church as a building, as a community of believers, and as the owner or possessor of material goods. He concluded that theologians were better equipped to govern the church under the first two meanings of the term, but that a jurist could perhaps do better in the third sense.[52] Augustinus Triumphus (†1328), an Austin Friar trained in theology at the University of Paris, where Godfrey of Fontaines had been among his teachers, likewise included in his *Summa de potestate ecclesiastica* (1312) a discussion that concluded that the College of Cardinals should elect theologians as popes in preference to lawyers or men trained in other fields.[53] Yet another theologian, this time a Sicilian also trained at Paris, Francesco Caraccioli (†1316), chancellor of the bishop of Paris, disputed a very similar question not long before his death, but approached it rather differently. For Caraccioli 'the church' meant solely the 'multitude of the faithful,' not a building or any other material property under their control. Since the primary task of those who governed the faithful was to guide them toward salvation by teaching them what they needed to believe and how they must behave in order to be saved, Caraccioli was able to conclude that a good theologian was far better prepared to fill that role than a jurist.[54]

49. Long, 'Utrum iurista vel theologus' 140, n. 3.

50. Jean Leclercq, 'Le magistère du prédicateur au XIIIe siècle,' *Archives d'histoire doctrinale et littéraire du moyen âge* 15 (1946) 107–45 at 139–42.

51. Manlio Bellomo, 'Giuristi cremonesi e scuole Padovane: Ricerche su Nicolà da Cremona,' in *Studi in onore di Ugo Gualazzini*, 2 vols. (Milan 1981) 1:81–112 at 101–2.

52. Martin Grabmann, 'Die Eröterung der Frage, ob die Kirche besser durch einen guten Juristen oder durch einen Theologen regiert werde, bei Gottfried von Fontaines (†nach 1306) und Augustinus Triumphus von Ancona (†1328),' in *Festschrift Eduard Eichmann zum 70. Geburtstag, dargebracht von seinen Freunden und Schülern* (Paderborn 1940) 1–19 at 5–13; Long, 'Utrum iurista vel theologus', 140.

53. Grabmann, 'Die Eröterung der Frage' 14–18. Long, 'Utrum iurista vel theologus' prints the relevant texts at 158–62.

54. Long, 'Utrum iurista vel theologus,' analyzes Caraccioli's argument in detail and edits his text at 152–58.

These polemical exchanges between theologians and canon lawyers were not an isolated phenomenon. They form part of a wider set of verbal disputes between members of medieval university faculties: civil lawyers quarreled with canonists, lawyers of both kinds belittled physicians, while members of the arts faculty, especially philosophers, stoutly defended the fundamental importance of their discipline against attacks from the other faculties. The battle of the faculties was something more than the proverbial inclination of academics to see their field of knowledge as the central key to understanding the universe.[55] It began to emerge, as we have seen, not long after universities themselves took shape, but it raged most vigorously in the late fourteenth and especially the fifteenth centuries. It is probably no coincidence that this was a time when many universities were experiencing a what turned out to be a temporary decline in attendance, following a period of spectacular growth—in 1300 Europe had somewhere between twenty and thirty universities; by 1500 there were about seventy of them.[56] Competition between faculties for available students accordingly increased, which probably accounts for much of the abrasiveness with which faculties trumpeted their claims to usefulness and intellectual eminence. Given the concurrent growth in the size and complexity of governments during this period and the need to recruit bureaucrats to manage them, it is no wonder that law faculties, whose alumni commonly fared better than those of other faculties in finding desirable positions, proved so attractive to students and so aggravating to their academic colleagues.

55. Isaiah Berlin, *The Hedgehog and the Fox: An Essay on Tolstoy's View of History* (New York 1970) 24.

56. Cobban, *The Medieval Universities* 116.

ELIZABETH MAKOWSKI

19 Canon Law and the Spirituality of Cloistered English Nuns

In 1459, worn down by a long property dispute which had depleted the community's resources, Abbess Joan Keteryche of Denny wrote a letter to her relative and patron, John Paston. It was an importunate letter that ended with this reminder: 'Consydre how we be closyd withynne the ston wallys, and may no odyr wyse speke with you but only be wrytynge.'[1] Hoping to persuade Paston to assist her, the abbess had needed to strike just the right rhetorical note and did so by mentioning the fact of her strict enclosure. It hardly signified that, by virtue of a papal mandate issued more than a century and a half earlier, every abbess in England as well as on the continent *should* have faced similar constraints. To remind her kinsman of the distinctive, the strict, nature of enclosure at Denny was to gain much needed leverage.

As Joan Keteryche knew well, the cloistered spirituality of the Minoresses of Denny was not typical of late medieval English nuns, notwithstanding a concerted papal attempt to make it so. That attempt had begun with the well-known 1298 decree of Pope Boniface VIII, *Periculoso*. Substituting the inflexible papal will for flexible local prerogative, in language reminiscent of his more famous decrees, *Periculoso* applied the law of enclosure to 'nuns of every community or order, in every part of the world, both collectively and individually'.[2] It sought to restrict both exit from and

1. *Victoria County History* (*VCH*), *The Victoria History of the County of Cambridge and the Isle of Ely*, ed. Louis F. Salzman (London, 1948 repr. 1967) 2.299. See also Paul Lee, *Nunneries, Learning, and Spirituality in Late Medieval English Society: The Dominican Priory of Dartford* (Suffolk, UK 2001) 37; Anne Francis Claudine Bourdillon, *The Order of Minoresses in England* (Manchester 1926) 30.

2. For a detailed account of the decree, including Latin text as an appendix, see Elizabeth Makowski, *Canon Law and Cloistered Women: Periculoso and Its Commentators, 1298–1545* (Washington, D.C. 1997).

entrance into monastic precincts—referred to respectively as active and passive enclosure. 'Reasonable and obvious cause' might mitigate claustration but only upon receipt of a 'special license' granted by the 'appropriate authority.'

Boniface VIII was not heedless of the fact that only the possession of adequate worldly goods could insure this level of separation from worldly affairs. He required nunneries to accept new members only if their communities could 'support them with goods or revenues and without penury.' He recognized that bishops, abbots, and other agents responsible for carrying out his measures would incur costs in doing so (for renovation of existing structures, sealing certain doors, constructing walls, etc.) and instructed them to 'meet expenses incurred therein from the alms procured from the faithful for this purpose.' This having been said, there could be no question that *Periculoso* was to be implemented. Invoking the 'threat of divine judgment and the prospect of eternal damnation,' he determined that the recalcitrant were to be 'constrained through ecclesiastical censure, with no right of appeal.'

Boniface included *Periculoso* as Title 16 in the third book of his official compilation of canon law, the *Liber Sextus*. He then sent copies of his collection to the law faculties of universities throughout Europe, since it would be the job of academic canon lawyers to interpret and to clarify the laws it contained. Despite its relatively straightforward mandate, the decree left these commentators with a wide range of issues that demanded such clarification.

The earliest interpreters, such as Joannes Monachus (d. 1313) and Johannes Andreae (d. 1348), author of the standard interpretation (ordinary gloss) of *Periculoso*, noted a number of questions that the decree had raised but not resolved. Who, for instance, was the 'appropriate authority' empowered to grant licenses to enter or leave the cloister? Were nuns who had already made their profession under a less strict rule of life to be compelled to accept enclosure? Could an abbess conduct visitations of the houses under her supervision without herself violating the law of enclosure? Were the 'ecclesiastical censures' which constrained the disobedient to be construed as excommunication?

In each instance, early commentators tended to a strict interpretation of the pope's words. Only the local official, usually a bishop, who had jurisdiction over a monastery of nuns could grant licenses lifting enclosure. A professed nun might indeed be compelled to abide by *Periculoso* even if that meant living under obligations stricter than those she had vowed to observe. Abbesses, as nuns, were bound by the rules of enclosure, and so could not possibly conduct visitations of houses under their jurisdiction. The ecclesiastical sanction with which the pope had threatened violators was to be understood as excommunication.[3]

Later commentators were not, however, so unequivocally supportive of Boniface VIII's hieratic aims; even those who were questioned *Periculoso's* practical impact. As in his more celebrated fiats, *Clericis laicos* (1296) and *Unam sanctam* (1302), Boniface had asserted comprehensive papal power over far-flung peoples and jurisdictions, and had utterly disregarded prevailing practice.[4] Academic lawyers could not help but debate the newly minted right of the papacy to impose a 'stricter way of life' on unwilling nuns. They also observed that the decree, whatever its intrinsic merits, was simply not being enforced in certain places—Venice being an often-cited example. Practicing canon lawyers, whose clients were occasionally the very nuns affected by *Periculoso*, sometimes went a step further than the theorists.[5]

Like their colleagues on the continent, noted English canonists began to interpret *Periculoso* shortly after its promulgation. In the fourteenth and fifteenth centuries, two of England's most famous canonists, John Acton and William Lyndwood, glossed *Periculoso* in light of previous, specifically English, legatine and episcopal statutes.[6] Both interpreted the papal mandate as augmenting earlier national legislation, and both noted the almost impossible task of enforcing it in England.

At the close of his 1348 commentary, John Acton wrote of that task with uncharacteristic verve:

> ... the nuns respond to these statutes, or to others concerning their lasciviousness, saying that those who made those laws were putting much confidence in their own highmindedness when they burdened them with these hard and intolerable restrictions. We see that these statutes are never, or badly, observed and so we might ask why the holy fathers bothered to labor so hard only to 'beat the air'.[7]

3. Makowski, *Canon Law* 53, 60–61, and 75–76.

4. Brian Tierney, *The Crisis of Church and State 1050–1300* (Toronto 1988; repr. of 1964 ed.) contains a succinct overview and translation of both famous decrees.

5. For specific examples see my article, 'Cloister Contested: *Periculoso* as Authority in Late Medieval *Consilia*,' *The Jurist* 71.2 (2011) 334–48.

6. Makowski, *Canon Law*, chapter 7. This chapter deals in greater detail with these English canonists. For essays on famous English canonists, see J. H. Baker, *Monuments of Endless Labours: English Canonists and Their Work, 1300–1900* (London 1998).

7. Cited and translated in Makowski, *Canon Law* 104.

Almost a century later, Acton's words were still relevant, echoed as they are in the *Provinciale* (1422–30) of William Lyndwood. *Periculoso* should have the force of a general law, opined Lyndwood, but it did not. English nunneries subject to monastic superiors were 'for the most part' compliant, but those supervised by bishops continued to disregard regulations, the legality of which they doubted. Less willing than Acton to concede the failure of the papal initiative, Lyndwood encouraged tepid bishops who had been swayed by recalcitrant nuns to renew their labors and so fulfill their enjoined responsibilities.

Lyndwood's characterization of both bishops and nuns was a negative one, but what in fact was going on? English episcopal registers show that some late medieval bishops were not the ineffectual figures depicted by Lyndwood. Beginning in 1299, Archbishop of Canterbury Robert Winchelsy (1293–1313), and his suffragans began sending copies of *Periculoso* to nunneries in their dioceses. A few hardy bishops even attended to its implementation by visiting the houses under their jurisdiction. None of these probably regretted his zeal more than Bishop Dalderby of London who, in 1300, was repaid for his eloquent explication of the details of their new cloistered life by having a copy of *Periculoso* hurled at his head by the unhappy nuns of Markyate.[8]

Throwing unwelcome papal directives in the air might get their attention, but bishops tended to respond better to reasoned objections, coupled with well-timed shows of local/legal opposition. Nuns who effectively resisted strict enclosure used both of these techniques, and their reasons for rejecting claustration were generally twofold. William Lyndwood had alluded to the first when he mentioned nuns ignoring a papal directive, 'the legality of which they doubted.'

Many sisters asked how they could be legally compelled, even by papal decree, to maintain strict active and passive enclosure when that meant living under obligations stricter than those they had vowed to observe at the time of profession? It was a good question since, as we have seen, even canon lawyers could not agree about the answer. For one thing, monastic profession produced some uniform, but by no means unilateral, results. Profession in an order created reciprocal obligations between regulars and their monasteries. By taking her vows, a nun bound herself inviolably to a religious community, and that community in turn, bound itself to her—each monastery being obliged to provide its members with food and other

8. Eileen Power, *Medieval English Nunneries, c. 1275 to 1535* (Cambridge 1922) 351–52. See as well Makowski, *Canon Law* 115.

necessities of life, in perpetuity. Nuns were quite well aware of the reciprocal obligations attached to profession, and they even took legal action when they felt themselves defrauded of the lifelong economic support they had a right to expect.[9] What specific obligations nuns bound themselves to by profession was not as clear-cut.

Although every statement of profession included the standard vows of poverty, chastity, and obedience, the particular words spoken and the attendant rituals differed widely, reflecting an order's characteristic vision of itself.[10] In Benedictine, Augustinian, Cluniac, and Gilbertine monasteries, profession formulae made no mention of enclosure. Even when mandates from general chapters required cloistering of communities that wished to be officially admitted to the Cistercian order, constitutions and house charters continued to avoid any mention of it in that order as well.[11]

9. For a particularly fine example see Dominicus de Sancto Geminiano, *Consilia* (ed. Lugduni 1541 fol. 15). In this case a professed nun sues to be readmitted to her monastery and reinstated into the community, with all of the rights that entails. Her suit for restitution is countered by her sister nuns on the grounds that the plaintiff had left voluntarily with all her belongings. There had been no forcible ejection, no spoliation; the plaintiff had renounced her rights, they claim, and therefore had no basis for a suit demanding restitution. Additionally, it is contended that the plaintiff had committed sexual indiscretions which should by themselves have been grounds for her expulsion. Dominicus argues forcefully that her suit stands.

10. Nancy Bradley Warren, *Spiritual Economies: Female Monasticism in Later Medieval England* (Philadelphia 2001). Chapters 1 and 2 deal particularly with such distinctions among Benedictine, Franciscan, and Bridgettine nuns. For a good example, see the record of the last profession (1528) of novices at the wealthy and prestigious Benedictine priory of Little Marlow, Buckingham County. The complete formula of profession, in English, is as follows. 'In the name of God, Amen. I, Sister Constance, in the presence of Almighty God and our blessed lady St. Mary, patron of this monastery and all angels and saints of heaven, and of you, reverend Father in God, John bishop of Lincoln and ordinary of this diocese, and in the presence of all this honourable witness, vow offer and fully give myself to serve Almighty God during my life natural in this monastery of Little Marlow, dedicated in honour of God and of our blessed lady St. Mary. And for this intent and purpose I here renounce forever and utterly forsake the world, and property of temporal substance and goods of the same and all other worldly delights and pleasures, taking upon me wilful poverty; vowing also and promising ever to live in pure chastity during my life: to change my secular life into regular conversation and religious manners, promising and vowing due and reverent obedience unto you, Reverend Father in God, John bishop of Lincoln and your successors, bishops; and unto my lady and mother Dame Margaret, now prioress of this monastery, and to her successors, prioresses of the same. And utterly from henceforth I forsake mine own proper will, and not to follow the same but to follow the will of my Superior in all lawful and canonical commandments. And to observe this holy order and religion according to the holy rule of St. Benedict and all the laudable constitutions of this monastery by the gracious assistance of Our Lord Jesus Christ. In witness whereof I do put and sign with mine own hand to this my profession.' Cited in 'Houses of Benedictine Nuns: The Priory of Little Marlow,' *A History of the County of Buckingham: Volume 1* (London 1905) 357–360, n. 18, available at http://www.british-history.ac.uk/report.aspx?compid=40308 (accessed: 10 June 2008).

11. Anne Winston-Allen, *Convent Chronicles: Women Writing about Women and Reform in the*

When professed nuns belonging to any of these traditional orders objected to *Periculoso*, or to later Observant reforms which incorporated its strictures, they often did so making explicit reference to such incontrovertible facts. This happened all over Europe.

According to the chronicler of Meaux Abbey, for instance, all Yorkshire nuns remained uncloistered nearly a century after attempts to enforce *Periculoso*, since they said that they 'refused to be bound by regulations stricter than those that they had undertaken to observe at their profession.'[12] When the Benedictine nuns of Rijnsburg Abbey solicited legal advice to bolster their opposition to the reforms of Nicholas of Cusa, they did so claiming that the cardinal could not impose upon them a stricter rule than that which they had followed 'as far back as human memory could recall.'[13] Similarly, the lawyer acting on behalf of a group of Perugian tertiaries in their struggle against attempts by Observant Franciscans to cloister them in 1469, argued that the tertiaries should keep their 'original and accustomed rule.'[14] And when the abbess of Santa Clara of Barcelona refused the observance of strict active and passive enclosure enjoined upon her in 1494, she claimed that it was 'contrary to the use, practice, and custom of the monastery.'[15]

Nuns in traditional orders throughout Europe also made a convincing case against enclosure on economic grounds. Without continued access to the larger world, they claimed, they would be impoverished. Since it had been anticipated by Boniface VIII, this claim might have been countered if more bishops had acted in accord with papal pragmatism and, like the zealous monastic reformer Johannes Busch, taken pains to secure an ample endowment for a house *before* expecting its members to realize the cloistered ideal.[16] Not that this was an easy task, since both nuns and their

---

Late Middle Ages (University Park, PA 2004) 132, reports that the proposed cloistering of the nominally Cistercian house of Rechentshofen was objected to as being against the wishes of the founders and as 'rustic and ignoble.' The earliest Cistercian foundations, including the well-known and aristocratic abbey of Las Huelgas, Spain were clearly not strictly cloistered foundations. See Louis J. Lekai, *The Cistercians: Ideals and Reality* (Kent, OH 1977) chapter 22; Constance Berman, *Women and Monasticism in Medieval Europe: Sisters and Patrons of the Cistercian Reform* (Kalamazoo, MI 2002).

12. John Tillotson, 'Visitation and Reform of the Yorkshire Nunneries in the Fourteenth Century,' *Northern History* 30 (1994) 2.

13. Winston-Allen, *Convent Chronicles* 137.

14. Katherine Gill, 'Scandala: Controversies Concerning *clausura* and Women's Religious Communities in Late Medieval Italy,' in *Christendom and Its Discontents*, ed. Scott L. Waugh and Peter D. Diehl (Cambridge 1996) 180.

15. Elizabeth Lehfeldt, 'Discipline, Vocation, and Patronage: Spanish Religious Women in a Tridentine Microclimate,' *Sixteenth Century Journal* 30 (1999) 1019.

16. See for example, Johannes Busch, *Chronicon Windeshemense und Liber de reformatione monasteriorum*, ed. Karl Grube (Halle 1886) 572, 588–91, and 671.

lay supporters had been used to very different sorts of economic arrangements.

At the Cistercian monastery of Marienkammer, near Halle, for example, Johannes Busch learned that kinsmen willing to provide private support for their daughters who had become nuns were not always willing to give bequests for general use. Providing endowments for a community as a whole sometimes required him to preach monitory sermons to the locals or to threaten to move all the nuns in a town to distant houses.[17]

In England too, such economic restructuring went against established custom as well as the desires of the laity, and nuns argued effectively that it need not be begun. When adequate endowments failed to materialize, English ordinaries agreed. Lay boarders, pensioners, and children schooled within cloister confines continued to supply needed income to nuns, while those nuns rendered the services which founders and patrons had long come to rely on.

At length, legal consultants, sympathetic bishops, and subsequent popes responding to the arguments and actions of nuns in traditional open monasteries all but undid the papal policy of enclosure that had been inaugurated by Pope Boniface VIII. Compromises between nuns, their diocesan overseers, and popes themselves soon became the norm.[18] Licenses to leave cloister precincts on monastic business or for reasons of health, and indults permitting outsiders to enter the cloister, were granted with such abandon that few of the restrictions set out in *Periculoso* were observed in the majority of late medieval English nunneries. An observation from the *Victoria County History*, citing the hapless Bishop Dalderby's attempts to impose those restrictions on the Benedictine nuns of Little Marlowe, nicely sums up the larger situation:

> There are no visitations of this house recorded in the episcopal registers except one of Bishop Dalderby in 1300, which was merely for the purpose of explaining to the nuns the Statute of Pope Boniface VIII. *Pro clausura monialium*. This statute was intended to compel the English nuns of all orders to observe a stricter enclosure; but though Bishop Dalderby did his duty conscientiously by explaining it to all the houses under his care—sometimes under rather trying circumstances—it seems to have been quite ineffectual. The English Benedictine nuns and Austin canonesses never had been strictly enclosed and quietly ignored the new regulations, even though they came from the pope himself. In later epis-

17. Busch, *Chronicon* 571–72. It is also reported in Power, *Medieval English Nunneries* 673–74.

18. Tillotson, 'Yorkshire Nunneries' 20–21; Makowski, *Canon* Law 115–21; Gill, 'Scandala' 191ff. She refers to the words which adorn so many fourteenth- and fifteenth-century papal exemptions: 'notwithstanding the decisions of our predecessor Boniface VIII,' as '*Periculoso*'s legal solvent.'

copal visitations the nuns of these two orders were often ordered not to go out without the consent of their superiors: but there was no established rule or custom before the Reformation to prevent them going out of the cloister at all.[19]

But, as Abbess Joan Keteryche's letter reminds us, there *were* strictly cloistered nuns in late medieval England. Those nuns closely approximated the Bonifacian ideal, although they were not the products of papal manipulation. They were the latecomers to the English scene, Franciscan, Dominican, and Bridgettine nuns whose spiritual ideal required, and whose economic circumstances allowed for, adherence to strict active, if not passive, enclosure.

The four nunneries of the Franciscan order in England were products of female initiative and linked to continental developments which accorded a distinctive place for religious women in monastic renewal.[20] The Minories, outside Aldgate in the parish of St. Botolph, London, was founded in 1293 by Blanche, Queen of Navarre, with the assistance of her husband Edmund, Earl of Lancaster.[21] The wealthy widow Denise de Munchensey founded Waterbeach in Cambridgeshire in the same year, and Denny was established only a mile away in 1342 by another widow, Mary of St. Pol, Countess of Pembroke.[22] Between 1364 and 1367, Bruisyard in Suffolk was founded by Lionel, Duke of Clarence, for the sake of his mother-in-law, Maud of Lancaster, granddaughter of Blanche of Navarre.[23]

The nuns in all of these houses observed a version of the Rule of St. Clare which was known as the Isabella rule. Isabelle, sister of King Louis IX of France and founder of the Abbey of Longchamp, outside of Paris, was responsible for its distinctive features. Among them was the specification that the nuns of Longchamp, and others who followed her rule, would be known as *Sorores minores* (Sisters Minor; Minoresses), a name suggesting the close relationship that Isabelle wished her nuns to have to the male Franciscan *Fratres minores* who would minister to them spiritually.[24] Like

19. 'Houses of Benedictine Nuns: The Priory of Little Marlow,' *A History of the County of Buckingham: Volume 1* (1905) 357–60, available at http://www.british-history.ac.uk/report.aspx?compid=40308 (accessed: 10 June 2008).

20. Warren, *Spiritual Economies* 13.

21. *VCH, The Victoria History of London*, ed. William Page (Folkestone, 1909) 1.516–19 for an overview of the history of the house; Bourdillion, *Minoresses* 16; Edward Murray Tomlinson, *A History of the Minories, London* (London 1907) 12.

22. *VCH Cambridge* 2.292–95; *VCH Cambridge* 2.295–302 for overviews; Bourdillon, *Minoresses* 14–21.

23. *VCH, The Victoria History of the County of Suffolk*, ed. William Page (London 1907) 2.131–32 for an overview. Bourdillon, *Minoresses* 22–25; Loveday Lewes Gee, *Women, Art and Patronage from Henry III to Edward III, 1216–1377* (Woodbridge, Suffolk 2002) 130.

24. Sean Field, *Isabelle of France* (South Bend, IN 2006). Chapters 3 and 4 discuss the compo-

all Franciscan nuns, however, the Minoresses were also referred to in the rule as *Sorores inclusae* (enclosed sisters), since they added a fourth vow at the time of profession, namely the vow to live *sub claustra*.[25] To this end, the Isabella rule provided substantial regulations for servants sent out of the abbey on behalf of the nuns, and it regulated the very limited conversations professed nuns might have with visitors. In the parlor there was to be a curtained grille to shield them from view and a *rota* or wheel set into a door to allow the sisters to take in food and other necessities without themselves being seen. Outsiders were required to secure papal and not merely episcopal permission for entry into the cloister precincts. In the words of the rule, each nun 'shall dwell all the days of her life enclosed, as a treasure kept to the sovereign king'.[26]

A firm understanding of, and adherence to, the Isabella rule in English houses was facilitated by the fact that the first nuns settling them came from Longchamp.[27] In the license granted to Denise de Munchensey for the establishment of Waterbeach we read of the Minoresses of the order of St. Clare, whom she is bringing there 'from beyond the seas,' and Joan de Nevers, fifth abbess of Longchamp, became the first abbess there.[28] Blanche of Navarre (whose uncle was Louis IX) brought Minoresses from Longchamp to her London foundation in the same year.[29]

Similar arrangements assured compliance with the monastic rules which governed life at the two other contemplative houses, Dartford and Syon. In 1346 four experienced Dominican nuns from the French priory of Poissy were the first settlers of Dartford Priory, and when Henry V laid the foundation stone of Syon in 1415, nuns from the Bridgettine motherhouse of Vadstena, Sweden, were recruited to live there.[30]

As was the case with all Dominican and Bridgettine communities, nuns

---

sition and content of the rule in detail and reference to its success in England. See also Gertrude Mlynarczyk, *Ein Franziskanerinnenkloster im 15. Jahrhundert* (Bonn 1987) 36–41; Bourdillon, *Minoresses* 8–9; Warren, *Spiritual Economies* 13.

25. Field, *Isabelle* 79. For the Rule of St. Clare, see Francis and Clare, *The Complete Works*, ed. Regis Armstrong and Ignatius Brady (New York 1982) 209–25.

26. Quoted in Bourdillon, *Minoresses* 62.

27. Field, *Isabelle* 119.

28. *Calendar of the Patent Rolls Preserved in the Public Record Office*, ed. H. C. Maxwell Lyte, J. G. Black, R. F. Isaacson, G. J. Morris, G. F. Handcock (London 1901) Edward I 1292–1301, 3.63.

29. Bourdillion, *Minoresses* 16.

30. Lee, *Nunneries* 20; *VCH, The Victoria History of the County of Kent*, ed. William Page (Folkestone 1974) 2.181–90 for an overview. George James Aungier, *The History and Antiquities of Syon Monastery* (London 1840) 21–31; Bridget Morris, *St. Birgitta of Sweden* (Woodbridge 1999) 171; *VCH, A History of the County of Middlesex*, ed. J. S. Cockburn, H. P. F. King, K. G. T. McDonnell (London 1969) 1.182–91 for an overview.

at Dartford and Syon observed the rule of St. Augustine, complemented by constitutions of their respective orders—a legal means of circumventing the Fourth Lateran Council's 1215 ban on new orders.[31] The Augustinian rule set down only very basic regulations for a monastic life, and it is in the constitutions that the peculiar features of the respective orders comes to life. The constitutions observed by the nuns of Dartford were those promulgated for all Dominican nunneries by the general chapter of the order in 1259.[32] These constitutions included regulations for maintaining strict enclosure: Two keys were to be used to lock the outer doors, communion was to be received through a grille, entrance into the cloister was restricted to monarchs, the highest ecclesiastical officials, and founders, and only the prioress, accompanied by 'three sisters of respectable age,' was allowed to speak with them.

The constitutions of the Bridgettines of Syon were even more detailed in their treatment of enclosure, Bridgettine spirituality being especially molded by the conviction that even the strictest monastic orders had lately succumbed to laxness.[33] Conversations with seculars were permitted on Sundays and great feast days, but then only with license of the abbess, in the company of other sisters, and at the grated windows designated for such visits. These windows might, again with permission, be opened if a nun requested that her relatives be able to see as well as to hear her. Such requests were to be made only after reflection upon the greater reward reaped in the hereafter by resisting the temptation to do so. As at Dartford, the nuns of Syon were to be heard, but not seen, even by their confessors. To ensure that all members of the community knew of these important specifications, the constitutions, in their entirety, were to be read aloud three times a year.[34]

From this brief overview it is apparent that when they took their vows of profession, English mendicant and Bridgettine novices knew that they would be expected to observe strict enclosure. In the case of the Minoresses, the addition of a fourth vow underscored the centrality of cloistering to

31. Lee, *Nunneries* 25–26; Roger Ellis, *Viderunt Eam Filie Syon: The Spirituality of the English House of a Medieval Contemplative Order from Its Beginnings to the Present Day* (Salzburg 1984) 3 and 40.

32. Lee, *Nunneries* 26.

33. Auke Jelsma, 'The Appreciation of Bridget of Sweden (1303–1373) in the 15th Century,' in *Women and Men in Spiritual Culture XIV–XVII Centuries*, ed. E. Schulte van Kessel (The Hague 1986) 163–75, provides a most lucid discussion of the spirit of the founder and her rule. Aungier, *History*, includes the constitutions of the order at 249. Ellis, *Viderunt Eam* 35, highlights those portions emphasizing enclosure.

34. Ellis, *Viderunt Eam* 3.

the Franciscan contemplative ideal. Among Bridgettines and Dominicans, profession formulae were worded to require a candidate's consent to the obligations enjoined not only by the rule of St. Augustine, but also by the constitutions of their respective orders.[35] These nuns, consequently, could never later assert that the cloister rules under which they were expected to live were outside additions 'stricter than the ones under which they had been professed.'

Different too was the 'community service' provided by these nuns. The appeal of the new orders to benefactors lay not in the regular involvement of religious women with their communities, but in their ascetic distance from it.[36] That is not to say that all traditional interaction with the laity was nonexistent. It was human nature to want to get closer to that field of sanctity that a house of ascetic women represented. Yet even as regards passive enclosure, expectations were not the same as for open monasteries.

When locals heard mass in the conventual church, they did so separated by a screen from the 'pure women who sing with their high and skillful voices.'[37] Although licenses allowing noble women to visit for various periods of time are documented, there was nothing like the press of visitors that often descended on traditional nunneries, and those who received such licenses seemed intent on more than a change of scene.[38] The pious Maud of Oxford, for example, chose to visit Bruisyard instead of Campsey Abbey because the latter monastery was too popular among well-to-do ladies.[39] With the exception of the Dominican priory of Dartford, (perhaps because it represented the female branch of the Friars Preacher) we find no evidence of schools for local children within any of these nunneries.[40] And save for the London community, lay boarders are almost nonexistent among the Minoresses.[41]

35. Aungier, *History* 317, reproduces the formulae.

36. Gee, *Women, Art and Patronage*. Chapter 1 discusses motives for patronage of the stricter orders, such as the Cistercians and Minoresses. Winston-Allen, *Convent Chronicles* 87, mentions the popular belief that the level of devoutness of religious increased the effectiveness of their prayers.

37. Lee, *Nunneries* 98–99, quoting Christine de Pisan, whose daughter was a Dominican nun at Poissy Priory.

38. Bourdillion, *Minoresses* 62–63, notes that papal permission was applied for in the case of houses of the Minoresses, and that visitors who went to the trouble to secure a costly license were 'almost all of high birth.' Lee, *Nunneries* 95–96, notes that the privilege afforded Dartford nuns to speak with visitors was an exceptional one, although school girls and laywomen did board at the house.

39. Marilyn Oliva, *Convent and Community in Late Medieval England* (Woodbridge, Suffolk, UK 1998) 137.

40. Lee, *Nunneries* 135 and 160–63.

41. Bourdillion, *Minoresses* 67. Oliva, *Convent and Community* 126, notes just three temporary or permanent residents at Bruisyard between 1350 and 1540.

The rewards that benefactors reaped for their investment in the new houses were less practical, but no less valued, than those provided by traditional communities. When patrons supported contemplative nuns, they nurtured enclaves of virtue in their midst. They could trust that they had secured particularly pious, and therefore particularly potent, prayers on behalf of themselves and their relatives, both alive and dead. By choosing to be buried at one of these houses, a practice especially favored by founders and their kin, they kept contact with these austere religious even in death.[42] Mary of St. Pol, for instance, was buried in the choir at Denny, dressed in the habit of a Minoress, and Mary's cousin Elizabeth de Clare was buried at the London Minories.[43] With these and other spiritual returns in mind, benefactors gave these communities what Pope Boniface VIII had correctly seen as the very cornerstone of the cloistered life, but what his diocesan officials had had so much trouble procuring: ample endowments.

42. Gee, *Women, Art and Patronage* 36 and 89 refers to the legal right of women to make independent decisions about where, and under whose auspices, they would be buried. Bourdillion, *Minoresses* includes a list of nineteen lay men and women who chose to be buried in Minoress houses.

43. Gee, *Women, Art and Patronage* 19, 37, 77, 107, and 150, for building and burial arrangements dictated by these women.

Bibliography of Robert Somerville's Publications

Books

The Councils of Urban II. Vol. 1: *Decreta Claromontensia* (Annuarium historiae conciliorum, Supplementum 1; Amsterdam 1972).

Law, Church, and Society: Essays in Honor of Stephan Kuttner, edited with Kenneth Pennington (Philadelphia 1977).

Pope Alexander III and the Council of Tours (1163) (Berkeley 1977).

Scotia pontificia—Papal Letters to Scotland before the Pontificate of Innocent III (Oxford 1982).

Florilegium Columbianum: Essays in Honor of Paul Oskar Kristeller (New York 1987), edited with Karl-Ludwig Selig.

Papacy, Councils and Canon Law in the 11th–12th Centuries (Variorum Reprints CS 312; London 1990; 2nd ed. 1993).

Paul Oskar Kristeller at Ninety (Columbia University, New York 1996).

Pope Urban II, the Collectio Britannica, and the Council of Melfi (1089), in collaboration with Stephan Kuttner (Oxford 1996).

Prefaces to Canon Law Books in Latin Christianity, Selected Translations, 500–1245, with Bruce C. Brasington (New Haven 1998).

Pope Urban II's Council of Piacenza, March 1–7, 1095 (Oxford 2011).

Articles

An Ordering Principle for Book VIII of Eusebius' Ecclesiastical History—A Suggestion, *Vigiliae Christianae* 20 (1966) 91–97.

Ordinatio "abbatis" in the Rule of St. Benedict, *Revue Bénédictine* 77 (1967) 146–63.

The Council of Beauvais, 1114, *Traditio* 24 (1968) 493–503.

The Council of Pisa, 1135: A Re-examination of the Evidence for the Canons, *Speculum* 45 (1970) 98–114.

The French Councils of Pope Urban II: Some Basic Considerations, 4 *Annuarium historiae conciliorum* 2 (1970) 56–65.

The So-called Canons of Nîmes (1096) (with S. Kuttner), *Tijdschrift voor Rechtsgeschiedenis* 38 (1970) 175–89.

Two Letters of Pope Innocent III, *Bulletin of Medieval Canon Law*, N.S. 1 (1971) 67–70.

The Case Against Berengar of Tours—A New Text, *Studi Gregoriani* 9 (1972) 144–65.

Pope Honorius II, Conrad of Hohenstaufen, and Lothar III, *Archivum historiae pontificiae* 10 (1972) 341–46.

An Unknown Letter of Pope Paschal II, *Speculum* 47 (1972) 737–41.

Lanfranc and Exeter, *Bulletin of the Institute of Historical Research* 45 (1972) 303–6.

Two Notes on Scotland and the Medieval Papacy, *Innes Review* 23 (1972) 149–51.

Baluziana, *Annuarium historiae conciliorum* 5 (1973) 408–23.

Pope Alexander III and King William I of Scotland, *Innes Review* 24 (1973) 121–24.

The Council of Clermont and Latin Christian Society, *Archivum historiae pontificiae* 12 (1974) 55–90.

The Canons of Reims (1131), *Bulletin of Medieval Canon Law*, N.S. 5 (1975) 122–30.

Pope Innocent II and the Study of Roman Law, *Colloques internationaux de La Napoule* 1 (1976) (= *Revue des Études Islamiques* 44 [1976]) 105–14.

The Council of Clermont and the First Crusade, *Mélanges Gérard Fransen* (= *Studia Gratiana* 20 [1976]) 2.325–37.

Cardinal Stephan of St. Grisogono: Some Remarks on Legates and Legatine Councils in the Eleventh Century, *Law, Church, and Society: Essays in Honor of Stephan Kuttner* (Philadelphia 1977) 157–66.

The Councils of Pope Calixtus II: Reims 1119, *Proceedings of the Fifth International Congress of Medieval Canon Law (Salamanca, 1976)* (Monumenta iuris canonici, Subsidia 6; Vatican City 1980) 35–50.

Anselm of Lucca and Wibert of Ravenna, *Bulletin of Medieval Canon Law*, N.S. 10 (1980) 1–13.

Luther, Erasmus, and the Thunderstorm of 1505, *Essays in Honor of J.A. Martin, Jr.* (= *Union Seminary Quarterly Review* 37 [1981–82]) 77–90.

The Councils of Pope Calixtus II and the Collection in Ten Parts, *Bulletin of Medieval Canon Law*, N.S. 11 (1981) 80–86.

Councils, Western (869–1179), *Dictionary of the Middle Ages* 3 (1983) 633–39.

The Beginning of Alexander III's Pontificate—*Aeterna et incommutabilis* and Scotland, *Miscellanea Rolando Bandinelli (Papa Alessandro III)* (Siena 1986) 355–68.

Mercy and Justice in the Early Months of Pope Urban II's Pontificate, *Chiesa, diritto e ordinamento della 'Societas christiana' nei secoli xi e xii* (Atti della nona Settimana internazionale di studio, Mendola 1983, Miscellanea del Centro di studi medioevali 11; Milan 1986) 138–58.

A Fragment of the *Passio sanctorum apostolorum Petri et Pauli*, *Vigiliae christinae* 40 (1986) 202–3.

On the Trail of a Lost Morningside Heights Manuscript, *Florilegium Columbianum: Essays in Honor of Paul Oskar Kristeller* (New York 1987) 95–105.

Scotia pontificia: Additions and Corrections (with Paul Ferguson), *Scottish Historical Review* 66 (1987) 176–83.

A Parisian Fragment of the *Collectio Lanfranci*, *Bulletin of Medieval Canon Law*, N.S. 16 (1987) 87–89.

Gregory VII, *The Encyclopedia of Religion* 6 (1987) 121–24.

The Letters of Pope Urban II in the *Collectio Britannica*, *Proceedings of the Seventh International Congress of Medieval Canon Law (Cambridge 1984)* (Monumenta iuris canonici, Subsidia 8; Vatican City 1988) 103–14.

"Pope Clement in a Roman Synod" and Pastoral Work by Monks, *Fälschungen im Mittelalter* (Monumenta Germaniae Historica, Schriften 33.2; Hannover 1988) 151–56.

Urban II, Pope, *Dictionary of the Middle Ages* 12 (1988) 302–4.

The Councils of Pope Gregory VII, *Studi Gregoriani* 13 (1989) 35–53.

The Origins of Columbia University's Collection of Medieval and Renaissance Manuscripts, *Renaissance Society and Culture: Essays in Honor of Eugene F. Rice, Jr.* (New York 1991) 289–300.

Some Remarks on the Origins of Columbia University's Collection of Medieval and Renaissance Manuscripts, *Medieval and Renaissance at Columbia University* (Rare Book and Manuscript Occasional Publication 1; New York 1991) 1–5.

Urban II and the Abbey of St. Antonin in Rouergue (with Giles Constable), *In lure Veritas: Studies in Canon Law in Memorv of Schafer Williams*, ed. Steven Bowman and Blanche Cody (Cincinnati 1991) 11–20.

Edmund Bishop and His Transcription of the *Collectio Britannica*, *Studia in honorem em.mi Card. Alfons M. Stickler*, ed. R. J. Card. Castillo Lara (Studia et textus historiae iuris canonici 7; Rome 1992) 535–48.

The Papal Bulls for the Chapter of St. Antonin in Rouergue in the Eleventh and Twelfth Centuries (with Giles Constable), *Speculum* 67 (1992) 827–64; also in *Miscellanea Domenico Maffei Dicata: Historia-Ius-Studium*, ed. Antonio García y García and Peter Weimar (Goldbach [bei Aschaffenburg] 1995) 1.33–69.

The Additions to the Canterbury *Decretum Ivonis* (Cambridge, Corpus Christi MS 19), *Cristianità ed Europa: Miscellanea di studi in onore di Luigi Prosdocimi*, 1.2 (Rome 1994) 405–15.

'Collecting Tidbits': Aulus Persius Flaccus and Bishop Burchard of Worms (with Anders Winroth), *De iure canonico medii aevi: Festschrift für Rudolf Weigand*, ed. Peter Landau (Studia Gratiana 27; Rome 1996) 507–16.

Pope Urban II and the Canons of St.-Jean-des-Vignes at Soissons, *From Byzantium to Iran: Armenian Studies in Honour of Nina Garsoian*, ed. Jean-Pierre Mahe and Robert W. Thomson (Columbia University Program in Armenian Studies, Suren D. Fesjian Academic Publications 5; Atlanta 1997) 229–42.

The Presentation of the Canons of Piacenza (March, 1095): An Overview, Baronius to Mansi, *Festschrift für Walter Brandmüller* (= *Annuarium Historiae Conciliorum* 27/28 [1995–96; appeared 1997]) 193–207.

Pope Nicholas I and John Scottus Eriugena: JE 2833, *Zeitschrift der Savigny-Stiftung für Rechtsgeschichte, Kan. Abt.* 83 (1997) (= Festschrift für Gérard Fransen) 67–85.

Papal Excerpts in Arsenal MS 713B: Alexander II and Urban II, *Proceedings of the Ninth International Congress of Medieval Canon Law* (*Munich* 1992), ed. Peter Landau and Jörg Müller (Monumenta iuris canonici, Subsidia 10; Vatican City 1997) 169–84.

Clermont 1095: Crusade and Canons, *La primera cruzada, novecientos años después: Il concilio de Clermont y los orígenes del movimiento cruzado*, ed. Luis García-Guijarro Ramos (Madrid 1997) 63–77.

Obituary for Stephan Kuttner, *Catholic Historical Review* 83 (1997) 181–84.

JL 5729 and Its Surroundings in Berlin MS Phillipps 1778, *Miscelanéa histórica en honor de Antonio García y García* (Studia Gratiana 29; Rome 1998) 815–24.

Pope Urban II "to the Beloved Sons in Christ C. and His Brothers", *Roma, magistra mundi. Itineraria culturae medievalis: Mélanges... Père L.E. Boyle*, ed. Jacqueline Hamesse (Textes et Études du moyen age 10.1; Louvain-la-Neuve 1998) 843–53.

An «Eighth Book» of the Collection in Seven Books (with Hartmut Zapp), *Grundlagen des Rechts: Festschrift fur Peter Landau*, ed. Richard H. Helmholz et al. (Paderborn 2000) 163–77.

Pope Urban II, a Pseudo-Council of Chartres, and *Congregato* (C.16, q.7, c.2 "palea"), *Reform and Renewal in the Middle Ages and the Renaissance: Studies in Honor of Louis Pascoe, S.J.*, ed. Thomas M. Izbicki and Christopher M. Bellitto (Studies in the History of Christian Thought 96; Leiden 2000) 18–34.

Urban II (1088–99), *The Great Popes through History: An Encyclopedia*, ed. Frank Coppa (Greenwood Press: Westport CT & London) 107–12.

Urban II's Privilege from April 16, 1097 for Hugh of Cluny and His Brothers (JL 5682), *"Ins Wasser geworfen und Ozeane durchquert": Festschrift für Knut Wolfgang Nörr*, ed. Friedrich Ebel et al. (Cologne 2003) 970–82.

A Letter from Archbishop Richard II of Bourges to Bishop Pons Stephani of Rodez concerning the Abbey of St.-Amans de Rodez *Scientia veritatis: Festschrift für Hubert Mordek zum 65. Geburtstag*, ed. Oliver Münsch and Thomas Zotz (Ostfildern 2004) 294–309.

Cardinal Deusdedit's *Collectio canonum* at Benevento, *Ritual, Text and Law: Studies in Medieval Canon Law and Liturgy Presented to Roger E. Reynolds*, ed. Kathleen G. Cushing and Richard F. Gyug (Aldershot 2004) 281–92.

Pope Calixtus II and Canon Law, *"Panta rei": Studi dedicati a Manlio Bellomo*, ed. Orazio Condorelli, 5 (Rome 2004) 235–43.

Canon Law, Inspired Law, and Papal Authority, *Studies Dedicated to David Weiss-Halivni*, ed. Ephraim Halivni (Orhot Press: Jerusalem 2005) 105–20.

A Fragment of *Compilato prima* at Columbia University, *Medieval Church Law and the Origins of the Western Legal Tradition: A Tribute to Kenneth Pennington*, ed. Wolfgang P. Müller & Mary E. Sommar (Washington, DC) 154–58.

Licit and *Illicit* in the Yarnall Collection at the University of Pennsylvania: Pages from the Decretals of Pope Gregory IX, *Law and the Illicit in Medieval Europe*, ed. Ruth Mazo Karras, Joel Kaye, and E. Ann Matter (Philadelphia 2008), 71–78.

Another Re-examination of the Council of Pisa, 1135, *Readers, Texts and Compilers in the Earlier Middle Ages: Studies in Medieval Canon Law in Honour of Linda Fowler-Magerl*, ed. Kathleen G. Cushing and Martin Brett (Ashgate 2008), 101–10.

Ivo in America, *Bishops, Texts and the Use of Canon Law around 1100: Essays in Honour of Martin Brett*, ed. Bruce C. Brasington and Kathleen G. Cushing (Ashgate 2008), 111–17.

The Crusade in the Councils of Urban II beyond Clermont, *Acts of the Segundas Jornadas Internacionales sobre La Primera Cruzada (Huesca, September 1999)*.

Adhemar of Le Puy, Papal Legate on the First Crusade, *Law as Profession and Practice in Medieval Europe: Essays in Honor of James A. Brundage*, ed. Kenneth Pennington and Melodie Harris Eichbauer (Farnham, U.K. 2011), 371–85.

Selected reviews

Review of H. E. J. Cowdrey, *The Epistolae Vagantes of Pope Gregory VII* (Oxford 1972), *Church History* 42 (1973) 279.

Review of Edward Peters, *The Shadow King: Rex inutilis in Medieval Law and Literature, 751–1327* (New Haven 1970), *Renaissance Quarterly* 26 (1973) 301–2.

Review of Richard Bruce Marks, *The Medieval Manuscript Library of the Charterhouse of St. Barbara in Cologne* (Analecta Cartusiana 21–22; Salzburg 1974), *Church History* 44 (1975) 249–50.

Review of Jean de Montclos, *Lanfranc et Bérenger: La controverse eucharistique du XIe siècle* (Études et Documents 37; Louvain 1971), *Speculum* 50 (1975) 106–8.

Review of John T. Gilchrist, *Diuersorum patrum sententie siue Collectio in LXXIV titulos digesta* (Monumenta iuris canonici, Series B: Corpus Collectionum 1; Vatican City 1973), *Speculum* 51 (1976) 750–52.

Review of Christopher P. Cheney, *Pope Innocent III and England* (Päpste und Papsttum 9; Stuttgart 1976), *American Historical Review* 83 (1978), 146.

Review of Rudolf Hüls, *Kardinäle, Klerus und Kirchen Roms, 1049–1130* (Bibliothek des Deutschen historischen Instituts in Rom, 48; Tübingen 1977), *Speculum* 55 (1980) 588–90.

Review of Wilfried Hartmann, *Das Konzil von Worms 868: Überlieferung und Bedeutung* (Abhandlungen der Akademie der Wissenschaften in Göttingen, Philologisch-historische Klasse, Dritte Folge 105; Göttingen 1977), *Speculum* 55 (1980) 578–80.

Review of Carlo Servatius, *Paschalis II. (1099–1118). Studien zu seiner Person und seiner Politik* (Päpste und Papsttum 14; Stuttgart 1979), *Catholic Historical Review* 68 (1982) 285–86.

Review of *Studies in the Collections of Twelfth-Century Decretals*, ed., revised and translated by C. R. Cheney and Mary G. Cheney from the papers of the late Walter Holtzmann (Monumenta iuris canonici, Series B: Corpus collectionum 3; Vatican City 1979), *Catholic Historical Review* 68 (1982) 135–36.

Review of Brian Tierney and Peter Linehan, eds., *Authority and Power: Studies on Medieval Law and Government Presented to Walter Ullmann on His Seventieth Birthday* (Cambridge 1980), *Church History* 52 (1983) 84–85.

Review of Hans-Eberhard Hilpert, *Kaiser- und Papstbriefe in den "Chronica Majora" des Matthaeus Paris* (Veröffentlichungen des Deutschen Historischen Instituts London 9; Stuttgart 1981), *Church History* 53 (1984), 435.

Review of Wilhelm Imkamp, *Das Kirchenbild Innocenz' III., 1198–1216* (Päpste und Papsttum 22; Stuttgart 1983), *American Historical Review* 90 (1985) 663–64.

Review of Jane E. Sayers, *Papal Government and England during the Pontificate of Honorius III.*

1216–1227 (Cambridge Studies in Medieval Life and Thought, third series 21; Cambridge 1984), *American Historical Review* 91 (1986) 1175.

Review of Günther Hödl and Peter Classen, *Die Admonter Briefsammlung nebst ergänzenden Briefen* (Monumenta Germaniae Historica: Die Briefe der deutschen Kaiserzeit 6; Munich 1983), *Catholic Historical Review* 72 (1986) 260–61.

Review of Henry Ansgar Kelly, *Canon Law and the Archpriest of Hita* (Medieval and Renaissance Texts and Studies 27; Binghamton, N.Y., 1984), *Church History* 55 (1986) 369–70.

Review of Wilfried Hartmann, *Die Konzilien der Karolingischen Teilreiche, 843–859* (Monumenta Germaniae Historica: Concilia 3; Hannover 1984), *Church History* 56 (1987) 269–70.

Review of Claudia Märtl, *Die falschen Investiturprivilegien* (Monumenta Germaniae Historica: Fontes Iuris Germanici Antiqui 13; Hannover 1986), *Catholic Historical Review* 76 (1990) 110–11.

Review of C. R. Cheney and John E. Jones, *English Episcopal Acta, 2: Canterbury 1162–1190* and 3: *Canterbury 1193–1205* (London 1986), *Journal of Ecclesiastical History* 39 (1988) 251–52.

Review of Joseph Avril, *Les conciles de la province de Tours (XIIIe–XVe siècles)* (Sources d'histoire médiévale publiées per l'Institut de Recherche et d'Histoire des Textes: Paris 1987), *Speculum* 65 (1990) 111–12.

Review of Mary Stroll, *Symbols as Power: The Papacy Following the Investiture Contest* (Brill's Studies in Intellectual History 24; New York 1991), *American Historical Review* 98 (1993) 848–49.

Review of Dietrich Lohrmann, *Papsturkunden in Frankreich: Diözese Paris 1. Urkunden und Briefsammlungen der Abteie Sainte-Geneviève und Saint-Victor* (Abhandlungen der Akademie der Wissenschaften in Göttingen N.F. 8, Göttingen 1989), *Journal of Ecclesiastical History* 43 (1992) 119–20.

Review of Alfons Becker, *Papst Urban II. (1088–1099)*, *Zeitschrift der Savigny-Stiftung für Rechtsgeschichte, Kan. Abt.* 80 (1994) 533–36.

Review of R.H. Helmholz, *Roman Canon Law in Reformation England* (Cambridge Studies in English Legal History; Cambridge 1990), *Renaissance Quarterly* 47 (1994) 201–3.

Review of Jörg Busch, *Der "Liber de honore ecclesiae" des Placidus von Nonantola: Eine kanonistische Problemerörterung aus dem Jahre 1111: Die Arbeitsweise ihres Autors und seine Vorlagen* (Quellen und Forschungen zum Recht im Mittelalter 5, Sigmaringen 1995), *Journal of Ecclesiastical History* 46 (1995) 560–61.

Review of Bernhard Schimmelpfennig and Ludwig Schmugge, *Rom im hohen Mittelalter: Studien zu den Romvorstellungen und zur Rompolitik vom 10. bis zum 12. Jahrhundert (Reinhard Elze zur Vollendung seines siebzigsten Lebensjahres gewidmet)* (Sigmaringen 1992), *Catholic Historical Review* 81 (1995) 644–45.

Review Essay: "Rescuing the Master of the Sentences: Marcia Colish's Peter Lombard," *The Historian* 58 (1996) 626–28.

Review of Giulio D'Onofrio, *Lanfranco di Pavia e l'Europa del secolo XI (nel IX centenario della morte [1089–1989]). Atti del Convegno internazionale di studi (Pavia, Almo Collegio Borromeo, 21–24 settembre 1989)* (Studi e documenti di storia ecclesiastica 51; Rome 1993), *Catholic Historical Review* 82 (1996) 526–27.

Review of Eamon Duffy, *Saints & Sinners: A History of the Popes* (New Haven 1997), *Church History* 67 (1998) 844–46.

Review of Herbert Schneider, ed., *Die Konzilsordines des Früh- und Hochmittelalters* (Monumenta Germaniae Historica: Ordines de celebrando concilio, Hannover 1996), *Journal of Ecclesiastical History* 50 (1999) 332–34.

Review of Pauline Henriette Joanna Theresia Maas, *The Liber sententiarum Magistri A.: Its Place amidst the Sentences Collections of the First Half of the 12th Century* (Middeleeuwse Studies 11; Nijmegen 1995), *Speculum* 74 (1999) 207–9.

Review of Frank M. Bischoff, *Urkundenformate im Mittelalter: Größe, Format und Proportionen von Papsturkunden in Zeiten expandierender Schriftlichkeit (11.–12. Jahrhundert)* (Elementa Diplomatica 5; Marburg an der Lahn 1996), *Speculum* 75 (2000) 893–95.

Review of Odette Pontal, *Les conciles de la France capétienne jusqu'en 1215* (Paris 1995), *Cahiers des civilisation médiévale* 43 (2000) 224–25.

Review of Francis Newton, *The Scriptorium and Library at Monte Cassino, 1058–1105* (Cambridge Studies in Palaeography and Codicology 7; Cambridge 1999), *Church History* 69 (2000) 879–80.

Review of Elke and Werner Goez, eds., *Die Urkunde und Briefe der Markgräfin Mathilde von Tuszien* (Monumenta Germaniae Historica, Laienfürsten- und Dynastenurkunden der Kaiserzeit, 2; Hannover 1998), *Journal of Medieval Latin* 12 (2002).

Review of Ann Freeman, in collaboration with Paul Meyvaert, *Opus Caroli regis contra synodum (Libri Carolini)* (Monumenta Germaniae Historica, Concilia 2, Supplementum 1; Hannover 1998), *Zeitschrift der Savigny-Stiftung für Rechtsgeschichte, Kan. Abt.* 89 (2003) 655–57.

Review of Brenda Bolton and Anne J. Duggan, eds., *Adrian IV the English Pope (1154–1159): Studies and Texts* (Church, Faith and Culture in the Middle Ages; Brookfield 2002), *Catholic Historical Review* 91 (2005) 143–45.

Review of Jason Taliadoros, *Law and Theology in Twelfth-Century England: The Works of Master Vacarius (c. 1115/1120–c. 1200)* (Disputatio 10; Turnhout 2006), *American Historical Review* 113 (2008) 1215–16.

Review of Ramsay MacMullen, *Voting About God in Early Church Councils* (New Haven 2006), *Church History* 77 (2008) 708–10.

Review of Wolfgang P. Müller & Mary E. Sommar, eds., *Medieval Church Law and the Origins of the Western Legal Tradition: A Tribute to Kenneth Pennington* (Washington, D.C., 2006), *Historian* 71 (2009) 656–57.

Review of *Gallia pontifica: Repertoire des documents concernant les relations entre la papaute et les monasteres en France avant 1198, III: Province ecclesiastique de Vienne, i: Diocese de Vienne* (Regesta pontificum Romanorum; Göttingen 2006), *Journal of Ecclesiastical History* 60 (2009) 341–42.

Review of Regula Gujer, *Concordia discordantium codicum manuscriptorum? Die Textentwicklung von 18 Handschriften anhand der D. 16 des Decretum Gratiani* (Forschungen zur kirchlichen Rechtsgeschichte und zum Kirchenrecht 23; Cologne 2004), *Francia* (2009), francia-online.net.

Review of Patrick Healy, *The Chronicle of Hugh of Flavigny: Reform and the Investiture Contest in the Late Eleventh Century* (Church, Faith and Culture in the Medieval West; Aldershot 2006), *Speculum* 84 (2009), 157–58.

Review of Jochen Johrendt and Harald Müller, eds., *Römisches Zentrum und kirchliche Peripherie: Das universale Papsttum als Bezeugspunkt der Kirchen von den Reformpäpsten bis zu Innocenz III* (Studien zu Papstgeschichte und Papsturkunden, N.F. 2, New York 2008), *Catholic Historical Review* 96 (2010) 790.

Contributors

Greta Austin
Associate Professor, University of Puget Sound, Department of Religion. She is the author of the book *Shaping Church Law around the Year 1000: The Decretum of Burchard of Worms* (Aldershot 2009) and ten articles, some of them very extensive, inluding "Authority in the Ivonian *Decretum* and Burchard's *Decretum*, "in *Readers, Texts, and Compilers in the Earlier Middle Ages* (Aldershot 2009) 35–58; "Freising and Worms in the Early Eleventh Century," *Zeitschrift der Savigny-Stiftung für Rechtsgeschichte*, Kan. Abt. 93 (2007), 45–108; and "Jurisprudence in the Service of Pastoral Care: The *Decretum* of Burchard of Worms," *Speculum* 79 (2004), 929–59.

Alison I. Beach
Assistant Professor of History, The Ohio State University, Columbus, Ohio, since 2011; Professor of Medieval History, Universität zu Köln, Cologne, Germany 2009–11; DAAD (German Academic Exchange Service) Guest Professor, University of Trier, 2008–9; Associate Professor of Religious Studies, College of William and Mary, Williamsburg, VA, 2001–9, Ph.D. Religion, Columbia University 1996. Besides six articles in either German or English she has published two books, *Manuscripts and Monastic Culture: Reform and Renewal in Twelfth-Century Germany* (Turnhout: Brepols 2007) and *Women as Scribes: Book Production and Monastic Reform in Twelfth-Century Bavaria* (Cambridge: Cambridge University Press, 2005). A third book is in preparation: *The Trauma of Reform: Religious Change in Twelfth-Century Constance*. She has been honored by prestigious awards and fellowships, including the Alexander von Humboldt Stiftung Trans-Coop Grant and the International Guest Professorship from the DAAD.

Uta-Renate Blumenthal
Professor of History Emerita, The Catholic University of America, Washington D.C. She is the recipient of major fellowships and grants and has published numerous articles on eleventh- and twelfth-century councils, manuscripts, papal biographies, and canonical collections. She has also published five books and edited two. Her *Der Investiturstreit* has been translated by the author into English and into Italian. She is one of the editors of this volume.

Bruce C. Brasington
Professor of History, Department of History and Geography, West Texas A & M University, Canyon, Texas. He was awarded the Ph. D. in History in 1990 at the

University of California—Los Angeles and has since published two books: *Ways of Mercy. The Prologue of Ivo of Chartres* (Münster, Hamburg, London: LIT Verlag, 2004) and with Robert Somerville *Prefaces to Canon Law Books in Latin Christianity: Selected Translations, 500–1245* (New Haven: Yale UP 1998); he is one of the editors of *Bishops, Texts and the Use of Canon Law around 1100, Essays in Honour of Martin Brett* (Aldershot: Ashgate 2008).

Martin Brett
Fellow of Robinson College Emeritus, Cambridge. He has published six books and innumerous articles. Among the books are *The English Church under Henry I* (Oxford 1975); *Councils and Synods of the English Church I (871–1204)* (Oxford 1981); *Hugh the Chanter: The History of the Church of York 1066–1127* (revised ed. Oxford 1990); *Acts of the Archbishops of Canterbury 1070–1161 I (1070–1136)* with Joseph Gribbin in the series English Episcopal Acta no. 28 (British Academy, 2004). He has two books in preparation, also in the same series of the British Academy. Honors clearly reflect his distinguished place among English medievalists: he is a Fellow of the royal Historical Society, of the Society of Antiquaries, and a Corresponding Member of the Monumenta Germaniae Historica. From 1992–2002 he was joint editor of the *Journal of Ecclesiastical History* and from 1993–2003 associate editor of the *New Dictionary of National Biography*. He is a member of numerous boards and committees of learned societies.

James A. Brundage
Ahmanson-Murphy Distinguished Professor Emeritus of History and Law, University of Kansas. He is the author of nine books, including *Law, Sex, and Christian Society in Medieval Europe* (Chicago 1987) and *The Medieval Origins of the Legal Profession: Canonists, Civilians, and Courts* (Chicago 2008) as well as *Medieval Canon Law* (London and New York 1995). Other titles are *Sex, Law and Marriage in the Middle Ages* (Aldershot 1993), *Richard Lion Heart* (New York 1974) and *Medieval Canon Law and the Crusader* (Madison 1969). His publications on the crusades are very numerous.

Giles Constable
This author of close to twenty books and well over a hundred articles has received at least four honorary degrees from the universities of Paris I, Georgetown, Longwood, and the Pontifical Institute of Mediaeval Studies, Toronto. A recipient of a Harvard Ph. D., he has taught at the University of Iowa, at Harvard (1958–85) and the Institute for Advanced Study, Princeton (1985–2003) where he is now professor emeritus. From 1977 to 1984 he served as director of Dumbarton Oaks, was visiting professor at The Catholic University of America (1978–84), at Georgetown, Princeton, and Arizona State University. He is a Fellow of the Medieval Academy and the American Philosophical Society and a Corresponding member of the Académie des Inscriptions et Belles-Lettres, Bayerische Akademie der Wissenschaften, British Academy, Accademia dei Lincei as well as others.

Kathleen G. Cushing

She is Reader in Medieval History at Keele University at Keele, Staffordshire, England and received her D. Phil in Medieval History at St. John's College, University of Oxford in 1992 and a Licentiate in Mediaeval Studies (post-doctoral), *summa cum laude* at the Pontifical Institute of Mediaeval Studies, Toronto in 1999. She has published two books: *Reform and the Papacy in the Eleventh Century: Spirituality and Social Change* (Manchester 2005), and *Papacy and Law in the Gregorian Revolution: The Canonistic Work of Anselm I of Lucca* (Oxford 1998); a third book, *Power, Discipline and Pastoral Care: Penance and Reform in Eleventh-Century Italy* is forthcoming. She is also the editor of three others with co-editors and adds numerous articles as well as websites to her achievements.

Charles Donahue Jr.

Paul A. Freund Professor of Law at Harvard Law School, is the author of at the latest count more than 55 publications, ranging from books to articles in encyclopedias. Among his books are: *Law, Marriage and Society in the Later Middle Ages* (2007), and with co-editors *Lex Mercatoria and Legal Pluralism: A Late Thirteenth-Century Treatise and its Afterlife* (1998); *Year Books of Richard II: 6 Richard II, 1382–1382* (1996); *Cases and Materials on Property* (1993); *The Records of the Medieval Ecclesiastical Courts, Part I: The Continent* (Berlin 1989); and *The Records of the Medieval Ecclesiastical Courts, Part II: England* (Berlin 1994); he was the editor of *Samuel Edmund Thorne: 1907–1994* (1995).

Detlev Jasper

Dr. Detlev Jasper's professional career is indelibly linked with the Monumenta Germaniae Historica, Munich, Germany, as *Wissenschaftlicher Mitarbeiter* from 1970 to 2007. His specializations were the history of the ecclesiastical reform of the eleventh and twelfth century and ecclesiastical history in general. His knowledge of manuscript sources and his editorial accuracy are legendary. Many of the MGH volumes will acknowledge his assistance in the preface. Besides numerous articles he published the monographs *Das Papstwahldekret von 1059: Überlieferung und Textgestalt* (1986); *The Beginning of the Decretal Tradition: Papal Letters from the Origin of the Genre through the Pontificate of Stephen V* (2001); as well as the much anticipated *Die Konzilien Deutschlands und Reichsitaliens 1023–1059* (Monumenta Germaniae Historica, Concilia 8, 2010).

Anna Trumbore Jones

Associate Professor of History at Lake Forest College, Lake Forest, Illinois, she received her Ph.D. in History at Columbia University in 2003. She has already published two books: *Noble Lord, Good Shepherd: Episcopal Power and Piety in Aquitaine, 877–1050* (Leiden 2009) and *The Bishop Reformed: Studies of Episcopal Power and Culture in the Central Middle Ages* (Aldershot 2007), edited with John S. Ott, as well as articles in *Annales du Midi* and *Viator*. The focus of her work is religion and culture in the south of France.

Peter Landau

Professor Dr. jur. emeritus of the Law Faculty of the Ludwig Maximilian University of Munich, Germany, has received multiple honorary doctorates and is president of the Stephan-Kuttner-Institute of Medieval Canon Law. His editions of the works of canonists of the twelfth and thirteenth centuries are very numerous with an emphasis on *summae* of Gratian's *Decretum*. But secular law is also very well represented among his more than a hundred publications, and he has made significant discoveries regarding the authorship of works like the German *Sachsenspiegel* or writings attributable to Anglo-Norman canonists. He is a co-editor of this volume.

Elizabeth Makowski

Professor of History Elizabeth Makowski of Texas State University has been widely acclaimed for her two books: *Canon Law and Cloistered Women: Periculoso and Its Commentators 1298–1545* (Washington D.C.: The Catholic University of America Press, 1997; paperback edition in 1999) as well as *A Pernicious Sort of Woman: Quasi-Religious Women and Canon Lawyers in the Later Middle Ages* (Washington D.C.: The Catholic University of America Press, 2005), described as "A must for the scholar as well as the general reader" (Elizabeth Cotter). She contributed several chapters in books and is equally well known for her articles.

Kenneth Pennington

Kelly-Quinn Professor of Ecclesiastical and Legal History at the Columbus School of Law and the School of Religious Studies of The Catholic University of America in Washington D.C., he is distinguished as a prolific author and editor. He is a Fellow of the Medieval Academy of America and has already been honored with a Festschrift *Medieval Church Law and the Origins of the Western Legal Tradition* (2006). He edited the *Apparatus glossarum in Compilationem tertiam* of Johannes Teutonicus (1981) and also published three major monographs: *Pope and Bishops: The Papal Monarchy in the Twelfth and Thirteenth Centuries* (Philadelphia 1984), *Popes, Canonists, and Texts 1150–1550* (Aldershot 1993) and *The Prince and the Law: 1200–1600: Sovereignty and Rights in the Western Legal Tradition* (Berkeley etc. 1993). He is the co-editor of six other books and has published more than 50 articles. He is the director of several major projects and series, including *Studies in Medieval and Early Modern Canon Law* of The Catholic University of America Press.

Edward Peters

Professor Edward Peters of the Department of History at the University of Pennsylvania, Philadelphia, has published more than one hundred books and scholarly articles between 1967 and the present, including *The First Crusade* (1971; 1998); *Witchcraft in Europe, 400–1700: A Documentary History* (2001); *Torture* (1985, rev. ed. 1996); and *Inquisition* (1989). His works have been translated into Spanish, Portuguese, Italian, and German. In addition to his activities as scholar and teacher, he was also the General Editor of the University of Pennsylvania Press series *The Middle Ages* from 1970 to 1995.

Roger E. Reynolds

In his distinguished career, Roger E. Reynolds, Professor Emeritus at the Pontifical Institute of Mediaeval Studies, Toronto, Canada, has published extensively on early medieval liturgy and canon law, with special attention to the transmission of texts. He has been honored by a Festschrift edited by Kathleen G. Cushing and Richard F. Gyug, *Ritual, Text and Law: Studies in Medieval Canon Law and Liturgy* (Aldershot 2004) reflecting the wide range not only of his own interests but also his influence and selfless dedication to students, colleagues, and the field. He has been a Senior Fellow at the Pontifical Institute since 1977 and is a corresponding Member since 1987 of the Monumenta Germaniae Historica. He has published six books, beginning with *The Ordinals of Christ from Their Origins to the Twelfth Century* (Berlin and New York 1978); *Law and Liturgy in the Latin Church, 5th–12th Centuries* (Aldershot 1994); and in the same series *Clerical Orders in the Early Middle Ages: Duties and Ordination* (Aldershot 1999); as well as *Clerics in the Early Middle Ages: Hierarchy and Image* (Aldershot 1999); and recently *The Collectio canonum Casinensis duodecimi saeculi (Codex terscriptus): A Derivative of the South-Italian Collection in Five Books* (Toronto 2001); and (with J. Douglas Adamson) *The Collectio Toletana: A Derivative of the South-Italian Collection in Five Books* (Toronto 2008). Both latter volumes are part of the series *Studies and Texts, Monumenta Liturgica Beneventana*, whose editor he is. His articles are too numerous to detail here.

Franck Roumy

The distinguished French jurist, ordinary professor of legal history at the University Panthéon-Assas (Paris II), has been honored with several prizes: the Prix de l'Institut de droit romain de Paris (1996); the Prix de thèse de l'Université de Paris (1996); and, a year earlier, the Prix Dupin-Aîné of the chancery of the University of Paris. He is a member of the boards of several legal associations and committees including the Advisory Board of the Stephan-Kuttner-Institute of Medieval Canon Law. He has published several books: in 1998 *L'adoption dans le droit savant du XIIe au XVIe siècle* (Paris 1998); in 2009 he edited (with Orazio Condorelli and Mathias Schmoeckel) *Der Einfluss der Kanonistik auf die europäische Rechtskultur, 1: Zivil- und Zivilprozessrecht* (Köln 2009) and with Bernard d'Alteroche, Florence Demoulin-Auzary, and Olivier Descamps *Mélanges en l'honneur d'Anne Lefebvre-Teillard* (Paris 2009). He has contributed more than thirty conference papers in addition to more than twenty articles and is currently working on a book on Abbo of Fleury.

Herbert Schneider

After his study of Catholic theology at the universities of Munich and Tübingen and at the Institut Catholique at Paris where he received a Diploma in Theology, Dr. Schneider's Ph.D. dissertation was written at the University of Regensburg under the guidance of Professor Horst Fuhrmann. The dissertation committee included Professor Joseph Ratzinger, now Pope Benedict XVI. Dr. Schneider became *Wissenschaftlicher Mitarbeiter* at the Monumenta Germaniae Historica, publishing his monumental and now famous *Ordines de celebrando concilio* in a new MGH series. He is currently at work on another critical edition for the Monumenta, the *Tractatus de ortu et fine Romani imperii* of Engelbert of Admont.

Charles R. Shrader

Dr. Shrader, who wrote his Ph.D. thesis on Vegetius's *De re militari* (1976) under the guidance of Robert Somerville, has a most unusual career—with special expertise in military history, particularly the history of U.S. Army logistics; strategy; political-military affairs; friendly fire; as well as European/NATO history and politics, psychological operation, and operations research. His distinguished career was entirely military: he was commissioned in the United States Army in 1964 as Distinguished Military Graduate from ROTC and retired from active duty as a Lieutenant Colonel in 1987. He frequently served overseas. He is currently an independent historical writer and consultant both for the military and the public in general. His many publications, however, are not exclusively military. He never lost his interest in manuscripts and liturgy. Among his articles are 'The False Attribution of an Eucharistic Tract to Gerbert of Aurillac,' *Mediaeval Studies* 35 (1973); 'A Handlist of Extant Manuscripts Containing the *De Re Militari* of Flavius Vegetius Renatus' *Scriptorium* 33 (1979); and 'The Influence of Vegetius' *De Re Militari*,' *Military Affairs* 45 (1981). The latter article received the 1982 Army War College Writing Prize.

Index of Manuscripts

Index of Papal Letters

General Index

Canon Law, Religion, and Politics: Liber Amicorum Robert Somerville was designed and typeset in Brioso by Kachergis Book Design of Pittsboro, North Carolina. It was printed on 60-pound Natures Natural and bound by Thomson-Shore of Dexter, Michigan.

www.ingramcontent.com/pod-product-compliance
Lightning Source LLC
LaVergne TN
LVHW040152080826
844660LV00014B/934/J

* 9 7 8 0 8 1 3 2 1 9 7 5 2 *